A TOUR GUIDE
TO THE
CIVIL WAR

A TOUR GUIDE
TO THE
CIVIL WAR

ALICE HAMILTON CROMIE

INTRODUCTION BY BELL IRVIN WILEY

FOURTH EDITION, REVISED AND UPDATED

RUTLEDGE HILL PRESS
Nashville, Tennessee

Published by Rutledge Hill Press, Inc., 211 Seventh Avenue North,
Nashville, Tennessee 37219. Distributed in Canada by H.B. Fenn and
Company, Ltd., 1090 Lorimar Drive, Mississauga, Ontario.

Typography by Bailey Typography

Library of Congress Cataloging-in-Publication Data

Cromie, Alice.
   A tour guide to the Civil War / Alice Hamilton Cromie :
introduction by Bell Irvin Wiley. — 4th ed., rev. and updated.
     p.   cm.
   ISBN 1-55853-200-5
   1. United States — History — Civil War, 1861-1865 — Dictionaries.
  2. United States — History — Civil War, 1861-1865 — Monuments —
Guidebooks. 3. United States — History — Civil War, 1861-1865 —
Museums — Guidebooks. 4. Historic sites — United States — Guidebooks.
  5. United States — Guidebooks. I. Title.
  E468.9.C8 1992
  973.7'03 — dc20   92-22746
                                        CIP

Printed in the United States of America
2 3 4 5 6 7 8 — 95 94 93

CONTENTS

INTRODUCTION

In 1862 while a group of Confederates was defending a bridge over the Tallahatchie River north of Oxford, Mississippi, the hobbled horse of Sam Jackson, First Mississippi Cavalry, wandered into a millpond and drowned. Sam's sad comment was: "Now, isn't this a hell of a tale to write home to Pap."

One would hardly expect to find a story of this sort in a tour guide of the Civil War. But it is the occasional tossing in of anecdotal tidbits such as Sam Jackson's misfortune that gives distinctiveness and sparkle to Alice Cromie's book. The story is found in the entry for Abbeville, Mississippi, a village located near Holly Springs, Mississippi, the scene of considerable fighting in the closing months of 1862.

The organization of the book is simple and sensible. A section is devoted to each of the forty-eight connected states and the District of Columbia, and within each state major entries—usually cities or forts—are arranged alphabetically. Sub-entries list, locate, and describe museums, monuments, homes, cemeteries, plantations, and other sites or objects which have a Civil War connection. The section on Mississippi, for example, begins with a brief statement giving the state's population in 1860, the number of men who entered Confederate service, how many of them survived the war, what major actions occurred within the state, and how many generals Mississippi contributed to Confederate service. Then come major entries for Abbeville . . . Beauvoir . . . Holly Springs . . . Iuka . . . Meridian . . . Natchez . . . Tupelo . . . Vicksburg . . . Yazoo City, and many other places, each locating the point on highways and telling briefly of Civil War events and persons connected with them. For a place of such importance as Vicksburg there are many sub-entries telling of Civil War happenings at such places as Anchuca, Christ Church, and McNutt House, giving the history of the gunboat *Cairo*, and describing the Old Court House Museum. Another principal entry locates and gives pertinent information about the Vicksburg National Military Park.

Sections for states like Arizona, North Dakota, and Wyoming are much shorter than those dealing with areas actively involved in the war. Material for Wyoming, like that for most other states far removed from the center of conflict, consists largely of location and description of forts having a Civil War connection, such as Fort Bridger, Fort Caspar, and Fort Reno. Sections treating of New York, Ohio, Pennsylvania, and other states which provided many troops for the Civil War contain descriptions of training camps, prisons, colleges, cemeteries, monuments, museums, historical societies, and parks, as well as homes of prominent people of the period.

Alice Cromie has done a vast amount of research, extending over a long period of time, to dig up interesting and accurate information about places throughout the nation that are related in any way to the great American conflict of the 1860s. Naturally, a work of such scope will be challenged in some of the details. Anyone who has worked with Civil War statistics, for example, will know that it is impossible to find agreement among so called "competent authorities" as to the number of troops mobilized, participants in the various battles, casualties, and desertions. Mrs. Cromie has not relied solely on perusal of printed works in her efforts to achieve accuracy but has called on experts in the various states to check the sections of the guide with which they are most familiar. The results are highly gratifying. Specialists in the details of the conflict will be pleased to find the name of Emma Sansom, the Alabama girl who assisted General Forrest, spelled correctly, and the statement made by Farragut at Mobile Bay precisely quoted.

Some readers doubtless will be disappointed at the omission of some object or site dear to their hearts. For example, I felt a twinge of regret when I found no entry telling of the monument erected by Pink Parker of Troy, Alabama, "in honor of John Wilkes Booth for killing old Abe Lincoln." But this is an unofficial memorial, conceived by a warped mind, and it probably has no place in a book of this sort. Certainly no one could list and describe *every* site or marker having to do with such a gigantic struggle as the American Civil War.

The *Tour Guide* is a very rich mine of information, and it will be of great assistance to the millions of people who delight in traveling over the country in pursuit of firsthand information about the Civil War. The use of the term *millions* in referring to such persons is no exaggeration. In 1973, over 35,000,000 people visited the thirty Civil War battlefields, monuments, and memorials administered by the National Park Service. Chickamauga-Chattanooga attracted 14,579,800 visitors that year; Kennesaw Mountain was second with 6,348,500; Gettysburg National Military Cemetery was third with 2,622,300; the Lincoln Memorial was fourth with 2,422,500; Gettysburg National Military Park was fifth with 1,489,400; and Fort Donelson National Military Park was sixth with 1,216,200. During the past ten years the annual total of visitors to Civil War shrines has more than doubled, and this trend seems likely to continue.

The question naturally arises: Why this deep and abiding interest of Americans in their conflict of a century ago? The answer is fairly obvious.

In the first place, it was "our war." It was fought by Americans, on American soil, over American issues. The heroes of the Civil War are ours, and they occupy a conspicuous place in the hall of our memories. Lincoln is the best known and the most revered of all Americans, both at home and abroad. According to Carl Sandburg, more books have been written about Lincoln than any other person in history except Jesus. Robert E. Lee, the military leader of the Lost Cause, is highly esteemed in both North and South, not only as a great general but also as a model of excellence in character and habits. Other outstanding heroes of the conflict are U. S. Grant, George H. Thomas, Winfield Hancock, David Farragut, Stonewall Jackson, Nathan Bedford Forrest, Jeb Stuart, and Patrick Cleburne, just to mention a few.

The Civil War is remembered because it was a transitional war. It was the last old-fashioned war, in which men charged in mass formation with the generals out in front. It was a "polite war," marked by many mutual acts of kindness on the part of the contestants. Yanks and Rebs often had friendly get-togethers between battles to talk, sing, drink, or gamble. It was also the first of the great modern wars, as witnessed by the use by both sides of railroads, the telegraph, ironclad battleships, submarines, land mines, rifled artillery, revolvers, and repeating shoulder arms. Moreover, it was the first war to be extensively reported by newspapers and to be sketched and photographed by artists and cameramen.

The Civil War is memorable because of its magnitude. It was far and away the biggest war ever fought on the American continent. In the Revolution of 1775–1781, American participants numbered less than half a million and in the Mexican War only 91,000. In the conflict of 1861–1865, over two million Northerners fought about a million Southerners. Civil War battles were much bigger than any that had ever been fought in the New World. At Shiloh the opposing forces aggregated 100,000 and at Fredericksburg 200,000. The Civil War was shockingly large in terms of casualties. A total of 618,000 men, North and South, died in that conflict from all causes. This exceeds by some 12,000 the aggregate of American deaths in our other wars from the Revolution through the Korean conflict.

We remember the Civil War because of its enormous impact on our history. The great conflict of the 1860s ended slavery. It determined the character of our nation. Before 1865 many people, North and South, thought that the states, individually or collectively, could withdraw from the Union when their rights or interests seemed to be imperiled. The Civil War established the superiority of national authority over local authority, save in areas explicitly reserved to the states. It decided that this country would be one great nation rather than a loose aggregation of competing entities each claiming to be sovereign.

Still another influence contributing to enduring recollection of the American conflict of a century ago is the presence among us of the parks, monuments, and other memorials established in memory of those who participated in this momentous struggle. Alice Cromie, by systematically locating these memorials and telling us of the men and events to which they pertain, has done much to enhance our knowledge of our past and deepen our appreciation of our heritage.

BELL I. WILEY

Emory University
Atlanta, Georgia

FOREWORD

Some years back at about two o'clock in the morning of a Labor Day week-end, my husband, Bob Cromie, suggested that someone really ought to compile a reliable list of signposts for Civil War buffs or, as he put it, Civil War nuts. We were on a Tennessee highway that parallels the Mississippi, heading north. One river, one sportswriter, one Civil War nut, countless night sounds, and an idea which at the moment seemed brilliant and now seems unforgivable.

We were returning to Chicago from an exhibition pro football game in Memphis when our headlights illuminated a painted board with an arrow pointing to the left and the stark lettering: FORT PILLOW. I mentioned loudly what a pity the hour was so late—I owned a slim volume entitled *Reports of the Committee on the Conduct of the War—Fort Pillow Massacre—* here was one place I'd truly like to see. "More than Jeff Davis's chin-whiskers? More than a piece of Stone Mountain?" he inquired, referring to a time when we'd headed, so to say, back to Chicago from Atlanta by way of Stone Mountain and the University of Georgia at Athens, where an archivist with great kindness allowed us to see the Confederate constitution and a blond wisp of whisker snipped from the chin of Jefferson Davis by the doctor who attended his last illness. This route, to no one's great surprise, took us through Asheville, North Carolina, and Lexington and Paducah, Kentucky.

On the present trip we had gone to Memphis on a round-about way not even a very old crow would be likely to fly, via Fort Donelson; the Surrender Room in Dover, Tennessee; Shiloh, Tennessee; and Corinth, Mississippi. Sportswriters, however, are an amiable lot, and we were soon following the arrow to the left on a bumpy country road which brought us to a modern prison equipped with floodlights, guardhouses, and tall fences not at all reminiscent of that 19th-century witticism: "As crooked as a Tennessee fence." I said, "I don't think Forrest was here exactly. It was on the river." A few more miles into the darkness convinced us that *the* Fort Pillow probably was now under the river (See HENNING, page 261).

The idea of a tour guide, born in Tennessee, grew stronger all across the land each time my driver eased out of traffic or backtracked for a historical marker only to hear an ungrateful "Forget it—it's the wrong war," or "Keep going, it's only something about a Mad Anthony Wayne."

Inevitably I wrote to my literary agent, explaining that Custer's pancake hat was in Chicago, that there was a Varina Howell Davis fan in Memphis, and that Sherman was buried in St. Louis; quite possibly there were others like me who would want to know what was still where and how to get there. My agent, the late Henry Volkening, despite a Union grandfather, responded: "Dear God! You sound like Samuel Johnson about to write his dictionary."

Time, and my own enthusiasm for so vast a chore, passed, but the need for a guide persisted, and still does. It is hoped that this new edition will not be as full of unsuspected flaws as CSS *Hunley* (for the story of one of its unfortunate crews, see South Carolina, CHARLESTON, *Magnolia Cemetery*). Maps and the best-intentioned informants have occasionally been in error, so that some directions may be as unfortunate as the wind direction at the battle of Perryville. Every effort has been made to eliminate mistakes. The manuscript has been checked and rechecked by historians of enviable credentials and by the dedicated travelers who still take the old roads as well as the new, and often the armchair route, back to the sites of the Civil War. These continuing scholars are as sharp-eyed and eager to find the undiscovered fact, or facet, of battles long silent as others are to dig up artifacts. As for the latter, one year on one of the three buses packed each spring with members and Camp Followers of the Chicago Civil War Round Table on its annual battlefield tour, John Hunter, of Madison, Wisconsin, an indefatigable walker and mountain climber (Lookout, Kennesaw, Stone, or South, etc.), settled an argument about where, these days, might be the place to find a minié ball—Stones River, Pea Ridge, the Wilderness? "I never have any trouble finding them," John said decisively, "in souvenir shops."

These same experts have spotted and will continue to pick out the errors that have evaded author, editor, and proofreader and gone into print. Daniel Hollis, of the University of South Carolina, protested one blooper I had typed absent-mindedly, wherein I substituted Benjamin Butler for Judah Benjamin as Confederate Secretary of State. Professor Hollis responded with admirable control: "No! He was a Yankee!" I astonished Dr. John Margreiter, of St. Louis, by assigning Brig. Gen. W. P. Sanders to the wrong army. He was a Yankee, too; but in locating the Knoxville, Tennessee, site where he was fatally wounded, I added injury more than a century later by listing him as CSA. The late Miner Coburn, a member of the Chicago Round Table, reminded me that Oliver Wendell Holmes, Jr., had never been Chief Justice of the Supreme Court although I had elevated him to that position, nor had Jefferson Davis served as Secretary of State in Pierce's cabinet. (Shelby Foote and other historians feel he may have been the best Secretary of War to have served to date.) So it goes. Any reader can join in the search to set the record straight, or what Charles Dufour of New Orleans aptly called the "speck-picking tournament."

The aim has been to include items most likely to be of general interest and availability. No effort was made to fill in historical background in areas where excellent free literature is available, e.g., all National Park Service sites. In states and territories well removed from what was popularly known as "the seat of war," the emphasis is on related materials which pertain to major participants in the conflict or which help to fill in the picture of what life was like in the years just prior to and during the war. The Indian uprisings of the West and Northwest were directly related to the withdrawal of regular troops for service in the war. California was greatly concerned with the activities of Napoleon III beyond its southern border. The content of the guide necessarily reflects the interests of the individual states as well as those of the author. Some areas have been especially active in erecting historically accurate markers; others have put time and funds into the development of museums, etc. A number of states have been able to carry out ambitious plans in designating sites and in restorations. Others have lacked funds to finish projects which may yet be completed.

The National Park Service has an extensive program for evaluating, designating, and preserving National Historic Landmarks. Members of both national and state centennial and historical commissions, archivists, librarians, and memorial societies have aided the location, documentation, and preservation of historical relics. It is as certain that more gunboats will be salvaged, more attics will yield letters and diaries to help identify landmarks or personnel, and more sod will be turned by plow or roadbuilder to yield articles of historical value, as it is that the controversy over who fired the first or last shot or raised the first Memorial Day flag will never cease. A tour guide to the Civil War cannot, therefore, be definitive but must follow a changing course like the Mississippi itself; another edition might bury an Island No. 10 or a Fort Pillow and reveal another ironclad. It is hoped that the present volume will aid and please some of the people, some of the time. Good hunting.

ACKNOWLEDGMENTS

I am unceasingly grateful to my husband, Bob Cromie, who trudged, climbed, and occasionally slid, over countless miles of Civil War terrain, when he would rather have been in a golf cart on better mowed turf. I am deeply grateful to my editors, who invariably have the same dedication for the job, with the same knack for making decisions and spotting errors, that Generals Lee, Grant, Jackson, and Sherman used in campaign plans.

My sincere thanks go to our National Park historians, guides, and personnel, who make *service* a meaningful word; the time spent in any area they maintain is a vastly pleasurable and informative occasion. Again I wish to thank the hundreds of persons whose aid was invaluable in compiling a state-by-state guide: the now dispersed but not forgotten members of the Civil War Centennial Commission, the members of the Society of American Travel Writers, the Travel Journalists Guild, the Midwest Travel Writers, state and local librarians, members of historical societies great and small, the United Daughters of the Confederacy, the Sons of the Loyal Legion, the National Council for Historic Preservation, the Western History Association, the Council on America's Military Past, the Westerners, members of chambers of commerce from Dade County, Florida, to Olympia, Washington, and all the fellow travelers of both beaten and lost paths who have shared experiences or corrected a turn in the road for me.

A special thanks to the many Civil War Round Tables who have given aid and encouragement to the author and a loud hurrah for the unblushing Number One Round Table, of Chicago, which no longer maintains its male-only status. The masthead of its valuable newsletter states: "The only requirement for membership is a genuine interest in the Civil War and its era." This group's annual battlefield tours are vastly popular and memorable, even though subject to occasional indignities. Once, our motley crew, arriving at an airport and struggling forth, with or without forage caps, kepis, battle flags, and maps, heard two observers remark.

"Who *is* that crowd?"

"Oh, they're just a bunch of Civil War bluffs."

To buffs everywhere, thanks—and "never sound retreat."

I would be remiss if I did not add a particular thank you to the following who in one way or another added much to the present volume: Margaret April, Edwin C. Bearss, Dr. G. P. Clausius, Miner T. Coburn, Brooks Davis, Shelby Foote, Philip Hohlweck, Marshall Krolick, E. B. Long, Dr. John Margreiter, Moore, Ralph Newman, Warren A. Reeder, Jr., Ver Lynn Sprague, Frank Welcher, Joseph L. Wisehart, and Bell I. Wiley. I regret that some of those to whom I am grateful no longer are with us.

ALABAMA

Alabama entered the Union on December 14, 1819, as the 22nd state. After the election of Lincoln, Gov. Andrew B. Moore called a state convention which met at Montgomery and on January 11, 1861, adopted the Ordinance of Secession. The Confederacy was organized and maintained at Montgomery, now known as "The Cradle of the Confederacy," for three and a half months before it was moved to Richmond. President Jefferson Davis was inaugurated on the portico of the State Capitol on February 18, 1861. There were no major land battles in Alabama, but more than 300 engagements, raids, and skirmishes took place. The state furnished 39 generals, several dozen general officers, and about 100,000 men to the service. A major contribution to the war effort was made in food, feed, arms, and cotton. The CSS *Tennessee* and other ironclads were made at the Confederate Naval Foundry at Selma, one of the most important military supply centers in the South.

The most important war action was the battle of Mobile Bay, won by Union forces under Adm. David G. Farragut in August 1864. Gen. J. H. Wilson and Union cavalry occupied Montgomery in April 1865, and the act of secession was revoked that year. The state was under military rule in 1867–1868 and in 1868, under a new constitution, was restored to the Union. Eight welcome centers are near major entrances to the state, with brochures and routing information.

ALEXANDRIA, Calhoun County. US 431. The hometown of Maj. John Pelham has a memorial monument. A Pelham Memorial Foundation has been organized to restore the birthplace of "The Gallant Pelham" who fought under Gen. J. E. B. Stuart in 60 engagements. His commission as lieutenant colonel had been signed and was on its way when he was killed by a stray shell at the battle of Kelly's Ford, Virginia, March 17, 1863.

ANNISTON, Calhoun County. US 431, north of US 78. A Confederate camp and sup-

ply base was established here in 1862; the Alabama and Tennessee River Railroad was built as far as the foot of Blue Mountain. In 1863, the Oxford Iron Works, a blast furnace, was erected a few miles south of the railhead to manufacture Confederate war supplies. The furnace and stores of cotton were demolished in 1865 by Union forces under Gen. John Thomas Croxton.

ATHENS, Limestone County. Off IS 65, US 31, 72. The town was occupied in 1862 by Federal forces under Gen. John Basil Turchin, sometimes known as the "Russian Thunderbolt." He commanded his brigade to burn the town in retribution for local resistance to occupation. Gen. Buell court-martialed and dismissed him for this action, but Turchin's wife persuaded Lincoln not only to pardon but to promote him. The Russian-born general's full name was Ivan Vasilevitch Turchininoff.

Athens College, Beaty and Pryor streets, founded in 1822, remained open during the Civil War. Campus tours.

Coleman Hill, southwest of courthouse square, is the site where Gen. Nathan B. Forrest's cavalry managed to convince Union Col. Wallace Campbell of the 110th U.S. Colored Infantry that 4,500 troops added up to 10,000. Forrest displayed his dismounted cavalrymen as infantry, then moved them to another part of the line of inspection to be presented as cavalry. His artillery was deployed in the same manner. Campbell, believing himself to be outnumbered, surrendered his troops.

ATTALLA, Etowah County. IS 59.

Oak Hill Cemetery has the grave of Cmdr. Ebenezer Farrand, an ardent secessionist who served in the U.S. Navy before the war and then in the Confederate navy.

AUBURN, Etowah County. IS 85, US 29.

Auburn University, southwest side of town. On campus near Langdon Hall is a lathe once used to make cannon in the Confederate munitions plant at Selma.

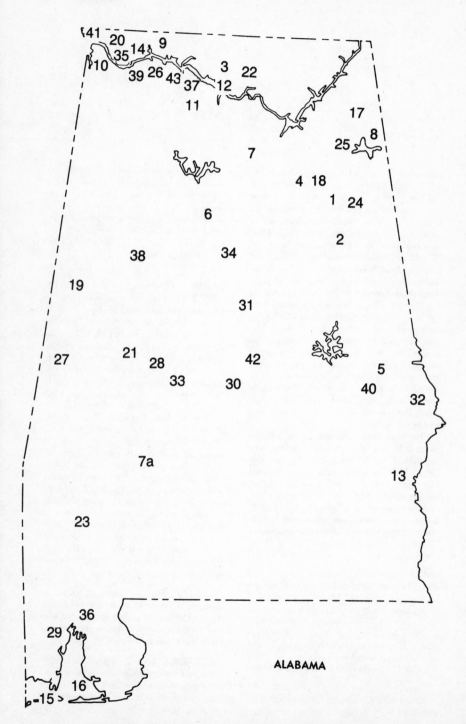

ALABAMA

Davis Monument, at railroad station, commemorates the site where Jefferson Davis reviewed the Auburn Guards on February 16, 1861. Davis was en route to Montgomery to be inaugurated.

Lane House, College and Thach St. The United Daughters of the Confederacy have placed a bronze tablet on the former home of Gen. James H. Lane, youngest brigadier general of the Confederate army. After the war he taught at Auburn.

Pine Hill Cemetery. Confederate monument commemorates the 98 Confederate soldiers buried here.

Presbyterian Church, Thach St. Erected 1850, used for wounded soldiers during the war.

BESSEMER, Jefferson County. IS 20.

Hall of History Museum, 1905 Alabama Ave., in restored railway depot, has war memorabilia in an eclectic display which includes a typewriter from Hitler's headquarters.

BIRMINGHAM, Jefferson County. IS 20, 59, 65.

Arlington Antebellum Home & Gardens, 331 Cotton Ave. SW. Antebellum home furnished in period with many antiques on display. Civil War items. Home was used as headquarters by Gen. J. H. Wilson in the spring of 1865.

Birmingham Library, 2100 Park Place, in Civic Center, has Civil War commemorative exhibits.

Tannehill State Historic Park, 12 miles southwest via IS 20 and IS 59, exit 100. There is an iron and steel museum at the site where the old ironworks once busily supplied Confederate munitions. Museum houses Civil War machinery and artifacts.

BLOUNTSVILLE, Blount County. US 231. On May Day, 1863, Col. A. D. Streight and Union cavalry came through town with Forrest's cavalry close behind. Streight set fire to his supply wagons in Blountsville and abandoned them; the Confederates arrived in time to save most of the supplies. There is a marker erected by the Alabama Historical Association about 10 miles east of town at the site of the Battle Royal, which took place at the "Royal Crossing" of the Black Warrior River. At this site, two Murphree sisters turned over to Gen. Forrest three Federal soldiers whom they had captured. Streight, in crossing the river, had lost two mules, each carrying two boxes of hardtack. Some of the Confederates waded into the stream to retrieve the packs from the dead mules. One remarked: "Boys, it's wet and full of mule hair, but it is a damned sight better than anything the old man's a-givin' us now."

BREWTON, Escambia County. US 29, 31.

Thomas E. McMillan Museum, in Fine Arts Center at Jefferson Davis College, has Civil War exhibits. Guided tours by appointment.

CAMDEN, Wilcox County, State 41, 28.

Courthouse has plaque for Pvt. Enoch Cook, who served in the army with ten sons and two grandsons. Five were killed in action.

CEDAR BLUFF, Cherokee County. State 9.

Lawrence House, about 4 miles east, has two markers for the site where Col. Streight surrendered to Gen. Forrest on May 3, 1863.

CENTER STAR, Lauderdale County. US 72.

Cunningham Plantation, Belview Rd. Benjamin Taylor house was built in 1850. Thomas J. Taylor, a son, enlisted in the Confederate army while a student at the University of Virginia, was killed at the battle of Baker's Creek in 1863. Ben's daughter refused to play the piano for Federal soldiers occupying the home. After the war Susannah married Capt. Jonathan M. Cunningham of the 27th Alabama Infantry.

CHEROKEE, Colbert County. US 72.

Cross Home, 1½ miles northeast, was the residence of Dr. William C. Cross, a surgeon in the Confederate service. Dr. Cross, who reached the rank of major and served at the battle of Shiloh, built this house in 1866 after Federal troops had burned his former home on the old stage coach road south of Cherokee.

Rutland Home, 2 miles southwest. Residence of John Watson Rutland. Secret hiding places built in the house held food and valuables during the war. Three of Rutland's sons served in the army. John, the eldest, was killed at Shiloh; Arthur was a La Grange cadet at the outbreak of war, went into active service; Hugh Watson served with the Franklin Blues, then the 2nd Alabama Infantry. The house was used to care for wounded and sick soldiers. Some skirmishes took place in the grove in front of the residence.

CHILDERSBURG, Talladega County. State 76.

DeSoto Caverns Park, 5 miles east on State 76. These onyx-marble caverns were discovered by Hernando de Soto in 1540. Confederates mined saltpeter here for gunpowder. Hour-long tours include a laster light and water show.

COURTLAND, Lawrence County. Alt. 72, State 33.

Rocky Hill Castle was built by James Saunders, later a colonel in the Confederate army. At one time the military court of the Army of Tennessee met here.

DECATUR, Morgan County. US 31, Alt. 72. The town was taken and retaken by both armies, until at war's end only a few buildings were intact. First known as Rhodes Ferry Landing, the town survived the war's devastation and later yellow fever. Old Decatur District, between the river and Lee St., is on site of wartime town, first settled in 1820. The Old Bank, 925 St. NE, served as a military hospital and guardhouse during the war; now houses the convention and visitors' bureau.

Hinds-McEntire House, 120 Sycamore St., about 1835. House served as headquarters for both armies. Local legend says Gen. Albert Johnston planned the battle of Shiloh here.

DEMOPOLIS, Marengo County. US 80.

Bluff Hall, 405 Commissioners Ave., and **Gaineswood,** Cedar and Whitfield streets, are antebellum mansions now open. Gaineswood was the center of a large plantation and was in construction from 1828 to the war.

EUFAULA, Barbour County. US 82, 431, at Georgia line.

Seth Lore Historic District has many historic buildings to be seen on self-guiding tours.

Chamber of Commerce is in the restored **Sheppard Cottage,** 504 E. Barbour, once the home of Dr. Edmund Sheppard who practiced medicine here when the town was known as Irwinton (1837). Brochures are available at **Shorter Mansion,** 340 N. Eufaula Ave., from the Heritage Association. Jefferson Davis once stopped at the **St. Julian Hotel. The Tavern,** 105 Front St., built in 1837 as an inn for steamboat traffic, used as a Civil War hospital, has war relics.

FLORENCE, Lauderdale County. US 43, 72.

Bounds Place, west end of Cypress Mill Rd. Confederate soldiers are said to have been hidden in the secret basement that is reached by a trap door. There are portholes in the outside walls that may have been used for rifles.

Confederate Monument, Courthouse lawn, Court and College streets. The gray stone figure of infantryman in marching equipment was made in Italy, dedicated in April 1903.

First Presbyterian Church, corner E. Mobile St. and N. Wood Ave. During the war Dr. William Mitchell, pastor, while praying for the success of the Confederacy, was arrested in the church by a Federal officer. He was sent to military prison at Alton, Illinois, for six months.

Florence Historical Board, 2207 Berry Ave., has a museum, historical sites information, and tours.

Forks of Cypress, Old Jackson Rd. about 5 miles from town. One of the state's finest examples of the temple type antebellum mansion. The mansion, struck by lightning, burned. Capt. James Jackson, son of the builder, served in Forrest's cavalry and was buried in the family cemetery near the house.

Irvine Place, 459 N. Court St. James Bennington Irvine, wealthy planter who lived here, was captured during the war and sent to Johnson's Island in Lake Erie. His diary is still in the family's possession.

Lambeth House, 203 Hermitage Dr., was used as a hospital during the war. First patients were casualties from a skirmish in Florence. Later several hundred sick and wounded soldiers were brought from Forts Henry and Donelson. Thirty-two who died here are buried in the Confederate section of the old Florence Cemetery. After the battle of Elk River, the home became a regularly designated hospital. Marker on home placed by United Daughters of the Confederacy.

Mapleton, 420 S. Pine St. Federal troops camped here and used the basement for concealing their horses. Later the house served as provost marshal's headquarters. Col. John Marshall Harlan of the 10th Kentucky Regiment occupied the house in 1862; it was Harlan who arrested the Presbyterian pastor for prayers not to the colonel's liking. Confederate Maj. Robert McFarland bought the house after the war.

McVay House, Mars Hill Rd. Gov. Hugh McVay filled the unexpired term of Gov. Clement C. Clay when Clay went to the U.S. Senate. About 1860, an iron foundry was established near the house; during the war, weapons and household wares were manufactured.

Monumental Park, S. Chestnut and Parkway, was built on the site of breastworks used by the Confederates in their stand against Col. A. D. Streight's cavalry.

O'Neal House, 468 N. Court St. Dr. Edward Asbury O'Neal was colonel of the 26th Alabama Regiment, later commissioned general under Hood's command. The house was occupied by Federal troops for a time. Gen. O'Neal served two terms as governor in the 1880s; his son Emmet also became governor.

Peters Plantation, about 5 miles west of town, on Gunwaleford Rd. Scene of a skirmish in April 1864. The "White Horse Company" of the 9th Ohio Cavalry had collected about 250 beef cattle at the plantation when Confederates led by Cols. James Jackson and Samuel Ives surrounded the camp, killed four Federals, and captured 42. Two who escaped went to Florence to report that Forrest was en route; Union troops then evacuated the town.

Pickett Place, 438 N. Seminary St. Home of Col. Richard Orrick Pickett of the 10th Alabama Cavalry.

Pope's Tavern, 203 Hermitage Dr., was a stage stop, served as a hospital during the war for both Confederate and Union wounded. Museum houses Civil War memorabilia. Guided tours are available.

Sweetwater Plantation, Sweetwater Ave. and Florence Blvd. Home of Gov. Robert Miller Patton who served from 1865 until 1868, when his administration was ended by a Congressional decree. Three Patton sons served in the Confederate army; two were killed in battle. Federal troops camped here for a time. It has been said the slave cabins were burned to cremate bodies of Federal soldiers who died of smallpox.

University of North Alabama, Wesleyan Ave. Wesleyan Hall quartered troops of both armies. Courtview, also known as Rogers Hall (north end of Court St. on campus), was inherited by Sallie Foster McDonald, wife of

Capt. Sterling Payne McDonald of the Confederate army.

Wakefield, 450 N. Court St. The home of Dr. W. H. Mitchell, pastor of the First Presbyterian Church, who was arrested by Federal authorities and imprisoned at Alton, Illinois. William L. Yancey and Gen. Stephen D. Lee were guests here.

Wilson Cemetery, 3 miles from town on the old Jackson highway near St. Florian. The graves of John W. and Matthew H. Wilson have identical inscriptions: "They were cruelly tortured and murdered by robbers." On a night in April 1865, a party of local citizens dressed in Federal uniforms and led by Lt. Tom Thrasher of the Union army robbed and shot John Wilson, his nephew Matthew, and a black overseer. Another nephew was wounded but fled to Sweetwater Plantation and survived.

FORT GAINES, on Dauphin Island, at entrance to Mobile Bay. The fort, now a state monument, guarded the port of Mobile directly opposite Fort Morgan. Inside the fort is a Confederate museum. Within the fort entrance are an anchor and chain from the USS *Hartford,* Adm. Farragut's flag ship in the battle of Mobile Bay. Museum has diorama.

FORT MORGAN, Baldwin County. At Mobile Point, east entrance of bay. During the battle of Mobile Bay, which began on August 5, 1864, Farragut is supposed to have said: "Dam [sic] the torpedoes! Four bells! Captain Drayton, go ahead! Jouett! Full speed!" The admiral had just been informed that the *Tecumseh* had been sunk by a submarine mine. Divers later located this monitor a few hundred yards offshore. A buoy marks the gravesite of 93 Union sailors. Torpedoes and smoke screens were used in this engagement for the first time in naval warfare. The fort is now a national historic landmark.

FORT PAYNE, DeKalb County. IS 59, US 11.

Memorial Park has a Confederate monument. Name of park was changed from Union to Memorial on Confederate Memorial Day, April 28, 1961.

GADSDEN, Etowah County. US 431, 278. Streight's forces sacked the town in 1863 and rode on, following the Coosa River, for Rome, Georgia, where a Confederate munitions base was in operation. Capt. John H. Wisdom, a Confederate mail contractor, made a 67-mile ride, arriving before midnight, to warn Rome of the enemy's approach.

Forrest Cemetery, west side of 15th St.,

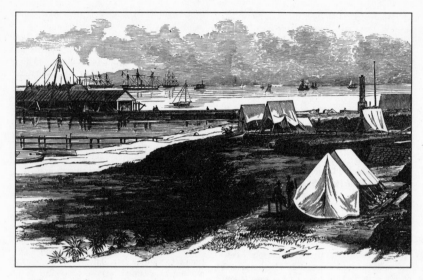

The water battery at Fort Morgan in Mobile Bay.

Walnut and Chestnut. Graves of Confederate soldiers are marked by iron Maltese crosses.

Site of Sansom Home, southeast corner of Kyle Ave. and 3rd St. Emma Sansom, 15-year-old guide for Gen. Forrest when he came through town in pursuit of Streight, once lived at this corner. The house burned in 1900. Emma just missed getting shot but waved her sunbonnet and may have shouted: "They've only wounded my dress!" Both sides cheered the girl and held fire until she had reached safety.

Emma Sansom Monument, 1st and Broad St. A bas-relief memorial erected by the United Daughters of the Confederacy shows Emma seated behind Forrest on his horse. She is pointing out the ford on Black Creek.

GAINESVILLE, Sumter County. State 39 near Mississippi line. Marker is on site of Gen. Forrest's surrender to Federal Gen. Canby on May 9, 1865. On the night before surrender, the men of the 7th Tennessee Cavalry cut their battle flag into souvenir pieces for all. It had been a gift made from the wedding dress of a young woman from Aberdeen, Mississippi.

GRAVELLY SPRINGS, Lauderdale County. Waterloo Rd., about 15 miles west of Florence. From this base, Gen. James H. Wilson began his raid into southern Alabama in March 1865. The camp extended from the springs to the Tennessee River. Gen. Hatch of Wilson's command had headquarters in the Cannon house.

GREENSBORO, Hale County. State 5.
Magnolia Grove, 1002 Hobson. The antebellum home is a state historical shrine. Original furnishings.

HALEYVILLE, Winston County. State 5, 13.

On the 4th of July, 1861, the residents seceded from Alabama, refusing to shoot at Old Glory. More than 2,000 men from town and county, planning to call their new "state" Nickajack, joined the Union forces after Confederates began to burn homes and jail or shoot seceders. This rebellious group became the First (and probably last) Alabama Cavalry in the Federal army.

HUNTSVILLE, Madison County. US 72, 431.
Church of the Nativity, southwest corner Eustis and Greene St., was saved from destruction reportedly by the inscription on the building: "Reverence My Sanctuary." In the memoirs of Mrs. Clement Clay, Jr., Dr. J. M. Bannister, pastor, was "quickly instructed as to the limited petitions with which he might address his God on behalf of his people."

Depot Museum, 320 Church St. Building walls still have Civil War graffiti. This was a hospital and prison after Federal troops took over the 1860 "passenger house" of the eastern division, Memphis & Charleston Railroad Co.

Logan Headquarters, 421 Adams Ave. Gen. John A. Logan of Illinois quartered here.

Madison County Courthouse, central plaza near Washington and Greene St. United Daughters of the Confederacy Room has Civil War relics.

Maple Hill Cemetery, east end of Eustis and California St. Five Alabama governors are buried here.

Morgan Birthplace, 558 Franklin St. John Hunt Morgan, Confederate raider, was born at this site in 1825.

Walker Home, Adams Ave. and McClung St. Home of Leroy Pope Walker who, as Confederate Secretary of War, gave the order to fire on Fort Sumter. When Federal soldiers occupied the town, they hoped to catch such a valuable prize as Walker. A friend who endured one of the search parties reported: "I remember distinctly seeing them look into preserve jars and cut-glass decanters, until my mother's risibles no longer could be repressed. 'You don't expect to find General Walker in that brandy bottle, do you?' she asked."

JACKSON, Clarke County. US 43, 84. The Salt Dome and Jackson Fault outside of town were important salt works used by the Confederate government.

JACKSONVILLE, Calhoun County. State 21.

Cemetery, S. Church and May St. Monument at the graves of Maj. John Pelham ("The Gallant Pelham") and Gen. John Forney, a professor of mathematics at West Point before the war who returned to Alabama to become aide to the governor.

Presbyterian Church, E. Clinton and Church streets. Marker in churchyard states that the building served as a Confederate hospital.

LEESBURG, Cherokee County. US 411.

Blount House, 7 miles west of town, was the site of a skirmish between Forrest and Streight. Wounded of both sides were cared for in the house.

LEIGHTON, Colbert County. State 20, Alt. 72.

Gregg's Tavern, 1 block west of traffic light on Alt. 72. The tavern was once a toll gate and social center on Alabama's first state highway. It was moved about 1 block west of original site.

Brig. Gen. John Gregg of the Confederate army once lived in the tavern.

La Grange College Site, 4 miles southwest of Leighton. Alabama's first college, opened in 1830. In 1860, it was renamed LaGrange Military Academy; it was burned by the 7th Kansas Cavalry, under the command of Col. F. N. Cornyn, April 28, 1863. Granite memorial on site.

The Preuit Oaks, on the Old Moulton Rd. southeast of Leighton. Col. Richard Preuit, wealthy slave owner, purchased the plantation in the 1850s. Federal soldiers plundered the home during a raid.

Presbyterian Church, 4½ miles north of Leighton on Byler Rd. and ¼ mile east on Mt. Pleasant Rd. The Old Brick Church was organized in 1820 by a Virginian. Present structure dates from 1827. Members of the congregation built the church assisted by slave labor. It closed during the war when all elders and deacons, except for one aged elder, went to war; none returned.

LIVINGSTON, Sumter County. State 11.

Confederate Monument on courthouse lawn. Names of Sumter County soldiers are inscribed.

MARION, Perry County. State 5, 14.

Judson College, north edge of town. Founded as the Judson Female Institute in 1839 by Milo P. Jewett, who later established Vassar College. Confederate Oak, near entrance of Jewett Hall, is the site where one of the original Confederate flags was presented to the Marion Light Infantry. Nicola Marschall, who designed the flag, taught at the college. Elmcrest, home of John Trotwood Moore, poet and historian who wrote of the plantation South, is now part of the college.

King House, Main St. Home of Capt. Porter King, reportedly the Confederate officer to whom Gen. Bee at First Manassas said: "Look at Jackson's brigade; it stands like a stone wall!" (Some authorities maintain that Bee's intent was to rally his troops, and therefore he shouted the remark to as many as were within earshot.)

Lea House, 318 Green St., is the site where Margaret Lea and Sam Houston were married in 1840.

Marion Military Institute. The institute's honorary military society, "The Morgan Raiders," wear authentic Confederate uniforms. "Old South Day," sometimes called "Raiders Day," is held annually with dress parade.

Monument to Nicola Marschall, just off main entrance of Perry County Courthouse,

Farragut's victory in Mobile Harbor: The Hartford engaging the C.S.S. Tennessee.

honors the artist and music teacher who designed the Confederate flag.

MOBILE, Mobile County. IS 10, US 98, 90. Gen. Joseph E. Johnston said Mobile was one of the best fortified cities in the Confederacy; it was a base for blockade running. The outer defense was commanded by Forts Morgan and Gaines, which were taken by the Federal navy in the battle of Mobile Bay, August 1864. In March 1865, Gens. Canby and Steele began a pincers move against the city. It surrendered April 12, three days after Gen. Lee had surrendered at Appomattox. The submarine *Horace L. Hunley* was built here. A Confederate torpedo plant and several small war industries were located here. Among noted citizens were: Adm. Raphael Semmes; Dr. S. P. Moore, surgeon-general and medical director of the Confederacy; Henry Hotze, Confederate propagandist in England; and John A. Campbell, assistant secretary of war of the Confederacy. Most historic homes are marked.

Bragg-Mitchell Mansion, 1906 Springhill Ave., was the home of John Bragg who willed it to his brother, Gen. Braxton Bragg. During the war, magnificent oak trees were sacrificed to allow Confederates free artillery range to shell

Union troops. Judge Bragg later replanted from acorns gathered from lost trees.

City Hall, Royal and Church streets, was originally used as a market place. William Howard Russell, British correspondent, stopping at Mobile in 1861, commented: "The market was well worthy of a visit—something like St. John's at Liverpool on a Saturday night. . . . The fruit and vegetable stalls displayed very fine produce, and some staples, remarkable for novelty, ugliness, and goodness. . . . We went into one of the great oyster saloons, . . . had opportunity of tasting those great bivalvians in the form of natural fish puddings, fried in batter, roasted, stewed, devilled, broiled, and in many other ways, *plus* raw. I am bound to observe that the Mobile people ate them as if there was no blockade, and as though oysters were a specific for political indigestions and civil wars." A Confederate soup kitchen was established at City Hall during the war.

Goldsby House, 452 Government St., was occupied by Union officers in the spring of 1865.

Magnolia Cemetery, George St. Southeast corner of burial ground is known as Confederate Rest, memorial to Confederate dead. National cemetery is in southwest corner, burial place of Federal soldiers who fell at Fort Blakely. Gen. Braxton Bragg is buried in the cemetery.

Museum of Mobile, 355 Government St., has Confederate relics and uniforms.

Oakleigh, 350 Oakleigh Pl. Mobile's official antebellum mansion is headquarters for the Historic Mobile Preservation Society. Period furnishings and museum. In one parlor is the Thomas Sully portrait of the famous belle, Octavia Walton LeVert. Mrs. Clement Clay, Jr., who grew up to be a belle in the 1850s, recalled her first Boat Club Ball and meeting with Madame LeVert, then the "reigning queen of every gathering at which she appeared," a person of whom Washington Irving said only one such was "born in the course of an empire." Mrs. Clay reported: "She wore a gown of golden satin, and on her hair a wreath of coral flowers, which her morocco shoes matched in hue. In the dance she moved like a bird on the wing."

Phoenix Fire Museum, 203 Claiborne, has Civil War fire-fighting equipment in an 1819 fire station.

Public Library, 701 Government St. Museum in east wing has Civil War items.

Father Ryan Statue, Spring Hill Ave., Scott and St. Francis streets. A life-size bronze of the noted priest-poet of the Confederacy.

Semmes House, 802 Government St. The former home of Adm. Raphael Semmes was presented to the First Baptist Church, which it adjoins. The church has converted the home for use as a small chapel; in the conversion the wall between the double parlors and the marble mantels were removed, otherwise house remains as originally built. Plaque marks the building. There is a monument to Adm. Semmes in Confederate Rest, Magnolia Cemetery.

USS **Alabama** *Battleship Park,* 1½ miles east on IS 10, Battleship Pkwy. exit. Cruises depart from the park docks for a 1½-hour sightseeing tour during which the captain narrates the Civil War battle of Mobile Bay and other harbor operations.

MONTEVALLO, Shelby County. State 25.

Brierfield Ironworks Park, 7 miles south just off State 25. A Civil War iron-producing furnace. Ruins in park.

MONTGOMERY, Montgomery County. IS 65, 85. Gen. James Wilson's Federal raiders occupied the city in April 1865. Public records had been removed to Eufaula; more than 100,000 bales of cotton were burned as Alabama's last gesture of rebellion.

Business Council of Alabama, 468 S. Perry

St. Gen. James Wilson's headquarters in 1865. From the porch the general read Lincoln's Emancipation Proclamation to a gathering of the newly emancipated blacks.

Exchange Hotel, northwest corner, Commerce and Montgomery streets. United Daughters of the Confederacy marker commemorates historic events which took place in the wartime hotel that once stood here. The first Confederate cabinet met in the building. William Yancey and Jefferson Davis spoke to the citizens of Montgomery from a balcony on the Commerce Street side of the hotel. Londoner William Russell, in 1861, found the service poor and suggested that "if the South secede, they ought certainly to take over with them some Yankee hotel keepers. This 'Exchange' is in a frightful state—nothing but noise, dirt, drinking, wrangling."

First White House of the Confederacy, 644 Washington Ave. The home of Jefferson Davis and his family when Montgomery was the capital. It was formerly located on the southwest corner of Bibb and Lee St. and was moved to its present location in 1921. War relics and Davis memorabilia.

Gerald House, 405 S. Hull St. The house where Herman F. Arnold lived when he wrote the orchestral score for "Dixie." The manuscript is in the Alabama Department of Archives and History.

Janney Foundry, N. Court and Randolph streets. Marker for Confederate munitions plant.

Lomax House, 235 S. Court St., was built about 1848 by James J. Gilmer, brother of Gov. George Gilmer and of Mrs. Sophia Bibb, who was an ardent war worker. Tennent Lomax, colonel of the 3rd Alabama, who was killed at the battle of Seven Pines, owned the house at the time of his death.

Montgomery Museum of Fine Arts, Lawrence and Highland. Period rooms, firearms, pioneer heirlooms among displays.

Oakwood Cemetery, 829 Columbus, has many memorials of historic interest.

Powder Magazine, west end of Eugene St.

St. John's Episcopal Church, northeast corner Madison Ave. and N. Perry St. Bronze tablet marks the Davis pew. During the war women met here to sew and knit for soldiers.

State Archives and History Department, Washington and Bainbridge St., in World War Memorial Building, has extensive newspaper and manuscript collections. Museum contains many Confederate relics.

State Capitol, east end of Dexter Ave. First Capitol of the Confederacy. On the main por-

10   ALABAMA

tico is the six-pointed bronze Davis Star, marking the spot where Jefferson Davis stood while Howell Cobb administered the presidential oath on February 18, 1861. The building has murals by Roderick MacKenzie depicting Alabama history. A case of Civil War relics is displayed in the governor's office. In the House of Representatives a marble shield commemorates the date of secession. On Capitol grounds are trees brought from battlefields where Alabama men fought during the Civil War. Near the west portico is a bronze figure of Jefferson Davis, 9 feet tall; it was given to the state by the United Daughters of the Confederacy. The Confederate monument at the north entrance to the Capitol was erected in memory of Southern soldiers and sailors. The cornerstone was laid by Jefferson Davis on April 26, 1886. On the south lawn, the bronze statue of Allen Wyeth, noted Confederate surgeon and founder of New York Polyclinic Medical School, was executed by Gutzon Borglum.

Winter Building, southeast corner Court Square. In 1861, the offices of the Southern Telegraph were located here. From a corner room on the second floor, Leroy Pope Walker sent the word giving Beauregard discretionary power to open fire on Fort Sumter.

Yancey Office Site, 109 Washington Ave. A bronze marker denotes site of law offices shared by John Archer Elmore and William Lowndes Yancey from 1848 to 1860. Yancey was considered one of the most voracious of Southern "fire-eaters." He penned the Ordinance of Secession, went to England and France to seek recognition for the Confederacy, returned to Alabama when Queen Victoria proclaimed neutrality, and served in the Confederate senate until his death in 1863. In his last days, Yancey was opposing centralized government in the Confederacy as he had in the Union.

MOORESVILLE, Limestone County. Off US 72 (AL 20), 6 miles east of Decatur. Alabama's oldest incorporated town is a national registered historic place. Andrew Jackson was a tailor's apprentice here. James Garfield is said to have preached during the war at the Community Church, built in 1820.

MOUNTAIN CREEK, Chilton County. Ten miles south of Clanton off US 31.

Confederate Memorial Park, just off highway. One of the few cemeteries dedicated solely to Confederate soldiers has a grave to the C.S.A. Unknown Soldier. Log cabin museum has uniforms and Civil War artifacts.

PHENIX CITY, Russell County. US 80 near Georgia line. Confederate breastworks

and rifle pits used during one of the last battles of the war, April 16, 1865, are still visible in outline by the Chattahoochee River.

Godwin's Cemetery has a monument to John Godwin, bridge builder, which was erected by Horace King, his former slave, in "remembrance of the love and gratitude he felt for his lost friend and former master."

SELMA, Dallas County. US 80, State 22. One of the most important supply depots in the Confederacy, the town had a naval foundry, rolling mill, armory, arsenal, and powder mill. During the last two years of the war, about half the cannon and two-thirds of fixed ammunition used by the Confederacy were made here. Government establishments covered about 50 acres, employed some 6,000 men and women; private industry employed about 4,000. Cavalry raiders under Gen. James H. Wilson won the battle of Selma, April 2, 1865.

Arsenal Place, Water Ave. and Church St. Site of the arsenal that covered three square blocks. Names of officers in charge are inscribed on monument.

Cahawba Ruins, about 9 miles southwest on State 22, then 5 miles south on dirt road. A Confederate prison was established here in 1864. Cahawba was the first state capital. Town was wiped out by flooding but interpretive signs mark sites.

Dawson-Vaughn House, 704 Tremont St., was the home of Col. N. H. R. Dawson, whose wife, Elodie Breck Dawson, was a half-sister of Mary Todd Lincoln.

Live Oak Cemetery, Valley Creek between Dallas and Selma Ave. Gen. Edmund Pettus, Gen. William Hardee, Gen. John Tyler Morgan, and Capt. Catesby ap R. Jones are buried here.

Mabry House, 828 Tremont St. Here in 1865 Capt. Catesby ap R. Jones married Miss Gertrude Tartt. Jones survived a number of naval engagements but in postwar years was fatally shot in a quarrel with one J. S. Harral.

Morgan House, 719 Tremont St. Home of Gen. John Tyler Morgan, who enlisted as a private in the Cahawba Rifles, served under Forrest at Stones River, fought at Chickamauga and Atlanta, was appointed brigadier general in 1863, and was raising black troops in Mississippi at war's end.

Naval Foundry, Water Ave. and Sylvan St. Monument on site of Confederate navy yard where the ironclads, *Tennessee, Gaines, Morgan,* and *Selma,* were built. The foundry was directed by Capt. Catesby ap R. Jones, who had commanded the *Merrimac* in the second day of battle with the *Monitor.*

Pettus House, 722 Alabama Ave. Home of Gen. Edmund Winston Pettus, whose brother, John, was governor of Mississippi during the secession crisis. Gen. Pettus commanded his brigade at Lookout Mountain, Atlanta, and Nashville, surrendered with Johnston in the Carolinas. After the war he served as U.S. senator for 12 years.

Philpot House, 603 Alabama Ave. Robert Philpot was killed in the battle of Selma.

Smitherman Historic Building, 109 Union St., began as a Masons' Hall and served as a Confederate hospital during the war. It has Civil War relics, furnishings, and other exhibits relating to Selma's history.

St. James Hotel, 1200 Water Ave., an early riverfront hotel served as headquarters for Confederate officers and arsenal and foundry personnel.

Sturdivant Hall, 713 Mabry, antebellum home, has war relics. The restored 1853 home was designed by Thomas Helm Lee, Robert E. Lee's cousin. Guided tours are available.

SHELBY SPRINGS, Shelby County. State 25.

Confederate Memorial Hospital and *Confederate Cemetery* are located here.

SMITHSONIA, Lauderdale County. County 6, west end of Gunwaleford Rd. on Tennessee River.

Cheathams Ferry was operated during the war by Columbus Smith. Ruins of his mansion remain; it was built when he became a merchant, ginner, and trader after the war.

SPANISH FORT, Baldwin County. IS 10. A land attack in March 1865 was led by Union forces under Maj. Gen. E. R. Canby. Confederate forces were commanded by Brig. Gen. Bryan M. Thomas, Col. I. W. Patton, and Brig. Gen. R. L. Gibson. Gunpits, trenches, and breastworks remain. Automobiles may be parked in Danner Circle, named for Capt. Albert C. Danner, Mobilian who won distinction during the siege of Vicksburg. From here walk over the lawn of Mrs. George Fuller's residence. This is the second highest point on the coast from Alabama to Maine. The second point of land is Point Clear. A house at Point Clear bore a direct hit during the battle of Mobile Bay. A metal plate with an inscription bearing the compliments of Adm. Farragut was used to cover the hole.

STEVENSON, Jackson County. State 72.

Railroad Depot Museum, 2 miles north of US 72 on State 117. The town was a vital strategic point because of location and railroad

junction. Federal forces eventually captured the area.

TOWN CREEK, Lawrence County. Alt. 72. Marker on highway ½ mile west of creek. On April 27, 1863, Gen. P. D. Roddey attempted to block the advance of Gen. G. M. Dodge. A detachment of Dodge's force, the 7th Kansas Cavalry, moved up LaGrange Mountain, burned LaGrange College and Lafayette Female Academy, as well as surrounding homes and barns.

TUSCALOOSA, Tuscaloosa County. US 82, 43. In April 1865, Gen. John T. Croxton and Union cavalry overcame the cadet defenders from the University of Alabama, captured the town, and burned all but three university buildings.

Battle-Friedman House, 1010 Greensboro, was the home of Virginia Clay-Clopton, author and wife of C.S.A. statesman Clement Clay. The 1835 mansion, built by planter Alfred Battle, is restored and furnished for city cultural center and house museum.

Cherokee, 1305 24th Ave., now Friedman Library, was built by Robert Jemison of the Confederate Congress.

Evergreen Cemetery has Confederate graves in the section designated as "Soldiers Rest."

Gorgas Home, northwest corner of Quadrangle on university campus, is a state shrine. It was the postwar residence of Gen. Josiah B. Gorgas, chief of ordnance for the Confederacy, after he retired as president of the university.

University of Alabama, US 11, has marker on campus. Little Round House was erected for the officer on duty when the institution adopted military discipline in 1860. It was fired on by Gen. Croxton's troops but not destroyed. A boulder nearby commemorates cadets who resisted the Union advance. The President's Mansion was built about 1840. Mrs. Langdon C. Garland, wife of the president, is said to have saved the residence from fire when she persuaded Federal invaders to leave the grounds. The blaze which they had already started was extinguished by black servants.

TUSCUMBIA, Colbert County. US 72.

Abernathy Home, 204 N. Main St. Dr. Robert Towns Abernathy was a surgeon with the 5th Alabama Regiment and served with Gen. P. D. Roddey's command until the surrender at Pond Springs.

Cloud House, 1001 E. 4th St. Robert Cloud bought this home in 1879 and lived here until his death in 1935. He served in the Confederate army, was wounded at Perryville and taken prisoner at Lookout Mountain, and spent 18 months in Rock Island prison.

Deshler Home and Institute, Main St. Maj. David Deshler founded Deshler Female Institute in 1874 in memory of his son, Gen. James Deshler, who was killed at Chickamauga. The Deshler Junior High School now occupies the site of the former home and school.

Johnson Home, north end of Mulberry St. on east side of North Commons. Headquarters for Federal officers during the war. Later the home of Col. W. A. Johnson.

Julian Home, 104 N. Dickson St. Main part of house was built at Cherokee Landing, later put on wheels and pulled by oxen to present site. A small door was cut in an upstairs bedroom during the war so that meat and valuables could be hidden. Lt. Col. William Reese Julian served under Gen. Roddey.

Helen Keller Birthplace, 300 W. North Commons. The home, which is known as "Ivy Green," was built in 1820. David Keller, grandfather of Helen Keller, and his wife, Mary, a second cousin of Robert E. Lee, were the first residents. Arthur M. Keller, Helen's father, was a captain in the Confederate army.

Locust Hill, 209 S. Cave St. Headquarters of Col. Florence N. Cornyn for a time in 1863. Damage during the Federal occupancy was estimated at $3,000. Col. Cornyn is said to have paid for "all the trouble and expense, then and there, in full," with $150 in Confederate money which he admitted he had taken from the tax collector. Unfortunately there seems to be no marker for the site where a tax collector relinquished funds.

St. John's Episcopal Church, 3rd and Dickson St. Federal troops camped near the church and stabled their horses inside the building.

TUSKEGEE, Macon County. US 80, 29.

Monument Square, center of business section, has a Confederate monument.

Tuskegee Institute National Historic Site, ½ mile northwest of town, was founded in 1881 through the efforts of Booker T. Washington. In 1896 Washington brought to the institute a young teacher, George Washington Carver, who had been born a slave just before the Civil War, later worked his way through school and received his master's degree in agriculture at Iowa State College. Dr. Carver's scientific experiments brought him international acclaim. The Carver Museum on campus has dioramas depicting black contributions to civilization, also Carver memorabilia. Booker T. Washington Monument on campus.

Varner-Alexander House, Montgomery St., was built in 1840 by William Varner. During the war the home, known as "Grey Columns," is said to have saved Tuskegee from fire when the commander of the Federal raiders found that Varner was a former fellow classmate at Harvard.

VALLEY HEAD, DeKalb County, east of IS 59. Dr. John S. Gardner, who tried to grow silkworms here, lived in Winston House, which later served as headquarters for Union Col. Jefferson C. Davis, a Kentuckian and cousin of the Confederate president. A perhaps apocryphal local story tells of an elderly fellow who happened upon the Federal encampment and is said to have asked Davis which paid the more, "Colonelin' the Bluecoats or Presidentin' the Confederates?"

WATERLOO, Lauderdale County. Waterloo Rd., about 30 miles east of Florence.

McCorkle's Drugstore, established in 1832, kept records showing numerous purchases made by the Federal army in 1863. After the war a claim was filed against the government, but was never paid.

Dr. Sullivan Home and Office, Waterloo Rd. The house was occupied by Federal troops who slept on the floor. Mrs. Sullivan spoke of having to step over sleeping soldiers in order to get to her kitchen to prepare breakfast for the family. A large square piano took up too much sleeping room and was tossed into the yard, but later was returned to the parlor.

Waterloo Methodist Church early in the war lost its pastor, Rev. J. B. Hardin, when he enlisted in the Confederate army.

WETUMPKA, Elmore County. US 231.

Elmore County Bridge, on Coosa River. West end of bridge has memorial in honor of Wetumpka Guards and other Confederate soldiers.

First Presbyterian Church was the point of departure for the Wetumpka Light Guard on April 27, 1861.

WHEELER, Lawrence County. State 20. Joe Wheeler State Park is named for Gen. Wheeler, who courted and married one of the Jones girls on the Jones Plantation, now the town of Wheeler. Park headquarters are just off State 101, 9 miles north of Town Creek.

ARIZONA

On December 30, 1853, James Gadsden, minister to Mexico, concluded the treaty which for $10,000,000 gave to the United States a considerable piece of real estate below the Gila River. Within three years this section of New Mexico petitioned for a separate territory. Tucson, the largest settlement in the Gadsden Purchase, was nearly 500 miles from Santa Fe, the territorial capital. Northern legislators, concerned with the extension of slavery into an area settled mainly by Southerners, managed to ignore petitions and bills introduced in behalf of Arizona.

In 1861 a Tucson convention declared the territory a part of the Confederacy. Granville H. Oury was elected delegate to the Confederate Congress. Capt. R. S. Ewell and other officers left their posts to enlist in the Confederate army. Forts were abandoned, buildings and military stores destroyed, and alert Apaches came in with a war whoop, harassing or killing all who did not escape to garrisoned Tucson or leave the territory.

In midsummer 1861, Lt. Col. John Baylor and Texas troops took possession of Mesilla Valley, proclaiming the Territory of Arizona to comprise all that part of New Mexico south of the 34th parallel with Mesilla the capital and Baylor the governor. The Confederacy, by dividing the area north and south, hoped to establish a path to California and to gain an open seaport on the Pacific, a port on the Gulf of California, and possibly the state of Sonora, Mexico. In any case, a continent-wide nation would have greater bargaining power in Europe.

Early in 1862, Texas cavalry under Capt. Sherod Hunter were sent to Tucson where they were welcomed by Southern sympathizers. Hunter saw Tucson as "a little old Mexican town built of adobe and capable of sustaining about fifteen hundred souls." Soon after arrival Hunter went into Pima country and confiscated 1,500 sacks of flour intended to help sustain Union troops based at Fort Yuma. A small squad of Union cavalry led by Capt. William McCleave from the Yuma base was captured. Col. J. H. Carleton, hoping to recapture McCleave, sent another cavalry detachment to the rescue. Lt. James Barrett and a cavalry detachment swung out to attack the Confederate flank while the main column was to strike simultaneously from the rear. Barrett caught up with the Texans before his support arrived. He and two of his men were killed. This action has by now acquired the prestigious title of "Farthest West Battle of the Civil War."

The Union, needing Arizona gold for a war-depleted treasury, got around to creating the Territory of Arizona in February 1863, dividing New Mexico east and west at 109 degrees longitude. The first territorial governor, John N. Goodwin, arrived the following year. By 1864 the white population was 4,573. Cochise and Geronimo had replaced the Confederates as the chief concern of the Union army in Arizona.

APACHE PASS, Cochise County. From junction of US 666, State 86, 9 miles east to Bowie. Marker is located beside State 86 at turnoff on Apache Pass Road.

Lt. George N. Bascom's unfortunate attempt to arrest Cochise at Apache Pass in February 1861, for a crime which he probably did not commit, made an important and implacable enemy of the Chiricahua Apache chief. In July 1862, 11 companies of Union infantry en route from Tucson to New Mexico were attacked here by Apaches led by Cochise and Mangas Coloradas. Hidden Indians surprised the soldiers with a musket volley, but they were routed by howitzer fire when the troops returned. This was the Apache introduction to cannon and they withdrew in short order. Lt. Albert J. Fountain, one of the victors, later reported a talk with Cochise who reminisced: "You never would have whipped us if you had not shot wagons at us."

Gen. James H. Carleton ordered Maj. T. A. Coult, 5th Infantry, California Volunteers, to build the fort with 412 feet of protecting stone walls, some 4½ feet high. Fort Bowie thereafter overlooked the only spring for miles and protected the Butterfield Stage Route. Foundations and fragments remain. The area is now a national historic site.

CALABASAS, Santa Cruz County. Two miles east of US 89 at a point about 10 miles north of Nogales. In 1856, U.S. Dragoons established a temporary camp here. Early in the war the California Volunteers reestablished the camp as Fort Mason, now a ghost town.

CAMP GOODWIN. *See* GERONIMO.

CAMP VERDE, Yavapai County. IS 17. A pioneer museum is maintained in a restored adobe building once part of the fort, now a state historic park 2 miles east of IS 17. Four restored buildings have military artifacts. Officers' quarters are furnished in period. Site first known as Camp Lincoln.

CANYON DE CHELLY NATIONAL MONUMENT, Apache County. US 66 at

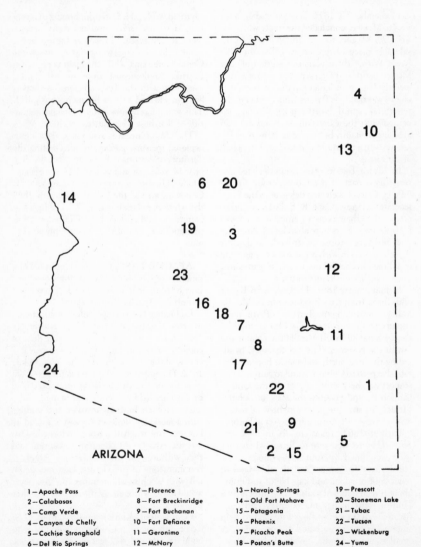

ARIZONA

1 — Apache Pass	7 — Florence	13 — Navajo Springs	19 — Prescott
2 — Calabasas	8 — Fort Breckinridge	14 — Old Fort Mohave	20 — Stoneman Lake
3 — Camp Verde	9 — Fort Buchanan	15 — Patagonia	21 — Tubac
4 — Canyon de Chelly	10 — Fort Defiance	16 — Phoenix	22 — Tucson
5 — Cochise Stronghold	11 — Geronimo	17 — Picacho Peak	23 — Wickenburg
6 — Del Rio Springs	12 — McNary	18 — Poston's Butte	24 — Yuma

Chambers, north on reservation road through Ganado, 3 miles east of Chinle. Navajos, like Apaches, took advantage of the Civil War's having drawn off state troops. Col. Kit Carson pursued warring Navajos throughout the summer and winter of 1863, until they holed up in Canyon de Chelly, once considered an impregnable fortress. On January 6, 1864, Carson's troops, in a state of near starvation, forced the surrender of nearly 7,000 Indians. From here they made the arduous "Long Walk" to a reservation at Bosque Redondo on the Pecos River in New Mexico.

CASA GRANDE, Pinal County. IS 10. *Casa Grande Valley Historical Society,* 110 W. Florence Blvd. Arizona's only Civil War battle at Picacho and the Mormon Battalion are depicted among historic displays. Museum is on both state and national historic registers.

COCHISE STRONGHOLD, Cochise County. Marker has been recommended for east side of US 80 between St. David and Tombstone. From this vantage point in the Dragoon Mountains, the great Apache led his warriors for 12 years of raids and was never dislodged from his stronghold. On the night of his death and burial, his followers raced their horses up and down the canyon until dawn to beat out every trace of his final hideout. *Cochise Visitor Center and Museum,* just east of jct., State 186 and IS 10, near Willcox.

COOLEY MOUNTAIN. *See* McNARY.

DEL RIO SPRINGS, Yavapai County. Marker on US 89 at road leading to the Del Rio Ranch in Little Chino Valley. Site of original Camp Whipple established December 1863. From January 22 to May 18, 1864, the offices of the territorial government of Arizona were operated from tents and log cabins here. Originally known as Camp Clark, it was renamed for Gen. Amiel W. Whipple, cartographer and army officer who had explored the area in 1853. Whipple was mortally wounded at Chancellorsville, May 1863.

Civil authorities accompanied by New Mexico Volunteers reached this site on January 22, 1864. Gov. Goodwin established executive offices, then set off with a military escort to inspect the area north of the Gila River. Richard McCormick carried on the operation of the government and in March began publication of the *Arizona Miner.* Six issues were printed before the government folded its tents and moved to Prescott.

FLORENCE, Pinal County. US 89, 80. Miss "Major" Pauline Cushman, actress and Union spy, once lived in a stucco adobe on West 6th St. Sentenced to death in Tennessee by orders of Gen. Braxton Bragg, she took to her bed, too ill to be hanged, and was rescued inadvertently by Rosecrans's advance guard. She survived to marry a Pinal County sheriff. *Pauline C. Tyler—Union Spy* is engraved on her headstone in the National Military Cemetery at the Presidio in San Francisco. The G.A.R. gave her a grand funeral.

Pinal County Historical Society Museum, 715 S. Main St., has no Civil War collection, but the barbed wire exhibit is worth a stop if you walk or drive around the fifth oldest town in the state which was settled in 1866 when war-seasoned troops were sent west to deal with Indians. Open afternoons only, Wed. to Sun., September to mid-July.

Visitor Center, 912 Pinal, in the restored Jacob Souter house, is a pleasant and informative small museum where you can pick up brochures and get directions to Cushman's former home.

FORT BRECKINRIDGE, Pinal County. At junction of State 77 with road to Aravaipa Canyon. Marker beside highway adjacent to ruins. The second military post in the Gadsden Purchase, garrisoned by troops from Fort Buchanan. Prevalence of malaria made duty here highly unpopular. The post was abandoned soon after the outbreak of the war. It was reestablished by California Volunteers as Camp Stanford in 1862. In 1866 it was renamed Camp Grant. Some foundations and walls remain.

FORT BUCHANAN, Santa Cruz County. State 82, 3 miles west of Sonoita. Established in 1857, it was abandoned shortly after the outbreak of war. Troops returning to the territory later built Fort Crittenden on a hill to the east.

FORT DEFIANCE, Apache County. State 264, 5 miles north of Window Rock in the Navajo Indian reservation. The fort was established in 1851, beat off an attack by some 1,000 Navajos in 1860, and was abandoned at the outbreak of war. The fort was reactivated in 1863 when Col. Kit Carson was assigned to conquer the Navajo. He established Fort Canby as a supply camp and base of operations, 28 miles southwest, between present-day Klagetoh and St. Michaels. It was abandoned in October 1864 after the defeat of the Navajo.

GERONIMO, Graham County. Site of Camp Goodwin on US 70 about 2 miles east of Geronimo. Established in 1864, it was the first U.S. Army post in the upper Gila Valley after Union troops returned to Arizona during the war. It was named for Gov. John N. Goodwin, who was then in office. The post was an important stopping point on the road from Fort Bowie to Forts Apache and Defiance.

McNARY, Navajo County. Cooley Mountain, on State 73 at Indian Pine, north of McNary. A landmark named for Lt. Corydon E. Cooley, a Virginian who served in the Union 1st New Mexico Cavalry. His ranch was a welcome stop for road-weary travelers. He is buried in the old army cemetery at Fort Apache.

NAVAJO SPRINGS, Apache County. Marker located on south side of US 66 at town of Navajo, where road turns off to Navajo Springs, 3½ miles. Site of first territorial government. During a snowstorm Gov. John N. Goodwin and other officials arrived from a four-month journey, via the old Santa Fe Trail, from Fort Leavenworth, Kansas; they took the oath of office December 28, 1863, and raised the Union flag at this spot. Government officials were not allowed to draw pay until they were within territory boundaries and performing the duties of office, so even though the party, escorted by Lt. Col. J. Francisco Chaves of the New Mexico cavalry, crossed what they took to be the Arizona-New Mexico line on December 27, they continued traveling to be quite sure. Lt. Col. Chaves took them some 40 miles farther west to Navajo Springs where water was available. The officials rode in three ambulances accompanied by cavalry and 66 mule-drawn wagons.

Chief Justice William F. Turner swore in the officials. A toast was drunk in champagne. Goodwin read a proclamation; Secretary Richard McCormick made a speech; cheers, prayer, and more speeches followed, and the snow-blown government was at last on salary.

OLD FORT MOHAVE, Mohave County. Site is beside the Colorado River, about 7 miles north of Topock, US 66. Marker is on north side of bridge approach. Western anchor of a military road across northern Arizona, the fort was among those abandoned at the start of the war. Buildings were burned and troops were withdrawn to Los Angeles. The post was reactivated in 1863, serving chiefly to protect a ferrying point on the road connecting Fort Defiance with California. Lt. A. W. Whipple, later killed at Chancellorsville, selected the site.

PATAGONIA, Santa Cruz County. Marker for Mowry Mine has been recommended for turnoff, State 82 and road leading to Lochiel. The Mowry Mine, about 14 miles south of Patagonia, was acquired by Lt. Sylvester Mowry in 1859. At the start of war the mine was producing about $1.5 million in silver and lead. Lt. Mowry, stationed at Fort Crittenden, was arrested by Union forces after the Confederates had retreated into New Mexico. He was jailed at Fort Yuma under charges that he had performed treasonable acts in making Confederate bullets at the Mowry. He was later acquitted and, though annoyed by the false arrest, he complimented his jailers on the brand of whiskey served and the hospitality of his guards.

PHOENIX, Maricopa County. IS 10, 17.

Arizona State Capitol Museum, W. Washington St. and 17th Ave. The inscription on the Confederate monument erected by the United Daughters of the Confederacy reads: "A nation who forgets its past has no future." Changing exhibits of early Arizona, artifacts, and documents are in wings. Guided tours of capitol.

Hall of Flame Museum, 6101 E. Van Buren St., has firefighting artifacts from 1725 with a number of pumpers, wagons, and other equipment of the 1860s.

Pioneer Arizona Living History Museum, 12 miles north of Bell Rd. via IS 17 at Pioneer Rd. exit. Some 20 original and reconstructed buildings of early days in Arizona. Costumed interpreters. A Civil War encampment occurs in late October.

PICACHO PEAK STATE PARK, Pinal County. Off IS 10 about 6 miles south of Picacho. The only Confederate-Federal engagement in Arizona took place at a spot with the redundant name of Peak Peak. On April 15, 1862, Texas troops under Lt. Jack Swilling were returning to Capt. Sherod Hunter's main base at Tucson when they were attacked by California cavalry led by Lt. James Barrett. Barrett and two of his men were killed; three were captured. A Confederate monument, about 2 miles north of battlefield, is dedicated to Capt. Hunter's Arizona Volunteers. Interpretative programs, seasonally.

POSTON'S BUTTE, Pinal County. Two miles northwest of Florence on Hunt Highway. Charles D. Poston, Arizona's first delegate to Congress, is buried atop this hill in accordance with his own wishes. Col. Poston was known as the "Father of Arizona" and was credited with influencing President Lincoln and Congress to create the Territory of Arizona. When Apaches increased their raids after regular troops were withdrawn, Poston's brother John was among the many victims. In 1863, Poston was made Superintendent of Indian Affairs for Arizona.

PRESCOTT, Yavapai County. US 89, State 69. Chamber of Commerce, 117 W. Goodwin St., has a leaflet for tours of historic sites.

City Hall has Pavi Coze murals depicting Fort Whipple and first legislature.

The Governor's Mansion, completed in 1864 for Gov. John H. Goodwin, is called a mansion in comparison with the shacks, tents, and wagons which housed most of Prescott's residents that year. The first permanent Capitol is said to have opened for business in a log cabin near here that proved too drafty. They soon moved to the newly built "mansion" where they convened before a roaring fire.

The John C. Frémont House, 1875, was the home of the once controversial "Pathfinder" while he served as fifth territorial governor. Furnishings and artifacts are of those years.

Old Fort Whipple, on US 89N, formerly Camp Whipple, was moved to site from Del Rio Springs and served as headquarters of the Military Department of Arizona. It was a command center during the Apache wars.

Sharlot Hall Museum, 415 W. Gurley St. On the grounds are the Sharlot Hall Building with artifacts of early days, clothing, tools, and weapons from 1864 on.

Site of the First Permanent Capitol, 1864–1867, on Gurley St. between Cortez and Montezuma streets. Arizona's first territorial legislature met on September 26, 1864.

QUARTZSITE, Yuma County. IS 10.

Hi Jolly Memorial, east on highway to old cemetery, is an interesting shrine remembering the Arab who came to Arizona with the camels which Jefferson Davis had hoped would be helpful in desert campaigns. Hadji Ali became Hi Jolly in soldier slang. The camels liked the desert but scared the horses, as well as mules, cattle, and probably gophers.

STONEMAN LAKE, Coconino County. State 87, south of Flagstaff. The site is named for the ingenious Gen. George Stoneman who was commanding in Fort Brown, Texas, at the outbreak of war, disobeyed orders to surrender

his troops to the Confederates, and escaped with his command by steamer to New York. He served with distinction throughout the war and was elected governor of California in 1883.

TUBAC, Santa Cruz County. Off US 89, about 20 miles north of Nogales. Marker in plaza. Tubac, a Pima word meaning "burned place," was the oldest white settlement in Arizona. When war service took the troops away in 1861, Apaches thinned the population to a point of no return.

The first Arizona newspaper began publication here on March 3, 1859. Its editor, Ed Cross, fought a bloodless rifle duel with Sylvester Mowry. No one was hurt, but the editor's luck ran out; he fell at Gettysburg while under recommendation for promotion to brigadier general.

Presidio State Historical Park has an underground display that shows the original foundations of the old presidio.

TUCSON, Pima County. IS 19, US 80.

Arizona Historical Society/Tucson Museum, near the entrance of the University of Arizona campus on Park Ave. at 949 E. 2nd St., has pioneer relics and extensive Southwest research material.

Armory Park, or *Plaza Militair,* S. 5th Ave. at E. 12th St., was used as camp and parade ground by the California Volunteers in 1862.

Fort Lowell Museum, 2900 N. Craycroft Rd., has old fort ruins. Reconstructed officers' quarters furnished in 1885. Changing military exhibits.

John C. Frémont House, 1858, 151 S. Granada Ave., is the community center. Another home used by Frémont during his service as territorial governor. Period furniture and changing exhibits.

WICKENBURG, Maricopa County. US 60, 70, 89. Marker is 2 miles west of town at the Vulture Road turnoff. The Vulture Mine is 12 miles southwest. One legend has it that Henry Wickenburg shot a vulture in 1863 and discovered gold nuggets when he went to pick up the dead bird. The mine, in any case, produced gold for the Union. Not open to public.

Desert Caballeros Western Museum, 20 N. Frontier St., has dioramas and artifacts showing the town's history.

ARKANSAS

Arkansas was admitted to the Union on June 15, 1836, as the 25th state, with its capital at Little Rock. Among the more than 435,000 inhabitants in 1860, some 111,000 were slaves. That year no one in the state voted for Abraham Lincoln; his name did not appear on the ballot. Sentiment, however, was fairly evenly divided at a March convention on the secession question which elected David Walker, an anti-secessionist, as president, and Elias C. Boudinot, a half-Cherokee slaveholder, as secretary. The delegates voted against secession but kept the gate on hinge by calling for a referendum to decide if Arkansas should take part in a conference of border states scheduled for Frankfort, Kentucky, in May.

Well before May, Sumter had fallen and President Lincoln had called for troops, assigning Arkansas a quota of 75,000. Gov. Henry M. Rector, without much fear of losing favor at home, sent Lincoln a flat no. A May convention in Little Rock passed the ordinance of secession by a vote of 69 to 1. On May 16, 1861, Arkansas became a Confederate state.

Fifty thousand Arkansans enlisted in the Confederate army. Thirteen thousand Arkansans, many of them blacks, served with the Union. The Confederate state government during its brief life had to move from Little Rock to Hot Springs, later to Washington, in Hempstead County, and briefly to Rondo, near the Texas border.

After Little Rock had fallen to Union forces commanded by Gen. Frederick Steele on September 10, 1863, Isaac Murphy, who had cast the sole dissenting ballot at the secession convention, was elected Union governor. Thereafter he presided in Little Rock while Confederate Gov. Harris Flanagin served at the provisional state capital in Washington. Roughly the line of the Arkansas River divided the opposing governments.

More than 450 military engagements (both land and naval battles) occurred within the state. The exceptionally bloody battle of Pea Ridge, or Elkhorn Tavern, was a major encounter of the war. While neither side managed to evict the enemy beyond state boundaries, Union forces soon gained an edge which was maintained to the end of hostilities.

In 1864 delegates again met at Little Rock, drew up a Unionist constitution, repudiated the Ordinance of Secession, and ratified the 13th amendment. The last skirmish took place at Monticello on May 24, 1865, 45 days after Lee surrendered at Appomattox. In 1868 Arkansas was readmitted to the Union.

ARKADELPHIA, Clark County. Off IS 40, US 67, State 8. A plaque has been dedicated at the site of the Confederate ordnance works. Once an important steamboat landing, the city has two colleges and a number of antebellum residences.

ARKANSAS CITY, Desha County. State 4, east of US 65, at Mississippi River. The earlier town of Napoleon had a lively if arduous existence. Nearly destroyed by fire when captured by Federal forces during the war, it was later captured by the Arkansas and Mississippi rivers. Its epitaph is given in Mark Twain's *Life on the Mississippi.*

ARKANSAS POST NATIONAL MEMORIAL PARK, Arkansas County. South of Gillett on US 165, State 169. The post was the first capital of the Arkansas Territory. Confederates built Fort Hindman here. On January 10, 1863, Gen. John A. McClernand's Federal troops, supported by Adm. David D. Porter's gunboat fleet, attacked the Confederates commanded by Gen. Thomas J. Churchill. After a two-day battle the post was held by Union forces. In 1960, Congress declared the post a national historic memorial.

AUGUSTA, Woodruff County. US 64, east of Bald Knob. In 1862, Gen. Steele's Federal forces occupied the town, camping on the lawn of the Woodruff County Courthouse, on 3rd St.

Augusta Cemetery, at the end of 3rd St., may just possibly contain the remains of

William Quantrill, rebel guerrilla. Quantrill reportedly died in prison; however, a Capt. L. J. Crocker, who moved to Augusta after the war, asserted before his death in 1917 that he was Quantrill and had escaped prison in a dress brought to him by his wife. Crocker, in any case, is buried here.

BENTON, Saline County. IS 30. *Kentucky Missionary Baptist Church,* State 5 off IS 30, exit 117, was occupied by both armies during the war.

BENTONVILLE, Benton County. US 71, State 72. Scene of a skirmish between Confederate Gen. Earl Van Dorn and Federal artillery led by Gen. Franz Sigel on March 6, 1862. Sigel retreated to the main Union force at Pea Ridge. The diary of Benjamin McIntyre, 19th Iowa Infantry, relates that, en route to camp at Sugar Creek near Bentonville in October 1862, the Missouri militia showed signs of disenchantment with carrying on the war: ". . . of which we were made aware by their comeing to a halt and declareing they could go no farther as the nature of their enlistment was such as did not compel them to go out of their state. But their Col was a man of emergencies, for mounting a stump he appealed to them in the name of God and patriotism and the state of Missouri." The appeal was successful.

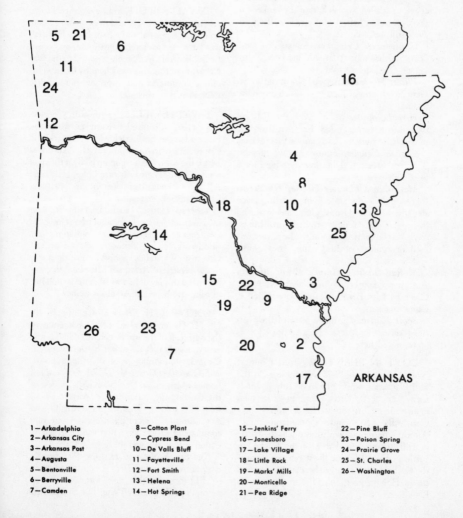

1 — Arkadelphia	8 — Cotton Plant
2 — Arkansas City	9 — Cypress Bend
3 — Arkansas Post	10 — De Valls Bluff
4 — Augusta	11 — Fayetteville
5 — Bentonville	12 — Fort Smith
6 — Berryville	13 — Helena
7 — Camden	14 — Hot Springs
15 — Jenkins' Ferry	22 — Pine Bluff
16 — Jonesboro	23 — Poison Spring
17 — Lake Village	24 — Prairie Grove
18 — Little Rock	25 — St. Charles
19 — Marks' Mills	26 — Washington
20 — Monticello	
21 — Pea Ridge	

BERRYVILLE, Carroll County. US 62, State 21.

Saunders Museum, 113 Madison, displays Col. C. B. Saunders's collection of firearms, among them the sidearms of Jesse James and Wild Bill Hickok. James took part in border guerrilla activities, and some sources give Hickok credit, if that's the word, for the death of Brig. Gen. Benjamin McCulloch at the battle of Pea Ridge.

CAMDEN, Ouachita County. US 79, State 24. During the Red River campaign, Camden was headquarters for both armies. Camden woolen mills turned out cloth for Confederate soldiers.

Bragg House, Rosston Rd., 4 miles west of town, was called "secesh harbor" by Yankee soldiers. A minor action took place in the yard. Wall still has a bullet.

Confederate Cemetery, Adams Ave. and Pearl St., has more than 200 markers for unknown Confederate soldiers.

Elliott-Meek House, 761 Washington St. Gen. Steele and officers were billeted here for a time.

Fort Lookout, off Gravel Pit Rd. on Ouachita River, guarded the town from the north. Rifle trenches and cannon pits remain.

Graham-Gaughan House, 710 Washington St. Gen. Steele had headquarters here for a brief time.

McCollum-Chidester House, 926 Washington St. Confederate Gen. Sterling Price slept here; later, Union Gen. Steele stayed overnight. War relics, original furnishings, Civil War bullet holes in walls. The setting was used for segments of the TV miniseries "North and South." Tours.

McRae-Godwin House, 305 California Ave., has cedar trees originally sent from Aquia Creek by John Powell who was later killed at Chickamauga.

Scott House, 2½ miles west of town on Rosston Rd. Confederate Brig. Gen. C. J. Polignac stayed here.

COTTON PLANT, Woodruff County. State 17, north of US 70 at Brinkley. On the Hill Plantation west of town on July 7, 1862, Gen. Samuel R. Curtis, planning a campaign against the Confederate-held capital, met Gen. Albert Rust and a Confederate force. After the battle, known variously as the battle of Hill's Plantation, battle of the Cache, or battle of Cotton Plant, Rust retreated across the Cache; Curtis changed his plans and moved toward Helena, postponing the attack on Little Rock.

CYPRESS BEND, Lincoln County. River moved, town died; site now in northeast corner of Cummins Prison Farm, but Henry M. Stanley, adventurer, once sold groceries, calico, and whiskey in a country store owned by Louis Altshul. Stanley enlisted in the 6th Arkansas Volunteers, survived a cholera epidemic in camp at Searcy, and was captured during the battle of Shiloh. He was released when he enlisted in the Federal artillery but was discharged for ill health, went to England, was wrecked off Barcelona, and returned to America where he joined the Union navy. Presumably, if the war had lasted longer he would have taken a tour of duty with the Confederate blockade-runners.

DEVALLS BLUFF, Prairie County. US 70 east of Little Rock. Federal troops camped here and built an arsenal and a large barracks which was later used as hotel, courthouse, and opera house. Federal Gen. Steele reported to the War Department that this was a healthy locality; his entire command had improved perceptibly since arrival in this area.

FAYETTEVILLE, Washington County. US 71, 62. Situated halfway between the Federal base at Springfield, Missouri, and the Confederate strongholds on the Arkansas River, the town was a common goal for the rival armies; consequently it often changed flags. All too often citizens lost homes, privacy, fences, horses, and salt meat.

Tebbetts House, 118 E. Dickson St., was used as headquarters by Federal troops in 1863. Confederate musket balls tore holes in interior woodwork. Judge Tebbetts was an ardent Unionist. War relics, period furnishings.

University of Arkansas Museum, on campus, has a display of historical material and furnishings from period Arkansas homes.

FORT SMITH, Sebastian County. IS 40, US 71. The city was taken by Confederates at the outbreak of the war but changed hands several times though no major battles occurred. Confederate monument on courthouse lawn.

Bonneville House, 318 N. 7th St., restored home of Mrs. Susan Neis Bonneville, widow of the dashing Gen. Bonneville, part of whose story was told by Washington Irving in *The Adventures of Captain Bonneville.* A onetime commander of the fort, Bonneville served as Union brigadier general.

Fort Smith National Historic Site, Rogers Ave. between 2nd and 3rd streets has remains of 1817 fort, and the "new" fort later used as supply depot in the Civil War. The city, named after Gen. Thomas A. Smith, dates back to 1817 when the first Fort Smith was established at the junction of the Arkansas and Poteau rivers. The second fort was established July 19, 1838. It was approved by the National Park Service as a historical monument in 1961. Museum has Indian, pioneer, and war relics.

Free Ferry Road is a street lined with antebellum mansions. Many early Fort Smithians owned large farms or plantations across the river. This road led to the free ferry that gave access to their holdings.

National Cemetery, Garland Ave. and S. 6th St., an enlargement of the old post cemetery. About 3,000 veterans, from the War of 1812 through the Korean War (both Federal and Confederate from the Civil War), are buried here.

Sebastian County Courthouse, east side of 6th St. between Parker and Rogers avenues. Confederate monument on lawn was placed here, it is said, rather than at the national cemetery because War Department officials objected to the inscription, which fails to recognize the Federal soldiers also buried at the cemetery.

HELENA, Phillips County. US 49 and Mississippi River. Known as Arkansas's only seaport, the city was a strategic prize during the war and was occupied by Union Gen. Samuel Curtis in 1862. On July 4, 1863, Confederate Generals Holmes, Marmaduke, and Walker attacked Curtis unsuccessfully. Marmaduke and Walker later settled a private quarrel by a duel in Little Rock. Walker lost the argument and his life.

Helena was the home of seven Confederate generals, most spectacular among them Maj. Gen. Thomas C. Hindman and Maj. Gen. Patrick R. Cleburne. Both led lively careers and died violently, although Cleburne was in his stocking feet at demise. Earlier that morning he had given his boots to a barefooted fellow Irishman from Little Rock, at the savage battle of Franklin, Tennessee.

Confederate Military Cemetery, north to Maple Hill Cemetery. About 100 soldiers are buried here in marked and unmarked graves.

Phillips County Museum, in public library, 623 Pecan St., has Civil War relics.

HOT SPRINGS, Garland County. US 70, 270. The war brought financial anguish to this famous spa, shutting off easy spenders from the North and sending Southerners to safer climates. Rather unexpectedly and unofficially, the city for three months in 1862 became the capital of Confederate Arkansas when Gov.

Rector, fearing a Federal invasion of Little Rock, took himself and state papers to the springs. The *Little Rock True Democrat* voiced a complaint as to the whereabouts of the government: "The last that was heard of it here, it was aboard the steamer *Little Rock* . . . stemming the current of the Arkansas River . . . decidedly inconvenient to those who have business to transact with the State."

JENKINS' FERRY STATE PARK, Grant County. State 46 about 12 miles from Sheridan. Here on April 30, 1864, Gen. Churchill and Gen. Walker led Confederate troops against Gen. Steele's Federal forces who were returning to Little Rock after an unsuccessful campaign into the southern part of the state. The encounter was bloody but indecisive. The battlefield became a state park in 1961.

JONESBORO, Craighead County. US 63, State 18. A skirmish occurred here in 1863 when Confederates drove out the Federal troops quartered at the Craighead County Courthouse. Present courthouse, South Main between Washington and Jackson streets, is on the site of the earlier structure built in 1859.

LAKE VILLAGE, Chicut County. US 65, 82. Town was occupied on June 7, 1864, by about 10,000 Federal soldiers recuperating from the battle of Ditch Bayou, which took place below the village. Gen. J. S. Marmaduke had harassed Union river traffic so successfully that Federal troops under Gen. A. J. Smith were sent against the Confederates at Ditch Bayou. The outnumbered Southerners withdrew after an all-day battle.

LITTLE ROCK, Pulaski County. IS 30, 40.

Albert Pike Home, 411 E. 7th St., was built in 1840 for Albert Pike, explorer, journalist, poet, and soldier. He served as Indian Commissioner for the Confederacy and led troops from the Five Nations in the battle of Pea Ridge. He quarreled with his superiors, sent a bitter letter to the Confederate Congress, and resigned his command.

Arkansas Territorial Restoration, 3rd and Cumberland St., a state-financed historical museum of eight original buildings. The Conway House is the former residence of Elias N. Conway, who was governor at the time of Lincoln's election.

City Park, entrance E. 9th and Commerce St., is on land acquired by the U.S. government for a military post in 1836. At the outbreak of war, the cantonment was seized by Confederate state militia who later tried unsuccessfully to burn the arsenal when they evacu-

Confederate forces were defeated at the battle of Pea Ridge.

ated the capital in 1863. The site remained a Federal army post until 1893. The arsenal, on the north side of the park, is the birthplace of Gen. Douglas MacArthur. Now a national historic landmark.

Mount Holly Cemetery, 12th & Broadway, has the graves of five Confederate generals; also has the grave of David Owen Dodd, who was hanged as a spy by Federal forces in Little Rock, January 8, 1864. Dodd was 17. He was captured in the woods near the Ten-Mile House on the old Southwest Trail by Gen. Steele's men and offered his freedom if he would reveal who in Little Rock had informed him about Union defenses. He chose death.

Old State House, W. Markham at Center St. The building, restored by the state, is an excellent example of fine antebellum architecture. It was Arkansas's first state capitol, the scene of the secession convention, and was much contested during the war. From this building the Confederate state government fled when Federal troops occupied Little Rock in September 1863. The United Daughters of the Confederacy Room contains lavish furnishings of the war period. On the lawn where Yankee soldiers were once photographed on dress parade stands the "Lady Baxter" cannon brought from New Orleans to help protect the city from Union gunboats.

MARKS' MILLS BATTLEFIELD, Cleveland County, north of New Edinburg, near the junction of State 8 and US 79. On April 25, 1864, Confederates led by Gen. James F. Fagan attacked and captured a 240-wagon Federal supply train, commanded by Lt. Col. Francis M. Drake and much needed by Gen. Frederick Steele at Camden. A number of prisoners were taken. Steele gave up his ambitions to advance his command toward Shreveport and returned to Little Rock.

MONTICELLO, Drew County. Junction of State 4 and 81. The last skirmish in Arkansas took place here on May 24, 1865.

PEA RIDGE NATIONAL MILITARY PARK, Benton County. US 62, 11 miles northeast of Rogers. The visitor center near entrance is open daily.

On March 7, 1862, some 16,000 Confederates opposed about 10,500 Federal troops here. Union forces under the quiet but able West Pointer, Gen. Samuel Curtis, had dug in at Pea Ridge. The daring and somewhat reckless Confederate Maj. Gen. Earl Van Dorn advancing from the south, decided to swing behind the Federals and launch a two-pronged attack. Historian Bruce Catton points out that Van Dorn's tactics had cut his own supply lines; his men were hungry and running out of ammunition by the following day when Curtis sent Franz Sigel's troops against them: "Sigel had one of his rare good days of the war, and the shattered Rebels were sent flying in all directions."

The Union victory, an exceedingly narrow one, saved Missouri for the Union and greatly influenced the course of the war in the Trans-Mississippi area. Losses were heavy on both sides. Confederate Gen. Benjamin McCulloch (who often wore a black velvet suit instead of a uniform) and Gen. James McIntosh were killed. Confederate Gen. William Y. Slack was mortally wounded. The battlefield was the first west of the Mississippi to be declared a national park; encompassing 4,278 acres, it is also the largest battle area west of the river. A seven-mile automobile tour of the field takes about an hour.

PINE BLUFF, Jefferson County, US 79, 65. In April 1861, several days before the attack upon Fort Sumter, a musket shot was fired across the bow of a Federal gunboat in the Arkansas River at this point. Because the act was carried out by regular troops acting under orders, and because Gov. Rector seized the cargo for the Confederacy, Pine Bluff citizens have a claim to the first shot of the war.

October 25, 1863, the town was occupied by Union troops who held their position by barricading the wharf with cotton bales, putting cannon into strategic locations, and spotting sharpshooters at upper-story windows. These efforts held off a Confederate attack led by Gen. John S. Marmaduke. The town remained in Federal hands thereafter. Homes on West Barraque St. date from the war period.

Purdom House is the restored 1851 medical office of Dr. James A. L. Purdom until his death in 1866. Medical artifacts exhibited.

Royston House, restored with period furnishings, was the home of Gen. Grandison D. Royston, who served in the Confederate Congress.

Weapons Museum has more than 600 firearms and sword weapons.

POISON SPRING BATTLEGROUND HISTORIC MONUMENT, Ouachita

County. State 24, 9 miles northwest of Camden. On April 18, 1864, Confederates under Gen. John S. Marmaduke routed a large Federal supply train commanded by Col. James M. Williams near Poison Spring. The battlefield, which is within a state forest, was made a state park in 1961.

PRAIRIE GROVE BATTLEFIELD PARK, Washington County. US 62, 10 miles

southwest of Fayetteville. On December 7, 1862, Maj. Gen. Thomas C. Hindman's Confederates, after a forced march across the mountains, attacked forces commanded by Gen. Francis J. Herron, en route to reinforce Gen. James G. Blunt's Federal troops who had skirmished at Cane Hill some days earlier. As matters worked out, Blunt reinforced Herron. Both sides laid at least tentative claim to victory. Hindman reported that the enemy fled the field at dark leaving dead, wounded, and regiment colors. When lack of food and ammunition forced the Confederates to retire to Van Buren, Herron reported, "the victory is more complete and decisive than I imagined." Battle lines are marked, buildings have been restored, and a museum contains relics. Exhibits and dioramas.

About 130 of the more than 3,000 acres of battleground are within the park. The visitor center has brochures for a 10-mile tour with 16 marked stops. A footpath leads to the Borden House that was used by Confederate snipers. The Morrow House at Cove Creek served as Hindman's headquarters, then as a hospital. Now a museum house with exhibits showing the "Effect of the Civil War on Ozark Culture." A number of other buildings also predate the war.

RONDO. *See* WASHINGTON.

SHERIDAN, Grant County. US 270W.
Grant County Museum, 409 W. Center, has Civil War exhibits.

ST. CHARLES, Arkansas County. State 1 at White River. During a battle on June 17, 1862, a cannon ball was shot through the open porthole of a Federal ironclad, the *Mound City,* on the White River. The ball, shattering a steam pipe, killed almost 150 soldiers on board and has been called the most destructive single shot of the war.

WASHINGTON, Hempstead County. State 4, north of US 67. Gov. Flanagin and his staff moved to this temporary capital when Union troops protected the town and it became a gathering place for Southern refugees. The *Telegraph,* one of the few newspapers in the Trans-Mississippi still publishing from a Confederate point of view, was occasionally printed on wallpaper.

Hempstead County Courthouse, now restored, was completed in 1833 and served as legal headquarters of the state from 1863 to 1865. State records were kept here until the end of the war, except for a time when the approach of Federal troops sent the temporary capital to Rondo, near Texarkana.

Old Washington Historic State Park, State 4, has several reconstructed or restored buildings. Among them:

Washington Tavern or Travelers' Inn, Franklin Ave. and State 4. The old Chihuahua Trail came down Franklin Ave. The inn (restored) was a stopover for many famous travelers, among them Jim Bowie. Legend has it that James Black, village smith, made the first of the popular Bowie knives much used in the war and elsewhere. In 1864, when Gen. Steele's forces threatened Washington, the state archives were removed to Rondo, in nearby Miller County, and were kept for three months in a general store. The old Rondo cemetery contains graves of 85 Confederate soldiers who died of disease while encamped there.

CALIFORNIA

In the national election of 1860, Abraham Lincoln carried California by a narrow margin. On May 17, 1861, the state formally pledged loyalty to the Union, although he received but one-third of the votes cast. Secessionists organized the Knights of the Golden Circle and the Knights of the Columbian Star. Gov. John G. Downey, who had taken office in January 1860, was thought to be sympathetic to the Confederacy. Unionists feared a possible uprising against the Presidio and Mint at San Francisco, the Monterey Custom House, the Mare Island Navy Yard, and the Benecia Arsenal. Authorities in Washington hastened to replace Gen. Albert Sidney Johnston, a Kentuckian commanding the Department of the Pacific. There were unfounded charges that Johnston would support secessionist plotters. Among fellow officers who spoke highly of the general's character and integrity was Ulysses S. Grant. The two generals led opposing armies in the bloody battle of Shiloh, Tennessee, where Johnston was mortally wounded.

The Far West was not asked to send troops to the eastern fighting front. Five hundred volunteers served with a Massachusetts unit. Regiments were raised to protect the overland mail and stage routes and to guard military and naval installations. California volunteers served to keep New Mexico and Arizona in the Union after these territories were invaded by Confederate forces from Texas, and they garrisoned Oregon and Washington posts. A principal contribution to the Union war effort was the steady supply of California gold.

A substantial number of California troops constituted a holding force north of Mexico to prevent incursions by the French-Austrian-Imperial Mexican troops; they maintained daily military patrols. U.S. Senator James A. McDougall, a former San Francisco lawyer, repeatedly introduced resolutions in Congress denouncing Napoleon III and the French intervention in Mexico. Ex-Senator W. W. Gwin, who left California in 1861, for a time represented the Confederacy at the court of Napoleon. Gwin's plan to colonize Sonora, Mexico, with Confederates was unsuccessful.

BENICIA, Solana County. West of IS 780 on north shore of Carquinez Strait.

Benicia Barracks and Arsenal was reinforced early in the war by a company of the 1st California Cavalry.

Benicia Capitol State Historical Park, First and West G streets, restored to the 1853–54 period when the Greek Revival building served as the third state Capitol. Furnished in period.

CAMP LINCOLN, Del Norte County. Off US 199, about 6 miles north of Crescent City. Marker on Smith's River Valley Road. Maj. James F. Curtis moved a temporary Camp Lincoln from Crescent City to this site on September 11, 1862. The commanding officer's quarters have been rebuilt on the original site.

COPPEROPOLIS, Calaveras County. State 4.

Federal Armory, south end of town. The building was headquarters for Union troops during the war. The massive iron doors are said to be the largest in the area.

FORT GASTON, Humboldt County. US 299. The fort, established in 1858, was the scene of an Indian skirmish on Christmas Day 1863. Officers' quarters adjoining the old parade ground are now used by staff members of the Hoopla Indian Agency.

FORT HUMBOLDT, Eureka County. US 101. Now a state historic park, 3431 Fort Ave., Eureka fort was headquarters for the Northern California District of the Humboldt. U. S. Grant served here in 1854 as captain of the 4th U.S. Infantry. The post was a group of log barracks and officers' cabins on a bluff above the harbor. Two companies, suffering from desertions, made up the garrison; Grant was relieved of his command on May 1, 1854. In 1862 several detachments of the 2nd California Infantry were posted here. The hospital, remodeled, has been moved a short distance from

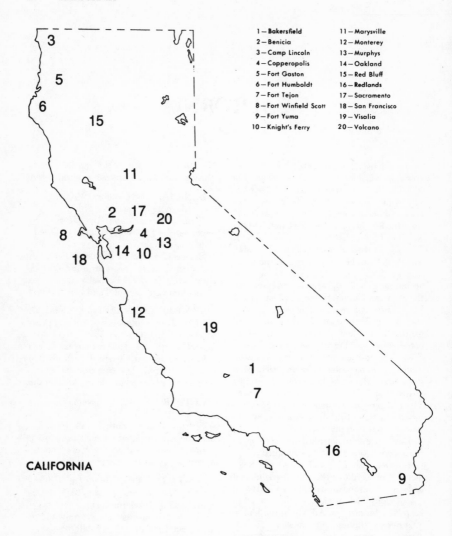

1 – Bakersfield	11 – Marysville
2 – Benicia	12 – Monterey
3 – Camp Lincoln	13 – Murphys
4 – Copperopolis	14 – Oakland
5 – Fort Gaston	15 – Red Bluff
6 – Fort Humboldt	16 – Redlands
7 – Fort Tejon	17 – Sacramento
8 – Fort Winfield Scott	18 – San Francisco
9 – Fort Yuma	19 – Visalia
10 – Knight's Ferry	20 – Volcano

CALIFORNIA

the original site. Officers' quarters are indicated by markers.

FORT TEJON, Kern County. US 99. The fort was established in 1854 to guard the pass through the Tehachapi Mountains. The famous "Camel Corps" was housed here, under the command of Edward F. Beale, then superintendent of Indian affairs for California and Nevada. Of 15 officers who served at the garrison, eight became Union generals, seven Confederate generals. The fort, now a state historic monument, was abandoned in September 1864. It has been restored and there is a visitor center on the grounds.

FORT YUMA, Imperial County. US 80, across the Colorado River from Yuma, Arizona. A strategic post on the southern transcontinental trail, the fort was garrisoned by California volunteers who, under the command of Col. James Carleton in the spring of 1862, moved against Confederate invaders of Arizona commanded by Capt. Sherod Hunter.

KNIGHT'S FERRY, Stanislaus County. State 120. The covered bridge over the Stanislaus River is said to have been copied after an earlier bridge designed by U. S. Grant. Lewis and John Dent, brothers of Mrs. Grant, operated a ferry here. Lewis Dent built the present bridge.

MARYSVILLE, Yuba County. Alt. 40, State 20. The *Marysville Express* saw the Federal troops as a "whining, runaway army" that disgraced the flag and "dishonored Republican chivalry all over the earth."

Mary Aaron Museum, 704 D St., has historical relics and documents.

Stephen J. Field Home, 630 D St. The residence of Marysville's first mayor, later appointed by Lincoln to the U.S. Supreme Court.

MONTEREY, Monterey County. State 1.

Larkin House, 510 Calle Principal, was built in 1835 by Thomas Oliver Larkin, U.S. consul to California. Sherman was a frequent visitor here during his stay in Monterey. Guided tours of the house and area, which is the Monterey State Historic Park, begin here. Visitors should register here.

Sherman's Quarters, Main and Jefferson St. In his recollections of California, Sherman wrote: "I had a small adobe-house back of Larkin's. Halleck [later Union Gen. Halleck] . . . not far off."

MURPHYS, Calaveras County. State 4.

Joaquin Miller Park, Miller Rd., is the site of the poet's former home. A mixed bag of monuments here honor Miller, Moses, and Robert Browning.

The Murphys Hotel, first called Sperry's, then Mitchler's, had Mark Twain, Gen. Grant, and Horatio Alger among its guests.

OAKLAND, Alameda County. US 50.

Oakland Public Museum, 1000 Oak St., has American and California history exhibits and Civil War items.

RED BLUFF, Tehama County. IS 5.

John Brown House, 135 Main St. In 1864 Red Bluff citizens raised money to aid John Brown's widow and three daughters, who lived here until 1870.

REDLANDS, San Bernardino County, IS 10.

Lincoln Memorial Shrine, Smiley Park at Grant and Eureka streets, has relics, photos, art, manuscripts, and books on Lincoln and the war.

SACRAMENTO, Sacramento County. IS 80.

Pony Express Building. 2nd and J St. Terminus of the Pony Express. In March 1861, Lincoln's inaugural address was carried from St. Joseph, Missouri, to Sacramento—1,966 miles—in seven days and 17 hours. Businessmen raised a purse of $300 for the star rider who brought a pouch of Chicago papers full of Southern war news a day ahead of schedule.

State Capitol, between 10th and 12th, L and N streets. Statuary, murals, and historical exhibits on the main floor and in the rotunda. Capitol Park has a collection of trees from Civil War battlefields. In February 1963, the legislature passed a resolution consenting to the placement of a memorial marker in Capitol Park honoring Californians, Union and Confederate. Marker was obtained by the Civil War Centennial Commission of California.

State Library, across from the Capitol, has murals depicting California history. The library was begun in 1850 with books donated by John C. Frémont, later a Union general. Extensive collection of early California newspapers, pictures, and relics.

Sutter's Fort State Historic Park, 2701 L St., has a bell which tolled for Lincoln's inauguration and for his assassination. In the fall of 1848, William T. Sherman, Edward Otho Cresap Ord (both of whom became Union generals), and a Capt. Warner camped abreast of the fort at what was known as the "Old Tan-Yard." Sherman recalled: "I was cook, Ord cleaned up the dishes, and Warner looked after the horses; but Ord was deposed as scullion because he would only wipe the tin plates with a tuft of grass, according to the custom of the country, whereas Warner insisted on having them washed after each meal with hot water. Warner was in consequence promoted to scullion, and Ord became the hostler."

SAN FRANCISCO CITY AND COUNTY. US 101.

Alcatraz Island, in the bay between San Francisco and Sausalito, was Gen. Albert Sidney Johnston's headquarters in 1861, when for a few months he was in command of the Department of the Pacific. Unionists feared a Confederate plot to take over military installations in California, and Brig. Gen. Edwin Vose Sumner relieved Johnston late in April. Gen. Johnston, whose high character was vouched for by U. S. Grant among other Union commanders, was killed at the battle of Shiloh. Alcatraz served as a military prison during the war. In 1863 it was garrisoned by 120 soldiers, having a barracks with accommodations for 600. Slide shows, tours. Part of Golden Gate National Recreation Area, headquarters at Bay and Franklin streets.

Fort Mason, also part of Golden Gate National Recreation Area. The commanding officer's house was built by Gen. John Frémont in 1853 when he served at the post.

Fort Point National Historic Site. Turn off Lincoln Blvd. at Long Ave. Built by the U.S. Army and completed in 1861, the fort was the main defense bastion on the coast and was constructed in a fashion similar to Fort Sumter. Now part of Golden Gate National Recreation Area.

Fort Winfield Scott, northern limits of the Presidio, near Golden Gate Bridge. The fort was reinforced in 1861 after the fall of Fort Sumter. It is the largest installation of its kind on the Pacific Coast.

The Presidio, Richardson Ave. and Lombard St. A U.S. military reservation, one of the oldest military stations in America. In April 1853, after surviving two shipwrecks in one day, William T. Sherman "footed it up to the Presidio." The commandant was not in, but his adjutant was. Sherman wrote: "I sent my card to him; he came out, and was much surprised to find me covered with sand, and dripping with water, a good specimen of a shipwrecked mariner. . . . Horses were provided, and we rode hastily into the city, reaching the office of the Nicaragua Steamship Company about dark. . . . " In the national cemetery is the grave of "Major" Pauline Cushman, actress and Union spy who was commissioned as honorary officer of the army. Museum.

Union Square, Post, Stockton, and Geary streets, derives its name from a series of lively pro-Union demonstrations staged here on the eve of the Civil War.

Wells Fargo Historical Collection, 420 Montgomery St. Historical relics, covering the period from the Gold Rush to the San Francisco Fire.

Western Business Headquarters, Pony Express, corner of Merchant and Montgomery St. A bronze plaque marks the site of the headquarters of the great Overland Freighting Firm of Russell, Majors, and Waddell, Founders, Owners, and Operators of the Pony Express. It is now a California State Historical Landmark.

VISALIA, Tulare County. State 63, 198. In the fall of 1862 a pair of Southerners, L. P. Hall and S. J. Garrison, bought the *Tulare Post* and converted it to the *Equal Rights Expositor.* Caring more for poetry than truth, they rewarded a group of women, who had raised $300 to support the gazette, with a fulsome tribute to "The Girls of Tulare":

"They are gentle and kind, yet with courage so rare,
They could whip all the Union men of Tulare. . . ."

The editors, no hair-splitters, saw Lincoln as a "long-shanked mule-countenanced railsplitter" and Congress as the most "corrupt crew that ever polluted the earth."

Tulare County Museum, in County Park, Mooney Grove, has relics of pioneer days.

VOLCANO, Amador County. State 88. Local legend says that Volcano's cannon, "Old Abe," helped to aid the Union; without firing a shot the formidable weapon held off a threatened Confederate uprising, else the area's gold might have gone to aid the Southern cause. There are a number of old buildings remaining.

COLORADO

Colorado Territory, established on February 28, 1861, was only six weeks old when the Civil War began, and neither the governor nor news of the shelling of Fort Sumter reached the area until May. The first legislature convened in Denver in August and selected Colorado City as capital. The second legislature met briefly in Colorado City in 1862 and adjourned back to Denver. Golden, offering a frame building and free firewood, became the next successful candidate for capital. Legislators met both in Golden and Denver until 1867, when the latter became permanent seat of the territory.

Colorado pledged loyalty to the Union but nearly as many Coloradans went to the Confederate army as to the Union. Gov. William Gilpin raised 11 Union companies, issued drafts for equipment without Federal authorization, and caused a temporary financial panic in the area; Gilpin was removed from office in 1862. Dr. John Evans of Chicago—a friend of Lincoln's—was appointed governor.

The territory exceeded by 30 percent her quota for enlistments; losses were heavy. Coloradans helped to defeat Confederate Gen. H. H. Sibley at Glorieta Pass in New Mexico, in the battle known as the "Gettysburg of the West." Some troops were garrisoned at frontier posts to protect settlers and wagon trains against increasingly active Indian raiders. The 2nd Colorado regiment was sent east, serving in the Oklahoma-Arkansas region. The 3rd Regiment went to Missouri where it fought in Gen. Schofield's Army of the Frontier, while the 2nd Colorado Volunteer Cavalry under Col. J. H. Ford patrolled eastern Kansas against guerrilla attacks led by Quantrill and other raiders. By 1864, Indian depredations had increased to such constancy that Gov. Evans called repeatedly on the War Department for the return of the cavalry. When his request went unanswered, he authorized the raising of a regiment known as "Hundred Days Men." These troops, led by Col. John M. Chivington, participated in the infamous "Sand Creek Mas-

sacre," during which Indian women and children were slaughtered in the attack on the Cheyenne and Arapaho village in southeastern Colorado. Chivington, born in Ohio, was a former minister. Far from subduing Indians, the affair aroused widespread protest, furious retaliation by united plains tribes, and endless controversy.

In May 1866, Congress passed a measure admitting Colorado to the Union. President Andrew Johnson vetoed it. Several other attempts to gain statehood were unsuccessful until August 1, 1876, 100 years after the nation began, Colorado became the 38th, the "Centennial," state.

BENT'S NEW FORT, Bent County. Off US 50, west of Lamar. The second fort built by William Bent was an Indian trading post, later sold to the government, named Fort Wise in 1860, renamed Fort Lyon in 1861. Volunteers known as "Gilpin's Pet Lambs" were posted here in 1861.

BENT'S OLD FORT NATIONAL HISTORIC SITE, Otero County. County 109, 194 E, northeast of LaJunta. Frémont used the fort as a base. Kit Carson was employed by Bent as a hunter. Confederate Gen. Sterling Price, en route to Mexico in 1847, stopped at Bent's Fort and hired William Bent as guide to Taos. The fort was a center of civilization on the Santa Fe Trail. Today's fort is a reconstruction.

BOGGSVILLE, Bent County. State 101, 2 miles south of Las Animas. Marker with bronze plaque. Last home of Kit Carson. Here on April 18, 1868, a daughter was born to Mrs. Carson, who died ten days later. Gen. Carson died not long after and was buried at Boggsville beside his wife. It was Carson's wish to be buried in Taos. More than a year after his death both Carsons were taken to Taos for reburial. Boggsville was named for Thomas O. Boggs, first settler, a friend of Gen. Carson and the executor of Carson's will.

BOULDER, Boulder County. US 36.

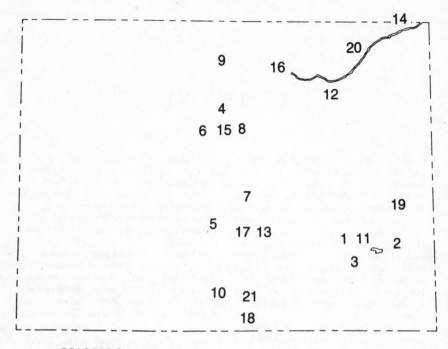

COLORADO

1 — Bent's Fort	7 — Colorado Springs	12 — Fort Morgan	17 — Pueblo
2 — Bent's New Fort	8 — Denver	13 — Fort Reynolds	18 — Raton Pass
3 — Boggsville	9 — Fort Collins	14 — Fort Sedgwick	19 — Sand Creek
4 — Boulder	10 — Fort Garland	15 — Golden	20 — Sterling
5 — Canon City	11 — Fort Lyon	16 — Greeley	21 — Trinidad
6 — Central City			

Boulder Historical Museum, 1206 Euclid Ave. The Boulder Historical Society displays relics from 1858 on.

BRECKENRIDGE, Summit County. State 9. After gold was panned here in 1861 in the Blue River, the community became a boom town. There were some 8,000 citizens when the war began. The town had been named for Vice President John C. Breckinridge who favored the Southern cause. Some townsfolk left to join the C.S.A.; those who remained changed the spelling of the town name.

CANON CITY, Fremont County. US 50. Joaquin Miller, poet, served as judge, mayor, and minister for Canon City at one period. During the war Miller was refused the use of the mails for a pro-Southern newspaper he was publishing in Oregon. Early in the war secessionists had a rendezvous at the A. C. Chandler Ranch near town on their way to Texas to join the Confederate army. In August 1861, Gov.

Gilpin appointed James H. Ford and Theodore H. Dodd to raise companies of infantry. They were assembled in Canon City and made up mainly from mining camp recruits.

Oldest House, Rudd Cabin in back of Municipal Building. One-room house built in 1860 has museum containing some original furnishings of the dwelling.

CENTRAL CITY, Gilpin County. State 279. Gold was discovered here in 1859, making the town one of the most important of the territory.

The Opera House, Eureka St. Edwin Booth, elder brother of John Wilkes Booth, performed here years after the war.

Teller House, Eureka St. In 1873, ex-President Grant walked along a path of solid silver bricks from his stagecoach to the hotel door.

COLORADO SPRINGS, El Paso County. IS 25, US 24.

Site of Colorado's First Capitol, Colorado
Ave. between 26th and 27th streets. The second territorial legislature probably met here
briefly in 1862; some authorities have put the
site elsewhere. Although the town advertised
its medicinal waters and the Garden of the
Gods, the governor and legislators soon returned to Denver.

DENVER, Denver County. IS 25, 70, US
40. Auraria and Denver City, mostly gambling
towns, joined as Denver in 1860, and became
the territorial capital in 1861 though its population was about 5,000 and Central City was
15,000.
Camp Weld, W. 8th Ave. and Vallejo St.
Marker indicates campsite. Denver Urban Re-
newal Authority has plans for a memorial at
this site. The camp was named for territorial
secretary Lewis L. Weld. Barracks cost $40,000
for materials; the labor was provided by soldiers. The 1st Regiment of Colorado Volunteers was organized with ten companies; John P.
Slough, a Denver lawyer, was commissioned
colonel.
City Park, between 17th and 23rd avenues,
has a plaque and memorial flagpole to Abraham Lincoln.
Civic Center, Colfax and Broadway, adjoining Capitol grounds. Monuments to prominent
pioneers and Col. Kit Carson and a memorial
colonnade. The Gettysburg Address is on a
bronze plaque on the north wall of the main
entrance lobby in City and County Building.
Colorado Historical Museum, 1300 Broadway. Exhibits include trophies of Col. Kit Carson; among regimental flags is the banner of
Gov. Gilpin's battalion known as the "Pet
Lambs." Two brass howitzers received in 1898
from New Mexico are on display. They were
buried in an Albuquerque garden in 1862 by
Gen. H. H. Sibley.
Colorado State Capitol, E. 14th Ave. and
E. Colfax. Gettysburg Address is on a bronze
plaque set in stone, south side of main west
entrance to the building. Here also is a plaque
with the full inscripton of Gen. Logan's Memo-
rial Day Order declaring the first Memorial
Day. In front of the Capitol is the Soldiers'
Monument, executed by Capt. John D.
Howland, a Civil War veteran. Four tablets on
the monument bear names of battles and of
Colorado soldiers who died in the war. Two
Civil War cannon flank the statue.
Likens Fountain, corner of Broadway and
Colfax, is dedicated to the memory of Sadie M.
Likens, who devoted years to aiding the sur-
vivors of the Civil War.

U.S. Post Office, 18th Ave. and Stout St.
The Gettysburg Address is on the wall of the
main corridor.

FORT COLLINS, Larimer County. US
287. A military post was brought here in 1864
from Laporte, and it was named for Lt. Col.
W. O. Collins, commanding officer at Fort
Laramie, Wyoming. The garrison protected
the Overland Trail and settlers in the Cache la
Poudre Valley. It has been said that many of the
settlers would have preferred the Indians to the
soldiers.
Fort Collins Museum, 200 Mathews St., has
a model of the old army post among displays.

FORT GARLAND, Costilla County. US
160. Established in 1858, replacing Fort Massachusetts. Volunteers arrived in December 1861
and were mustered into Federal service. They
soon departed to join Canby in New Mexico.
During the war, volunteers manned the garrison. Most regulars had gone to war.
The restored adobe fort is a state monument
with dioramas and frontier relics. Two of the
four howitzers buried by Gen. Sibley in Albuquerque in 1862, and later given to Colorado
by New Mexico, are displayed here. Col. Kit
Carson commanded the fort from 1866 until
1867. Carson and Gen. Sherman held a council here in 1866 with Ouray, Ute chief.

FORT LYON, Bent County. US 50. The
building in which Kit Carson died is now a
museum with Carson mementoes on display.
(*See* BOGGSVILLE.)

FORT MORGAN, Morgan County. IS 76.
One of the forts established in 1865 when In-
dian hostility increased to the point where
overland travel was virtually stopped.
Fort Morgan Museum, 400 Main St., in
City Park.

FORT REYNOLDS, Pueblo County. There
is a marker for the old fort on US 50, 1 mile east
of Avondale. The post was named for Gen.
John F. Reynolds, who was killed at Gettysburg
in 1863.

FORT SEDGWICK, Sedgwick County. US
138. The post was established in 1864 by volunteer troops to protect the overland route to
Denver. It was known as Camp Rankin until
September 1865. Outlines of buildings may be
seen. Julesburg, a Pony Express station, stood
east of the fort. In 1865 it was burned by Indians in retaliation for the Sand Creek Massacre.
Monument on site of old Julesburg.

GOLDEN, Jefferson County. IS 70. Territorial capital from 1862 to 1867.

Colorado Railroad Museum, 17155 W. 44th Ave. Displays of early railroad artifacts, cars, and records.

Lookout Mountain, Lariat Trail. Five miles west off US 6. At the summit, the tomb of Buffalo Bill Cody and the Cody Memorial Museum, which has relics and exhibits of Cody's life.

GREELEY, Weld County. US 85, 34. The editor of the *New York Tribune,* Horace Greeley, who advised young men to go west (and the Union army to go to Richmond), helped to establish a colony here, sending his agricultural editor, Nathan Meeker, to do the job. Meeker lived at 1324 9th Ave.

PUEBLO, Pueblo County. IS 25.

El Pueblo Museum, 905 S. Prairie Ave. Historical exhibits, dioramas, and reproductions of old Fort Pueblo.

Federal Building has four cannon balls on stone base in park adjoining building. The 15-inch shells were used by the U.S. Army and Navy from 1861 to 1865.

Roselawn Cemetery has Civil War memorial and cannons and shells with marker, erected in 1902 by the Women's Relief Corps, G.A.R.

RATON PASS, Las Animas County. US 85. Stone monument with plaque on mountain branch of Santa Fe Trail crossed by Kearney's Army of the West in the Mexican War, and by the 1st Regiment Colorado Volunteers in the Civil War.

SAND CREEK, Kiowa County. State 96, 10 miles north of Chivington. Site of massacre on November 29, 1864. Col. J. M. Chivington and Colorado Volunteers attacked Black Kettle and the Southern Cheyennes without warning. The Indians had assumed themselves to be under the protection of nearby Fort Lyon. Of 300 slain, more than 200 were women and children. No prisoners were taken. White losses: 10 killed, 38 wounded. Marker on the ridge overlooking site of Indian encampment.

STERLING, Logan County. IS 80S, US 6.

Overland Trail Museum, east of Platte River bridge on US 6. Historical exhibits.

TRINIDAD, Las Animas County. IS 25, US 350.

Kit Carson Park has equestrian statue of Col. Carson.

Old Baca House and Pioneer Museum, across from Post Office on Main St. Mementoes of Kit Carson and the Santa Fe Trail. Museum is maintained by the State Historical Society.

CONNECTICUT

Connecticut became the fifth state on January 9, 1788. At the outbreak of the Civil War, Gov. William A. Buckingham issued a proclamation calling for troops. Within the week, two regiments of 780 men each were enrolled and equipped. The Hartford Volunteer Rifles was the first volunteer company accepted.

In 1855 the Know-Nothings, who were predominantly anti-foreign and anti-Catholic, had succeeded in electing a governor, William T. Minor. During his administration an act was passed which forbade state courts to naturalize aliens; other legislation restricted suffrage. Minor ordered the dissolution of six militia companies composed of foreign-born (Irish) men. In 1861, however, the state suddenly marched to a different drummer. A bill was hastened through the Assembly to repeal the 1855 act of dissolution; the Irish were welcomed back to the service; and old grievances for the time forgotten, they came in vast numbers. Before war's end, 8,000 Connecticut Irish served the Union. In all, more than 50,000 Connecticut men joined the Union army.

BERLIN, Hartford County. US 5A, State 72.
Soldiers Monument, near the Congregational Church, Robbins St., is one of the memorials said to be the first erected to Civil War soldiers.

BRIDGEPORT, Fairfield County. IS 95.
Barnum Museum, 820 Main St. Memorabilia of Phineas T. Barnum and of "General" Tom Thumb. The Great Showman, Barnum, was 51 years old in 1861 but paid for four substitutes and also contributed heavily to the war chest. Barnum and his friend, Elias Howe, Jr., once fought a small skirmish with pacifists at Stepney, 10 miles north of town. The two gentlemen took to the Stepney peace rally two buses loaded with Union soldiers home on leave. A preacher was haranguing the North for aggression when he was chased into a nearby cornfield and Barnum was carried to the platform on his troops' shoulders. He gave a pa-

triotic speech. Howe also spoke briefly. "If they fire a gun, boys," he told the soldiers, "burn the whole town, and I'll pay for it." No shots were fired.
City Hall, State and Broad St. Bronze tablet commemorates site where Lincoln spoke on March 10, 1860.
Seaside Park, end of Main St. Entrance at Perry Memorial Arch on Park. Just beyond arch is the Elias Howe, Jr., statue. Howe, inventor of the sewing machine, had a large factory in Bridgeport. At the outbreak of war, he organized the 17th Connecticut Volunteers, was offered a commission but enlisted as a private. Crippled by a leg disability, he could not march with the regiment and was appointed regimental postmaster. When payday was late, he learned the amount of two months' pay for the regiment, $31,000, sent home for the money, advanced it to the paymaster, then stood in line with his fellow privates and gave his receipt for his share, $28.65. He died in Bridgeport soon after the war. The monument is located at the site where he camped with the 17th Connecticut when it was organized. A generous man, particularly to soldiers and their dependents, his estate was found to be quite small. There is a statue of Barnum in the park by the sea wall. Modeled by Thomas Ball and cast by Von Müller in Munich, it was unveiled July 4, 1893.
Tom Thumb Statue, Mountain Grove Cemetery, North Ave. and Dewey St., is as large (or as little) as Tom Thumb in life. The newly married Thumbs once lived on North Ave. after their New York wedding. It is said that Abraham Lincoln, receiving the couple at the White House, said: "My boy, God likes to do funny things; here you have the long and short of it." And Tom Thumb, when asked if he had any advice to offer on the conduct of the war, said, "My friend Barnum would settle the whole affair in a month."

CANTERBURY, Windham County. State 169.

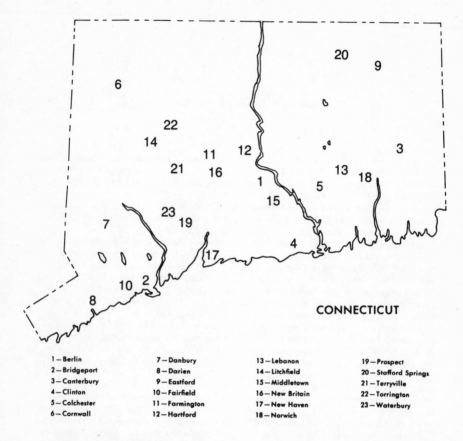

CONNECTICUT

1 — Berlin	7 — Danbury	13 — Lebanon	19 — Prospect
2 — Bridgeport	8 — Darien	14 — Litchfield	20 — Stafford Springs
3 — Canterbury	9 — Eastford	15 — Middletown	21 — Terryville
4 — Clinton	10 — Fairfield	16 — New Britain	22 — Torrington
5 — Colchester	11 — Farmington	17 — New Haven	23 — Waterbury
6 — Cornwall	12 — Hartford	18 — Norwich	

Prudence Crandall's School, known also as the Elisha Payne House, at southwest corner of village crossroads, at Jct. Routes 14 and 169. In 1832, Miss Crandall opened a school for young women, admitted Sarah Harris, a 17-year-old black girl who had attended District School with an excellent record for scholarship. So many parents withdrew their daughters that the school fell into financial straits and Miss Crandall elected to conduct classes exclusively for black girls. On April 1, 1833, 20 girls, recruited by abolition leaders from all over the East, were admitted to the school. As a result of community uproar, the legislature passed the "Black Law," prohibiting the establishment of a school for non-resident African-American pupils without the consent of local civil authorities. Miss Crandall spent a night in jail and was tried twice by jury and found guilty; then the Connecticut supreme court reversed the decision and ended her legal, if not social, difficulties. Miss Crandall and her schoolhouse suffered

continued abuse; rowdies attempted to burn her house, filled her well and smeared her walls with refuse, while presumably self-respecting merchants and physicians refused to serve her or her pupils. In 1834 she closed the school. In 1886, the Connecticut legislature voted that a pension of $400 be paid to Miss Prudence Crandall, then an elderly woman living in Kansas. Changing exhibits. Period furnishings.

CLINTON, Middlesex County. US 1, 81.
Wright Birthplace, 95 E. Main St. Gen. Horatio G. Wright was commander at the battle of Winchester where his rallying of his troops made Sheridan's famous ride possible. Fort Wright on Fisher's Island was named for him. Period furnishings.

COLCHESTER, New London County. State 2.
Soldier's Monument, on the village green, differs from many as it depicts an older man.

CORNWALL, Litchfield County. US 4, State 4.

Sedgwick Monument. Gen. John Sedgwick was born here in 1813. It is said he was offered command of the Union armies a number of times but declined. He often acted as commander-in-chief in Gen. Meade's absence. He served in the Peninsular campaign, was wounded at Antietam, and was killed by a sniper at Spotsylvania on May 9, 1864. Gen. Grant said his loss was "greater than a whole division."

DANBURY, Fairfield County. IS 84, exit 5.

Wooster Cemetery, Ellsworth Ave. The Soldiers' and Sailors' Monument is dedicated to unknown soldiers of the Civil War; it was modeled by Solon Borglum.

DARIEN, Fairfield County. IS 95, exit 13.

Civil War Cemetery, in Noroton Heights. The former Fitch Home for Soldiers has been razed, but the cemetery remains with numerous monuments to Connecticut soldiers.

EASTFORD, Windham County. Route 198.

Eastford Cemetery has monument to Gen. Nathanial Lyon, born in Eastford in 1818. Lyon was killed at the battle of Wilson's Creek, Missouri, August 10, 1861. He was the first Union general to die in action, and his funeral in Connecticut was attended by thousands.

FAIRFIELD, Fairfield County. IS 95.

Pulpit Rock, Unquowa Rd., across from high school. Dr. Samuel Osgood preached from this rock to open-air audiences during the Civil War. His home, Waldstein, was nearby on the rock ledge.

FARMINGTON, Hartford County. IS 84, exit 39.

Riverside Cemetery, Maple St., has monument in honor of Civil War dead.

HARTFORD, Hartford County. IS 84, 91, 86.

Bushnell Park, adjoining Capitol grounds on north, has two Farragut cannons, the "Dahlgren Guns," from the flagship *Hartford,* also "Andersonville Prison Boy," by Bela Lyon Pratt, honoring soldiers who died in Southern prisons. Over Trinity St., which bisects the park, is a Civil War Memorial Arch, monument to the 4,000 Hartford soldiers who served the Union.

Connecticut Historical Society, 1 Elizabeth St. Museum and library.

Harriet Beecher Stowe House, 73 Forest St.

Mrs. Stowe lived here during the last 23 years of her life.

Mark Twain House, 351 Farmington Ave., has many Twain items and a memorial library.

Museum of Connecticut History, in State Library, 231 Capitol Ave., has historical exhibits, Colt firearms collection, and portraits of governors.

State Capitol, Capitol Hill, has battle flags and historical relics, including the figurehead of Adm. Farragut's flagship. On the grounds is the "Petersburg Express," a mortar used by the 1st Connecticut Heavy Artillery during the siege of Petersburg.

IVORYTON, Middlesex County. State 9, exit 3N.

Museum of Fife & Drum, 62 N. Main St., has a Civil War musical exhibit.

LEBANON, New London County. Route 87.

Buckingham Houses, faces the Common. The birthplace and the original family homestead of the wartime governor, William Buckingham.

Liberty Hill Cemetery, on State 87, has the grave of Capt. S. L. Gray, whaling skipper who was killed when his ship was shelled off Guam by the Confederate raider *Shenandoah.* The captain's body, preserved in spirits, was brought home by his wife and buried in the cask instead of the casket.

LITCHFIELD, Litchfield County. State 63.

Stowe Birthplace, North and Prospect St. Harriet Beecher Stowe was born here on June 14, 1811. *Uncle Tom's Cabin* or *Life Among the Lowly* sold 300,000 copies the first year, and is selling yet. Dr. Oliver Wendell Holmes said in a poem: "All thru the conflict up and down, Marched Uncle Tom and old John Brown."

MIDDLETOWN, Middlesex County. State 9.

Mansfield House, 151 Main St. Gen. Joseph King Fenno Mansfield was born in New Haven, educated at Middletown and West Point. The general, who had served with distinction in the Mexican War, was far from young in 1861 but was determined to serve again. He commanded the Department of Washington, where he was responsible for engineering and building the defense of the Capitol. As commander of the 12th Corps he was mortally wounded at Antietam. He was buried at Middletown on September 22, 1862.

South College, High St. Chapel has com-

Connecticut foragers return to Baton Rouge with captured supplies.

memorative windows honoring Wesleyan men who were killed in the Civil War.

Union Green, Main St. at Pleasanton, has a Civil War Soldiers' Monument.

MYSTIC, New London County. IS 95.

Mystic Seaport Museum, IS 95, exit 90, State 27. The largest maritime museum in America preserves 19th-century vessels and artifacts of sea-going craft and shipyards. Living history demonstrations in some exhibits.

NEW BRITAIN, Hartford County. IS 84, State 72.

Fairview Cemetery, Smalley St., between Gladden and East streets. Joseph H. White, nine-year-old-drummer boy of the Civil War, is buried here.

Kensington Congregational Churchyard has Civil War monument, dedicated July 28, 1863.

NEW HAVEN, New Haven County. IS 91, 95.

East Rock Park, 1½ miles northeast at foot of Orange St. Soldiers' and Sailors' Monument, dedicated in 1887.

Fort Nathan Hale, Woodward Ave., is a reconstructed Civil War fort.

Gowie-Normand House, 317 Bassett St. Two miles north on State 15, exit 60. Private home built in 1840 has James A. Garfield memorabilia. Open all year by appointment.

Grove Street Cemetery, Grove and Prospect St. Among those buried here are Theodore Winthrop, one of the first officers killed in action in the Civil War; Rev. Lyman Beecher, father of Harriet Beecher Stowe; and Eli Whitney.

Monitor Square, Chapel St., Derby, and Winthrop Ave. Monument to Cornelius Scranton Bushnell, who was chiefly responsible for the successful building of the *Monitor,* using plans made by John Ericsson.

United Church-on-the-Green, formerly North Church. In 1855, Henry Ward Beecher preached to Capt. Lines's antislavery company starting out for Kansas. The congregation donated funds for Sharps rifles. Reportedly the rifles traveled to Kansas packed in crates marked *Bibles*. Beecher's Brooklyn congregation is also said to have contributed to the Kansas migration.

NORWALK, Fairfield County. IS 95, exit 14N.
Lockwood-Mathews Mansion Museum, 295 West Ave. America's "first chateau" was built during the busy year of 1864. A 50-room palace, now a National Historic Landmark. Restoration in progress.

NORWICH, New London County. IS 95.
Buckingham Memorial, 307 Main St. The home of Gov. William A. Buckingham from 1858 to 1860. The house served as headquarters for the Grand Army of the Republic for a number of years.

PROSPECT, New Haven County. Routes 68, 69.
Civil War Monument, on village green, was erected by the state in recognition of Prospect's having contributed a larger proportion of soldiers to the Union cause than any other Connecticut town; the number was greater than that of the registered voters.

SOMERS, Tolland County. IS 91, exit 47E.
James F. King Indian Museum, 332 Turnpike Rd., has Civil War memorabilia.

STAFFORD SPRINGS, Tolland County. Routes 190, 32.
Civil War Memorial, in business center, is a bronze statue of "Remembrance."

TERRYVILLE, Litchfield County. US 6.
Atwater Memorial, Baldwin Park. Dorance Atwater was captured at Hagerstown, Maryland, on July 6, 1863. Before he was 21, he had passed through six Confederate prisons: Libby, Smith Building, Pembertons, Belle Isle, Andersonville, and Columbia. At Andersonville

he was assigned to keep the death roll; he took the record with him, concealed in the lining of his uniform. It is now in the state library at Hartford. After the war Clara Barton and Atwater went to Andersonville to identify and mark Union graves.

TORRINGTON, Litchfield County. State 8.
John Brown Birthplace. House was destroyed by fire but marker denotes site where Brown was born on May 9, 1800. In 1805, Owen Brown migrated with his children to the town of Hudson in the Western Reserve of Ohio.

WATERBURY, New Haven County, IS 84, State 8.
Soldiers' Monument, on the green, was executed by George E. Bissell.

WESTBROOK, Middlesex County, IS 95, exit 65.
Military Historians Museum, N. Main St., has some Civil War uniforms including a nurse's cape. Also an extensive Civil War library.

WINSTED, Litchfield County. State 44.
Simon Rockwell House, 225 Prospect St. Civil War memorabilia.

WOODSTOCK, Putnam County. Route 169.
Roseland Cottage, Route 169, is an intriguing mixed bag of 19th-century memorabilia. The 1846 "cottage" is pink outside and even more astonishing indoors. Henry Brown, merchant and publisher, who was the builder, hosted presidents Grant, Hayes, Harrison, and McKinley, and Henry Ward Beecher. Brown was an abolitionist.

DELAWARE

In Delaware, first of the 13 colonies to ratify the Constitution, the law from 1776 onward made it illegal to import or export slaves. By 1860 less than one black resident in twelve was still a slave. Quakers maintained a branch of the Underground Railroad helping fugitives escape to the North. In the 1860 national election, John Breckinridge, proslavery candidate, received a majority of Delaware votes, but when war came, the state, though bitterly divided in feeling, supported the Union. Two wartime governors, Democrat William Burton and former Democrat William Cannon, who ran on the Union ticket, remained loyal to the Federal government.

There were few abolitionists or secessionists, but there were substantial numbers of neutralists. Although an undetermined number of citizens joined the rebellion, there were no organized Delaware troops sent to the Confederacy. Union units included nine infantry regiments, one of cavalry, and one of artillery; many volunteers joined the regular army, the navy, and regiments of other states. Gen. H. H. Lockwood, Gen. A. T. A. Torbert, Gen. Thomas A. Smyth, Rear Adm. Samuel F. du Pont, and Col. Henry A. du Pont were Union officers. Gen. Smyth, a former Wilmington coachmaker, was the last general officer killed in the war. He was wounded by a Virginia sharpshooter on April 4, 1865, and died two days later. The du Pont powder mills made a major contribution to the Union war effort. A newly developed du Pont powder gave a longer range to naval guns.

CHESAPEAKE AND DELAWARE CANAL, New Castle County. US 13. The canal, which may be crossed in the village of St. Georges, was of strategic importance in the war. Troops and supplies were brought from Philadelphia to Washington via the waterway, which was then a lock canal of relatively shallow draught.

DELAWARE CITY, New Castle County. On Delaware River. Site is reached by a 10-minute boat ride. Museum and audio-visual presentation.

Fort Delaware, on Pea Patch Island. Now a state park, the fort was completed in 1860 and served as a Federal prison during the war. There were 12,500 prisoners on the island in August 1863. Among generals imprisoned here on occasion were: Joseph Wheeler of Alabama; Basil Duke of Kentucky; Franklin Gardner of Louisiana; G. H. Steuart and J. J. Archer of Maryland; Jeff Thompson of Missouri; J. J. Pettigrew and Robert Vance of North Carolina; and E. S. Johnson of Virginia.

DOVER, Kent County. US 13.

Delaware State House, east side of village green on S. State St. The second oldest state house still in use. Portraits of war heroes and statesmen are in the corridors. The Capitol was occupied by Federal troops.

Delaware State Museum, 316 S. Governor's Ave. US 13A. Historical exhibits include costumes, furnishings, silverware, and early fire-fighting and woodworking tools.

Woodburn, 151 Kings Hwy., was a legendary station on the Underground Railway, now the governor's mansion.

GEORGETOWN, Sussex County. US 113. Birthplace, January 30, 1841, of George Alfred Townsend, Civil War correspondent, author of *Campaigns of a Non-Combatant.* Also the birthplace of Gen. A. T. A. Torbert.

LEWES, Sussex County. (Pronounced Lewis) State 14.

Memorial Park, on the Canal Basin, has a 6-pound gun which was fired during the war to celebrate Union victories; when Lincoln was reelected in 1864, Southern sympathizers reportedly hid the gun so well it was not recovered for 50 years.

NORTH MILFORD, Kent County. US 113.

Christ Episcopal Church, southwest corner 3rd and Church St. Gov. William Burton, who served from 1859 to 1863, is buried here.

Old Methodist Episcopal Cemetery, North and 3rd St. Maj. Gen. A. T. A. Torbert is buried here. He was drowned in a shipwreck in 1880.

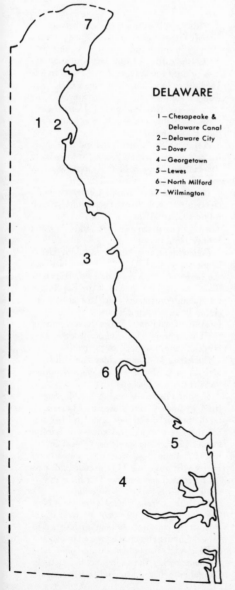

DELAWARE

1 — Chesapeake &
    Delaware Canal
2 — Delaware City
3 — Dover
4 — Georgetown
5 — Lewes
6 — North Milford
7 — Wilmington

Torbert House, southwest corner N. Walnut and 2nd St. Gen. Torbert was graduated from West Point in 1855, served in the Indian campaigns before the Civil War, led his regiment in the Peninsular campaign, and was wounded at Antietam. He was made major general in 1864, and later became U.S. minister resident to Central America and consul general at Havana and at Paris.

ODESSA, New Castle County. US 301. The town was a major station on the Underground Railroad before the war.

WILMINGTON, New Castle County. IS 95.

Admiral Samuel F. Du Pont Statue, south of Rockford Tower at Tower Rd. and W. 19th St. S. F. du Pont received the rank of rear admiral for a naval victory at Port Royal. He was defeated at Charleston in 1863, having followed orders with which he did not agree, and was relieved at his own request. He served on boards and commissions thereafter until his death in June 1865.

Hagley Museum, Barley Mill Rd. and Brandywine Creek, northwest of city. Early industrial buildings include E. I. du Pont's first powder mills. Dioramas and recordings illustrate powder-making operations. Shortly after the outbreak of the Civil War, Henry du Pont, a West Point graduate, canceled orders for Virginia business in the event that Virginia might secede and let Lincoln know he could count on the du Pont powder mills. Henry became major general commanding Delaware's Volunteers, although he took no active part in military action. His eldest son, Henry Algernon, also a West Point graduate, served with the artillery. Throughout the war, permanent guards were posted in the Brandywine area to protect the vitally important supply center. Du Pont furnished the Union about 4 million pounds of powder, some of which—known as du Pont's Mammoth Powder—provided naval guns with a range greater than any previously known.

Old Town Hall, 512 Market St. The museum has historical relics; the library has maps, newspapers, and documents on Delaware history.

Soldiers and Sailors Monument, Delaware Ave., W. 14th and N. Broom St. Monument to Delaware's Civil War dead was unveiled in 1871.

University of Delaware, Goodstay Center, Pennsylvania Ave., has more than 2,000 items pertaining to Abraham Lincoln's life.

Wilmington and Brandywine Cemetery, Delaware Ave., Madison and Adams St. Gen. Thomas A. Smyth is buried here.

DISTRICT OF COLUMBIA

The population of Washington in 1860 was slightly more than 61,000; temporary wartime population nearly doubled that. Late in April 1861, the capital was wild with rumors of Southern invasion, of plots to kidnap the president and cabinet. Kentuckian Cassius Clay and Kansan James Lane organized companies of vigilantes who were placed under the command of Maj. David Hunter; one was stationed at Willard's Hotel and the other, the Frontier Guards, at the executive mansion where they drilled and bedded down in the East Room. The first troops to arrive were a company of regulars from Minnesota and 460 Pennsylvania volunteers. The Pennsylvanians were billeted in the Capitol. Maj. Irvin McDowell directed the defense of the building: paintings, sculpture, and windows were boarded over, doors were blockaded with planks, stones, and cement casks; iron plates intended for the unfinished dome were used to protect the porticoes. Guards were posted at the Treasury and similar precautions were taken to defend the building; even so, Lincoln, thinking he'd heard a cannon boom, walked out to have a look at the Arsenal, found the doors open, no guards posted, and the arms available to the passerby.

When secessionist rioters in Baltimore attacked the 6th Massachusetts en route to Washington and seized the telegraph office, the capital was isolated without communication and without much hope of getting expected reinforcements. Maryland railroad bridges were being burned. Lincoln is said to have told the Massachusetts Volunteers: "I don't believe there is any North. The Seventh Regiment is a myth. Rhode Island is not known in our geography any longer. You are the only Northern realities." Next day the New Yorkers arrived, with kid gloves and crossbelts and feeling they'd already experienced the hardships of war, having had to leave a thousand velvet-covered campstools at Annapolis. After a parade, they took up quarters in the Capitol, calling it the Big Tent and explaining that the top was left open for ventilation.

Although Washington soon became an armed camp—even the Patent Office became a military hospital and cowsheds became bakeries—the threat of Confederate invasion was present until the latter part of the war. In July 1864, Gen. Jubal Early and some 19,000 Confederate soldiers attacked Fort Stevens. The garrison, commanded by Gen. Horatio Gouverneur Wright, repulsed the Southerners and the city was saved.

American Red Cross, 17th and D St. NW. Inscription over portico reads: "In Memory of the Heroic Women of the Civil War." A museum has Civil War exhibits.

Battleground National Cemetery, 6625 Georgia Ave. NW, has the graves of 41 Union soldiers killed at the battle of Fort Stevens. There are monuments for New York, Ohio, and Pennsylvania troops.

Blair House, now known as the President's Guest House, 1651 Pennsylvania Ave. NW, was the home of Missouri's statesman, Francis P. Blair, one of the founders of the Republican party, and Montgomery Blair, Postmaster General in Lincoln's administration. In this house Lincoln offered Robert E. Lee the command of the Union army. House reserved for visiting heads of state, not open to the public.

Buchanan Monument, Meridian Hill Park, 16th St. and Florida Ave. Memorial honors President James Buchanan.

Capitol Prison, 1st and A St. SE. Site of the Old Brick Capitol, used by Congress after the British burned the Capitol in 1814; during the Civil War it was known as Capitol Prison. Confederate spies Rose O'Neal Greenhow and Belle Boyd were imprisoned here. Henry Wirz was hanged in the courtyard, having been tried and sentenced for his maltreatment of prisoners at Andersonville.

DuPont Circle, Massachusetts, New Hampshire, and Connecticut avenues, P and 19th streets converge. A fountain designed by Daniel Chester French was erected in memory of Rear Adm. Samuel Francis du Pont.

Emancipation Statue, in Lincoln Park on E. Capitol St. between 13th and 14th streets NE.

Sculptor Thomas Ball depicted Lincoln liberating a slave and was paid by donations from former slaves, dedicated in 1876, with Frederick Douglass in attendance.

Ericsson Memorial, west end of West Potomac Park, Constitution Ave., honors John Ericsson, inventor of the screw propeller who designed and built the *Monitor* in 1861.

Farragut Square, I, K, and 17th streets, has heroic bronze statue of Adm. David G. Farragut cast from metal taken from the flagship *Hartford.*

Ford's Theatre, 511 10th St. NW, where Lincoln was shot by John Wilkes Booth on the evening of April 14, 1865, has been restored. Museum contains artifacts relating to the assassination. Talks given 9:30 A.M. to 4:30 P.M., except when live productions are in rehearsal or performance. A National Historic Site.

Fort Dupont, Alabama Ave. SE, was one of the defenses erected in 1861 for protection of the capital. It has been restored.

Fort Stevens, Piney Branch Rd. and Quackenbos St. NW. Originally called Fort Massachusetts, the fort, in conjunction with Fort Slocum, commanded the northern approach to the capital. It was enlarged in 1862 and renamed Fort Stevens April 1, 1863, after Brig. Gen. Isaac Ingalls Stevens, who was killed in the battle of Chantilly in 1862. Emory Chapel now stands on the site of the eastern magazine; the western magazine has been reconstructed. The garrison under Gen. Wright repulsed Confederates under Gen. Early on July 11–12, 1864. Losses totaled nearly 900 killed and wounded. Lincoln stood on a parapet watching the battle; this was the only occasion on which an American president has been under fire of enemy guns while in office.

Frederick Douglass Home National Historic Site, 1411 W St. SE, has period furnishings. This was the last home of the former slave who became a black leader and minister to Haiti. Visitor center and film.

Garfield Monument, 1st St. and Maryland Ave. SW. Memorial honors President James G. Garfield, Union general from Ohio during the Civil War.

Grant Memorial, on the Mall at 1st St. SW, is one of the largest equestrian statues in the world. The monument has 12 horses, 11 soldiers, and four lions; Sculptor Henry M. Shrady took 22 years to complete the memorial, which was dedicated on April 27, 1922, 100th anniversary of Grant's birth.

Hancock Monument, 7th St. and Pennsylvania Ave. NW. Equestrian statue honors Gen. Winfield S. Hancock, who served in many

campaigns and was one of 15 officers given the thanks of Congress for service at Gettysburg.

Holt House, northeast corner of New Jersey Ave. and C St. SE. Site of home of Judge Joseph Holt, Buchanan's Secretary of War, later presiding judge at the trial and execution of Mary E. Surratt, conspirator in Lincoln's assassination.

Lafayette Square, across from the White House. Among notables who once lived on the square: John C. Calhoun, William H. Seward, and James G. Blaine. A sculptured Andrew Jackson, on his horse, has occupied the center spot since 1853. *Decatur House Museum,* 748 Jackson Pl., has been the home of many statesmen; now operated by the National Trust for Historic Preservation. During President John F. Kennedy's administration, plans were made to raze the old houses for the construction of an executive office building and court of claims. Mrs. Kennedy managed to have new plans drawn up so that many of the finest small structures could be spared.

Library of Congress, 10 1st St. SE. The library contains more than 12 million books and pamphlets; more than 17 million manuscripts; extensive collections of maps, prints, photographs, periodicals, and music. Among the many notable exhibits are the first and second drafts of Lincoln's Gettysburg Address.

Lincoln Memorial, W. Potomac Pk. at 23 St. NW, at the Washington approach to the Arlington Memorial Bridge. The 36 columns of the memorial symbolize the Union; there were 36 states in Lincoln's time. The seated Lincoln was designed by Daniel Chester French; it was carved from 28 blocks of Georgia white marble by the Picirilli brothers of New York; the pedestal is of Tennessee marble. The building is of white Colorado-Yule marble; interior walls are Indiana limestone, panels of Alabama marble. Lincoln's Gettysburg Address is carved on the south wall; north wall has the Second Inaugural Address.

Lincoln Statue, Judiciary Park, H and 5th streets. Also in the park is the Pension Building which has a frieze depicting Civil War troops.

Lincoln Under Fire Plaque, Fort Stevens Park, Piney Branch Rd. and Quakenbush St. (*Also see Fort Stevens.*)

Manger-Hay-Adams Hotel, 16th and H St. NW. Henry Adams and John Hay once lived at this site.

Marine Corps Museum, 9th and M streets SE, Bldg. 58 in the Navy Yard, has exhibits depicting the corps' history for more than 200 years, with dioramas, flags, uniforms, firearms, etc.

The 7th Regiment (New York) en route to Washington, D.C.

McClellan Monument, Connecticut Ave. and California St. NW. Equestrian statue of Gen. George E. McClellan.

McPherson Square, 15th and I St. NW, has statue of Gen. James Birdseye McPherson, who was killed at the battle of Atlanta.

Meade Statue, Union Square, 1st St. opposite Capitol, honors Gen. George G. Meade.

Museum of History and Technology, Constitution Ave., 14th and 12th streets. The building has exhibits formerly housed in the Smithsonian.

National Archives, Constitution Ave., between 7th and 9th streets NW. The Exhibition Hall has the Declaration of Independence, the Constitution, the Bill of Rights, and other documents on display.

National Firearms Museum, 1600 Rhode Island Ave. NW. Civil War weapons among exhibits.

National Gallery of Art, 7th and 4th streets, Constitution Ave. and Madison Dr. An illustrated catalog with map is available free at the information desk. Conducted tours are available.

National Historical Wax Museum, 500 26th St. NW. Among tableaux are Lee and Grant at Appomattox and the assassination of Lincoln at Ford's Theater. Among figures are Thomas J. Jackson, George Washington Carver, Harriet Beecher Stowe, and Clara Barton.

National Portrait Gallery, in the S wing of the Old Patent Office Bldg. between 7th, 9th, G and F streets, is part of the Smithsonian Institution. The building served as a Civil War hospital. Lincoln's second inaugural ball was held here. Now restored. A gallery devoted to Civil War exhibits includes the last photograph taken of Lincoln and Mathew Brady photographs.

Navy Museum, Bldg. 76, Washington Navy Yard, 9th and M streets SE, has the history of the Navy from the Revolution to the present.

New York Avenue Presbyterian Church, New York Ave. and H St. The building was completed in 1861. Presidents Buchanan, Lincoln, and Andrew Johnson attended services here. The Lincoln pew has been preserved; the tower chimes were a gift of Robert Todd Lincoln. Lincoln's hitching post and the original manuscript of his proposal to abolish slavery are on display.

Nuns of the Battlefield, Rhode Island Ave. and M St. NW. One of the nuns honored by the bas-relief memorial is Mother St. Pierre Harrington, mother superior of the Ursuline Convent at Galveston when it was shelled by the Union navy, which mistook it for a Confederate base.

Oak Hill Cemetery, 28th, 29th, and 30th streets in Georgetown, has the graves of Edwin Stanton, Lincoln's Secretary of War, and James G. Blaine. During part of the war Blaine was representative from Maine.

Petersen House, 516 10th St. NW, across from Ford's Theater. Lincoln was carried here after being shot by John Wilkes Booth on the night of April 14, 1865, and he died here the following morning. Rooms are restored to original appearance.

Pike Monument, Indiana Ave. and 3rd St. NW. Memorial honors Confederate Gen. Albert Pike, who helped to win the Five Nations of Indian Territory to the Confederate cause.

President's Park, Pennsylvania Ave. One part of the park is the 18 acres within the iron fence of the executive mansion; the other is a 52-acre area which includes the Ellipse. There is an equestrian statue of Gen. William T. Sherman in the park.

Rawlins Square, E St., has a statue of Gen. John A. Rawlins.

Robert Lincoln House, 3014 N St., Georgetown. Robert Lincoln bought the house of Judge Dunlop, Supreme Court member who was deposed by President Lincoln because of Southern leanings. Robert Todd Lincoln lived here until his death in 1926.

Rock Creek Park, in northwest Washington following Rock Creek, contains the remains of *Fort De Russy,* one of the 68 forts that circled the city for defense. Near Oregon Ave. and Military Rd., it can be reached by foot. Civil War battlefield hikers can call park headquarters at (202) 426-6832.

St. John's Church, 3240 O St. NW. Every president since Madison has attended services. Windows honor statesmen.

Scott Circle, Massachusetts Ave. and 16th St. NW, has statue of Gen. Winfield Scott, who was a year older than the Constitution and general-in-chief of the army in 1861.

Sheridan Circle, Massachusetts Ave., honors Gen. Philip Sheridan.

Smithsonian Institution, the Mall north of Independence Ave. between 12th and 9th streets. Many historical exhibits are in the new Museum of History and Technology on the north side of the Mall. The Medical Museum and Library was founded in 1862 with specimens from Civil War battlefields.

Thomas Circle, two blocks east on Massachusetts Ave. at Vermont, 14th, and M St. NW, is dedicated to the memory of Maj. Gen. George H. Thomas, the "Rock of Chickamauga."

United States Capitol, between Constitution and Independence avenues. The 258-foot dome was erected during the Civil War. Lincoln was said to have announced: "If people see the Capitol going on it will be a sign to them that we intend the Union shall go on." The Statue of Freedom was placed atop the dome on December 2, 1863. It was executed by Thomas Crawford in Rome and had a rough passage to America, so much so that most of the cargo had to be thrown overboard in a storm that damaged the vessel carrying the statue. The ship was condemned and sold in Bermuda where the statue was placed in storage. After it finally reached Washington the war was in progress and work was delayed until late 1863. The Capitol served as a barracks during the early days of the war; later it was a hospital for wounded. Basement committee rooms were bricked into ovens to provide bread for the forts and batteries surrounding the city. Capitol vaults were packed with foodstuffs against a possible siege of the city. Many Civil War personages are portrayed in sculpture and art throughout the Capitol. Among statues in the rotunda are those of Lincoln, Grant, and Edward D. Baker, who was killed at Balls Bluff. Lincoln, Garfield, McKinley, and Kennedy lay in state in the Rotunda. In 1864, states were invited to send statues of their favorite citizens to stand in Statuary Hall, formerly the Hall of Representatives. Eighty-four statues came, and the overflow was placed in adjacent rooms and corridors. Among Civil War military or legislative persons in the hall: Gen. Joseph Wheeler, Alabama; Confederate Vice President Alexander H. Stephens, Georgia; Gen. Lew Wallace, Indiana; Gov. Samuel J. Kirkwood, Iowa; Sen. John J. Ingalls, Kansas; Vice President Hannibal Hamlin, Maine; Confederate President Jefferson Davis, Mississippi; Vice President John C. Calhoun, South Carolina; and Gen. Robert E. Lee, Virginia.

Washington Cathedral, Wisconsin Ave., between Massachusetts Ave. and Woodly Rd. The Lee-Jackson Memorial windows, given by the United Daughters of the Confederacy, memorialize incidents in the lives of Gens. Robert E. Lee and T. J. Jackson, in stained glass.

The White House, 1600 Pennsylvania Ave., has many Civil War associations. In his diary for April 18, 1861, John Hay wrote: "The White House is turned into barracks. Jim Lane marshalled his Kansas Warriors today at Willard's and placed them at the disposal of Maj. Hunter, who turned them tonight into the East Room. It is a splendid company— worthy such an armory . . . The Major has made me his aide, and I labored under some uncertainty as to whether I should speak to privates or not." The East Room was the scene of a gay reception for Gen. Ulysses S. Grant— and later of sorrow when Lincoln's body lay in state. A Healy portrait of Lincoln is in the state dining room; Mrs. Robert Todd Lincoln willed it to the Executive Mansion. "Cannonading on the Potomac," painted by A. Wordsworth Thompson, a *Harper's Weekly* war correspondent, depicts a war scene near Ball's Bluff, Virginia. It hangs in the Red Room. The Lincoln Bedroom was originally Lincoln's Cabinet Room. Here he signed the Emancipation Proclamation. The Lincoln Sitting Room, in the southeast corner of the second floor, has engravings, prints, and mementos of the Lincoln administration. One of five copies of the Gettysburg Address in Lincoln's handwriting is in this room. President Truman first collected Lincoln pieces from other parts of the White House to create this room as a Lincoln shrine. Mrs. John F. Kennedy and her aides discovered one of the chairs in the government storehouse at Fort Washington; a duplicate was then given to the collection by a resident of Arlington. The Treaty Room was President Andrew Johnson's Cabinet Room. Healy's painting of "The Peacemakers," showing Lincoln conferring with Gens. Grant and Sherman and with Adm. Porter on the *River Queen*, is in this room.

Willard Hotel, 14th St. and Pennsylvania Ave. Lincoln and Buchanan both lived at the Willard at one time. Lincoln left without paying his bill, having his mind on the impending inauguration. He sent a note of apology promising payment. Now the Willard-Inter Continental Hotel.

FLORIDA

Florida came into the Union on March 3, 1845, and seceded on January 10, 1861. Most Floridians held that secession was legal and logical. The majority hoped to have separation without war; some young bloods looked forward to a "bout with the North."

By 1860 cotton was the basis of the Florida economy. As the blockade became more effective, Florida morale, which had been high to the point of jubilation at the time of secession, rapidly deteriorated. Some 15,000 Floridians served in the Confederate army—more than the number of registered voters. Except for the first gay days of the war, clothing and weapons were a problem. Arms, equipment, even tents and clothing were purchased anywhere they could be had. The legislature appropriated $100,000 for weapons; but purchasing in an inflated market soon exhausted the funds without supplying sufficient arms for the troops. In the summer of 1861, Gov. Madison Starke Perry petitioned the governor of North Carolina for additional arms. Gov. John W. Ellis felt he could not send military supplies out of state but suggested that Florida troops travel to Virginia by way of Raleigh. He felt that tender-hearted North Carolinians would surely help to equip unarmed soldiers on their way to war. North Carolina mercy, however, was never put to the test: The government at Richmond refused to accept the unequipped Florida troops. Blockade runners found it highly profitable to bring in arms and ammunition, but as late as the fall of 1863, the state quartermaster general had only 19 rifles and 25 percussion pistols in his warehouse.

The battle of Olustee in northern Florida was the major engagement fought in the state. Confederate forces under Gen. Joseph Finegan routed Union troops under Gen. Truman A. Seymour. Florida forts were of prime importance throughout the war. Two minor forts were taken by state troops before the ordinance of secession had been passed. Confederates took over Forts Barrancas and McRee and the Pensacola Navy Yard. The Union reinforced Fort Pickens and soon occupied Pensacola.

Brig. Gen. Edward M. McCook received the surrender of Florida troops in Tallahassee, the only Confederate capital east of the Mississippi River which had not been captured during the war. The Union flag was raised over the capitol on May 20, 1865.

APALACHICOLA, Franklin County. US 98.
Old Chestnut Street Cemetery has Confederate graves, including those of seven veterans who were with Pickett at Gettysburg.

Orman House, 5th St. During the war Mrs. Sarah Orman placed a large keg on the house roof to warn Confederates that Federal troops were in town.

Raney House, southwest corner of Market and Ave. F, was the home of former mayor David G. Raney, who had three sons in Confederate service: David, Jr., a marine; Edward in the cavalry; and George P. in the infantry. The house has been restored.

Trinity Church, Gorrie Square, gave its bell to be melted down for cannon; its carpets and cushions were donated to Confederate soldiers.

BRADENTON, Manatee County. US 41.
Manatee Burying Ground, 15th St. E. Soldiers from both forces are buried here, including Brig. Gen. John Riggin, aide to Grant.

South Florida Museum, 201 W. 10th St., Memorial Pier, has a variety of displays pertaining to the war.

CEDAR KEY, Levy County. State 24. During the war this was a strategic point from which blockade runners exported lumber and cotton and brought in supplies for the Confederacy.

Cedar Key Historical Society Museum, on State 24 at 2nd St., displays historic photos dating from the 1850s.

DAYTONA BEACH, Volusia County. IS 4.
Halifax Historical Society Museum, 252 S. Beach St., has Civil War memorabilia.

DE FUNIAK SPRINGS, Walton County. US 90.
Confederate Monument, courthouse lawn,

FLORIDA

1 — Apalachicola	15 — Lee Monument
2 — Bradenton	16 — Madison
3 — De Funiak Springs	17 — Mandarin
4 — Ellenton	18 — Marianna
5 — Fort Clinch	19 — Miami
6 — Fort De Soto	20 — O'Leno
7 — Fort George Island	21 — Olustee
8 — Fort Jefferson	22 — Palatka
9 — Fort Pickens	23 — Pensacola
10 — Fort Walton	24 — St. Augustine
11 — Gainesville	25 — St. Petersburg
12 — Homosassa	26 — Tallahassee
13 — Jacksonville	27 — Tampa
14 — Key West	28 — White Springs
14a — Lake City	29 — Woodville

was the first Florida memorial to Confederate soldiers; it was erected in 1871.

ELLENTON, Manatee County. IS 75.

Gamble Mansion, 3708 Patten Ave., off highway on Manatee River. The mansion, which is designated the Judah P. Benjamin Memorial, was built between 1845 and 1850. It was leased to W. A. Griffin in 1858. When Griffin enlisted in the Confederate army in 1862, Capt. Archibald McNeill and family moved in. McNeill was a Confederate commissary agent who salvaged uncut cane, made it into sugar, and stored it away. A Federal party from the *James L. Davis* destroyed the sugar refinery in August 1864 but did not harm the mansion except for looting. In May 1865, Judah P. Benjamin took refuge here. While he was in residence, Federal forces made a surprise raid. Benjamin and McNeill hid out in a palmetto thicket. Now a Confederate Memorial Historic Site, it has been restored. It has many period furnishings and relics placed by the United Daughters of the Confederacy.

FORT CLINCH STATE PARK, Nassau County. State A1A, the "Buccaneer Trail to Fernandina Beach." Confederates occupied the fort at the beginning of the war. It was not completed nor well equipped. Col. Robert E. Lee attempted to make it workable. The 3rd Regiment of Florida Volunteers was stationed here; it was evacuated in March 1862 and occupied by Federal forces thereafter. Visitor center with exhibits. Park attendants present living history wearing Union uniforms of 1864.

FORT DE SOTO PARK, formerly Mullet Key, off St. Petersburg. The fort may be reached by the new Pinellas County Bayway. It was designed by Robert E. Lee when he was a lieutenant colonel in the U.S. Army. Guns were set up to guard the entrance to Tampa Bay but were never used for defense.

FORT GADSDEN HISTORIC SITE, Franklin County. US 98, State 65. In 1814 the British built a fort here, soon abandoned. Andrew Jackson's Lt. James Gadsden later built a supply base at the site. In 1862 the Confederates moved in until the following year when malaria drove them inland. There are some remains and a miniature replica of the fort.

FORT GEORGE ISLAND, Nassau County. State 105, east of Jacksonville.

Kingsley Plantation, on north bank of river, is the oldest plantation house in Florida. Guided tours.

Yellow Bluff Fort, on Heckscher Dr., about 1 mile south of State 105. Earthwork on the north bank of the St. Johns River was used at various times by both Federal and Confederate troops. Confederates built it to aid the batteries established across the river at St. Johns Bluff. The National Park Service has made restorations of walls.

FORT JEFFERSON, on Dry Tortugas Key, 68 miles west of Key West. Known as the "Key to the Gulf of Mexico," the fort hampered Confederate blockade runners. Dr. Samuel A. Mudd, who set Booth's leg during his flight after the assassination of President Lincoln, was confined at the fort. It is now a national historic monument, reached by boat or seaplane. Though occupied by the Union throughout the war, the fort never saw battle but fired upon any Confederate vessels that ventured within range. Its unstable foundations of coral and sand caused the walls to crack. Nevertheless, in 1863 it held some 2,400 prisoners. Visitor center and guided tours.

FORT PICKENS STATE PARK, on Santa Rosa Island, near Pensacola. A U.S. artillery company under Lt. Adam J. Slemmer was stationed at Barrancas Barracks, Pensacola, in January 1861. At the Navy Yard, Commodore James Armstrong had less than 100 ordinary seamen, 38 marines, plus one steamer with a crew of 78 and a supply ship with 36 men. The two Union commanders conferred. Slemmer's company, reinforced by 30 ordinary seamen from the Navy Yard, occupied Fort Pickens which could be reinforced from the sea. Armstrong surrendered the Navy Yard on January 12, but Slemmer refused to surrender Fort Pickens. Southern senators advised against attacking the fort, which was held to be "not worth one drop of blood." In October, however, it became the target during the battle of Santa Rosa Island. A force of about 2,600 Confederates under Gen. Richard H. Anderson landed on the island early in the morning of October 9 and attacked a camp occupied by the 6th New York. Regulars from the fort drove off the invaders. Artillery duels were held a number of times during the war between the fort and Confederate shore batteries. When Confederates withdrew from Pensacola in May

1862, the Federals moved in. Fort Pickens became a prison for military and political prisoners. It is now part of the Gulf Islands National Seashore under the stewardship of the National Park Service, an agency within the Department of the Interior; there is an exhibit room in the old headquarters building, and the grounds have explanatory markers.

FORT WALTON, Okaloosa County, US 98. The fort was occupied by Confederates during the war. A large mound here was excavated in 1861; skeletons, which were found lying on their backs with their hands crossed, were wired together and displayed by the soldiers in one of the fort buildings. A Federal gunboat shelled the area sometime later and destroyed the exhibit along with the building.

GAINESVILLE, Alachua County. IS 75, State 24. A skirmish took place in February 1864 when Federal raiders tried to capture two trains but were repulsed. The battle of Gainesville occurred in August 1864 when some 300 Union troops occupying the town were driven out by Florida cavalry.

Florida State Museum, Museum Rd. and Newell Dr. Collections contain relics of state history.

HOMOSASSA SPRINGS, Hernando County, US 19.

Yulee Sugar Mill Ruins State Historic Site, in old Homosassa, off State 490. At Yulee's home, Cottonwood Plantation, the trunks and papers belonging to the fleeing Jefferson Davis, which were seized near Waldo, were hidden, but later taken to Waldo and put in the care of a railroad agent.

JACKSONVILLE, Duval County. IS 10, 95. Blockade runners used the St. Johns River. The city was occupied four times by Union forces.

Battle of the Brick Church, Myrtle Ave. and Monroe St. Federal and Confederate troops skirmished here in 1862. Marker at the south entrance to main waiting room of the Union Terminal Station on Bay St.

Confederate Monument, in Hemming Park, given to the city by Charles G. Hemming, a member of the Jacksonville Light Infantry.

Confederate Park, Main and Hubbard St. Site of the eastern end of Confederate trenches which extended to the Union Terminal.

KEY WEST, Monroe County. State 1, at extreme end of Florida Keys. The only Southern city which has always flown the Union flag.

Fort Zachary Taylor State Historic Site, west end of United St., was held by Federal forces during the war. The East Gulf Block-

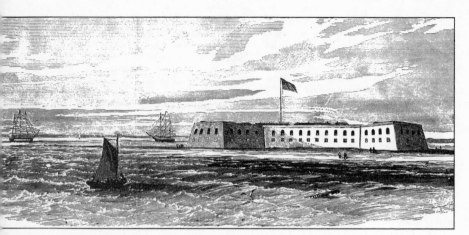

Fort Pickens on Santa Rosa Island, Pensacola Bay.

ading Squadron was located here. In 1862, Federal Flag Officer J. L. Lardner was in command. Excavations have uncovered part of a long-buried arsenal. Fort claims the largest collection of Civil War cannons in the U.S.

Key West Lighthouse Museum, 938 Whitehouse St., in former lighthouse keeper's quarters. Displays lighthouse history. An 1847 lighthouse is in the garden.

LAKE CITY, Columbia County. IS 10.

Live Oak Cemetery has the graves of 151 Confederates killed in the battle of Olustee.

LEE MONUMENT, Nassau County. US 1. On highway south of bridge over the St. Mary's River is a memorial to Robert E. Lee.

LIVE OAK, Suwannee County, IS 10, US 90, is bordered on three sides by the river Stephen Foster made famous in "Old Folks at Home," which begins, "'Way down upon the Swanee River."

Suwannee River State Park, 13 miles west on US 90, has Confederate earthworks.

MADISON, Madison County. US 90, State 145. The town was a Confederate stronghold.

Oak Ridge Cemetery, 601 NW Washington, has the graves of 31 Confederates killed at the battle of Olustee.

MANDARIN, Duval County. State 13. A Union gunboat shelled the village during the war. The town was Harriet B. Stowe's winter home. Tiffany window in Episcopal Chapel honors her.

MARIANNA, Jackson County. IS 10, US

90. Hometown of wartime governor, John Milton.

Battle of Marianna Memorial, in Confederate Park, commemorates the engagement of September 27, 1864, between Federals and the Home Guards—boys, elderly men, and invalids known as the "Cradle and the Grave" detachment.

Torreya State Park, south off State 12, has Confederate gun pits, antebellum house.

MIAMI, Dade County. IS 95, US 1.

Lummus Park, 404 N. River Dr. and NW 3rd St., has stone barracks of long-gone Fort Dallas, once commanded by Gen. Sherman well before the war. The fort was at the river in 1835–38.

MONTICELLO, Jefferson County. US 19.

Old Cemetery, E. Madison St., has the graves of Confederate soldiers who died in Monticello after being brought some 94 miles from the battle of Olustee. The grounds are being restored.

O'LENO STATE PARK, Suwannee County. US 41.

Natural Bridge, east side of highway between Lake City and High Springs, over the Santa Fe River. Part of the Bellamy Road which John C. Breckinridge, Confederate Secretary of War, and his party, which included Col. John Taylor Wood, grandson of Zachary Taylor and aide of Jefferson Davis, followed on May 16, 1865, en route to the east coast in their escape to Cuba.

OLUSTEE BATTLEFIELD STATE HISTORIC SITE, Baker County. US 90, 3 miles east of Olustee. The greatest Florida engagement took place here on February 20, 1864.

Federals commanded by Gen. Truman A. Seymour hoped to break up communications between east and west Florida and to capture the supply base at Lake City. Confederates under Gen. Joseph Finegan routed the Federals. A museum has interpretive displays.

PALATKA, Putnam County. US 17. The town was occupied by Union troops in March 1864. After skirmishes, the Federals withdrew but landed another force some miles south in May from the steamer *Columbine.* When the Union troops moved toward Volusia, Confederates at Palatka fired on the steamer, which surrendered.

St. Marks Church, Main and 2nd, was used as Federal barracks. In 1838 when Fort Shannon was built as garrison, supply depot, and hospital for the area, Winfield Scott, Zachary Taylor, and William Sherman were here.

PENSACOLA, Escambia County. IS 10, US 98. The city was captured by the Union and served as a base for the Federal blockade of the coast.

Fort Barrancas, in harbor, was held by Confederates until 1862.

Mallory House, Palafox Parkway, between Gregory and Wright. Home of Stephen Mallory, Confederate Secretary of Navy.

Pensacola Historical Museum, 405 S. Adams St. at Zaragoza St., in the Old Christ Church, which was used as a barracks by Union forces.

Perry House, northeast corner of N. Palafox and E. Wright St. The home of Brig. Gen. E. A. Perry, later governor.

ST. AUGUSTINE, St. Johns County. IS 95, US 1.

St. Augustine Historical Society Library and Museum, St. Francis St., south end of the Sea Wall, adjoining Oldest House. Local history relics.

State Arsenal, 108 Marine St., was occupied by Union troops.

ST. MARKS, Wakulla County. State 363.

San Marcos de Apalache, Canal St., has Civil War artifacts. The old army post was occupied by the Confederates. A Federal naval attack was repulsed in 1865.

TALLAHASSEE, Leon County. IS 10, US 19, 27.

Historic Old Capitol, S. Monroe. Here the secession convention met in 1861. The capital was never captured but troops were surrendered here in 1865. Susan Bradford, daughter of Dr. Edward Bradford, wealthy planter, wrote: "Capitol Square was so crowded you could see

nothing but heads. . . . As the old town clock struck one, the Convention, headed by President McGehee, walked out on the portico. In a few moments they were grouped about the table on which someone had spread the parchment on which the Ordinance of Secession was written. It was impossible for me to tell in what order it was signed, the heads were clustered so closely around the table, but presently I heard Col. Ward's familiar voice. There was a little break in the crowd and I saw him quite plainly. He dipped his pen in the ink and, holding it aloft, he said, in the saddest of tones, 'When I die I want it inscribed upon my tombstone that I was the last man to give up the ship.' Then he wrote slowly across the sheet before him, 'George T. Ward'. . . . .When at length the names were all affixed, cheer after cheer rent the air; it was deafening. Our world seemed to have gone wild." An announcement for June 1862 let it be known that Gen. Beauregard had issued an urgent request for pickles and cordials. The gifts were to be deposited in the "sewing room" of the Capitol. The *Florida Sentinel* was critical of the lax way in which prisoners of war were treated by the military; the editor pointed out there was such familiarity between the guard and the guarded that it was sometimes "impossible, except for the dress, to designate the prisoners."

Museum of Florida History, Bronough and Pensacola streets. Displays and the state archives are here.

Presbyterian Church, N. Adams St. and W. Park Ave., has been remodeled except for slave gallery. During the war, services were held alternately here and at the Methodist church, but it was pointed out that neither meeting was "as largely attended by the male portion of our city as they might be."

TAMPA, Hillsborough County. IS 4. Four companies enlisted in the Confederate army; the town was blockaded and shelled in 1863 and then occupied. In 1862, however, the doughty Confederate commander of the Oklawaha Rangers, on being ordered by the commander of the USS *Sagamore* to surrender the city, sent back the message: "We have no such thing in the books as surrender."

WHITE SPRINGS, Hamilton County. US 41.

Stephen Foster State Folk Cultural Center, on banks of Suwannee River, honors the composer of Florida's state song, "Old Folks at Home," and many other ballads that were wartime favorites. Museum has dioramas.

WOODVILLE, Leon County. US 319.

Battle of Natural Bridge, 6 miles east of town. On March 6, 1865, Confederate regulars, Home Guards, and West Florida Seminary cadets turned back a Federal army and navy amphibious operation bent on capturing St. Marks and Fort Ward in an advance on Tallahassee. Monument, markers, and earthworks are on the battlefield. Now a state historical site.

GEORGIA

Georgia, the fourth state to enter the Union (January 2, 1788), seceded on January 19, 1861. A number of prominent Georgians had opposed secession, among them Alexander Stephens, who became Vice President of the Confederacy, and Judge Garnett Andrews, whose daughter Eliza said of his efforts to hold the state in the Union that he might as well have tried to "tie up the northwest wind in the corner of a pocket handkerchief."

Georgians quickly responded to Gov. Joseph E. Brown's call for troops; not only the young bloods of the gentry but students, clerks, farmers, and veterans of the War of 1812 came forward. By May 1861 the governor had organized six regiments and two battalions; by October about 25,000 Georgia troops were in service. This number had increased to 75,000 a year later.

The path of war in Georgia, on paper, looks to be one of the simplest of any of the leading Confederate states. The darting cavalry raiders were busy elsewhere—part of Sherman's strategy was aimed at keeping Forrest occupied and well out of the way. The state, then, is not heavily dotted with scattered cavalry skirmishes and guerrilla incidents; the major battle lines cut a swath about 60 miles wide from Chattanooga through Atlanta and Milledgeville to Savannah and the sea. The path, it should be said, represents countless lives and more than a million dollars in property damage.

ALBANY, Dougherty County. US 19, 82, State 300.

Bridge House, Front St. at Flint River. During the war the bridge was burned and the building used as a meat packing house for Confederate troops. It was later remodeled for a theater. Laura Keene, whose performance Lincoln was watching at the time of his assassination, appeared here in *Our American Cousin.*

ALLATOONA, Bartow County. US 41, State 20. Sherman was familiar with Allatoona Pass from his army service in 1843. Early in the Atlanta campaign he decided to swing around

Johnston's army at this point, a pattern he followed to Kennesaw Mountain, where he made the costly error of changing his footwork. In the words of the historian Bruce Catton: "Johnston side-stepped and retreated . . . . and the two armies went down through northern Georgia in a series of movements that were almost formalized, like some highly intricate and deadly dance." The battle of Allatoona Pass was fought in October 1864 between Hood's forces and Union troops led by Gen. J. M. Corse. After heavy fighting, in which Corse was wounded, the Confederates were forced to withdraw. After the battle Sherman signaled from Kennesaw Mountain to ask about Corse and received the reply: "I am short a cheekbone and one ear but am able to whip all hell yet." When the two met later, Sherman looked at the general's rather unimpressive scar and remarked: "Corse, they came damn near missing you, didn't they?"

ANDERSONVILLE NATIONAL HISTORIC SITE, Macon County, State 49.

Andersonville National Cemetery is on the site used by Confederates for burial of Union prisoners. Many of the 13,000 soldiers buried here died at the prison.

Andersonville Prison Park, site of Camp Sumter, one of the largest of Confederate prisons. Providence Spring is on the grounds. Reportedly, the Yankee prisoners prayed for rain and got it in abundance; the downpour also providentially opened up an old spring that had been clogged. More than 33,000 prisoners were packed into a stockade built for 10,000. Some escape tunnels and wells remain. A sundial monument honors Clara Barton for her postwar work marking graves. Also on grounds: Confederate earthworks, state monuments, and a visitor center with interpretive programs. Walking tours and informative talks offered on weekends in summer months. The museum not only pertains to this hopelessly overcrowded site of the Civil War but comprises exhibits relating to prisoners of other wars from the Revolutionary through Vietnam.

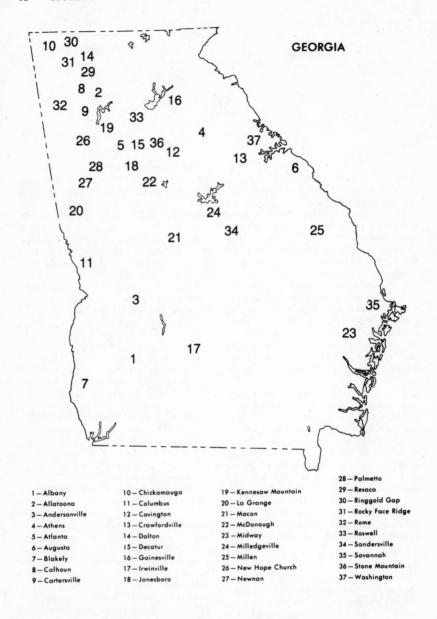

GEORGIA

1 — Albany	10 — Chickamauga	19 — Kennesaw Mountain	28 — Palmetto
2 — Allatoona	11 — Columbus	20 — La Grange	29 — Resaca
3 — Andersonville	12 — Covington	21 — Macon	30 — Ringgold Gap
4 — Athens	13 — Crawfordville	22 — McDonough	31 — Rocky Face Ridge
5 — Atlanta	14 — Dalton	23 — Midway	32 — Rome
6 — Augusta	15 — Decatur	24 — Milledgeville	33 — Roswell
7 — Blakely	16 — Gainesville	25 — Millen	34 — Sandersville
8 — Calhoun	17 — Irwinville	26 — New Hope Church	35 — Savannah
9 — Cartersville	18 — Jonesboro	27 — Newnan	36 — Stone Mountain
			37 — Washington

Monument to Capt. Henry Wirz. The statue in the center of town honors the Confederate commandant who was in charge of the Andersonville Prison. He was seized in 1865, tried in Washington, and hanged on November 10. The memorial was erected by the United Daughters of the Confederacy in protest against his execution.

ANDREWS' RAID: On April 12, 1862, the Western & Atlantic locomotive, the General, had stopped at Big Shanty (now Ken-

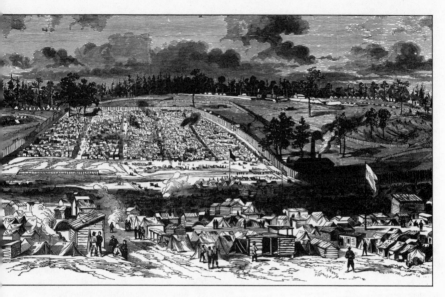

The great prison pen at Andersonville.

nesaw). Passengers went into the Lacy Hotel for breakfast; the engineer, conductor, and a railroad foreman also went to the dining room, and James J. Andrews, a Union secret service agent, with 21 men, 18 of whom were Union soldiers dressed as civilians, stole the locomotive. Their plan was to set fire to bridges on the W & A while heading north. The three railroad men gave chase, running part of the way, then borrowing a push car at Moon's Station and a locomotive at Etowah. Their progress was slowed by barricades and missing rails, but by foot and engine-hopping they reached a point near Adairsville where they were picked up by a southbound locomotive, the Texas (which had been shunted to a siding to make way for the General). From this time on they were running backwards, north, through Resaca, Tilton, Dalton, and Ringgold. The General was abandoned near Graysville, below Chattanooga. Within a week all the raiders had been captured and imprisoned. On June 7, 1862, Andrews was hanged at public execution in Atlanta. Seven others were hanged on June 18. Eight escaped from prison in Atlanta on October 16, 1862; the remaining six were paroled on March 17, 1863.

ATHENS, Clarke County. US 29, 78. A Confederate double-barreled cannon, City Hall Plaza, was a flop; the chained-together balls never fired at the same instant. A popular legend says the chain broke at the first firing and the cannonballs, set free, destroyed a cabin and a cow.

Chapel, University of Georgia campus. Union soldiers camped on the grounds and used the front columns for target practice.

Chicopec Building, 1180 Broad St., was a gunsmith's shop. Marker.

Gilmer Hall, Prince and Oglethorpe Ave., served as a hospital and a rehabilitation center for Confederate soldiers.

Howell Cobb House, 689 Pope St. Gen. Cobb was Secretary of State in Buchanan's administration and was president of the Confederate congress.

Ilah Dunlap Little Memorial Library, university campus, has the Confederate constitution and a wisp of chin-whiskers snipped from Jefferson Davis by his doctor; they are kept in the archives vault, however, and are not on display. The library has many valuable documents.

Old College, on campus. Plaque marks room of Alexander H. Stephens and Crawford W. Long. The college roommates represent Georgia in the Hall of Fame in Washington.

Welcome Center, 280 E. Dougherty St., in restored historic house, has maps for self-guiding tours and booklets.

ATLANTA, Fulton County. IS 20, 75, 85.

Atlanta History Center, 3101 Andrews Dr. at W. Paces Ferry Rd., has handsomely landscaped grounds surrounding an impressive Palladium-style building. Tours on the hour and half-hour. The headquarters in Walter McElreath Hall contain archives, a research library, and a museum with permanent exhibits that include "Atlanta and The War: 1861–1865" and "Atlanta Resurgens," which deals with Reconstruction. In the 32-acre complex are gardens, trails, and two restored houses. In the collection is the only Confederate States Marine Corps uniform known to have survived the war. The Wilbur G. Kurtz maps of the campaign of and battle for Atlanta are particularly fine. McElreath Hall houses the Margaret Mitchell Memorial Library.

Atlanta History Center Downtown, 140 Peachtree St., has changing exhibits, history videos, and information on historical events in the city.

Battle of Atlanta, on July 22, 1864, was fought partly on a line along Moreland Ave. SE, to Flat Shoals Ave. and southeast to Glenwood Ave. Severe fighting took place at Leggett's Hill, near 282 Moreland Ave. SE. For details of the engagement in which Confederates under Gen. John B. Hood, who had relieved Joseph Johnston, fought against Sherman's army, tourists are advised to visit the Cyclorama in Grant Park.

Battle of Ezra Church, on July 28, occurred in the vicinity of the Lickskillet Rd. The site is between Simpson St. and West Lake Dr. Logan and his 15th Corps held off five Confederate attacks.

Battle of Peachtree Creek, on July 20, north of the creek between Peachtree St. and Piedmont Rd. The Confederates learned here as at Chickamauga that Gen. George Thomas never gave ground easily. Hood attacked the Federals while they were astride the creek and weakened them further by a gap of nearly 2 miles between Thomas and Schofield. The Union line "sagged," but Thomas brought up his guns and repulsed the furious assault. Much of the fighting occurred in an area now occupied by the Bobby Jones Municipal Golf Course. Two bridges put across Peachtree Creek were built by engineers under Gen. John Geary, first mayor of San Francisco, who turned down the governorship of Utah, accepted the governorship of Kansas, and after the war was governor of Pennsylvania.

Ben W. Fortson, Jr., State Archives and Records Building, 330 Capitol Ave. SE, has an extensive file of Civil War records. In the collection are service records, Confederate pension applications, original muster rolls of Confederate units, rosters of Georgia soldiers, and personal papers. The history of the Confederacy is beautifully depicted in stained-glass windows.

Candler Building, southeast corner Peachtree and Houston St. High relief heads in a frieze at grand staircase, Houston St. entrance, are those of Alexander H. Stephens, Charles J. Jenkins, Gens. John B. Gordon and Joseph E. Wheeler, Sidney Lanier, Joel Chandler Harris, and Eli Whitney.

City Hall, 56 Mitchell St., is on the site of headquarters occupied by Sherman in 1864 when the John Neal mansion stood here. Observation tower offers panoramic view of city.

Cyclorama, 800 Cherokee Ave. SE, depicts the battle of Atlanta in a panoramic painting measuring 50 feet in height, 400 feet in circumference, and weighing 18,000 pounds. The building also contains a museum of Civil War relics and the *Texas,* the locomotive engine which took part in the 87-mile chase after the Andrews raiders on April 12, 1862.

Fort Walker, in Grant Park, was a Confederate battery constructed by slave labor for the city's defense in 1864. It was named for Gen. W. H. T. Walker, who was killed in the battle of Atlanta, July 22.

Georgia State Capitol, Washington St. between Mitchell and Hunter St., houses the state library. Building contains battle flags, paintings, and statuary of Civil War interest. A statue of Gen. John B. Gordon is on Capitol grounds. It is the work of Solon Borglum. Statue of wartime governor, Joseph E. Brown, also on grounds.

Grady Monument, on Marietta and Forsyth St., honors Henry Woodfin Grady, renowned Georgia editor and orator of the war years.

Grant Park, Atlanta Ave., Sidney St., Cherokee Ave., and the Blvd., comprises 144 acres including Old Fort Walker and the Atlanta Cyclorama, as well as breastworks from the battle of Atlanta. (Grant Park is *not* named for Ulysses S. but for Col. L. P. Grant, who helped to fortify the city against Sherman's army.)

Huff House, 70 Huff Rd. NW, was headquarters for Confederate Maj. Charles T. Hotchkiss; later Gen. Thomas had headquarters here. Reportedly, still later a neighbor saved the house by saying it belonged to an Englishwoman and hoisted the Union Jack to help the story. It was known as the House of Three flags.

Johnston's Headquarters, Marietta St. and Lewis Ave, NW. At this site on July 18, 1864, Gen. Joseph Johnston transferred command of the Army of Tennessee to Gen. John B. Hood.

McPherson Monument, McPherson and Monument Ave., was erected on the spot where Gen. James Birdseye McPherson was killed on July 22, 1864. The death of McPherson was a personal loss to Sherman as well as a military loss to the North. The able Ohioan had been hoping to return home to marry Miss Mary Hoffman, but Sherman had felt he could not be spared from the Atlanta campaign. McPherson's inconsolable fiancée remained in seclusion for more than a year after his death.

Oakland Cemetery, 248 Oakland Ave. SE. The Lion of Atlanta, carved from a single block of Georgia marble, was dedicated to the unknown Confederate dead on April 26, 1894. Among those buried in the cemetery is Gen. Clement A. Evans, who served in a number of campaigns under Stonewall Jackson, led a brigade in Early's Washington raid, and was wounded at Monocacy. He became a Methodist minister after the war. Also buried here is Gen. John B. Gordon, who planned and led the assault on Fort Stedman at Petersburg. His wife, Fanny, left the children with her mother-in-law and traveled with her husband in all his campaigns, to the vast displeasure of Gen. Jubal Early who was said to have yearned for the Federals to capture her. Margaret Mitchell, author of *Gone With the Wind,* is also buried at Oakland.

Old Lamp Post, northeast corner of Whitehall and Alabama St., was damaged in the battle of Atlanta; it has been repaired. An eternal light burns for the Confederacy. It still has a bullet hole in its base.

Piedmont Park, Piedmont Ave., north of 10th St., has the Peace Monument near 14th St. entrance. It is the work of Allen Newman, was unveiled in 1911; both Federal and Confederate soldiers attended the ceremonies. A memorial to Sidney Lanier also is in the park.

Sutherland, 1940 DeKalb Ave. NE. The home of Gen. John B. Gordon stood at this site, but burned down soon after the war. *See also Oakland Cemetery.*

Walker Monument, Glenwood Ave., 1½ miles from Moreland Ave., was erected on the site where Confederate Gen. W. H. T. Walker was slain by a Federal picket, July 22, 1864.

ATLANTA CAMPAIGN: Markers interpreting the campaign of spring and summer 1864, are located on five small tracts of land under state jurisdiction which provide parking and viewing areas. A number of other sites have been marked; however, those designated for special treatment by an act of Congress in 1937 are: Ringgold Gap, Rocky Face Ridge, Resaca, and Cassville, all on US 41, and New Hope Church on State 92, 13 miles southwest of Acworth.

AUGUSTA, Richmond County. IS 20, US 1, 25, 78.

Augusta-Richmond County Museum, 540 Telfair St., is in an 18th-century building that served as a Civil War hospital. Confederate relics.

Confederate Monument, Broad St. between 7th and 8th streets, is an impressive memorial of Italian marble. The heroic statue at the peak is a likeness of Berry Greenwood Benson, Georgia scout and sharpshooter who served throughout the war, was captured and escaped more than once (*Also see* ELMIRA, NEW YORK), and lived till New Year's Day 1923, never having surrendered his rifle. Life-size figures of Gens. Lee, Jackson, Walker, and Cobb are a part of the memorial.

Confederate Powder Mill, 1717 Goodrich St. Augusta was an ordnance center of the Confederacy. The great chimney of the powder works at the Sibley Mill remains.

Magnolia Cemetery, 702 3rd St. Poets Paul Hamilton Hayne, Richard Henry Wilde, and James Ryder Randall are buried here.

Monument of Confederate Dead, 439 Greene St.

Poets' Monument, center of green, between McIntosh and Jackson St., honors four Georgia poets: Sidney Lanier, James Ryder Randall, Paul Hamilton Hayne, and Father Abraham Ryan, poet-priest of the Confederacy.

Randall Monument, center of Greene St., between McKinnie and the canal, honors James Ryder Randall, author of "Maryland, My Maryland."

U.S. Arsenal, 2500 Walton Way, on Augusta College campus, was surrendered in 1861, five days after Georgia seceded. Capt. Arnold Elzey, commanding the arsenal, served in the Confederate army.

BLAKELY, Early County. US 27, State 62.

Confederate Flagpole and Monument, Courthouse Square. The flagpole, erected in 1861, is the only Confederate relic of its kind in existence. The monument was added years later by the United Daughters of the Confederacy.

Review of the Clinch Rifles in front of the Augusta Arsenal.

CALHOUN, Gordon County. IS 75. Town was in Sherman's path but was not destroyed.

CARTERSVILLE, Bartow County. IS 75. George Ward Nichols, Sherman's aide who kept a diary of the Great March, recorded for November 13, 1864: "At Cartersville the last communications with the North were severed with the telegraph wire. It bore the message to General Thomas, 'All is well.' And so we have cut adrift from our base of operations, from our line of communications, launching out into uncertainty at best . . . . The history of war bears no similar example, except that of Cortez burning his ships." Only two houses escaped destruction.

Walnut Grove, off State 61, was the home of Confederate Gen. Pierce Manning Butler Young, who in 1861 was at West Point expecting to be graduated in June. Reluctantly he resigned in March to go with his state. He was wounded at South Mountain and at Ashland, took part in the defense of Augusta. Toward the end of the century he was Consul General at St. Petersburg.

CHICKAMAUGA, Walker County. US 27.

Gordon-Lee House, on Cove Rd., southwest of Battlefield, was headquarters for Gen. Rosecrans in 1863 when he ordered the Gordon family to vacate the main house which was then used as a hospital. James Garfield, later President, was chief of staff when the Union troops were here. The Confederates retook the house in September 1863. Museum on second floor of restored mansion.

CHICKAMAUGA AND CHATTA-NOOGA NATIONAL MILITARY PARK, Catoosa County, US 27. *Also see* CHATTANOOGA, TENNESSEE. The visitor center is on US 27 about 9 miles south of Chattanooga. Trained historians are on duty; a museum has exhibits. Free information for self-guided tours available; salient points are well marked. In September 1863, Rosecrans with 58,000 men forced the Confederates to withdraw from Chattanooga. Bragg established headquarters at LaFayette, Georgia, where he awaited reinforcements. After driving the

Federals back from Chickamauga, Bragg bottled them up in Chattanooga with most of their supplies cut off. Union reinforcements saved the besieged troops in November; Confederates again withdrew to the south and Bragg was replaced by Joseph Johnston.

COLUMBUS, Muscogee County. IS 185, US 80, 280, 27. The town was an important Confederate supply depot captured by Union troops on April 16, 1865. The Confederate ironclad *Muscogee* has been raised from the Chattahoochee River; its hull and other relics in museum at 101 4th St.

Columbus Iron Works, southwest corner of Front Ave. and Dillingham St., was known as Naval Iron Works during the war; in 1863, it produced a breech-loading cannon made from the wheel shaft of a sunken river steamer.

Confederate Naval Museum, 202 4th St., displays remains of the Gunboat CSS *Chattahoochee* and the ironclad ram CSS *Jackson/Muscogee,* which were raised from the Chattahoochee River. Also artifacts and ship models.

Fort Benning Infantry Museum, Ingersoll St., Bldg. 396 on Baltzell Ave. History of the foot soldier. The fort was named for Confederate General Henry L. Benning, nicknamed "Rock," a successful lawyer before and after the war.

Historic Columbus Foundation, 700 Broadway, has details for self-guiding tours of the 26-block historic district. The Historic Riverfront Industrial District takes in several areas from 800 Front St. to 38th St. along the east bank of the river.

Muscogee County Courthouse, 9th and 10th streets, and 1st and 2nd avenues. On grounds is a cannon captured by Federals at Shiloh. It was cast at the local iron works from household metal contributed by Columbus women and was known as the "Ladies Defender." Also on grounds, "Red Jacket," a brass salute gun which saluted each state's secession and Jefferson Davis's inauguration.

COVINGTON, Newton County. IS 20 State 12.

Henderson House, 2 blocks east of square, left of Floyd St., was the home of Gen. Robert J. Henderson, who served under Gen. Joseph Johnston.

CRAWFORDVILLE, Taliaferro County. IS 20.

Alexander H. Stephens Memorial State Park, 2 miles north of IS 20 via State 22 exit. The site contains Liberty Hall, former home of the Confederate vice president. It has been restored. Stephens, who never weighed more than a hundred pounds and seldom had a really well day in his life, was arrested here soon after the war and taken to Fort Warren in Boston Harbor for several months. Although his health never improved greatly, even after parole, he became governor of Georgia in 1882 and died in office the following year. In the library at Liberty Hall he wrote *A Constitutional View of the Late War Between the States.* The house contains many Confederate mementoes. Park also has Stephens's grave. Museum.

CUTHBERT, Randolph County. US 82.
Greenwood Cemetery, graves of 24 Confederate soldiers who died at Hood Hospital, later Andrew College. Confederate monument.

DALTON, Whitfield County. IS 75. Plaque on highway describes this segment of the Atlanta campaign.
Crown Garden and Archives, 715 Chattanooga Ave. Historical society has changing Civil War exhibits.
Huff House, 71 Selvidge St. Headquarters for Gen. Joseph Johnston in the winter of 1864. Bronze marker on lawn.

DECATUR, DeKalb County. Off IS 285, US 29. McPherson's troops destroyed the railroad here just before he was killed in the battle of Atlanta.

FITZGERALD, Ben Hill County. US 129.
Blue and Gray Museum, in Old Depot, has relics of Confederate and Union veterans from many states. A Southerner and a Northerner founded the town in 1894.

FORT GORDON, Richmond County. South of US 1 and Augusta.
Signal Corps Museum, 37th St. and Ave. of the States, includes exhibits of signal devices and field artillery from the Civil War.

GAINESVILLE, Hall County. US 23.
Altavista Cemetery has the grave of Gen. James Longstreet.

IRWINVILLE, Irwin County. State 107.
Jefferson Davis Memorial State Park, 1½ miles north of town. Museum has war relics. A bronze bust of Jefferson Davis marks the spot where he was captured in 1865. Davis heard firing just before daylight and snatched up his wife's cloak by mistake. As he left the tent, Mrs. Davis threw her shawl over his head. These items and the spurs he wore when captured have been turned over by the National Archives to the Jefferson Davis Memorial at Biloxi, Mississippi. Confederate museum here.

JONESBORO, Clayton County. US 41. The battle of Jonesboro occurred August 21–September 1, 1864, when Hood sent Hardee and two corps to protect the railroad at this point. They engaged the Union 15th Corps outside of town. Hood, learning that Schofield was on the railroad at Rough and Ready, a point halfway between Jonesboro and Atlanta, brought half of Hardee's men back to Atlanta. Sherman then sent Schofield and Thomas to Jonesboro to bag Hardee. Sherman said later it was the only time in the campaign Thomas had ever urged his horse to a gallop. Even so, Hardee escaped the net and dug in farther south at Lovejoy's Station.

The town also has claim to its boast as "Home of *Gone With the Wind.*" There is a long list of Tara's in the phone book. Devoted readers can find likely background places. Tara may have been based on a house at the corner of Tara and Folsom roads, which when last seen was far less imposing than the movie's version.

KENNESAW, Cobb County. IS 75.
Battle-rama, scale model of the battle of Kennesaw Mountain, housed in a replica of the Troup Hurt House. Narration and an exhibit pertaining to the battle of Atlanta.
Big Shanty Museum, 2829 Cherokee, houses the much-traveled locomotive the General; other relics. Slides and films.

KENNESAW MOUNTAIN NATIONAL BATTLEFIELD PARK, Cobb County. Two miles northwest of Marietta, Exit 116 from IS 75; follow the brown signs leading to the entrance gate and the visitors center on Old US 41. Kennesaw Mountain is the federal government's memorial commemorating the entire 1864 Atlanta campaign. The visitor center offers an orientation program of the battle, exhibits, and a bookstore. The mountaintop features a panoramic view of the surrounding area, including downtown Atlanta and Stone Mountain, weather permitting. General Sherman, for debatable reasons, diverted from his maneuver strategy of swing-around flanking tactics in favor of a direct assault. This decision played into the hands of Gen. Joe Johnston's waiting entrenched Confederates. "Hell broke loose in Georgia," yelled one Rebel above the gunfire of June 27, 1864. Nearly 3,000 Union troops fell that morning, compared to a Confederate loss of about 800. Defensive forticiations accounted for the lopsided Confederate victory.

The battlefield has approximately 16 miles of interpretive trails, troop movement maps, monuments, historical markers, and cannon emplacements. Special programs are presented on weekends during peak season. Free shuttle bus operates on weekends to the mountaintop. Picnicking areas are available. Recreational fields for ball playing, kite flying, or family fun are available in designated areas only. No overnight facilities are available in the park.

For seasonal park hour changes, contact the visitor center at (404) 427-4686 or the Superintendent at P.O. Box 1610, Marietta, GA 30061.

LA GRANGE, Troup County. IS 85, US 29. Legend says that all the men in the town went to war.
Bellevue, 204 Ben Hill St., was the home of Col. Benjamin H. Hill, who served in the Confederate Senate, 1861–1865. Period furnishings.

MACON, Bibb County. IS 75, US 80, 41.
City Hall, Poplar and 1st streets and Cotton Ave. The building served as state capitol from November 18, 1864, until March 11, 1865, which was the last session of the general assembly of Georgia under the Confederate government.
First Presbyterian Church, 1st and Mulberry streets. After Appomattox when the city was still occupied by Gen. James Wilson and troops, the general ordered that the U.S. flag be hung over the front door. The minister refused to hold the service and was replaced by a colleague who read a Psalm: "For they that carried us away captive required of us a song and they that wasted us required of us mirth." The congregation departed by the back door to avoid Old Glory.
Green-Foe House, Washington Ave. James Mercer Green was surgeon-general in charge of Macon hospitals during the war.
Harriet Tubman Center, 340 Walnut St., presents history of black Americans and cultural achievements.
Hay House, 934 Georgia Ave. During the war Confederate gold supposedly was hidden in a secret room off the stairs. A treasure house of antebellum architecture.
Johnston House, southwest corner of Georgia Ave. and Spring St., was the home of William B. Johnston who had charge of the Confederate Treasury's depository at Macon.
Lanier Birthplace, 835 High St. Sidney Lanier was born here in 1842. The poet served with the Macon Volunteers in Virginia, was captured on a blockade runner and imprisoned at Point Lookout, Maryland, for several months.

Municipal Auditorium, 1st and Cherry St., has historical murals by Don Carlos du Bois and Wilbur G. Kurtz.

Old Cannonball House and Macon Confederate Museum, 856 Mulberry St. Built in 1853, this house was struck by a cannonball during an attack on July 30, 1864, and now houses a United Daughters of the Confederacy museum.

Overlook, on Coleman Hill, was the residence of Gen. James H. Wilson, who captured Macon on April 20, 1865.

Rosehill Cemetery has graves of Confederate soldiers.

Washington Memorial Library, southeast corner of College St. and Washington Ave., has exhibits pertaining to Sidney Lanier and genealogical and Civil War collections.

MARIETTA, Cobb County. IS 75, US 41.
National Cemetery has 10,000 Union graves; *Confederate Cemetery* has 3,000 graves. Henry Cole, in a pacific gesture in 1866, donated land for the cemetery so that North and South could share a final resting place, but prideful citizens created the separate Confederate burial grounds nearby.

McDONOUGH, Henry County. US 23. One division of Sherman's army burned the town after the fall of Atlanta.

MIDWAY, Liberty County. US 17.
Midway Church was erected in 1792. Gen. Judson Kilpatrick and cavalry camped here and made raids about the countryside in 1864. Among early pastors were Abiel Holmes, father of Oliver Wendell Holmes, and Jedidiah Morse, father of Samuel F. B. Morse.

MILLEDGEVILLE, Baldwin County. US 441. The town, which was state capital until 1867, was spared the worst of Sherman's scorched earth policy. The state penitentiary was burned but not the entire town. George Nichols, Sherman's aide, noted in his diary that surgeons at the hospitals, the principal of the insane asylum, and others expressed their gratitude that order was maintained. Sherman slept in his bedroll on the floor of the executive mansion, from which the furnishings had been evacuated along with the governor. Eliza Frances Andrews, in *The War-Time Journal of a Georgia Girl,* saw the city after Sherman had gone: "Before crossing the Oconee at Milledgeville we ascended an immense hill, from which there was a fine view of the town, with Gov. Brown's fortifications in the foreground and the river rolling at our feet. The Yankees had burnt the bridge, so we had to cross on a ferry. There was a long train of vehicles ahead of us, and it

was nearly an hour before our turn came, so we had ample time to look about us. On our left was a field where 30,000 Yankees had camped hardly three weeks before. It was strewn with the debris they had left behind, and the poor people of the neighborhood were wandering over it, seeking for anything they could find to eat, even picking up grains of corn that were scattered around where the Yankees had fed their horses. We were told that a great many valuables were found there at first,—plunder that the invaders had left behind, but the place had been picked over so often by this time that little now remained except tufts of loose cotton, piles of half-rotted grain, and the carcasses of slaughtered animals, which raised a horrible stench. Some men were plowing in one part of the field, making ready for next year's crop."

Old State Capitol, Wayne, Elberton, Franklin, and Greene streets, housed the secession convention of 1861. Here, Sherman's troops held a mock session of the legislature "repealing" the ordinance of secession. Building is now occupied by the Georgia Military College.

St. Stephens Episcopal Church, S. Wayne St. Union horses and rowdy soldiers occupied the church, the soldiers doing more damage than the animals. It is said that soldiers poured sorghum down the organ pipes to prevent their being used to signal Southern sympathizers in the area.

MILLEN, Jenkins County. US 80.
Camp Lawton, a Confederate prison camp, was located near here in the winter of 1864. It was intended to relieve the congestion at Andersonville. As matters worked out, Sherman's army relieved the congestion. The troops were particularly vengeful on Millen, burned the attractive railroad station and the hotel, and looted houses. The prison stockade was abandoned before their arrival.

NEW HOPE CHURCH MONUMENT, State 92, 4 miles northeast of US 278 at Dallas. Tablet at site describes the battle of May 25, 1864. Johnston took up a position protecting the Atlanta roads in this area. The Federals made a series of unsuccessful assaults on the Confederates.

NEWNAN, Coweta County. IS 85, US 29.
College Temple, 73 College St. A now defunct college for women was used as hospital for both armies during the war.

PALMETTO, Fulton County. US 29. In September 1864, Gen. Hood, with 40,000 men, planned to cut the Federal lines of communication from a base here. Jefferson Davis visited Hood, reviewed the troops, and gave an encouraging speech. A Yankee commentator said he prayed a little, threatened much, and promised more.

RESACA, Gordon County. IS 75. Parking and overlook area, with tablet descriptive of Federal assault in this section of the Confederate defense line. The Confederates were entrenched on a semicircle of hills about the town, with the Oostanaula River to the rear. *Confederate Cemetery* has 500 graves.

RINGGOLD GAP, Catoosa County. US 41. Descriptive bronze tablet at site where Sherman began his campaign to win Atlanta on May 7, 1864. The Union army had maintained an advance position here during the winter.

ROCKY FACE RIDGE, Whitfield County. US 41. Marker for Confederate stronghold in spring of 1864, evacuated on May 12 as Sherman threatened the line of communication.

ROME, Floyd County. US 27. In May 1863, the town entertained Nathan Bedford Forrest's troops after their capture of Col. Abel D. Streight nearby in Alabama. This was the terminus of John H. Wisdom's long ride from Gadsden, Alabama, to warn the town of Streight's approach. There is a large cannon lathe on Civic Center Hill, with sledge hammer marks made by Sherman's men, who tried to destroy it. There are some 377 Confederate graves in a cemetery on Myrtle Hill.

Forrest Memorial, Broad and 2nd Ave.

Noble Foundry, between railroad tracks and the Etowah River, manufactured Confederate supplies, including cannon. Sherman sent a small cavalry force to hold the town during the summer of 1864; in October he had headquarters here, and when he withdrew to Kingston early in November he destroyed the foundry and all factories that might be helpful to the Confederacy.

ROSWELL, Fulton County. US 19. Cotton mills were destroyed when Federal forces occupied the town after the battle of Kennesaw Mountain. Descriptive marker at site of former mills.

SANDERSVILLE, Washington County. State 24. Wheeler's cavalry engaged Sherman's army here in November 1864, delaying the march only slightly. Wheeler's men dismounted and fought in hand-to-hand combat.

SAVANNAH, Chatham County. IS 95, US 17, 80. The end of the Georgia line of march was occupied after the reduction of Fort McAllister, in time for Sherman to offer the city to Lincoln as a Christmas present. There was some carping in Washington that he had allowed Hardee to escape, but Savannah was a magnificent prize and Lincoln sent his thanks.

Confederate Memorial, Forsyth Park, Gaston St. to Park Ave. Monument surmounted by the bronze figure of a Confederate soldier. Enclosure also has memorial busts of Gen. Lafayette McLaws and Brig. Gen. Francis S. Bartow.

Fort Jackson Maritime Museum, 3 miles east via Islands Expressway, has naval history of area.

Fort McAllister State Historical Park, 10 miles east on US 17, then left on State 144. On the bank of the Great Ogeechee River. Confederate earthworks and visitor center with exhibits. When Union gunboats attacked in March 1863, the only fatality was a cat, the mascot.

Fort Pulaski National Monument, on Cockspur and McQueens islands, at the mouth of the Savannah River. US 80E. The fort was the first command of Gen. Robert E. Lee and became a landmark in artillery history during the war. The structure, enclosing the parade ground, is surrounded by a moat with drawbridges. It was designed by a veteran of Napoleon's staff, Gen. Simon Bernard. With the exception of Bernard, who died in 1831, every army engineer who worked on the construction of the fort became either a Union or a Confederate general. Georgia occupied the fort, without resistance, on January 3, 1861, and armed it for protection of the port. Most Confederates, including Lee, considered it impregnable, in the belief that no existing weapons could penetrate the brick walls. Union Capt. Quincy A. Gillmore believed otherwise and with rifled cannons proved his point. Some projectiles are still embedded in the walls. Numbered markers are at significant points. Attendants are on duty; a historian gives lectures at frequent intervals.

Juliette Gordon Low Birthplace, 142 Bull St. and 10 Oglethorpe Ave. The future founder of the Girl Scouts was a quick-tempered Confederate girl in 1865. She is said to have told Gen. Howard, whose sleeve had been empty since Seven Pines: "I shouldn't wonder if my papa did it! He has shot lots of Yankees." Sherman visited the Gordon house a number of times. Juliette's mother was Nellie Kinzie Gordon, Chicago born and bred. The Lows also lived for a time at 329 Abercorn St. Among guests were Gen. Lee and William Makepeace Thackeray.

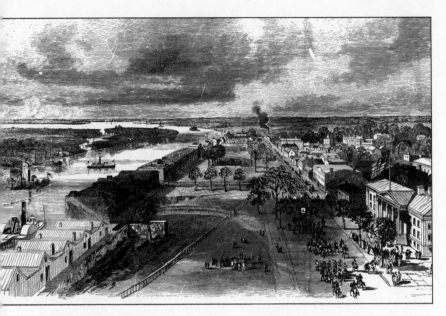

A view of Savannah, looking east toward Fort Jackson.

The Pink House, 23 Abercorn, was headquarters for Union soldiers in 1865. It is now a restaurant.

Sherman Headquarters, 14 W. Macon St. The Green-Meldrim mansion was occupied by the general in December 1864. While here he learned that a son, Charles, his seventh child, whom he had never seen, was dead of pneumonia. The general had never fully recovered from the loss of his young son and namesake, Willy, who died in Memphis in 1863. Sherman spent a lonely New Year's Eve in this house, wrote to his brother John " . . . were it not for General Grant's confidence in me, I should insist upon a little rest. As it is, I must go on." Building is now the parish house of St. John's Episcopal Church.

Ships of the Sea Museum, 503 E. River, on river, has many ship relics.

STONE MOUNTAIN MEMORIAL STATE PARK, DeKalb County. Off US 78.
The 3,200-acre park is dedicated to Confederate soldiers and sailors. The granite mass rises 825 feet from a base that is 7 miles in circumference. The deep relief carving depicts Generals Lee and Stonewall Jackson, and Confederate President Jefferson Davis. The figure of Lee is said to be as high as a 9-story building.

The carvings on the north face of the mountain were begun by Gutzon Borglum; work was discontinued in the mid-1920s when the sculptor and the monument association had a dispute. Augustus Lukeman continued the carving but completed only one section. Walker Hancock, of Gloucester, Massachusetts, finished the massive work. The area has been extensively developed. There is a cable-car lift which rises 2,600 feet to the summit of the mountain. A museum has extensive relics and exhibits, including a 60-foot relief map of Sherman's march to the sea. An antebellum plantation, including the plantation house and nineteen outbuildings, has been moved to the area, refurnished, and restored. Early in April the park hosts the Antebellum Jubilee, a living history celebration.

THOMASVILLE, Thomas County. US 19, 84.

Chamber of Commerce, 401 S. Broadway, has a visitor center with information on self-guiding tours, brochures, maps. You might inquire if the mansion that served as the background for Ashley's home, the picnic scene where Scarlett first met Rhett Butler in the film *Gone With the Wind*, is open for viewing. In recent years it was the home of John Hay Whitney; private.

TYBEE ISLAND, Chatham County, reached by a causeway and US 80.

Tybee Museum, north end of beach, has a Civil War room with relics of both forces.

VALDOSTA, Lowndes County. IS 75.

Lowndes County Historical Society and Museum, 305 W. Central Ave., has an original Confederate secession decree among its exhibits.

WASHINGTON, Wilkes County. US 78. Courthouse square has five descriptive markers for last Confederate cabinet meeting, May 5, 1865.

Toombs House, Robert Toombs Ave., was the home of Robert Augustus Toombs, Confederate statesman and army officer. For a time after the war Toombs went to England rather than take the oath of allegiance.

Site of Haywood, W. Robert Toombs Ave. Eliza Frances Andrews, author of *The War-Time Journal of a Georgia Girl,* once lived here. Her memoirs of the last days of the Confederacy are among the best accounts of the period.

Washington-Wilkes Historical Museum, 308 E. Robert Toombs Ave. On US 78, has Confederate relics. Washington was on the itinerary of the flight of Jefferson Davis. The United Daughters of the Confederacy have his camp chest among their collections. The shrine is maintained by the Georgia Historical Commission.

IDAHO

Gold was discovered in 1860, bringing a rush of everything including prospective governors to Idaho. When the territory was organized in 1863, Lincoln had difficulty finding anyone to take the office. William H. Wallace became governor and a legislature convened at Lewiston in December 1863. By 1864, Idaho City in the gold-rich Boise basin was a boom town. The capital was moved to Boise and two stage lines were established. The transcontinental telegraph reached Boise in 1875. On July 3, 1890, Idaho became the 43rd state.

BOISE (Pronounced *Boy*-see), Ada County. IS 80N.

Fort Boise, 5th and Fort St. A troop of Oregon cavalry built barracks for five companies in 1863. Soldiers garrisoned here patrolled the area, keeping in check the Shoshone Indians of the Snake River.

State Historical Museum, 610 N. Julia Davis Dr., has mementos of early Idaho.

COEUR D'ALENE, Kootenai County. IS 90. In 1877 General Sherman chose this site where the Spokane River flows out of Coeur d'Alene Lake as the place for an army post and asked Congress to appropriate 1,000 acres. The post was called Fort Sherman when he retired. Now North Idaho College occupies the area.

Fort Sherman Museum, Fort Sherman Chapel, Hubbard and Woodland Dr.

FORT HALL, Bingham County. Eleven miles west of US 91–191 at Evans' Trading Post. A lava monument marks the site of the post which was once an Oregon Trail stopping place, garrisoned by regular and volunteer troops at various times during the 1850s and early 1860s. It was destroyed by flood in 1863.

IDAHO CITY, Boise County. State 21. A visitor in 1864 described the town as "full of saloons and gambling houses, dance houses of evil repute, and hurdy-gurdys of fair repute." Many buildings remain, including an early Masonic Hall, the first Idaho Odd Fellows Hall. Boot Hill Cemetery has the graves of 200 persons buried in 1863, and the rumor is that only 28 died naturally.

Boise Basin Museum, Montgomery St. at Wall St., was built as a post office in 1863, then served as a Wells Fargo station. Renovated. Museum exhibits begin with 1862 gold rush days. Historical relics include mining equipment of Civil War period.

LEWISTON, Nez Perce County. US 95.

Fort Lapwai, on Lapwai Creek east of town, was established in 1862; it remained active throughout the war.

SODA SPRINGS, Caribou County, US 30N.

Camp Connor was established here May 30, 1863, by the California Volunteers under Col. Patrick Connor, after nearly wiping out the Cache Valley Shoshone in the battle of Bear River late in January.

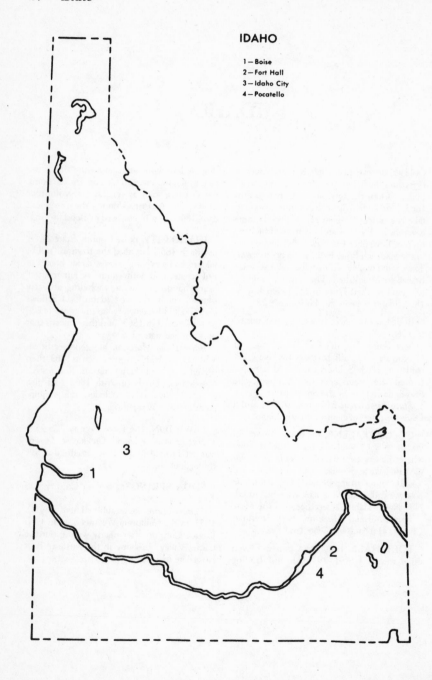

IDAHO

1 — Boise
2 — Fort Hall
3 — Idaho City
4 — Pocatello

ILLINOIS

Illinois entered the Union on December 3, 1818, as the 21st state. From the beginning slavery was a point of argument between abolitionists in the north and pro-slavery men in the downstate area. As late as 1862 a convention, meeting to revise the state constitution, approved overwhelmingly the sections prohibiting blacks from migrating to Illinois or to vote.

In the great debates of 1858, Abraham Lincoln and Stephen A. Douglas argued the question of equality. Douglas held that the founding fathers had meant that British subjects on this continent were equal to those living in Great Britain. Lincoln maintained that the declaration of equality was drafted to promote the "happiness and value of life to all people of all colors everywhere."

After the outbreak of war, Douglas made a valiant and successful effort to unite Illinois citizens in the cause of national strength. Downstate, John A. Logan and John A. McClernand, later Civil War generals, also worked to gain support for the Union. In the spring of 1861, Illinois had no effective militia nor any considerable amount of arms. Within five days after the call for volunteers, more than 62 companies were formed. Gov. Richard Yates called a special session of the legislature and organized six regiments of infantry. About 257,000 men served in the Union army. It has been estimated that one out of seven Illinois soldiers died in the war.

ALTON, Madison County. US 67, State 140.

Confederate Cemetery, Rozier and State St., North Alton, is the burial place of several thousand Confederate soldiers who died of illness in the state prison.

Elijah Lovejoy Monument, north end of Monument Ave. at entrance to cemetery. Lovejoy's newspaper plant was sacked three times by a mob and the abolitionist editor was fatally shot while defending his press, November 7, 1837.

Site of Lincoln-Douglas Debate, Broadway at end of Market St. The last of the great debates took place October 15, 1858, on a platform erected at the east side of the old City Hall. Lincoln said the fundamental conflict was between those who believed and those who did not believe that slavery was wrong. "That is the issue that will continue in this country when these poor tongues of Judge Douglas and myself shall be silent."

Site of the First State Prison in Illinois, Broadway and Williams St. Part of one cell tier remains. The prison opened on February 1, 1861, and was reported crowded by the twelfth of the month. The prison was quarantined for a time during a smallpox epidemic.

AMBOY, Lee County. US 52.

Lincoln Boulder, 106 Main St., marks the site where Lincoln spoke on August 26, 1858, on the eve of his Freeport debate with Douglas.

AURORA, Kane County. US 34.

Aurora Historical Museum, 304 Oak Ave., has Civil War items and local historical material. The 17-room antebellum mansion has two rooms furnished as they were when William Tanner, merchant, built the house in 1856–1857.

BEARDSTOWN, Cass County. US 67.

City Hall, W. 3rd and State St., has the original courtroom where Lincoln defended William "Duff" Armstrong in a murder trial in the spring of 1858. Among the salient points made by the young lawyer was the fact that the moon was down on the night an eyewitness claimed to have seen the fatal blows struck from a distance of 150 feet at eleven P.M. The case was known thereafter as the "Almanac Trial." A museum has antique guns and Indian artifacts.

City Square. Granite memorials mark sites where Lincoln and Douglas spoke from opposite ends of the square during the senatorial campaign.

Volunteer Site, in recreation park near river. Marker commemorates the spot where Lincoln

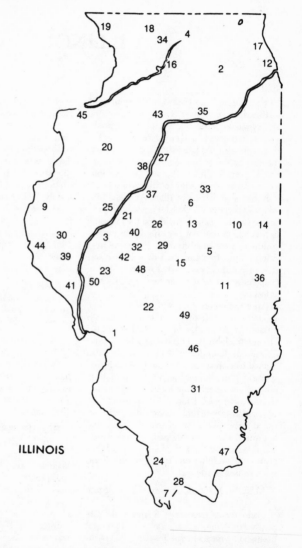

ILLINOIS

led the volunteers from Clary's Grove to be mustered into service as part of the 4th Regiment of Mounted Volunteers of the Brigade of Samuel Whiteside, April 28, 1832.

BELVIDERE, Boone County. US 20. Among the several women who seem to have taken up arms in the Civil War was Jennie Hodgers of Belvidere, who is said to have en-

listed as Pvt. Albert D. J. Cashier in August 1862, 95th Illinois Volunteer Infantry. While working as a handyman in 1911, Jennie broke her/his leg and the secret was discovered. She is buried, as Albert, in Saunemin Cemetery, Livingston County.

Belvidere Cemetery has the grave of Gen. Stephen A. Hurlbut, first national commander of the G.A.R. A marker in his honor was erected in Boone in 1953 by the Illinois State Historical Society.

BEMENT, Piatt County. State 105.

Bryant Cottage State Museum, 146 E. Wilson St. Francis E. Bryant, cousin of poet William Cullen Bryant, was a friend of Stephen A. Douglas. In this house, on the night of July 29, 1858, Lincoln and Douglas made arrangements for their debates. Marker on State 105.

BENTON, Franklin County. IS 57, State 37. The home of Gen. John A. Logan. Stephen A. Douglas campaigned here. The county historical society has a Lincoln file.

BERWYN, Cook County, US 42A. Heroic statue of "Lincoln, the Friendly Neighbor," on southeast corner of Cermak Rd. and Riverside Dr. Statue, by Avard Fairbanks of Salt Lake City, shows Lincoln with two children and a dog.

BLOOMINGTON, McLean County. IS 55, 74, US 51.

David Davis Mansion, Monroe and Davis St. Home of the former state senator and Supreme Court justice who was one of Lincoln's closest friends is under the custody of the Illinois State Historical Society and is open to the public.

Majors Hall. Monument commemorates site where Lincoln made his "Lost Speech" against slavery and where the first state convention of the Illinois Republican party was held. The speech was lost because reporters were so engrossed, it is said, they forgot to take notes.

McLean County Historical Society Museum, 201 E. Grove. War relics and local historical material.

The Pantagraph, published since 1846, printed Lincoln's famous "Lost Speech," which advocated preservation of the Union, sentiments that helped Lincoln win the presidency.

Soldiers' Monument, Miller Park, W. Wood and Summit St., is a memorial to McLean County's Civil War dead as well as soldiers of other wars previous to the World War.

BUNKER HILL, Macoupin County. State 112.

Lincoln Statue, Main St. Erected in 1904 and paid for by Capt. Charles Clinton of Cincinnati in memory of Macoupin County soldiers who served under him in the 1st Missouri Cavalry.

BYRON, Ogle County. State 2.

Soldiers' Monument, Chestnut and 2nd St., erected in 1866 in memory of Illinois Civil War soldiers.

CAIRO, Alexander County. IS 57, US 51. (Pronounced *ay*-ro.) Charles Dickens, in *American Notes,* called the town a "detestable morass" and further abused the community by making it the "Eden" of his *Martin Chuzzlewit.* Albert D. Richardson, Horace Greeley's ace correspondent, said he suspected Cairo babies were born with fins; others said babies were born web-footed. Wet or damp, Cairo was a strategic point of great importance to the Union. Cairo was the site of a Union training camp and supply depot, the base for operations against Forts Henry and Donelson.

Cairo Point—Fort Defiance State Park, US 51, south edge of town. A Riverboatman's Memorial observation tower gives an excellent view of the area. Site of the former fort.

Magnolia Manor, 27th and Washington Ave. Built by Charles A. Galigher in 1872, the home was the scene of a gala reception for President and Mrs. Grant on their return from a world tour in 1880. It is now a museum, maintained by the Cairo Historical Association.

Site of Civil War Post Office, southwest corner of Commercial Ave. and 6th St. The post office was once housed at this corner in a store whose slogan was: "Our store will be kept open Day and Night for the accommodation of steamboats."

Site of Grant's Headquarters, 609 Ohio St. During part of his stay in Cairo, Grant's family lived in rooms opposite his office on the second floor.

Site of St. Charles Hotel, Ohio and 2nd St., remains known as the Halliday Hotel. It burned in 1943; one wing remains. Grant stayed here at one time, as did many officers and war correspondents. War reporter Franc Wilkie complained that all correspondents were assigned to Room 45, third floor back, overlooking a yard full of refuse and a section of the country mostly under water. There were two beds in the room and usually a sleeping, fully-clothed-even-to-his-boots drunk in each. Saddles, bridles, and horse blankets were heaped about the room, but no water, towels, or soap could be found.

The Tigress Flagpole. A memorial was erected by the city of Cairo and the Illinois State Historical Society in 1961 to the flagpole recovered from the river packet *Tigress,* commandeered by the Union army, which carried Gen. Grant up the Tennessee River to Shiloh on April 6, 1862. The *Tigress* was sunk a year later while running batteries at Vicksburg. The crew survived and returned the flagpole to Cairo.

CARBONDALE, Jackson County. US 13, 127.

Woodlawn Cemetery was the scene of an early Memorial Day service. A number of Civil War soldiers are buried here.

CARLINVILLE, Macoupin County. US 54.

Lincoln Memorial, S. Broad and 1st South St., is a boulder with the address, in bronze, which Lincoln delivered here on August 31, 1858, to a scattered and not overly sympathetic audience.

CARMI, White County. US 460, State 1. The Lincoln Heritage Trail passes just northeast of town.

Ratcliff Inn, restored by the White County Historical Society, is now a museum. Lincoln stayed here in 1840.

CARTHAGE, Hancock County. US 136.

Site of Lincoln Speech, south of courthouse entrance on the square. In his senatorial campaign against Douglas, Lincoln spoke here on October 22, 1858. The *Chicago Tribune* reporter noted: "Mr. Lincoln was in admirable spirits and voice and gave us the best speech ever made in Hancock County." Stone marker on site.

CHAMPAIGN-URBANA, Champaign County. IS 57, 74, US 45.

County Courthouse, Main St. and Broadway. Memorial at north entrance states that Lincoln came this way when he rode the 8th Judicial Circuit. In 1853 he argued a railroad case, receiving $25 for his client, the Illinois Central. In 1854 he spoke against Sen. Douglas and the Nebraska Bill. Marble tablet on second floor commemorates the speech.

CHARLESTON, Coles County. State 16. The Charleston Heritage Trail is marked by a silhouette of Lincoln as a circuit rider.

Coles County Courthouse, public square, has replaced the building where Lincoln practiced law. The square in March 1864 was the scene of a riot when armed Copperheads attacked members of the 54th Illinois Infantry. Nine persons were killed and 12 wounded. Of the slain, six were soldiers, two Copperheads, and one unlucky chap was a Republican accidentally hit by a shot intended for a Copperhead who was trying to escape after capture.

Dennis Hanks Gravesite, west end of town in old cemetery.

Lincoln Log Cabin State Site, nine miles south of town. The Lincoln cabin, reconstructed, is furnished in period. The original cabin disappeared from the Columbian Exposition in 1893 and hasn't been found yet. The reconstruction stands on the original stone foundation. Thomas and Sarah Bush Lincoln lived here from 1837 until death and are buried in Shiloh Cemetery, northwest of park. Museum and summer interpretive program.

The Moore House, 4th St., 1 mile north of park. Lincoln paid a last visit to his stepmother before leaving for his first inauguration. Legend has him riding on the caboose of a freight train—having missed connections for the passenger train at Mattoon.

Site of Fourth Lincoln-Douglas Debate, marker on fairgrounds at west side of town, State 16. In the debate of September 18, 1858, Lincoln apparently kept well in mind that he was speaking to southern Illinoisans. His rebuttal speech began with: "I am not in favor of Negro citizenship."

CHICAGO, Cook County. IS 57, 80, 94.

Camp Douglas Site, Douglas Plaza, 3232 Dr. Martin Luther King, Jr, Dr. There is now a Civil War Memorial Wall at the Griffin Funeral Home which is situated on the former campsite. It honors both Federal and Confederate soldiers buried in nearby Oak Wood Cemetery and Ernest Griffin's grandfather, Pvt. Charles H. Griffin, who enlisted at Camp Douglas and served in the "Fighting 29th" of the U.S. Colored Infantry. Camp Douglas also served as an induction center.

Centennial Park, 18 E. Chestnut St., possibly was the smallest area ever dedicated as a Civil War memorial. A 400-pound boulder was dedicated during the centennial year, October 6, 1965. The area then fronted the Abraham Lincoln Book Shop, the original home of the Number One Civil War Round Table, founded here in 1940 and now located at 357 W. Chicago Ave., where the boulder is on display.

Chicago Historical Society, Clark St. at North Ave., has outstanding Civil War and Lincoln collections. Period rooms, dioramas, relics, paintings, and sculpture, as well as an extensive library. The Lincoln Parlor is a replica of the Springfield parlor. Peterson Bedroom has the actual bed on which Lincoln died, and much to the envy of custodians at Appomattox Court House, the Society has the table on which the Grant-Lee surrender terms were signed, also the table on which the Emancipation Proclamation was signed, and the pen and holder used to sign it. Such personal items as Lincoln's watch, spectacles, pocket knife, and nail file are in Lincoln Hall.

Five of Ellsworth's Chicago Zouave cadets.

Chicago Public Library Cultural Center, Washington and Randolph St. G.A.R. Memorial Hall on second floor has a fine collection of uniforms, flags, weapons, musical items, and documents.

Douglas Tomb State Historic Site, east end of 35th St. A bronze figure of Douglas sculptured by Leonard Volk surmounts a 100-foot shaft. Tomb is at the base of the shaft.

Du Sable Museum of African History, 740 E. 56th Pl., has many artifacts, paintings, sculpture, and a Hall of the Immortals.

Garfield Park, Central Park Ave. and Washington Blvd. "Lincoln, the Rail Splitter" by Charles J. Mulligan, and a plaque, "Peace," dedicated to the Illinois G.A.R. are in the park.

Graceland Cemetery, Irving Park and Clark St. Allan Pinkerton, master detective, and Timmy Webster, hanged as a spy, are here.

Grant Park, Randolph and E. 14th St., has the seated statue of Lincoln by Augustus Saint-Gaudens; also the Saint-Gaudens monument to General John A. Logan. Grant, however, is in Lincoln Park; moving the general to his own park, it is said, would be too expensive.

"Here's Chicago," a multimedia show in the Water Tower Pumping Station at E. Pearson and N. Michigan Ave., includes an audio-animatronic Abraham Lincoln telling his life story.

Libby Prison, 14th Pl. and Wabash Ave. Only bricks remain of the onetime Richmond, Virginia, prison, which later became a part of the old Coliseum.

Lincoln Park, North Ave. to Hollywood Ave., has an Abraham Lincoln monument by Saint-Gaudens; architect was Stanford White. "The Chicago Lincoln" statue by Avard Fairbanks is in Lincoln Square, at Lincoln and Lawrence Ave.

McKinley Park, 38th St. and Western Ave., has McKinley Monument by Charles J. Mulligan.

Newberry Library, Clark, Walton, and Dearborn St., has periodic exhibitions of rare books, prints, and maps. There are 34 G. P. A. Healy portraits in the building, which were a gift from the artist. Portraits of Lincoln, Grant, Sherman, Sheridan, Beauregard, and Porter are in the collection.

Oak Woods Cemetery, 1035 E. 67th St. About 6,000 Confederates are buried here, most of whom died while prisoners of war at Camp Douglas. The cemetery contains a Confederate monument and a statue of "Lincoln, the Orator" by Charles Mulligan.

Regenstein Library, Department of Special

Collections, University of Chicago, 1100 E. 57th St., has one of the largest Lincoln collections in the area, including original manuscripts, letters, diaries, books, and prints.

Rosehill Cemetery, 5800 Ravenswood Ave., has a memorial to Leonard Wells Volk, who created the life masks of Lincoln and Douglas; also memorials to "Long John" Wentworth, the Edwin T. Bridges Battery, the Ezra Taylor Battery, Gen. Thomas E. G. Ransom, and the Board of Trade G.A.R. Long John, who was 6 feet, 6 inches, and weighed 300 pounds, according to some estimates, was said to have made the shortest stump speech ever heard in Illinois when he was running for the office of mayor of Chicago in 1860. Reportedly Wentworth said: "You damn fools—you can either vote for me for mayor or you can go to hell."

Sheridan Monument, Sheridan Rd. and Belmont Ave. The memorial to Gen. Philip Sheridan was executed by Gutzon Borglum.

Site of the Wigwam, southeast corner of Lake St. and Wacker Dr. The building in which Lincoln was nominated for the presidency stood on land owned then and now by the Garrett Biblical Institute of Evanston. The widow of Augustus Garrett, an early Chicago mayor, gave the property to the Institute in 1856.

St. James Episcopal Church, Huron St. and Wabash Ave. Lincoln and Isaac Arnold attended services here November 25, 1860.

Tremont House, where Lincoln spoke and where politicians slept— by Murat Halstead's count, "near fifteen hundred"—during the 1860 convention, is long gone from the southeast corner of Lake and Dearborn St.

Volk Studio, southeast corner of Washington and Dearborn St. A bronze memorial plaque commemorates the site where sculptor Leonard W. Volk had a studio in 1860 when he made the life mask of Abraham Lincoln.

CLINTON, DeWitt County. US 51, 54.
Courthouse Lawn has a statue of Lincoln by Van den Bergen, quoting Lincoln's remark on fooling all of the people some of the time, some of the people all of the time, but not all of the people all of the time. The village of Clinton may or may not be fooling some of the people some of the time into believing the remark was made in a speech at this site on September 27, 1858. Authorities disagree as to when, where, or if, Lincoln ever spoke the lines. Historian Paul Angle, Lincoln scholar, *did* say on February 20, 1964, that in his opinion Lincoln could have made the remark at Clinton; but Angle remained puzzled about one thing: "It's so good, if he said it once, why didn't he keep repeating

it? I'd have kept saying it to the ends of the earth." To this, Lincoln scholar Ralph Newman added, rather thoughtfully: "And it *is* a fact Lincoln had a habit of repeating his best remarks."

The Homestead, 219 E. Woodlawn, was built in 1863, later became the residence of Clifton H. Moore, a law partner of Abraham Lincoln. Other buildings on grounds include a general store, farm and railroad museum, carriage barn, and a covered bridge.

DANVILLE, Vermilion County. IS 74, US 150, 136.
Danville Soldiers Monument, Main and Gilbert streets, by Lorado Taft.

Hooton House, 207 Buchanan, supposedly is the home where Lincoln came close to being tipsy on homemade wine. Hooton had fine vineyards and crushed his own grapes.

Site of Lincoln-Lamon Law Office, northwest corner of Redden Square, Main and Vermilion St. Ward Hill Lamon and Abraham Lincoln, then making the rounds of the 8th Judicial Circuit, formed a law partnership in 1852.

Site of McCormick House, 103 W. Main. Lincoln and other circuit riders lodged here during their visits to Danville.

Vermilion County Museum, 116 Gilbert St. The home of Dr. William Fithian is marked by a boulder on the lawn with a plate stating that Lincoln delivered an impromptu speech from the balcony of this house while a guest here in 1858.

DECATUR, Macon County. IS 72, US 51.
Lincoln had many associations with Decatur, his first home in Illinois. His first political speech was made here; a Republican convention here coined the slogan "Honest Abe, the Rail Splitter," and a special train brought him en route to his inauguration. G.A.R. Post #1 was founded here in 1866.

Lincoln Homestead State Park, 10 miles west on County 27 at Sagamon River. Direction marker on US 36. Site of first Illinois home of Lincoln family. Here in 1830 the 21-year-old Abraham worked for his father on the farm, often splitting rails expertly as he had done in Indiana.

"Lincoln the Lawyer," bronze statue at entrance of Macon County Building. Figure was sculpted by Lovet Lorski.

Lincoln Square is the site where Lincoln practiced law and made his first political speech. Bronze tablet on building at southeast corner commemorates arrival of Lincoln family by ox cart in 1830.

Log Cabin Courthouse, Fairview Park, Mc-
Clelland and W. Eldorado St., has been restored and moved from original site in
midtown. Lincoln's cousin, John Hanks,
helped to build the structure that served as the
first courthouse in Macon County.

Millikin University, W. Main St., has a
statue of the young Lincoln, by Fred Torrey, on
campus.

"Wigwam" Bronze Marker, on Millikin
Bank Building. In 1860, at Decatur's
"Wigwam," the Illinois Republican convention
endorsed Lincoln as its candidate for President
of the United States and gave him the sobriquet
of "Rail Splitter." Another statue is in front of
the courthouse. A replica of the courthouse of
Lincoln's day is in Fairview Park.

DIXON, Lee County. Alt. 30.

Lincoln Monument State Memorial, between Galena and Hennepin on Lincoln
Statue Drive, site of the Dixon blockhouse.
Here Jefferson Davis, Zachary Taylor, and Lincoln met during the Black Hawk War in 1832.
The bronze statue, by Leonard Crunelle, depicts Lincoln as a young captain of volunteers.

DWIGHT, Livingston County. IS 55, US
66. The Keeley Institute for the treatment of
alcohol and drug addiction was started by Dr.
Leslie Keeley, a Civil War surgeon, who was
continuing a study of alcoholics begun among
Union soldiers.

ELKHART, Logan County. US 66. Home
town and burial place of Richard J. Oglesby,
who served as Republican legislator before he
was commissioned a colonel of the 8th Illinois
in April 1861. He was promoted to major general in 1862 and served until May 1864, when
he resigned to serve as Governor of Illinois.

EQUALITY, Gallatin County. State 13.

General Michael K. Lawler Monument.
Lawler, who was born in Ireland, served as captain in the 3rd Illinois Infanty and as a cavalry
captain in the Mexican War, raised the 18th
Illinois Infantry in April 1861, was promoted to
brigadier general in 1863.

EVANSTON, Cook County. IS 94, US
14–41.

Calvary Cemetery, Chicago Ave. The Irish
Brigade Monument honors the grave of its
commander, John Mulligan.

Evanston Historical Society, 225 Greenwood St., has Civil War relics, including costumes, equipment, and surgical instruments,
which, at this writing, are in storage.

White House, 2009 Dodge. Only part of the

house remains. In 1860, Lincoln stayed overnight at the home of his friend Julius White,
harbor master of Chicago and member of the
Board of Trade, who resigned to raise the 37th
Illinois Volunteers.

FLORENCE, Pike County. South of US
36–54. A marker for the 99th Illinois Infantry,
the first regiment out of the state under call of
1862, embarked at this spot for St. Louis; it was
62 days under fire, lost 187 men.

FREEPORT, Stephenson County. US 20.

Civil War Monument, Courthouse lawn,
US 20 and State 75. Names of Stephenson
County soldiers and battles in which they
fought are recorded on a monument which has
life-size figures of a Civil War sailor, infantryman, cavalryman, and artilleryman.

Lincoln the Debater, by Leonard Crunelle,
in Taylor's Park, 1 mile east of courthouse on
State 75. The bronze figure, donated by W. T.
Raleigh, was unveiled August 27, 1929, on the
71st anniversary of the Lincoln-Douglas debate
in Freeport. A number of survivors who heard
one or more of the debates were present at the
ceremony.

Site of Second Lincoln-Douglas Debate, N.
State Ave. and E. Douglas St., is marked by a
memorial boulder. It was here Lincoln said:
"This government cannot endure permanently
half slave and half free." The Douglas admission that local legislation could practically
counteract any Federal law on slavery in a territory became known as the "Freeport Doc-
trine."

Stephenson County Historical Society,
1440 S. Carroll Ave., has a fine collection of
historical items and memorabilia, much of it
from the home of Jane Addams.

GALENA, Jo Daviess County. US 20.
Galena sent nine generals to the Civil War:
U. S. Grant, John A. Rawlins, William
Rowley, Augustus L. Chetlain, J. E. Smith, Jas-
per Maltby, Ely S. Parker, J. C. Smith, and
John Duer. An annual tour of historic homes is
conducted the last weekend in September.
Tourist information at DeSoto House.

DeSoto House, Main and Green St. Lincoln
spoke from a balcony in 1856. Grant had headquarters here for his 1868 and 1872 presidential
campaigns. Restored and still a hotel.

Galena Historical Museum, 211 S. Bench
St., has an unusually varied collection of historical items; many were donated by persons
living far from Galena who wanted to honor
Gen. Grant. The life-size painting "Peace in
Union," by Thomas Nast, depicting the surrender at Appomattox, is featured.

Grant Memorial Home, 500 Bouthillier. Now a state memorial, the home was presented to Gen. Grant on August 19, 1865. The whole town and plenty of visitors met Grant at the depot, 36 young women in white dresses welcomed him to a DeSoto House reception, E. B. Washburne made a speech, and Grant was presented with a handsome new home on the east side of town. The rooms display period furnishings, Grant trophies, souvenirs, and family heirlooms. Many visitors are interested in a bowl of fruit artifically preserved with an Indian formula by Mrs. Grant. The china and silver used by the Grants in the White House are so invitingly displayed in the dining room that one young housewife, more practical than historically inclined, recently exclaimed: "Oh, I think it's terrible all those nice dishes are being wasted!"

Grant Park, Park Ave. and Jackson St. Bronze memorial statue, "Grant—Our Citizen," by Johanes Gelert. The park has a granite shaft to Civil War soldiers, also cannons from the war.

Grant Store Site, 120 S. Main. Marker shows site where Grant worked for his father in 1860. There is a reconstructed Grant Leather Store at 211 S. Main.

Illinois Central Railroad Depot, foot of Bouthillier St. Gen. Grant came home in August 1865, arriving at this station. From here he departed to take office as 18th president. During a furlough in the early part of the war, Grant remarked to a friend, "I would like to be mayor of Galena, then I might get a sidewalk built from my home to the depot." On his triumphal return in 1865, one of the many garlanded arches over Main St. had the message: "General, the Sidewalk Is Built."

Jo Daviess County Courthouse, 312 N. Bench St. Capt. Grant volunteered for duty at a mass meeting here in April 1861.

Kittoe Home, 105 High St. Dr. Edward Kittoe was surgeon and medical director of the Army of Tennessee. He served as lieutenant colonel on Grant's staff.

Methodist Church, 125 S. Bench St. Grant pew in the First Methodist Church has a plaque.

Rawlins Home, 515 Hill St. Gen. John A. Rawlins served as head of Grant's staff and, according to Charles A. Dana, who spent some time with Grant in the Vicksburg campaign, Rawlins "bossed everything" at headquarters. During Grant's presidency, Rawlins was Secretary of War.

Rowley Home, 515 Hill St. Gen. William R. Rowley was a brigadier general and provost marshal on Grant's staff.

Smith Home, 807 S. Bench St. John E. Smith was a major general on Grant's staff. At the outbreak of the war he was a jeweler with a shop on Main Street.

Turney House, 612 Spring St., is the restored home of Galena's first lawyer. Furnished in Federal period. Tours.

Ulysses S. Grant Home State Historical Site, 101 Bouthillier Street. Grant and his family lived here in 1861 and his family remained throughout most of the war. D.A.R. marker.

United States Post Office, Green St., was built as a customs house for river traffic in 1858 under the direction of Ely S. Parker, a Seneca Indian, son of a famous chief. Parker was refused admission to the bar because he was not a citizen, was graduated from Rensselaer as an engineer, and became a friend of Grant, who was then a clerk in his father's leather store; Parker later served on Grant's staff.

Washburne Home, 908 Third St. Elihu B. Washburne was in Congress for 18 years, served as Secretary of State, and was minister to France during Grant's administration. Capt. Grant drilled recruits on the Washburne lawn in 1861.

GALESBURG, Knox County. IS 74, US 150, 34.

Beecher Chapel was an Underground Railroad station.

Carl Sandburg State Historical Site, 331 E. 3rd., has Lincoln Room, with memorabilia.

Henry M. Seymour Library has the Ray D. Smith Civil War collection of more than 5,000 volumes, also the Donna Workman collection, "Books That Lincoln Read."

Knox College, E. South between Cherry and Cedar, scene of the Lincoln-Douglas debate of October 7, 1858, later a training center for Union cadets. On campus:

Old Main, east end of building, site of Lincoln-Douglas debate. The speakers entered the front door of "Old Main" and stepped out on the platform through a window. A banner reading "Knox College for Lincoln," which appears in many drawings of the event, had been hung on the belfry facing the south front of the building. High winds had changed plans and platform to the east. The banner was rehung, torn by the wind and with some of the lettering turned inward so that a good many sketches made from memory are inaccurate, possibly proving that an audience for once was more intent upon listening than looking. Two students who lived in a dormitory known as "East Bricks" had just bought a ton of coal, which had been delivered to their door on the day of debate. Next morning they found it had been so trampled into the earth by the crowd they had to mine it again. In Old Main classrooms, cadets were trained in military science and drilled on the grounds by Maj. Julius Sandau of the Union army.

Whiting Hall was a center for women's aid work. Surgical bandages were made, food and clothing assembled and sent to the armies.

GIANT CITY STATE PARK, Jackson County. Off US 51, near Makanda. The park, which has curious stone formations, reportedly was once headquarters for the Illinois Knights of the Golden Circle, who promoted draft resistance and carried on espionage for the South.

HAVANA, Mason County. US 136, State 78.

Mason County Courthouse is a replica of the original structure in which Lincoln practiced law.

Rockwell Park has marker commemorating a Lincoln speech in August 1858, during his senatorial campaign against Douglas.

HIGHWOOD, Lake County. Sheridan Rd.

Fort Sheridan Museum, Bldg. 33, in the guardhouse, has Civil War medical equipment and mementos of Gen. Philip Sheridan.

HILLSBORO, Montgomery County. State 16, 127.

Beckemeyer School, once the county fairgrounds, site of Lincoln speech in September 1858.

Blockburger Inn, Main and Tilson St. Lincoln often stayed here overnight on trips to Vandalia, then the capital.

Eccles Home, corner of Berry and Water St. Lincoln was often a guest at the home of Joseph T. Eccles.

Hillsboro Courthouse is site where Lincoln spoke in July 1844.

JACKSONVILLE, Morgan County. US 67, 36-54. An abolitionist center in prewar days. Both Lincoln and Douglas gave speeches here. Douglas began the practice of law here in 1834, later received the title of the "Little Giant" from Jacksonville friends and supporters. Wartime Governor Richard Yates lived here and was graduated from Illinois College.

Civil War Memorial, public square, was erected by Morgan County.

Duncan Park, 4 Duncan Pl., built in 1835 by Gov. Duncan, was a home where such notables as Daniel Webster, Martin Van Buren, and Abraham Lincoln were entertained.

East Cemetery has a Civil War monument.

Fair Grounds, W. State St., has marker for site where Grant's troops camped en route to Missouri.

Grierson Memorials, on E. State St. and at the American Legion Home, W. College. Memorials to Gen. Benjamin Grierson, a former music teacher who became famous for a raid into Mississippi with a cavalry corps, covering 600 miles in 16 days, April 17 to May 2, 1863.

Illinois College, 1101 W. College Ave. The Rev. Edward Beecher, brother of Harriet Beecher Stowe, was first president. Richard Yates was in first graduating class. Lincoln spoke here in February 1859, and was an honorary member of the Phi Alpha Society.

JONESBORO, Union County. State 127, 146.

Fair Grounds, N. Main St., is the site of the third Lincoln-Douglas debate, September 15, 1858. Marker near town square.

KANKAKEE, Kankakee County. IS 57, US 54.

Kankakee Historical Museum, Water St. and 8th Ave., has Civil War relics.

LAWRENCEVILLE, Lawrence County. US 50.

Lincoln Trail State Memorial, on US 50 east of town, marks site where Lincoln family entered Illinois from Indiana. They then turned northeastward toward Palestine where the land office was located. It seems ironic that almost everywhere Lincoln set foot is commemorated when he never spoke of his family background or early struggles if he could avoid it. The bronze figure of the young Lincoln at the head of a covered wagon is most impressive.

LEWISTOWN, Fulton County. US 24. The town made famous by Edgar Lee Masters in *Spoon River Anthology* was often visited by Lincoln and Douglas. In a now-vanished courthouse, Lincoln, Robert Ingersoll, and Edward D. Baker appeared as lawyers, and Stephen Douglas as judge. Pillars from old courthouse are now a memorial in the Protestant Cemetery.

Major Newton Walker House, 1127 N. Main St. Home of Maj. Walker who served with Lincoln in the state legislature at Vandalia. Lincoln was often Walker's guest.

Proctor's Grove, southwest part of town. Douglas spoke to 5,000 persons here in August 1858; next day Lincoln answered in a speech at the courthouse.

Ross Mansion, 409 E. Milton Ave., was built by Col. Lewis Ross. The architect was said to be a Southern sympathizer, and a cannon was pointed toward the building during draft riot days. The building was restored after being damaged by fire, not by a cannonball.

LINCOLN, Logan County. IS 55, US 66. The only town named for Lincoln with his knowledge and consent was christened by him with watermelon juice in August 1853.

Lincoln College, Ottawa and Keokuk St., founded in 1865, was the first and only college named for Lincoln during his lifetime. On campus are the Lincoln Room and Presidential Museum and the memorial statue, "Lincoln, the Student."

Logan County Courthouse, in midtown, stands on site of building where Lincoln once practiced law.

Old Alton Depot, on Broadway adjoining present depot. Site where first Logan County volunteers left for the war in April 1861, where Douglas spoke April 26, 1861, and where the Lincoln funeral train stopped briefly on May 3, 1865.

Old Postville Hotel, 5th and Madison St., formerly Duskin's Inn, where Lincoln often stayed overnight during court sessions.

Old Prim Store and Postoffice, northeast corner of 5th and Washington St. Store often visited by Lincoln in 1837.

Postville Courthouse State Historic Site, 5th St. off US 66. The building is a replica of the 1839 structure that was the first courthouse in the 8th Circuit Court District when Lincoln rode the circuit. Museum has relics and documents of that era.

Postville Park, 5th and Washington St. Lincoln engaged in "town ball," horseshoe pitching, and throwing the maul here. In downtown area is site where a conspiracy to steal Lincoln's body from its tomb was plotted in 1876.

LOCKPORT, Will County. State 7, 171.

Illinois & Michigan Canal Museum, 803 S. State St. (State 171), in the original home of the canal commissioner (1837), has one of the two known scale models of Lincoln's Tomb.

Lockport Township Civil War Days, Delwood Park, State 171, are reenactments of infantry, cavalry, and artillery engagements taking place the last weekend in September.

LOVINGTON, Moultrie County. State 32, 133. The Lincoln family camped 2½ miles south of town (on State 32, intercepting the Paris to Springfield road).

MARION, Williamson County. IS 57, State 37. Home town of Robert G. Ingersoll and John A. Logan, lawyers who organized regiments at the outbreak of the war and became colonels. Ingersoll commanded the 11th Illinois Cavalry, Logan the 31st Illinois Infantry.

MARSHALL, Clark County. IS 70, State 1.

Lincoln Trail State Park, 2 miles south off IS 70, on State 1, a site on the Lincoln family's journey from Indiana.

MATTOON, Coles County. US 45. U. S. Grant mustered in the 21st Illinois Infantry here in June 1861. Marker on Illinois Central depot. The Camp Grant flagpole now stands in front of the U.S. Grant Motor Inn.

Lincoln Log Cabin State Park, 12 miles southeast on US 36. (*See* CHARLESTON.)

METAMORA, Woodford County. State 116.

Metamora Courthouse State Historic Site, 113 E. Partridge, displays original furnishings in courtroom where Lincoln practiced law from 1844 to 1856. Museum with period relics. Guided tours.

MORRIS, Grundy County. IS 80, US 6.

Grundy County Courthouse has a memorial commemorating Grundy County's contribution to the siege of Vicksburg.

MOUND CITY, Pulaski County. IS 57, US 51, State 37.

Marine Ways. Marker erected by the Illinois State Historical Society commemorates the naval depot of the western river fleet located at Mound City during the Civil War. Keels of three Eads ironclads were laid here; the marine ways are still in operation.

U.S. Military Hospital, Ohio levee. Marker erected by the Illinois State Historical Society in 1961 indicates the site of an 1861 hospital. Following the battle of Shiloh, 2,200 Union and Confederate wounded were patients in the southern portion of the brick building, 150 yards east of the marker.

MOUNT PULASKI, Logan County. US 54, State 121.

Mount Pulaski Courthouse State Historic Site, on the town square. Restored. Lincoln practiced law here in his circuit riding days, from 1847 to 1853.

MOUNT STERLING, Brown County. US 24, State 99. Both Lincoln and Daniel Boone had relatives here. The spot where Lincoln spoke in October 1858 is marked by a boulder on the North Grade School campus. Stephen Douglas held court here when serving as circuit judge.

MOUNT VERNON, Jefferson County. IS 64, US 460, State 15, 37.

Lincoln Medallion on courthouse, public square.

Supreme Court House, head of Main St. Lincoln won one of his biggest corporation law cases and fees in this building. In November 1859, he visited here with nine railroad officials including George B. McClellan, later to become commanding general of the Army of the Potomac. In 1888 Clara Barton used the building as a hospital after a tornado.

NAPERVILLE, DuPage County. IS 55, US 34.

Civil War Monument, Washington St. east of library, erected by the G.A.R. in 1870 in memory of Civil War soldiers.

NEW SALEM STATE PARK, Menard County. State 97, 18 miles northwest of Springfield. The state park is a complete restoration of the village Lincoln lived in from 1831 to 1837. Early maps and family archives were followed in the reconstruction. Guides are available; buildings are well marked for a walking tour of the settlement. The *Onstat Cooper Shop* is the only original building in the park, but 13 cabins, the *Rutledge Tavern,* ten shops, and a school have been faithfully reproduced. The park is open year-round.

Heroic statue of "Lincoln from New Salem" by Avard Fairbanks, at top of hill, was gift to Illinois from the Sons of the Utah Pioneers.

A replica of an 1832 riverboat *Talisman* makes hourly trips in season on the Sangamon River, with narration during the 2½ mile cruise.

NORMAL, McLean County. IS 55.

Jesse Fell House, 502 S. Fell Ave., moved from original site. Lincoln often visited his friend Fell, who was a founder of the town and one of the three men who helped to make Lincoln a candidate for president. Owen Lovejoy, David Davis, and John and Cyrus Bryant, brothers of the poet William Cullen Bryant and friends of Lincoln, also were frequent visitors at the Fell home.

Richard Hovey House, 202 W. Mulberry Ave. The home of Charles Edward Hovey, major general in the Civil War, commanding the 33rd Regiment of Illinois Volunteers, which was made up largely of teachers and students from Illinois State Normal University, where Hovey had been principal. The outfit was sometimes known as the "Brains Regiment." Poet Richard Hovey was born here on May 4, 1864, at a time when his father was recovering from war wounds.

OAK BROOK, Du Page County. US 34.

Old Graue Mill and Museum, York Rd. and Ogden Ave., is one of the few authentic Underground Railroad stations in Illinois. The water-wheel gristmill has Civil War relics on the ground floor.

OREGON, Ogle County, State 2.

Lincoln Boulder, on highway, site of speech, August 16, 1856.

Ogle County Historical Society, 111 N. 6th St., has war items.

Soldiers' Monument, in town square, is by Lorado Taft.

OTTAWA, LaSalle County. IS 80.

Washington Park, Columbus and LaFayette St., has boulder marking site where the first Lincoln-Douglas debate was held, August 21, 1858.

PARIS, Edgar County. US 150, State 1. The Alexander home, where Lincoln often visited, is now an office building. In behalf of presidential candidate John C. Frémont, Lincoln spoke here in 1856; in his own behalf, he spoke in 1858 when a candidate for the U.S. Senate.

PEKIN, Tazewell County. State 29. Lincoln practiced law here during his years on the circuit. Another lawyer described a bat eviction: Lincoln, in a "bob-tail sack coat" and jeans that came within 16 inches of his feet, took a broom to a bat loose in the courtroom. Someone else tried a cattle whip, but Lincoln's broom proved the best weapon.

PEORIA, Peoria County. IS 74, US 24, 150.

Courthouse Square, Main and Adams St. South portico of courthouse commemorates site of Lincoln's Peoria speech, October 16, 1854, in which reportedly he denounced slavery for the first time publicly. Southeast corner of square has the Soldiers' and Sailors' Monument, by Fritz Triebel.

Peoria Historical Society Museum, 942 Glen Oak Ave., is housed in restored Judge Flanagan mansion, built in 1837.

PERRY, Pike County. State 107.

Grant Campsite, on Perry-Naples Rd., north of Valley City and east of Perry. Marker dedicated May 19, 1963, by the Pike County Historical Society, for site where U. S. Grant camped with the 21st Regiment Illinois Volunteers, July 8, 1861.

PETERSBURG, Menard County. State 97.

Farmers Point Cemetery, 5 miles south on State 96-123. Mentor Graham grave. Graham was Lincoln's schoolteacher at New Salem.

Menard County Courthouse has Lincoln papers on display.

Oakland Cemetery, in southwest section of Petersburg, has the grave of Ann Rutledge. The

headstone has lines written by Edgar Lee Masters, who is buried north of the Rutledge site:
Out of me unworthy and unknown
The vibrations of deathless music;
'With malice toward none, with charity for all.'

Rosehill Cemetery, east of town, has memorial erected by the Illinois State Historical Society in honor of Dr. Benjamin Franklin Stephenson, founder of the G.A.R.; the former surgeon of the 14th Illinois Volunteers the G.A.R.'s first adjutant general.

PITTSFIELD, Pike County. US 36, 54. John Hay, Lincoln's secretary, later ambassador, Secretary of State, and Lincoln biographer, spent two years here as a student.

Central Park has boulder marking site of Lincoln speech on October 1, 1858.

East School, built during the war, a registered historic landmark.

Worthington House, 626 W. Washington, was the home of Dr. Thomas Worthington who was host here to Lincoln, Hay, and Nicolay.

PLEASANT PLAINS, Sangamon County. State 125.

Clayville Tavern, on highway, 12 miles west of Springfield. The stagecoach stop where Lincoln frequently stayed has been restored. Clayville was once a local rallying place for members of Lincoln's political party.

PRINCETON, Bureau County. IS 80, US 6, 34.

Cyrus Bryant House, 1110 S. Main St., has boulder in yard marking site where Cyrus and John Bryant, brothers of the poet William Cullen Bryant and friends of Lincoln, had a log cabin when they appropriated the land.

John Bryant House, 1518 S. Main St., was reportedly an Underground Railroad Station.

Owen Lovejoy House, east side of town, was the residence of the abolitionist minister, friend of Lincoln and brother of Elijah Parish Lovejoy, Alton editor killed by a pro-slavery mob. Also an Underground Railroad Station.

QUINCY, Adams County. US 24.

All Wars Museum, 1701 N. 12th St. on the grounds of the Illinois Veterans Home, is one of the nation's oldest and largest institutions for veterans. Exhibits include Civil War memorabilia.

Lincoln-Douglas Debate, east side of Washington Park. The site of the sixth debate is marked by a bronze plaque designed by Lorado Taft. It is the only commemorative marker of the seven debate sites that depicts Douglas as a participant.

Quincy Historical Society, 425 S 12th St., in John Wood restored mansion, has changing exhibits. Among them have been items from Andersonville Prison and items belonging to George Atzerodt and Lewis Paine, who plotted with Booth to assassinate Lincoln.

ROCK ISLAND, Rock Island County. IS 80, US 67, 6.

Rock Island Arsenal, on Rock Island in Mississippi River, has the John M. Browning Museum with an extensive collection of weapons. The arsenal was one of the largest Northern prisons during the Civil War. The old stone bridge marks a former boundary. Confederate cemetery.

ROSEMONT, Christian County, has Lincoln monument just west of town, on State 16.

SALEM, Marion County. IS 57, State 37. Lincoln made an important speech here that helped to bring about the election of William Henry Harrison as president in 1840. Houses in which Lincoln once stayed are at 321 S. Franklin and in the 300 block of W. Schwartz.

SHAWNEETOWN, Gallatin County. State 13.

First Bank of Illinois, established in 1816 in the home of John Marshall, was reportedly visited by Lincoln when he came to Shawneetown on a law case.

Old Slave House, 1 mile south of State 13 on State 1. John H. Crenshaw, who owned salt mines, was permitted to own slaves, it is said, because the state received 14 percent of its revenues from his taxes. Stories about the establishment seem to grow worse over the years. It is said that documents prove he kept a stud slave for breeding purposes and himself sired more than 300 children—a performance which today would assure him tabloid headlines and guest appearances on many TV shows.

The third floor of the house apparently had a curious arrangement of cells with wooden bunks and chain anchors imbedded in the floor.

SPRINGFIELD, Sangamon County. IS 55, 72, US 66.

Abraham Lincoln Memorial Garden, 60 acres on the shores of Lake Springfield.

Benjamin Edwards Home, 700 N. 4th St., now houses the Springfield Art Association. Judge Benjamin S. Edwards was host here to Lincoln, Grant, John Hay, and other notables. House has period furnishings, sculpture, and paintings.

Camp Butler National Cemetery. Marker for the camp erected by the Illinois State Historical Society. Butler was a concentration camp for Illinois Volunteers, also a prison camp for captured Confederates. Now a national cemetery, it contains the graves of 1,642 Union and Confederate soldiers.

Executive Mansion, 4th, 5th, Jackson, and Edwards. Lincoln was among those who watched the brickmasons at work on the house in the 1850s. The Lincolns were later guests of Gov. William H. Bissell.

First Presbyterian Church, 7th and Capitol Ave., has the pew once occupied by the Lincolns.

Globe Tavern, 315 E. Adams St. Site of the tavern in which the Lincolns lived for a time.

Great Campsite, on the old Jacksonville Rd., west of Springfield. U. S. Grant campsite marker erected in 1961 by the D.A.R.

Great Western Station, 10th and Monroe St. Depot where Lincoln said farewell to Springfield. Complete text of his speech is on a tablet. Lincoln never came back alive, as his stepmother predicted. Depot has been vividly restored to depict that poignant day.

Illinois State Capitol, 2nd St. Information and guide service available in rotunda. The building contains sculpture and paintings of prominent Civil War participants, among them: Lincoln, Douglas, Grant, and Logan. Lincoln, Douglas, and Yates are represented among statuary on east front of building.

Illinois State Historical Library in the Old State Capitol has an extensive collection of Abraham Lincoln and Civil War materials, manuscripts, photographs, and so forth. Lincolniana, historical documents, portraits.

Lincoln Circuit Marker, northeast corner Lincoln Square, bronze tablet.

Lincoln Home National Historic Site, 426 S. 7th. The only home Lincoln owned has some original furnishings and personal memorabilia. Lincoln and his family lived here for 17 years before moving to Washington. Visitor center offers films, exhibits, and a bookstore and issues free tickets required for tours of the Lincoln Home. The surrounding historic neighborhood includes residences of neighbors of the Lincoln family that are being preserved and restored.

Lincoln-John F. Stuart Law Office, 109 N. 5th St., near Washington. Site of Joshua Speed's store above which Lincoln and Speed lived for several months.

Lincoln-Herndon Law Office, southwest corner, 6th and Adams St. Offices were on the third floor. Building restored in 1968; Lincoln's office and a 2nd floor courtroom, where he often tried cases, are carefully refurbished. Before forming a partnership with Herndon, Lin-

coln and Stephen T. Logan were partners at this address.

Lincoln Marriage Home, 406 8th, home of Ninian Wirt Edwards, son of Gov. Ninian Edwards. Abraham Lincoln and Mary Todd were married in her uncle's house; Mary Lincoln died here in 1882.

Lincoln Nomination, 116 N. 6th St. Lincoln received notice of his nomination for the presidency in a second-floor room here.

Lincoln Tomb, Oak Ridge Cemetery, north part of city. The tomb and monument are state maintained; Mrs. Lincoln and three of their four sons are in crypts south of the cenotaph: Edward Baker, William Wallace, and Thomas. Robert Todd Lincoln, eldest son, is buried in Arlington National Cemetery.

Old State Capitol State Historical Site, City Square, has been restored as a permanent shrine to Lincoln, Douglas, Grant, and others. Here Lincoln made his "House Divided" speech. The building, which is more than 100 years old, served from 1876 as the Sangamon County courthouse. It was purchased by the state in 1961. North side of building has memorial to Abraham Lincoln as commander-in-chief, erected by National Society, Daughters of the Union, 1947. South side of building has the Stephen A. Douglas "Protect the Flag" speech on a plaque erected by the Springfield Historical Monuments Commission, 1961.

Smith Store, 528 E. Adams St., the original building in which Lincoln wrote his First Inaugural Address.

Vachel Lindsay Home, 603 S. 5th St., was owned in the 1850s by Clark M. Smith, who married Anna Maria Todd, younger sister of Mary Todd Lincoln. The Lincolns often visited here.

TROY GROVE, LaSalle County. US 52.
Wild Bill Hickok Monument, on highway. Birthplace of Hickok who served as a Union scout.

UNION, McHenry County. Off IS 90.
McHenry County Historical Society Museum, 6422 N. Main St. Civil War relics and a research library.

Seven Acres Antique Village and Museum of Civil War Days, 8512 S. Union Rd. One hundred participants stage twice-a-day battles during the two-day event held the first weekend in July.

UTICA, LaSalle County. US 178.
La Salle County Historical Museum, Canal and Mill streets, has a Lincoln carriage and other relics.

VANDALIA, Fayette County. IS 70, US 51.

Little Brick House Museum, 621 St. Clair St., has Lincoln items.

Old State Burial Ground, 2 blocks south of Old Capitol. In the cemetery is the grave of Col. Lucien Greathouse, killed at age 22 at the head of his regiment during the battle of Atlanta, also the grave of Gustav Stahl, who served in the campaign at Vicksburg.

Vandalia State House State Memorial, 315 W. Gallatin. Lincoln and Stephen A. Douglas both served in the House of Representatives in this building. Period items are featured in the furnishings of this historic building, which was the state Capitol between 1820 and 1839. It has been handsomely restored. In the Supreme Court Room, young Abraham Lincoln received his license to practice law. The date was September 9, 1836.

WAUCONDA, Lake County, State 176.

Lake County Museum, Lakewood Forest Preserve, State 176, has a small but excellent display of Civil War memorabilia.

WEST DUNDEE, Kane County. State 31.

Site of Pinkerton's Cooperage, 3rd and Main. Allan Pinkerton came from Glasgow, Scotland, in 1843, establishing a cooper shop at this corner, later organized Chicago's first detective agency, and became Secret Service chief during the early part of the Civil War.

WINCHESTER, Scott County. US 36, 54.

Scott County Courthouse has tablet denoting site of Aiken Tavern, where Lincoln stayed in 1854. A boulder marks site of Lincoln speech in which he first referred to the Kansas-Nebraska issue.

Stephen A. Douglas Monument, public square. Douglas moved to Winchester from Vermont in 1833, taught school and began his law practice here.

WOODSTOCK, McHenry County. US 14.

Civil War Monument, City Park, erected by the Woodstock Woman's Relief Corps.

INDIANA

Indiana was the 19th state to enter the Union; the date was December 11, 1816. During the controversial 1850s members of both Republican and Democratic parties held that states should be allowed to secede if they so desired. In southern Indiana, many were sympathetic to the South. Gov. Oliver P. Morton, however, was strongly pro-Union and worked effectively for Northern support. He collected arms throughout the state, put them in readiness, and went to Washington to make arrangements for additional weapons. Lewis Wallace was named adjutant general. On April 15, Gov. Morton wrote Lincoln that he had 10,000 men ready for service. In all, the state furnished 208,367 men to the Union army; nearly 25,000 were killed or died of disease in service. Indiana troops took part in more than 300 engagements, from Philippi, now in West Virginia, on June 3, 1861, to Palmetto Ranch, Texas, the last battle of the war, on May 13, 1865.

The state was invaded once, for five days in July 1863, by Gen. John H. Morgan and his raiders. Gov. Morton wired Gen. Boyle at Louisville: "You have all our regular troops. Please state what steps have been taken to arrest the progress of the rebels." It took two more wires to elicit a reply that managed to beg all three queries: "He [Morgan] has no less than 4,000 men and six pieces of artillery . . . . Your cities and towns will be sacked and pillaged if you do not bring out your State forces." Morton issued a general order for all able-bodied men south of the National Road to arm themselves and form home guard companies; Gen. Lew Wallace was called back from a fishing trip; Morgan and the Harrison County militia skirmished at Corydon, which was then occupied by the Confederates. After raiding the former state capital, Morgan moved on to Salem, Dupont, and Versailles, then crossed into Ohio, ending the invasion.

BEDFORD, Lawrence County. US 50, State 37.

Lawrence County Historical Society, in county courthouse, has historical material. Civil War items.

BLOOMINGTON, Monroe County. US 37.

Lilly Library, on the Indiana University campus at 7th St., has an impressive collection of rare books and documents and Abraham Lincoln's desk and chair.

BROOKVILLE, Franklin County. US 52.

Hackleman Monument, in courthouse yard, honors Gen. Pleasant A. Hackleman, the only Indiana general killed at the battle of Corinth, October 1862.

Lew Wallace Birthplace, 3rd St. Site is marked at the rear of Catholic church. Gen. Wallace was born here in 1827.

BRUCEVILLE, Knox County. State 67, 550.

Site of Lincoln Speech. Lincoln spoke in a grove of walnut trees opposite Christian Church on a night in 1844. He was speaking in behalf of Henry Clay. A group of Democrats tried to break up the meeting but were quieted. Lincoln spent the night at the home of Maj. William Bruce, at the corner of Washington and Back Street. The major had 25 children.

CANNELTON, Perry County, State 66, has marker for a raid by Confederate Capt. Thomas Henry Hines.

CENTERVILLE, Wayne County. US 40.

Morton Home, western edge of town, has marker. Wartime Gov. Oliver P. Morton served in the U.S. Senate in 1867, was re-elected in 1873, and served until his death in 1877.

CONNORSVILLE, Fayette County, State 1, 44.

Reynold's Museum of Science and Industry, S. Vine St., has Civil War relics.

CORYDON, Harrison County. IS 64, US 460, State 62.

Battle of Corydon took place about a mile

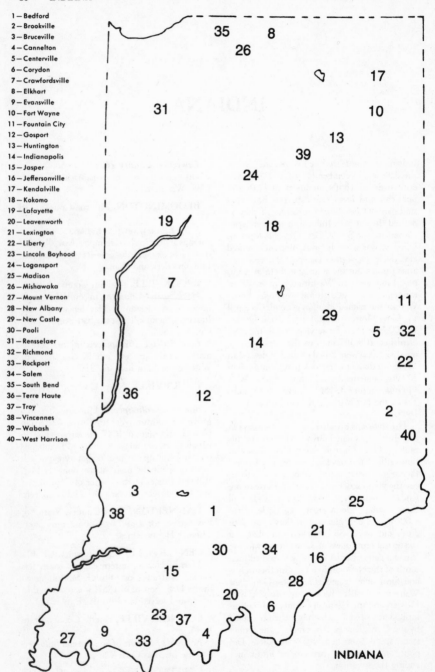

1 — Bedford
2 — Brookville
3 — Bruceville
4 — Cannelton
5 — Centerville
6 — Corydon
7 — Crawfordsville
8 — Elkhart
9 — Evansville
10 — Fort Wayne
11 — Fountain City
12 — Gosport
13 — Huntington
14 — Indianapolis
15 — Jasper
16 — Jeffersonville
17 — Kendalville
18 — Kokomo
19 — Lafayette
20 — Leavenworth
21 — Lexington
22 — Liberty
23 — Lincoln Boyhood
24 — Logansport
25 — Madison
26 — Mishawaka
27 — Mount Vernon
28 — New Albany
29 — New Castle
30 — Paoli
31 — Rensselaer
32 — Richmond
33 — Rockport
34 — Salem
35 — South Bend
36 — Terre Haute
37 — Troy
38 — Vincennes
39 — Wabash
40 — West Harrison

INDIANA

south of town on July 9, 1863. Home guards fought gallantly but were outnumbered. They surrendered and were held captive during the raiders' occupation of the village. Marker on State 135 Business.

Posey House Museum, 225 Oak St., has a Civil War drum and rifle among displays.

CRAWFORDSVILLE, Montgomery County. US 136, 231.

Gen. Lew Wallace Study, E. Pike St. and Wallace Ave., has Wallace memorabilia, including correspondence with Lincoln.

Henry S. Lane Home, 212 S. Water St. Col. Lane was governor and a U.S. senator during the war. He helped to secure the nomination of Abraham Lincoln. His possessions are preserved as a memorial to Indiana Civil War history. The house is an 1814 Greek Revival mansion.

ELKHART, Elkhart County. US 20, 33.

Ambrose Bierce House, 518 W. Franklin St. The mysterious Bierce once lived at this site. He enlisted in 1861, wrote vividly of his experiences at Shiloh and elsewhere. After the war he joined a surveying expedition into Indian Territory and disappeared into Mexico in 1913. Among his most memorable works is the short story "An Occurrence at Owl Creek Bridge."

EVANSVILLE, Vanderburgh County. US 40, 41. Has marker for site of U.S. military hospital.

Evansville Museum, 411 S.E. Riverside, has a Civil War display.

Soldiers and Sailors Memorial Coliseum, 1st and Court St.

FORT WAYNE, Allen County. IS 69, US 30.

Louis A. Warren Lincoln Library and Museum, 1301 S. Clinton St. Among many Lincoln relics are the flag that draped his box at Ford's Theatre, photographs, letters, and manuscripts. A bronze heroic statue of Lincoln as a Hoosier youth, in the plaza, was dedicated September 16, 1932. It is the work of Paul Manship. The library contains some 9,000 volumes pertaining exclusively to Lincoln; association books, collateral publications, clippings, and periodicals are also available to students. The museum has paintings, photographs, prints, broadsides, and sculpture; archives department has Hanks family genealogy, Kentucky and Indiana history.

FOUNTAIN CITY, Wayne County. US 27. Almost the entire community took part in helping slaves escape along the Underground Railroad under the direction of the Levi Coffins, who were the prototypes of Simon and Rachel Halliday in Stowe's *Uncle Tom's Cabin.*

The Levi Coffin House State Historic Site, US 27, north of IS 70 exit, was often called the Grand Central Station of the Underground Railroad. Coffin and his wife, known as "Aunt Katie," were Quakers.

FRANKLIN, Johnson County. IS 65.

Franklin County Historical Museum, 150 W. Madison St., has Civil War relics.

GOSPORT, Owen County, State 67. On east side of White River, farm and grave of David Vanbuskirk, at 6 feet, 10½ inches, the tallest Union soldier of Co. F, 27th Indiana, which enlisted only six-footers.

Camp Hughes was located here during the war. Marker.

HUNTINGTON, Huntington County. Off IS 69, US 24.

Mount Hope Cemetery, on highway, has the grave of Lambdin P. Milligan, a Huntington attorney who was a leader in the Knights of the Golden Circle. He was once arrested with others and taken to military court in Indianapolis where, with Dr. William Bowles of French Lick and Stephen Horsey of Shoals, he was accused of a plot to kidnap Gov. Morton and hold him as hostage during an insurrection. All three men were convicted and sentenced to be hanged, but were taken out of the state by friends before the sentence could be carried out. The U.S. Supreme Court eventually reversed the decision.

INDIANAPOLIS, Marion County. IS 65, 69, 70, 74.

Camp Morton, site of the old Indiana State Fairgrounds, between Talbott and Central from 19th to 22nd St. Soldiers were quartered in stables and pens used for livestock. The race track became a drill field. On September 12, 1861, the 27th Indiana Volunteer Regiment was mustered into service. One of the privates was B. W. Mitchell of Company F, who found the famous Lost Order giving directions for Lee's plans just before the battle of Antietam. The order was wrapped around three cigars, taken to Gen. McClellan's headquarters, and was of such importance that for once even McClellan moved quickly, overtaking the Southern army at South Mountain the next day.

Camp Robinson, Thomas Taggart Riverside Park. South end of the park was the site of a Union camp.

Indiana Zouaves resting in Camp McGinnis the day after the battle of Romney.

Crown Hill Cemetery, 3402 Boulevard Pl., has graves of Benjamin Harrison and Oliver P. Morton.

Garfield Park, Raymond St. and Garfield Dr. A granite shaft was moved here from Greenlawn Cemetery. It was erected as a tribute to the Confederate prisoners who died in the Indianapolis prison camp.

Harrison Home, 1230 N. Delaware St. Benjamin Harrison, 23rd president, was a brigadier general in the Civil War in the Army of the Cumberland. Home has been restored, has original furnishings.

Lincoln Monument, southwest corner of University Park, New York and Vermont St. The bronze statue of Abraham Lincoln is by Henry Hering. Also in the park, at the south entrance, is a statue of Benjamin Harrison.

Soldiers' and Sailors' Monument, Monument Circle. One of the first monuments erected to the private soldier. A 38-foot statue of Victory surmounts the shaft; an observation platform is just below the statue. Elevator service is provided. Stone sculpture is by Rudolph Schwartz; bronze by George T. Brewster. Civil War picture gallery. Recently an $11 million restoration was completed.

State Capitol, Capitol at Market. Washington and Ohio St. Portraits, sculpture, and battle flags. Marker on grounds at site of Civil War arsenal.

State Library and Historical Building, N. Senate and Ohio St. Extensive collection of Indiana history.

JASPER, DuBois County. US 231.

Enlow's Mill, southeastern edge of town. The Lincolns once lived between here and Hoffman Mill on Anderson Creek. Thomas Lincoln is said to have exchanged a desk he had made for a bag of meal. The desk was used at the mill for many years, later on display at the Jasper Desk Factory. Mill razed after 1964 flood.

JEFFERSONVILLE, Clark County. IS 64, 71, US 42.

Howard Steamboat Museum, 1101 E. Market St. Steamboat models, photographs, equipment, and a library.

United States Army Quartermaster Depot, 10th St. and Meigs Ave. During the Civil War, this was the base from which troops and supplies were sent to points south.

KENDALVILLE, Noble County. US 6. Camp Mitchell was located here during the war.

KOKOMO, Howard County. US 35, 31. Hometown of Gen. Thomas Jefferson Harrison, captain of the 6th Indiana and later colonel of the 8th Indiana Cavalry.

Howard County Historical Society, 1200 W. Sycamore, has collections from 1840.

Pioneer Cemetery, Wildcat Creek and Purdue St., has graves of Civil War soldiers.

LAFAYETTE, Tippecanoe County. IS 65, US 52. Camp Tippecanoe was established here during the war.

Reynolds Home, 622 Main St. At this site stood the home of Gen. Joseph Reynolds, classmate of U. S. Grant at West Point. Grant was visiting at the home when he learned he had been offered the commission of colonel of the 21st Illinois Regiment. Reynolds and his older brother, William, were in the grocery business when Joseph was commissioned colonel of the 10th Indiana on April 25, 1861. On May 17, he was made brigadier general, long before his classmate Grant rose in rank. He served in many campaigns, chiefly in the western theater of war, was made major general in 1865. In 1876, while serving in the far West, he captured Crazy Horse's winter camp, took ponies, but withdrew without destroying the dismounted warriors and was condemned by many of his contemporaries for thus having contributed to the Little Big Horn massacre. Reynolds resigned after a court-martial.

Tippecanoe County Historical Society Museum, 909 South St., has local historical items.

LA PORTE, La Porte County, US 35, south of IS 80.

La Porte County Historical Society, in county complex, has the Jones Collection of firearms, regimental memorabilia, and other Civil War relics.

LEAVENWORTH, Crawford County. US 62-66. In 1863, a detachment of Morgan's men under Capt. Thomas Hines raced through town. Townspeople joined the Union cavalry trying to retrieve stolen horses.

LEXINGTON, Scott County. State 336. The Indiana Civil War Centennial Commission has been placing markers along the line of Morgan's Raid. One of the sites is here; among others are: Harris, Madison, Ohio River crossing, Salem, Vernon, Versailles, and Vienna. (*Also see* CORYDON.)

LIBERTY, Union County. US 27.

Site of Burnside House, Seminary and Fairground St. Ambrose Burnside lived here from 1824 to 1854.

LINCOLN BOYHOOD NATIONAL MEMORIAL, Spencer County, on State 162, south of Lincoln City. Lincoln lived here from 1816 to 1830. He was nine years old when his mother died. The memorial visitor center, which includes a 24-minute film, has exhibits, Nancy Hanks Lincoln Hall and Abraham Lincoln Hall is open daily except Thanksgiving Day, Christmas Day, and New Year's Day. Sculptured panels on the adjoining wall depict scenes and people in Lincoln's life. Nancy Hanks, who died at 35, is buried on the site. Also here is a Lincoln Living History Farm open mid-April thru mid-September.

LINCOLN CITY, Spencer County. State 162. An outdoor musical drama, *Young Abe Lincoln,* is performed on summer evenings in Lincoln State Park.

LOGANSPORT, Cass County. US 35, 24.

Camp Logan, 3rd and Ottawa St. Site of 1861 camp occupied by the 46th Indiana Infantry.

Cass County Historical Society, 1004 E. Market, has Civil War items.

MADISON, Jefferson County. US 421, State 7.

James F. D. Lanier State Historic Site, Elm and W. 1st St. The home of James Lanier, who financed the state during difficult times in the Civil War. He advanced $1,000,000, as an unsecured loan for much needed equipment. Home has many of its original furnishings. The River Days Festival, held the third weekend in May, celebrates Madison's Civil War heritage with crafts and antiques, at the Lanier House.

MISHAWAKA, St. Joseph County. US 31. Camp Rose was located here during the war.

MOUNT VERNON, Posey County. State 69.

Leonard Cemetery, 6th and Canal St., has the grave of Gen. Thomas Gamble Pitcher, friend of Lincoln, who was wounded at Cedar Mountain. After the war he served for a time as superintendent of West Point.

Soldiers' and Sailors' Monument, Main St., honors soldiers of Posey County. It was executed by Rudolph Schwartz, who also helped to design the Indianapolis monument.

NEW ALBANY, Floyd County. IS 64, US 150.

Anderson Female Seminary was located on the southwest corner of LaFayette and Market St. Established in 1841 by Col. John Anderson and his wife, the school soon was divided—the Anderson Collegiate Institute being established for male students. Confederate Gen. John Hunt Morgan was a pupil here.

Floyd County Museum, 201 E. Spring St., has Civil War displays among changing exhibits.

National Soldiers' Cemetery, 1943 Ekin Ave., has graves of Civil War soldiers.

Willson Home, 520 Culbertson Ave. Byron Forceythe Willson was an editorial writer on the *Louisville Journal.* His poem, "The Old Sergeant," was written for distribution by the newspaper carrier boys as a Christmas souvenir; it attracted the attention of Lincoln, who asked Oliver Wendell Holmes who had written it. Holmes learned of the author through the *Journal* editor, George D. Prentice, and the poem was widely circulated.

NEW CASTLE, Henry County. State 3, 38.

Henry County Historical Society Museum, 606 S. 14th St., is housed in the home of Civil War Gen. William Grose. Pioneer and war relics.

PAOLI, Orange County. US 150.

William Bowles House, 2 blocks south of courthouse. Bowles was a leader in the Copperhead organization, the Knights of the Golden Circle.

RENSSELAER, Jasper County. US 231.

Memorial Park, on Iroquois River opposite business section, has bronze statue of Gen. Robert Houston Milroy. Milroy was commissioned captain of the 9th Indiana in April 1861, and colonel four days later. Promoted to major general in November 1862, he commanded in Virginia, retreating before Ewell's advance to Pennsylvania. High casualties in the withdrawal brought him before a board of investigaton, which exonerated him. Later in the war he was so effective against guerrillas in West Virginia that the Confederacy put a price on his head. After the war he served for a time as Indian agent.

RICHMOND, Wayne County. IS 70, US 40. Camp Wayne was located here during the war.

Wayne County Historical Society Museum, 11th and A St. Historical and Indian items.

ROCKPORT, Spencer County. US 231.

Lincoln Pioneer Village, City Park, has log buildings, a museum of early transportation, stockade, and a pioneer museum.

SALEM, Washington County. State 135, 60.

John Hay Birthplace, 307 E. Market St. Hay, who became one of Lincoln's secretaries and biographers, was born here October 8, 1838. A national historic site.

Morgan Marker, on S. Main St., for raid of July 10, 1863.

SOUTH BEND, St. Joseph County. US 20, 31.

Northern Indiana Historical Society, 112 S. Lafayette Blvd. The museum, which is located in the old county courthouse, has memorabilia on Schuyler Colfax, vice president under Ulysses S. Grant.

Studebaker National Museum, 525 S. Main St., has among its displays carriages belonging to Presidents Grant and McKinley and the carriage in which Lincoln rode to Ford's Theatre on his last night.

TERRE HAUTE, Vigo County. IS 70, US 41-150. Camp Vigo was located here during the war.

Highland Lawn Cemetery, US 40, east of town. Senator Daniel Wolsey Voorhees is buried here. His defense of John Brown for the burning of Harpers Ferry brought national attention. His oratory was so persuasive that a judge once set aside a jury verdict in his favor on the grounds that the jurors had been "unduly influenced."

Historical Museum of the Wabash Valley, 6th and Washington St., exhibits and library.

Memorial Hall, Ohio St. between 2nd and 3rd St., has war exhibit.

TROY, Perry County. State 66. Occasionally Lincoln operated a ferry across Anderson River for a farmer named James Taylor. Reportedly, the enterprising Lincoln then built a scow to take passengers to steamers. He was taken to court on the complaint that he was operating without a license. Lincoln held that he merely conveyed passengers to midstream, and Justice of the Peace Samuel Pate ruled that Lincoln was not guilty, that taking passengers halfway was not "setting them over."

VERNON, Jennings County, State 3, 7. The town, which was founded in 1816, was a major stop on the Underground Railroad and is on the National Register of Historic Places. Maps at the Chamber of Commerce, 44 Short St.

VINCENNES, Knox County. US 50.

Lincoln Memorial Bridge, Vigo St., was built in 1931 and links the highway from Hodgenville, Kentucky, to Springfield, Illinois.

WABASH, Wabash County. US 24. Camp Wabash was established here during the war.

Lincoln of the People Statue, courthouse square, is the work of Charles Keck.

Wabash County Historical Museum, 89 W. Hill St., is in the 1899 Memorial Hall Bldg., which was constructed as a memorial to Civil War veterans. Civil War items.

WEST HARRISON, Dearborn County. US 52, State 46.

Morgan Marker, US 52 and State St. Morgan's final stop in Indiana was at the American Hotel on Harrison Avenue, on July 13, 1863.

ZIONSVILLE, Boone County. State 49. This is a northern suburb of Indianapolis. En route to his first inauguration in Washington, Lincoln spoke to the people from the platform of his train. The site of the former railroad station is marked by a monument in Lincoln Park.

IOWA

Iowa entered the Union on December 28, 1846, as the 29th state. In prewar years a number of Quakers and followers of John Brown helped fugitives escape to the North. On the first call for volunteers in 1861, Iowa's response was overwhelming. The state quota of one regiment was soon filled, and Gov. Samuel J. Kirkwood organized two additional regiments. He reported to the War Department that he could raise 10,000 men but had no arms. A general assembly, called in special session in May, voted $800,000 worth of bonds and pledged the "faith, credit, and resources of Iowa" to the Union cause.

Iowa sent 75,000 volunteers into the army; more than one-sixth were killed in service. There were 48 infantry regiments, nine cavalry regiments, and four artillery companies. Iowa had four major generals: Samuel R. Curtis, Grenville M. Dodge, Francis J. Herron, and Frederick Steele; many Iowans were brigadier generals and colonels. The Congressional Medal of Honor was awarded to 27 Iowans.

ALGONA, Kossuth County. US 169.
Kossuth County Museum, Dodge and Nebraska streets, has Civil War artifacts.

BURLINGTON, Des Moines County. US 34, 61.
Crapo Park, River Road, has a monument to Gen. John M. Corse.
Hudson House, northwest corner of Columbia and 5th St. Abraham Lincoln stayed here when he visited Burlington in 1858 and gave a speech on October 5 at the Grimes Opera House, which stood on the northeast corner of Valley and Main St.
Marion Hall, northeast corner of 4th and Washington St. Site of fugitive slave trial of 1855. Judge David Rorer dismissed the slave, Dick, who went to Canada. During the war the hall was a recruiting center.

CEDAR RAPIDS, Linn County. US 151, US 30-218.

Iowa Masonic Library, 813 1st Ave., on square named for Stephen Douglas, who spoke here in 1858. Museum has historical displays.

CHARITON, Lucas County, US 34.
Lucas County Historical Museum, 17th and Braden, has period rooms, Civil War items, and a relocated schoolroom.

CORYDON, Wayne County, State 14.
County Museum on highway has excellent period shops, many relics.

COUNCIL BLUFFS, Pottawattamie County. IS 29, 80.
Dodge House, 605 S. 3rd St. Residence of Gen. Grenville M. Dodge, who was serving on Gov. Kirkwood's staff as a member of the Home Guard when Fort Sumter fell. He was commissioned colonel of the 4th Iowa, wounded at Pea Ridge and at Atlanta. The house has been designated as a historic landmark.
Dodge Memorial, 1512 S. Main St. Brown stone marker, at Rock Island station, commemorates the survey Gen. Dodge made in 1852 to select the route of the railroad across Iowa.
Fairview Cemetery, east end of Lafayette Ave., has a memorial in honor of Mrs. Grenville Dodge sculpted by Daniel Chester French. Amelia Jenks Bloomer, pioneer woman suffragist, is also buried here.
Lincoln Monument, Oakland Dr. and Lafayette Ave., commemorates Lincoln's visit of August 12–14, 1859.
Public Library, southwest corner Willow Ave. and Pearl St., has Gen. Grenville Dodge documents.

CROTON, Lee County. On Des Moines River, south of State 2. The Benning house here has a cannonball from the battle of Athens across the river in Missouri. The Sprouse house served as temporary hospital; it has been presented to the Iowa Society for the Preservation of Historic Landmarks.

DAVENPORT, Scott County. IS 80, US 6. In pre-Civil War days Dred Scott lived here for

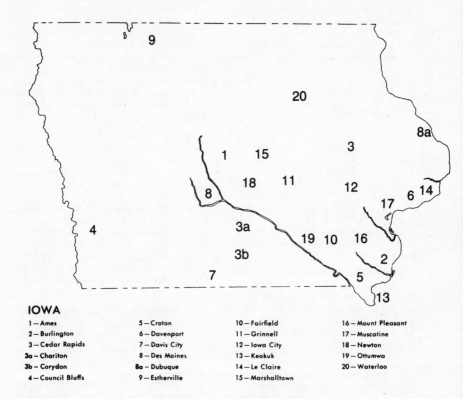

IOWA

1 — Ames	5 — Croton	10 — Fairfield	16 — Mount Pleasant
2 — Burlington	6 — Davenport	11 — Grinnell	17 — Muscatine
3 — Cedar Rapids	7 — Davis City	12 — Iowa City	18 — Newton
3a — Chariton	8 — Des Moines	13 — Keokuk	19 — Ottumwa
3b — Corydon	8a — Dubuque	14 — Le Claire	20 — Waterloo
4 — Council Bluffs	9 — Estherville	15 — Marshalltown	

a time. John Brown organized provisions here before his attack on Harpers Ferry. The village of East Davenport holds a Civil War muster and Mercantile Exposition in September. Battle re-enactments take place at McClellan parade ground in the riverfront park, once the Union army's Camp McClellan.

Site of Camp Roberts, 2800 Eastern Ave. This training camp for Civil War recruits was later known as Camp Kinsman. Still later the Iowa Soldiers' Orphans' Home was established here to care for Civil War orphans.

City Cemetery, Rockingham Rd. and Sturdevant-Harris St., has the grave of Dr. John Emerson, owner of the slave Dred Scott. In northeast corner of burial ground are graves of more than 200 Union soldiers who died at Camp Black Hawk, a cavalry training camp.

Soldiers' Monument, Main St. Memorial to Civil War participants.

The Annie Wittenmyer Home was established during the Civil War for the orphans of soldiers. Mrs. Wittenmyer was famous for her diet kitchens in army hospitals.

DAVIS CITY, Decatur County. US 69.

Lt. Col. George Pomutz, of the 15th Iowa Infantry, lived in a Hungarian settlement south of Davis City in New Buda township. He was wounded at Shiloh, brevetted brigadier general in 1865, later wrote a history of his regiment. After the war he was appointed consul to Russia and died at St. Petersburg.

DES MOINES, Polk County. IS 235, US 65.

Hoyt Sherman House, Woodland Ave. at 15th St. Maj. Hoyt Sherman, brother of Gen. William T. Sherman, lived here in the 1870s. Presidents Grant and McKinley were visitors.

Soldiers' and Sailors' Monument, Capitol Park. A 145-foot granite shaft.

State Capitol, Grand Ave. between 9th and 12th, has battle flags of Iowa regiments; included are banners of First Regiment, Iowa Colored Infantry, and 37th Infantry, known as the Graybeards—all were over 45 years old.

The Iowa State Historical Museum and Archives, 600 E. Locust, has exhibits of military history among its collections.

DUBUQUE, Dubuque County, US 61.
Old Shot Tower, River and Tower St., produced three tons of shot daily during the war.
The River Adventure, 3rd St. Ice Harbor comprises six sites which depict 300 years of river history. The complex includes two paddle wheelers as well as the National Rivers Hall of Fame.

ESTHERVILLE, Emmet County. State 17, 9.
Fort Defiance, 1½ miles southwest of town. After the Sioux outbreak in Minnesota in July 1862, a series of forts was built in northwest Iowa. Fort Defiance was the largest of the group. Gov. Kirkwood sent Col. S. R. Ingham to take charge of the area. The Sioux abandoned plans to sweep down the Des Moines Valley and the Little Sioux by way of the lakes in Dickinson County, and after the battles north of the Iowa line they moved toward the West. A state park.

FAIRFIELD, Jefferson County. US 34.
Evergreen Cemetery has monument to Mrs. M. E. Woods, who took a commissary wagon to war and traveled among Iowa troops with supplies and a soldier escort. Gov. Kirkwood gave her an honorary commission as major.

FORT DODGE, Webster County. US 169, along both banks of the Des Moines River.
Fort Museum and Frontier Village, 1¼ miles southwest on Bus. 169. A replica of an 1862 militia fort housing two original cabins are within the stockade. Exhibits include military artifacts.

GRINNELL, Poweshiek County. US 6, 3 miles north of IS 80.
Site of Grinnell Home, 1019 Broad St. Bronze tablet marks home of Josiah Bushnell Grinnell, to whom Horace Greeley said: "Go West, young man, go West and grow up with the country." Grinnell established the town and set aside land for Grinnell College. The home was once a station on the Underground Railroad.

IOWA CITY, Johnson County. IS 80, US 6, 218.
Camp Fremont, 1861 camp of the 10th Iowa Infantry, is now part of the city airport.
Jefferson Hotel, southwest corner Washington and Dubuque St., reportedly is on the site where a small mob planning to lynch John Brown gathered, but Brown, warned in time, escaped.
Kirkwood Home, 1028 Kirkwood Ave. Iowa's wartime governor, Samuel J. Kirkwood, lived in a small frame house at this site.

Oakland Cemetery, Governor and Brown St., has the grave of Gov. Kirkland.
Old Capitol National Historic Landmark, on university campus, was built in the 1840s and served as the permanent seat of government for Iowa's territorial, then state, governments until 1857. Restored.
State Historical Society, 402 Iowa Ave., has Civil War letters, rosters, journals, and other manuscripts.

KEOKUK, Lee County. US 218. The town was an important embarkation point for Civil War regiments. A number of hospitals were established here during the war. There is an equestrian statue of Gen. Samuel R. Curtis near the river.
National Cemetery, S. 18th & Ridge streets, is a 4,205-acre burial ground containing graves of soldiers from eight wars. Established in 1861, the cemetery has the graves of eight Confederates who died as prisoners among the 750 Civil War dead. This is one of the twelve original national cemeteries and was designated by Congress at the same time as Arlington.

LE CLAIRE, Scott County. IS 80, US 67. Col. William F. Cody and Capt. James B. Eads lived here. "Buffalo Bill" was born on what was known as the Wilson farm, 1½ miles northwest of town. The home is three miles southwest of McCausland; follow signs. The house was built by Cody's father in 1847. There is a monument dedicated to him at the Green Tree Hotel on the banks of the Mississippi. The elm tree, 13 feet in circumference, stood here long before the Civil War. River men down on their luck often stayed here for weeks. Col. Cody played here as a boy.

MARSHALLTOWN, Marshall County. US 30. The Bowen Guard of Marshalltown became Company D, 5th Iowa Infantry, in July 1861. W. P. Hepburn, prosecuting attorney, organized a cavalry company and served as its captain.
Public Library, State and N. Center St., has museum.

MISSOURI VALLEY, Harrison County. IS 29, US 30. Relics salvaged by the National Park Service from the steamboat *Bertrand,* sunk April 1, 1865, en route to Fort Benton, are on display. De Soto Wildlife Refuge. Boat site can be visited most of the year. Visitor center.

MOUNT PLEASANT, Henry County. US 34.
Harlan-Lincoln Museum, 4 blocks north of US 34 on Iowa Wesleyan College campus. The

home of Sen. James Harlan and his son-in-law, Robert Todd Lincoln. Restored, original furnishings. By appointment only.

MUSCATINE, Muscatine County. State 22.

Civil War Veterans' Memorial, southwest corner of square.

OTTUMWA, Wapello County. US 63, 64.

Civil War Veterans' Memorial, Central Park. The monument, designed by David Edstrom, was financed by school children's savings.

WATERLOO, Black Hawk County. US 63, 20.

Grout Historical Museum, Park Ave. at South St., has a variety of historical and Indian exhibits.

KANSAS

Kansas became the 34th state on January 29, 1861. When Fort Sumter was attacked, U.S. Senator James H. Lane, fearing Lincoln would be kidnapped or assassinated, recruited 120 Kansas men in Washington and formed the "Frontier Guard," which was billeted in the White House to protect the President.

Gov. Charles Robinson and Senator Lane were soon recruiting troops within the state. Kansas had a quota of 16,654 to be filled; however, more than 20,000 Kansans enlisted. Out of 30,000 men of military age, the state furnished 23 regiments and four batteries to the Union army. About 8,500 were casualties.

A few skirmishes took place along the Missouri border in 1861. Kansas units fought in the western theater of the war from Missouri to Mississippi, and Kansas regiments, both white and black, were used in Indian territory in 1862 and 1863. As in prewar years, guerrilla raiders were a major problem. The destruction of Lawrence, Kansas, on August 21, 1863, by Quantrill's raiders caused the deaths of about 150 men and boys and the loss of $1.5 million in property.

ATCHISON, Atchison County. US 73.

Lincoln Plaque in courthouse square commemorates a speech which Lincoln gave here.

Massasoit House, 210 Main St. Site of a hotel where Lincoln once spent the night after making a campaign speech. Horace Greeley also stayed here on a western visit. Fugitive slaves were hidden in the basement during Underground Railroad days.

BALDWIN CITY, Douglas County. US 56.

In 1856 proslavery Missourians invaded the town, took several abolitionist captives, and destroyed property until order was restored by antislavery forces.

Baker University received a donation of $100 from Abraham Lincoln in 1864; museum on campus in Old Castle.

BAXTER SPRINGS, Cherokee County. US 66.

Site of Baxter Springs Massacre, end of E. 7th St. A Federal garrison of white cavalry and colored infantry was attacked on October 6, 1863, by Quantrill's men. Part of the garrison was away from the post at the time. Nine were killed. Quantrill lost two men. Maj. Gen. James G. Blunt, with his staff and a detachment of troops, was approaching the garrison en route to Fort Gibson, mistook the raiders for a welcoming escort, and was soon surrounded. Quantrill captured all but Blunt and seven or eight men; 87 were killed.

Baxter Springs National Cemetery has a monument in memory of Quantrill's victims, most of whom are buried here.

Library Park, 10th and Park Ave., has a Confederate cannon, made in Macon, Georgia, captured at Pea Ridge, Arkansas, in 1862.

BUFFALO, Wilson County. US 75.

Site of Old Fort Belmont, a military post and stagecoach station until after the war. Hapo, Chief of the Osage, who fought for the Union during the war, is buried near the fort in an unmarked grave.

CONCORDIA, Cloud County. US 81. Sgt. Boston Corbett, who claimed to be the slayer of John Wilkes Booth, had a dugout a few miles to the southeast. Corbett, a member of the 16th New York Cavalry, had been a hatter's apprentice and later an evangelist. He was quoted as saying that God had directed him to shoot Booth.

A Secret Service man reportedly replied to this: "I guess He did, or you could never have hit Booth through that crack in the barn." For a time, Corbett lectured to Kansas farmers and showed magic lantern slides of Booth and of himself and the four conspirators on the scaffold.

DODGE CITY, Ford County. US 50, 283.

Fort Dodge, 5 miles east on US 154, was established in 1865 by Gen. Grenville Dodge to protect the Santa Fe Trail. In addition to Gen. Dodge, Civil War participants Custer, Sheridan, Hancock, Hickok, and Cody were

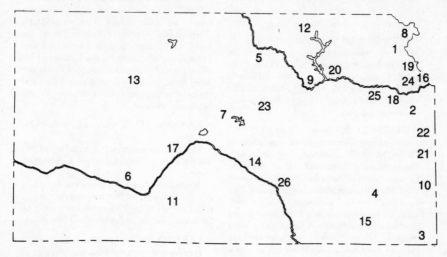

KANSAS

associated with the fort. Several stone buildings are still in use. Now a state home for veterans. Museum and library open daily.

Santa Fe Trail, marker on northwest corner of 2nd Ave. and Trail St. The trail was used from 1821 to 1872.

ELLSWORTH, Ellsworth County. US 40.
Mother Bickerdyke Home. A home for Civil War nurses and female relatives of veterans was established on the south edge of town by the Civil War nurse, Mary Bickerdyke. Mrs. Bickerdyke was one of the few persons connected with Sherman's army who had no awe of the leader. On one occasion she asked him to change an order, he said he was busy, and Mrs. Bickerdyke said: "Fix this thing as it ought to be fixed. Have some sense about it. . . . I can't stand here fooling all day." The order was changed.

ELWOOD, Doniphan County. US 36. Lincoln, campaigning in 1859, chose Elwood as his first stop in Kansas.

FORT RILEY, Geary County. *See* MANHATTAN.

FORT SCOTT, Bourbon County. US 69, 54. The fort, established in 1842, was abandoned in 1853, regarrisoned as Union headquarters during the Civil War. During the years it was not in use as an army post, it was a rendezvous spot for Free Staters John Brown, Charles Jennison, and others. A number of original buildings remain.

Fort Blair, a Civil War blockhouse, has been rebuilt and moved to its present site in Blair Park.

Fort Scott Museum, 101 Blair St., has Civil War mementos and pioneer relics. It is housed in the former headquarters building.

Fort Scott National Cemetery, E. National Ave., established in 1862, is one of the original twelve national cemeteries.

Fort Scott National Historic Site, Old Fort Blvd. at business jct. US 69, 54. The buildings have been restored and reconstructed to the look of the early fort. Visitor center and museum are in the restored post hospital. The museum has audio-visual, living history, and interpretive programs, guide service.

FORT ZARAH SITE, Barton County. US 56. The fort was one of a chain that guarded the Santa Fe Trail. It was established by Gen. Samuel R. Curtis, September 6, 1864, and named for the general's son, Maj. H. Zarah Curtis, who was killed at Baxter Springs. No buildings remain at the site.

GREENSBURG, Kiowa County. US 54.
Greensburg Cemetery has a monument to Dudley Mitchell, a veteran who served with Sherman's army. A hardtack biscuit sent home from the South was kept by the family and mortised into the face of Mitchell's tombstone after his death. The hardtack issued to the Pennsylvania Dragoons apparently could have served in place of a tombstone. One of the recruits recalled: "The kind issued to our regiment were old navy crackers . . . doubtless left over as a surplus from previous wars. . . . If you attempted to crush one with your fist, you were likely to injure your knuckles more than you would the cracker. Artificial teeth were pronounced unreliable, and some, we know, sent theirs home for safekeeping."

HANOVER, Washington County. State 15E.
Hollenberg Pony Express Station Historic Site, 2 miles east on State 243, is the only unaltered pony express depot in its original location. The downstairs served as family quarters, tavern, store and stage station; upstairs was a common sleeping room for express riders and stage line employees. Museum.

HAYS, Ellis County. IS 70, US 40.
Fort Hays Historic Site, on US 183 Alt. south of IS 70, has the stone guardhouse, blockhouse, and officers' quarters of the original Fort Fletcher which was renamed Fort Hays in 1866. Buffalo Bill Cody supplied the post with meat. Its first troops were known as Galvanized Yankees, former Confederate prisoners of war. The post served as headquarters for Indian campaigns led by Civil War Gens. W. S. Hancock and Philip Sheridan. The buildings have exhibits. Visitor center.

HUTCHINSON, Reno County. US 50.
Soldiers' Monument, 1st Ave. Park, 1st Ave., and Walnut St. The Civil War memorial is surmounted by a figure of Abraham Lincoln. It was dedicated in 1919.

INDEPENDENCE, Montgomery County. US 75, 160.

Site of Rebel Creek Battle, 1 mile east on US 160. On May 15, 1863, 22 Confederate officers led by Col. Charles Harrison and Col. Warner Lewis, nephew of explorer Meriwether Lewis, had a skirmish with a band of Osage Indians. In a running fight, one Indian and two officers were killed. On a gravel bar in the Verdigris River, 18 Confederates were killed and their bodies multilated. Colonel Lewis and one other man escaped.

KANSAS CITY, Wyandotte County. IS 29, 35, 70.
Oak Grove Cemetery, north end of 3rd St., has the grave of Mary A. Sturges, Union army nurse.
Wyandotte County Historical Museum, 631 N. 126th St. in Bonner Springs. Among relics are a captain's commission signed by President Lincoln and other Civil War items.

LARNED, Pawnee County. State 156.
Fort Larned National Historic Site, on US 156, west of town, was built in 1859 to guard the Santa Fe Trail. It is one of the best preserved of all forts that once protected the Overland Route; workshops, stone barracks, and warehouse remain. Former officers' quarters are now stocked with historical displays. Visitor center has exhibits, slide program, and guided tours in summer or by request.

LAWRENCE, Douglas County. IS 70, US 40, 59. The town was plundered and burned on August 21, 1863. Although accounts disagree, it seems likely William Clarke Quantrill had the sour cream of the outlaw crop among the nearly 500 men who rode with him into Lawrence: Thomas Coleman (Cole) Younger, Frank James (brother Jesse Woodson James was not along that day), Bloody Bill Anderson, George Todd, John Jarette, and Bill Gregg. Some of the men had lists of persons they wanted to kill (Quantrill hoped to murder Seth Lane), but lists were soon abandoned in wholesale slaughter which spared only women. Larkin Skaggs was the only guerrilla lost in the raid. Historian Paul I. Wellman reports that Skaggs was "killed, and also scalped, by White Turkey, a Delaware Indian, who seems not to have been caught up in the general panic. . . ."
Eldridge Hotel, southwest corner of 7th and Massachusetts. The hotel that stood here in 1863 was burned by Quantrill's raiders; although the besieged guests had waved a sheet in peaceful surrender, all were robbed and the hotel vandalized.
First Methodist Church, 724 Vermont St.

Stone marker denotes site of church which was used as a morgue on August 21, 1863.

Oak Hill Cemetery, 13th St. Buried here are the victims of the Lawrence Massacre; Sen. James Lane; wartime governor Charles Robinson; and John P. Usher, Lincoln's Secretary of the Interior.

Site of Massacre of Recruits, 935 New Hampshire St. Stone marker near spot where Quantrill's men shot down 20 unarmed boys.

Snyder House, south of intersection of 19th and Haskell St. A well marks the site where the Rev. S. S. Snyder of the United Brethren Church was killed as the raiders entered town. Snyder, a lieutenant in the 2nd Colored Regiment, was milking a cow when shot.

Speer House, 1024 Maryland St., is the site where Larkin Skaggs was killed by White Turkey.

Watson Library, on University of Kansas campus, west of Fraser Hall, has historical relics.

LEAVENWORTH, Leavenworth County. IS 29, US 73. There were many border conflicts before the war and the town was largely proslavery but remained loyal to the Union when the conflict began.

Fort Leavenworth, 7th St. and US 73 3 miles north off US 73, is one of the oldest army posts in the country. It was established in 1827 to protect the Santa Fe Trail. During the Civil War, volunteers were mustered and trained here. A monument to U. S. Grant stands at the intersection of Scott and Grant Ave. It was sculptured by Lorado Taft and dedicated in 1889. There are a number of Union graves in the 15-acre national cemetery.

Frontier Army Museum, Gibbon and Reynolds avenues, opposite Bert Hall. Exhibits depict the history of the fort and include Civil War artifacts. The carriage in which Lincoln rode when here is among the vehicle displays.

MANHATTAN, Riley County. Off IS 70, U.S. 24, State 13.

Beecher Bible and Rifle Church, east of town at Wabaunsee, was built in 1862 by a colony of northern emigrants who went to Kansas during the prewar slavery conflicts. Henry Ward Beecher's Brooklyn church donated money to buy rifles; these were packed in crates marked "Bibles" and shipped to Kansas.

Custer House, on Sheridan Ave., Quarters 24A, was named for the future general but he did not live here. The first territorial Capitol of Kansas State Historical Park, 3 miles from exit 301 off IS 70, was built in 1853 during the "Bloody Kansas" days. The legislature was mainly a body of proslavery Missourians who had crossed into the state to sway the elections. They removed the Capitol to Shawnee Methodist Mission in Fairview and the settlement of Pawnee vanished. The Capitol, restored, is a museum with period items. The U.S. Cavalry Museum, Bldg. 205, displays the history of the cavalry from the Revolutionary War to the mid-20th century.

Fort Riley, 9 miles southwest off IS 70, was first known as Camp Center, established to protect the Santa Fe Trail. By 1855 it was renamed Fort Riley and converted to a cavalry post. Custer was second in command.

Hartford House, 2309 Claflin Rd., in Pioneer Park, is one of ten buildings brought here in 1855 on a riverboat by a group of Free Soilers. Restored, with period furnishings.

MARYSVILLE, Marshall County. US 36, 77.

Original Pony Express Home Station No. 1 Museum, 106 S. 8th St., was headquarters for postal riders before the telegraph reached Kansas. Exhibits of frontier memorabilia.

MOUND CITY, Linn County. State 52.

Site of Battle of Mine Creek, also known as the battle of Round Mound. A Civil War monument is in the Federal cemetery at Mound City. Late in October 1864, Gen. Sterling Price, having been defeated at Kansas City, Missouri, crossed into Kansas and camped at Trading Post. On the morning of October 25, Union troops under Gens. Pleasonton, Blunt, and Curtis engaged the Southern forces and ended the threat of Rebel invasion of Kansas.

OSAWATOMIE, Miami County. US 169.

Samuel Adair (John Brown) Cabin Historic Site, 10th & Main streets. Adair was pastor of the Old Stone Church, at 6th and Parker, and was Brown's brother-in-law. The site has the log cabin Brown once lived in. The cabin has been moved from its original site and has period furnishings. Statue of John Brown in the park.

PAWNEE ROCK, Barton County. US 156. Kit Carson camped here and Indians waited for vulnerable wagon trains. The signatures of Carson, Robert E. Lee, John Sherman, and others were on the rock; some may still be found.

PLEASANTON, Linn County. US 69. (*Also see* MOUND CITY.) The Mine Creek Civil War Battlefield is two miles south. On October 25, 1864, one of the last significant conflicts west of the Mississippi took place on Mine Creek. Some 7,000 Confederates were defeated by the Union's better weapons.

Linn County Historical Museum, six blocks west of the US 69 bypass at 107 S. Park St., has exhibits and audio-visual displays to highlight Civil War activities in the area.

SALINA, Saline County. IS 70, US 40.

Oakdale Park, Oakdale Dr., has memorial gate at north entrance, erected by the county in honor of Civil and Spanish-American War soldiers.

SHAWNEE, Johnson County. US 50, 56. The first settlement was Gum Springs. Later a mission for Indian children was established here from 1839 to 1862. During the bloody prewar years this was the capital for proslavery forces. Still later it was raided by Quantrill's guerrillas. Some prewar buildings remain in Old Shawnee Town, 57th St. and Cody.

TOPEKA, Shawnee County. IS 70.

Kansas Museum of History, 6425 W. 6th St., has exhibits from prehistoric times to the present. The Pottawatomie Baptist Indian Mission State Historic Site is next to the museum. It was built in 1848 and has been restored.

Kansas State Historical Society and Museum, Memorial Building, 10th and Jackson St. Displays featuring Kansas history and John Brown memorabilia. Original Kansas constitution is in lobby of building. Also has a bronze Abraham Lincoln by Merrill Gage.

Kansas State House, Capitol Square, Jackson and Harrison St. The famous John Steuart Curry murals depicting the days of "Bleeding Kansas" are on the second floor in the rotunda. Curry was born near Dunavant, Jefferson County, Kansas.

Site of Old Stockade, 6th and Kansas Ave. A sidewalk plate marks the site of "Fort Folly," a roofless log affair erected in 1864 as protection against Price's Confederate raiders.

Topeka Cemetery, Lafayette and 10th St., has a monument to Kansas soldiers who fell at the battle of the Blue. It was dedicated May 30, 1895, by Col. George Veale, who led the 2nd Kansas Militia in the battle.

KENTUCKY

In 1860, Kentucky voted against native sons Abraham Lincoln and John C. Breckinridge, giving support instead to John Bell of Tennessee, a Whig of long standing who represented the Constitutional Union party and was in some ways the most conservative of the four candidates. Although the state was hopelessly divided at the outbreak of war, many Kentuckians hoped to maintain neutrality. In May 1861, the legislature formally announced the state's neutrality. Meanwhile, both armies were beginning to recruit within the area. Both Union and Confederate presidents were Kentuckians and hoped to gain the state's loyalty and support. Lincoln was quoted as saying that he hoped God was on his side, but he absolutely had to have Kentucky. In the summer of 1861, Confederates under Maj. Gen. Leonidas Polk occupied Columbus. Two days later, Grant occupied Paducah. By September the legislature had created a military force to expel the Confederates. On September 11, a resolution was made that Gov. Magoffin, who was pro-Southern, be instructed to "inform those concerned that Kentucky expects the Confederate or Tennessee troops to be withdrawn from her soil, unconditionally." Another resolution requesting the governor to expel both Federal and Confederate troops was defeated. Kentucky, by this act, seemed to be safely in the Union camp; nevertheless some 35,000 Kentuckians volunteered for the Confederate army and the state was regarded as a Rebel state by many Northerners throughout the war.

More than 75,000 Kentuckians joined the Union army, and more than 400 engagements took place in the state. The battle of Perryville, in October 1862, was the most severe. After Perryville there was no serious Confederate threat, but numerous cavalry raids and guerrilla strikes were maintained.

The Kentucky Historical Highway Markers Commission has followed an extensive program to designate sites worthy of recogniton. Because of the frequent scattered raids, skirmishes, and incidents, nearly every county has a point of Civil War interest.

ALBANY, Clinton County. State 90. Federals took the town in 1863 for ten months. There was much guerrilla activity in the area. Thomas E. Bramlette, U.S. district judge in 1862, elected governor in 1863, was born near here. Descriptive marker at courthouse, which was burned.

AUGUSTA, Bracken County. State 8, 19, on Ohio River. "Augusta in Civil War" marker on State 8. Gen. Basil Duke of Morgan's cavalry engaged the Federal Home Guards under Col. Joshua T. Bradford on September 27, 1862. Capt. Sam Morgan, cousin of the general, was among the 21 killed. Duke later wrote that most of his casualties occurred in the first few minutes of street fighting when the Federals were taking aim from houses. "Some of the women came [while the fight was raging] from the part of the town where they had retired for safety, to the most dangerous positions, and waited upon the wounded, while the balls were striking around them."

BARBOURVILLE, Knox County. US 25 E. Marker for action here on highway 1½ miles north of town. Home Guards and Confederates skirmished at the Barbourville Bridge, September 9, 1861.

BARDSTOWN, Nelson County. US 62. After Perryville, Morgan's cavalry captured and destroyed a train of 51 wagons at Cox's Creek Bridge, 6 miles north of town, October 20, 1862.

Camp Charity. Marker on US 62, 10 miles east. Established by Morgan for recruiting troops into the 2nd Kentucky Confederate Cavalry, September 1861.

Lincoln Homestead State Park, 5 miles north on State 528, has replica of cabin built by the president's grandfather. Thomas Lincoln lived here until he was 25. Some furnishings were made by him. Also here is the Berry

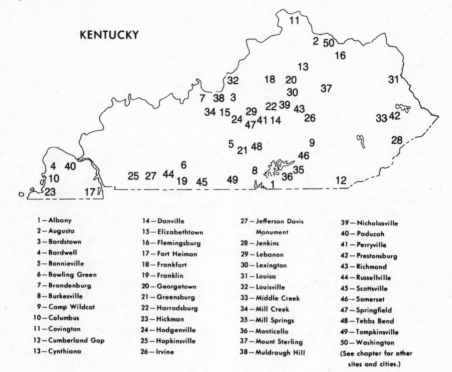

KENTUCKY

1 — Albany	14 — Danville	27 — Jefferson Davis	39 — Nicholasville
2 — Augusta	15 — Elizabethtown	Monument	40 — Paducah
3 — Bardstown	16 — Flemingsburg	28 — Jenkins	41 — Perryville
4 — Bardwell	17 — Fort Heiman	29 — Lebanon	42 — Prestonsburg
5 — Bonnieville	18 — Frankfort	30 — Lexington	43 — Richmond
6 — Bowling Green	19 — Franklin	31 — Louisa	44 — Russellville
7 — Brandenburg	20 — Georgetown	32 — Louisville	45 — Scottsville
8 — Burkesville	21 — Greensburg	33 — Middle Creek	46 — Somerset
9 — Camp Wildcat	22 — Harrodsburg	34 — Mill Creek	47 — Springfield
10 — Columbus	23 — Hickman	35 — Mill Springs	48 — Tebbs Bend
11 — Covington	24 — Hodgenville	36 — Monticello	49 — Tompkinsville
12 — Cumberland Gap	25 — Hopkinsville	37 — Mount Sterling	50 — Washington
13 — Cynthiana	26 — Irvine	38 — Muldraugh Hill	(See chapter for other sites and cities.)

Home, where Nancy Hanks lived before her marriage. Blacksmith and carpenter shops are replicas.

The Mansion, 1003 N. Third St., is said to be the site where the Confederate flag was first raised. Guided tours.

"My Old Kentucky Home State Park," one mile east on US 150, has Stephen Foster memorabilia in a handsomely preserved antebellum home. *The Stephen Foster Story* is presented in an outdoor theater during summer months.

Old Bardstown Village and Civil War Museum, east of 1st on E. Broadway. The Old Bardstown Village is a reproduction. Museum has medical, cavalry, and infantry relics.

Spalding Hall, 114 N. 5th, was used as a hospital during the war. Houses the Historical Society Museum. Civil War artifacts and Lincoln mementos.

BARDWELL, Carlisle County. US 62–51. In this area chains were used across the Mississippi River to hamper Union gunboats. (*Also see* COLUMBUS.) Confederate fortifications

and trenches were established here early in the war. Descriptive marker at junction of highways.

BENTON, Marshall County. US 641. Forrest skirmished here two days before the battle of Paducah, March 1864. Marker.

BIG HILL, Madison County. US 421, Old Wilderness Road marker on highway. Several sharp skirmishes occurred in the area. Grant stopped here in 1864 on his way north from Knoxville.

BONNEVILLE, Owsley County. State 28, 30. Marker on courthouse lawn.

On April 15, 1864, some 78 guerrillas attacked the town but were driven off by the citizens.

BONNIEVILLE, Hart County. IS 65.

Glen Lily, on Green River, was the birthplace of Simon Bolivar Buckner, who surrendered to Gen. Grant at Fort Donelson and much later was pallbearer at Grant's funeral.

Louisville & Nashville Railroad Bridge, over Bacon Creek, was burned by Morgan's cavalry and 100 Union prisoners were taken, December 26, 1862.

BOWLING GREEN, Warren County. IS 65, US 31W. In November 1861, Gen. Buckner occupied the town; a division led by Gen. Albert Johnston then fortified the area as permanent headquarters. Plans were changed by the Federal reduction of Forts Henry and Donelson; Confederates evacuated and Union troops, moving in, completed the fortifications.

Civil War Defense Line, marker on US 31W, 2 miles northeast of town. Western Kentucky University is on the site once occupied by a fort known as College Heights. Trenches are now campus walkways.

Kentucky Building, on Western Kentucky University campus, has a large collection of historical exhibits. The university was built around a Civil War battle site.

Kentucky Building, at state college (*see above*), has an extensive collection of Kentucky history. Museum has pioneer and Indian relics.

Kentucky Confederate Capitol, marker on US 68. Gen. Johnston fortified the area which served as Capitol for four months until Union forces took over and finished fortifications.

BURKESVILLE, Cumberland County. State 90. Markers in public square and on State 61 at state line. Morgan and his men crossed the Cumberland River at this point on July 2, 1863, for his longest raid north. The courthouse was burned during the war.

BURNSIDE, Pulaski County. US 27. The town was named for Gen. Ambrose Burnside, who had headquarters here in 1863 at what was then Port Isabel, head of navigation on the Cumberland River.

CAMPBELLSVILLE, Taylor County. State 55. Markers on highway bypass south of town for battle of Green River Bridge on Independence Day, 1863. The courthouse was burned during the war.

CAMP WILDCAT, Laurel County. Marker on US 25, north of London, denotes site. In October 1861, Zollicoffer with seven regiments and a light battery attacked Union troops under the command of Brig. Gen. Albion Schoepf. Historian Benjamin Lossing described the scene: "It was in a most picturesque region of one of the spurs of the Cumberland Mountains, on the direct road from Cumberland Gap. . . . The invader moved swiftly, swooping down

from the mountains like an eagle on its prey." The prey, in this instance, repulsed the eagle.

CANTON, Trigg County. State 80. On October 26, 1861, Forrest's cavalry shelled and drove off the Union gunboat *Conestoga,* which had come upriver to bombard the town.

CASEYVILLE, Union County. State 130. Marker. Everyone in town was taken prisoner by a Union gunboat crew after a shelling on July 26, 1862. Most of the crowd was released. Nineteen hostages were taken to Evansville, Indiana.

CATLETTSBURG, Boyd County. Off IS 64, US 23. Marker. The town served as an army base. In September 1863, home guard troops skirmished with guerrillas.

CLOVERPORT, Breckinridge County. US 60. Marker for Lincoln Family Trail. In 1816, Thomas Lincoln and family ferried across the Ohio at this point when moving from Hodgenville to Indiana.

COLUMBIA, Adair County. US 23.

Wolford Monument, on courthouse lawn, honors Col. Frank L. Wolford, colonel of the First Kentucky Union Cavalry and one of the most picturesque cavalry officers in the West. He defeated Gen. John H. Morgan in the battle of Lebanon, Tennessee, 1862. He chased Morgan across Kentucky, Indiana, and Ohio in July 1863. Morgan tried to surrender to Wolford, realizing that Wolford was a gallant and humane officer.

COLUMBUS, Hickman County. State 80. Marker on highway and at battlefield. In the fall of 1861, J. G. Deupree of the 1st Mississippi Cavalry was stationed here under Leonidas Polk. The camp was situated on the river bank about one mile south of the railroad depot. It was still a young war in September when Deupree wrote: "When off duty, we enjoyed nothing more than to gather on the bluff just north of Columbus to see gun-boats pursue Capt. Marsh Miller as he returned from his daily scouts up the river. . . . Sometimes the Grampus was gone so long we feared she had been captured; but at length she would be seen in the distance under a full head of steam and with her shrill whistle doing its utmost to be heard all down the river; and beyond were the gunboats, firing as they came. After getting under protection of our land batteries, the Grampus never failed to turn and 'pop away' with her six-pounder, much to our amusement and doubtless to the amusement of the Federals

General Grant's troops cross Mayfield Creek on their way to Columbus.

as well." Polk occupied the fortifications on the bluff, putting in 140 cannons.

Columbus-Belmont Battlefield State Park, comprising 156 acres 2 miles west on State 58, has a museum, housed in a building which was used as an infirmary during the war. There are trenches and a section of the great chain which was stretched across the river; also the six-ton anchor to which the chain was attached. This was known as the "Gibralter of the West." The battle was the opening of the Federal's western campaign. Audio-visual program on the battle.

COVINGTON, Kenton County. IS 71, 75, US 25. Hills behind town were fortified to protect Cincinnati. In September 1862, Confederates under Gen. Henry Heth came within three miles of the city, but Union troops came across the Ohio on a pontoon bridge made of coal barges and Heth withdrew after a light skirmish near Fort Mitchell. Descriptive marker at Fort Mitchell Country Club. A newspaper account emphasized the "unparalleled excitement" in Cincinnati and the fact that no able-bodied men, including squirrel hunters, were allowed to leave town except in a southerly direction.

CUMBERLAND GAP NATIONAL HISTORICAL PARK, west end of park, near Middlesboro, US 25E. The gap was twice taken and evacuated by Confederates. "Long Tom," the largest gun then in use, was installed by the Southerners to command the lowlands on either side. Union troops captured the gap on June 18, 1862, had to evacuate three months later. It was recaptured by Burnside on September 9, 1863. A visitor center has historical exhibits, observation deck, and literature. The park covers about 32 square miles in three states; Cumberland Gap runs into Bell County, Kentucky, from Tennessee.

CYNTHIANA, Harrison County. US 27. Marker on highway.

Battle of Cynthiana. On July 17, 1862, Morgan's raiders defeated home guards. The depot and military supplies were burned. Camp Frazier was destroyed. Much of the fighting took place around an old covered bridge over the Licking River. Morgan again defeated a Federal force here June 10–11, 1864, but Union reinforcements arrived next day, driving off the raiders. Most of the business section was destroyed. On June 12, 1864, Morgan was disastrously defeated by Union troops under Maj. Gen. Stephen Burbridge.

Battle Grove Cemetery, on Millersburg Rd., was the site of June 12, 1864, engagement. Confederate monument here was erected in 1869.

DANVILLE, Boyle County. US 150. A holier-than-thou announcement was in the "Civil War Annals of Kentucky" for October 10, 1862: "Confederate forces refuse to occupy or use, for hospitals or otherwise, the dwellings at Danville of Gen. Jerry T. Boyle and Rev. Dr. Robert J. Breckinridge—in striking contrast with the Federals occupation, for hospital purposes, of Provisional Governor Richard Hawes' residence at Paris."

Centre College, west end of Main St., had Beriah Magoffin, Civil War governor, and Maj. Gen. John C. Breckinridge among its graduates.

DIXON, Webster County. US 41.
Site of Prison Pen, courthouse square. Confederates were confined here after the battles of Slaughtersville in 1862 and Providence in 1864.

EDDYVILLE, Lyon County. IS 24, US 62. Marker. Home town of Brig. Gen. Hylan Benton Lyon, who was taken prisoner at the Fort Donelson surrender and after his exchange led a brigade under Forrest.

ELIZABETHTOWN, Hardin County. IS 65, US 31W. Thomas Lincoln, Abraham's father, lived in the town or nearby from 1796 to 1816. He moved to Indiana but when his wife, Nancy, died, he returned here and married Sarah Bush Johnston. A number of skirmishes took place here. In December 1862, the town was shelled by Morgan's troops, who took 600 prisoners. The Visitors Commission, 24 Public Square, has self-guiding tours.

Brown-Pusey Community House, N. Main and Poplar St., was a stagecoach inn. Gen. Custer lived next door on Main St. while serving as military governor after the war.

Helm House, marker at site, was the home of Gen. Ben Hardin Helm of the 1st Kentucky Cavalry, known as the Orphan Brigade, which he commanded in the absence of Maj. Gen. John C. Breckinridge. Helm was married to Mrs. Lincoln's sister Emily. Lincoln offered him the position of Union paymaster; Helm declined the offer. He was killed at Chickamauga, September 20, 1863.

Lincoln Heritage House, 2 miles northwest on US 31W, then east at Freeman Lake Park. One of the two log structures here was built in part by Thomas Lincoln, who was a skilled carpenter and cabinet maker. House has period furnishings.

FLEMINGSBURG, Fleming County. State 57. Marker for Morgan's last raid. On September 2, 1863, 70 guerrillas robbed the bank and townspeople.

Andrews Home, south of courthouse square, has marker. Capt. James J. Andrews, who led the famous Andrews Raid, capturing the Confederate locomotive the General, was a resident here for a time.

FORREST MARKERS. Gen. Nathan Bedford Forrest fought his first Kentucky skirmish near Sacramento, McLean County, late in December 1861. At that time a Kentucky belle, mounted on a handsome horse, temporarily joined his raiders. The sight of her "untied tresses floating in the breeze, infused nerve" into the general's arm, as he noted in his official report. Confederates came off winners in the skirmish with Federals under Capt. Robert G. Bacon. From July to October 1862, Forrest operated throughout central Kentucky, as well as in Tennessee; in the spring of 1864 he invaded western Kentucky as far as Paducah. There are numerous state markers pointing out routes taken by his troops. Some of them will be found at:

Gold City, Simpson County.
Greenville, Muhlenburg County.
Madisonville, Hopkins County.
Marion, Crittenden County.
Morganfield, Union County.
Paducah, McCracken County.
Providence, Webster County.
Sacramento, McLean County.
Sturgis, Union County.

FORT HEIMAN, Calloway County. Junction of State 121 and Fort Heiman Rd. Marker at New Mount Carmel Church. A Confederate defense on the Tennessee River fell to Union forces in February 1862. Area was again occupied by Confederates for a short time in 1864. Site is now flooded by Kentucky Lake.

FORT KNOX, Hardin County. US 60.
Patton Museum, Bldg. 4554, has Civil War hand weapons.

FRANKFORT, Franklin County. IS 64, US 60. The only capital of a state remaining in the Union which was captured by Confederates during the war. Gen. Kirby Smith occupied the town on September 3, 1862, until October 4. When Richard Hawes was being installed as governor, Federal troops cut the ceremony short.

Frankfort Cemetery, E. Main St., has monument honoring soldiers of all wars. Theodore O'Hara, who served in the Mexican and Civil wars, author of "The Bivouac of the Dead," is buried here.

Kentucky Military History Museum, US 60, Old State Arsenal, E. Main, has weapons, flags, and uniforms of several wars, including the Civil War.

Old State Capitol, Broadway and St. Clair St., was the seat of government in Civil War years. Kentucky History Museum, next to the old Capitol, has a taped presentation of Kentucky's role in the war.

Old State House, Broadway and St. Clair Mall. In the annex is the Museum of the Kentucky Historical Society. Among documents and manuscripts are personal and official papers of Lincoln and Jefferson Davis. The Confederate Room has artifacts from the Civil War. Gun collection has Civil War cannon and a machine gun used particularly at covered bridges; by killing the first horses of a regiment, a gunner could effectively block the bridge.

State Capitol, south end of Capitol Ave., has a statue of Lincoln and of Jefferson Davis in the rotunda. Murals and paintings depict Kentucky history.

FRANKLIN, Simpson County. US 31W. Marker for Sue Mundy's grave. The Franklin County outlaw joined forces with Quantrill in the spring of 1865. He was captured with two companions at Webster on May 12, had one of the briefest trials this side of Deadwood, and was hanged at Broadway and 18th St. in Louisville on May 16, 1865.

GEORGETOWN, Scott County. IS 75, US 62.

City Cemetery has grave of Confederate Gov. George Johnson, killed at Shiloh.

Georgetown College, College St. Giddings Hall was the scene of a campus riot in 1861. Southerners attempted to raise the Confederate flag but were repressed by Northerners. A fistfight took place. One account of the affair says that the college president lined up the Confederates on the south side of lawn, the Unionists on the north, and at a signal both groups turned about face and the entire student body marched off to war.

GLASGOW, Barren County. US 68. On October 10, 1861, Federal troops were ambushed by ten Confederates and routed; 11 men were killed; equipment and 30 horses were cap-

tured. When Gen. Braxton Bragg moved into Kentucky in 1862, Glasgow was the first town occupied.

GOOSE CREEK, Clay County. Southeast of Manchester, off State 80. In October 1862, the 1st and 20th Kentucky Infantry fell upon the rear guard of Gen. Kirby Smith's forces near the Goose Creek salt works, taking 90 prisoners.

GREENSBURG, Green County. State 70. Home town of two Union generals, E. H. Hobson and W. T. Ward. Hobson was wounded at Shiloh, pursued Morgan in the summer of 1863 and again in 1864. He was wounded and captured at Cynthiana, later was commander at Lexington. Ward led a brigade in the Army of the Cumberland, served at Atlanta and on the March to the Sea, was severely but not mortally wounded at Resaca. Marker honoring generals is located in Old Courthouse square. Six Confederate prisoners were shot here on November 19, 1864, on orders given by Gen. Stephen G. Burbridge, military governor, in retaliation for the slaying of two Union men.

HARDINSBURG, Breckinridge County. US 60. Marker for courthouse burned during the war. On October 15, 1864, Capt. McCarroll's guerrillas attacked the town and were driven off by citizens. McCarroll was killed.

HARRODSBURG, Mercer County. US 127.

Old Fort Harrod State Park has replicas of pioneer cabins, first schoolhouse, Mansion Museum, and the Lincoln Marriage Temple which houses the log cabin in which Abraham Lincoln's parents were married. It was moved here from the original site at Beech Fork settlement. Tom and Nancy Lincoln were married on June 2, 1806, by the Rev. Jesse Head. The Mansion Museum has Lincoln and Confederate rooms.

Presbyterian Church of Harrodsburg had a dispute about whether to take care of Confederate or Federal wounded; the congregation split on the problem, founded a Northern and Southern branch of the church, later reunited.

St. Philips Episcopal Church, marker at site. Gen. Leonidas Polk conducted services here on the eve of the battle of Perryville. Church is still in use.

HARTFORD, Ohio County. US 231. Another town that lost a courthouse in the war. On January 22, 1865, Quantrill's guerrillas, dressed as Federal soldiers, made a strike here, killing two men.

HENDERSON, Henderson County. US 60. Marker on courthouse lawn. The town was seized on July 22, 1862, by Federals coming from Evansville.

HICKMAN, Fulton County. State 125. Marker on highway. On September 3, 1861, Confederate troops from Tennessee fortified the town. In January 1865, Quantrill crossed into Kentucky en route to Washington, reportedly to assassinate President Lincoln. Frank James was one of the 30 guerrillas with Quantrill. A news item of the times said a "party of rebel cavalry" pillaged all the stores in town.

HODGENVILLE, Larue County. US 31E, State 61.

Abraham Lincoln Birthplace National Historic Site, 3 miles south on US 31E, State 61. Visitor center contains exhibits, diorama, an audio-visual program pertaining to Lincoln's boyhood travels, and literature. Memorial building houses a log cabin which may have been the one in which Lincoln was born on February 12, 1809. The original Thomas Lincoln Sinking Spring farm is included in the historic site.

Hodgenville Courthouse, marker, was burned by Quantrill on February 22, 1865.

Knob Creek, marker on US 31E, northeast of Hodgenville, site of first home Lincoln remembered. There is a reconstructed cabin on the site where Lincoln lived from 1811 to 1816.

The Lincoln Museum, 66 Lincoln Sq., has wax figures depicting a dozen significant episodes in Lincoln's life. Memorabilia and art exhibited also.

Lincoln Statue, in square, was executed by A. A. Weinmann, a student of Saint-Gaudens.

HOPKINSVILLE, Christian County. US 41. One of N. B. Forrest's stops.

Courthouse has marker. Town was occupied by Federal forces and the courthouse burned during war.

Pennyroyal Area Museum, 217 E. 9th St. Civil War exhibits and Jefferson Davis memorabilia.

IRVINE, Estill County. State 89, ½ mile north of town, has marker. Junction of State 52–499 has marker. Sharp skirmish on July 30, 1863, between the Union Kentucky cavalry under Col. Lilly and Scott's Confederates. On October 13, 1864, the jail was burned by 40 guerrillas who released four prisoners, then plundered the town.

JEFFERSON DAVIS MONUMENT, Todd County. US 68, in Fairview. Birthplace of

Jefferson Davis has been commemorated by a 351-foot obelisk. Museum at top of monument. Elevator service. Twenty-two-acre park contains a replica of the cabin in which Davis was born on June 3, 1808.

JENKINS, Letcher County. US 23, 119.

Pound Gap, on summit of Cumberland Mountain, was the site of Confederate camp attacked by Gen. Garfield on March 14, 1862. Barracks, huts, and stores were burned; Confederates retreated into Virginia with a loss of seven men.

LAKELAND, Jefferson County. State 22.

Kentucky Military Institute, founded in 1845, furnished officers to both armies.

LANCASTER, Garrard County. State 52. Harriet Beecher Stowe is said to have visited the Gen. Thomas Kennedy family here when gathering material for *Uncle Tom's Cabin.* Gen. Kennedy is buried in nearby Paint Creek Presbyterian Church graveyard.

LAWRENCEBURG, Anderson County. US 62, east of US 127. Marker on Board of Education building. A hand-to-hand cavalry skirmish took place here on October 6, 1862, between Col. Scott's Confederates and Col. R. T. Jacob's 9th Kentucky.

LEBANON, Marion County. US 68. Markers on highway and at courthouse and railroad station, both of which were burned. Lt. Tom Morgan was killed here. The battle of Lebanon was fought on July 5, 1863, between Morgan, with two cavalry brigades, and Col. Charles S. Hanson, with the 20th Kentucky Union Infantry Regiment. Hanson, outnumbered, took refuge in the Louisville and Nashville Railroad depot, was able to delay Morgan's advance for some seven hours. The delay was costly for the CSA, greatly hindering the expedition across the Ohio River, although military supplies and medicines were captured.

LEXINGTON, Fayette County. IS 64, 75, US 68, 27.

Breckinridge Statue, Cheapside Park. John Cabell Breckinridge was Buchanan's vice president. He left Kentucky in October 1861 to avoid arrest as a traitor. He served under Gen. Albert Johnston at Shiloh, later served in Louisiana, at Stones River, Chickamauga, and the Shenandoah Valley. In the last months of the conflict he was Confederate Secretary of War. He was Gen. Joe Johnston's advisor during surrender negotiations in North Carolina. Two Breckinridge cousins stayed with the Union. The Breckinridge home is at 429 W. 2nd St.

Ellerslie, US 25, 1 mile south of town. Marker for home of Levi Todd, grandfather of Mary Lincoln.

Ficklin House, 102 W. High St. Jefferson Davis roomed at the home of Joseph Ficklin, Lexington's postmaster, when Davis was a student at Transylvania University, 1821–1824. Marker at site.

Fort Clay, marker at west end of W. High St. viaduct, for Civil War fortification.

Hopemont, the Hunt-Morgan House, 201 N. Mill St. Last home of Gen. John Hunt Morgan, the "Thunderbolt of the Confederacy." A Morgan statue is in the courthouse square.

Lexington Cemetery, US 421, 833 W. Main St. Among those buried here are members of Mary Todd Lincoln's family; James Lane Allen, Kentucky author; Gen. John Hunt Morgan; Col. W. C. P. Breckinridge; Henry Clay; Gen. Basil Wilson Duke; Gen. Gordon Granger; and 500 Confederate soldiers. The national cemetery is also located here.

Mary Todd Lincoln House, 578 W. Main, was the girlhood home of Mary Todd. Restored with personal items from the Lincoln and Todd families. She was born at 501 W. Short, December 13, 1818. Lincoln was a guest here three times.

Transylvania College, W. 3rd St., is the oldest college west of the Alleghenies. Among former students: Jefferson Davis, John C. Breckinridge, Albert Sidney Johnston, and John Hunt Morgan. Library has Jefferson Davis letters. "Old Morrison" was used as a hospital during the war. Medical museum.

Waveland, Higbee Mill Rd., off US 27S. The antebellum mansion has been handsomely restored. The military relics room has Civil War items. Guide service is provided. In addition to the mansion, the tour includes former slave quarters, an icehouse, fireplace, kitchen, and smokehouse. Now a state historic shrine.

LOUISA, Lawrence County. US 23. Guerrillas under Bill Smith raided nearby Peach Orchard on November 5, 1864, captured two steamers, and plundered the town. Marker on courthouse lawn.

Fort Bishop marker on US 23 Bypass.

LOUISVILLE, Jefferson County, IS 64. US 31, 150. The city was a depot for the transfer of Rebel prisoners to the North, a hospital center (by 1863, 19 military hospitals were here), and a base of supplies for the Army of the Cumberland. Confederate Gen. Richard Taylor, son of President Zachary Taylor, was born here, as was Union Gen. Robert Anderson, the "hero of Fort Sumter."

Confederate Monument, S. 3rd and Shipp St., was erected by the Kentucky Women's Confederate Monument Association.

Farmington, 3033 Bardstown Rd., was designed by Jefferson, built by John Speed in 1810. Lincoln visited here in 1841. Rooms have period furnishings.

The Filson Club, 1310 S. Third, has Kentuckiana library and museum. The club, named for historian John Filson, is one of the country's outstanding historical societies.

Galt House, 2nd and Main St. Marker at site of famous hotel where Sherman once had his headquarters. Grant and other generals also were guests here in war years, but Sherman probably had the worst time of it. It was at the Galt House, during a conference with Secretary of War Simon Cameron and other Washington officials that the Ohio general gave some observers the impression he was insane, wildly overestimating the strength of the enemy, and subject to unreasoning fears. It was many months before he lived down the newspaper stories, even in his home state of Ohio.

Jefferson County Courthouse, 5th and Jefferson. During Confederate occupancy of Frankfort in 1862, the state legislature met here.

Lincoln Monument, west lawn of library on 4th St. Heroic statue is the work of George Grey Barnard.

Louisville Defense Forts. A ring of 12 forts built in August 1864 protected the city against an invasion that never came. The line, some 10 miles long, went from Beargrass Creek and the Ohio River on the east, to Paddy's Run and the Ohio on the west; it was angled to cover all turnpikes. Forts were named for Union officers killed in battle. Fort McPherson was in the center, at Preston St., Barbee, Brandeis, Hahn, and Fort St.; from east end, Fort Elstner was between Frankfort Ave. and Bronsboro Rd., near Bellaire, Vernon, and Emerald Ave.; Fort Engle near Spring St. and Arlington Ave.; Fort Saunders in Cave Hill Cemetery; Fort Hill between Goddard Ave. and St. Louis Cemetery; Fort Horton at junction of Shelby and Merriweather St.; Fort Philpot near 7th St. and Algonquin Pkwy.; Fort St. Clair Morton, 16th and Hill; Fort Karnasch, Wilson Ave. between 26th and 28th St.; Fort Clark at 26th and Magnolia; and Fort Southworth, on Paddy's Run at the Ohio. Time marches on: the city incinerator occupies Fort Horton; the sewage disposal plant covers Fort Southworth.

MADISONVILLE, Madisonville County. US 41

Historical Library and Museum, 107 Union St., has Civil War relics among its more than 4,000 displays.

MAYFIELD, Graves County. US 45. Marker on highway.
Camp Beauregard was captured by Union Gen. C. F. Smith on January 7, 1862.

MAYSVILLE, Mason County. US 68.
Camp Kenton was established by Union Lt. William Nelson in the fall of 1861, after Gen. George Thomas succeeded him in command at Camp Dick Robinson.

MIDDLE CREEK, Floyd County. State 114. Marker on highway west of Prestonsburg. Battle of Middle Creek was won by Gen. James A. Garfield on January 10, 1862, gaining control of the Big Sandy country.

MIDWAY, Woodford County. IS 64, US 62. Morgan and Mundy markers on highway and railroad. On February 2, 1865, guerrillas captured the town, robbed residents, and burned depot.

MILL CREEK, Hardin County. US 31W.
Mill Creek Cemetery has graves of Lincoln family members: Bersheba Lincoln (Abraham Lincoln's grandmother) and two aunts, Mary Lincoln Crume and Nancy Lincoln Brumfield.

MILL SPRINGS, Wayne County. State 90, Marker on highway east of town as roadside park. Battle also has been called Logan's Cross Roads, Fishing Creek, Somerset, and Beech Grove. Confederate defense positions were located here. Eight thousand Confederates under Gen. Felix Zollicoffer were defeated by the same number of Federals under Gen. Thomas on January 19, 1862. Site where Zollicoffer was killed (*see also* MEMPHIS, TENNESSEE) and 106 Confederate dead were buried in one grave is enclosed in small cemetery off State 80 near Nancy.

MONTICELLO, Wayne County. State 90.
Monticello Park is dedicated to soldiers killed in the Civil War. Gen. Morgan's raiders came this way in late May 1863; to be specific, in the words of Gen. Basil Duke: "When General Morgan reached Monticello, which the enemy had evacuated . . . he found . . . a superior Federal force in Horseshoe bottom on Greasy creek, in the western end of Wayne County."

MORGAN MARKERS: Gen. Morgan's biographer, Basil Duke, reported that the general once met a straggler near the Kentucky-Tennessee line and demanded sternly why he

was absent from his regiment. The fellow answered, "Well, General, I'm scattered." Morgan himself was scattered at these among other places:

Augusta, Bracken County.
Bardstown, Nelson County.
Brandenburg, Mead County.
Cynthiana, Harrison County.
Elizabethtown, Hardin County.
Flemingsburg, Fleming County.
Harrodsburg, Mercer County.
Hindman, Knott County.
Jackson, Breathitt County.
Lebanon, Marion County.
Midway, Woodford County.
Monticello, Wayne County.
Morehead, Rowan County.
Mt. Sterling, Montgomery County.
Muldraugh Hill, Meade County.
Pikeville, Pike County.
Prestonsburg, Floyd County.
Tompkinsville, Monroe County.
Winchester, Clark County.

MOUNT STERLING, Montgomery County. IS 64, US 60. On March 21, 1863, Confederate forces took the town, gaining 428 prisoners, plus wagons and mules. On December 1, Confederates burned the courthouse. Marker near building. Morgan captured town and approximately $60,000 from the Farmer's Bank on June 8, 1864. He was badly defeated the following day, June 9, by Maj. Gen. Stephen T. Burbridge and his cavalry regiment.

MULDRAUGH HILL, Meade County. US 60. Between Christmas and New Year's Day of 1862–1863, Morgan was busy burning railroad trestles. The town, now on north edge of Fort Knox Military Reservation, was also known as Muldrow's Hill. Gen. Sherman gave a newspaper correspondent a few hours to depart from this spot, although the reporter came armed with a letter from the general's brother-in-law, Thomas Ewing, Jr. (What might be considered invincible proof of Sherman's courage was his handling, or mishandling, of newspapermen. Others may claim this as final proof of his madness.) In any case, Sherman ordered the mild-mannered Florus B. Plimpton of the *Cincinnati Commercial* to take the next train out of Muldraugh's Hill, after which the general suggested the best restaurant in case the reporter cared for dinner before train time.

MUNFORDVILLE, Hart County. IS 65, US 31 W. Confederates won a victory here after a three-day siege in September 1862.

Earthworks and forts remain. Marker on highway denotes site of Glen Lily, home of Confederate Gen. Simon Bolivar Buckner. House was destroyed by fire. Munfordville was also the home town of Union Maj. Gen. Thomas J. Wood, an able division commander in the Army of the Cumberland.

NEW CASTLE, Henry County. US 421. Marker. A Confederate cavalry detachment overcame the home guard here on September 21, 1862, taking 170 men and a sizable number of rifles and horses.

NICHOLASVILLE, Jessamine County. US 27.
Camp Dick Robinson, south of town. Marker on highway. The first Federal recruiting station south of the Ohio River.
Camp Nelson Federal Cemetery has 3,000 Union graves.
Fort Brannaum, US 27, was set up to stop Confederates at river.

OWENSBORO, Daviess County. State 54. On January 8, 1865, the courthouse was burned by Confederate guerrillas under Davidson and Porter. Marker at site.

OWENTON, Owen County. US 227, State 22.
Civil War Recruiting Camp, marker at highway junction.
Owen County Courthouse was occupied by Federal forces.

OWINGSVILLE, Bath County. IS 64, US 60. Gen. John Bell Hood was born here. The courthouse was burned during the war; the mishap was said to be carelessness of Federal soldiers. Seven Union soldiers were killed by guerrillas on October 6, 1863.

PADUCAH, McCracken County. IS 24, US 60. Grant fortified the city in September 1861. Forrest made a last attempt to take the city in March 1864.
Confederate Flag Marker, 3rd St. between Broadway and Kent Ave. Site of first public showing of Confederate flag in 1861 in Paducah.
Fort Anderson, Trimble St. between 4th and 5th. Site of fortifications built by Grant in 1861. Marker.
Grant Landing, 1st and Broadway on wharf. Marker is at site where Grant arrived in the fall of 1861 and proclaimed a state of martial law.
Tilghman Statue, 17th and Madison St., honors Gen. Lloyd Tilghman, who organized the 3rd Kentucky Regiment and was killed during the battle of Champions Hill in 1863.

Monument was erected by members of the family and the United Daughters of the Confederacy. Gen. Tilghman lived at 7th St. and Kentucky Ave.
Wallace Headquarters, northwest corner of 6th and Clark St. Grant was a guest here at the headquarters of Gen. Lew Wallace.

PAINTSVILLE, Johnson County. US 23-460. Markers on highway for Civil War actions in the Big Sandy area.

PERRYVILLE BATTLEFIELD STATE HISTORIC PARK, Boyle County. Two miles north off US 150. The major engagement fought in Kentucky took place here on October 8, 1862. It is also sometimes called the battle of Chaplin Hills. About 58,000 (only about 22,000 actually were involved) Federals under Gen. Don Carlos Buell opposed 16,000 Confederates led by Gen. Braxton Bragg. The Crawford house, Bragg's headquarters, and the Squire H. P. Bottom house, which was in the midst of the fighting, are still standing. The conflict began almost by accident and was characterized by odd circumstances. Bragg thought Buell had fewer troops at Perryville; Buell thought Bragg had more. Buell had been thrown from a horse that morning and had remained at headquarters where Gen. Gilbert dined with him. Because of the terrain and the direction of the wind, no sound of battle reached them until 4 in the afternoon. Later in that much confused day, Polk mistook Union troops for Confederates and ordered the commander to cease firing into his own men. Col. Keith of the 22nd Indiana responded that he was sure his fire was aimed at the enemy and asked who Polk might be. Polk realized his error and rode away before it was costly. Both commanding generals were severely criticized—Bragg for his failure to hold Kentucky, Buell for allowing the Confederates to withdraw safely. Buell was relieved of command after Perryville.

PEWEE VALLEY, Oldham County. State 146.
Confederate Cemetery is located here. Marker at site.

PIKEVILLE, Pike County. US 23-460.
City Park has plaque commemorating the spot where James A. Garfield was sworn in as Union brigadier general in January 1862.

PRESTONSBURG, Floyd County. US 23-460, State 114.
Battle of Ivy Mountain, marker on highway 12 miles south of town. Federals under Brig. Gen. W. O. Nelson defeated Confederates un-

der Brig. Gen. John S. Williams, November 8, 1861. Nelson was promoted to major general on July 17, 1862.

Battle of Middle Creek, marker on State 114, east of town. Col. Garfield commanded a brigade of Ohio and Kentucky troops and carried out a campaign which drove the Confederates under Gen. Humphrey Marshall from the Big Sandy Valley.

Garfield's Headquarters, off Main St. Marker at site.

REID VILLAGE, Montgomery County. US 60. Marker locates site of birthplace of John Bell Hood, Confederate general.

RICHMOND, Madison County. Off IS 75, south of Lexington. Scene of engagement in 1862 between Maj. Gen. E. Kirby Smith's Confederates and 7,000 Federals led by Gen. M. D. Manson. The Southerners drove the Union troops, under the overall command of Gen. Nelson, back to the Kentucky River.

Courthouse, Courthouse square, Main St., in downtown historic district, was used as a hospital during the war.

Richmond Cemetery has the grave of statesman Cassius M. Clay, known as the "Lion of White Hall." Clay died on the night of July 22, 1903; a few hours later a bolt of lightning knocked the head off Henry Clay's statue in Lexington Cemetery. Kentuckians declared that "old Cash" had done it.

White Hall State Shrine, 5 miles north on IS 75. The restored home of emancipationist Cassius Clay who published an antislavery newspaper among other achievements, has period furnishings. Clay was a friend of Lincoln's.

Woodlawn was occupied by troops of both armies. John Fox, Jr., wrote of this house in his novel, *Crittenden.*

ROYALTON, Magoffin County. State 7. Marker on highway 3 miles south of town, describes the battle of Puncheon Creek.

RUSSELLVILLE, Logan County. US 431, 68.

Coke House, southeast corner of 4th and Winter St. Delegates from 64 counties met here November 18, 1861, to form a provisional Confederate government of Kentucky. Bowling Green was named capital and George W. Johnson elected governor. Three weeks later Kentucky was admitted to the Confederacy as the 12th state. Confederate Gen. George B. Crittenden and his brother, Union Gen. Thomas L. Crittenden, were natives of Russellville.

SCOTTSVILLE, Allen County. US 31E. Confederate guerrillas led by Cols. Hughes, Hamilton, and Dougherty raided the town on December 27, 1863. Maj. Johnson's company caught up with the band in Tennessee and recovered most of the plunder.

SHELBYVILLE, Shelby County, IS 64. Civil War blockhouse replica in midtown. Battle markers.

SOMERSET, Pulaski County. US 23.

Dutton's Hill, scene of engagement on March 30, 1863. More than 1,000 Federals under Brig. Gen. Q. A. Gillmore met 2,600 Confederate cavalry under Gen. Pegram. Confederates retreated after five hours.

SPRINGFIELD, Washington County. US 150, State 528.

Lincoln Homestead State Park, State 528, has the actual home of Nancy Hanks, Lincoln's mother, and the site of her marriage to Thomas Lincoln. (*Also see* BARDSTOWN.)

Mordecai Lincoln House, next to state park, was built by Abraham's uncle in 1797 and is the only remaining residence in Kentucky on its original site in an unaltered condition known to have been owned and occupied by a member of the Lincoln family. And we can be sure no log has been left unturned in a search for these structures.

Springfield County Clerk's Office has the marriage bond of Thomas Lincoln, signed by him and Richard Berry, Jr. Also the certificate of Rev. Jesse Head, who performed the ceremony. Other Lincoln family documents are in the collection.

TEBBS BEND, Taylor County. State 55. Marker and monument just off highway, south of Green River, for engagement of July 4, 1863, in which Morgan's cavalry tried to rout the well-fortified 25th Michigan Infantry, commanded by Col. O. H. Moore. Morgan suffered heavy losses including some of his best officers.

TOMPKINSVILLE, Monroe County. US 100. On July 8, 1862, Morgan defeated Federal forces occupying the town. Among those taken prisoner was Maj. Jordan, commanding the 3rd Pennsylvania Cavalry. Confederate Col. Hunt of Georgia was mortally wounded. April 22, 1863, Confederates burned the courthouse.

VANCEBURG, Lewis County. State 10. *Union Memorial* on courthouse lawn.

WAKEFIELD, Spencer County. State 55. Quantrill was ambushed by home guards in a barn near here on May 1, 1865; the guerrilla leader was mortally wounded and died in Louisville.

WASHINGTON, Mason County. US 68. *Johnston Birthplace,* on US 62-68, is now a shrine to Gen. Albert Sidney Johnston, who was killed at Shiloh.

Slave Block, in courthouse square, is the place where Harriet Beecher Stowe saw a slave auction while visiting friends here in 1833.

WEBSTER, Breckinridge County. Off US 60. Sue Mundy, Billy Magruder, and Henry Metcalfe were captured near here on March 12, 1865. (*See* FRANKLIN.)

WEST LIBERTY, Morgan County. State 172. On October 23, 1861, Federal troops routed a Confederate force here.

WILLIAMSBURG, Whitley County. IS 75, US 25W. Marker on courthouse lawn. On November 1, 1864, Confederates raided the town hoping to seize the U.S. government payroll. The money had been removed, but raiders found 30 stands of muskets.

LOUISIANA

Louisiana came into the Union on April 30, 1812, with a constitution modeled after that of Kentucky. Present boundaries were fixed in 1819 when Spain relinquished its claim to territory east of the Sabine River. On January 26, 1861, the state seceded. It existed as an independent republic for six weeks before joining the Confederacy.

From a white population of some 350,000, Louisiana sent about 65,000 to the Confederate army; at least 15,000 were killed in the war. The conflict was brought within the state in 1862 when Flag Officer David Farragut sailed up the Mississippi River, ran by the forts of St. Philip and Jackson, and occupied New Orleans on May 1. Soon after, Farragut forced the surrender of Baton Rouge; thereafter, all southeast parishes were held by the Union.

Shreveport became the capital of the Trans-Mississippi Confederacy. The Union Red River campaign of 1864, led by Gen. N. P. ("Nothing Positive") Banks, was part of a pincers movement against Shreveport; another Federal force was moving south from Arkansas. Gen. Richard Taylor attacked Banks at Mansfield and again at Pleasant Hill, driving the Federals to Alexandria, where, as a Louisiana girl noted in her diary, Banks could have a little breathing space in the shadow of his gunboats. The Union commander, however, was not breathing too easily. The Red River was low, and the gunboats could not get through the rapids until a Wisconsin colonel found the solution: building wing dams out from the banks would deepen the channel. Although the Union forces escaped, Banks's army was unable to take part in other Federal campaigns of 1864.

Among leading Louisiana Confederates was Judah P. Benjamin, who served successively as attorney general, secretary of war, and secretary of state. John Slidell, diplomat, was involved in the famous *Trent* case when he was taken prisoner from an English ship while en route to England. The Creole Gen. P. G. T. Beauregard was known as the "Napoleon in Gray." Gen.

Leonidas Polk was Episcopal bishop of Louisiana. Gen. John B. Hood lived in New Orleans after the war and is buried there. Gens. Braxton Bragg and Richard Taylor were Louisiana plantation owners. Taylor was one of three civilians who became lieutenant generals.

The state had both Confederate and Federal governments during the war years. Thomas O. Moore and Henry W. Allen governed from Opelousas and later Shreveport; military governor Gen. George Shepley, succeeded by Michael Hahn, had offices at New Orleans. Military governors remained in office until 1868, when Louisiana was readmitted to the Union.

ALEXANDRIA, Rapides Parish. US 71. The Federal forces constructed Bailey Dam here to deepen the river channel so their ships could escape. Confederate fortifications may still be seen on outskirts of town.

Many antebellum buildings and homes were lost when Union troops burned most of the town, as well as Pineville across the Red River, in 1864. During Reconstruction days, Gen. George Custer's troops are said to have mutinied at 4th and Beauregard streets, where a cathedral now stands.

Alexandria City Hall, De Soto St., between 2nd and 3rd St. Confederate Monument is on the grounds.

Pineville National Cemetery, Shamrock St., Sanders, Reagan, and Main St., has a monument marking trench where 1,537 Federal soldiers are buried. They were removed from Brownsville, Texas, in 1911. (*Also see* PINEVILLE.)

BATON ROUGE, Baton Rouge Parish. IS 10, 12, US 61.

Allen Tablet, Dufrocq and Spain St. Memorial tablet denotes site where Col. Henry Watkins Allen was wounded during the battle of Baton Rouge. As Allen, commanding the 2nd Brigade, rode forward in charge, he seized the colors of Boyd's Battalion to inspire his

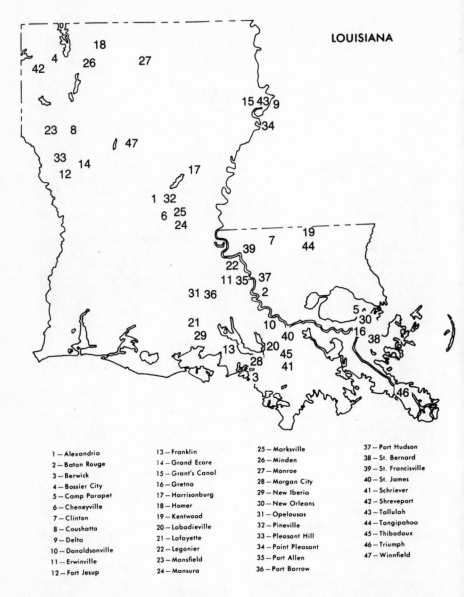

LOUISIANA

1 — Alexandria	13 — Franklin	25 — Marksville	37 — Port Hudson
2 — Baton Rouge	14 — Grand Ecore	26 — Minden	38 — St. Bernard
3 — Berwick	15 — Grant's Canal	27 — Monroe	39 — St. Francisville
4 — Bossier City	16 — Gretna	28 — Morgan City	40 — St. James
5 — Camp Parapet	17 — Harrisonburg	29 — New Iberia	41 — Schriever
6 — Cheneyville	18 — Homer	30 — New Orleans	42 — Shreveport
7 — Clinton	19 — Kentwood	31 — Opelousas	43 — Tallulah
8 — Coushatta	20 — Labadieville	32 — Pineville	44 — Tangipahoa
9 — Delta	21 — Lafayette	33 — Pleasant Hill	45 — Thibodaux
10 — Donaldsonville	22 — Legonier	34 — Point Pleasant	46 — Triumph
11 — Erwinville	23 — Mansfield	35 — Port Allen	47 — Winnfield
12 — Fort Jesup	24 — Mansura	36 — Port Barrow	

men. Promoted to brigadier general, he was elected governor of Confederate Louisiana in 1864. (*Also see Old State Captiol.*)

Battle of Baton Rouge State Monument, 330 S. 19th St. Site of the engagement on August 5, 1862. Confederates under Gen. John Breckinridge attacked the Union forces under Brig. Gen. Thomas Williams. Williams had been expecting the attack, but a thick fog covered troop movements. Gen. Williams, former mathematics professor at West Point and a veteran of the Seminole and Mexican wars, was killed. Confederate Lt. Alexander H. Todd, half-brother of Mrs. Lincoln, also was killed.

Confederate Monument, North Blvd. and 3rd St., was erected in 1886.

Burning of the Louisiana state capitol on December 30, 1862.

Louisiana Hotel stood at the northeast corner of Layfayette and Main St., received a direct hit from a Federal battleship during Farragut's attack on the city; a cannon ball went through both walls of the building. The hotel later was used as a Federal hospital.

Louisiana State Capitol, Riverside Mall. The 48 steps are inscribed with the names of states in order of their admission to the Union; Hawaii and Alaska at the top level flank "E Pluribus Unum." The observation tower, 450 feet high, gives a panoramic view of some 30 miles distance. State history is reflected in sculpture and murals. Memorial Hall is an important feature of the building.

Louisiana State University, 3 miles south on Highland Rd., began as the Louisiana Seminary of Learning in Pineville. William T. Sherman was its first president. He resigned with regret after the state seized the U.S. arsenal at Baton Rouge and before the ordinance of secession was signed. Sherman wrote to Gov. Thomas O. Moore: "If Louisiana withdraw from the Federal Union, I prefer to maintain my allegiance to the Constitution as long as a fragment of it survives." All cadets and professors except three joined the Confederate army; one cadet enlisted in the Union forces. The school was closed until after the war. The institution was moved here after the war.

Magnolia Cemetery, N. Dufrocq and Main St. The battle of Baton Rouge took place here in August 1864. One of the famous diaries of the war was written by Sarah Fowler Morgan, *A Confederate Girl's Diary.* In May 1861, her brother Harry was killed in a duel; her father, Judge Morgan, died six months later. Three brothers served the Confederacy. Capt. Gibbes Morgan, 7th Louisiana, was wounded at Sharpsburg and later died as prisoner at Johnson's Island, Ohio. Capt. George Morgan, 1st Louisiana, died in Virginia. James Morgan served in the Confederate navy. His excellent war memoirs were entitled *Recollections of a Rebel Reefer.* A number of Morgans are buried in this cemetery.

National Cemetery, N. Dufrocq St., Convention and Florida St. About 2,000 Union soldiers are buried here.

Old State Capitol, North Blvd. at River Rd.

The building was burned in 1862 when it was serving as a Federal prison; it was rebuilt in the 1880s. Monument on grounds marks the gravesite of Henry Watkins Allen, Confederate governor of Louisiana and brigadier general. During the Federal occupation of the city, Sarah Morgan made a Confederate flag, flew it from her shoulder, and walked about the State House terrace. Next day she.was embarrassed and shamed by what she decided had been an unladylike display of defiance. Some 15 or 20 Union officers standing on the terrace had been "stared at like wild beasts by the curious crowd." Sarah decided they were fine and noble-looking, even if Yankees. "I came home wonderfully changed in all my newly acquired sentiments, resolved never more to wound their feelings, who were so careful of ours, by such unnecessary display. And I hung my flag on the parlor mantel . . ."

BERWICK, St. Mary Parish. US 90. Detachments of the 4th Louisiana Infantry were stationed here in the fall of 1861. The town was an important center for blockade runners. Confederate soldier Robert Patrick was stationed here in 1862. "We built good quarters at Berwick City and got along very well there. We got as many oranges as we knew what to do with. They grew in the greatest abundance." Brashear City, east of Berwick Bay, was captured by Federal forces in June 1863 and used as a naval base for operations up Bayou Teche and along the coast.

BOSSIER CITY, Shreveport Parish. US 71, 80.
Fort Smith, Coleman St., between Monroe and Mansfield St. A bronze tablet on a concrete model of the original fort marks the site of Confederate garrison.

CAMP PARAPET, Jefferson Parish. US 90. The powder magazine was one of the Confederate defenses for the city of New Orleans. Union forces took over the area and completed the earthworks in 1862. The parapet extended in an irregular line for a distance of two miles.

CHENEYVILLE, Rapides Parish. US 71. Gen. Leroy A. Stafford is buried near here at Greenwood. Stafford was mortally wounded in the Wilderness, May 5, 1864.

CLINTON, East Feliciana. State 35. Federals burned buildings on St. Helena St. in 1862; it was raided a number of times later in the war.
Marston House, Bank St., served as a Confederate hospital.

Silliman College, Bank St. south of Marston House, was also a hospital. Robert Patrick noted, for December 15, 1862: "There is a great deal of sickness among the soldiers now and they are dying right fast at the hospitals in Clinton."

COUSHATTA, Red River Parish. US 71, 84.
Springfield Cemetery has the grave of Gen. Henry Gray, who was colonel of the 28th Louisiana. Gray fought under Gen. Taylor during the Vicksburg siege, was wounded at Bayou Teche, and led a brigade in the Red River campaign.

DELTA, Madison Parish. US 80. In this area Grant attempted to change the course of the Mississippi River during the Vicksburg campaign. Part of "Grant's Canal" was later made into a park. (See GRANT'S CANAL.)

DONALDSONVILLE, Ascension Parish. State 22. Francis R. T. Nicholls, Confederate general and Reconstruction governor, was born here. He lost his left arm at Winchester and his leg at Chancellorsville. Gen. James Patrick Major is buried here. He was a veteran Indian fighter, became an officer on Van Dorn's staff, commanded a cavalry battalion at Wilson's Creek, and fought in the Red River campaign of 1864. Also buried here is Gen. Allen Thomas, who took over Prince Polignac's division when the Frenchman went home to seek aid for Louisiana.

ERWINVILLE, West Baton Rouge Parish. US 190. The Confederate ram *Arkansas* was blown up by her crew to prevent capture by the Federal *Essex,* not far east of Erwinville.
Randall Oak Marker. In 1861, James R. Randall, a Marylander teaching at Poydras College, wrote "Maryland, My Maryland," which became a favorite song of the war among Southern troops. Yankees undoubtedly must have preferred the tune to the lyrics, in which hum and drum are rhymed with "Northern scum." Randall was seated under the oak tree when he composed the song. Marker is on US 190. Tree is north on State 93.

FORT JESUP STATE COMMEMORATIVE AREA, Sabine Parish. State 6, 6 miles east of Many. The fort was a major post on the Southwestern frontier. Many who served here later became Civil War generals.

FRANKLIN, St. Mary Parish. US 90. Many settlers were from the North and sympathized with the Union. Federal gunboats patrolled the Teche, but homes were spared, including beautiful Arlington Plantation, which has been handsomely restored. 56 E. Main, on the Teche.

Battle of Franklin. Marker is at site where the Confederates fought a delaying action against Federals in the spring of 1863. The Confederates retreated toward Opelousas.

Grevemberg House, St. Mary's Parish Museum, City Park on Sterling Rd., is a mid-century home with Civil War relics.

GRAND ÉCORE, Natchitoches Parish. State 6.

Russell Cemetery has the grave of Col. Louis De Russy, a veteran of the Mexican and Civil wars.

GRANT'S CANAL, Lake Providence. US 80. Marker is at site of the last project in a number of Union attempts to get safely past the Vicksburg batteries by changing the course of the Mississippi River. All efforts, including the plan to connect the Mississippi with Lake Providence, were unsuccessful. A series of markers has been erected on the line of Grant's march through Louisiana. A number of these will be found on US 80 and 65. Among important sites: Young's Point, Milliken's Bend, Richmond, Trinidad Plantation, New Carthage, Ione Plantation, Davis Island, Choctaw Bayou, and Hard Times Landing, where, on the morning of April 29, 1863, Grant concentrated his troops. On April 30, Grant's army, supported by Adm. Porter's fleet, made an unopposed landing at Bruinsburg, Mississippi.

GRETNA, Jefferson Parish. Off IS 10, State 23.

Bellechasse, south of town, was the home of Judah P. Benjamin, secretary of state and of war for the Confederacy. Furnishings were confiscated by Federal troops. House has disappeared.

Memorial Arch, Huey P. Long Blvd., honors the Jefferson Parish dead of all wars.

HARRISONBURG, Catahoula Parish. State 8.

Fort Beauregard, established here, was one of four Confederate forts guarding the Ouachita River. Lt. Col. Fremantle, of the Coldstream Guards, who toured in the Confederacy in 1863, found the fort much more formidable in appearance than expected. In May 1863, it was heavily shelled by Union gunboats; it was evacuated by the Confederates in September.

HOMER, Claiborne Parish. US 79.

Claiborne Parish Courthouse was a point of departure for Southern troops in the war.

KENTWOOD, Tangipahoa Parish. US 51.

Roncal. Marker indicates site of the Charles E. A. Gayarré home. Gayarré held a number of public offices and wrote a four-volume history of the state. (*Also see* NEW ORLEANS.)

LABADIEVILLE, Assumption Parish. State 1.

Bragg Plantation House, south of town, across Bayou Lafourche Bridge, about ½ mile from highway. Gen. Braxton Bragg was a sugar planter in antebellum times in Lafourche Parish.

Leighton Plantation Site, southeast toward Thibodaux, was the home of Leonidas Polk from 1842 to 1854. The "Fighting Bishop" was killed near Marietta, Georgia, in the Atlanta campaign.

White Home, 8 miles south on Bayou Lafourche. Birthplace of Edward Douglass White, who served as a Confederate officer in the war, later became Chief Justice of the United States Supreme Court.

LAFAYETTE, Lafayette Parish. US 90. Two Confederate generals are buried here: Franklin Gardner commanded a cavalry brigade at Shiloh, took command of Port Hudson in 1863, was captured but later exchanged. After the war he was a planter. Alfred Mouton, who was christened Jean Jacques Alexandre Alfred, was killed at Mansfield, April 8, 1864; his oldest son was also killed in the war. Gen. Louis Hebert, cousin of Gen. Paul Hebert, is buried at Breaux Bridge, a short distance northeast on State 347. Hebert was captured at Pea Ridge, exchanged, fought at Corinth and Vicksburg. At war's end he was in charge of heavy artillery at Cape Fear, North Carolina.

Chretien Point Plantation, 5 miles west on IS 10 to State 93, 11 miles north to Parish Rd. 356, west one block to Chretien Point Rd., is a 20-acre cotton plantation, the site of a Civil War battle. The house is Greek Revival with a stairway copied for Tara in the filming of *Gone With the Wind.*

Lafayette Museum, 1122 Lafayette, has Civil War relics. Former governor and U.S. senator Alexandre Mouton, who lived here, presided over the Secession Convention in Baton Rouge in 1861. His son Alfred (see next entry) was the eldest of four offspring.

Mouton Monument, Jefferson St. and Lee Ave., honors Brig. Gen. Jean Jacques Alexandre Alfred Mouton. At the beginning of the war he was made captain of the Acadian Guards, the first company recruited in the parish. Monument was erected by the United Daughters of the Confederacy.

University of Southwestern Louisiana, E. University Ave. An engagement was fought in the woods near the campus in 1863, when Confederates were retreating from Gen. Banks's Federals.

LEGONIER, Pointe Coupee Parish. State 1. Gen. Banks crossed the Atchafalaya River at this point in the spring of 1864, in his retreat after the Red River campaign. Banks occupied White Hall, the home of Gen. B. B. Simms.

MANSFIELD, De Soto Parish. US 171.

Mansfield State Commemorative Area, 4 miles south on State 175. On April 8, 1864, the Red River campaign climaxed here as Confederates under Gen. Dick Taylor met and defeated the Northerners. Banks retreated to Pleasant Hill, next day fought another engagement there. Banks then retreated south. The park has a museum with relics, exhibits, and maps of the battle.

MANSURA, Avoyelles Parish. State 1.

Battle of Mansura. Confederates attempted to bar the Federals retreating from Mansfield but had to withdraw. Marker at site.

MARKSVILLE, Avoyelles Parish. State 1.

Fort De Russey. A Confederate stronghold on the lower Red River fell to the Union advance toward Shreveport in March 1864.

MINDEN, Webster Parish. IS 20. En route to Monroe from Texas in 1863, Fremantle encountered a number of planters taking their families, slaves, and household possessions away from the advance of Federal troops. "At 5 p.m. we reached a charming little town called Mindon, where I met an English mechanic who deplored to me that he had been such a fool as to naturalize himself, as he was in hourly dread of the conscription."

Confederate Memorial is at south end of City Park.

MONROE, Ouachita Parish. IS 20. A number of skirmishes took place here. During the siege of Vicksburg, Adm. Porter's gunboats came up the Ouachita and shelled the courthouse and other buildings.

MORGAN CITY, St. Mary Parish. US 90. During the war the town was known as Brashear City; the name was changed in honor of Charles Morgan, president of the New Orleans, Opelousas and Great Western Railroad. (*Also see* BERWICK.)

NAPOLEONVILLE, Assumption Parish.

State 1. Federal troops stabled their horses in Christ Episcopal Church and used the stained glass windows for target practice.

Madewood Plantation, 2 miles south on State 308, faces Bayou Lafourche. Among elegant furnishings in the 1846 mansion is a Mathew Brady photograph of Gen. Robert E. Lee.

NEWELLTON, Tensas Parish. State 4, 608.

Winter Quarters State Commemorative Area, State 608. Grant's headquarters en route to Vicksburg siege were in this mansion. Civil War relics displayed.

NEW IBERIA, New Iberia Parish. US 90.

Church of the Epiphany, 301 W. Main St., was used as a military hospital.

Shadows-on-the-Teche, opposite post office, has antebellum furnishings and garden. It was headquarters for Gen. N. P. Banks during part of the war. The widow of David Weeks, the builder, died during Banks's occupancy and is buried on the grounds.

NEW ORLEANS, Orleans Parish. IS 10. In spring 1862, David Farragut's fleet consisted of 24 wooden vessels with about 200 guns. Late in April he ran past the forts of St. Philip and Jackson, which defended the entrance to the Mississippi, engaged the Confederate river fleet, and destroyed it with the loss of only one Union vessel. After New Orleans surrendered to Farragut, Gen. Benjamin Butler's troops arrived on transports and occupied the city on May 1.

Battle Abbey, behind the Cabildo, on St. Peter St., has war relics. Gen. Butler made use of the building in 1862.

Beauregard Houses and Monument. The house at 1113 Chartres St. was the birth place in 1837 of Paul Morphy, master chess-player. Gen. Beauregard lived here for a time. After the war, Beauregard lived for a number of years at 934 Royal St. At City Park, at the Esplanade Ave. entrance, is the equestrian statue of the general. The statue by Alexander Doyle was unveiled in 1913 by the general's granddaughter, Hilda Beauregard. House was restored by a later owner, the novelist Frances Parkinson Keyes, who frequently wrote about the house and area.

Benjamin House, 327 Bourbon St. Statesman Judah P. Benjamin, often called the "brains of the Confederacy," lived here at one time.

The Cabildo, on Jackson Square, has a variety of portraits and exhibits pertaining to the

Federal troops arrive under a flag of truce to demand the surrender of New Orleans.

Civil War period. In this building Louisiana was formally transferred from France to the United States. Part of the Louisiana State Museum, the Cabildo was being restored when it was closed indefinitely because of a fire in 1988. Phone (504) 523-6722.

Cable House, 1313 8th St. George Washington Cable, author and lecturer, wrote vividly of antebellum and war days. Joaquin Miller, California poet, occupied the house for a winter in the 1880s. Miller was once denied the use of the mails during the war years for his pro-Southern views in a Union-minded western town.

Caffery House, 1228 Race St., was built during the war by John T. Moore, in what might qualify as the nick of time. The foundation was laid by slave labor; the house was partly paid for with Confederate money.

Chalmette Monument and National Cemetery, 6 miles east on State 46. At the site of the 1815 battle of New Orleans, Confederate batteries attempted to stop Farragut in 1862. In the national cemetery are more than 14,000 Union soldiers; about half are unknown.

Christ Church Cathedral, St. Charles Ave. Bishop-Gen. Polk is buried here.

Church of Our Lady of Guadalupe, N. Rampart and Conti St. Father Turgis, soldier-priest of the Confederacy, served here after the war.

City Hall Site, 543 St. Charles. The lowering of the Louisiana flag at City Hall was an occasion of great emotion in a city not disposed to take defeat quietly. Farragut sent two officers to demand immediate surrender from the mayor, who refused. Julia LeGrand recorded the scene, and the general sentiment, in her diary for May 1862: "Four days we waited, expecting to be shelled . . . so he [Farragut] marched in his marines with two cannons and our flag was taken down and the old stars and stripes lifted in a dead silence. We made a great mistake here; we should have shot the man that brought down the flag, and as long as there was a house-top in the city left, it should have been hoisted."

Confederate Museum, 929 Camp St. Among an extensive collection of Confederate relics are clothing and possessions of Jefferson

Davis, Gen. Beauregard's original uniform, the battle flag of the Louisiana Tigers, and the sword carried by Gen. Albert Sidney Johnston when he was killed at Shiloh.

Customs House, 423 Canal St., was begun in 1848 with P.G.T. Beauregard, the young engineer, in charge. Later Gen. Ben ("Beast") Butler had headquarters here.

Cypress Grove Cemetery, City Park Ave. and West End Blvd., has the remains of William B. Mumford, a professional gambler who was hanged by Gen. Benjamin Butler after having been convicted of treason. Mumford pulled down a United States flag that had been raised over the U.S. Mint.

Davis Monument, Jefferson Davis Pkwy. Jefferson Davis died in New Orleans in 1889; his body lay in state in City Hall and for two years reposed in the mausoleum of the Army of Northern Virginia at Metairie Cemetery. The monument was unveiled on February 22, 1911, the 50th anniversary of the Davis inauguration. The statue was designed by Edward Valentine.

Dreux Monument, Canal St. at Jefferson Davis Pkwy., opposite Davis statue, honors Charles Didier Dreux, the first New Orleans officer to be killed in action. Col. Dreux organized the Orleans cadets. The monument, designed by Victor Holm, is of Stone Mountain granite.

Forsyth House, 1134 First St. Jefferson Davis died here in 1889 while visiting Judge Charles Erasmus Fenner. Mr. Davis occupied the guest room on the ground floor.

Fort Pike State Commemorative Site, 23 miles east via US 90. Federal forts guarding the entrance to Lake Pontchartrain were taken over by the state forces in January 1861. Self-guiding tours of exhibits.

Gallier House Museum, 1118–1132 Royal St., is restored to its 1860s look.

Gayarré Home, 601 Bourbon St. Charles Gayarré was a noted Louisiana legislator and historian. His principal work was a four-volume history of the state. (Also see KENTWOOD.)

Greenwood Cemetery, City Park Ave. and Canal Blvd., across from Cypress Grove Cemetery. Monument to the Confederate dead has life-size busts of Jackson, Lee, Leonidas Polk, and A. S. Johnston. Gen. Thomas Scott is buried in the cemetery; he was mortally wounded at the battle of Franklin.

Hermann-Grima House, 820 St. Louis St. Creole cooking demonstrations in former slave quarters of restored 1831 historic home.

Historic New Orleans Collection, 533 Royal St. The museum center has tours of several buildings, and changing displays.

Hood House, 1206 3rd St. Gen. John B. Hood and two members of his family died here in the yellow fever epidemic of 1879.

Jackson Barracks, Delery St. and Mississippi River. When Louisiana seceded, Confederates took over the post; it was later retaken and garrisoned by Union troops.

Jackson Square, Decatur St. Gen. Benjamin Butler had an inscription cut on the base of the Jackson statue when he occupied the city in 1862: "The Union Must and Shall Be Preserved."

Kaul House, 904 Orange St. Sir Henry Morton Stanley, who served variously in the Civil War in both armies and in the Union navy, lived here as a boy. His foster father was a New Orleans merchant.

Lee Monument, in Lee Circle, St. Charles and Howard Ave. The memorial, sculptured by Alexander Doyle, was unveiled in 1884. Jefferson Davis, Gen. Beauregard, and other friends of Gen. Lee were present at the ceremonies.

Liberty Monument, Canal St. near N. Front St., commemorates the citizens' challenge to carpetbagger rule in September 1874. Monument was designed by Charles R. Orleans.

Metairie Cemetery, Pontchartrain Blvd. and Metairie Rd. The Army of Northern Virginia Monument honors Gen. Thomas J. Jackson and the Louisiana Brigade that fought under him. There are 2,500 men buried in the mausoleum. The Jackson statue was executed by Achille Perelli. Monument to the Louisiana Division of the Army of Tennessee has an equestrian statue of Gen. Albert Sidney Johnston, depicted as he led the charge at Shiloh. Gen. P. G. T. Beauregard is buried in the mausoleum. The memorial was executed by Alexander Doyle and Achille Perelli. The Washington Artillery Monument is the work of George Doyle. Among other tombs in the cemetery are those of Gens. John B. Hood and Richard Taylor.

New Orleans Public Library, 219 Loyola Ave., has a sizable collection of Civil War material.

St. Charles Hotel, St. Charles St. A model of the original hotel is in the Cabildo. It was one of the finest hotels in the country. The author of the humorous *Squibob Papers*, under the pseudonym of John Phoenix, observed: "The St. Charles Hotel is a lively and bustling village of about one thousand inhabitants. . . . On arriving at the St. Charles the planter's party are supplied with a parlor and the necessary sleeping apartments, and commence living at the rate of about five bales of cotton a week." Slaves were auctioned off in the hotel's exchange. Albert D. Richardson, Horace Greeley's "spy" in the early months of 1861, witnessed a slave sale: "The auction was in the great bar-room of the St. Charles Hotel, a spacious, airy octagonal apartment, with a circular range of Ionic columns. The marble bar, covering three sides of the room, was doing a brisk business. Three perturbed tapsters were bustling about to supply with fluids the bibulous crowd, which by no means did its spiriting gently." Gen. Butler is said to have been miffed at being refused the use of the choice parlor, and settled the matter by taking over the whole hotel.

St. Louis Cemeteries: No. 1, Basin St., between St. Louis and Toulouse, has the tombs of Charles Gayarré and Paul Morphy; Gen. Albert G. Blanchard, of the 1st Louisiana, who served at Seven Pines and Drewry's Bluff; and Gen. John B. Grayson, who was commanding the Department of Middle and Eastern Florida when he died at Tallahassee in October 1861. No. 2, N. Claiborne Ave. and Bienville St., has the tomb of Pierre Soulé, statesman and Confederate provost marshal. Also in the cemetery is the tomb of Oscar J. Dunn, mulatto lieutenant governor of the Reconstruction period.

St. Patrick's Church, 712 Camp St. Father James Mullon, pastor, was an ardent Confederate who seems to have waged a successful war of nerves with Gen. Benjamin Butler. When Butler ordered the congregation to discontinue public prayers for the Confederate cause, Father Mullon conducted silent prayers. On another occasion, Butler accused the priest of having refused to bury a Union soldier. Father Mullon responded that he was ready to bury the entire Union force, Butler included.

Slidell House, 312 Royal St. John Slidell, a New Yorker, became a Louisiana politician in the years before the war. He was captured en route to England on a Confederate mission in 1861.

Thornhill House, 1420 Euterpe St. Gen. Butler made the house headquarters for the Freedman's Bureau.

Trinity Church, 1329 Jackson Ave. The "Fighting Bishop," Leonidas Polk, served here in prewar years, left in 1861 to enlist in the army, and was killed in the Atlanta campaign, June 14, 1864. There is a stained-glass memorial behind the altar dedicated to Bishop Polk.

U.S. Customs House, Decatur and Canal St. The much-disliked Gen. Ben "Beast" Butler used part of the unfinished building for headquarters, part for prisoners.

U.S. Mint, Esplanade and Decatur St. The old mint building was the scene of the Mumford hanging in 1862. William Mumford had seized the U.S. flag from the building and dragged it through the muddy street. He was hanged from a gibbet erected just below the flagstaff. The building, now part of the state museum, was renovated in the 1850s by Gen. Beauregard when it was still a Federal mint. Briefly in 1861 it was the C.S.A.'s only mint.

Washington Avenue Cemetery, at Prytania St., has the tomb of Gen. Harry Hays, who commanded the Louisiana Brigade. After the war he was New Orleans sheriff for a year.

PINEVILLE, Rapides Parish. US 71.
Bailey's Dam. Marker on highway indicates site of wing dam suggested by Col. Joseph Bailey, a Wisconsin lumberman before the war. The engineering feat was successful in allowing the Union fleet, which could not get through the shallow waters here, to escape. Most of town was destroyed in 1864, but Mount Olivet Church on Main St. survived and served as Union barracks during occupation. (Also see ALEXANDRIA.)

PLEASANT HILL, Sabine Parish. State 1. On the day after the battle of Mansfield in April 1864, another engagement was fought here. Federals then retired to Alexandria.

POINT PLEASANT, Iberville Parish. State 30.
Cemetery has the tomb of Gen. Paul O. Hebert, who was governor in the 1850s. Hebert fought at Galveston, Milliken's Bend, and had the last command of the Trans-Mississippi Department, surrendering it to Gen. Granger after Lee's surrender at Appomattox.

PORT ALLEN, West Baton Rouge Parish. IS 10, State 1.
Allendale Plantation, home of Henry Watkins Allen, war governor, was burned in the war; Allen exiled himself to Mexico.
Allen Statue, in front of courthouse, was sculpted by Angela Gregory of New Orleans.

PORT BARROW, Ascension Parish. State 30. The area was bombarded during Farragut's operations after taking New Orleans. It became a center for guerrillas. Gen. Ben Butler sent troops to subdue the area; they established a small fort which was later retaken by Confederates, who evacuated the fort when Union gunboats opened fire.

PORT HUDSON STATE COMMEMORATIVE AREA, East Baton Rouge Parish. US 61. Port Hudson surrendered, after a long siege, on July 8, 1863; it was the last link between the eastern part of the Confederacy and the Trans-Mississippi. The area takes in only part of battlefield, has viewing towers, trenches, guns, and an interpretive program. In the area is a national cemetery with more than 3,000 Union soldiers, most of whom are unknown. Confederates are buried in Port Hudson. At Mount Pleasant Landing, off State 272, Confederate statesman Judah P. Benjamin owned a plantation. The Union sloop of war *Mississippi* exploded opposite Profit Island, south of Mount Pleasant, having been set afire by Confederate artillery at Port Hudson.

ST. BERNARD, St. Bernard Parish. State 46.

Kenilworth Plantation was once owned by Confederate soldier Leonidas Montgomery Thermopylae McClung. It is said that Pierre Gustave Toutant Beauregard once received a golden dress sword in this house; the sword was in honor of his Mexican War campaign. Beauregard's birthplace was at nearby Contreras; the house has been destroyed.

St. Bernard Cemetery, opposite St. Bernard Catholic Church, has the tomb of M. A. Laure Villere, first wife of Gen. Beauregard.

ST. FRANCISVILLE, East Feliciana Parish. US 61.

Fairview Plantation, which occupied a hill overlooking Thompson's Creek, was used for a time by Gen. Grant and as a hospital.

Locust Grove, 4 miles east, is the burial place of Sarah Knox Taylor, daughter of Gen. Zachary Taylor and first wife of Jefferson Davis.

SCHRIEVER, Terrebonne Parish. State 1, 20.

Magnolia served as a Federal hospital. Troops are said to have used the grand piano for a horse trough.

SHREVEPORT, Caddo Parish. IS 20, US 71, 80.

Caddo Parish Courthouse, McNeil, Milam, Marshall, and Texas St., has a Confederate monument at the Texas St. entrance. Busts of Lee, Jackson, Beauregard, and Allen are a part of the memorial.

Cane-Bennett Bluff was Gen. Kirby Smith's headquarters when he was commander of the Trans-Mississippi Department.

Centenary College, 2911 Centenary Blvd. Among former students, during a period when the college was located at Jackson: Jefferson Davis and Judah P. Benjamin. In October 1861, all the students had gone to war and the college closed until hostilities were over. It was moved here in 1907.

Fort Humbug Memorial Park, foot of Stoner Ave. One of three forts built during the war when Gen. Banks was rumored to be headed this way. Confederates put up charred logs to resemble cannon.

Louisiana State Exhibit Museum, 3015 Greenwood Rd., has Civil War relics and records.

TALLULAH, Madison Parish. IS 20, US 80. An important supply depot for the Confederates was destroyed by Union troops under Col. William D. Bowen in 1862.

TANGIPAHOA, Tangipahoa Parish. IS 55, US 51.

Camp Moore was a training area for Confederates during the early part of the war. It was named for Gov. Thomas O. Moore, whose home Mooreland, near Alexandria, was burned by Federals in 1864. About 400 Confederates are buried in the camp cemetery.

THIBODAUX, Lafourche Parish. State 1. Gen. Francis Redding T. Nicholls is buried here. Wounded at Chancellorsville, he had a foot amputated, later served in the Trans-Mississippi Department, was twice governor and chief justice of the Louisiana Supreme Court.

Edward Douglas White State Commemorative Area, 5 miles north on State 1. White, who became a U.S. Supreme Court Justice, was 15 years old when the war began, was taken prisoner by the Federals after the fall of Port Hudson, but was paroled because of poor health (if you had to be a POW, this sometimes was the right war for it) and later studied law in New Orleans. His birthplace was built in 1790 by slaves using hand-hewn cypress. Nineteenth-century furnishings.

St. John's Episcopal Church, State 1. The Confederacy's "Fighting Bishop," Leonidas Polk, served here.

TRIUMPH, Plaquemines Parish. State 23.

Fort Jackson. Forts Jackson and St. Philip guarded the mouth of the Mississippi River until Farragut steamed past them on April 24, 1862.

WHITE CASTLE, Iberville Parish. State 1.

Nottoway Plantation, 2 miles north off State 1 (follow signs), was completed two years before the war began and survived it without destruction. Restored, with period furnishings, it is representative of the best of antebellum mansions. At its completion it was the largest dwelling in Louisiana and stood on a 7,000-acre plantation.

WINNFIELD, Winn Parish. US 167.

Drake's Salt Works were a major source of salt for the Confederacy.

MAINE

Maine entered the Union in 1820 with a constitution that prohibited slavery; this gave an edge in Congress to the free states and led to the Missouri Compromise. Even in Colonial days most blacks in Maine were paid servants. Abolitionism was strong, except in coastal areas where prosperity depended in part upon Southern trade. Most counties had antislavery societies; Republicans gained and held political supremacy. Hannibal Hamlin of Maine was Vice President under Abraham Lincoln.

From a population of just over 600,000, the state sent about 72,000 men to the Union forces. Of these, some 6,700 served in the navy and marines. Five Maine regiments fought at Bull Run. Maj. Gen. Hiram Berry of Rockland was killed at Chancellorsville. Over 6,000 Maine men fought at Gettysburg. On June 26, 1863, Confederates under the command of Lt. Charles W. Read captured the revenue cutter *Caleb Cushing* in Portland Harbor. The Confederates were pursued and captured next day; the cutter was set on fire and blown up. Read, considered one of the South's most distinguished naval men, was imprisoned but was back in action in the last months of the war, at New Orleans.

In July 1864 an attempt was made to raid Calais, Maine. Three of the Southerners, captured while attempting to rob the Calais Bank, were sent to Maine State Prison for three years. Many other Southerners were in the vicinity to assist in the raid on Calais, but after the failure of the first attempt, they did not show themselves. At Appomattox, Gen. Joshua Chamberlain was designated by Grant to receive the surrender of Lee's army. Chamberlain ordered his troops to give the marching salute.

AUGUSTA, Kennebec County. IS 95.

Executive Mansion, State St., is the former home of James G. Blaine, Congressman from Maine in 1863. Historical relics are displayed.

State Hospital, end of Arsenal St. Site of the former National Arsenal. Gen. O. O. Howard and Lt. Robert Anderson were among commanders stationed here.

State House, State and Capitol St., houses the state library and has an exhibit of battle flags. The library has an extensive collection of books on all phases of the war, including regimental histories.

State Park, Capitol and Union St. Maine regiments encamped here during the war.

BATH, Sagadahoc County. Off IS 95, US 1. Pvt. Joe Pepper of Bath was the first man killed in the Army of the Potomac.

Maine Marine Museum, 243 Washington, has a rare collection of items pertaining to local shipbuilding, including the Civil War period. The 10-acre site includes two former shipyards, an early schooner that can be boarded, and the Sewall House, 963 Washington, which has paintings, models, dioramas, and artifacts.

BREWER, Penobscot County. IS 95, US 2. Gen. Joshua Lawrence Chamberlain, who lived at 80 Chamberlain St., was a professor at Bowdoin College in 1862 when he changed his plans to study abroad and joined the Union army. He received the Congressional Medal of Honor for his service at the battle of Gettysburg, in which he helped to defend Little Round Top. He later served as governor of Maine and president of Bowdoin College.

BRUNSWICK, Cumberland County. IS 95, US 1.

Bowdoin College, Maine St., has among its alumni William Pitt Fessenden, Secretary of the Treasury in Lincoln's cabinet, Hannibal Hamlin, vice president, and Franklin Pierce, 14th president. Tours.

First Parish Church, Maine and Bath Sts. Dr. Calvin Stowe, husband of Harriet Beecher Stowe, was professor of religion at Bowdoin and preached here. Mrs. Stowe reportedly had a vision of "Uncle Tom" during a service here. Her pew, and the pulpit from which Longfellow spoke, are still here.

MAINE

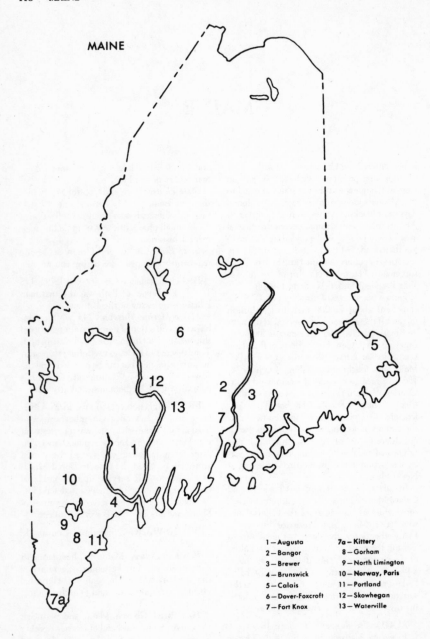

6

12

13

2   3

7

5

1

10

4

9

8   11

7a

1 — Augusta
2 — Bangor
3 — Brewer
4 — Brunswick
5 — Calais
6 — Dover-Foxcroft
7 — Fort Knox

7a — Kittery
8 — Gorham
9 — North Limington
10 — Norway, Paris
11 — Portland
12 — Skowhegan
13 — Waterville

Harriet Beecher Stowe House, 63 Federal St. The house where *Uncle Tom's Cabin* was written is now a restaurant and motor inn.

Joshua L. Chamberlain Civil War Museum, 226 Maine St., has memorabilia of the Union general who became president of Bowdoin. He was honored as the only officer to receive a battlefield promotion from Gen. Grant and was chosen to accept the Confederate surrender at Appomattox. (*Also see* BREWER.)

Pejepscot Historical Society Museum, 159 Park Row. Regional Americana. Civil War Museum.

DOVER-FOXCROFT, Piscataquis County. State 150, 153. The first Maine enlistee was John Colby Weston of Foxcroft.

FORT KNOX STATE PARK, Waldo County. US 1, near Prospect. Civil War troops trained here. The fort commands a view of the Penobscot River and Bay. The fort was never finished.

KITTERY, York County, IS 95.

Fort McClary State Historic Site, 3½ miles east of US 1, in Kittery Point. The blockhouse was built in the 1840s and modified in the 1860s. The fort was garrisoned during the war.

Kittery Historical and Naval Museum, north of junction of US 1 and State 236 on Rogers Road, has displays for more than three centuries of naval history.

LIMINGTON, York County. State 11.

McArthur House, Maine St. Gen. William McArthur organized the 8th Maine Regiment when 73 Limington men enlisted.

NORWAY, Oxford County. State 117, 118. The town sent eight companies and two generals to the Civil War: Maj. Gen. George L. Beal and Gen. Benjamin B. Murray. Artemus Ward and Hannibal Hamlin both worked for the local newspaper.

PARIS, Oxford County, State 26, birthplace of Hannibal Hamlin.

Old Brick, Main St., home of Gen. William King Kimball, 2nd Maine.

POPHAM BEACH, Sagadahoc County. South of US 1 on waterfront.

Fort Popham State Historic Site is a brick and granite fort started in 1861 but never completed. Circular staircases lead to towers. Interpretive signs on grounds.

PORTLAND, Cumberland County. IS 95.

Fort Allen Park, Fort St. and Eastern Promenade, has Civil War cannon.

Fort Knox State Historic Park, west of the Waldo-Hancock Bridge, on the west bank of the Penobscot River, was used for troop training during the Civil War.

Monument to Portland Soldiers of the Civil War, in Market Square, was executed by Franklin Simmons.

ROCKLAND, Knox County. On Penobscot Bay, US 1.

Shore Village Museum, 104 Limerick St., has a Civil War collection.

SEARSPORT, Waldo County. US 1.

Penobscot Marine Museum, corner of US 1 and Church St., comprises seven buildings including a captain's home built in 1860. Two houses and the old town hall were built before the war. Displays include paintings, navigational equipment, and models of early ships.

SKOWHEGAN, Somerset County. US 201. Abner Coburn, one of Maine's Civil War governors, lived here as did the peripatetic humorist Charles Farrar Browne (Artemus Ward).

WATERVILLE, Kennebec County. IS 95.

Colby College, Mayflower Hill. Guided tours available. Elijah Parish Lovejoy, born near Albion and an honor graduate of Colby, was killed by a proslavery mob in Alton, Illinois, where he edited an abolitionist newspaper. Memorial Hall, on campus, was erected in honor of students killed in the Civil War and contains many historical items.

Redington Museum, 64 Silver, has Civil War relics.

MARYLAND

Maryland had a conflict of loyalties and economic interests by 1860 which made the state favor compromise. In general the eastern shore, Baltimore, and southern counties were in favor of secession when compromise was no longer possible; northern and western counties supported the Union. It was no accident that John Brown's raid was launched from a northwestern Maryland base and that the Massachusetts troops marching to the defense of Washington in 1861 were attacked by angry citizens of Baltimore.

After the Baltimore rioting, Gen. Benjamin Butler was sent to occupy Annapolis and Baltimore. Other key points were put under guard and the state remained closely supervised for the rest of the war. In September 1861, influential members of the General Assembly were arrested to prevent the possible passage of an Act of Secession. Although the state remained in the Union, many Marylanders served in the Confederate army.

In August 1862, Gen. Robert E. Lee moved the Army of Northern Virginia into Maryland. There were battles at Harpers Ferry, South Mountain, and Antietam, or Sharpsburg. The following year Maryland was crossed by Confederates en route to Gettysburg. After the battle of Monocacy in the summer of 1864, Southern forces threatened Baltimore and Washington. Minor incidents and raids occurred until the last days of the war.

ANNAPOLIS, Anne Arundel County. US 50-301.

Banneker-Douglass Museum of Afro-American Life and History, 84 Franklin St. Displays focus on African-American life in Maryland.

Naval Academy Museum, King George St. and Severn River. Among displays are the sword of Franklin Buchanan, first superintendent of the academy, who became a Confederate admiral, his portrait by Rembrandt Peale, an oil painting of Commodore Matthew Fontaine Maury, presented by the United Daugh-

ters of the Confederacy, Maury's epaulettes, given by Lowndes Maury, weapons, battle flags, Adm. Semmes's navy uniform buttons, and models of Civil War vessels.

St. John's College, College Ave., was used as camp and hospital during the war.

State House, State Circle. In the Flag Room are flags carried by Maryland troops in the Confederate service. Also displayed in the building is an oil painting of James Ryder Randall and a holograph of his song, "Maryland, My Maryland," which was popular with Southern troops and was adopted in 1939 as the official state song.

United States Naval Academy. Capt. Blaker, superintendent, asked Gen. Butler, in command of the 8th Massachusetts, to protect the academy and the *Constitution,* which soon sailed to Newport, Rhode Island, arriving there on May 9, 1861. The faculty and administration were transferred to Newport and the academy closed at Annapolis until 1865.

ANTIETAM NATIONAL BATTLE-FIELD, Washington County. East of junction of State 34 and 65. (Also known as the battle of Sharpsburg.) Probably more men died in the battle of September 17, 1862, than in any other single day of the war. About 41,000 Confederates under Gen. Lee fought against 87,000 Federals under Gen. McClellan. Lee hoped to gain Maryland supplies and men to help fill his depleted ranks. The Union assault began at Dunker Church and ended above the bridge, now known as Burnside Bridge, with the defeat of Burnside. Church has been reconstructed by the park service; visitor center has a museum and orientation facilities for an understanding of the battle. Exhibits are well marked for an auto tour of the 782-acre site. There are also markers in the surrounding area. (It might be noted that the North named armies and battles after rivers or creeks: [Army of *the* Cumberland, Army of *the* Tennessee, Bull Run, Antietam Creek], whereas the South chose names of states or towns [Army of Tennessee, Army of

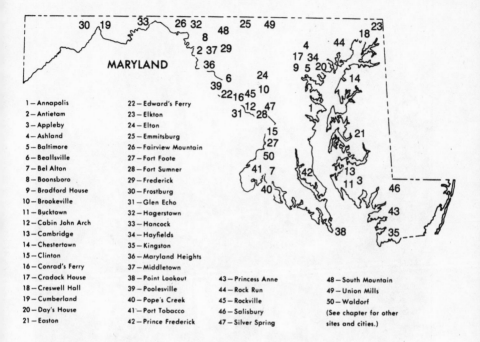

1 — Annapolis
2 — Antietam
3 — Appleby
4 — Ashland
5 — Baltimore
6 — Beallsville
7 — Bel Alton
8 — Boonsboro
9 — Bradford House
10 — Brookeville
11 — Bucktown
12 — Cabin John Arch
13 — Cambridge
14 — Chestertown
15 — Clinton
16 — Conrad's Ferry
17 — Cradock House
18 — Creswell Hall
19 — Cumberland
20 — Day's House
21 — Easton

22 — Edward's Ferry
23 — Elkton
24 — Elton
25 — Emmitsburg
26 — Fairview Mountain
27 — Fort Foote
28 — Fort Sumner
29 — Frederick
30 — Frostburg
31 — Glen Echo
32 — Hagerstown
33 — Hancock
34 — Hayfields
35 — Kingston
36 — Maryland Heights
37 — Middletown
38 — Point Lookout
39 — Poolesville
40 — Pope's Creek
41 — Port Tobacco
42 — Prince Frederick

43 — Princess Anne
44 — Rock Run
45 — Rockville
46 — Salisbury
47 — Silver Spring

48 — South Mountain
49 — Union Mills
50 — Waldorf
(See chapter for other
sites and cities.)

Northern Virginia, Sharpsburg, etc.]. Cannons mark sites where six generals died.

Antietam National Cemetery was established in 1865, contains graves of 5,032 Union soldiers, of whom 1,836 are unidentified. Probable date of Civil War interments was 1862.

APPLEBY, Dorchester County. State 343 west of US 50. The home of Gov. Thomas Holliday Hicks, who was in office during the indecisive weeks of 1861. Hicks had opposed Butler's occupation of Annapolis but finally took a stand for the Union. He was elected to the U.S. Senate in 1862, served until his death in 1865. He is buried in Cambridge; a monument marks his grave.

ASHLAND, Baltimore County. State 45 near Cockeysville. A railroad bridge over the Gunpowder River was destroyed April 20, 1861, under orders of Baltimore officials who hoped to prevent recurrence of street rioting caused by troops passing through town. Confederates destroyed the bridge again in July 1864.

BALTIMORE (Independent City). IS 70, 83, 95, US 140.

Baltimore Camps of the Civil War. Fifteen camps were established in and around the city; among them: Camp Andrew, on property of Confederate Gen. George H. Steuart, near intersection of Baltimore St. and Fulton Ave.; Camp Belger, on Eutaw St., built by the 37th Regiment, New York National Guard; Camp Bradford, also called Camp Cattle Grounds, near Charles and 25th St., on fairgrounds of Maryland Agriculture Society; Camp Carroll, Carroll Park beside mansion (also called Camp Chesebrough; Pennsylvania and later Connecticut cavalry units were located here); Camp Hoffman, occupied by Maryland Public Guard, was located in present LaFayette Square; Camp Patterson Park (the 110th New York Volunteers were here in 1862); and Camp Small, Cold Spring Rd. at Jones' Falls, Melvale, guarded the Northern Central Railroad—the Ellsworth Zouaves and Pennsylvania Volunteers were also here at one time.

Baltimore Forts. At least 13 forts were garrisoned during the war; among these were: Fort Carroll, opposite Sollers Point flats, protecting the harbor; Fort Federal Hill, Battery St. and Key Highway, built by the 5th New York Volun-

The Bouquet Battery commanded the railroad viaduct over the Patapsco River.

teers in 1861 (the regiment was known as Duryea's Zouaves); Fort Marshall on Smoke Hill, Foster Ave. and 3rd St. guarding the Philadelphia, Wilmington, and Baltimore Railway; and Fort Worthington, northeast of Baltimore Hospital and behind the Baltimore Cemetery, guarding the Bel Air Rd.

Baltimore Military Hospitals were numerous; hotels as well as houses and churches were used for the wounded. Among these were the National Hotel, across from Camden Station, and Fountain Hotel, at Howard and Camden St. Steuart's Grove, also known as Jarvis U.S. General Hospital, built on the property of Confederate Gen. Steuart, was one of the largest.

Baltimore Riot, Pratt near Gay St. The 6th Massachusetts arrived at President Street Sta-

tion on April 19, 1861. The men were loaded into horse-drawn cars to be taken to the Camden Station; the tenth car was stopped by blocked tracks, the men returned to President Station to march to Camden and were attacked in Pratt St. In the melee four soldiers and 12 civilians were killed.

Camden Station, Camden and Howard St., was used by Lincoln on his way to his first inaugural, en route to Gettysburg, and on his Baltimore trip of 1864. His funeral train passed through in April 1865. The Baltimore & Ohio was the only railroad connecting Baltimore and Washington.

Federal Hill, Warren Ave., near Key Hwy., was an observation point during the war.

Fort McHenry National Monument and Historic Shrine, east end Fort Ave., was built in 1794; its resistance to the British inspired "The Star Spangled Banner." The garrison was increased at the outbreak of the Civil War. Military and political prisoners were kept here, some without trial. Francis Key Howard was arrested at his Baltimore home in September 1861 and brought to the fort where his father, Charles Howard, was already confined, 47 years to the day since his grandfather had been inspired to write "The Star Spangled Banner" while watching the fort.

Front Street Theater, northwest corner of Front and Low St. Lincoln was renominated, with Andrew Johnson as vice president on the ticket, in June 1864. In this building John C. Breckinridge had been nominated in 1860.

Great Blacks in Wax Museum, 1601 E. North Ave., has life-size wax figures portraying blacks in the Civil War and Reconstruction.

Green Mount Cemetery, Greenmount and Oliver St. Among the famous, and infamous, buried here: John Wilkes Booth, Confederate Gen. Joseph Eggleston Johnston, Confederate Maj. Gens. Arnold Elzey, Benjamin Huger, and Isaac Ridgeway Trimble, Confederate Brig. Gens. Joseph Lancaster Brent, Lewis Henry Little, George Hume Steuart, and John Henry Winder, Union Maj. Gen. John Reese Kenly, Union Brig. Gen. Richard Neville Bowerman.

Loudon Park Cemetery has a Confederate monument designed by Adelbert J. Volck. Among those buried here are Confederates Maj. Gen. Charles W. Field, Brig. Gen. Bradley Tyler Johnson, and Lt. Col. Harry Gilmor.

Lincoln Visit, 702 Cathedral St. When President Lincoln spoke at the Sanitary Fair at the Maryland Institute in 1864, he stayed overnight in the house now at this address. In April 1865, Lincoln lay in state at the Merchants Exchange, at Gay and Water St.

Maryland Historical Society, 201 W. Monument St. Museum has extensive displays of Maryland history. The Confederate Room has a fine collection of uniforms, including one that belonged to Adm. Buchanan. Also Gen. Lee's camp chair and other rare items.

Monument to Confederate Dead, Mount Royal Ave., between Lafayette and Mosher St., was sculptured by J. Wellington Ruchstuhl, on a commission from the United Daughters of the Confederacy. Dedicated May 2, 1903. Confederate veterans from the Pikesville Confederate Soldiers' Home participated. Winged Glory holds aloft the laurel of History as she supports a dying standard-bearer, in whose hand the flag droops in defeat but does not fall.

Monument to Confederate Women, Charles and University.

Mount Clare Station, Pratt and Poppleton in the B&O Railroad Museum. Here are Civil War baggage cars and many other rare items.

Peale Museum, 225 N. Holliday St., has historical portraits and prints. Rare photographs.

President Street Station, President, Canton, and Aliceanna St. On February 23, 1861, Lincoln and detectives arrived here before daylight and were taken by horse car to the Camden Station. The detectives were anticipating trouble along this route; the 6th Massachusetts Infantry was not, but it was the latter group going from Camden to President St. that ran into violence.

St. Paul's Graveyard, Redwood St. near Pine. Plaque on wall honors Brig. Gen. Lewis A. Armistead, C.S.A.

Sam Smith Park, Pratt St. Plaque on sea wall adjacent to park reproduces the cover of "Maryland, My Maryland," given by the Baltimore Civil War Round Table, the Civil War Centennial Committee of Baltimore, and the Maryland Civil War Centennial Commission; it was dedicated April 23, 1961. The site is near the area where the Baltimore riot, which inspired the James Ryder Randall poem, took place.

Shot Tower, Fayette and Front streets. About 500,000 25-pound bags of shot were produced here annually from 1828 to 1892. Audio-visual program.

Sidney Lanier Statue, Charles St. at Johns Hopkins University. Bust by Ephraim Keyser. The work was a gift of the poet's cousin, Charles Lanier, in 1888.

Statue of Lee and Jackson, Wyman Park at corner of Howard St. and Park Dr. The memorial, which depicts the last meeting of the Confederate generals at Chancellorsville, is said to be the only double equestrian statue in the world. Laura G. Frazier, sculptress. Dedicated May 1, 1948, and given through a bequest of $100,000 in the will of Henry Ferguson.

U.S. Frigate Constellation, Pier 1, Pratt St. The nation's oldest warship saw action in the Civil War. It is now a maritime museum and a national historic shrine.

BEALLSVILLE, Montgomery County. State 28, 109. During Antietam campaign, the 8th Illinois Cavalry captured the battle flag of the 12th Virginia Cavalry here. In October 1862, J.E.B. Stuart, escaping from Union troops, left the road at a point north on State 109 about halfway to Barnesville and marched to White's Ford.

BEL AIR, Harford County. State 22. Edwin and John Wilkes Booth were born at Tudor Hall, 3 miles northeast of town.

Tudor Hall, 3 miles northeast, was built by

Junius Brutus Booth; birthplace of Edwin and John Wilkes Booth.

BEL ALTON, Charles County. Near junction of US 301 and State 427. Marker for path of J. Wilkes Booth. Booth and David Herold, unable to cross the Potomac, hid in nearby meadows.

BOONSBORO, Washington County. US 40A. Gen. Jackson camped about 1 mile east of town along the road from Turner's Gap on the night of September 10, 1862. While walking his horse, Jackson was almost captured by Federal cavalry. Headquarters were across the road from the Murdock house. Gens. Lee, Longstreet, and D. H. Hill came through Boonsboro during the course of the war. Four days after the battle of South Mountain, Fitzhugh Lee's cavalry had a skirmish in Boonsboro streets with Federal troops. On July 8, 1863, Federal cavalry engaged J. E. B. Stuart here. Churches and homes served as emergency hospitals after the battle of Antietam.
Boonesborough Museum of History, 113 N. Main St. Civil War relics.
Washington Monument State Park, 3 miles southeast, off US 40A, has a history center with Civil War artifacts.

BRADFORD HOUSE, Baltimore County. Charles St. Ave. Home of Gov. Augustus W. Bradford was burned July 11, 1864, by Confederates in retaliation for the burning of Gov. Letcher's home in Virginia. State Roads Commission marker puts this as the closest point to Baltimore reached by Confederate troops during the war; they were part of Jubal Early's force which moved to attack Washington.

BRIDGEPORT, Carroll County. IS 81, State 97, 3 miles northwest of Taneytown. Sickles' 3rd Corps camped here June 30, 1863, then moved to Emmitsburg.

BROOKEVILLE, Montgomery County. State 97, south of US 40. J. E. B. Stuart, heading north to join Ewell and Lee in Pennsylvania, arrived here on June 28, 1863, paroled the majority of 400 prisoners at Brookeville, paroled the remainder next day at Cooksville.

BUCKTOWN, Dorchester County. Eight miles south of US 50.
Harriet Tubman Birthplace. Born of slave parents about 1820, Harriet grew up to marry John Tubman, a free black. She was helped to escape by Quaker Thomas Garrett of Wilmington, Delaware. She later helped her parents and about 300 others to escape north. During the war she worked as cook, nurse, laundress, scout, and spy.

BUDD'S FERRY, Charles County. West of State 224, inaccessible by car. Joe Hooker's division camped at the ferry during the winter of 1861–1862.

BURKITTSVILLE, Frederick County. US 340. Civil War correspondent George Alfred Townsend, whose pen name was Gath, built five houses here after the war with royalties from his novels. His estate, Gapland, was host to many celebrities of the day. He built a memorial to war correspondents on South Mountain, now in Gathland State Park. (*See* SOUTH MOUNTAIN.)
Gathland State Park, 1 mile west at Crampton Gap, has a visitor center with Civil War artifacts and a collection of Townsend's mementos. The park is crossed by the Appalachian Trail.

CABIN JOHN ARCH, Montgomery County. McArthur Blvd., 3 miles west of Washington. The arch, now part of the Washington water conduit system, was completed in 1863. It was begun when Jefferson Davis was U.S. Secretary of War and bore his name as well as that of President Franklin Pierce. In 1862, Secretary of the Interior Caleb had the name of Davis removed.

CAMBRIDGE, Dorchester County. State 343 west of US 50. Home town of James Wallace and Clement Sulivane. Wallace raised the 1st Eastern Shore Regiment; Sulivane served with the 21st Virginia, was captured at Saylor's Creek.
Camp Wallace was organized here in 1861. The Eastern Shore Regiment fought against the 2nd Maryland Infantry, C.S.A., at Gettysburg.
Old Trinity Church, State 16. Buried in the adjoining cemetery is Anna Ella Carroll, of the illustrious Carroll family, who was known as Lincoln's "other cabinet member." She was a fine strategist and helped to plan the Tennessee campaign.

CHESAPEAKE AND OHIO CANAL NATIONAL HISTORIC PARK, Cecil County. Visitor center is in the western Maryland Station Center, Canal St., Cumberland. Towpath extends 184.5 miles from Georgetown to Cumberland. Last three lift-locks about 5 miles from the town near Canal Boat replica, which features captain's cabin, hay house, and mule-stable on board tours.

CHESTERTOWN, Kent County. US 213.
Vickers Birthplace. Maj. Gen. George Vickers opposed secession, served with the Eastern Shore Militia, had two sons who fought

for the Union and one in the Confederate army. After the war he was one of 19 senators to vote "not guilty" in the impeachment trial of President Johnson.

War Monument, in front of Kent County Courthouse, was erected in 1917 by Judge James Alfred Pearce, honors Kent County soldiers who fought for either side. Federal inscription faces north, Confederate south.

CLARYVILLE, Allegany County. US 40A.

Claryville Inn, US 40A, was built to host travelers on the old National Road and served as military hospital during the war. Open for dining. The Claryville bridge on highway at State 55 is believed to be the last of its kind on the old National Road.

CLINTON, formerly Surrattsville, Prince Georges County. Off IS 95, junction of State 223 and 381.

Surratt House & Tavern, 9110 Brandywine Rd. The town was Surrattsville, on the main road to Washington, in 1854 when John Surratt was postmaster. Later the house served as tavern as well as post office and sheltered John Wilkes Booth in his flight south after assassinating Abraham Lincoln. He was accompanied by fellow plotter David Herold. Mrs. Mary Surratt was given a controversial death sentence for her aid to the men involved in the tragic affair. Guides in period costumes conduct tours and discuss Booth's stop here on his flight from Washington.

CONRAD'S FERRY, Montgomery County. About 4½ miles beyond Poolesville at State 107 and Potomac River. Name was changed to White's Ferry after the war. The point was garrisoned by Union troops to protect the Chesapeake and Ohio canal. *White's Ford* was 3 miles north of Conrad's Ferry (inaccessible by car). Confederates crossed the Potomac here three times: Lee in September 1862, moving toward Frederick and Antietam; Gen. J.E.B. Stuart in October 1862, after Chambersburg raid; Jubal Early in July 1864, retreating from Washington. The Maryland Civil War Centennial Commission, Hagerstown, published a booklet which lists and describes state historic places and persons of the Civil War period. It contains an excellent list of bridges, ferries, and fords across the Potomac River; most of the bridges were destroyed during the war.

COOKSVILLE, Howard County. State 97, 114. Stuart's cavalry captured the "Seven Hundred Loyal Eastern Shoreman" here on June 29, 1863.

CRADOCK HOUSE, Baltimore County. State 130 near junction with US 140. While Gilmor's raiders rested here in July 1864 after burning the Gunpowder River bridge, Maj. Gen. William B. Franklin escaped; he had been taken prisoner from a train stopped at the bridge. Franklin had been wounded at Sabine Cross Roads in the Red River expedition, was on sick leave when captured.

CRESWELL HALL, Cecil County. US 40, near Delaware line. Legislator John A. J. Creswell was influential in keeping Maryland in the Union. In 1862, as assistant adjutant general, he was responsible for raising the state quota of Union troops. He introduced penny postcards during his service as Postmaster General in Grant's administration.

CUMBERLAND, Allegany County. US 40, 220.

Barnum House, corner of George and Baltimore St. On the night of February 20, 1865, Union Maj. Gen. Benjamin F. Kelley was captured while sleeping at the hotel that stood at this site. Sgt. Joseph Kuykendall, of McNeill's Rangers, bagged the sleeping general.

Dent House, 118 Green St., was the home of Frederick Dent, who became the father-in-law of Gen. U. S. Grant. Dent, the first white child born in Cumberland, died in the White House.

Revere House, 184 Baltimore St., was the hotel where Gen. George Crook was captured by Sgt. Vandiver, also on the night of February 20, 1865. After the war he became a renowned Indian fighter, called "Gray Fox" by the Indians.

Rose Hill, 512 Dunbar Dr. Col. Lew Wallace and the 11th Indiana occupied the grounds in 1861.

DARNESTOWN, Montgomery County. State 28. Headquarters of Gen. Nathaniel P. Banks, August–December 1861.

DAY'S HOUSE, Baltimore County. Junction of US 1 and Kingsville-to-Fork Rd. On July 11, 1864, William Fields, one of Harry Gilmor's raiders, pulled down Ishmael Day's Union flag; Day shot him, then escaped to the woods; the raiders burned house and barn.

EASTON, Talbot County. State 309, 331.

Buchanan Home, State 370 west of town on south shore of Miles River. The Rest was the home of Franklin Buchanan, Confederate admiral. Buchanan had served under Oliver Perry; in 1861 he was commandant of the Navy Yard at Washington. After the Baltimore riot he resigned his commission, later changed his mind but was dismissed from U.S. service. In March 1862, he sank the *Cumberland* and the *Congress*, on which his brother McKean Buchanan was acting paymaster. He was given top Confederate naval rank in August 1862. He died here in 1874 and is buried in Wye Cemetery.

Foxley Hall, Aurora and Goldsborough St., was the home of Confederate Col. Oswald Tilghman.

Talbot Monument, opposite courthouse on S. Washington St., honors "The Talbot Boys," Confederate soldiers of Talbot County. The name of Adm. Buchanan heads a list of 20 officers.

Tuckahoe, 12 miles southwest of Easton, was the birthplace of Frederick Douglass. In his autobiography, which became a best-seller of its day, Douglass wrote: "I was born in Tuckahoe, near Hillsborough, and about twelve miles from Easton, in Talbot County, Maryland. I have no accurate knowledge of my age, never having seen any authentic record containing it. By far the larger part of the slaves know as little of their age as horses know of theirs . . . . I do not remember to have ever met a slave who could tell of his birthday. They seldom come nearer to it than planting-time, harvest-time, cherry-time, spring-time, or fall-time." Douglass was the son of a slave, Harriet Bailey, and a white father, possibly his master. He worked as field servant, then as house servant in Baltimore. In later years, after he'd escaped to the North, he published a weekly paper in Rochester, New York. A memorial to Douglass is on the campus of Morgan State College in Baltimore.

Wye Cemetery, about 15 miles northwest of Easton, east of State 370, has graves of Charles Sidney Winder, Confederate brigadier general, killed at Cedar Mountain, August 9, 1862, and Adm. Franklin Buchanan.

EDWARD'S FERRY, Montgomery County. Road to southwest from junction of State 107 and 109 at Poolesville. Stone's Corps garrisoned the crossing of the river in the winter of 1861–1862. In June 1863, Gen. Hooker crossed part of his army at Edward's Ferry, moving north so speedily as to force Lee to change his plans for moving upon Harrisburg. Lee turned toward Gettysburg instead. *Harrison Island,* which lies 2 miles above the ferry, was the spot from which Union forces crossed into Virginia for the Ball's Bluff engagement.

ELKTON, Cecil County. US 40. A mass meeting here in April 1861 pledged to remain

in the Union even if all the rest of Maryland seceded.

Stump Farm, 3 miles south of highway and Susquehanna River Bridge. A Union depot and cavalry staging area were located at the mouth of the Susquehanna River. Perry Point Hospital now occupies site.

Wilna, on Blue Ball Rd. 3 miles north of town, was the home of William Whann Mackall, Confederate brigadier general, captured at Island No. 10 in April 1862. Later Mackall served on the staff of Braxton Bragg, a West Point classmate.

ELTON, Montgomery County. At Sunshine on State 97. Marker erected by the United Daughters of the Confederacy for birthplace of Ridgely Brown, who helped organize the 1st Maryland Cavalry, May 15, 1862. He was killed at South Anna River, Virginia, June 1, 1864.

EMMITSBURG, Frederick County. Junction of US 15 and State 97. Gen. O. O. Howard's 11th Corps camped here June 30, 1863; the following day Sickles's 3rd Corps marched through town. Both were en route to Gettysburg.

FAIRVIEW MOUNTAIN, Washington County. US 40.

Federal Signal Station, marker on highway. Station near this point was taken October 10, 1862, by Stuart's cavalry. Messages from here to South Mountain were relayed via Catoctin to Sugar Loaf to Washington.

FORT FOOTE, Prince Georges County, off State 414. The fort, built in 1863, was garrisoned throughout the war. It is well preserved. Two 15-inch Rodman naval guns are on the grounds.

FORT FREDERICK, Washington County. South of US 40A, southeast of Big Pool. Ancient stone fort was garrisoned by Union troops in 1861–1862. Restored, with museum.

FORT SUMNER, Montgomery County. One mile west of Washington on McArthur Blvd. at intersection of Sangamore Rd. and Westpath Way. The fort was western anchor of Washington defenses. Only Battery Baily on the east side of Little Falls Branch remains on the Montgomery County defenses of Washington.

FREDERICK, Frederick County. IS 70, 270, US 40, 340.

Battle of Monocacy, 3 miles south on State 355. On July 9, 1864, Gen. Lew Wallace's forces delayed Early's Confederates who were marching toward Baltimore and Washington. Wounded were taken to Arcadia and the Markell estate. Federals lost about 1,800 out of 6,000; Confederates lost less than 700 out of 14,000 troops.

Confederate Headquarters, State 240 east of Frederick. Marker by State Roads Commission. At Best's Grove, near Monocacy Junction, Lee, Jackson, and Longstreet had quarters in September 1862. The famous lost order No. 191 and the proclamation to the people of Maryland were written here.

Evangelical Lutheran Church, Church St. between Market and Middle Alley. A false floor was built over pews so that sick and wounded soldiers could be tended here.

Evangelical Reformed Church, 9–13 W. Church St. Gen. Jackson slept through a service on a Sunday evening in September 1862, while the Rev. Daniel Zacharias prayed for the success of Union troops. Jackson had attended the service to prevent any trouble from his troops. Barbara Fritchie was a church member.

Frederick Barracks, 242 S. Market St., were used as hospitals during Civil War.

Frederick City Hall, Market St. On July 9, 1864, Gen. Jubal A. Early, C.S.A., demanded and got $200,000 when he threatened to burn down the town. Three days earlier, he had used the same threat successfully in Hagerstown.

Frederick County Courthouse, Record and Church St. The Maryland general assembly met here to consider secession but moved to another building. Conferences were still going on when the courthouse burned. Present building was completed during the war.

Fritchie House, 154 W. Patrick St. The house has been reconstructed but not as often as the story of Barbara Fritchie. She was 95 years old and may well have waved a flag at Jackson's troops—but Jackson went down Mill and Bentz streets and rejoined his men at some distance from the Fritchie home. Historical relics are in the home.

Historical Society of Frederick County, 24 E. Church St., has exhibits and relics collection.

Kemp Hall, southeast corner of Church and Market St. The legislature called to consider secession met here on April 26, 1861. Plaque on building was dedicated February 15, 1961, as part of the Maryland Centennial Commemorative program.

Mt. Olivet Cemetery, south end of Market St., has graves of Barbara Fritchie and more

General Bank's division recrossing the Potomac from Williamsport.

than 400 unknown Confederate soldiers killed at South Mountain, Monocacy, and Antietam.

Ramsey House, 119 Record St., was site where Gen. George L. Hartsuff recuperated from a wound received at Antietam. He was visited here by Abraham Lincoln. Hartsuff later served at Petersburg.

Taney House, 121 S. Bentz St. Chief Justice Roger Brooke Taney handed down the Dred Scott decision, also administered the presidential oath to Abraham Lincoln. House has original furnishings and mementos, but is open only by appointment. Taney monuments are situated in front of the State House at Annapolis and in Baltimore, on Washington Place. He is buried in St. John's Roman Catholic Cemetery.

Union Headquarters, marker at southwest edge of town marks site where Gen. Hooker was relieved and Gen. Meade took command in June 1863, before Gettysburg.

GLEN ECHO, Montgomery County.

Clara Barton National Historic Site, 5801 Oxford Rd. The restored home of the Civil War nurse who served gallantly at a field hospital on the bloody battlefield of Antietam and nearly twenty years later founded the Red Cross. Barton memorabilia.

HAGERSTOWN, Washington County. IS 70, 81. The town lay in the routes taken to many battles. In June 1863, Gens. Lee, Longstreet, A. P. Hill, and Ewell came this way. After defeat at Gettysburg, Longstreet's 1st Corps camped about 2 miles south toward Sharpsburg. Hill's 3rd Corps was encamped here from July 7 to 13. The following year some of Early's troops stopped here en route to Washington and demanded $20,000 not to burn the town. The editor of the *Hagerstown Mail,* Daniel Deckart, was arrested in September 1861 for pro-Southern views; in May 1862, the newspaper office was sacked by citizens angry with the defeat of the Union 1st Maryland Infantry by the Confederate 1st Maryland Infantry at Front Royal, Virginia.

Kennedy Farm, at Potomac River and US 340. Marker near Maryland entrance to old Harpers Ferry Bridge. John Brown stayed at a farm here, posing as Isaac Smith, and gathered arms and men for the attack on Harpers Ferry.

Lee at Hagerstown, US 40A. Marker on highway. Lee with Longstreet's corps arrived here September 11, 1862, before the battles of South Mountain and Antietam.

Miller House, 135 W. Washington, has Civil War relics.

Mount Prospect, on West Washington St.

After the battle of Antietam, Mrs. Howard Kennedy and her small daughter, Annie, saw a wounded Union officer collapse in the road; they cared for him in the house. He was Oliver Wendell Holmes, Jr., who later became a Justice of the U.S. Supreme Court. His father's search for him was commemorated in the poem, "My Search for the Captain."

Rose Hill Cemetery, Potomac St. and Willow Lane. Statue of Hope marks the graves of more than 2,000 Confederate soldiers who died at Antietam and South Mountain. Confederate Monument was erected in 1877,

Zion Reformed Church, Potomac and Church St. Gen. George Custer once climbed to the bell tower to have a look at the terrain. Sharpshooters chased him from the roost.

HAMPTON NATIONAL HISTORICAL SITE, Baltimore County. 535 Hampton Lane, Towson. The antebellum mansion still has original furnishings, restored gardens, outbuildings, including overseer's and slave cabins on 48-acre tract.

HANCOCK, Washington County. IS 70, US 40.

St. Thomas Church was used as hospital by the 39th Illinois Volunteers, 5th Connecticut, 46th Pennsylvania, and 29th New York. Batteries around and behind building opposed Confederate batteries on opposite shore of Potomac.

HAYFIELDS, Baltimore County. Northwest corner of State 145 and US 111 Expressway. Home of John Merryman when arrested by Union troops in May 1861. He was taken to Fort McHenry and released later without trial, although Judge Roger Brooke Taney had issued a writ of habeas corpus directing the provost marshal to bring Merryman to court. Taney protested to Lincoln when this was not complied with; Lincoln did not intercede. In July 1864, Gen. Bradley T. Johnson had lunch here en route to destroy the Gunpowder bridges.

HYATTSTOWN, State 355 just south of Frederick County line. Scene of September 1862 skirmish between Stuart's cavalry and Federal infantry. Town also was on Early's route to Washington in July 1864.

KINGSTON, Somerset County. State 413.

Kingston Hall, east of highway, was the birthplace of Anna Ella Carroll, a tireless worker for President Lincoln. It is said she gave the War Department a plan for the capture of Vicksburg which resembled the one eventually carried out by Grant. Long after the war Congress voted her a pension for her services to the Union. She is buried in Old Trinity Graveyard, Church Creek, Dorchester County.

MARYLAND HEIGHTS, Washington County. Northwest of State 340, opposite Harpers Ferry. Jackson occupied the area in May 1861. Union troops were here in September 1862. Gen. Lafayette McLaws seized the heights and occupied the site until the surrender of Harpers Ferry. Union troops here in 1864 delayed Gen. Early on his trip to Washington.

MIDDLEBURG, Carroll County. East of junction of State 194 with Westminster Rd. Gen. George Meade had headquarters here just before Gettysburg. U.S. government marker locates army positions for June 29, 1863.

MIDDLETOWN, Frederick County. Off IS 70, US 40A, 8 miles west of Frederick. Gen. Jacob Cox camped here on September 13, 1862. During the battle of South Mountain, homes and churches were used as hospitals. Rutherford B. Hayes was among the wounded. After Gettysburg, Meade concentrated forces here on July 7, 1863. Early, who seemed to like dollars better than Sherman's bummers liked chickens, came through town on July 8, 1864, asked for $5,000 instantly, but agreed to take $1,500 in cash by 7 A.M. and the remainder by 6 P.M., to be paid by the election district. Early did not wait around for the second payment, however. Middletown's Barbara Fritchie was Nancy Crouse, who flew the Union flag from the second story of her father's house to the annoyance of neighbor Samuel D. Riddlemoser. Southern cavalrymen en route to South Mountain stopped at Riddlemoser's and decided to bring down the "Yankee rag," but Nancy draped herself in it, true to poetic tradition. With a pistol at her head she announced: "You may shoot me, but never will I willingly give up my country's flag into the hands of traitors," or so the story goes. For some reason she had a change of heart and handed over the flag. The Rebel captain, Edward S. Motter, wrapped it around his horse's head as he rode out of town. Yankees gave pursuit and returned the flag to Miss Crouse.

OAKLAND, Garrett County. Junction of US 219 and State 39. On April 26, 1863, Confederate Gen. William E. Jones captured Union troops guarding the B & O Railroad.

Church of the Presidents, 2nd and Liberty streets. President U. S. Grant attended services here while vacationing.

PIKESVILLE, Baltimore County. IS 695, US 140. State police headquarters is located in an armory built in 1812, later a Confederate soldiers' home, housing more than 150 veterans.

POINT LOOKOUT, St. Mary's County. State 5. Hospital and prison camp during the war. A Confederate monument here is said to be the only memorial erected by the U.S. government to Civil War POWs (3,384) who died in the prison camp. Bartlett Yancey Malone, of the 6th North Carolina Regiment, was here in 1864. For January 1, he noted: "The morning was plesant but toward evening the air changed and the nite was very coal. was so coal that five of our men froze to death befour morning . . . . too of our men was so hungry to day that they caught a Rat and cooked him and eat it." The fare and weather were somewhat better by July 1: "It is very plesant to day We had pical Pork for breakfast this morning and for dinner we will have Been Soop."

POOLESVILLE, Montgomery County. Junction of State 107 and 109. The town was usually occupied by Union troops, and at times 20,000 were camped here. Occasionally Confederate troops were encamped. J.E.B. Stuart's right flank was here in September 1862 and skirmished with Federals. In June 1863, Gen. Joe Hooker had headquarters here. In July 1864, Gen. Jubal Early retreated through town. *Poole House,* south side of Main St. near Willard Rd., was the home of Frederick Poole, where funeral services were held for Lincoln's friend Col. Edward Baker, killed at Ball's Bluff.

POPE'S CREEK, Charles County. Two miles southwest of US 301, just north of Potomac River Bridge. Thomas A. Jones, signal agent for the South, lived here and helped to conceal Booth and Herold in April 1865 when they were fleeing from Washington. Jones sold Booth the boat in which the assassins escaped across the river on April 22.

PORT TOBACCO, Charles County. US 301, now ½ mile from river. A port for Civil War smugglers. George Atzerodt, one of the plotters against Lincoln, lived in the area. At Rose Hill, northwest of town, lived Annie Olivia Floyd, agent in the Confederate underground mail service. Commissions for the Confederates who raided St. Albans were hidden in a hollow andiron here. Annie Floyd is buried in the cemetery of St. Ignatius Roman Catholic Church on State 427.

PRINCE FREDERICK, Calvert County. State 2. Marker on highway.

Taney Birthplace. Justice Roger Brooke Taney was born here March 17, 1777. He administered the oath of office to Van Buren, Harrison, Polk, Taylor, Pierce, Buchanan, and Lincoln.

PRINCESS ANNE, Somerset County. US 13.

Chaille-Long Birthplace, junction of US 13 and State 363. Charles Chaille-Long was born here July 2, 1842. He was a student at Washington Academy when war broke out. He became a captain in the 11th Maryland Infantry and served in the defense of Washington.

Elmwood, 7½ miles west of town near State 363, was the home of Arnold Elzey, who was born here December 18, 1816, christened Arnold Elzey Jones. He dropped the Jones before his graduation from West Point in 1837. He served under Stonewall Jackson, was twice wounded; by September 1864 he was chief of artillery in the Army of Tennessee.

ROCK RUN, Harford County. Between US 40 and 1, south of Susquehanna River. The home of Confederate Brig. Gen. James J. Archer, who was wounded and captured at Gettysburg; he was exchanged in August 1864, returned to service, and died in Richmond, October 24. The estate is now a state park.

ROCKVILLE, Montgomery County. IS 270. Ten miles northwest of Washington on State 355. McClellan had headquarters here in September 1862. Jeb Stuart occupied town in June 1863; Jubal Early was here in July 1864; a cavalry skirmish took place on July 13 between the 2nd Massachusetts and Bradley T. Johnson's men, retreating with Early.

Confederate Monument, opposite courthouse, erected by United Confederate Veterans and United Daughters of the Confederacy in 1913, honoring Montgomery County Confederate soldiers.

SALISBURY, Wicomico County. Junction US 13 and 50.

Camp Upton, established by Brig. Gen. Henry H. Lockwood in November 1861, was center for control of the eastern shore. The 4th Wisconsin was dispatched from here to Snow Hill, mistook a welcoming committee for Southern sympathizers, and made them repair a bridge over which the regiment had passed with difficulty. Camp site is now occupied by the *Salisbury Times.*

SILVER SPRING, Montgomery County. IS 495, US 29, north of Washington. Early halted here on his march to Washington, July 11, 1864.

Grace Church, on Georgia Ave., has marker in churchyard to unknown Confederate soldiers buried by Federal troops after Early turned back to Virginia.

SOUTH MOUNTAIN, Frederick County. State 572, 17, 67. Markers for the battle of September 14, 1862, in which Maj. Gen. William Franklin routed Confederates and gained control of Crampton's Gap, are located at top of Gap and on eastern face of mountain. Site where Gen. Jesse L. Reno was killed about sundown that day is on the Old Sharpsburg Road, 12½ miles west of Frederick. Gathland, at southern end of South Mountain, is the site where George Alfred Townsend, Civil War correspondent who used his initials to make up the greater part of his pen name "Gath," was responsible for what may be the worst looking memorial of the era, a memorial to correspondents. Someone who *admired* it said: "Above a Moorish arch he [Townsend] super-imposed three Roman arches, and these flanked with a square crenellated tower, producing a bizarre and picturesque effect. Niches shelter a carving of a horse's head and symbolic statuettes of Mercury, Electricity and Poetry. Tablets bear the suggestive words, 'Speed' and 'Heed,' and quotations appropriate to the art of war correspondence from a variety of sources beginning with the Old Testament. . ." At Turner's Gap, on US 40A, 13 miles west of Frederick, is a series of markers erected by the U.S. Government and by the State Roads Commission, pertaining to the battle of South Mountain, which was a part of the Antietam campaign.

UNION MILLS, Carroll County. US 140. Marker on highway. The Shriver family was divided by the road and by politics. Gen. Stuart camped on the southwestern side of the road in a Shriver home, on June 29, 1863. The next night Gen. James Barnes, of the 1st Division, 5th Corps, USA, was a guest of Shrivers on the northeastern side of the road.

WALDORF, Charles County. East of town at junction of State 232 and 382. Marker on highway.

Samuel Mudd Home, Ste. Catherine, just off State 382 on State 232. Dr. Samuel Mudd set the broken leg of John Wilkes Booth on April 14, 1865, and was later sentenced to Dry Tortugas prison, off the coast of Florida, where he aided many a yellow fever victim as he had aided the caller in the night.

MASSACHUSETTS

Massachusetts, sixth of the original 13 states, was the birthplace of abolitionism and was the first state to respond to Lincoln's call for arms on April 15, 1861. Within a few days, 1,500 men were en route to Fort Monroe. Baltimoreans, who rioted against Massachusetts troops on April 19, 1861, gave Massachusetts editors and orators a ready-made parallel. The Baltimore shooting came 86 years to the day after the shot heard 'round the world at Concord. The men of Massachusetts rallied around the flag via pulpit, press, and recruiting center. A fifth regiment reported in Boston for active duty on April 19. By the middle of May, the Secretary of War had to request the governor of Massachusetts not to send more troops than requested. In July, Lincoln would explain to Congress: "One of the greatest complexities of this government is to avoid receiving troops faster than it can provide for them."

Massachusetts troops were reorganized to conform to U.S. Army requirements. Each new regiment had ten companies and, for the first year of the war, a 24-piece band. Some 3,000 volunteers, left over after the quota was filled, enlisted in other states. Six companies helped to fill the New York quota. The state took pride not only in the valor of her men but in their modesty of apparel. There were no Zouaves, Turkish or Swiss Guards, or Mozart Regiments; however, the regimental flags were as colorful as any. Tara's harp and the Irish green figured prominently in at least two. Massachusetts sent more men to the Union navy than any other state except New York, and furnished about 160,000 men to the army.

AMESBURY, Essex County. IS 95, State 110.

Whittier House, Friend and Pickard St. The home of John Greenleaf Whittier from 1836 until 1892. Whittier manuscripts and memorabilia. The Quaker poet was an active member of the Anti-Slavery Society, edited the *Pennsylvania Freeman,* and contributed editorials to the *National Era,* a Washington antislavery paper.

AMHERST, Hampshire County. State 9. Young men from Amherst College enlisted in groups during the war, forming the nucleus of several companies. Henry Ward Beecher, brother of Harriet Beecher Stowe, was an Amherst graduate.

BOSTON, Suffolk County. IS 93, 95.

Adams Home, 57 Mount Vernon St. Charles Francis Adams, Sr., served as Civil War ambassador to England. His son, John Quincy Adams, served on Gov. Andrew's staff, helping to dispatch regiments to the front. Henry Adams became confidential secretary to his father in London. Charles Francis Adams, Jr., served as lieutenant with the 1st Massachusetts Cavalry, was brevetted brigadier general in 1865. In June 1861, Charles Francis Adams, Jr., wrote to his mother about his drilling fellow Bostonians too old for regular duty but willing for home guard service: "Imagine a line of potbellied, round-shouldered respectabilities of fifty or thereabouts standing in two rows and trying to dance. . . . I saw Mr. Robertson and Captain Crane side by side in the front rank with Mr. Gill and poor old Flint vainly struggling to cover them in the rear. That was too much and I almost smiled right out loud. The only man I saw who could by any possibility be converted into a soldier was, unfortunately, our worthy pastor, Mr. Wells, who, however, in case of emergency would probably have other duties to perform. There he was, however, with his musket in his hand and it was so refreshing to see a man who seemed able to bend his back that I asked John to make him a sergeant."

African Meeting House, 46 Jay St. It is believed to be the oldest church building for blacks in the country. On this site the New England Anti-Slavery Society was established in 1832. Changing exhibits. Guided tours on the hour. Now the starting point for the Black Heritage Trail. Information also at the National Park Visitor Center, 15 State St.

Booth Home, 29A Chestnut St. Edwin Booth, brother of John Wilkes Booth, lived

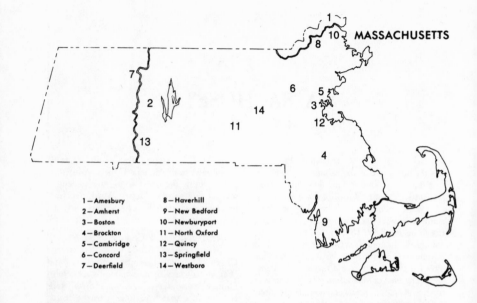

MASSACHUSETTS

1 — Amesbury   8 — Haverhill
2 — Amherst   9 — New Bedford
3 — Boston   10 — Newburyport
4 — Brockton   11 — North Oxford
5 — Cambridge   12 — Quincy
6 — Concord   13 — Springfield
7 — Deerfield   14 — Westboro

here. His first acknowledged stage appearance was at the Boston Museum in 1849; he had once previously stuttered through a part in Baltimore and chose ever after to forget the whole thing. Adam Badeau, friend of Booth and military secretary to Gen. Grant, related an incident that happened on a railway platform in Jersey City in March 1865, when Booth was on his way to Philadelphia. A young man was shoved by the crowd against a sleeping car, lost his footing as the train began to move, and was pulled back from the wheels by Edwin Booth, who caught him by the coat collar. The young man was Robert Lincoln.

Boston Common, Soldiers' and Sailors' Monument on highest point of Common honors Civil War dead.

Boston Public Garden, statue on Boylston St. Mall honors Col. Thomas Cass, commander of 9th Massachusetts.

Boston Public Library, Copley Square, has a major Civil War collection.

Emancipation Statue, Park Square, commemorates Lincoln's freeing the slaves.

Everett Birthplace, Boston St., Edward Everett Square, Dorchester. Site of birthplace is marked by a tablet across the square from the Edward Everett statue, by W. W. Story. Everett, eminent statesman and renowned orator, was the "other man" who spoke at Gettysburg on November 19, 1863.

Faneuil Hall, Merchants Row, is known as the Cradle of Liberty. The hall was the scene of many Anti-Slavery Society meetings and demonstrations in prewar years. One of the great speeches made here was by Wendell Phillips in denunciation of William Austin, state attorney general, who had defended the slayers of abolitionist Elijah Parish Lovejoy. He finished to a "whirlwind of applause"—when the question of the murderer's guilt was put to a vote, the hall resounded with a unanimous "Aye!" The museum has an extensive collection of relics.

First Corps Cadet Armory, 105 Arlington St., has collection of battle flags, uniforms, documents, and one of the most complete collections of Civil War pictures outside the National Archives.

Forest Hills Cemetery, Morton St. Among notables buried here are William Lloyd Garrison and Edward Everett Hale.

Fort Warren, Georges Island, in Boston Harbor Islands State Park, reached by ferry from Long Wharf, has a memorial marker erected by the United Daughters of the Confederacy in honor of Confederate soldiers imprisoned here in 1861–1865.

Garrison Monument, Commonwealth Ave. Mall. William Lloyd Garrison edited the famous antislavery *Liberator,* from 1831 to 1860. In 1832 he founded the American Anti-Slavery Society and later served as its president.

This funeral cortege was for four Massachusetts soldiers killed in Baltimore en route to Washington.

Garrison was considered a crank by many contemporaries, including some who were also opposed to slavery but felt that the editor confused the issue with too many unrelated causes. He was interested in women's rights and tried to see that women had a chance to serve on National Anti-Slavery Society committees. Some of his opponents held that putting a woman on a committee was "contrary to the usages of civilized society." Garrison felt that slavery could not be destroyed by political means but only by moral persuasion; he opposed the war until after the Emancipation Proclamation.

Hooker Monument, on State House lawn. Gen. Joseph Hooker never cared much for his nickname of "Fighting Joe," which was given to him by the press. He retaliated, just before Chancellorsville, when he ordered that all news dispatches sent from the Army of the Potomac should be signed, to some extent thereby curbing irresponsible reporting.

Howe Home, 13 Chestnut St. Julia Ward Howe, author of "The Battle Hymn of the Re-

public," lived here. Mrs. Howe, with her husband, Samuel Gridley Howe, was a leader in the abolition movement.

Massachusetts Historical Society, 1154 Boylston St. The oldest historical society in America has an extensive collection of Americana.

Old Corner Book Store, School and Washington streets. Once a meeting place for Longfellow, Emerson, Harriet Beecher Stowe, Oliver Wendell Holmes, and other literati. Massachusetts authors supported the Union in prose and poetry. Whittier's verses were said to be a favorite with Lincoln. One of his war poems, set to an old hymn, became a popular song in Northern family circles. James Russell Lowell, in a new series of *Biglow Papers*, exhorted his countrymen to renounce slavery. Julia Ward Howe wrote patriotic verses for the *Atlantic Monthly*.

Park Street Church, 1 Park St., is located on "Brimstone Corner"—because brimstone was stored here during the War of 1812. When

Henry Ward Beecher preached, parishioners said it was well named. Garrison delivered his first antislavery address here in 1829.

Phillips Monument, Boylston St., was sculpted by Daniel Chester French. Wendell Phillips was as prominent an abolitionist orator as Garrison was a writer. He succeeded Garrison as president of the American Anti-Slavery Society. A plaque marks the Phillips home at 26 Essex St. Phillips was 50 years old when the war began. He was unable to take political office because of his refusal to take an oath under the Constitution, and he was too old for active duty, so he made speeches. In the first winter of the war he lectured in New York and Washington, addressed the troops in Alexandria, and took a speaking tour of western states. He was hit by an egg in Cincinnati. Police protection was nonexistent; Phillips's friends held off members of the audience who wanted to tar and feather the speaker. News of the riot, however, brought him packed audiences during the rest of his tour.

Shaw Memorial, facing the State House from the Common. The group statue, executed by Augustus Saint-Gaudens, depicts Col. Robert Gould Shaw, his horse, and his black troopers. Shaw's regiment, the 54th Massachusetts, became the first black unit to be recruited under state authority. One of the finest memorials in the country, it is a bronze bas-relief.

State House, Beacon St. The Hall of Flags on second floor has Civil War battle flags. Doric Hall has busts and statues of Civil War leaders, together with a Healy portrait of Lincoln. Underground Archives Building contains documents, letters, and relics of Civil War period, available to scholars and historians only. Gov. John A. Andrew, who served here in wartime, was an enlightened leader, championed black soldiers, and fought for fairness.

Sumner Monument, Boylston St. Mall, was executed by Thomas Ball. Charles Sumner was a leading abolitionist senator. He was injured when caned in the Senate by Rep. Preston Brooks in 1856.

BRAINTREE, Norfolk County. State 3.
General Sylvanus Thayer Birthplace, 786 Washington St., has Civil War memorabilia.

CAMBRIDGE, Suffolk County. IS 93, US 3.
Longfellow National Historic Site, 105 Brattle St. Henry Wadsworth Longfellow lived here from 1837 until his death in 1882. The house contains manuscripts, books, and furnishings. Longfellow, who lost his wife tragically in a fire in 1861, wrote far less about the war than most of his contemporaries; his few writings on the conflict were dejected in tone.

Mount Auburn Cemetery, Mount Auburn St., has the graves of Longfellow, James Russell Lowell, Oliver Wendell Holmes, and Edwin Booth.

CENTERVILLE, Barnstable County. State 3 on Cape Cod.
Centerville Historical Society Museum, 513 Main St., has Civil War artifacts and guided tours.

CONCORD, Middlesex County. State 2.
Alcott House, Lexington Rd. Louisa May Alcott, who served as a volunteer nurse in the Union hospital in Georgetown, wrote a vivid account of her experiences in *Hospital Sketches.* In one month of duty she contracted typhoid and had to be sent home. The home, which is also called Orchard House, is open to the public.

Emerson House, Cambridge Turnpike and State 2A, opposite Antiquarian House, was the home of Ralph Waldo Emerson from 1835 until his death in 1882. Emerson wrote and spoke eloquently against slavery, made a fiery address on the subject at the Smithsonian Institution in Washington in January 1862.

Sleepy Hollow Cemetery, Bedford St., contains the graves of Emerson, Hawthorne, Thoreau, the Alcotts, and Daniel Chester French.

CUMMINGTON, Hampshire County. State 9.
William Cullen Bryant Homestead, State 112 off State 9. The poet and editor of the New York *Evening Post* was born here in 1794 and bought the house in 1865 as a summer home. Original furnishings. Tours on weekends and holidays.

DEERFIELD, Franklin County. US 5.
Memorial Hall, Memorial St., has the Sheldon collection of colonial, Indian, and Civil War relics.

HAVERHILL, Essex County. State 110.
Haverhill Historical Society, 240 Water St., has Civil War relics.

Whittier House, 3 miles east on highway. John Greenleaf Whittier, who has been called the Poet Laureate of the Union, was born here in 1807. House has period furnishings.

HINGHAM, Plymouth County. State 3A.
Samuel Lincoln House, State 3A. Ancestors of Abraham Lincoln lived here. Capt. Sam's house dates from 1750. Also in town, Gen. Benjamin Lincoln House, built in 1667.

LYNN, Essex County. State 1A.

Grand Army of the Republic Museum, 58 Andrew St., has Civil War weapons, artifacts, and exhibits.

MARBLEHEAD, Essex County. State 1A.

Fort Sewall, at the northeast end of Front St., was built in the 18th century and manned through the Spanish-American War. Open from dawn to dusk.

NEWBURYPORT, Essex County. US 1.

Garrison Monument, in Brown's Park, Pleasant and Green St., honors the "Great Liberator," William Lloyd Garrison.

NEWTON, Suffolk County. IS 95, State 30.

Jackson Homestead, 527 Washington St., is an 1809 brick building with hand-hewn beams, which was a station on the Underground Railroad before the war. Slaves were hidden in the basement.

NORTH OXFORD, Worcester County. Off IS 395, State 12.

Clara Barton Birthplace, off State 12, is the birthplace of Union nurse Clara Barton, who founded the Red Cross. Period furnishings and memorabilia of the "Angel of the Battlefield."

QUINCY, Suffolk County. IS 93, State 3.

Adams National Historic Site, 135 Adams St. The home of the Adams family for nearly a century and a half has original furnishings used by four generations. Charles Francis Adams, Jr., wrote to his mother in June 1861 of the town's reaction to the battle at Big Bethel, in which a Quincy man was killed. The Federals had been repulsed and retreated in disorder. "Our flags . . . were hung at half mast for a day and loud swearing there as elsewhere, was heard at and about Brigadier General Pierce [E. H. Pierce]. It was a bad affair and John Palfrey writes that two companies of regulars would have carried the battery with ease, but this is the beginning of our militia generalship and, alas, that this should have been a Massachusetts man. In fact our good old State, which began this war so well, is likely after going up like a rocket to come down like a stick, and she is now rapidly falling behindhand." Young Adams voiced more complaints about the quality of officers being sent to the war and apparently concluded in the next several months to have a hand at the job himself. By November he was in the army.

SPRINGFIELD, Hampden County. IS 91.

Springfield Armory National Historic Site, Federal St., comprises several museums and exhibits. The fence around the armory was made of recast Revolutionary and Civil War cannons. In 1864 over 3,000 men were employed at the armory, turning out 1,000 rifles a day.

STOCKBRIDGE, Berkshire County. State 102, 183.

Chesterwood, off State 183, 1 mile south of jct. State 102, was the summer home and studio of Daniel Chester French, who was the sculptor for the Abraham Lincoln statue in Washington's Lincoln Memorial. His plaster cast of that work is here. Changing exhibits in the barn gallery. Guided tours.

MICHIGAN

When Southern states left the Union, Michigan did not endorse the sentiment of "wayward sisters depart in peace." In January 1861, both Gov. Moses Wisner, who was leaving office, and the incoming governor, Austin Blair, emphasized loyalty to the Union. Secession was held to be an overt act of treason. In February, Senator Zachariah Chandler wrote to the governor: "Some of the manufacturing states think a fight would be awful. Without a little bloodletting, this Union will not, in my estimation, be worth a rush."

A special session of the legislature in May authorized the governor to raise ten regiments and to borrow $1,000,000. By 1862, with the increase of factory pay at home and the discouraging progress of the war, Michigan men were unresponsive to calls for recruits. Bounties were necessary in order to raise enough troops for new companies. By 1865, as much as $150 was offered in an effort to fill the quotas. In all, Michigan sent 31 regiments of infantry, 11 of cavalry, and one each of artillery, engineers, and sharpshooters. George A. Custer became a brigadier general at 23. Michigan troops captured President Jefferson Davis near Irwinville, Georgia, on May 10, 1865, and delivered the famous prisoner to Fortress Monroe.

ALLEGAN, Allegan County. State 40, 89. The home and grave of Gen. Benjamin D. Pritchard, captor of Jefferson Davis, are here. The home has remained in the Pritchard family and has not been open to the public. The grave is well marked, near the center of Oakwood Cemetery. Pritchard served with the 4th Michigan Cavalry, 1862–1865.

ANN ARBOR, Washtenaw County. IS 94, US 94.
University of Michigan. The William L. Clements Library of American History has original photographs of Michigan Civil War soldiers, posters, and many manuscripts. The Stearns Collection of Musical Instruments, Hill Auditorium, has bugles, horns, flutes, etc., of the Civil War period throughout the

displays, which are arranged according to type rather than date of use. The Michigan Historical Collection in the Rackham Building has a vast number of Civil War diaries and letters, soldier and civilian; also many photographs and printed materials. This is a research library, as is the Clements Library.

BATTLE CREEK, Calhoun County. IS 94, US 94, 27.
Oak Hill Cemetery, South Ave. and Oakhill Dr., has the grave of Sojourner Truth, who gained her freedom in New York State in the 1820s. The former slave, who was six feet tall, traveled through New England and the West speaking against slavery; her platform manner is said to have had a curiously mystic effect. She abandoned her given name of Isabella for a name more representative of her journey to preach truth.

BAY CITY, Bay County. IS 75, State 25, 81.
Bay County Historical Museum, 321 Washington Ave. Exhibits contain weapons, maps, diaries, and other manuscripts, also presidential campaign material.

COPPER HARBOR, Keweenaw County. US 41.
Astor House Museum, Minnetonka Resort, corner of US 41 and State 26, has Civil War memorabilia.

DEARBORN, Wayne County. IS 94, US 12.
Dearborn Historical Museum, 915 Brady and 21950 Michigan Ave. The three buildings of the complex were part of the original U.S. Government Arsenal. The Exhibit Annex has shops and vehicles. The Commandant's Quarters and the McFadden-Ross House contain period furnishings. Commandant's headquarters and McFadden-Ross House have Civil War displays: uniforms, weapons, medals, letters, and diaries.
Henry Ford Museum and Greenfield Village, Village Rd. and Oakwood Blvd. Among

MICHIGAN

1 — Ann Arbor	17 — Ludington
2 — Battle Creek	18 — Mackinac
3 — Bay City	19 — Manistee
4 — Belding	20 — Marquette
5 — Cassopolis	21 — Marshall
6 — Dearborn	22 — Midland
7 — Detroit	23 — Monroe
8 — East Lansing	24 — Muskegon
9 — Escanaba	25 — Niles
10 — Fort Wilkins	26 — Onsted
11 — Garden City	27 — Plymouth
12 — Grand Rapids	28 — Pontiac
13 — Hastings	29 — Port Huron
14 — Holland	30 — Presque Isle
15 — Kalamazoo	31 — Traverse City
16 — Lansing	

buildings on the village green is the Logan County Courthouse from Illinois, where Lincoln practiced law before becoming President.

DETROIT, Wayne County. IS 75, 275, 94, 96. Mayor William C. Duncan called a war meeting for July 15, 1862, to assemble at what is now the Campus Martius intersection of Michigan and Woodward Ave. Elder statesman Lewis Cass, who had been Buchanan's Secretary of State, was on hand. The mayor and other leading citizens spoke in behalf of the Union war effort before the grandstand was smashed by a mob that also ripped up the patriotic bunting. The rioters seemed to be under the misapprehension that they were about to be drafted. They pursued two Union leaders and local businessmen, Eber B. Ward and Duncan Stewart, to the Russell House hotel, at the corner of Woodward Ave. and the Campus Martius, where Sheriff Flanigan and a deputy held off the attack with drawn revolvers. There was some talk that the "melancholy spectacle" had been inspired by Confederates infiltrating the city from Canada. Loyal Union men set to work to erase the blot on the state's honor, sent out a call to the men of Detroit, proclaiming "the fair fame of your city is at stake." Detroiters responded, many of them thoughtfully bringing clubs to the meeting; the rally was conducted without violence on July 22, and recruiting continued.

Children's Museum, 67 E. Kirby St. A Civil War display contains items that belonged to a Michigan soldier; among them are canteen, bootjack, bedding, uniform, and gun.

Detroit Historical Museum, Woodward at Kirby St. The exhibits include Civil War artifacts, equipment, and weapons. Michigan life during wartime is also a part of the display.

Detroit Public Library, 5401 Woodward, has the Burton Historical Collection, with many negatives of J. Jex Bardwell's Civil War photographs. Bardwell documented the home front, photographing war meetings, the training of infantry, the return of the 1st Michigan Infantry in August 1861, and the memorial service for President Lincoln in 1865. The collection, which also has the papers of Gov. Austin Blair and many other wartime figures, is for research only. Changing exhibits.

Fort Wayne Military Museum, 6325 W. Jefferson. The fort was used as training grounds and headquarters during the war. In May 1861, J. Jex Bardwell made an outstanding series of stereoscope views of the 1st and 2nd Michigan Infantry in training at this site. The cards, which sold for fifty cents each and are priceless now, were titled: "Coldwater Artillery," "Col. Israel Richardson and the Officers of the 2nd Regiment," "Dress Parade," etc., and are considered some of the finest photographs of the war period. The museum displays weapons, uniforms, equipment, and artifacts. A series of maps illustrates battles in which Michigan regiments participated, one for each year of the war. The fort has been restored to its look of the Civil War period. Displays are of military history from 1701 to 1890. The 83-acre complex includes original barracks, tunnels, a museum, and a military bridge.

Museum of African-American History, 301 Frederick Douglass. The Culture Center has artifacts and documents tracing the history of black people in America. One exhibit is "An Epic of Heroism: The Underground Railroad in Michigan 1837–1870."

Soldiers' and Sailors' Monument, in Cadillac Square, was designed by Randolph Rogers.

EAST LANSING, Ingham County. IS 96.

Michigan State University Museum has interpretive Civil War displays which are changed at intervals; exhibits include maps, models, military equipment, and many Civil War manuscripts.

ESCANABA, Delta County. US 41, State 35.

Delta County Historical Society, Ludington Park. Exhibits include medical supplies, photographic equipment, maps, photographs, and documents. Museum is open June to September only.

FORT WILKINS STATE PARK, Keweenaw County. US 41.

Fort Wilkins Museum, Copper Harbor, attempts to reproduce the typical prewar garrison. Much of the material, including weapons and utensils, was used by soldiers of the Civil War period.

GALESBURG, Kalamazoo County. IS 94.

Shafter Monument, Main and Battle Creek St., honors William Rufus Shafter who was born in a log cabin here in 1835, served in the Civil and Spanish-American wars, and was retired as major-general in 1901.

GRAND RAPIDS, Kent County. IS 96, 196.

Grand Rapids Public Museum, 54 Jefferson Ave. SE. Exhibits feature local participation in the war; uniforms, rifles, small arms, musical instruments, and lithographs. A maul used by Lincoln as a rail splitter is in the collection, also a silver cigar box given to the president by the actor John McCullough, and a piece of the vest worn by Lincoln at the time of his assassination.

HANOVER, Jackson County. Off State 60.

Hanover-Horton Area Historical Society, 105 Fairview St., has rare reed organs dating back to the Civil War.

HASTINGS, Barry County. State 37.

Barry County Memorial Museum, Charlton Park. Exhibits are displayed in cases located throughout the building. There are collections of clothing, weapons, miscellaneous equipment, and maps and documents.

KALAMAZOO, Kalamazoo County. IS 94, US 131. Travelers on the interstate highway of today may find it difficult to picture the Michigan seen by Auguste Laugel, a 30-year-old Frenchman who crossed the state during the Civil War: "Nothing catches the eye on this fertile plain . . . you pass at one bound all the phases of civilization; here fire slowly burns the last trunks of a part of the forest about to be put under cultivation; cows still stray about the pastures, full of china-asters and golden-rods . . . The first shelters are shanties . . . the emigrant, grown richer, builds a larger house, the woodwork is painted yellow or white, and green blinds are at every window . . . . The railway follows for a long time the sleeping waters of the harmonious Kalamazoo, which creeps along between woods of yellow maples. At nightfall the bare prairie assumes the aspect of a black and motionless lake, without reflections."

Kalamazoo Public Museum, 315 S. Rose St. Exhibits emphasize Michigan's role in the war; uniforms, guns, flags, documents, musical instruments, and photographic equipment. The draft box used in Kalamazoo is in the collection. On March 3, 1863, Congress had passed the draft act which put single men 20 to 45 years of age and married men 20 to 35 subject to call. A drafted man could hire a substitute or pay $300 for exemption. By 1865, Michigan had authorized counties to pay $100 in bounties for enlistees.

LANSING, Ingham County. IS 69, 96.
Michigan Library and Historical Museum, 717 W. Allegan St., is an impressive new center which opened in 1989. The Civil War gallery has permanent displays which include a full-size photo mural of the antislavery leader, Laura Haviland, who is holding slave manacles. Sojourner Truth also is given proper attention for her years of antislavery efforts. Battle flags, portraits, broadsides, and photographs are a part of the collection.
State Capitol, Capitol Ave. between Allegan and Ottawa St. On grounds is a statue of Michigan's war governor, Austin Blair, designed by Edward C. Potter, and monuments to the 1st Michigan Engineers and Mechanics Regiment and the 1st Michigan Sharpshooters Regiment.

LUDINGTON, Mason County. US 10, 31.
Rose Hawley Museum, 115 W. Loomis, has displays of 19th century settlers, effects and Civil War artifacts, and an extensive library available for research.

MANISTEE, Manistee County. US 31.
Manistee County Historical Museum, 425 River St. The museum has Confederate money, exchanged by pickets for tobacco, including some now-rare bills; a copy of the Wallpaper edition of the *Vicksburg Citizen* for July 2, 1863; documents, clothing items, equipment, and weapons. In the permanent collection, also, is the diary of Col. E. W. Muenscher, Ohio Volunteers, which is complete except for parts lost overboard on the Mississippi. Mrs. Virginia Stroemel, director, mourns the loss of several hundred letters written by the highly literate colonel who had a gift for description and a "fanatic regard for detail." The letters were destroyed by a short-sighted administrator of the estate on the grounds that they were "personal."

MARQUETTE, Marquette County. US 41.
Marquette County Historical Society Museum, 231 N. Front St. Weapons, diaries, newspapers, and G.A.R. items, including convention medals.

MARSHALL, Calhoun County. IS 69, 94.
Honolulu House, off IS 94, Marshall exit, on the Fountain Circle, was built in 1860 by the former U.S. consul to the Hawaiian Islands. Restored with period furnishings.
Marshall Historical Society, Honolulu House. Among exhibits is a fairly rare item, a pair of Civil War shoes. The society also has an exhibit in the town hall.
Triangle Park, east end of Michigan Ave. and Mansion St. Marker locates site of cabin of Adam Crosswhite, a fugitive slave. In 1847, Marshall citizens prevented his being returned south. This action helped to bring about passage of the Fugitive Slave Act of 1850.

MIDDLEVILLE, Barry County. State 37.
Historic Bowens Mills, 11691 Old Bowens Mills Rd., is an 1864 working water-powered grist and cider mill, now a State Historic Site. Mill buildings include the 1860 Bowens home.

MONROE, Monroe County. IS 75. George Armstrong Custer met Elizabeth Bacon, daughter of Judge Daniel Bacon, while he was visiting a married sister in Monroe. Miss Bacon turned her suitor down but later relented and they were married on February 28, 1864.
Custer Equestrian Statue, Elm Ave. and N. Monroe St., was designed by Edward C. Potter.
Monroe County Historical Museum, 126 S. Monroe. Displays include Civil War items, such as weapons, flags, medical kit; a large amount of the material pertains to Gen. George A. Custer.

MUSKEGON, Muskegon County. IS 196.
Evergreen Cemetery, Pine and Irwin St., has the grave of Jonathan Walker, who was arrested for helping fugitive slaves before the war. He was convicted by a federal court and the letters SS, for slave stealer, were branded on his hand. Whittier made the occurrence the subject of his poem, "The Man With the Branded Hand." A fellow abolitionist, Photius Fisk, erected the monument which marks the grave.
McKinley Monument, Webster Ave., between 3rd and 4th St. The figure of William McKinley was sculpted by Charles Henry Niehaus.
Muskegon County Museum, 430 W. Muskegon, has rifles, small arms, sabers, and musical instruments of the Civil War.

Soldiers' and Sailors' Monument, W. Clay Ave. between 3rd and 4th St., is the work of Joseph Carabelli. Statues are in four corners of the park; Lincoln and Farragut are by Charles Niehaus, Grant, and Sherman by J. Massey Rhind.

PONTIAC, Oakland County. IS 75.

Governor Moses Wisner Historic House, 401 Oakland Ave. Exhibits pertain to Pontiac's participation in the war at home and in the field. Many items relate to the 22nd Michigan Regiment, of which Wisner was colonel.

PORT HURON, St. Clair County. IS 69, 94, US 25, State 21.

Soldier's Monument, 1104 Grove Ave., was erected in 1893. At the base of the shaft are cannon used in the siege of Vicksburg.

PRESQUE ISLE, Presque Isle County. US 23.

Old Presque Isle Lighthouse and Museum, 5295 Grand Lake Rd., 23 miles north of Alpena, has rifles, cannon, sabers, miscellaneous equipment. Museum in keeper's restored home. The picturesque lighthouse was designed by Jefferson Davis in 1840. Visitors can climb hand-hewn steps to the top of the tower.

TRAVERSE CITY, Grand Traverse County. US 31.

Con Foster Museum, Clinch Park. Civil War dental tools are part of the collection which includes other weapons and documents.

MINNESOTA

When Minnesota became the 32nd state on May 11, 1858, the population was more than 150,000. Henry H. Sibley was elected first governor. In April 1861, Gov. Alexander Ramsey was in Washington when news came of the Fort Sumter surrender. The governor hastened to the War Department to offer 1,000 Minnesotans for service; these were the first Union troops offered for the Civil War. Acting Gov. Ignatius Donnelly issued a call for troops; the 1st Regiment was organized rapidly and reached the east in time to participate in the battle of Bull Run.

With more than 20,000 Minnesota men away from the state, the Sioux Nation went on the warpath. On August 18, 1862, they set out from the Lower Agency at Redwood Falls on a devastating raid across the Minnesota River. Soldiers from Fort Ridgely were ambushed and all but wiped out. The settlement of New Ulm was virtually destroyed and was evacuated for several weeks after the attack.

Lincoln came in for sharp criticism when he commuted the death sentence of all but 38 Indians when 400 were brought to trial and 303 condemned to death. Settlers were paid compensations from Sioux trust funds; title to reservation lands was revoked, and all payment of annuities ended.

The Minnesota Outdoor Recreation Resources Commission, in cooperation with the state historical society, highway department, and state parks conservation department, has developed and identified historic sites, adding museum and descriptive markers to aid self-guided tours.

BIRCH COULEE BATTLEFIELD, Renville County. US 71, 1½ miles north of Morton. Sioux Indians ambushed Minnesota troops commanded by Maj. Joseph R. Brown on September 2, 1862. Thirteen men were killed and many more wounded. Reinforcements were sent by Gen. Sibley on September 3, and the Indians withdrew. The area is now a state park. Interpretive markers have been rec-

ommended. A 52-foot granite shaft on State 19 at Morton commemorates the soldiers and citizens who fought in the battle. Another shaft nearby honors six Indians who remained loyal during the uprising.

CAMP RELEASE, Lac Qui Parle County. US 212. Site where the Sioux Indians released prisoners to Gen. H. H. Sibley on September 26, 1862. A 50-foot granite shaft marks the north edge of former parade ground where the women and children were set free. The area is now a state memorial wayside.

CANNON FALLS, Goodhue County. US 52, State 19.

City Cemetery has a granite shaft with statue of William Colvill, who led the 1st Minnesota Regiment at Gettysburg in 1863. It was erected in 1928.

FORT RIDGELY, Brown County. State 4, 5 miles south of Fairfax. The fort was the major military post associated with the Sioux uprising of 1862; its successful defense was a turning point in the Sioux War. On August 20, the post was attacked by some 400 Sioux Indians under Little Crow, and on August 22 by about twice that number. About 180 civilians and volunteers were able to hold the fort until the attackers withdrew. Sgt. John Jones and crew manned the few cannon expertly. The fort had been garrisoned by regular U.S. Army troops until the outbreak of the war when they were replaced by volunteers. Until the summer of 1862 it was a training camp for newly enlisted Union soldiers. In 1863 and 1864, the post again was used for training troops and as an embarkation point for western wagon trains. It was regarrisoned by army regulars in 1865. Most of the area is now within a state park. Archaeologists have uncovered eight building sites. The stone warehouse has been restored and houses a museum and assembly hall. A log powder magazine has been restored and the battlefield marked. In the cemetery southeast of the fort are monuments to Capt. John S.

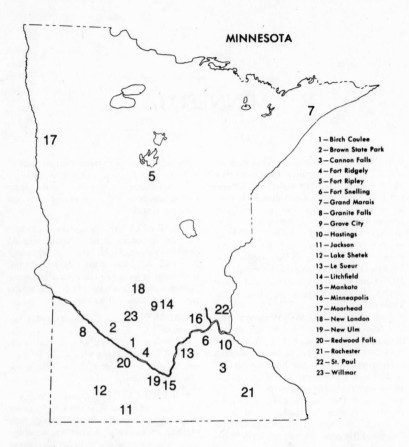

MINNESOTA

1 — Birch Coulee
2 — Brown State Park
3 — Cannon Falls
4 — Fort Ridgely
5 — Fort Ripley
6 — Fort Snelling
7 — Grand Marais
8 — Granite Falls
9 — Grove City
10 — Hastings
11 — Jackson
12 — Lake Shetek
13 — Le Sueur
14 — Litchfield
15 — Mankato
16 — Minneapolis
17 — Moorhead
18 — New London
19 — New Ulm
20 — Redwood Falls
21 — Rochester
22 — St. Paul
23 — Willmar

Marsh, commander of the fort, and the more than 20 soldiers who were ambushed and killed with Marsh at Redwood Ferry on August 18, 1862; to Mrs. Eliza Muller, wife of Dr. Alfred Muller, post surgeon (Mrs. Muller cared for the wounded during the siege); and to Chief Mouzoomaune and the Chippewa Indians who remained loyal during the uprising. There are 17 restored buildings. Costumed guides present a living history program. History center has a film and exhibits.

FORT RIPLEY, Crow Wing County. US 371, State 115. Marker on US 371 across Mississippi River from site. The state's second military post was established in 1848–1849. The site is on Infantry Rd., within the grounds of Camp Ripley. Visitors must stop at the administration building near the main gate. From 1861 to 1865, regular army troops were replaced by Minnesota volunteers. The 1st Minnesota Reg-

iment did frontier duty in June 1861. The 5th Minnesota built an additional stockade in 1862 when it was feared the Chippewa Indians would join the Sioux in revolt. Troops of the 7th Minnesota reinforced the post. Ruins of a brick powder magazine are all that remain of the garrison. Three steel-rifled cannon near the Camp Ripley administration building were presented to the 1st Minnestoa in 1862 by Henry S. Sanford, then U.S. minister to Belgium, in honor of the regiment's service at Bull Run and Ball's Bluff.

FORT SNELLING, Ramsey County. State 5, 55, in Fort Snelling State Park. State's first military post was garrisoned during the Civil War. After the Sioux uprising it served as an Indian prison camp for a time. Foundations have been located by excavations. There is a museum in the Round Tower, which formerly served as a lookout.

GRAND MARAIS, Cook County. US 61. Marker for site of William Colville homestead; he was colonel of the 1st Minnesota.

GRANITE FALLS, Yellow Medicine County. US 212.

Wood Lake Battlefield, 7 miles south on State 67. H. H. Sibley defeated Little Crow here on September 23, 1862, and was commissioned a brigadier general soon after. The engagement ended the Minnesota uprising. Granite shaft is in memory of seven soldiers who died here. Battle Marker on State 67, north of Echo. Upper Sioux Agency marker on State 67, southeast of Granite Falls.

GROVE CITY, Meeker County. US 12, State 4. Marker on State 4, 3 miles south of town.

Sioux Uprising Monument, at Acton, southwest of town. Shaft is on site of Howard Baker cabin where the uprising began in August 1862. This marker may be relocated, as it stands on lawn of a farmhouse.

HASTINGS, Dakota County. US 61.

William Le Duc House, 1629 Vermillion St., was built during the Civil War by Gen. Le Duc, who had attended Lancaster Academy in Ohio with Gen. William Sherman and served under Sherman, McClellan, Hooker, and Thomas in the war. The octagonal ice house is an unusual feature. Restored.

HUTCHINSON, McLeod County. State 15. The town was founded by three abolitionist brothers, Asa, John, and Judson Hutchinson, who traveled widely and sang antislavery songs from the 1840s through the war. The town charter called for women's suffrage, temperance, and the abolition of slavery. When the Sioux attacked here during the wartime uprising, a farmer killed their leader, Chief Little Crow. A statue marks the spot where he was killed, on Main Street.

JACKSON, Jackson County. IS 90, US 16.

Ashley Park, State St. and Riverside Dr., has monument to 19 settlers killed by the Sioux in 1857 and 1862.

JOSEPH R. BROWN STATE MEMORIAL WAYSIDE PARK, Renville County. County Road 15, about 1 mile east of junction with County Road 9, 8 miles south of Sacred Heart. Former Indian agent, editor, politician, and inventor, Joseph Brown was in New York on business pertaining to his invention of a steam wagon when his Sioux wife and 12 children learned of the Indian uprising. Mrs. Brown, in an ox-drawn wagon, with her family and neighbors, headed for Fort Ridgely and was overtaken by Sioux warriors who threatened to kill the group. Mrs. Brown threatened them in their own language that the wrath of her Sisseton relatives would strike the war party if any harm befell her family. The Browns were taken to the home of Chief Little Crow and later were set free at Camp Release. While they were away the 19-room Brown home, known as "Farther and Gay Castle," was ransacked and burned by Indians. A plaque and ruins of the house mark the site.

LAKE SHETEK STATE PARK, Murray County. State 30. Monument to settlers slain in the Sioux uprising of August 1862 was erected in 1925.

LE SUEUR, Le Sueur County. US 169.

Mayo House, 118 N. Main St. Dr. William W. Mayo cared for the sick and wounded who survived the Sioux uprising. In 1863 he served as examining surgeon of the 1st Minnesota district board, examining prospective Civil War soldiers. Guided tours begin in the History Center next door at 112 N. Main St.

LITCHFIELD, Meeker County. US 12. Monument in Ness Lutheran Cemetery, southwest of town, marks mass grave of five settlers killed in Sioux uprising.

G.A.R. Hall and Meeker County Museum, 308 N. Marshall St., has Civil War memorabilia and research materials.

MANKATO, Blue Earth County. US 169.

Blue Earth County Historical Society Museum, 606 S. Broad St., has historical displays featuring Indian and pioneer artifacts.

Sioux Execution Site, N. Front and E. Main St. Thirty-eight Sioux warriors were put to death here for their part in the great uprising which took the lives of 640 settlers. The mass execution took place on December 26, 1862. A Fort Snelling military tribunal had sentenced 303 Indians to death; Lincoln had commuted the sentence of all but the 38. Stone marker on site.

MINNEAPOLIS, Hennepin County. IS 35W, 94, US 10, 2.

Hennepin County Historical Society, 2303 3rd Ave. S. Historical exhibits feature pioneer days in Minnesota.

NEW LONDON, Kandiyohi County. US 71, State 23.

Lebanon Swedish Cemetery has monument to 13 members of the Anders P. Lundborg and Anders P. Broberg families, killed by the Sioux in the August 1862 uprising.

NEW ULM, Brown County. US 14, State 15.

Brown County Historical Museum, Center St. and Broadway, has relics of the great Sioux uprising of 1862 which reached its high point in New Ulm.

Milford Monument, 8 miles northwest of town on Brown County Road 4, has names of 52 victims of Sioux attack that took place on the night of August 18, 1862.

Monument, Center St., commemorates the two Sioux uprising battles fought here, August 19 and August 23, 1862. Forty persons were killed, many wounded.

REDWOOD FALLS, Redwood County. US 71, State 19.

Lower Sioux Agency and Interpretive Center, ½ mile east on County Rd. 26 from junction with County Rd. 29. The Sioux uprising began here. Exhibits and audio-visual programs depict the history of the eastern Dakotah Indi-ans since the 1700s. An 1861 stone warehouse remains at the site. Granite markers indicate other buildings.

ST. PAUL, Ramsey County. IS 35E, 94, US 61, 52.

Minnesota Historical Society, 690 Cedar St. Historical exhibits.

Ramsey House, 265 S. Exchange St. Home of Gov. Alexander Ramsey, who offered the first troops to the Union Army in Washington in April 1861. Guided tours available.

Sibley House, 218 River St. in Mendota, 6½ miles southwest via State 5, 55. Home of Henry H. Sibley, first governor and Civil War general. Period furnishings, museum.

WILLMAR, Kandiyohi County. US 71.

Vikor Lutheran Cemetery, north of town, has a red granite monument marking the grave of Guri Endreson Rosseland, a heroine of the Sioux uprising.

MISSISSIPPI

Admitted to the Union in 1817 as the 20th state, Mississippi was the second to secede. A Jackson convention adopted the Ordinance of Secession on the morning of January 9, 1861. No actual fighting took place on Mississippi land during the first year of the war, with the exception of the Ship Island occupation by Union forces in December and a raid on Biloxi by the Union navy on December 31. The battle of Shiloh in April 1862 brought the war across the state line. Confederates withdrew to Corinth where another engagement was fought. From that time until May 4, 1865, when Gen. Richard Taylor surrendered his decimated forces to Gen. Edward Canby, there were few days without bitter fighting. The fall of Vicksburg, a stronghold known as the "Gibraltar of the Confederacy," was a major turning point of the war.

Although the 1860 census showed a total of 70,295 white males of military age, the state sent 80,000 men, boys, and elders to the war; no more than 20,000 returned. Jefferson Davis, Mississippi planter, soldier, and statesman, was the Confederacy's only president; five Mississippians were major generals, 25 were brigadier generals. The Reconstruction period was a time of continuing struggle and hardship marked by violence. In March 1867 the state was put under military rule. In February 1870 Mississippi was readmitted to the Union.

ABBEVILLE, Lafayette County. State 7. The town was the scene of two skirmishes in 1864. Two years earlier it provided the background for errors large and small. At one point in the back-and-forth struggle for north Mississippi, Gen. Grant—based at Oxford—wired Col. Robert Murphy at Holly Springs that Confederate cavalrymen were to spend the night at Rocky Ford; therefore Murphy should send Union cavalry to locate the camp and stop the Confederates from advancing upon the Union stronghold at Holly Springs. Murphy promptly ordered Lt. Col. Quincy McNeil of the 2nd Illinois Cavalry to proceed to Rocky Ford; unfortunately, neither Murphy nor McNeil had the least notion where that might be. By the time they had telegraphed Grant, "Where is Rocky Ford?" and got back the reply that it was 20 miles east of Abbeville on the Tallahatchie, Confederate cavalrymen were closing in on Holly Springs from the east.

When Gen. Van Dorn's Confederates raided Holly Springs sometime later, Grant sent several infantry regiments from Oxford to Abbeville by rail to defend the Tallahatchie bridge. A purely private mishap befell Sam Jackson of the 1st Mississippi Cavalry when camped near town. The boys were in the habit of hobbling their horses and turning them loose to graze in the fields. Sam's sorrel pony wandered into a millpond to have a cool drink but, with his head tied close to his forefoot, drowned before anyone could rescue him. Sam bemoaned: "Now, isn't this a hell of a tale to write home to Pap?"

ABERDEEN, Monroe County. US 45, State 8.

Reuben Davis Home, Commerce St. west of railroad station. Gen. Davis was first a Whig, then a Union Democrat, then an ardent secessionist. He was a member of the Confederate Congress and continued active in state affairs after the war. He was defeated in a congressional race in 1876, where he was the National Party candidate. Late in life he wrote *Recollections of Mississippi and Mississippians,* an important contribution to state history.

Monument to the Confederate Dead was erected by the United Daughters of the Confederacy in 1901. It was sculpted in Italian marble in Italy at a cost of more than $1,000. Names of Monroe County soldiers are inscribed on the sandstone base.

Old Cemetery, Cemetery Road, has a plot containing graves of 30 unknown Confederate soldiers who were fatally wounded in the battle of Egypt, Mississippi, where Union forces under Gen. Grierson defeated Confederate troops on December 28, 1864.

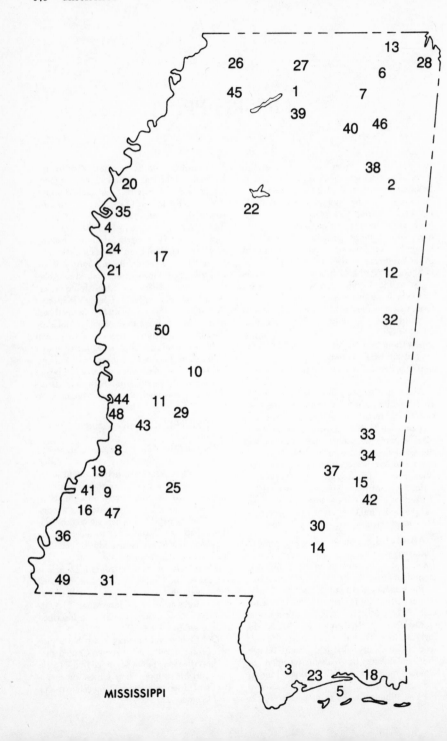

26 27 13
        6 28
45 1 7
   39 40 46
      38
       2
20
35
4
24 17 12
21
        32
50
10
44 11
48 29 33
43 34
8 37
19 15
41 9 25 42
16 47
36 30
      14
49 31
      3 23 18
        5

BEAUVOIR, Harrison County. US 90, on Gulf. Marker on highway. The last home of Jefferson Davis. The 1850 house and pavilions have been handsomely restored. The spacious grounds are landscaped. Many original furnishings remain. The Confederate Museum, in the old Veteran's Hospital, has war relics and Davis memorabilia. The cemetery has 700 Confederate graves, including the Tomb of the Unknown Soldier of the Confederate States of America.

BEULAH, Bolivar County. State 1.

Doro Plantation, marker on highway, 1 mile south of town. The home of Charles Clark, governor from 1863 to 1865, was received as a fee in an Indian lawsuit in the 1840s. Gov. Clark's arrest on a charge of "high treason" at a special session of the legislature in May 1865 touched off hostilities of the Reconstruction era. He is buried on the plantation.

BILOXI, Harrison County. IS 10, US 90.

Biloxi Lighthouse, US 90 and Porter Ave. near the end of Benachi Ave. This famous landmark was painted black after the assassination of Lincoln. Though legend was that the black paint was to commemorate the tragic event, later accounts say it was because of rust.

Church of the Redeemer, Bellman St. and E. Beach Blvd. Jefferson Davis worshiped and served as vestryman in a building which had four memorial windows honoring the Davis family and a pew marked with a silver plate. This was "smashed to bits" in 1969, as a witness relates, by Hurricane Camille, but some of the window bits were rescued and reconstructed for use in the rebuilt church.

BOONEVILLE, Prentiss County, US 45, State 30. An engagement between Gen. J. R. Chalmers's cavalry and Sheridan's horsemen took place here on July 1, 1862. A marker at the junction of US 45 and State 2 indicates the site of a Council of War which was held on the night of June 9, 1864, when Gens. S. D. Lee and Nathan Bedford Forrest met to plan the battle of Brices Crossroads.

Citizens' Cemetery has a monument to Confederate soldiers buried here. Two were killed in the Booneville battle; most of the more than 70 others were with Beauregard at Corinth.

BRICES CROSSROADS NATIONAL BATTLEFIELD SITE, Lee County. State 370, 6 miles west of Baldwyn and US 45. On June 10, 1864, Nathan Bedford Forrest won a tactical victory against larger Union forces under Gen. S. D. Sturgis, forcing them to withdraw to Memphis. Markers on the one-acre battlefield identify landmarks by the text and maps. Additional information may be obtained from the superintendent, Natchez Trace Parkway, Tupelo. The historic site is maintained by the National Park Service and is open daily. Adjacent to the site, a cemetery has 102 Confederate graves, each identified and marked in 1989.

BRIERFIELD, Warren County. US 61. Marker on highway south of Vicksburg at road leading to Palmyra Island. Hurricane and Brierfield were plantations belonging to Joe and Jefferson Davis at Davis Bend, now Davis Island. Accessible only by boat and airplane. (*Also see* MOUND BAYOU.)

BRUINSBURG, Claiborne County. US 61. Marker on highway in Port Gibson is at turn of road to Bruinsburg. Gen. Grant landed forces here, April 30, 1863. The day before, a detachment of Grant's men had temporarily kidnapped a local black to use as a guide to Port Gibson. When Grant, pointing to a map, inquired about a road, his informant said he wouldn't advise using that one because it was "plumb full of backwater." He advised the general to try the Rodney Road, which had the best houses and plantations in all the country. As part of the centennial commemoration of the war, Claiborne County erected ten historical markers along the line of Grant's march. These give the story of the Federal invasion that led to the siege of Vicksburg. Among them, in this area: the landing at Bruinsburg, the march past Windsor mansion (now in ruins because of an 1890 fire, though used for the motion picture *Raintree County* as a war relic), and the fight for the Bruinsburg Rd. during the battle of Port Gibson. A 20-car ferry operates from St. Joseph, Louisiana, to a point near Bruinsburg.

CANTON, Madison County. IS 55, US 51. The city was occupied by both Confederate and Union forces during the course of the conflict. Late in May 1863 about 12,300 Confederates were camped here.

Confederate Cemetery contains graves of 350 soldiers, mostly from the Army of Tennessee, who were killed or mortally wounded at Shiloh or Corinth. A monument here commemorates the servants who followed the men of Harvey's Scouts during the war.

Luckett Home, E. Academy, was headquarters of Gen. Joseph Johnston.

Mosby Home, Center St., was used by Sherman and Union mules.

CHAMPION HILL, Hinds County. Marker on US 80 at Bolton. Site of the most severe engagement in the Vicksburg campaign, May 16, 1863. In contributing to an article on Confederate cemeteries forty years after the battle, the Hon. H. Clay Sharkey, Confederate veteran, said: "In the battle of Baker's Creek, or Champion Hill, our dead were buried by the Federals in trenches, no separate graves being made. This spot has been so long neglected that there is nothing now discernible by which the burial trenches can be identified."

COLUMBUS, Lowndes County. US 45, 82.

Billups Home, southeast corner 9th St. and 3rd Ave. N, was modeled after Jefferson's Monticello when built by Gov. James Whitfield about 1854. During a session of the refugee legislature in 1863, Jefferson Davis was a guest here. Legend says he was serenaded by the townspeople.

Blewett-Harrison-Lee House, 7th St. between 3rd and 4th Ave. N. Marker on N. 7th St. The home of Lt. Gen. Lee, legislator, historian, and first president of A & M College, is now a museum exhibiting the general's personal belongings and papers. Gen. Lee, who was born in Charleston, South Carolina, was one of two officers sent by Gen. Beauregard to demand the surrender of Fort Sumter. He served

in both the eastern and western theaters of the war; his last campaign was in North Carolina, where he was paroled with Gen. Joseph Johnston's army.

Christian Church, northwest corner of 6th St. and 2nd Ave. N. The refugee legislature was housed in this small Gothic Revival church next to the courthouse. The Senate met here while the House of Representatives convened in the courthouse.

C.S.A. Arsenal, 10th Ave. N. Marker. The legislature came to Columbus soon after Jackson fell into Federal hands. In 1862 the arsenal employed more than 1,000 persons. Later, one of the buildings became the site of Union Academy, first free public school for blacks in Columbus.

First United Methodist Church, Main at 6th St., was begun in 1860, building interrupted by the war. Parts of tin roof were used to provide canteens. Building later served as hospital.

Friendship Cemetery, formerly Odd Fellows Cemetery, 4th St. at 13th Ave. S. A onetime park was converted into a cemetery with burials of Federal and Confederate soldiers killed at the battle of Shiloh. Confederate Decoration Day began here on April 26, 1866.

Kenneth Gatchell Home, 2nd Ave. at 15th St. S., was used as a prison, with its French doors bricked over.

Taynor, 3rd Ave. N., was the home of Rev. Thomas Cox Teasdale, a friend to both Lincoln and Jefferson Davis during the Civil War.

Whitehall, 3rd St. S and 6th Ave. S, is an 1843 mansion that once occupied the entire block. It served as a Confederate hospital during the war.

Visit the Chamber of Commerce, 318 7th St. N, for narrative maps of a driving tour past many historic homes. Sites are marked with blue and white directions.

CORINTH, Alcorn County. US 45, 72. Marker at junction of US 45 and State 2, for the battle of Corinth of October 3-4, 1862.

Confederate Park, Battery Robinett, Polk and Linden streets, has a monument to Col. William Rogers of the 2nd Texas, who was killed attacking the fort. Restored.

C.S.A. Rifle Pit, marker on State 2 at 7th St. The pit, one of a series built in 1862 as a second line of defense against the Federals advancing from Shiloh, has a circular design and is about 50 feet in diameter.

Curlee House, 301 Childs St., was used as headquarters for both sides in the Civil War. Confederate generals Braxton Bragg and Earl

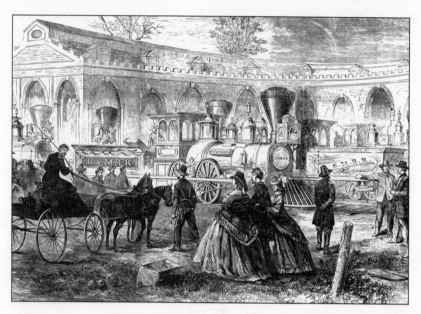

Locomotives built at Vicksburg by Federal soldiers.

Van Dorn resided here in 1862. Later Union general Halleck was there. The Greek Revival dwelling is furnished in period.

Grant's Headquarters, marker on US 45. The Elgin House, at southeast corner of Fillmore and Bunch St., served as Union quarters. In *The Lost Account of the Battle of Corinth,* edited by Monroe F. Cockrell, an eyewitness of the events noted: "Into the very heart of town rushed the Confederates, driving the Federals before them from house to house. They soon passed Rosecrans' headquarters, which were at the house now occupied as a residence by Mr. Fred Elgin. Onward they swept to the Tishomingo House at the railroad crossing. Near this point the brave Col. W. H. Moore, of the 43rd Mississippi, commanding Green's brigade, fell pierced by a bullet and mortally wounded. The Confederates had by this time become badly scattered and were in no condition to meet the attack made upon them by Sullivan's fresh brigade. . . . Broken and disordered the Confederates . . . began to fall back, slowly and stubbornly firing backward as they retired."

Johnston's Headquarters, marker on US 45 at Fillmore St. Gen. Albert S. Johnston stayed at Rose Cottage, the home of Mr. and Mrs.

W. M. Inge, before the battle of Shiloh. His body was brought here to lie in state after the battle.

Jones Boarding House, 815 Waldron St. Site of a temporary Confederate prison.

National Cemetery, 1 mile southwest of courthouse, on Meiggs St. More than 6,000 Union soldiers are buried here, casualties of the fighting in and around Corinth.

Polk Headquarters, southeast corner of Fillmore and Bunch St. The A. K. Weaver home was occupied by Gen. Leonidas Polk when the Federals invaded the town.

ELLISVILLE, Jones County. IS 59. The question of whether or not Jones County seceded with the rest of the state has entertained or annoyed countless outsiders ever since 1861. Alexander L. Bondurant, writing on the ticklish subject in 1898, furnished a sample of the supposed Jones County Ordinance of Secession: "Whereas, the State of Mississippi, for reasons which appear justifiable, has seen fit to withdraw from the Federal Union; and, Whereas, We, the citizens of Jones County, claim the same right, thinking our grievances are sufficient by reason of an unjust law passed by the Confederate States of America forcing us to go into distant parts, etc. . . . ." After which, Bondurant quoted a number of persons who attested the whole matter was a fiction and that Jones County sent as many men to the service as might be expected. Both sides of the controversy seem to have agreed that an area of rural folk who had no slaves did protest what they construed as a "planters' war," and that some of those eligible for military service took to the swamps to avoid enlistment.

ENTERPRISE, Clarke County. IS 59, US 11. Marker on highway ½ mile north of town. The town served during the war as the location of a hospital and camp for exchanged Confederate prisoners and the temporary refuge for the state government. W. O. Hart, son of an officer of the 8th Louisiana Artillery, recalled that as a boy in 1861, stationed at Enterprise: ". . . we were located in an abandoned schoolhouse. This building was so large that tents were put in it for sleeping quarters. . . . It was here that I saw baseball played for the first time. My father, who had been an active amateur baseball player in New Orleans, organized two teams, which played in the large grounds near the schoolhouse."

FAYETTE, Jefferson County. US 61, State 28.
Fayette Memorial Park. Park and monument are dedicated to the memory of Confederate soldiers.

FORT PEMBERTON, Leflore County. US 82. Marker on highway at Greenwood, near US 49E turnoff. Site of fort at which Adm. D. D. Porter's gunboats, en route to Vicksburg early in 1863, were halted by shore batteries and by the sunken hulk of the *Star of the West* in the river channel.

GAUTIER, Jackson County. (Pronounced Go-*chay*). IS 10, US 90. Marker on highway about 2½ miles from town indicating the site of Adm. David Glasgow Farragut's boyhood home about 2 miles north. Not long ago Wes Lawrence, a Cleveland newspaperman, inquired at the nearest crossroads trading center for exact directions to Farragut's home. No one had ever heard of it and one gentleman, scratching his head, said, "Tell you the truth, I don't believe I am acquainted with the gentleman." The admiral's father was the first justice of the peace for Pascagoula. There is a romantic legend that an orphan girl living with the family first cursed the land and then drowned herself in Farragut Lake because David did not return her love. Crop failures have been attributed to her.

GRAND GULF MILITARY PARK, Claiborne County. Seven miles northwest of US 61 at Port Gibson. Union Adm. David Dixon Porter once said, "Grand Gulf is the strongest place on the Mississippi." Point of Rock is the highest elevation in the area; the Confederates fortified this vantage point with Fort Cobun, 40 feet above water level, and established Fort Wade about ½ mile from the river. Grand Gulf was shelled and partially burned in the spring of 1862 and again in April 1863. The military park, opened in 1962, has two well-preserved forts and some of the best preserved trenches and gun emplacements still in existence. A museum has displays, maps, and models.

GREEN GROVES, Coahoma County. State 1. Marker on highway for the 1,900-acre plantation home of Gen. Nathan B. Forrest.

GRENADA, Grenada County. IS 55, US 51. Marker on US 51 at intersection with State 8. Federal plans to attack were stopped at this point by Gen. Van Dorn's raid on Holly Springs, December 1862. In the fall of 1862, Gen. Pemberton made his headquarters here.
Confederate Cemetery has 160 unknown soldiers and one whose name is given as "----- Jacoby."
Confederate Fort, marker on US 51 at Grenada Dam. Main defensive position on the Yalobusha River line occupied by Gen. Pemberton against Grant's forces in the fall of 1862.
Price's Headquarters, 217 Margin St. When Gen. Sterling Price occupied the Bruce Newsome home, President Jefferson Davis reviewed Pemberton's army here.
Walthall Home, College Blvd., opposite Grenada College. The home of Edward Cary Walthall, who first enlisted as a lieutenant in the 15th Mississippi Regiment, later was elected colonel of the 29th Mississippi; in June 1864 he was made major general. After the war, he served in the U.S. Senate.

GULFPORT, Harrison County. IS 10, US 90. Fort Massachusetts is located on west Ship Island, 10 miles offshore, in an area designated *Gulf Islands National Seashore,* comprising 135,000 acres. Boats for the island leave Gulfport and Biloxi twice daily. The U.S. War Department began construction of the fort in 1858; 48 large cannon were shipped from Pittsburgh late in 1860. The outbreak of war left the Union garrison isolated; they partially destroyed the fort hoping to prevent Confederates from taking possession. Southern forces occupied and rearmed the garrison in July, and evacuated and fired it in September. Gen. Benjamin Butler and a garrison of about 7,000 Union troops moved in at year's end and named the fort for Butler's home state. It was used as a prison for captured Confederates.

HAMPTON PLANTATION, Washington County. Marker at intersection of State 1 and 446. The part-time residence of Gen. Wade Hampton III. The general, who served throughout the war, lost much of his South Carolina property during Sherman's march through the Carolinas. This Mississippi plantation was purchased by the Hampton family in 1840.

HAZLEHURST, Copiah County. IS 55, US 51. Marker on highway in center of town, which was raided by Gen. Benjamin Grierson and his cavalry in 1863.

HERNANDO, De Soto County. IS 55. At the home of Confederate Col. T. W. White (known later as the Farrington Home), both Confederate and Federal prisoners were exchanged. The Baptist Cemetery and the Spring Hill Cemetery have Confederate graves.

HOLLY SPRINGS, Marshall County. US 78, center of town, has marker. Grant's southern advance was halted 48 miles south of here by Gen. Van Dorn's raid of December 1862. Van Dorn destroyed Grant's winter stores and took about 1,500 prisoners. Before the war ended the town had endured 62 Union raids. Many historic homes are open during an annual spring pilgrimage.

Clapp-Fant Place, 221 Salem Ave., was the home of Judge J. W. Clapp, a member of the Confederate Congress. Reportedly the judge had a price on his head but twice eluded capture. Once he escaped through the orchard while his son held the enemy at the front of the house by offering them buttermilk; again under pursuit, the judge, a small man, climbed to the attic, crept along the eaves and hid in the capital of a Corinthian pillar. A. M. West lived here after the war when Judge Clapp moved to Memphis. West had served as commissary, quartermaster, and paymaster of the Confederate army.

Grant's Headquarters, 330 Salem Ave. Grant occupied a home designed like a Swiss chalet. Marker on Salem Avenue.

Hull House, southeast corner of E. Falconer Ave. and Randolph St. The former town house of Maj. Dabney Hull, later a part of the Mississippi Synodical College. Capt. Edward H. Crump, the major's nephew, was sitting on the veranda, with his horse tied nearby, when he heard a shout, "The Yankees are coming!" Mrs. Hull invited Ed and his horse into the parlor and thus saved them both.

Marshall County Historical Museum, College and Randolph streets, has Civil War artifacts and a military uniform collection.

Methodist Church, southeast corner Van Dorn Ave. and Spring St. Grant stabled his mules in the basement, after thoughtfully removing the stained glass windows for safekeeping. The windows have been replaced. During the war, court sessions were held in the church basement after the courthouse had been burned by Union troops.

Ord Headquarters, 411 Salem Ave. Gen. Edward Otho Cresap Ord, a veteran Indian fighter and career officer, occupied the home of Dr. Charles Bonner after the war, while Ord commanded the 4th Military District.

Polk Place, 300 Craft St., was built in the 1830s by Thomas Polk, brother of Confederate Gen. Leonidas Polk, who was known as the "Fighting Bishop."

Presbyterian Church, northwest corner of S. Memphis St. and Gholson Ave. Soon after the church's dedication the Federal army arrived and used the lower floor for a stable.

The Rufus Jones House, 800 E. Falconer Ave. When Van Dorn raided the city, a Union surgeon was quartered here with his family. The doctor supposedly disappeared when the troops dashed in, his wife mourned his absence loudly, and one of the Jones's boys advised her not to be scared: "*Our* soldiers don't fight *women.*" When she explained she was concerned not for herself but for her husband, her son added that Confederate soldiers didn't fight doctors either.

Strickland House, 800 Van Dorn Ave., was often visited by Jefferson Davis. When Confederates recaptured the town, the owners of the home are supposed to have hidden a Yankee officer to repay him for not allowing his fellow officers to convert the house into a hospital.

Walter Place, 331 W. Chulahoma Ave. Mrs. Grant awaited the general in this house when Van Dorn captured the city; she asked him to protect the privacy of her room, thereby saving her husband's papers. Grant, in return, made the house off-limits for Union soldiers when the town was retaken by the North. Thus he created an oasis for Confederates slipping through town.

IUKA, Tishomingo County. US 72. Marker on highway at entrance to Minerals Springs Park. The battle of Iuka took place on September 19, 1862. Historian Earl Schenck Miers has dubbed it the "Battle of the Wrong Wind."

The wind that day blew the battle sounds away from Gen. Ord in the field and from Grant, waiting at Burnsville, so that Rosecrans without support met the Confederates under Gen. Sterling Price and paid heavily in casualties. Confederate Gen. Henry Little was killed in the fighting, which continued until dark. Nearly all homes and buildings of the town were converted into hospitals in the aftermath of the battle. Dead were separated by uniform color and buried in trenches. About 300 Confederates, half of them Texans, the rest Missourians and Arkansans, were buried in Shady Grove Cemetery. Union soldiers were reburied in the National Cemetery, Corinth. C.S.A. Gens. Price, Forrest, Kelly, Van Dorn, and Whitfield, and U.S. Gens. Grant, Rosecrans, Hurlbut, and Ord had quarters in the town at some time during the war.

Brinkley Home, Eastport St., served as Grant's headquarters.

Coman House, Quitman St., opposite courthouse, was the home of Maj. J. M. Coman, whose daughter married John M. Stone. Stone, who lived here until his death in 1900, was active in the Reconstruction period, becoming governor in 1876.

Confederate Marker, in front of courthouse, commemorates soldiers killed in the battle of Iuka.

Matthews House was on southwest corner of Main and Quitman St. and served as Gen. Forrest's headquarters. During the battle of Iuka, women, children, and men too old to fight gathered in the basement. An elderly man went forth with a white sheet nailed to a broomstick as a truce flag to ask Gen. Rosecrans to protect the women and children of Iuka.

JACKSON, Hinds County. IS 55, 20. Marker on US 80 at west city limits for the state capital, which was originally known as LeFleur's Bluff. It was chosen for the seat of government in 1821 and named for Andrew Jackson. The first battle of Jackson was fought May 14, 1863, when Union forces led by Gen. Sherman occupied the city. After the fall of Vicksburg, the city was again besieged July 10–16, 1863, and so nearly destroyed, again by Sherman's men, it was known as Chimneyville. The governor's mansion and a few private homes were not burned. Sherman said that for 30 miles around the city the land was "terrible to contemplate." The city was occupied twice by Federals in 1864—once in February and again in July.

Battlefield Park, formerly known as Winter Woods, Langley St. and Terry Rd. Earthwork trenches and cannon.

City Hall, S. President St., 4 blocks south of capitol. One of the few buildings to escape destruction in 1863. A now vanished cupola served as a Confederate lookout. The building served as a hospital during the war.

Fortification Street, running east and west through the modern section of town, was the line of Confederate defense. The line extended west between Raymond and Clinton roads.

Governor's Mansion, Capitol St., was built in 1842 and served as headquarters for Sherman and Grant during the war. Guided tours.

Greenwood Cemetery, N. West St. at Davis St. Two Confederate brigadier generals, four colonels, and more than 100 soldiers are buried here. Also buried here is John R. Lynch, secretary of state after the war.

Manship Home, 420 E. Fortification St. Confederate defense fortifications crossed the front lawn. A fire bell on the lawn was the only bell in the city to escape being melted for ammunition during the war. It was rung for curfew, funerals, fires, and battle news. This was the home of Civil War mayor C. H. Manship. Period furnishings.

The Oaks, 823 N. Jefferson St., was occupied by Gen. Sherman during the siege in 1863. Period furnishings.

Old Capitol, State and Capitol St., houses the Mississippi State Historical Museum. The building, which was completed in 1840, has been restored. The Secession Convention took place in this building, and here Jefferson Davis made his last public address to the legislature in 1884. The State Historical Museum in the building has Civil War and Davis memorabilia, and dioramas and offers self-guiding tours.

Site of Bowman Hotel, Amite St. between N. State and North St. The hotel, burned between the May and July 1863 occupation of Jackson, was a favorite gathering place for state politicians.

State Capitol, Mississippi and President St., houses the state hall of fame and the state library as well as legislative chambers and supreme court.

LIBERTY, Amite County. State 24-48. The town, founded in 1809, claims to have the first Confederate monument in the state. It was made in New Orleans, brought part of the way by oxen, and erected in 1871, at a cost of more than $3,000. Four tablets are inscribed with the names of Amite County soldiers who died in the war. Marker on State 28.

MACON, Noxubee County. US 45. Marker

on highway at north city limits. J. G. Deupree, a member of the Noxubee Squadron of the 1st Mississippi Cavalry, recalled the intensity of war spirit in Macon after Lincoln's election: ". . . a meeting was held in the Court House. After some discussion, Hon. J. L. Hunter, past sixty years of age, . . . undertook to organize the troopers. . . . Meeting the volunteers in the open field not far from Purdy's Corner, he soon brought order out of chaos, drilling the men briefly in evolutions by fours and platoons. After marching several times up and down Main Street, he halted the company, had them dismount, hitch horses, and repair to the Town Hall for the election of officers. The old Captain declined to allow his own name to be voted on . . . by unanimous vote, Judge H. William Foote was elected Captain with three efficient lieutenants, three sergeants, and four corporals . . . also, a bugler, Mr. J. J. Hunter, who . . . could sound a cow's horn to perfection." When Union forces burned Jackson, Macon became the temporary capital. Gov. Clark set up his offices in the Calhoun Institute, then a private school for girls. The legislature met here for two sessions.

Confederate Cemetery has the graves of 300 soldiers, 274 of whom have been identified. Buried here as well are 216 unidentified Union soldiers.

MARION, Lauderdale County. US 45. Marker on highway for C.S.A. Cemetery. Seventy unknown Confederate soldiers who died at field hospitals after various battles from Shiloh to Vicksburg are buried here.

MERIDIAN, Lauderdale County. IS 20, 59, US 11, 80. Marker on US 80 at east city limits. At the outbreak of war, the town was made a military camp and division headquarters. State records were brought here for safekeeping in 1863; the town served as temporary capital for a month. Sherman's troops destroyed the town in February 1864.

Merrehope, 905 Martin Luther King, Jr., Drive, one of four homes saved.

MOUND BAYOU, Bolivar County. US 61. Marker on highway in front of hospital. The town was settled by ex-slaves. One of the founders, Isaiah T. Montgomery, bought the plantation of his former master, Joe Davis, at Davis Bend and lived there until he moved to Mound Bayou. He was the only black delegate to the Constitutional Convention of 1890.

NATCHEZ, Adams County. US 61. A part of Flag Officer Farragut's fleet moved up the Mississippi in the spring of 1862 demanding the surrender of river towns. Cmdr. James S. Palmer sent a note to the city of Natchez, but no one would accept it. Palmer went ashore with seamen, marines, and a pair of howitzers. Two council members appeared, accepted the note, departed, and brought back a reply from the mayor: "An unfortified city, an entirely defenseless people, have no alternative but to yield to an irresistible force, or uselessly to imperil innocent blood. Formalities are absurd in the face of such realities." Cmdr. Palmer thought that this arrogance, and a similar retort he'd received from Baton Rouge, were unmatched until he forwarded his surrender demands at Vicksburg. Military Gov. James L. Autry wrote in reply: "I have to state that Mississippians don't know, and refuse to learn, how to surrender to an enemy. If Commodore Farragut or Brigadier-General Butler can teach them, let them come and try." Vicksburg, to be sure, proved how costly it was to try, and its civic pride has remained as unscarred as—a Vicksburgian points out—the town of Natchez remained when the heat was on.

The Briars, west end Irvine Ave., facing the Mississippi River, was the home of Varina Howell, who married Jefferson Davis here in 1845.

The Burn, 712 N. Union St., served as Union hospital during the siege of Vicksburg.

D'Evereux, D'Evereux Drive, just off Business Route 84–61. Federal soldiers camped on the lawn, chopping down oaks and magnolias for kindling, but not disturbing the house.

Green Leaves, Washington and S. Rankin St., has autographed albums of Confederate generals and other Civil War memorabilia.

Lansdowne, Martin Luther King Rd., was invaded by Union raiders who slapped the mistress of the house for refusing to hand over the keys to the storage room. George Marshall of Lansdowne was wounded at Shiloh.

Longwood, Lower Woodville Rd. Construction was interrupted by the war. The ground floor was completed; upper floors remained unfinished. The story is that workmen left tools, paint cans, and brushes as they went off to answer the call to arms.

Magnolia Hall, Pearl at Washington, was damaged by the Union gunboat *Essex* in 1862. Costume museum.

Memorial Park, Auburn and Duncan Ave. Stephen Duncan, a slaveholder, was a Unionist whose beliefs alienated so many of his Confederate friends that he went north during the war and never returned to Natchez. His heirs gave the property to the city. It is maintained as a park and memorial.

Monmouth, John A. Quitman Pkwy., restored, has a Civil War museum.

Montaigne, Liberty Rd., was the home of Confederate Gen. William T. Martin. Local legend says Union troops used the drawing room as a stable, the grand piano as a feed box.

Ravenna, 601 S. Union St., was the home of Zuleika Metcalfe, who was arrested by Federal soldiers while she was smuggling supplies to the Confederates.

Rosalie, S. Broadway at Canal, served as Union headquarters in 1863. Soldiers camped on the lawn. Gen. Grant and his family later stayed here for a brief time. Mrs. Andrew Wilson, mistress of Rosalie, and her children remained in residence while Union Gen. Walter Q. Gresham and his family also occupied the house. The two families got on well enough, although Mrs. Wilson proved to be a member of the Confederate secret brigade and was later banished from her own house (after the friendly Greshams had moved on) and became a Confederate nurse.

Weymouth Hall, 1 Cemetery Rd., on a bluff overlooking the river, was occupied during the war but survived without harm. It has been restored and furnished in period. Tours available.

Visitor Information is available at Canal St. Depot, corner of Canal and State streets.

NEWTON, Newton County. US 80, State 15. On April 24, 1863, Col. Grierson's raiders attacked the Southern Railroad of Mississippi at Newton Station and then headed for Baton Rouge.

Doolittle C.S.A. Cemetery. Marker on US 80 north of town. About 100 Confederate soldiers are buried in the Doolittle family cemetery.

OKOLONA, Chickasaw County. US 45. Marker on highway at south city limits. The 1st Mississippi Cavalry was organized here by Col. James Gordon, an 1855 graduate of the University of Mississippi who armed and equipped the company at his own expense. The cost was $32,000. The town was raided three times. In the raid of December 1862, Confederate Col. C. R. Barteau was wounded in defending the town. Early in 1864, Federal troops burned the College Hospital and the depot, which contained 100,000 bushels of corn, then set fire to surrounding cornfields. In February, Gen. Nathan Forrest recaptured the town by a victory over Union forces under Gen. Smith, although Forrest's brother Jesse was mortally wounded by retreating Federals. The third successful Union raid occurred early in December 1864 when the town was virtually destroyed.

Confederate Cemetery, in the southwest section of town, has the graves of 1,000 soldiers who either were killed in the raids or died of disease.

OXFORD, Lafayette County. State 6, 7. Marker on State 6. The university town was chartered in 1837, burned by Federal troops in 1864. After the battle of Shiloh, the University of Mississippi buildings were used as a hospital. Students went to war as the University Grays. No major battles took place in the town, but it was partly burned in August 1864.

Isom Home, 1003 Jefferson Ave. The residence of Dr. T. D. Isom, who was chief surgeon at the university Confederate hospital.

Lamar House, 616 N. 14th St. The home of Lucius Quintus Cincinnatus Lamar, former university teacher who became Confederate Commissioner in Europe during 1862 and 1863.

Rowan Oak, Old Taylor Road, ½ mile south of town square, was the home of novelist William Faulkner, whose fictional Col. Sartoris was based on his great-grandfather, C.S.A. Col. William Falkner.

St. Peter's Cemetery, east end of Jefferson Ave., has the graves of many illustrious Southerners, among them: L. Q. C. Lamar, Dr. T. D. Isom, and A. B. Longstreet, author of *Georgia Scenes.*

University Museums, University Ave., at 5th St., have a permanent collection of more than 6,000 relics, including Civil War items.

University of Mississippi, University Ave. Students organized a company known as the University Grays. In the fall of 1861 only four students showed up for classes and the faculty resigned. Dr. A. J. Quinche was retained as custodian. A Minnesotan, Dr. Quinche had known the Grant family during years spent in Illinois. Some townspeople believed it was partially because of this that the university property was spared by the invading army. About 800 soldiers who died in the university hospital were buried in a Confederate cemetery on ground belonging to the university.

PONTOTOC, Pontotoc County. State 6, 15. Marker at State 6 and N. Congress St.

Pontotoc Cemetery. Soldiers from all wars since 1812, including 123 Confederates.

PORT GIBSON, Claiborne County. US 61. Marker on highway at south city limits. (*Also see* BRUINSBURG and GRAND GULF.) The story of Grant's march through Claiborne County is well told in ten historical markers placed along the route. On April 30, 1863, Grant put 22,000 soldiers and 60 guns ashore at Bruinsburg, thus gaining an important foothold on the Mississippi side of the river below Vicksburg. Confederate brigades under Gens. Martin Green, William Baldwin, E. D. Tracy, and Col. F. M. Cockrell were defeated after an all-day fight at Port Gibson on May 1. Gen. Tracy was killed. Gen. J. B. McPherson pursued the retreating Southerners to Hankinson's Ferry, and Sherman crossed the Mississippi at Grand Gulf.

Cary Birthplace, northwest corner of Church and Walnut St. Constance Cary, who made the first Confederate battle flag, reputedly was born here.

Claiborne County Courthouse, built in 1845, was enlarged and remodeled in 1903; however, original walls and relics of the past remain. A Confederate monument faces the courthouse.

The Hill, south end of town near railroad. Gen. Earl Van Dorn was born in a large brick house built early in the 19th century by his father. He is buried in the Port Gibson cemetery north of his birthplace.

Lookout Point, on hill overlooking Bayou Pierre, marks the extreme right of the Confederate line during the battle of Port Gibson. A replica of a log meeting house has been built by the Port Gibson-Claiborne County Historical Society on the site of the original log cabin.

Old Bethel Church, near Bruinsburg, was riddled with bullets as Gen. J. A. McClernand's troops used the belfry for target practice in passing.

Irwin Russell Memorial, southeast corner of College and Coffee St. Formerly the Port Gibson Female College, used as a Confederate hospital, the building is dedicated to the poet Russell, born in Port Gibson and author of "Christmas Night in the Quarters." City Hall and County Library are housed here. Museum has Civil War exhibits.

QUITMAN, Clarke County. US 45. The Confederate Cemetery was discovered when a farmer plowed up a handful of uniform buttons.

RAYMOND, Hinds County. State 18. Marker on highway. The courthouse, built 1854–1857 with skilled slave labor, served as a Confederate hospital after the battle of Raymond, May 12, 1863.

REDWOOD, Warren County. US 61, State 3. Marker on State 3 for Snyder's Bluff. Entrenchments built for the defense of Vicksburg repelled Union gunboats, December 27–28, 1862, and demonstration by Gen. Sherman, April 30 and May 1, 1863.

RODNEY, Jefferson County, southeast of Alcorn.

Presbyterian Church was shelled by a Union gunboat, the *Rattler.*

SENATOBIA, Tate County. IS 55, US 51. Marker on highway at south city limits. Federal troops burned the town after a skirmish.

TUPELO, Pontotoc County. State 6.

Tupelo County Museum, State 6 at Westwood Park, has Civil War displays.

TUPELO NATIONAL BATTLEFIELD, Lee County. State 6, 1 mile west of US 45B. When Gen. Forrest had chased Gen. S. D. Sturgis's troops from the Brices Cross Roads area, Gen. Sherman wrote: "Forrest . . . whipped Sturgis fair and square, and now I will put against him A. J. Smith and Mower, and let them try their hand." The battle began early on July 14, 1864, and continued through the following day. Neither side had a complete victory: Forrest could say the Union forces had turned back after the battle; Smith could take credit for saving the railroad over which supplies were being rushed to Sherman's "Army Group" as it closed in on Atlanta. The one-acre battlefield site, maintained by the National Park Service, has a marker with text and maps.

UNION CHURCH, Jefferson County. State 28. Marker on highway at west city limits indicates site where Grierson's raiders were checked April 28, 1863.

VICKSBURG, Warren County. IS 20, US 61. The reduction of Vicksburg, Confederate stronghold, was the main Federal objective in the western theater of war after Grant was given command of the Department of the Tennessee in October 1862. The city withstood land and naval attacks and prolonged siege until Gen. Pemberton was forced to surrender on July 4, 1863. The Vicksburg Chamber of Commerce, lobby of the Hotel Vicksburg, offers a free map with descriptive log of historic sites. Trained guides are available for tours daily, including holidays; arrangements for group or private tours may be made.

Anchuca, 1010 First East St., was once owned by Joseph Davis, elder brother of Jefferson Davis. President Davis once addressed the people of Vicksburg from the balcony of the mansion. Restored.

Balfour House, 1002 Crawford. On Christmas Eve a ball was interrupted as the battle of Vicksburg opened. The house later was headquarters for Union Gen. James B. McPherson. Restored.

The Federal army embarks on the banks of the Mississippi River near Vicksburg.

Cedar Grove, 2200 Oak St. Federal warships of Farragut's squadron shelled the house as they passed shore batteries on their way up-river. The front door is patched where a shell entered. The ball is now lodged in the door casing between twin parlors. The home was purchased for restoration by the Vicksburg Little Theatre Guild.

Christ Church, northwest corner of Locust and Main St. The fourth oldest Episcopal church in Mississippi. The cornerstone was laid in April 1839 by Leonidas Polk, who as a general in the Civil War was known as the "Fighting Bishop." (Polk also laid the cornerstone of the University of the South at Sewanee, Tennessee, in 1860.) He was killed at Pine Mountain, Georgia, in the Atlanta campaign.

Cook-Allein House, 1104 Harrison St., was built by Col. A. J. Cook during the war. After the fall of Vicksburg, it was converted into a Federal hospital. Soldiers left their insignia stamped on the living room floor.

Duff-Green House, 1114 First East St. The mansion, considered one of the most magnificent in town, was shelled and later served as a Confederate hospital.

Luckett House, 1116 Crawford St., built in 1830, was shelled in 1863. After the city surrendered, Union officers were quartered upstairs while their horses were stabled on the ground floor.

Lum House, on US 61. Marker is misleading. House is postwar. The William Lum house was destroyed during Union occupation of the city because Capt. Cyrus Comstock wished to erect a battery on site.

McNutt House, northwest corner of Monroe and First East St., is said to be the oldest house in town. A Confederate soldier, Lt. D. N. McGill, who died June 4, 1863, from injuries received in the city's defense, is buried in the side yard.

McRaven, east end of Harrison St., is little changed from war times and has the battle scars to prove it. In 1864, John Bobb, owner, ordered a group of Federal soldiers out of his garden, speeding them along with a brickbat. They returned later with muskets and murdered him. The garrison commander had the soldiers court-martialed and hanged. Guided tours.

Newman House-Candon Hearth, 2530 S. Confederate Ave., only antebellum house on a battle line, has many shrapnel scars, relics, trenches in garden.

Old Court House Museum, 1008 Cherry St., was built in 1858 by slave labor on land given to the county by the family of Rev. Newit Vick. On July 4, 1863, Gen. Grant had the Union flag run up on this building. The museum, managed by the Vicksburg and Warren County Historical Society, houses one of the largest collections of Civil War Americana. Open daily.

"The Vanishing Glory," shown at 717 Clay St., is a multimedia presentation of the siege of Vicksburg, drawn from letters and diaries.

Toy and Soldiers, a museum at Cherry and Grove streets, contains more than 30,000 toy soldiers from several wars, as well as Civil War artifacts.

USS Cairo Museum, opposite National Cemetery entrance, has artifacts and a film. The vessel was sunk in the Yazoo River in 1862. The salvage efforts took years with navy ordnance experts assisting in the operations. Ninety-four years after the sinking, Edwin C. Bearss, historian at the Vicksburg National Park Service, Don Jacks, park employee, and Warren Grabau, geologist, found the *Cairo.* A human bone found inside the vessel has created a puzzle, as Lt. Comdr. Selfridge reported no loss of life in the sinking. Walter E. H. Fentress, commanding a detail of sharpshooters on the tinclad *Marmora,* described the *Cairo's* unlucky encounter with an "infernal machine": "I saw her anchor thrown up several feet in the air. In an instant she commenced to settle, and was run to the bank and a hawser got out; but shortly she slid off the bank and disappeared below the water." According to historian Virgil Carrington Jones, a contemporary of Lt. Cmdr. Selfridge reported sardonically: "Selfridge of the *Cairo* found two torpedoes and removed them by placing his vessel over them." In reporting his loss to Adm. Porter, Selfridge said he supposed a court would be held. Porter responded: "I have no time to hold courts. I can't blame any officer who puts his ship close to the enemy. Is there any other vessel you would like to have?"

Vicksburg Marker, US 61 and Cherry St., near Old Courthouse. Site of Spanish Fort Nogales, later U.S. Fort McHenry.

Willis-Cowan House, 1018 Crawford St. Built in the 1840s, the house was lent to Gen. Pemberton during the siege and served as his headquarters until the fall of the city.

VICKSBURG NATIONAL MILITARY PARK, entrance at eastern edge of town on US 80 and IS 20. A 16-mile tour of the nearly 1,800 acres of battlefield is well marked; guided tours, however, may be arranged through the Vicksburg Convention and Visitors Bureau. The visitor center, adjacent to park entrance, has exhibits, sales area, and audio-visual program. It is open daily. For more information, write park superintendent, 3201 Clay St., Vicksburg, MS 39180. The National Cemetery in the northern section of the park was established in 1866 for the burial of more than 16,000 Federal soldiers. Admission fees: $3.00 per vehicle; $1.00 per person (bus); 62 or over, free.

WOODVILLE, Wilkinson County. US 61, State 24.

Rosemont, 1 mile east of US 61 on US 24, is the restored boyhood home of Jefferson Davis. On October 5, 1864, Union cavalry routed Confederates and burned Bowling Green, home of Judge Edward McGehee, prototype of Stark Young's planter in *So Red the Rose.* He is buried on estate. Roses planted by Davis's mother, Jane Davis, still bloom in season. Guided tours include taped narratives of the Confederate president's life and that of the plantation.

YAZOO CITY, Yazoo County. US 49. Marker on highway. Site of Confederate navy yard established in 1862. The ironclad ram *Arkansas,* which engaged two Union fleets on the Mississippi, was completed here.

Yazoo Historical Museum, 322 N. Main, has Civil War relics.

MISSOURI

Missouri entered the Union on August 10, 1821, the 24th state. In the 1850s about 24,000 planters and farmers owned the 115,000 slaves in the state; most of the population wanted compromise in peace, neutrality in the event of the war. When Lincoln called for volunteers after the fall of Fort Sumter, Governor Claiborne Fox Jackson shot back a fiery response which started out loud and clear but fizzled at the end like a damp firecracker: "[the] requisition is illegal, unconstitutional, revolutionary, inhuman, diabolical, and cannot be complied with." Jackson was a not-too-secret friend of the South. Unionists in St. Louis prepared to defend the small arsenal there, Francis Blair asked Washington to send extra troops, and Capt. Nathaniel Lyon brought an 80-man detachment from Fort Riley. Both the Wide-Awakes, a Union home guard composed mostly of Germans, and the pro-Southern Minute Men drilled in St. Louis. One of the first skirmishes of the war took place at Camp Jackson in Lindell's Grove on May 10, 1861, when Lyon's men took the secessionist state militia into custody and marched them to the arsenal as prisoners of war. Both Grant and Sherman were in the crowd that day, neither in uniform. Sherman was serving as president of the Fifth Street Railroad, having resigned as superintendent of the Louisiana Military Academy.

In June, Lyon's forces routed Confederates at the Boonville skirmish and gained control of northern Missouri. In October, Confederates defeated Federals in the bloody battle of Wilson's Creek and Gen. Lyon was killed. Lyon was an exceedingly able commander; his loss to the Union is incalculable. Politically the state remained divided. A convention in March 1861 had voted to remain in the Union. Jackson called a meeting of the legislature in October which voted to secede, although not enough members were present to constitute a legal session. However, Missouri was admitted as the 12th Confederate state in November 1861. In midsummer, a state convention had voted to oust the secessionist administration

and had installed a pro-Union government with Hamilton R. Gamble as governor. The Jackson contingent controlled southern Missouri until March 1862, when the Union victory at Pea Ridge, Arkansas, sent them further south. (See MARSHALL, Texas, for Confederate capital of Missouri.)

There were more than 1,160 battles or skirmishes fought within the state; this was 11 percent of all fought within the nation and more than any other state except Virginia and Tennessee. Missouri sent 40,000 men to the Confederate army and 110,000 to the Union. The last important action took place at Westport in what is now Kansas City when Gen. Sterling Price was defeated by Gen. S. G. Curtis's Army of the Border, October, 23, 1864. The following year Missouri adopted a new constitution which included a Test Oath clause denying former secessionist sympathizers the franchise. The highly unpopular clause was repealed five years later.

ARROW ROCK, Saline County. State 41.
Arrow Rock Tavern, 2 blocks north of State 41, was built in 1834. It has been restored with ballroom, taproom, dining room, and lodgings furnished in the style of more than a century ago. Also in Arrow Rock State Park is the home of George Caleb Bingham, artist.

BELMONT BATTLEFIELD, Mississippi County. State 77. Now under the river; in 1861 Grant's forces, numbering about 3,000, landed 3 miles above Belmont. Five companies were left to guard the transports; the rest moved against six Confederate regiments under Gen. Gideon J. Pillow. After a four-hour engagement the Confederates retreated. While Grant's men were looting the camp, Polk sent reinforcements in an attempt to cut the Union troops off from their transports. In an all-day battle the South lost 642 of 4,000 men; Grant lost 607 of 3,114. Grant also lost his horse and bay pony, saddle, and equipment.

BLUE SPRINGS, Jackson County. IS 70, US 40. If any copy of the *Jackson County Demo-*

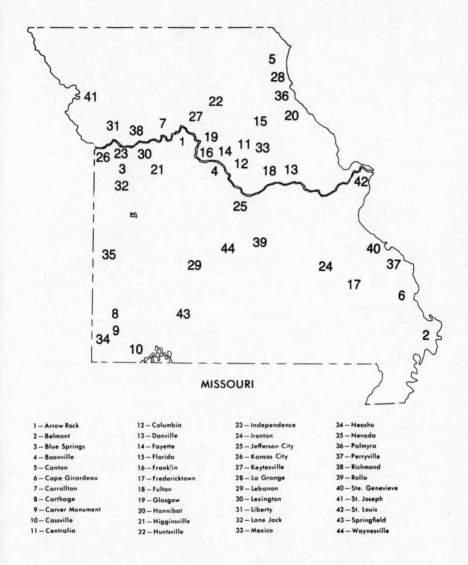

MISSOURI

1 — Arrow Rock	12 — Columbia	23 — Independence	34 — Neosho
2 — Belmont	13 — Danville	24 — Ironton	35 — Nevada
3 — Blue Springs	14 — Fayette	25 — Jefferson City	36 — Palmyra
4 — Boonville	15 — Florida	26 — Kansas City	37 — Perryville
5 — Canton	16 — Franklin	27 — Keytesville	38 — Richmond
6 — Cape Girardeau	17 — Fredericktown	28 — La Grange	39 — Rolla
7 — Carrollton	18 — Fulton	29 — Lebanon	40 — Ste. Genevieve
8 — Carthage	19 — Glasgow	30 — Lexington	41 — St. Joseph
9 — Carver Monument	20 — Hannibal	31 — Liberty	42 — St. Louis
10 — Cassville	21 — Higginsville	32 — Lone Jack	43 — Springfield
11 — Centralia	22 — Huntsville	33 — Mexico	44 — Waynesville

crat for September 27, 1901, reached Lawrence, Kansas, it must have been read with mixed (which is to say stirred, not blended) emotions. Headlines read: "Quantrell's Men Meet, The Annual Reunion Brought Twenty-five Survivors Together. Frank James Here, Too. Remembered All the Boys and Exchanged Jokes With Them." The aged raiders met on the grounds of the old Blue Church, near the place where the organization was formed in 1863, and where many picnics were held later.

Frank James gave a speech and offered a resolution asking that a monument be erected to the "noble women" who stood by them in the dark days of the war, stating that he would start the fund with $50. Frank's home address was given as St. Louis. Most of the one-time marauders, whose activities once caused the border counties to be depopulated by the famous Order No. 11, came from the same old neighborhood: Kansas City, Independence, Lexington, Blue Springs, and Oak Grove. The 25 were photographed, grouped behind a massively framed portrait of their lost leader Quantrill, whose name seems to have been spelled about an equal number of times with an *e*. The society reporter concluded an account of the day's doings: "One social feature . . . was a little band of Blue Springs ladies trying their luck on throwing the balls at a bell for the cigars. Some of them managed to hit the frame in which the bell hung, others would miss it by ten feet, while others kept the crowd back of them dodging. Until these ladies took charge of the balls the blue looking old man had not seen a nickel all day; but the wild, uncertain throws of the ladies created such an excitement that the whole picnic were trying to throw at once. The old bell man was so full of joy that he set up the cigars to the ladies and bade them goodbye in the smoothest style." In 1901 most of Quantrill's bones were in Ohio; the man sent by the raider's mother to bring back his body from the old Portland Catholic Cemetery in Louisville had stolen souvenir pieces of the skeleton. A Kansas collector acquired some of it. Bill Anderson lay in an unmarked grave in Richmond, and Jesse James in Clay County, while Frank James, Sam Whitset, and the Webb boys, among others, were throwing balls at a bell for free cigars.

BOONVILLE, Cooper County. IS 70, US 40.

First Battle of Boonville was fought June 17, 1861, 4 miles east of town. Pro-Southern state troops commanded by Col. John S. Marmaduke were routed by Federal forces led by Capt. Nathaniel Lyon.

Kemper Military Academy, 3rd St. and Center Ave., is the oldest boys' school and military academy west of the Mississippi, founded June 1844.

Old Cooper Jail, built in 1848, has been renovated.

Second Battle of Boonville, east end of Morgan St., on St. Joseph's Hospital grounds. Line of trenches can be traced. The Chamber of Commerce reports that bullets and cannonballs can still be found. The battle took place in the fall of 1863.

Thespian Hall, northeast corner of Main and Vine St., now known as the Lyric Theater, is the oldest surviving theater building west of the Alleghenies. It was used as a hospital and military prison during the conflict.

Vest Home, 745 Main St. Sen. George G. Vest served as representative to the Missouri general assembly in 1860, later served in the Confederate Congress and in the U.S. Senate.

Home has been altered but much of the interior is unchanged.

CANTON, Lewis County. US 61. Hometown of Jesse Barrett, preacher and teacher who established the *Canton Press* in 1862. The Democratic weekly stated its policy as "Pledged but to truth, to liberty and law, no favor swings us and no fear shall awe."

Culver-Stockton College, west side of town, was headquarters for Union army.

CAPE GIRARDEAU, Cape Girardeau County. IS 55, US 61.

Court of Common Pleas, Themis and Spanish St. Civil War prisoners were kept in basement cells. Civil War relics in museum on second floor. A Confederate memorial fountain is northwest of the building.

Fort A, one of four forts built by Union troops in 1861, was located at the east end of Bellevue St; *Fort B* was on grounds of present Southeast Missouri State College, Normal and Henderson Ave.; *Fort C,* at end of Sprigg St.; *Fort D,* on northeast corner of Locust and Fort St. Fort D was one of the major defenses of the town when Gen. Marmaduke attacked on April 17, 1863. After being repulsed, Marmaduke retreated to Jackson.

CARROLLTON, Livingston County. US 65.

St. Mary's Cemetery, northeast edge of town, has the grave of Gen. James Shields. It is marked by a Federal monument.

Shields Monument, east side of courthouse lawn, is a life-size bronze honoring the general. Shields once challenged Lincoln to a duel, but the two resolved their differences and became good friends. Shields was appointed governor of Oregon Territory and served as first U.S. senator from Oregon when it attained statehood. He commanded a division in the Shenandoah Valley campaigns, later was U.S. senator from Illinois, Minnesota, and Missouri.

William Baker House, 5 miles south of town on Missouri River. Baker, a river captain, built a mansion which became a hotel for steamboat travelers known as River House. In 1865 three former Union soldiers crashed a New Year's Eve party and, when ordered to leave, challenged all present to a duel. In the fracas, James McMurtry, one of the trio, was killed and his opponent seriously wounded. Local legend says McMurtry's ghost haunts the house—possibly still in hopes of getting one more for the road.

CARTHAGE, Jasper County. Off IS 44, US 71, 66. Four markers for the battle of Carthage, July 5, 1861, begin 8 miles north of town and 1 mile west of US 71. The battle of Carthage, between pro-Southern state guardsmen and a Federal force of 3-month volunteers from St. Louis, was the first of 13 skirmishes in the town. Col. Franz Sigel met the state troops 8 miles north of town on what was called the "Lower Bridge Road." One of the series of rear-guard actions fought by Sigel took place in mid-town; the last, toward sundown, occurred near the southwest corner of Carter Park on East Chestnut and River St. Sigel then retreated to the east. The courthouse was burned in October 1863 by Confederate guerrillas; the remainder of town was destroyed in September 1864 and not resettled until the summer of 1865. There are statues of Gen. Sigel and Confederate Gen. Jackson, by Carl Moses. Carthage was the hometown of Belle Starr (Myra Belle Shirley), daughter of an innkeeper. Contrary to legend, neither Belle nor her brother Ed rode with Quantrill's raiders. Ed was a bushwhacker. The inn burned in 1863; the Shirleys then went to Texas.

County Courthouse has a mural, "Forged in Fire," by Lowell Davis, that shows the county history, including the tumultuous Civil War days.

Kendrick House, US 66 and 71, north of town, was occupied by both Union and Confederate troops during the war.

Self-guiding tour of historical area is marked by green signs. About four miles in business and residential districts are covered.

CASSVILLE, Barry County. State 37. The town served as Confederate capital of Missouri when Confederate members of the Missouri general assembly held a session here early in November 1861. The ordinance of secession was rewritten by Senator George Vest; the ordinance and an act of affiliation to the Confederate states were signed by the legislators.

CENTRALIA, Boone County. The Centralia Massacre of September 1864 took place when 30 Confederate guerrillas led by Bill Anderson plundered the town, held up the Columbia stagecoach, then put ties across the tracks of the North Missouri railroad and held up the St. Louis train. Union soldiers on the train were forced to strip off their uniforms, then were lined up and shot. That same day another group of Union soldiers, under Maj. A. V. E. Johnson, was nearly wiped out and captured by the guerrillas. Johnson, believing Anderson had only 30 men, divided his command, leaving half of it to guard the town, which was still in shock. Johnson's cavalry was actually mostly mounted infantry—recruits

who had been trained to fight on foot; when they rode into the guerrilla ambush Johnson coolly ordered them to dismount and to face the foe as best they could. Maj. Johnson was killed by 17-year-old Jesse James. The guerrillas rode back to Centralia and finished off all but 19 who managed to reach the blockhouse at Sturgeon. The 39th Missouri was decimated in little more than an hour. The guerrillas had lost three men, but the James boys, George Todd, Anderson, Archie Clements, and John Thrailkill rode off to spread more terror.

COLUMBIA, Boone County. IS 70, US 40. *University of Missouri, Ellis' Library,* in Lowry Mall on campus, houses the State Historical Society collections of historical material, including 13 original George Caleb Bingham paintings. The State Historical Society owns the original Bingham painting of Order No. 11. The artist, who was far from unbiased, expressed his views in oil but produced one of the masterpieces of Civil War art. (*Also see* KANSAS CITY.)

DANVILLE, Montgomery County. US 40. On October 14, 1864, Anderson's men razed and plundered Danville, killed militiamen and civilians, and burned many of the buildings.

FAYETTE, Howard County. State 5. *Central College,* north end of Main St. Brannock Hall was occupied by Federal troops who stabled their horses on the first floor and used second and third floors for barracks.

Jackson Home, north of town, on State 5. Gov. Claiborne Fox Jackson had three wives who were daughters of Dr. John S. Sappington; when Jackson asked for the hand of the third daughter, Sappington is supposed to have replied, "You can take her but don't come back after the old woman."

FLORIDA, Monroe County, State 154. *Twain's Birthplace* was moved from here to the Mark Twain State Park, State 107, on the Salt River. There is a Mark Twain monument in the center of town.

FRANKLIN, Howard County. IS 44, US 40, State 87. *Old Franklin* was once the head of the Santa Fe Trail. Among those who lived here at one time: Meredith Marmaduke, a Missouri governor; Claiborne F. Jackson, Marmaduke's brother-in-law, also a governor; Kit Carson, Union scout; and George Bingham, artist. On an old road near here the boys of the community armed hastily to help Confederates in the battle of Boonville.

Construction of floating mortar batteries at the Upper Ferry near St. Louis.

FREDERICKTOWN, Madison County. US 67. The last Trans-Mississippi invasion by the Confederates was made in September 1864, when Sterling Price assembled troops here hoping to take Fort Davidson at Pilot Knob.

An unmarked field just south of town was the site of an engagement here October 21, 1861, between State Guard men under Brig. Gen. M. Jeff Thompson (later called "The Bootheel Swamp Fox") and Union troops under Col. J. B. Plummer.

FULTON, Callaway County. Off IS 70, US 54.

Callaway County seceded from both sides and is still called the "Kingdom of Callaway." The Kingdom of Callaway Historical Society and the St. Louis Civil War Round Table placed a monument on County Z near Calwood, formerly Moore's Mill, on the same day Americans first landed on the moon. The marker was of the places where irregulars under Joseph Porter skirmished with Federals led by Gen. Odon Guitar.

State Hospital, E 5th and State St., was established in the late 1840s as the first hospital for mental patients west of the Mississippi. Federal troops occupied the buildings.

GEORGE WASHINGTON CARVER NATIONAL MONUMENT, Newton County, 2 miles west of Diamond on County V,

½ mile south. Visitor center displays Carver memorabilia. On the grounds are the home and family burial plot and the figure of "Boy Carver" by Robert Amendola. George Washington Carver was born of slave parents about 1864, grew up to be a distinguished scientist with international acclaim.

GLASGOW, Howard County, State 5, is in an area settled mostly by people from Virginia and Kentucky. Howard, Boone, and Callaway counties are still known as "Little Dixie."

City Hall was occupied by Capt. J. Vance during the battle of Glasgow, October 15, 1864. Col. Chester Harding had fortified a hill and posted about 200 men in rifle pits; Maj. J. W. Lewis had deployed 310 men in the north part of town. Confederates under Joseph Shelby were entrenched across the Missouri River; Confederate Gen. John B. Clark occupied a ridge south of town. Confederate bombardment began about dawn; the Federals surrendered about 1:00 P.M. The city hall was burned and a good many buildings destroyed. Many prewar homes here have plugged walls because of that morning's severe bombardment. The present city hall replaced the one occupied during the Civil War. It was built immediately after the war.

Methodist Church served as a temporary hospital after the battle in which some 200 persons were killed or wounded.

HANNIBAL, Marion County. US 61, 36.

Civil War Fort, US 61N, 2nd exit to Huck Finn Shopping Center. Union troops here guarded the Hannibal-St. Joseph Railroad Bridge at South River crossing. Museum has cavalry equipment and memorabilia.

Mark Twain Home and Museum, 208 Hill St. Exhibits include many items once owned by Samuel Clemens, who became famous as Mark Twain—but not for his war service, which amounted to a few months in the Confederate army in 1861. Twain became a friend and admirer of Gen. Grant and was responsible for easing the general's widow's financial situation. The *Memoirs* which Grant lived just long enough to finish were published by Twain's firm, sold thousands of copies, and Twain turned over about $450,000 in royalties to Mrs. Julia Grant.

HIGGINSVILLE, Lafayette County. Off IS 70, State 13, 20.

Confederate Memorial State Park, 1 mile north on State 20. A Confederate Home was established here in the 1890s. Confederate monuments and cemetery at site.

HUNTSVILLE, Randolph County. US 24. Birthplace of "Bloody Bill" Anderson, who may have been the most infamous guerrilla of the war. He went into raids with his own piercing Anderson yell, which from all accounts must have made the Rebel yell sound like a love song. Anderson was out to avenge his father's death in a border skirmish and the death of his sister in the collapse of a Federal prison in Kansas City by killing every Federal soldier or sympathizer he could. (*See* CENTRALIA.)

INDEPENDENCE, Jackson County. IS 70, 435, US 24. A starting point for both the Oregon and Santa Fe trails, the historic town became a battle site in August 1862 and again in October 1864. Twice the Confederates held the town for one day only.

Bingham-Waggoner Estate, 313 W. Pacific, was the home of George Caleb Bingham from 1864 to 1870. He painted one of his most famous works here, "Order No. 11," based on the 1863 directive that ordered residents to leave their property unless they signed an oath of allegiance to the Union. House restored. Guided tours.

Harry S Truman Library, on US 24, has some Civil War items in its collections. There are exhibits pertaining to the history of the presidency.

Jackson County Jail and Museum, 217 N. Main St., The building served as provost marshal's headquarters during the war; the living area has been authentically restored with period wallpaper, carpeting, and furnishings. The jail was a cooling-off spot for Frank James and William Quantrill at one time. Families of Southern sympathizers were herded into custody here following the issuance of Order No. 11. The museum has an extensive collection of Civil War items. An antebellum schoolhouse has been moved to the museum patio; it has not been rebuilt but remains as it was when in use.

IRONTON, Iron County. State 72. Brig. Gen. U. S. Grant and the 21st Illinois arrived here in August 1861; Grant was soon relieved by Gen. B. M. Prentiss and placed in command of the District of Southeast Missouri. A statue commemorates the site of Grant's headquarters when he was commissioned brigadier general.

Courthouse, center of town, was used as a refuge for Union forces retreating before the battle of Pilot Knob. Walls are scarred. A pair of 3-inch ordnance rifles stand in front of the building.

Fort Davidson State Historic Park, an earthwork north of town on State 21, was occupied by Union forces under Brig. Gen. Thomas Ewing to protect the Pilot Knob and Iron Mountain ore. In September 1864, 1,200 Federals held off Price's full charge and stopped the Confederate drive on St. Louis.

JEFFERSON CITY, Cole County. US 50, 54. The closest sound of battle came in 1864 when Gen. Price moved within 4 miles, intending to sack the town. A few cannonballs fell within the city limits, but Union troops were reinforced and Price turned toward Kansas City.

Cole County Historical Society Museum, 109 Madison St., has war relics and other historical items.

Jefferson Landing State Historic Site, Jefferson St. at the river, has restored 1850s buildings, museum, and audio-visual presentation.

Lincoln University, 1820 Chestnut St. The idea of the university was conceived by members of the 62nd Colored Infantry around a Civil War campfire—at least legend puts the planners around the fire—at Camp McIntosh, near Galveston, Texas. Maj. Gen. Clinton B. Fisk, of the 65th Colored Infantry, is said to have supported the idea. Fisk University in Nashville was named for the general. Lincoln was opened September 17, 1866, with Lt. Foster of the 62nd as first president.

National Cemetery, 1042 E. McCarty St.,

has graves of 78 Union soldiers killed in battle near Centralia. Woodland Cemetery, which adjoins the National, has a plot allotted to the state with the grave of Confederate Gen. John S. Marmaduke.

State Capitol, on bluff overlooking Missouri River. In June 1861, *New York Tribune* correspondent Albert D. Richardson followed Capt. Lyon to Jefferson City: "The soldiers were cooking upon the grass in the rear of the Capitol, standing in the shade of its portico and rotunda, lying on beds of hay in its passages, and upon carpets in the legislative halls. They reposed in all its rooms, from the subterranean vaults to the little circular chamber in the dome. Governor and Legislature were fled." Richardson also visited the executive mansion, found cigar boxes, champagne bottles, ink stands, private letters, and family knickknacks scattered. One letter had accompanied a gift, reassured the governor that the "Old Bourbon Whiskey Cocktail" had been made in St. Louis and was not even tainted with "B. Republicanism." Richardson saw a disparity between the evidences of sudden flight and the governor's pronouncement which lay upon the piano: "Now, therefore, I, C. F. Jackson, Governor of the State of Missouri, do issue this my proclamation, calling the militia of the State, to the number of FIFTY THOUSAND, into the service of the State. . . . Rise, then, and drive out ignominiously the invaders!"

Richardson concluded: "As we walked through the deserted rooms, a hollow echo answered to the tramp of the colonel and his lieutenant, and to the dull clank of their scabbards against the furniture." The present building is the third Capitol; two earlier structures were destroyed by fire. The subject of all decorations is the history of Missouri. Thomas Hart Benton murals are in the west wing.

State Museum, Capitol Building, includes the History Hall with historical exhibits, Civil War trophies, battle flags, weapons.

KANSAS CITY, Jackson County. IS 29, 35, 70, US 69, 24. After Quantrill's raid on Lawrence, Kansas, in 1863, Gen. Thomas Ewing, with headquarters in Kansas City, issued the controversial Order No. 11, intended to depopulate Missouri border counties so that Federal forces could combat guerrillas. The counties of Jackson, Cass, Bates, and half of Vernon were affected. Rebel sympathizers were forbidden to carry on business and many were jailed, including women. Wives and children of known guerrillas were ordered to leave Missouri and the District of the Border. George Caleb

Bingham, artist, born a Virginian, was a foe of Ewing both during and after the war. His painting of Order No. 11 helped to keep Ewing from political positions he aspired to in later years. In August 1863, a three-story building on Grand Avenue between 14th and 15th streets, which was used as a prison for women known to be associated with Confederate guerrilla leaders, collapsed; many inmates were seriously wounded; "Bloody Bill" Anderson's sister was killed. George Caleb Bingham's wife owned the building.

Battle of Westport. Marker in Loose Park, 51st and Wornall Rd. In 1864, Confederate Gen. Price, commanding the District of Arkansas, made a last gamble to drive the Union forces from Missouri. In October the Kansas militia was driven back from the Little Blue River to a position behind the Big Blue. Jo Shelby crossed the Big Blue and the Union line withdrew to Westport and Kansas City. About 29,000 troops engaged in the battle of Westport on Sunday, October 23. Gens. Samuel Curtis and Alfred Pleasanton commanded Federal troops. Shelby, Marmaduke, and Price led the Confederates who fought valorously but were repulsed, driven back down the border and beyond the Arkansas River. The Civil War was virtually over in Missouri.

Other markers will be found at the battle of Blue site, 60th St. and Manchester Trafficway, which was the beginning of the Westport battle; Confederate artillery action, 445 W. 56th St.; a Union flanking movement, Sunset Dr. and Rockwell Lane; heavy fighting, 63rd and the Pasco; site where Gen. Samuel Curtis watched the fighting along Brush Creek, Westport Rd. and Pennsylvania Ave.

Forest Hill Cemetery, 6901 Troost, has Confederate statue and the graves of Gen. Jo Shelby and his men of the Iron Brigade.

Union Cemetery, 227 E. 28th St. Terrace, has the graves of George Caleb Bingham; Alexander Majors, organizer and superintendent of the Pony Express; and Confederate soldier Spencer McCoy, son of the founder of Westport, killed at 18 in the battle of Springfield. A granite shaft marks the graves of 15 Confederate soldiers who died in Kansas City as prisoners of war. About 1,200 unknown soldiers are also here.

Wornall Home, 61st Terrace and Wornall Road, was used as a hospital by both armies. Handsomely restored with period furnishings.

KEYTESVILLE, Chariton County. US 24, State 5.

Hill House, 100 W. North, was home of

unlucky William Reading, shot by Union soldiers as he ran out the back door.

Price Park, in midtown, has heroic bronze statue of Gen. Sterling Price, sculptured by Allen G. Newman. Correspondents of the day, from both Northern and Southern papers, often referred to the general as "courtly" or "knightly." After the battle of Lexington he gave seats in his own carriage to the captured Col. and Mrs. Mulligan, a bride of 19.

KIRKSVILLE, Adair County. State 6.

Northeast Missouri State University has a fine Abraham Lincoln collection in Pickler Memorial Library.

LA GRANGE, Lewis County. US 61.

Marshall House, 3rd and Jefferson St. Daniel M. Marshall was a country doctor and abolitionist who returned to Indiana after antagonizing Southern sympathizers in this area. His son, Thomas Riley Marshall, lived here in 1860, was later governor of Indiana, Vice President under Woodrow Wilson, and clichémaker who said: "What this country needs is a good five cent cigar."

Soldiers' Monument, in public square, was erected in 1864.

LEBANON, Laclede County. IS 44.

The highway was an important military road used by both armies. The Union installed a telegraph line with stations at St. Louis, Rolla, Lebanon, Springfield, and Fort Smith, Arkansas. It was known as the Wire Road. Confederates cut the wires as often as possible.

McClurg Memorial, in cemetery at north edge of town. Joseph W. McClurg was a colonel in the war, later served in Congress and as governor.

LEXINGTON, Lafayette County. US 24, State 13.

Anderson House, State 13, stood in the midst of battle and changed hands several times. It served as a hospital and has been restored with some original furnishings. Guided tours.

Battle of Lexington State Historic Site, off US 24. The "Battle of the Hemp Bales" was fought September 18, 1861, between Confederates under Price and Federals under Mulligan. Firing was maintained for 52 hours; then on the morning of September 20, Confederates constructed movable breastworks of hemp bales soaked in water to withstand heated shot, advanced toward the Union lines, and won the battle by day's end. Memorial Building in College Park has a map of battle and historic scenes. Markers denote Price and Mulligan headquarters.

Lafayette County Courthouse has cannonball imbedded in east column.

Lexington Historical Museum, 13th and Main St. Civil War and Pony Express relics.

LIBERTY, Clay County. IS 35, US 69.

A U.S. Arsenal, south of town on the Missouri River bluff, was held up twice. In 1855, about 100 Clay countians raided the arsenal, in aid of proslavery Kansans. The government recovered all but $400 worth of supplies. The second raid came on April 20, 1861, when 200 secessionists from Clay and Jackson counties, led by Col. Henry L. Routt, demanded surrender of the garrison. The Federal forces were held prisoner, stores were removed and distributed to Southern sympathizers. Public meetings were held on the question of secession; the town voted first one way and then the other. Guerrilla warfare grew so rife the citizens finally condemned the marauders in a public meeting on July 20, 1864, as "ravenous monsters of society." The following spring Dr. Reuben Samuels and his family were asked to leave the county for "treason and notoriously disloyal practices." Dr. Samuels was the stepfather of Frank and Jesse James.

James Homestead, northeast of town and 3 miles from Kearney. Alexander Franklin James was born here in 1843; Jesse Woodson James in 1847. In June 1863, a band of volunteers hanged Dr. Reuben Samuels until he was near death and gave Jesse a beating with a rope. On trips home after the war Jesse posed as a tombstone salesman. On his last trip here he was buried in the front yard; in 1882 his body was reinterred at Mount Olivet Cemetery, Kearney. Guides narrate stories about the outlaws; in summer an outdoor dramatization is presented, evenings.

Jesse James Bank Museum, on Old Town Square, is the restored site of the first daylight bank hold-up in the United States. Frank and Jesse James are reputed to have made a withdrawal of $60,000 in February 1866. James memorabilia.

Liberty Tribune, in the spring of 1862, published lists of men who were rejoining the Union cause. Among those who took the oath of allegiance and posted a $1,000 bond was 19-year-old Alexander Franklin James, of Quantrill's guerrillas.

William Jewell College, established in 1849, was occupied by Federal troops during the war. Horses were stabled on the first floor of Jewell Hall; second and third floors were used as hospital.

LONE JACK, Jackson County. US 50.

Battle of Lone Jack took place August 16, 1862. Maj. Emory Foster and Union cavalry opposed Confederates who were supported by Quantrill's guerrillas, including the Younger brothers. The Federals retreated. The Union and Confederate dead were buried in separate trenches at Soldiers Cemetery. The Confederate burial ground was near a solitary blackjack tree. There is now a marble shaft at the site. The Union gravesite is marked, but the soldiers who fell here have been reinterred at Leavenworth. The new museum has a diorama and historical displays.

MEXICO, Audrain County. US 54. Grant was stationed here in the summer of 1861.

Audrain County Historical Museum, 501 Muldrow St. The 1857 home, Graceland, was visited by Grant during the early days of the war. Period rooms.

NEOSHO, Newton County. US 60, 71. Secessionist members of the Missouri legislature met here on October 21, 1861, adopted an act declaring "the ties heretofore existing between the United States and the State of Missouri dissolved." Federal troops arrived, causing the session to adjourn. They met ten days later at Cassville. In 1863 the town was garrisoned by Federal troops. Gen. Joseph Shelby attacked the Union forces in October 1863 and shelled the courthouse; Capt. McAfee surrendered the Federal garrison.

NEVADA, Vernon County. US 71, 54. The town was known as the "Bushwhackers' Capital." In May 1863, Capt. Anderson Norton with Kansas troops burned the town.

Bushwhacker Museum, 231 N. Main, in 1861 former jail. Civil War relics in collection.

NEW MADRID, New Madrid County. IS 55, US 62. At the top of the New Madrid bend of the Mississippi River.

The New Madrid Historical Museum, Main and Waters streets, has exhibits relating to the Civil War engagements here. On March 13, 1862, Brig. Gen. John Pope and his Union troops won a hard day's fighting, forcing the C.S.A. commodore, George Hollins, to withdraw.

PALMYRA, Marion County. US 61.

Greenwood-Palmyra Cemetery, north edge of town, has the grave of William H. Russell, one of the founders of the Pony Express.

Palmyra Massacre Monument, on courthouse lawn. In September 1862, Confederates under Col. Joseph C. Porter raided the town

and captured Andrew Allsman, Union spy. Soon after, Union forces under Col. John McNeil sent word to the Confederates that unless Allsman was returned ten prisoners from Porter's command would be shot. Allsman was not returned; his fate has never been determined, but the ten unlucky Confederates were put to death at the fairgrounds by an inept firing squad of 30 who made a slaughter of the execution.

PERRYVILLE, Perry County. IS 55, US 61.

Union Memorial, courthouse lawn, honors 1,800 Perry County soldiers who served in the war.

RICHMOND, Ray County. State 13.

Richmond Cemetery, N. Thornton St., has the grave of Capt. Bill Anderson ("Bloody Bill") who was killed—fittingly enough—in ambush in Ray County, October 27, 1864. Most historians agree that Anderson was a psychopath; it seems likely he would have been a desperado even if his father and sister had died peacefully in their beds. Though photographs belie the statement, he is said to have been "an extremely handsome man, tall, sinewy and lithe." He had curly, dark, shoulder-length hair and blue eyes that "literally blazed." He attacked his victims crying and screaming; most of them, however, were soon beyond the range of sound—he seldom if ever took a prisoner. It is true that Cole Younger came to town with a Wild West show some ten years after the war, learned that Anderson had been buried without a funeral, and straightway hired a preacher, had the traveling show band provide music, and conducted a ceremony. Headstone finally placed in 1967.

ROLLA, Phelps County. IS 44, US 63. Fort Wyman was located here during the war. Outside log walls were slanted to make minié balls glance off. The original structures were surrounded by trenches and a moat. The fort was one of a series to protect Rolla, where 20,000 troops were quartered.

STE. GENEVIEVE, Ste. Genevieve County. US 61.

Historical Museum, Merchant and Third streets, has Civil War relics.

ST. JOSEPH, Buchanan County. IS 29, US 59.

Jesse James Home, 12th and Penn. Jesse James was living here as "Mr. Howard" when he was killed for reward money, April 5, 1882. The former fellow outlaw, Bob Ford, who shot

James, was sentenced to be hanged as was his brother who assisted him; both were pardoned. Some original furnishings. Guided tours.

Pate House Museum, 12th and Penn St. The onetime "luxury" hotel was headquarters for the Pony Express. It contains 1860s railroad memorabilia as well as Pony Express relics. The James house is on the grounds.

Pony Express Stables and Museum, 912-914 Penn St. The Overland Mail by pony service began April 3, 1860. Copies of Lincoln's inaugural address made the trip to Sacramento in 7 days and 17 hours. The stables were rebuilt in 1886.

St. Joseph Museum, 11th & Charles, has Civil War relics.

ST. LOUIS, St. Louis County. IS 44, 55, 70.

Bellefontaine Cemetery, 4947 W. Florissant Ave. Among those buried here are: Francis P. Blair, Union statesman and general; Confederate Gen. Sterling Price; and Capt. James B. Eads, engineer and builder of ironclads.

Calvary Cemetery, 5239 W. Florissant Ave., has the graves of Gen. William Tecumseh Sherman and Gen. Don Carlos Buell.

Campbell House, 15th and Locust St., has costumes and historical relics. Grant, as president, once spoke from the balcony of the Double Parlor.

Camp Jackson, known as Lindell Grove, is not marked at present. It is now part of the campus of St. Louis University. Lyon and Blair lined up their guns along the height which is now Grand Ave. and Olive St. Historian and St. Louis journalist Ernest Kirschten has observed that an unexpected benefit of urban redevelopment is that it gives the visitor a better view of the terrain as it was in 1861. In the course of redevelopment, Gen. Lyon—half statue and half high relief—was moved to Lyon Park, Broadway and Arsenal St., near the old arsenal. The general in sculpture has often caused comment because he appears to be on the verge of falling off his horse, which is about half his size.

City Art Museum, 10501 Gravois Rd., has George Caleb Bingham paintings. Northwest of museum is a bronze statue of Edward Bates, by J. Wilson McDonald. Bates served as Attorney General for Lincoln. A bronze statue of Francis P. Blair is also in the park.

Eads Bridge, on the riverfront, was designed by Capt. James B. Eads, the engineer who opened and maintained the channel at the mouth of the Mississippi and built the Civil War gunboats used on the river. He worked in the shipyards at the foot of Marceau St. in south St. Louis.

Grant's Farm, Gravois Rd. at Grant Rd. The farm known as "Hardscrabble," once owned by U. S. Grant, is now on a tract of land maintained by Anheuser-Busch brewery.

Jefferson Barracks Historical Park, 10 miles south on IS 55, S. Broadway exit, S. Broadway at Kingston and Bypass 50, southeast of Kirkwood. Among Civil War participants once stationed here were Jefferson Davis, Robert E. Lee, Ulysses S. Grant, William T. Sherman, Don Carlos Buell, John C. Frémont, W. S. Hancock, James Longstreet, Joseph Johnston, and a number of others who became generals during the war. There is a national cemetery west of the parade grounds. A museum is situated in a restored powder magazine. Visitor center.

Jefferson National Expansion Memorial, 11 N. 4th St. This National Park Service facility is now distinguished by the Gateway Arch designed by Eero Saarinen. Elevator service to the observation area has been provided for visitors, affording the sort of view Blair, Halleck, Sherman, and Grant had to imagine when planning campaigns at the Planters Hotel in the late fall of 1861. The Museum of Western Expansion is in visitor center.

Old Courthouse, 11 N. 4th, has dioramas and films. The Dred Scott case was heard here. Slaves were once auctioned from the east steps, and U. S. Grant freed his only slave here in 1859. Grant also made application for St. Louis city engineer and was turned down. The old courthouse is part of the Jefferson National Expansion Memorial on the riverfront.

Old National Hotel, southeast corner of 3rd and Market St., where "A. Lincoln and family, Illinois" once registered, has been razed but marker denotes site.

St. Louis Arsenal, southeast corner of 2nd and Arsenal. During the troubled months early in 1861, the largest supply of ammunition in the West was stored here.

Soldiers' Memorial Military Museum, 1315 Chestnut St., has memorabilia from pre-Civil War through Vietnam.

SILVA, Wayne County. US 67.

Rebel Cave, ½ mile west of US 67 on State 34, then ½ mile north. An ancient limestone cave is thought to have been a Confederate hideout. There is a 45-minute interpretive program.

SPRINGFIELD, Greene County. IS 44.

Drury College, 900 N. Benton, between Central and Calhoun, has cannon used in war.

The first charge of Frémont's bodyguard at Springfield.

Near the administration building are rifle pits made by the Union army.

Springfield National Cemetery, 1702 Seminole St., has the graves of soldiers lost at the battle of Wilson's Creek, Forsyth, Newtonia, Carthage, Pea Ridge, and Springfield. There are more than 700 unknown soldiers here. By 1868 a total of 1,514 Union soldiers were buried here. The Confederate Cemetery was established in 1870. There are 463 gravesites in the Confederate section; some are unknown soldiers. A flagpole and a memorial stone have been erected by the United Daughters of the Confederacy. A monument honors Gen. Sterling Price and another marks the burial place of Henry Walters, a scout with John Singleton Mosby, the "Gray Ghost." Union monuments commemorate Federal soldiers and Gen. Nathaniel Lyon, who was killed at the battle of Wilson's Creek but is not buried here. Gen. Ben McCulloch captured Lyon's body twice: in the field where he returned it under a truce flag; again in its coffin in the courthouse left by fleeing Union troops.

Wilson's Creek National Battlefield, about 10 miles southwest via US 60, State M and M ZZ. Visitor center has film and displays, maps for self-guided tours. There are wayside exhibits and walking trails. On August 10, 1961, the 100th anniversary of the battle, the park was dedicated. It is the second national battlefield west of the Mississippi; ridges and hollows are much as they were at the time of the battle, which was fought between Federal forces under Gen. Lyon and the combined forces of Gen. Sterling Price's Missouri units and Arkansas Confederates under Gen. McCulloch. The Union lost one who might well have become a leading general when Nathaniel Lyon was killed on Bloody Hill. Thirty of the Union officers who took part in the battle became generals before the end of war.

WAYNESVILLE, Pulaski County. IS 44. The town was prosecession and flew the Stars and Bars until Federals marched down the Wire Road and took over the village on June 7, 1862. A small fort was erected as a federal supply base on the route between Rolla and Lebanon. When Benjamin McIntyre, of the 19th Iowa, was camped nearby on the Big Piney, he noted in his diary: "Waynesville is one of those necessary little towns which are needed in certain counties as a place for horse racing, quarrels & fights."

MONTANA

Parts of Montana have been included at various times in the territories of Dakota, Idaho, Louisiana, Missouri, Nebraska, and Oregon, and a northwestern section was acquired in 1846 by a treaty with England. Lewis and Clark were the first white men known to have crossed the area. Fur traders and missionaries were followed by prospectors. When gold proved plentiful and as the Civil War dragged on, both Confederate and Union soldiers headed west, establishing settlements known as Yankee Flat and Jeff Davis Gulch.

The Organic Act of May 26, 1864, created Montana Territory. Sidney Edgerton was chosen governor and the legislature met at Bannack. In 1865 the capital was moved to Virginia City. Acting Gov. Thomas Francis Meagher (pronounced Marr), a Union general and territorial secretary, called for a constitutional convention. Eight delegates missed the meeting and the constitution, which was dispatched to St. Louis, got lost somewhere down the river. Gen. Meagher himself was lost when he fell from a steamer deck into the Missouri and was drowned in 1867.

Another constitutional convention was held, in Helena in 1884, but it was five years before Montana was admitted to the Union as the 41st state.

BANNACK, Beaverhead County. Southwest of Dillon between State 278 and State 324. Montana's oldest town and first capital was named for the Bannack Indians. A party of prospectors from Colorado hit a placer bonanza on Grasshopper Creek. Someone helpfully tacked up a signpost at the confluence of Rattlesnake Creek and Beaverhead River. It was merely a rough board inscribed in axle grease, and the message looked Chaucerian, but it was the only road guide in miles of wilderness:

Tu grass Hop Per digins
30 myle
Kepe the trale nex the bluffe
The reverse had the added information:
To Jonni Grants
one Hundred & twenti myle

Bannack was "grass Hop Per digins"; Jonni Grant was a Deer Lodge Valley rancher; and some thousand gold-minded adventurers soon followed the trail next to the bluff. An Akron lawyer, Sidney Edgerton, had been appointed chief justice of the Idaho Territory. En route to Lewiston, Idaho, in the fall of 1863, he paused at Bannack with his family, stayed the winter, and returned to Washington in the spring to advocate a new territory. Montana Territory was established that May; Lincoln appointed Edgerton governor and named Bannack as temporary capital. It has been said the capital should have been on wheels; when gold was discovered at Alder Gulch, most of Bannack called it Moving Day and resettled at the new diggings at Virginia City where the legislature, following the crowd, convened for its second session. Bannack is now a state monument. Among the remaining buildings: Skinners Saloon and the Hotel Meade, once the county courthouse. Marker on US 91, 11 miles south of Dillon.

BILLINGS, Yellowstone County. IS 90, 94.
Boothill Cemetery. East end of Black Otter Trail. Some of the slowest gunmen in the Old West are here.

Also here is the grave of Muggins Taylor, the scout who spread the word of Custer's Last Stand.

BOZEMAN, Gallatin County. IS 90. John M. Bozeman guided the first immigrant train into the Gallatin Valley in 1864. Later in the year Jim Bridger led in another wagon train. By year's end the settlement consisted of six cabins and one hotel and was known unofficially as Missouri, from the many Missourians among the settlers. Bozeman is buried here.

BOZEMAN PASS, seat of Park County. US 10, 13 miles west of Livingston. A Shoshone squaw first guided the Lewis and Clark expedition through this pass in 1806. John M. Bozeman, a Georgian, brought his first party through the pass in 1863. Marker on highway. Fourteen miles east of Livingston is a marker on

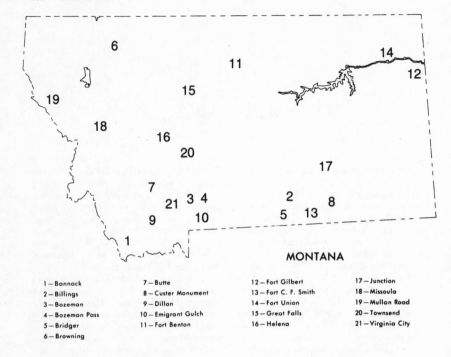

MONTANA

1 – Bannack	7 – Butte	12 – Fort Gilbert	17 – Junction
2 – Billings	8 – Custer Monument	13 – Fort C. F. Smith	18 – Missoula
3 – Bozeman	9 – Dillon	14 – Fort Union	19 – Mullan Road
4 – Bozeman Pass	10 – Emigrant Gulch	15 – Great Falls	20 – Townsend
5 – Bridger	11 – Fort Benton	16 – Helena	21 – Virginia City
6 – Browning			

US 10 at the campsite where Bozeman was killed by Blackfeet Indians in 1867.

BRIDGER, Carbon County. US 310. Marker on highway 2 miles south of town honors Jim Bridger, guide and scout for wagon trains and Federal troops.

BROWNING, Glacier County. US 89, 2. *Museum of the Plains Indians,* ½ mile west, 13 miles from Glacier National Park. Dioramas, murals, exhibits of costumes, artifacts, and maps. Conducted tours arranged by appointment.

CUSTER BATTLEFIELD NATIONAL MONUMENT, Big Horn County. The main entrance is 1 mile east of US 87, IS 90, on US 212. Park rangers conduct historical talks. The national cemetery here was established in 1876. Four days after the battle of Little Big Horn, Gen. Terry's troops buried officers in shallow graves and partially covered enlisted men. When a detail from Fort Keogh arrived nearly a year later, many skeletons had been exposed by weather and then picked clean by wolves and coyotes. Custer's remains were sent to West Point for reburial.

DILLON, Beaverhead County. IS 15, US 91.

Beaverhead County Museum. 15 S. Montana St. Pioneer and Indian historical displays. Artifacts and relics.

EMIGRANT GULCH, Park County. US 89, 29 miles north of Gardiner. State marker on site where a wagon train stopped in August 1864, made a strike in the gulch, and launched a mining boom. Flour was about as expensive here as in the Confederacy that winter; and tobacco was worth its weight in gold.

FORT BENTON, Chouteau County. US 87. The last navigable port on the upper Missouri was an important post and trading center. The adventurer and prospector, Herman Francis Reinhart, noted in his recollections: "There was a great rush to the mines right after the War, and the route from St. Louis up the Missouri to Fort Benton was a favorite. . . . It only took the steamer from 30 to 50 days to go down the river to St. Louis, as they were light-loaded and ran with the current. It was a pleasant trip to go down, but fearful hard sometimes to come up." Coming upriver, the passengers were lucky if Indians had not wiped out the wood-chopping stations, in which case all hands were laid to the axe. The fort site is east of town, just off the highway. The original blockhouse and adobe wall remain. Marker off US 87.

Museum, 1800 Front, has dioramas and displays.

FORT GILBERT, Richland County. State 20. Marker at site of Old Fort Gilbert is on highway 5 miles north of Sidney. The fort was named for Col. Gilbert, one-time commanding officer at Fort Buford Military Reservation, which was situated to the north of this site. Fort Gilbert was established in 1864.

FORT C. F. SMITH, Big Horn County. Near State 313, on Big Horn River. It is said the fort was manned by the 27th Infantry in 1866, because the regiment's colonel had provoked Secretary of War Stanton by asking for an easy post. Stanton supposedly asked his clerk, "Which place next to hell is the worst place to send a regiment?" The reply was, "To the Powder River country." Marker on US 87, 1 mile south of Lodge Grass. (A marker on US 10, 35 miles east of Miles City, says of Powder River: "This is the river that exuberant parties claim is a mile wide, an inch deep, and runs up hill. The statement is exaggerated.")

FORT UNION, Roosevelt County. US 2. The fort was established in 1828 by John Jacob Astor's fur company, 3 miles up the Missouri from the mouth of the Yellowstone. It was an important post for 40 years, but whiskey was sold to Indians against Federal law. To protect the post against drunken customers, a 20-foot stockade with two blockhouses was constructed. By 1864, Gen. Alfred Sully found conditions so deplorable he recommended government control of the fort. It was dismantled in 1886 and its materials used to build Fort Buford across the North Dakota line. Now a national historic site.

GREAT FALLS, Cascade County. IS 15.
Charles M. Russell Museum Complex, 400 13th St. Russell's paintings of the Old West, wax models, Indian costumes, and relics. Browning weapon collection.

HELENA, Lewis and Clark County. IS 15. In 1864 four Georgians prospected in an area they named "Last Chance Gulch." It is now Helena's main street and, with surrounding gulches, has yielded more than $20 million in gold.
Montana Historical Society Museum, Roberts St. and 5th Ave. Relics, dioramas, and historical displays. The Russell Art Gallery has bronzes and paintings by Charles M. Russell.
Pioneer Cabin, 218 Park, some authentic 1863 furnishings.
State Capitol, 6th and Montana. In front of

the Capitol is a statue of Gen. Thomas Francis Meagher, who raised the Irish Brigade of New York, fought in the Peninsular campaign, later served with Sherman, and was acting governor of Montana. On US 91, 1 mile north of town, is a marker for Last Chance Gulch. On US 91, 6 miles south, is a marker for the Prickly Pear Diggings, where the Northern Overland Expedition camped in September 1862. The train of 125 emigrants came from St. Paul, under the guidance of Capt. James L. Fisk, to open a wagon route to connect at Fort Benton with the Mullan Road from Walla Walla.

JUNCTION, Yellowstone County. US 10, ¼ mile east of Custer. Marker for a stage station, once a stop for outfits bound for old Fort Custer, which was about 30 miles south on the Crow Reservation. Calamity Jane spent some time here.

MISSOULA, Missoula County. IS 90. Gen. Isaac I. Stevens, later killed at Chantilly, led a railroad survey party here in 1853. The trading post was originally called "Hell Gate"; it became the county seat.
Missoula County Courthouse, W. Broadway between Harris and Higgins St., has murals.
Missoula Public Library, 301 S. Main St. has a collection of historical works on Montana and the Northwest.
State Marker on US 10, 2½ miles east of town.
University of Montana, University and Arthur avenues, has a mountain on its campus (Mount Sentinel) and a historical museum in the Fine Arts Building.

MULLAN ROAD, Mineral County. US 10. Markers on US 12, 21 miles west of Helena and on US 10, 2 miles east of DeBorgia, for the military road built by Capt. John Mullan, 2nd Artillery, U.S.A. The road, completed in 1862, was 624 miles long, connecting Fort Benton with Fort Walla Walla. Congress authorized construction under supervision of the War Department. The winter camp, east of DeBorgia, was known as Cantonment Jordan.

TOWNSEND, Broadwater County. US 12, southeast of Helena. Confederate soldiers, who hit a pay streak here in the fall of 1864, named the site Confederate Gulch. Marker on US 12, 8 miles west of town.

VIRGINIA CITY, Madison County. State 287. Southerners reportedly named the town Varina for the wife of Jefferson Davis, but a Northern judge refused to write the name on a legal document and substituted Virginia in compromise. Gold was found in Alder Gulch in May 1863, bringing a population boom; the capital was moved here. The town remained a haven for Southern sympathizers. The Virginia City newspaper habitually referred to the rest of the United States as "America"; an expedition heading down the Yellowstone River was said to be "weighing anchor to sail to America." Much of the town has been restored. Markers on State 34, near Virginia City and near Nevada City.

NEBRASKA

Early bills to create a Nebraska Territory failed because members of Congress could not agree on the slavery question. In 1854, Senator Stephen A. Douglas of Illinois introduced a bill which became the Kansas-Nebraska Act, providing that Kansas and Nebraska should decide for themselves whether to remain free or allow slavery. President Pierce appointed a South Carolinian, Francis Burt, as governor. Burt died soon after taking office and was succeeded by Secretary of State Thomas B. Cuming. As acting governor, Cuming took a census (there were 2,732 residents), and held an election for a legislature, which convened on January 16, 1855, at Omaha City. From the first, opposing factions from the north and south Platte regions argued about the capital's location. By 1864 the territory had been reduced to approximately its present size, and Congress passed an act permitting the area to become a state whenever its citizens were ready. In February 1866, a constitution was ratified by the state but failed to pass Congress inasmuch as the document restricted the franchise to "white men." A special session of the territorial legislature arrived at the conclusion that white meant any color whatever. Congress then passed the bill to admit Nebraska as a state over President Andrew Johnson's veto. The new state was proclaimed 37th in the Union on March 1, 1867. A commission headed by David Butler, first state governor, selected a small village on the prairie between Salt and Antelope creeks for the capital, changing its name from Lancaster to Lincoln.

There were a few slaveholders in Nebraska but no large-scale controversy between abolitionists and proslavery factions as in Kansas. Here, as in other Northwest territories, the outbreak of war created fear of Indian uprisings. Regular troops were withdrawn from Fort Kearny and Fort Randall. The territory was asked to contribute one regiment and was assured that part of the force would remain within the area to defend the frontier. However, the regiment was ordered to service in the South,

with no further mention of home defense. John Milton Thayer, later governor of Wyoming Territory and of Nebraska, was commissioned colonel of the First Volunteer Infantry in July 1861.

Cheyenne, Sioux, and Arapaho made periodic raids on stage coaches and freight and wagon trains along the Platte and Little Blue rivers. Many stage stations and ranches were burned and property looted. When the 1st Nebraska Cavalry rendezvoused at Omaha in August 1864, it was reorganized as the 1st Nebraska Veteran Volunteer Cavalry and dispatched to Fort Kearny, thereafter guarding military substations on the Oregon Trail. The Nebraska Battalion, recruited mostly in Omaha, served throughout the war with the 5th Iowa Cavalry. The 2nd Nebraska Cavalry, under Gen. Alfred Sully, led expeditions against the hostile Sioux in the Dakota Territory. About 3,300 Nebraskans served in the war.

ADAMS, Gage County. State 41, 43.
Adams Cemetery has a Civil War memorial erected by Sergeant Cox Post, G.A.R.

AINSWORTH, Brown County. US 20, 37.
City Park, near US 20. A memorial erected to Union veterans of the Civil War. Funds were donated by Lewis K. Alder, a pioneer attorney.

AURORA, Hamilton County. IS 80, US 34, State 14. Civil War Memorial on courthouse lawn.

BEATRICE, Gage County. US 136, 77. (Pronounced Be-*at*-triss.)
Gage County Historical Museum, 2nd and Court streets, has Civil War memorabilia.

Homestead National Monument of America, 3½ miles northwest of town on State 4, accessible from State 3 or US 77. Monument administered by the National Park Service, commemorating the first homestead claim under the act of Congress signed by President Lincoln, May 20, 1862. Daniel Freeman made the claim on January 1, 1863. Graves of Freeman

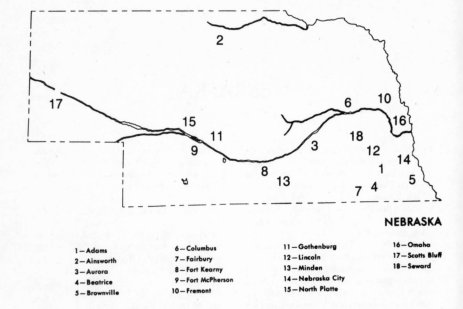

NEBRASKA

1 — Adams	6 — Columbus	11 — Gothenburg	16 — Omaha
2 — Ainsworth	7 — Fairbury	12 — Lincoln	17 — Scotts Bluff
3 — Aurora	8 — Fort Kearny	13 — Minden	18 — Seward
4 — Beatrice	9 — Fort McPherson	14 — Nebraska City	
5 — Brownville	10 — Fremont	15 — North Platte	

and his wife are marked by a granite stone taken from the old state capitol at Lincoln. The visitor center has a museum.

BELLEVUE, Sarpy County, IS 29, US 34. Historic Bellevue has a pre-Civil War bank, church, and settler's cabin.

Sarpy County Historical Society, 2402 Clay Street.

BROWNVILLE, Nemaha County. US 136. This once-important trading center on the Missouri River has been restored by the Brownville Historical Society on Main Street. The society museum and a number of old homes are open to visitors.

Site of Enlistment of Company C, 1st Regiment of Nebraska, 1st and Main St., has an All Wars Monument, erected at the place where Company C enrolled on June 8, 1861. A Civil War cannon is nearby. It was presented to Brownville by the government.

Walnut Grove Cemetery has the graves of Civil War soldiers.

COLUMBUS, Platte County, US 81, was the home town of Maj. Frank North and Capt. Luther North. Luther North enlisted in the 2nd Nebraska Cavalry in the fall of 1862, was mustered in at Omaha, and spent the winter stationed on the Pawnee Reservation. In the spring of 1863 his company joined the expedi-

tion against the Indians led by Gen. Alfred Sully. That fall North took part in the battle of White Stone Hill, in what is now North Dakota; the regiment was mustered out in December and North came home to Columbus.

The summer of 1864 proved the bloodiest for Nebraska. In August Indians struck every stage station and ranch between Julesburg and Fort Kearny. A number of settlers in the Platte and Little Blue valleys evacuated to the east. Gen. Samuel R. Curtis, veteran of Pea Ridge, took over command of the Department of Kansas in 1864, came through Columbus en route to Fort Kearny, and took Frank North with him as interpreter. As boys, both Norths had learned the Pawnee language from Indian youths who lived in skin lodges not far from the North home. Gen. Curtis gave Frank North permission to enlist a command of 100 Pawnees to serve as scouts. Frank soon signed up the quota, but, as Luther recounted in his memoirs: " . . . there was some hitch about mustering them in, and Frank went to Omaha. He was gone a couple of weeks, and when he got back the Pawnees had gone on their annual fall hunt and the men that he enlisted had gone with them, except perhaps ten or fifteen young fellows that had no horses." Horseless scouts were fairly worthless although the tribe claimed some of the fastest runners in the world; however, the brothers North rounded up enough Pawnees to muster the group at Columbus in January 1865 as Company A, Pawnee Scouts, Frank North, captain.

DORCHESTER, Saline County. US 6.
Saline County Historical Society has Civil War collection.

FAIRBURY, Jefferson County. US 136.
City Park has the homestead log cabin of Edward Hawkes. It has been moved from original site near Endicott. Except for base and floor the cabin is unchanged from 1864.
County Courthouse has a replica of the watering well which stood at the spot where Wild Bill Hickok killed David Colbert McCanless in 1861. Site is also marked, 2 miles east of Quivera Park.
Jefferson County Historical Society Museum, 712 5th Street.
Quivera Park, 7 miles southwest of town, has a marker for John C. Frémont and Kit Carson who carved their names in sandstone here in June 1842.
Rock Creek Station State Historical Park, 6 miles southeast. The Pony Express stopped here. Restored post office and Visitor Center.

FALLS CITY, Richardson County. US 73.
Richardson County Historical Society, Museum, 2114 Harlan St.

FORT CALHOUN, Washington County. US 73.
Washington County Historical Society Museum, 14th and Monroe streets.

FORT KEARNY STATE HISTORICAL PARK, Kearney County. State 410, south of IS 80. The fort, which served as a base for frontier defense against hostile Indians during the Civil War period, was manned by volunteers, including former Confederate soldiers known as Galvanized Yankees. It has been restored.

FORT McPHERSON NATIONAL CEMETERY, Lincoln County. South of Maxwell on State 330. The post was known as Cantonment McKean in 1863, renamed Fort Cottonwood in 1864 for nearby Cottonwood Springs, and renamed in 1866 for Gen. James Birdseye McPherson, killed at the battle of Atlanta. A statue is dedicated to the 7th Iowa Volunteer Cavalry. There is a Pony Express marker near the mouth of Cottonwood Canyon.

FORT MITCHELL. *See* SCOTTS BLUFF.

FORT OMAHA. *See* OMAHA.

FREMONT, Dodge County. US 30, 77.

Once a station on the Overland Trail, the city was named for Gen. John C. Frémont. There are many markers here and throughout the state for Overland and Morman trails and the old Military Road.
City Park, Main St., has a Lincoln monument.

GOTHENBURG, Dawson County. IS 80, US 30. A log cabin that served as a Pony Express station 6 miles west of Cottonwood Springs has been moved to the Ehman Park near the highway.

HASTINGS, Adams County. US 6, 34, 281.
Hastings Museum, 1330 N. Burlington Ave., is headquarters for the Adams County Historical Society.

KEARNEY, Buffalo County. IS 80.
Fort Kearny Museum, 131 S. Central, has a variety of historical relics.
Fort Kearney State Historical Park, State 10. The 1846 fort was at Nebraska City and was moved here to protect the Oregon Trail. There is a museum, as well as a restored 1864 blacksmith-carpenter shop.

LINCOLN, Lancaster County. IS 80.
Antelope Park, 23rd to 33rd, M and Sheridan streets, has a war memorial northeast of Garfield Street entrance. Figures designed by Ellis Burman represent soldiers of four American wars.
Lincoln Monument, west entrance to capitol. A heroic-size bronze figure of Lincoln, by Daniel Chester French, stands before a granite tablet on which the Gettysburg Address is engraved. The original model is in the Lincoln Tomb at Springfield, Illinois.
New State Museum of History, 15th and P streets, has displays of state history from prehistoric days to the present.
Wyuka Cemetery, in soldier burial section, has a statue of Gen. John M. Thayer, Civil War soldier and later governor of Nebraska.

MINDEN, Kearney County. US 34. For a Civil War coffee break, try the *Pioneer Village.* Mr. Harold Warp, founder, avowedly prefers not to display anything pertaining to war or liquor. The exhibits show the progress made in American living from 1800 to present times. More than 30,000 historic items are housed in 22 buildings. In Minden itself there is a Civil War marker placed in 1914 by the G.A.R.

NEBRASKA CITY, Otoe County. IS 29, US 34, 73-75.
John Brown's Cave, S. 19th St., north of

cemetery. The cave-cabin reputedly was used by John Brown as a station for runaway slaves. Fugitives crossed the Missouri River at this point into Tabor, Iowa.

Morton Home, Arbor Lodge State Historical Park, 1 mile northwest on US 73, has the pioneer home of J. Sterling Morton, advocate of Arbor Day. Morton came to Nebraska City in 1855 to edit the *News,* the only newspaper in the territory at that time. Museum. The original structure was expanded to a 52-room mansion.

NORTH PLATTE, Lincoln County. IS 80, US 83.

Buffalo Bill State Historical Park, 3½ miles northwest via US 30 and Buffalo Bill Ave. Cody's 18-room ranch, barn, and outbuildings are still standing. Buildings open; interpretive films.

Lincoln County Historical Museum, 2403 N. Buffalo Bill Ave., has furnished rooms and exhibits depicting the history of the country. In the rear of museum is a re-created early railroad village.

Sherman's Camp, on the Oregon Trail, has marker where Gen. Sherman camped in 1872.

OMAHA, Douglas County. IS 29, 80.

For anyone who wonders what tribe Ak-Sar-Ben belonged to, after seeing the name frequently on field or coliseum, it's Nebraska spelled backward.

Fort Omaha, 30th St. between Fort St. and Laurel Ave., was established as Sherman Barracks in 1868 in honor of the Civil War general who completed arrangements for acquiring the land. A plaque on building No. 1 states that Sherman stayed here; he thought Omaha so far removed from hostilities that he referred to the post as "hindquarters."

The General Crook House Museum, on US 75 at 30th and Fort streets, on the Fort Omaha campus of the Metropolitan Community College. This was Quarters 1 of Fort Omaha and was the residence of Gen. George Crook, who helped to bring about a major decision making the Indian "a person" entitled to constitutional rights and protections. Presidents Grant and Hayes were old friends and guests at the residence. Period furnishings and memorabilia.

Great Plains Black Museum, 2213 Lake St. Exhibits, early photographs, film, and slides show the history of black Americans from 1850 onward.

Union Pacific Museum, 1416 Dodge St., has a museum with exhibits depicting development of the railroad. A replica of Lincoln's funeral car, papers, and portraits.

Union Pacific Shops, 13th and Webster. At this site the first locomotive in the area, the General Sherman or Engine #1, arrived by packet from St. Louis in 1865. Engine #2 was the General McPherson, which also came by steamer from St. Louis. The first train from Omaha to Salings' Grove had Sherman and 20 leading citizens riding on flat cars using nail kegs for seats.

PLATTSMOUTH, Cass County. IS 29, US 34.

Cass County Historical Society, 646 Main St., has museum with collections from 1850.

RUSHVILLE, Sheridan County. US 20.

Sheridan County Historical Society Museum, E. US 80, has collections from prehistoric times to present.

SCOTTS BLUFF NATIONAL MONUMENT, Scotts Bluff County. State 92. A landmark on the Oregon Trail. There is a museum at the visitor center featuring history of the trail. Fort Mitchell, originally known as Camp Shuman, is nearby. It served as an outpost from 1864 to 1867, was renamed for Gen. Robert B. Mitchell, who first served with the 2nd Kansas, was later assigned to the Nebraska District, later appointed governor of New Mexico territory by President Andrew Johnson.

SEWARD, Seward County. US 34, State 15. The county was first named for Gen. Greene of Missouri but was renamed when Greene enlisted in the Confederate army. There is a Civil War memorial in the courthouse square erected by the G.A.R.

YORK, York County. Off IS 80, US 81.

Anna Bemis Palmer Museum, 211 E. 7th St., has a variety of historical displays pertaining to city, county, and state.

NEVADA

Nevada has been called the Battle Born state because it was admitted to the Union during the Civil War. Lt. John C. Frémont, later a Union general, explored and mapped the area between 1843 and 1845, with Col. Kit Carson as guide. The United States acquired the region in the treaty of Guadalupe Hidalgo at the close of the Mexican War in 1848. It was then part of Utah Territory and remained sparsely populated until a pair of prospectors in 1859 discovered silver at Virginia City. Henry Comstock laid claim to what he thought was a good outcrop of gold which happened to have some "black stuff" mixed in. The strange ore was found to be one of the richest veins of silver in the world. The Comstock lode touched off another foot and mule race over the mountains; the population increased from a scant 1,000 in 1859 to seven times that in 1860.

Congress continued to ignore petitions for a separate territory throughout 1860, but in 1861 it passed a territorial organic act which President Buchanan signed on March 2. One of Lincoln's first official acts was to commission James W. Nye, a New York politician, as governor of the Nevada Territory. In November the legislature convened at Carson City, which was selected as capital.

In *Roughing It*, Mark Twain—whose brother was first territorial secretary—describes the state palace of Gov. Nye as ". . . a white frame one-story house with two small rooms in it and a stanchion-supported shed in front—for grandeur. . . . It compelled the respect of the citizen and inspired the Indians with awe. The newly arrived Chief and Associate Justices of the territory, and other machinery of the government, were domiciled with less splendor. They were boarding around privately, and had their offices in their bedrooms."

The territory in quest of statehood had no less a friend at court than Lincoln himself. He was much in need of another certain antislavery vote in Congress to push through a constitutional amendment to abolish slavery. Although the area had fewer than the number of residents required by Congress for statehood, an enabling act to set up the new state was passed, and a constitutional convention met in November 1863. Unfortunately, the proposed constitution had a taxation section that proved unpopular with miners who managed to defeat it in election. A new enabling act was put through; a second convention met and managed to settle its arguments in a record four months, and therewith telegraphed the approved constitution to Washington. The tab was $3,416.77; but everyone, including Lincoln, was in a hurry and the sum, in any case, must have seemed piddling to a territory producing $24 million a year. On October 31, 1864, Nevada was proclaimed a state. Henry G. Blasdel, a mining engineer originally from Indiana, was elected governor.

The state sent one company of troops to join a California regiment in 1861; in 1863 raised six companies of infantry and six of cavalry. Neither saw service against the Confederates but were active in protecting the area against hostile Indians. Nevada's most famous contribution to the war was a 50-pound sack of flour.

AUSTIN, Lander County. US 50, State 8A. Reuel Colt Gridley, a grocer with Southern sympathies, lost a mayoral election bet with Dr. H. S. Herrick, Unionist. The penalty was to carry a 50-pound sack of flour about a mile down the canyon to the village of Clinton. On an April morning a parade formed with the city's officers-elect on horseback in the lead, followed by Herrick, carrying Gridley's coat and cane, and followed by Gridley and the sack of flour decorated with ribbons and Union flags. Gridley's young son marched alongside carrying a flag while the Austin band played "Dixie." Amid cheers and mill whistles, the flour was delivered to the Bank Exchange Saloon in Clinton where other whistles were dampened, speeches made, and the procession re-formed to return to Austin. At the Grimes and Gibson Saloon in Austin, the day being young and the flour no worse for travel, the sack

177

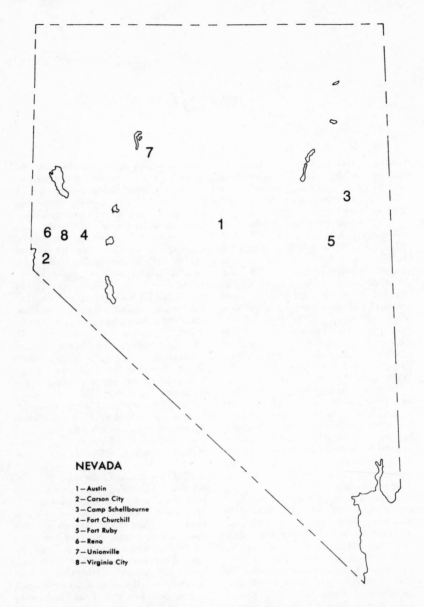

NEVADA

1 — Austin
2 — Carson City
3 — Camp Schellbourne
4 — Fort Churchill
5 — Fort Ruby
6 — Reno
7 — Unionville
8 — Virginia City

was auctioned off, returned and auctioned again, until more than $10,000 had been collected in behalf of the Sanitary Commission fund for war relief. Not too long later, Austin adopted the flour sack design for the city seal. Gridley, converted to helping the Union cause for this or other reasons, auctioned the flour at Virginia City and points east and west. Before

the show closed, the sack had toured both coasts. Its final appearance took place in St. Louis; then Gen. Lee surrendered at Appomatox, and Gridley went home, personally broke after having bagged more than $200,000 for the aid of war wounded. The sack is in the Nevada State Historical Society at Reno. Gridley is buried in Stockton, California, with a G.A.R. monument in Carrara marble to commemorate his salesmanship. Austin was also the final home of camels used in the "arid-region experiment." As Secretary of War, Jefferson Davis had been interested in trying out a scheme to use camels in desert areas of the American West. In 1864 some of the camels were sold at auction in southern California; nine were bought by a former keeper and brought to Austin where for years they carried salt from marshes to quartz mill.

The Reese River Reveille began publishing in May 1863. Files are preserved in the courthouse.

US 50, which has been called the loveliest road in America, was once the Pony Express route. Legend has it that the settlement began after a Pony Express horse kicked over a rock that had hidden the mouth of a cavern where silver was found. Some horse, some rock, to be sure, but in 1864 at least 10,000 hopefuls were in town ready to stake mining claims.

CARSON CITY, Ormsby County. US 50, State 88. The smallest capital in the lower 48 states is located in Nevada's smallest county. It was first known as Eagle Valley, so named by Maj. William Ormsby when the townsite was laid out in 1860. Later known as Eagle Ranch, its present name honors Kit Carson.

Nevada State Museum, N. Carson and Robinson St. Exhibits of guns, coins, and pioneer relics.

State Capitol, N. Carson St. The building, completed in 1871, has an excellent oil painting of Abraham Lincoln by Charles W. Shean at north end of second floor. The Capitol has been restored at the cost of $6 million. Tours in both this building and the governor's mansion.

FORT CHURCHILL STATE HISTORIC PARK, Lyon County. Seven miles south on US 95, then one mile west on Old Fort Churchill Road. The fort was established in 1860 to subdue the Paiutes and to protect the mail routes. It was headquarters for the U.S. Military District of Nevada and was garrisoned from 1860 to 1869. Supporters of the Confederacy were numerous in Nevada in 1861, and on June 7 of that year Maj. George Blake, commanding at the fort, dispatched Capt. T. Moore and 20 dragoons to take possession of all public arms in

Carson City. The transaction was carried out without incident and the arms were later dispatched to Virginia City to protect Union interests against citizens who were threatening to raise the secession flag. Skeleton walls of the old adobe barracks are still standing.

FORT RUBY, White Pine County. (Also known as Camp Ruby.) Eight miles south of Cave Creek at the Fort Ruby Ranch. In 1862 and 1863, Goshute and Paiute Indians repeatedly harassed the overland mail. Two companies of California Volunteers stationed here were kept busy with skirmishes. In 1864, Nevada Volunteers took over the post.

RENO, Washoe County. IS 80, US 395. The town was named for Gen. Jesse Lee Reno, a Union officer killed at the battle of South Mountain; he was the fellow who tried to buy Barbara Fritchie's flag, an incident which led to Whittier's erroneous poem.

Nevada Historical Society Museum and Research Library, 1650 N. Virginia Street, has pioneer relics and artifacts.

UNIONVILLE, Pershing County. State 50, south of Mill City. Ardent Northerners founded the town in 1861, but a number of equally fervent Southerners settled in the area. Like all Gaul, the community was divided in three parts: Lower Town (or Dixie), Centerville, and Upper Town (or Unionville). During the war Centerville served as the Mason-Dixon line with an hourly shuttle stage connecting the separated sections.

VIRGINIA CITY, Storey County. State 17, southeast of Reno. Sentiment favored the Union, and two regiments were sent to Fort Churchill. But Southern sympathizers were still active and raised a Confederate flag. Mark Twain worked as a reporter on the *Territorial Enterprise.* Edwin Booth was among the number of stars who appeared at Piper's Opera House, B and Taylor streets.

U. S. Grant stayed at the Savage Mansion in 1879. Built in 1861 with a mine office on the first floor and the superintendent's living quarters on two upper floors, it has been restored and in recent years has been open for tours or overnight stops.

NEW HAMPSHIRE

New Hampshire, ninth of the original 13 states, opposed slavery from the early years of the 19th century. John P. Hale, born in Dover, broke with the Democratic party in 1845, became the first important antislavery U.S. senator, and was one of the founders of the Republican party. On the contrary, Franklin Pierce, the only New Hampshire native to become president, was a States' Rights advocate, opposing Hale both in policy and public debate.

When Lincoln called for volunteers after the fall of Fort Sumter, mass meetings were held throughout the state; 28 recruiting offices were opened. A landslide of volunteers enlisted—three times the quota called for. In all, the state raised 18 regiments; about 39,000 men served in the war. Three women attempted to enlist as soldiers, two others served outstandingly as nurses; and one impatient patriot, from Littleton, took up his gun and headed for Washington ready to defend the capital on his own if need be.

The 5th New Hampshire Volunteers had more casualties than any other Union regiment. The 13th New Hampshire led the Union troops into Richmond when the Confederacy was overcome.

AMHERST, Hillsboro County. State 101, southwest of Manchester. A memorial to Horace Greeley, war-time editor of the controversial *New York Tribune,* is on the common. Greeley's birthplace is at Mount Vernon, a few miles northwest of Amherst on State 13.

BEDFORD, Hillsboro County. Off IS 293, State 101, near Manchester. Birthplace of Zachariah Chandler, known as a Radical Republican, who was a U.S. senator and a member of the Committee on the Conduct of the War.

BETHLEHEM, Grafton County. IS 93, US 302. Gen. Grant, as president, took what was called the "wildest ride of his life" from Bethlehem to the Profile House in Franconia Notch in August 1869. In a coach drawn by fine horses and with speedster Edmund Cox at the reins, Grant made a normal two-hour trip in a record 58 minutes. He is said to have sent Cox a driving whip the following Christmas.

BOSCAWEN, Merrimack County. US 3, north of Concord. Birthplace of John Adams Dix, who served as Secretary of the Treasury during the latter part of the Buchanan administration and as major general in the war. When he was informed on January 29, 1861, that the captain of the revenue cutter *McClelland* refused to surrender the vessel to the Federal government in New Orleans, Dix issued a dispatch which concluded with the now famous dictum: "If anyone attempts to haul down the American flag, shoot him on the spot."

Birthplace of William Pitt Fessenden, Main St., is marked by a granite tablet. Fessenden was U.S. senator from Maine and Secretary of the Treasury in Lincoln's cabinet.

BRADFORD, Merrimack County. Off IS 89, State 103, 114, was the hometown of Mason Weare Tappan, a lawyer and member of Congress, who served as colonel of the 1st New Hampshire Regiment of Volunteers. Tappan had no previous military experience but was regarded by those who knew him as "the proper person to take command."

CANAAN, Grafton County. US 4, State 118. James Furber's house was an Underground Railroad station as early as 1830. Furber's father-in-law, James Harris, also helped fugitives on toward Canada. Furber is said to have made trips to Lyme, on the Connecticut River, about once a fortnight with fugitives received from Concord stations. From Lyme they were sent north via the Connecticut Valley.

The Ball House, 31 Myrtle St., was the home of inventor Albert Ball, who at Worcester, Massachusetts, in 1863 devised the combined repeating and single-loading rifle known as the Springfield.

Soldiers' Monument, in Broad Street Park,

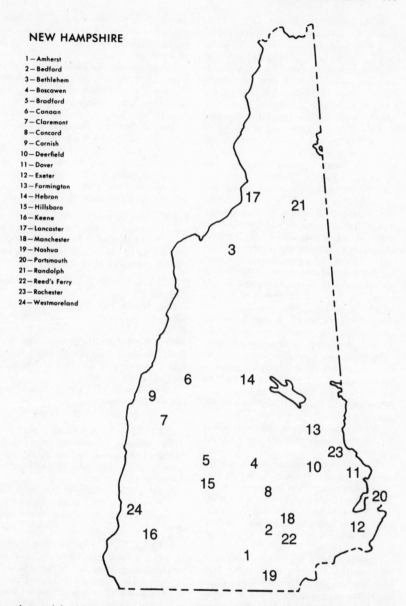

NEW HAMPSHIRE

1 — Amherst
2 — Bedford
3 — Bethlehem
4 — Boscawen
5 — Bradford
6 — Canaan
7 — Claremont
8 — Concord
9 — Cornish
10 — Deerfield
11 — Dover
12 — Exeter
13 — Farmington
14 — Hebron
15 — Hillsboro
16 — Keene
17 — Lancaster
18 — Manchester
19 — Nashua
20 — Portsmouth
21 — Randolph
22 — Reed's Ferry
23 — Rochester
24 — Westmoreland

was designed by Martin Milmore. Peterborough has a duplicate in its town common.

CLAREMONT, Sullivan County. IS 91, State 103, 120.

Birthplace of Salmon P. Chase, State 12. Chase, who became Lincoln's Secretary of the Treasury, was born here January 13, 1808, the eighth of 11 children of Ithamar Chase. So many of the houses in the area were built by Chases, a story is told that one of them informed a member of the populous Bellows family in Walpole that there were enough Chases in town to chase all others into Walpole. The other replied there were enough Bellows in Walpole to blow them all back again.

CONCORD, Merrimack County. IS 93. Responding to Lincoln's call for troops, 75,000 soldiers came to Concord, the capital. The 1st New Hampshire has been called the first Union regiment to go to the front fully equipped with uniforms, arms, baggage, hospital, and supply train. On May 25, 1861, it departed from the Concord railroad station amidst cheers and tears. It might also be claimed it was the first back—still fully equipped and in the best of health. The 1st had been ordered to invade Virginia, under Gen. Robert Patterson, to prevent Gen. Joseph Johnston from reinforcing Beauregard at Bull Run. Patterson failed to engage the enemy, explaining that he had not received orders to attack. Whether or not he supposed the 18,000 men in his command were merely to remonstrate with Johnston, he was mustered out on July 27, and the 1st New Hampshire went home on the cars to a grand reception at the state capitol, with Concord's loveliest young women serving as waitresses at the banquet. More than half reenlisted in other units. The 2nd New Hampshire acquired a spinster in her mid-forties, Miss Harriet Patience Dame of Concord, as army nurse. She camped with the regiment even on the battlefield, providing medicine, warm extra clothing, coffee, and beef tea. Joseph A. Gilmore of Concord was elected governor in 1863. Reelected in 1864 when patriotism and war spirits were running low, he managed to raise additional troops without invoking the draft.

New Hampshire Historical Society, 30 Park St., has historical museum and library. Changing exhibits.

Pierce Manse, 14 Penacook St., was the home of President Franklin Pierce in the 1840s. It has been moved from its original site on Montgomery St., restored and furnished in period. The former president died October 8, 1869, and is buried beside his wife and three children in old North Cemetery. Granite memorial at gravesite.

Statehouse, Main St., has a display of battle flags in the rotunda. Portraits of New Hampshire officers who served in the Civil War are displayed throughout the building. Statues of Franklin Pierce and John P. Hale are on the Plaza.

CORNISH, Sullivan County. State 120, north of Claremont. At the battle of Bull Run, John L. Rice of Cornish fell with a bullet through his lungs. A memorial service was held at home; but friends found him in a corner of the field, cleaned his wound and fed him for ten days until he was removed to a Confederate hospital. He survived to become lieutenant colonel of a black Union regiment and a lawyer after the war.

Saint-Gaudens National Historic Site, State 12A, home of sculptor Augustus Saint-Gaudens. He is buried on the estate. Among noted Civil War memorials executed by Saint-Gaudens are those of Adm. Farragut, Gen. Logan, Gen. Sherman, President Lincoln, and Robert Gould Shaw, a young Bostonian who died while leading the first black regiment in the war. It is said Saint-Gaudens was attracted to Cornish, while at work on his "Standing Lincoln," by a friend who assured him there were plenty of "Lincoln-shaped men up there."

DEERFIELD, Rockingham County. State 107. Birthplace of Gen. Benjamin Butler in 1818. Butler grew up to be the least popular man in New Orleans, but in 1882 he was elected governor of Massachusetts.

DOVER, Strafford County. Spaulding Turnpike.

Hale House, 192 Central Ave., was the home of John Parker Hale, noted statesman. He was so ardently opposed to slavery he was sometimes called the "Hale Storm." Vice President Calhoun declared he would sooner argue with an inmate of Bedlam than with Hale on the question of slavery.

Lincoln House, 107 Locust St., was a frame cottage where Lincoln slept in 1860 after making a political address at the old city hall.

EXETER, Rockingham County. State 101. Gilman Marston of Exeter was colonel of the 2nd New Hampshire Volunteers. A lawyer and a member of Congress, he learned soldiering at the age of 49.

Boarding-Place of Robert Lincoln, corner of High and Pleasant St. Lincoln visited his son here while Robert was a student at the academy.

FARMINGTON, Strafford County. State 11, off US 3. Birthplace of Jeremiah Jones Colbath, who changed his name to Henry Wilson. In 1862, as U.S. senator from Massachusetts, he introduced a bill to create a national award for valor to be known as the Medal of Honor. Twenty New Hampshire men won it during the war. Wilson was vice president 1873–1875.

HEBRON, Grafton County. State 3A. Birthplace of Nathaniel S. Berry who became governor in 1861 and served until June 1863. Berry was an ex-Free Soil Democrat and a friend of President Lincoln. During his admin-

Morning detail of the 4th New Hampshire on Hilton Head Island.

istration, the 2nd through 17th New Hampshire regiments were mustered into service.

HILLSBORO (formerly **HILLSBOROUGH**), Merrimack County. State 31.

Franklin Pierce Homestead, junction of State 9 and 31. Family home of the 14th president. It was built in 1804 and is now a state historic site. Pierce, considered one of the most personable presidents, believed that slavery was protected by the Constitution; he was estranged from many of his friends during the war because of his attitude. Nathaniel Hawthorne was his lifelong devoted friend. Mrs. Jefferson Davis, who with her husband had known Pierce in prewar years, remembered him with fondness. In his last public speech, May 1869, the year of his death, he reaffirmed his loyalty to the Union and his belief that the Constitution should have been strictly adhered to. The house, restored by the New Hampshire Federation of Women's Clubs, has furniture and carpeting that were brought from Boston when young Franklin was a student at Bowdoin College. The French block-wallpaper was hung in 1824.

JEFFERSON, Coos County. State 2. Thaddeus S. C. Loewe, balloonist of the war, was born at Riverton. A marker on US 302 just west of town commemorates the inventor. He organized and directed a Union balloon force during the war, later invented useful devices for atmospheric observation.

KEENE, Cheshire County. State 10, 12. The 6th New Hampshire Regiment staged and trained here. Assigned to Burnside's expedition to North Carolina, the 6th arrived on Hatteras Island in March 1862 with 150 cases of measles. Col. Simon Goodell Griffin took over as commanding officer. His new command suffered no battle casualties, but only 300 were well enough for duty.

LANCASTER, Coos County. US 3. Charles Farrar Browne, known as Artemus

Ward, spent his apprenticeship on the *Coos County Democrat*. Ward, who wrote humorously of war meetings and the draft, described one editor as a man of great pluck who would most certainly enlist as a brigadier general if it weren't absolutely necessary for him to remain at home and announce in his paper from week to week that the government was about to take "vig'rous measures to put down the rebellion."

MANCHESTER, Hillsboro County. IS 93. Frederick Smyth of Manchester became governor in March 1865; he supervised demobilizing.

NASHUA, Hillsboro County. IS 93.
Monitor Marker, 25 E. Hollis St. A bronze tablet was placed here in commemoration of the gunboat *Monitor,* at the site where porthole stoppers were made in the old iron and steel works.

NEWPORT, Sullivan County. State 10, 11. Sarah Josepha Hale, a native, was the successful editor of the popular magazine *Godey's Lady's Book*. She persuaded President Lincoln to proclaim Thanksgiving a national holiday.

PORTSMOUTH, Rockingham County. IS 95. New Hampshire Turnpike. The USS *Kearsage*, which destroyed the Confederate cruiser *Alabama* and *New Hampshire*, were built in navy yards (partly in Kittery, Me.). Home of Civil War governor Ichabod Goodwin at Strawberry Banke has been restored. In the commandant's quarters at the Navy Yard, the first admiral of the U.S. Navy, David G. Farragut, died on August 14, 1870.

Fort Constitution, 4 miles east on State 1B in New Castle, built on the site of an earlier fort, has granite walls added during the Civil War. Museum.

REED'S FERRY, Hillsboro County. US 3. Birthplace of Walter Kettredge, author and composer of the wartime ballad "Tenting on the Old Camp Ground."

ROCHESTER, Strafford County. Spaulding Turnpike. A bronze memorial on the common, S. Main and Hancock St., is dedicated to soldiers and sailors of the Civil War.

WESTMORELAND, Cheshire County. State 12. Corp. Isaac W. Derby of this village was typical of New Hampshire troops in hardiness if not, fortunately, in experience. He survived an amputation without anesthetic, refused to go to the hospital, and was soon back on duty with the regiment. It was said of him, in understatement, "Derby was a nervy man."

NEW JERSEY

New Jersey, the third state, entered the Union on December 18, 1787. The state provided 88,000 troops and $23 million to the Federal Civil War effort. In April 1861, the state legislature appropriated the first $2 million and by May 4, regiments had left for Annapolis. Maj. Gen. Philip Kearny, who led the first New Jersey troops into war, was killed at Chantilly, in the battle of Ox Hill.

In 1863 a Copperhead movement had gained enough strength to elect Joel Parker, Democrat, as governor. Parker's success was also partly due to the fact that many New York bankers who lived in the state had a mistrust of Lincoln. There was no fighting except political on New Jersey soil, and the state began a great period of prosperity soon after the war's end.

BARNEGAT LIGHTHOUSE STATE PARK, on the tip of Long Beach Island, surrounds the old lighthouse, which was built in 1857–58 by Gen. George Meade, who later led the Union forces at Gettysburg.

BORDENTOWN, Burlington County. Off IS 195, US 130.

Clara Barton Schoolhouse, 142 Crosswicks St. Miss Barton, who became a Union nurse and founder of the Red Cross, established one of the first free public schools here in 1851. She resigned when townspeople insisted that her work be supervised by a male principal.

BURLINGTON, Burlington County. US 130.

Grant House, 309 Wood St. Gen. Grant, who kept his family here during part of the war, is said to have been at the house on the night Lincoln was assassinated.

CAMDEN, Camden County. IS 95, US 130.

Harleigh Cemetery, Haddon Ave. and Vesper Blvd. Walt Whitman's vault was designed by himself. The poet's parents, brothers, and sisters are also buried here. The heavy stone doorway is always left open.

Walt Whitman Home State Site, 330 Mickle. Residence occupied by Walt Whitman from 1884 until his death in 1892. It is now a museum, with original furnishings and mementos. Whitman served as a Christian Commission volunteer and hospital aide in the war.

CAPE MAY, Cape May County, southernmost tip of the state, was a holiday place for presidents Lincoln, Grant, Pierce, and Buchanan, and Horace Greeley, among other famous 19th-century persons. The whole community is now a National Historic Landmark.

FINN'S POINT NATIONAL CEMETERY, Salem County. State 49. Used as a burial ground for Confederate prisoners of war who died in the prison camp at Fort Delaware on Pea Patch Island. Monuments to the 2,436 Confederate and 300 Union soldiers buried here.

FORT MOTT STATE PARK, Salem County, State 49. Used during the Civil War for the defense of the Delaware River and the Port of Philadelphia. Gun mounts and underground facilities.

FREEHOLD, Monmouth County. Off US 39.

Monmouth County Historical Museum, 70 Court St., has Civil War weapons.

HACKENSACK, Bergen County. State 17. Scene of a print shop raid during the war. An abolitionist editor's plant was ransacked and the Union flag was burned on the public green.

War Memorial Monument, at south end of Main St., was dedicated in 1924.

LONG BRANCH, Monmouth County. State 36.

Long Branch Museum, 1260 Ocean Ave., has Civil War relics. Town was a spa for Grant, Hayes, Harrison, and Garfield, who came here to die.

NEWARK, Essex County. IS 78.

Essex County Courthouse, Springfield Ave. and Market St. The famous seated Lin-

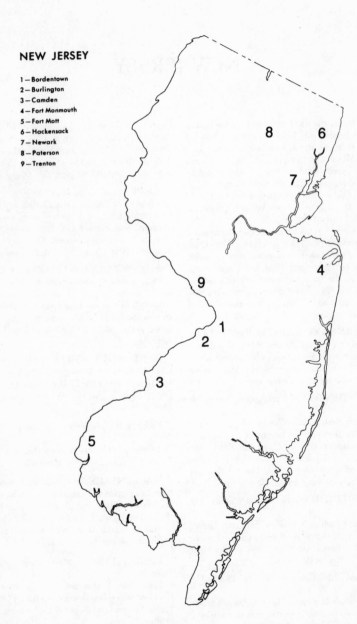

NEW JERSEY

1 — Bordentown
2 — Burlington
3 — Camden
4 — Fort Monmouth
5 — Fort Mott
6 — Hackensack
7 — Newark
8 — Paterson
9 — Trenton

Volunteers leaving the Jersey City railroad depot en route to Washington, D.C.

coln bronze by Gutzon Borglum is in the plaza. It was unveiled in 1911.

Military Park, Broad St. and Park Pl., has Gutzon Borglum statue, "The Wars of America." In northeast corner of park is a statue of Maj. Gen. Philip Kearny.

Site of Crane House, 14 Mulberry Pl. Stephen Crane, author of *The Red Badge of Courage,* often said to be the best novel ever written about the Civil War, once lived at this address. Crane is buried at Hillside, New Jersey.

PATERSON, Passaic County. IS 80.

Old Gun Mill, Mill and Van Houten streets, was built by Samuel Colt, who designed a re-

volver he thought was a failure; legend says he sold it to an Indian trader. When the U.S. sent a large order, Colt had no model. He remade the gun—and history—in Hartford, Conn.

TRENTON, Mercer County. IS 295. Lincoln spoke to the two houses of the legislature on February 21, 1861, when en route to his inauguration.

State Capitol, 121 W. State St., has collection of battle flags. State museum and library are in the Capitol annex. During the war, tents were pitched on the ground. Rooms were turned over for the use of military officers; the rotunda and corridors were filled with recruits.

NEW MEXICO

Southern influences were strong in New Mexico territory in the prewar years. Abolition leaders in Congress defeated a bill for statehood in March 1861, and New Mexico did not become a state until 1912. Most New Mexicans remained loyal to the Union throughout the war, partly because their ancient rival and enemy, Texas, was in the Confederacy. At the outbreak of war, Confederates under the command of Brig. Gen. H. H. Sibley marched up the Rio Grande Valley and occupied the Capitol at Santa Fe. Sibley seems to have lost more battles with the bottle than with the Union; his soldiers blamed his drinking for their failure to capture Fort Craig during an engagement at Valverde. By establishing headquarters at Santa Fe, Sibley extended his lines so far it was impossible to maintain them. Federal forces, strengthened by Colorado Volunteers, surprised the Confederates en route to Fort Union in Apache Canyon and won a decisive battle at Glorieta and also at Pidgin's Ranch in March 1862. The Union reoccupied Santa Fe in April. Union troops caught up with retreating Confederates at Peralta on April 15, hastened the rebels on their way, and ended the Confederate invasion of New Mexico.

ALBUQUERQUE, Bernalillo County. IS 25, 40.

Casa de Armijo, east side of plaza, served as headquarters for both Union and Confederate officers during the Civil War. Although partly remodeled, much of the original building remains. The battle of Albuquerque in April 1862 was little more than a skirmish. Both sides fired their cannons but stopped when townspeople complained.

BOSQUE REDONDO, Valencia County. US 60, 84. Site of old Fort Sumner. Col. Kit Carson in 1863 captured Mescalero Apaches and kept them in a new reservation on the Pecos River. The Navajos captured by Carson's troops in Canyon de Chelly, Arizona, made their famous "Long Walk" to Bosque Redondo.

FORT CRAIG. *See* VALVERDE.
FORT FILLMORE. *See* MESILLA.

FORT STANTON, Lincoln County. South of State 48, off US 380 at Capitan. The fort was established in 1855. In 1861 the fort was destroyed by Confederate troops, reoccupied by Federal forces in 1863.

FORT THORN, Doña Ana County. US 85, near Salem. Post was established in 1853 and later abandoned. Gen. Sibley and Confederate troops occupied it in 1862 on their march north. This fort as well as others in the area had been abandoned by Federal forces under Maj. Isaac Lynde early in the war when Texas troops under Col. Baylor invaded New Mexico. Lynde was called "cowardly and pusillanimous" by irate fellow officers.

FORT UNION NATIONAL MONUMENT, Mora County. State 161, 8 miles northwest of Watrous. Established in 1851, the fort was a major supply depot and military post. John Van De Bois, a young New Yorker stationed at the fort in 1861, wrote of the secession talk prevalent at the post in February and March. He had received inducements to join the Southern army but recorded in his diary: "The soldiers are loyal, though most of the officers are going south themselves, and all the West Pointers except Longstreet urge their soldiers to remain true." James Longstreet later became a Confederate general. Confederate forces were hoping to capture the post when Union troops cut them off at Glorieta Pass in March 1862. Adobe walls and foundations remain. Visitor center has a museum. There is a self-guiding, 1¼-mile tour trail through the 100 acres of adobe ruins.

FORT WINGATE, McKinley County. US 66. The fort was named for Capt. Benjamin Wingate, who was killed at the battle of Valverde in 1862. An earlier Fort Wingate is near Grants. This post was garrisoned by Brig. Gen. James H. Carleton in 1862. Col. Kit Carson was based here for a time.

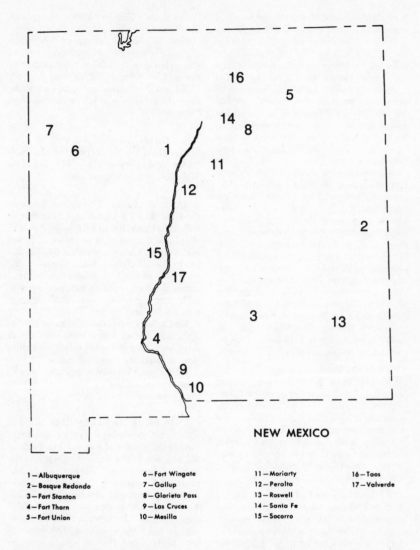

NEW MEXICO

1 — Albuquerque	6 — Fort Wingate	11 — Moriarty	16 — Taos
2 — Bosque Redondo	7 — Gallup	12 — Peralta	17 — Valverde
3 — Fort Stanton	8 — Glorieta Pass	13 — Roswell	
4 — Fort Thorn	9 — Las Cruces	14 — Santa Fe	
5 — Fort Union	10 — Mesilla	15 — Socorro	

GALLUP, McKinley County. IS 40, US 66. *Kit Carson Cave,* 8 miles east on US 66, 3½ miles north on side road. Carson reportedly spent some time in the cave during his roundup of Navajos in 1864.

GLORIETA PASS, Santa Fe County. US 84, 85. On March 28, 1862, Maj. Chivington succeeded in destroying the Confederate ammunition and supply train without Union loss. Confederates retreated to Santa Fe. Johnson's Ranch, where the supply train was demolished, has disappeared but other battle positions can

be identified. The site has been granted historic landmark status.

LAS CRUCES, Doña Ana County. IS 10, 25, US 85.

Amador Hotel, Amador St., was a favorite rendezvous point for soldiers from Forts Seldon and Fillmore. The dining room sometimes served as a courtroom, the kitchen as a jail.

LA MESILLA STATE MONUMENT, Doña Ana County. US 85. An important stop on the El Paso-Fort Yuma stage line and the

Butterfield Overland Mail route, the town was captured in July 1861 by Lt. Col. John R. Baylor, who declared himself governor of Confederate Arizona and Mesilla the capital. Fort Fillmore, the Union garrison at Mesilla, was commanded by Maj. Isaac Lynde, accused of "brainless imbecility" by the post surgeon who saw that no preparations were made to defend the fort against the Texans. When Confederates occupied the town, Lynde more or less politely, certainly calmly, demanded their surrender. When it was refused, Lynde sent the cavalry in a frontal attack which was brief and highly unsuccessful; the troops withdrew to Fort Fillmore and the next day retreated to Fort Stanton. Historian Paul Horgan quotes the Fort Fillmore surgeon on Lynde's defense of Mesilla: ". . . one of the most extraordinary, imbecile, and childish military movements ever perpetrated." In August 1862, California Volunteers under Gen. James H. Carleton took possession of the town and made it headquarters of the Military District of Arizona. The plaza remains much the same as in the days when it was the seat of a county that included Arizona and a goodly piece of New Mexico.

Gadsden Museum, Boutz-Barker Rd., just east of State 28, has such historical items as guns, bugles, and flags of the Civil War period.

PERALTA, Valencia County. Off IS 25, US 85. Gov. Henry Connelly had a store and home here. Confederate forces occupied Connelly's house and destroyed goods and furniture amounting to $30,000. The last skirmish in the state took place here April 18, 1862, when Federal forces succeeded in forcing Confederates to cross the Rio Grande, abandoning supply trains; some 60 wagons were left in the river or on the banks.

SANTA FE, Santa Fe County. IS 25, US 84-85. In 1848 Gen. Stephen Watts Kearny led his troops here and put up the Union flag. During the war Confederate soldiers occupied the town for only two weeks before being driven out by Federals.

Kit Carson Monument, south entrance of Federal Building, erected by the G.A.R.

San Rosario Cemetery has the grave of wartime Gov. Connelly.

Santa Fe National Cemetery, US 64, north of plaza. Formerly the post cemetery, the burial ground has graves of soldiers killed in the battles of Pidgin's Ranch and Valverde.

Soldiers' Monument, on plaza, commemorates the soldiers who fell at the battle of Valverde.

SOCORRO, Socorro County. IS 25.
Park Hotel Site, west of plaza. Headquarters for the Union forces in 1861-1862. Gen. Lew Wallace stayed here at one time.

TAOS, Taos County. US 64, State 3. During the Civil War, Kit Carson and other citizens nailed the Union flag to a cottonwood pole in the plaza and stayed in the area to see that it was not removed. Carson gave orders that the flag was to fly day and night. Today Taos is one of a few places in the U.S. where the flag flies around the clock. In Taos it has flown continuously since Carson and Capt. Smith Simpson nailed it to the cottonwood.

Kit Carson House, east of plaza on US 64. The colonel's home from 1843 to 1868. Period furnishings and historical relics, including guns, saddles, and household items.

Kit Carson Memorial State Park, 2 blocks north of plaza on State 3. Carson's grave is in the 17-acre tract.

VALVERDE BATTLEFIELD, Socorro County. US 85. Marker for Fort Craig on highway, 37 miles south of Socorro. The battle of Valverde was fought across the river from the fort in February 1862. Texans under Gen. H. H. Sibley routed the Federals after a two-hour engagement and captured a battery. Col. Kit Carson commanded part of the Federal force. The Confederates went on to take Albuquerque and Santa Fe while the Federals withdrew to Fort Craig. Parts of walls of 18 adobe buildings and earth mounds remain at the fort. The post, active in the Apache wars, was abandoned in 1885.

NEW YORK

New York became the 11th state on July 6, 1776. New York City served as United States capital from 1785 to 1790. Long before the Civil War, factional groups with a diversity of European heritage and interests made state politics a highly controversial affair. Although many New Yorkers opposed slavery, not all were unsympathetic toward the South and the states' rights cause. The spectacular newspaper editor, James Gordon Bennett, of the *New York Herald,* usually spoke for the Democrats; Horace Greeley, of the *Tribune,* gave unceasing support to the abolitionists.

In spite of draft riots, the state sent its full quota of men and supplies to the war effort. Probably the worst riot of the Civil War took place in New York City in July 1863. Gov. Horatio Seymour, a leader of states' rights forces, challenged the constitutional right of the government to enforce the draft. On July 11, the provost marshal drew the first names from a lottery wheel. These were published the following day, a Sunday, and mobs began to gather; on Monday when the drawing resumed, rioting broke out. A mob of some 50,000 protestors wrecked property to the extent of $1.5 million damage; more than a dozen persons lost their lives before Federal troops from the Army of the Potomac restored order. By the time rioters were dispersed, more than 1,000 had been killed or wounded. By war's end, New York had sent about 500,000 troops to the Union army; one-tenth were killed in service.

ADAMS, Jefferson County, off IS 81, exit 41.
Historical Association of South Jefferson, 9 E. Church St., is a Civil War period house-museum.

ALBANY, Albany County, IS 90, 87,
New York State Capitol, State St., Washington Ave., Swan, and Eagle St. There is a Military Room. Daily tours. On Capitol grounds in eastern section is an heroic equestrian statue of Gen. Phil Sheridan, who was born in Albany. The monument was designed by J. Q. A. Ward and finished by Daniel Chester French.

The Capitol and state museum are now in the *Governor Nelson A. Rockefeller Empire State Complex,* which comprises 65 acres and 10 buildings. The museum has more than 200 battle flags and one of the largest collections of Civil War relics in the country.

Washington Park, State and Willet St., S. Lake and Madison Ave. At north end of park is the Soldiers' and Sailors' Memorial.

AUBURN, Cayuga County. US 20.
Cayuga Museum of History and Art, 203 W. Genesee St., has William H. Seward memorabilia.

Fort Hill Cemetery, 19 Fort St., has the grave of Seward, Lincoln's secretary of state.

Harriet Tubman Home, 180 S St., has been restored. Using the Underground Railroad, the former slave helped some 300 others to escape. During the war she also served as a Union spy and scout. Tours by appointment.

Seward Home, 33 South St. on State 34. William H. Seward was born in Orange County in 1801, was graduated from Union College, and practiced law in Auburn. The house was built in 1816 by his father-in-law, Elijah Miller. During the war years, Seward entertained leading political figures here. An attempt was made on his life as part of the Lincoln assassination conspiracy; he was wounded but lived until 1872. In 1867 he was chiefly responsible for the purchase of Alaska, a transaction which was derided as "Seward's Folly" or "Seward's Frog Pond." The mansion contains many of the original furnishings. A National Historic Landmark.

BATAVIA, Genesee County. IS 90, State 63.
Holland Land Office, 131 W. Main St., has Civil War artifacts.

BUFFALO, Erie County. IS 90, 190, 290.
Buffalo and Erie County Historical Society,

NEW YORK

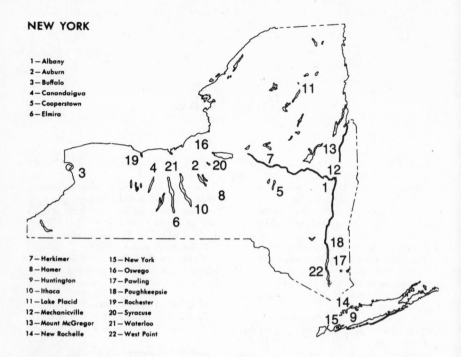

1 — Albany
2 — Auburn
3 — Buffalo
4 — Canandaigua
5 — Cooperstown
6 — Elmira

7 — Herkimer	15 — New York
8 — Homer	16 — Oswego
9 — Huntington	17 — Pawling
10 — Ithaca	18 — Poughkeepsie
11 — Lake Placid	19 — Rochester
12 — Mechanicville	20 — Syracuse
13 — Mount McGregor	21 — Waterloo
14 — New Rochelle	22 — West Point

25 Nottingham Court off Elmwood Ave., has period rooms and shops.

Soldiers' and Sailors' Monument, center of Lafayette Square, was designed by George Keller and executed by Caspar Buberl.

CANANDAIGUA, Ontario County. US 20.

Ontario County Historical Society, 55 N. Main St., has historical displays and manuscripts. A Lincoln life mask is in the collection. Changing exhibits.

CHERRY CREEK, Otsego County, US 20. Civil War monument downtown. Walking tour brochures at the Chamber of Commerce, Village Hill. The Cherry Valley Museum, 49 Main St., has women's costumes of the Civil War period.

COOPERSTOWN, Otsego County. State 28. Gen. Abner Doubleday, West Point graduate, served in the Shenandoah campaigns and helped to defend Washington against Jubal Early's attack in 1864.

Fenimore House, 1 mile north on State 80. Headquarters of the New York State Historical Association, the house has a Hall of Life Masks and other historical displays.

ELMIRA, Chemung County. State 17. Berry Greenwood Benson, a sharpshooter from South Carolina, was captured near Washington and sent to Elmira Prison. Maj. Henry V. Colt, brother of the pistol maker, broke up an escape attempt on August 29, 1864. Colt reportedly said: "I must keep those fellows close, or they'll get away yet. If we hadn't caught them, they'd be halfway to Dixie by now. Well, I feel sorry for them, they deserved to succeed." The tunnelers were nicknamed the "Engineer Corps" and relieved of some of the harder chores. In October, Benson succeeded in tunneling to freedom: "I ran until exhausted, then stopped and looked back. There lay the prison under its bright lights, white with tents, populous with a sleeping multitude. And there were the pickets, the blind pickets, calmly walking their beats. Is it to be wondered at that I should give vent to my joy in unseemly ways, jumping up and cracking my heels together, throwing my hat in the air? . . . It was all I could do to keep from shouting 'The Bonnie Blue Flag' at the top of my voice."

Chemung County Historical Center, 415 E. Water St., has Mark Twain mementos, records of Confederate soldiers, POWs buried in Woodlawn Cemetery.

Mark Twain Study, Elmira College Campus, Park Pl., is built in the form of a Mississippi riverboat pilothouse.

Park Church, 208 W. Gray St. Rev. Thomas K. Beecher, brother of Harriet Beecher Stowe and friend of Twain, was catalyst in the building of this midcentury structure.

Woodlawn Cemetery, 1200 Walnut St. Samuel Clemens (Mark Twain) and family are buried in the Langdon family plot.

Woodlawn National Cemetery, 1825 Davis St., has graves of 3,000 Confederates who died as prisoners of war at Elmira.

ESPERANCE, Schoharie County, US 20.
Esperance Historical Museum, Church St., has memorabilia pertaining to Capt. George A. Turnbull, Civil War officer.

HERKIMER, Herkimer County. IS 90, State 28.
Herkimer County Historical Society, N. Main and Court St., has Civil War relics.

HOMER, Cortland County. IS 81, State 41.
Carpenter House, north edge of town. Francis Bicknell Carpenter was born here in 1830. His most noted painting, "Lincoln Reading the First Draft of the Emancipation Proclamation," hangs in the U.S. Capitol. Carpenter's account of his Washington stay, entitled *Six Months at the White House With Lincoln,* is a memorable comment on many of the nation's leaders in wartime. On one occasion, fellow New Yorker William Seward (who is seated stiffly in the foreground of the famous painting) said to Carpenter: "I've told the President you are painting your picture upon a false presumption . . . you appear to think in common with many other foolish people that the great business of this Administration is the destruction of slavery. Now allow me to say slavery was killed years ago. Its death knell was tolled when Abraham Lincoln was elected President. The work of this Administration is the suppression of the Rebellion and the preservation of the Union . . . Restoration of National Authority is of vastly more consequence than the destruction of slavery."
Homeville Museum, 49 Clinton St., has 7 rooms of military displays, including Civil War items.

HUNTINGTON, Suffolk County. State 25.
Whitman Birthplace, off State 110, 246 Old Walt Whitman Rd. Poet Walt Whitman served in military hospitals during the war. The home has period furnishings. Now a historic site.

ILION, Herkimer County, IS 90.
Remington Firearms Museum, on Barge Canal. Antique firearms.

JAMESTOWN, Chautauqua County. State 394.
Fenton Historical Center, 67 Washington St. Civil War memorabilia in the mansion home of Gov. Reuben E. Fenton, who visited wounded soldiers when he was a congressman, franked their letters, and took family members behind lines to find their wounded.

KINGSTON, Ulster County. IS 87.
Bevier House, Route 209, 3½ miles south. Stone house with period rooms has Civil War items.

LAKE PLACID, Essex County. State 86, 73.
John Brown's Farm, 4 miles south via State 73. Site is ½ mile south of highway. Abolitionist Brown lived here in 1849. Monument marks gravesite. When Brown's widow, his second wife Mary, brought the abolitionist's body from Virginia, the five-day journey was made partly in secret, with an empty hearse to delude the emotional crowds. Wendell Phillips paid a funeral tribute in the Brown cabin at North Elba. Among Browns buried are Watson and Oliver, both killed at Harpers Ferry. Now a state historic site.

LITTLE VALLEY, Cattaraugus County. State 169.
Cattaraugus County Memorial and Historical Museum, Court St., has Civil War relics.

MECHANICVILLE, Saratoga County. State 32.
Hudson View Cemetery has a monument in honor of Col. E. E. Ellsworth, first Northern officer killed in the war. He was shot after removing a Confederate flag from a hotel roof in Alexandria, Virginia, May 24, 1861.

MONROE, Orange County. State 17M or exit 129 off State 17.
Museum Village of Orange County, 1¼ miles west off State 17M, depicts a crossroads town of the 19th century. There are 33 buildings with Americana of the period.

MORRISTOWN, St. Lawrence County, State 37.
Red Barn Museum, River Rd. on Seaway Trail. Civil War military display, re-created blacksmith shop and icehouse.

NEW YORK, York County. IS 78, 80, 87, 95. The New York Convention and Visitors Bureau, 2 Columbus Circle, has free maps and visitors' guides.

Colors presentation of the 20th U.S. Colored Infantry at the Union League clubhouse in New York.

Battery Park, lower Manhattan, has statue of John Ericsson, designer of the *Monitor.*

Brady Studio, Broadway at Fulton. Mathew Brady, the best known photographer of the Civil War, opened a studio here in 1844. He learned photography from Samuel F. B. Morse, who invented the telegraph. Nearby at 115 Nassau St. was the shop of Currier & Ives, who produced many colorful, if inaccurate, lithographs of Civil War scenes.

Central Park, from 59th to 110th St., 5th Ave. to Central Park West. Near park entrance at Grand Army Plaza and 59th St. is the Saint-Gaudens statue of Gen. William Tecumseh Sherman. Also in the park is the 107th Regiment memorial by J. Q. A. Ward.

Cooper Union, 3rd Ave. at 7th. Lincoln spoke here on February 27, 1860. The speech is said to have contributed more than any other single event to Lincoln's nomination for president. In April 1861 the Women's Central Association of Relief was organized in the Great Hall; out of this group came the Sanitary Commission. U. S. Grant, William Lloyd Garrison, Henry Ward Beecher, Harriet Beecher Stowe, and Mark Twain were among the many notable speakers here. The lectern used by Lincoln is still in use.

Cypress Hills National Cemetery, in Brooklyn, has the graves of more than 3,000 soldiers who died in hospitals.

Draft Riots. Plaques mark sites of mob action: 5th Ave., between 43rd and 44th streets, site of black orphanage burned by rioters; on the northeast corner of 3rd Ave. and at 46th St., at the site of a district enrollment office in which the names of draftees were picked from a lottery wheel; and 46th St. and 10th Ave., site of the home of Willy Jones, a laborer whose name was the first drawn in the draft on July 11, 1863.

Fort Wood, Liberty Island, was an ordnance depot during the Civil War.

Foster Home, 6 Greenwich St. The site of lodgings where songwriter Stephen Collins Foster spent his last days in 1864.

General Grant National Memorial, Riverside Dr. and 122nd St. Gen. and Mrs. U. S. Grant are buried in the sarcophagus. Since 1957 the monument has been administered by the National Park Service.

Governor's Island, off Battery Park in Upper

New York Bay, was an embarkation point for Civil War troops.

Grace Protestant Episcopal Church, Broadway and 10th St., was the scene of Gen. Tom Thumb's wedding. The bride and groom were later received by President Lincoln.

Greeley House, 124 Greenwich St. The abolitionist editor boarded here with Dr. Sylvester Graham, minister and dietician who favored unsifted flour.

Hall of Fame for Great Americans, on New York University Campus, University Ave. and W. 181st St., in the Bronx. Among those of the Civil War period who are represented in bronze busts are: Lincoln, Grant, Farragut, Lee, Sherman, Whittier, Harriet Beecher Stowe, Oliver Wendell Holmes, James B. Eads, Walt Whitman, Matthew F. Maury, and Thomas J. Jackson.

"Little Church Around the Corner," Church of the Transfiguration, 1 E. 29th St. The Rev. Dr. George H. Houghton sheltered escaped slaves in the rectory basement; during the draft riots he maintained a bread line for the unemployed.

Madison Square, Madison Ave. and W. 23rd St., has a statue of William H. Seward at the corner of 23rd and Broadway, and statue of Adm. David Farragut, on the 24th St. side. The Seward monument is an anomaly, composed of the secretary's head on Lincoln's body, the latter handily having already been cast when the Seward committee ran out of memorial funds.

Museum of the City of New York, 1220 5th Ave. Dioramas on the history of the city and other displays. A multimedia presentation depicts the history of the city.

New York Historical Society, Central Park West 77th St., has a temporary "Behind the Lines" exhibit of life and activity in the army and on the home front during the Civil War. Exhibits are changed at intervals. The library has Civil War manuscripts, maps, and newspapers. Permanent exhibitions include a gallery of military and naval history.

New York Public Library, 42nd St. and 5th Ave., has letters, clippings, and other manuscripts pertaining to the war, including the contents of a Confederate mailbag.

Plymouth Church of the Pilgrims. Orange St. near Hicks, Brooklyn, was antislavery. Henry Ward Beecher served as minister. Lincoln twice attended services in 1860. The Grand Army Plaza, at north entrance to Prospect Park, has a commemorative arch honoring Civil War heroes.

St. John's Episcopal Church, 9818 Fort Hamilton Pkwy., was founded in 1834 by army officers stationed at Fort Hamilton. Gens. Lee and Jackson were members of the congregation. Jackson was baptized here. Lee was a vestryman. There is a memorial tablet erected by the United Daughters of the Confederacy.

Sheridan Square, 2 blocks west of Washington Square in Greenwich Village, has the Joseph Pollia statue of Gen. Phil Sheridan.

Soldiers' and Sailors' Monuments are located on Riverside Drive and 89th St., and in Prospect Park, Brooklyn.

Union Square, 4th Ave., has a statue of Abraham Lincoln near the 17th St. entrance.

OSWEGO, Oswego County. US 104.

Fort Ontario State Historic Site, E. 7th St., 3 blocks north of highway. The fort was an active post in all wars until 1946; it has been restored to its appearance in the Civil War period. A museum has exhibits pertaining to the fort's history and a slide program.

PAWLING, Dutchess County. State 22.

Pawling Cemetery, south of the Pawling School for Boys, has the grave of Adm. John Lorimer Worden, commander of the *Monitor* in the battle with the *Merrimac* in 1862. Worden commanded the *Montauk* in the attack on Charleston in 1863, and destroyed the Confederate raider *Nashville.*

POUGHKEEPSIE, Dutchess County. US 9.

Soldiers' Fountain, South Ave. and Montgomery St., is a fanciful cast iron monument to Civil War soldiers.

Young-Morse Historic Site "Locust Grove," 370 South Rd. This 1853 Tuscan-style villa was the home of Samuel F. B. Morse, inventor, whose telegraph was widely used during the war. Exhibits.

ROCHESTER, Monroe County. IS 490, 590.

Frederick Douglass Monument, Central Ave. and St. Paul St., was designed by Sidney W. Edwards and dedicated by Gov. Theodore Roosevelt in 1899. Douglass, who was born a slave in Easton, Maryland, escaped in 1838. During the war he helped to organize black troops, later served as minister to Haiti.

George Eastman House, 900 East Ave., is a museum of photography.

Mount Hope Cemetery, 791 Mt. Hope Ave., has the grave of Frederick Douglass. The former slave moved to Rochester in 1847 when he was already famous as the author of *Narrative of the Life of Frederick Douglass,* which sold 5,000 copies in four months.

SYRACUSE, Onondaga County. IS 81, 90.
Museum of Local History, 321 Montgomery St., has Civil War displays.
Onondaga Historical Association Museum, 3211 Montgomery St., has changing exhibits on area history. Some Civil War items.

TROY, Rensselaer County. IS 787. Home of Herman Melville and of meat packer Sam Wilson, who became the national symbol "Uncle Sam." Also the home of Rensselaer Polytechnic Institute, founded in 1824, one of the first schools to grant degrees in science and engineering, and the Emma Willard School, the oldest academy for women in the nation. Many leading females of the Civil War period were graduates.

WARSAW, Wyoming County. Alt. 20.
Gates House Museum, Perry Ave., was the home of Seth M. Gates, U.S. Congressman and a leading abolitionist. Military artifacts and period furnishings.

WATERLOO, Seneca County. US 20.
Memorial Day Museum, 35 E. Main St., is a mansion filled with Memorial Day memorabilia. The town (among others) claims the first Memorial Day was observed here.
Scythe Tree, 2 miles west of town on Route 5-21. The blades of scythes hung by farm boys leaving for enlistment in the Civil War are imbedded in a Balm of Gilead poplar.

WATERTOWN, Jefferson County. State 12.
Jefferson County Historical Society, 228 Washington St., has Civil War memorabilia.

WELLSVILLE, Allegany County. State 19.
David A. Haws Library, 155 N. Main St., has Lincoln pictures and Currier & Ives lithographs.

WEST POINT, Orange County. IS 87.
United States Military Academy. Visitor center is just outside Thayer Gate (Bldg. 2107). Battle Monument, at Trophy Point, is dedicated to the men of the regular army who died in the Civil War. West Point Museum, on Thayer Rd., has a variety of displays pertaining to the war, including weapons used by men of both armies, flags, accouterments, and a diorama showing the close of the third day at Gettysburg; Gen. Lee is in the foreground talking to Gen. Pickett as Confederate soldiers return from the famous charge. At the northwest corner of the parade ground is a monument dedicated to the memory of Maj. Gen. John Sedgwick, USMA, Class of 1837, who was killed by a sharpshooter at the battle of Spotsylvania in 1864. The statue was made from bronze cannon tubes captured by Gen. Sedgwick's corps. At Trophy Point, which faces the Hudson River near the parade ground, are many cannon tubes, ranging from small six-pounders to a section of the barrel of the 700-pound Blakley cast iron rifled seacoast gun which exploded in the test firing. Nearby is a 150-pound English-made Armstrong rifled muzzle-loader, captured at Fort Fisher, North Carolina, in 1864. Across the Hudson River at Cold Spring, a large iron foundry was known as the Arsenal of the North during the war. It was managed by Robert P. Parrott, a USMA graduate. The foundry produced more than 1,700 guns and more than 3,000,000 projectiles during the war.

WILTON, Saratoga County, Off IS 87W.
Grant Cottage, a state historic site, off Route 9, 8 miles north of Saratoga Springs. President Grant and family stayed here when he wrote his memoirs. They were achieved during the agonizing days of his final illness and are invaluable to anyone interested in the 19th century and/or in great literature. Despite the author's travail, the work is inspiring reading.

NORTH CAROLINA

Although Union sentiment was relatively strong in North Carolina, one of the original 13 states, the call for men after the fall of Fort Sumter brought the response from Gov. John W. Ellis: "You can get no troops from North Carolina." After the proclamation blocking Southern ports, all Unionist papers in the state supported the Secessionist party. A number of North Carolinians felt they had been forced into secession by the warlike measures taken in Washington. The flamboyant governor, Zebulon Vance, who served from 1862 to 1865, described himself as having been pleading for the Union cause with hand upraised when the news came of the events in Charleston harbor and Lincoln's call for volunteers: "When my hand came down from that impassioned gesticulation," Vance recalled, "it fell slowly and sadly by the side of a Secessionist." In any case, a convention met at Raleigh and on May 20, 1861, adopted the ordinance of secession and ratified the constitution of the Confederacy.

North Carolinians are proud of the claim that they were "First at Bethel, farthest at Gettysburg and Chickamauga, and last at Appomattox." Although this fails to encompass the first, last, or even farthest point of the war, it catches the North Carolina spirit.

The state sent 125,000 men, here as in some other areas a larger number than the voters. Nearly 20,000 North Carolinians died in battle, another 20,000 from disease. Nearly 100 battles or skirmishes were fought within the state. The first encounter occurred on August 28, 1861, when forts at Hatteras Inlet were fired upon by Federals commanded by Gen. Benjamin Butler and Flag Officer Silas Stringham. Forts Hatteras and Clark were captured, and Roanoke Island was attacked on February 8, 1862. Federal forces held most of the Sound region throughout the war. The largest North Carolina engagement took place at Bentonville, March 20–21, 1865, when Gen. William T. Sherman defeated Gen. Joseph E. Johnston. On April 26, 1865, Gen. Johnston surrendered to Sherman at Bennett House near Durham.

ASHEVILLE, Buncombe County. IS 26, 40.

Civic Center, Haywood St., has monument to Zebulon Baird Vance, wartime governor of North Carolina.

Lee's School, US 70 east of town. Boys school was conducted by Confederate Col. Stephen Lee, a West Point graduate.

Riverside Cemetery, Birch St., has the graves of Gov. Vance and of Brig. Gen. Thomas L. Clingman, who fought in the Wilderness, was wounded at Cold Harbor, again wounded after the Petersburg siege, and rejoined his command only a short time before the final surrender. (Thomas Wolfe, who wrote a memorable story about Chickamauga among other renowned works, is buried here as is O. Henry, who qualifies as a war baby; he was born William Sydney Porter in 1862.)

Zebulon B. Vance Birthplace Historic Site, north on US 23, then 6 miles east on Reems Creek Rd. The log cabin houses many original furnishings and relics. Vance, born here on May 13, 1830, went to the University of North Carolina in homemade shoes and homespun breeches. He pulled himself up by his homemade boot straps to become one of the most colorful statesmen of his day and wartime governor of his state. He was arrested by President Johnson on his 35th birthday and imprisoned at the Old Capitol in Washington until paroled. Later he again served as governor and as U.S. senator. Visitor center, museum.

BENTONVILLE BATTLEGROUND STATE HISTORIC SITE, Johnston County. US 701. Marker at junction with Bentonville Rd. On March 19–21, 1865, some 25,000 Confederates under Gen. Joseph Johnston opposed 60,000 Federals under Gen. Sherman. This was the last major action in North Carolina. The site, maintained by the State Department of Archives and History, has been restored. The 6,000-acre battlefield has well-

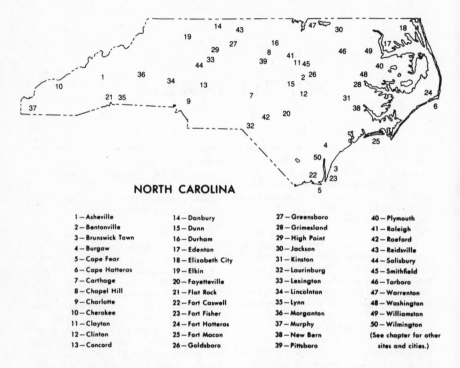

NORTH CAROLINA

1 — Asheville	14 — Danbury	27 — Greensboro	40 — Plymouth
2 — Bentonville	15 — Dunn	28 — Grimesland	41 — Raleigh
3 — Brunswick Town	16 — Durham	29 — High Point	42 — Raeford
4 — Burgaw	17 — Edenton	30 — Jackson	43 — Reidsville
5 — Cape Fear	18 — Elizabeth City	31 — Kinston	44 — Salisbury
6 — Cape Hatteras	19 — Elkin	32 — Laurinburg	45 — Smithfield
7 — Carthage	20 — Fayetteville	33 — Lexington	46 — Tarboro
8 — Chapel Hill	21 — Flat Rock	34 — Lincolnton	47 — Warrenton
9 — Charlotte	22 — Fort Caswell	35 — Lynn	48 — Washington
10 — Cherokee	23 — Fort Fisher	36 — Morganton	49 — Williamston
11 — Clayton	24 — Fort Hatteras	37 — Murphy	50 — Wilmington
12 — Clinton	25 — Fort Macon	38 — New Bern	(See chapter for other
13 — Concord	26 — Goldsboro	39 — Pittsboro	sites and cities.)

preserved earthworks. The Harper House was used as a hospital by both armies. A guide is available in the summer months.

BLOWING ROCK, Wautaga County. US 321. Stoneman's cavalry came through here on a raid, March 28, 1865, fought a skirmish with the home guard at Boone on the same day.

BRAGGTOWN, Durham County. US 501. Marker denotes site of Fairntosh, the antebellum plantation of the Cameron family, who were among the state's largest slave-holders until 1865.

BRUNSWICK TOWN-FORT FISHER STATE HISTORIC SITE, Brunswick County. South of Wilmington on State 133. A Confederate fort was built diagonally across the old town which had lain in ruins for nearly a century. The garrison held out for 30 days after the fall of Fort Fisher. Earthworks are well preserved. Reconstructed gun emplacements. Visitor center has exhibits and audio-visual program.

BURGAW, Pender County. US 117. On highway is marker for home of S. S. Satchwell, head of the Confederate hospital at Wilson.

Pender Monument, on courthouse lawn, honors Gen. William Dorsey Pender, youngest major general of the Confederacy. Memorial erected by the United Daughters of the Confederacy.

CAPE FEAR, Brunswick County. Off Southport, State 133. Fort Caswell was manned during the Civil War. A swimming pool fed by warm springs has been built into the fortifications.

CAPE HATTERAS NATIONAL SEASHORE, between Pamlico Sound and Raleigh Bay.

Cape Hatteras Lighthouse. Visitor center in keeper's cottage has exhibits. Federal naval forces took the cape after bombardment early in the war. The Old Hatteras Light, dating from 1798, was destroyed. Ruins remain.

CAROLINA BEACH, New Hanover County, US 421.

Blockade Runner Museum (*also see* FORT FISHER) features the history of Fort Fisher and the wartime blockade. There is a 40-foot diorama and a narration of events to accompany slides.

CARTHAGE, Moore County. US 15-501.
Moore County Courthouse has marker honoring Andrew Johnson, who once worked as a tailor here.

CHAPEL HILL, Orange County. IS 40, US 15.
University of North Carolina is the oldest state university in the country. The library has an outstanding manuscript division, the Southern Historical Collection, available for reference only. Among the more than 3,000,000 items, the Civil War comprises a substantial proportion.

CHARLOTTE, Mecklenburg County. IS 77, 85, US 74.
Confederate Cabinet Meeting, US 29, State 49. President Jefferson Davis held his last full cabinet meeting here on April 22–26, 1865.
Confederate Navy Yard, 226 E. Trade St. Site is marked by a plaque. In May 1862, the center of naval ordnance was moved here from Norfolk for greater security.
Julia Jackson Birthplace, 834 W. 5th St. Mrs. Thomas J. Jackson came from Virginia to live with her sister, Mrs. James P. Irwin; Julia Jackson was born here on November 23, 1862. Two of Mrs. Jackson's sisters also were wives of Confederate generals, D. H. Hill and Rufus Barringer.
Mint Museum, 2730 Randolph Rd., was used as Confederate headquarters and hospital. It now houses a museum with art and historical exhibits.
Shipp Monument, S. Mint and W. 4th St., commemorates the military reinstatement of the former Confederate states. Lt. William Shipp was the first Southerner to be graduated from West Point after the war.

CHEROKEE, Swaim County. US 19.
Cherokee Marker, 2 miles north on US 441, honors Cherokee Indians who served in the Confederate army. It was erected by the United Daughters of the Confederacy.
Museum of the Cherokees, at junction of US 19 and 441, has historical displays.

CLAYTON, Johnston County. US 70.
There was a skirmish here following the battle of Bentonville in March 1865. Confederates installed two cannon on a hill at the Ellington House and fired upon Federals coming up from Smithfield.

CLINTON, Sampson County. US 701.
Holmes House, marker on highway about 4 miles north of town. Home of Gabriel Holmes, governor and congressman, and his son, Con-

federate Gen. Theophilus H. Holmes, stood about 2 miles southeast.
Moore Birthplace, State 403 northeast of Clinton. Thomas O. Moore, wartime governor of Louisiana and secession leader, was born about 4½ miles northwest of marker.

CONCORD, Cabarrus County. IS 85, US 29A.
Houston House, 25 N. Union St. President Jefferson Davis stayed overnight on April 18, 1865.

CRESWELL, Washington County. US 64.
Marker on highway denotes site of grave of Confederate Gen. James Johnston Pettigrew, who was wounded at the battle of Gettysburg.

DANBURY, Stokes County. State 89. Marker on highway.
Moody Tavern, adjacent to courthouse, was headquarters for Gen. Stoneman on a raid through western North Carolina on April 9, 1865, the day after Lee had surrendered.

DAVIDSON, Mecklenburg County. IS 77, US 21. Confederate Lt. Gen. D. H. Hill is buried here. He was a West Point graduate and served in the Mexican War.

DEEP GAP, Wautauga County. US 421. Stoneman's Federal forces erected a palisaded fort here in April 1865.

DOBSON, Surry County. IS 77, US 601. Gen. George Stoneman and cavalry came through here on a raid, April 2, 1865; also through Mount Airy.

DUNN, Harnett County. IS 95, US 301. Marker about 2 miles south. Another marker will be found on State 82, south of Erwin.
Battle of Averasboro. On March 15, 1865, Hardee's Confederate troops delayed the march of Gen. Sherman's army toward Goldsboro. Breastworks are about ½ mile east of marker on State 82. Chicora Confederate cemetery has the graves of 55 soldiers killed in the action.

DURHAM, Durham County. IS 40, 85.
Bennett Place State Historic Site, 4 miles northwest off US 70. The house where Gens. Sherman and Joseph Johnston met on April 26, 1865, to perfect surrender terms, has been reconstructed. Only the chimney remains of the original building. Sherman was sharply criticized by the radical North for his leniency in the negotiations. Most historians agree he was following Lincoln's wishes, which had been made known to Grant and Sherman in the City Point conference. Gen. Johnston was a pallbearer at Sherman's funeral in 1889. Exhibits

related to North Carolina in the Civil War are in the visitor center. Guided tours available and an audio-visual presentation shown on request.

Duke University, West Campus, library has a large Confederate imprint collection.

EDENTON, Chowan County. US 17.

Blair House, E. Church St., was the home of Brig. Gen. Thomas C. Manning, later chief justice of the Louisiana Supreme Court.

Confederate Monument, north edge of village green, honors the Chowan County men of the Civil War. The crosswalks are laid out in the pattern of their flag.

Wingfield, 10 miles west of town on banks of Chowan River, is the site of a fort built by Union sympathizers, known as Buffaloes, in the fall of 1862. The fort and plantation house were later destroyed by a detachment sent by Lt. Gen. D. H. Hill.

ELIZABETH CITY, Pasquotank County. US 17.

Charles House, 701 W. Colonial Ave., was used as a hospital.

Confederate Monument, in public square.

Judge Small House, 204 E. Colonial Ave., served as Federal army headquarters.

ELKIN, Surry County. IS 77, US 21.

Richard Gwyn House, W. Main St., was built in 1861–1862. Union Gen. Stoneman stayed overnight in 1865; reportedly, he was in love with a Gwyn relative in California, and either because of this or as a gift to his hostess, spared the house.

FAYETTEVILLE, Cumberland County. IS 95, US 301, 401. Sherman's bummers came into town ahead of the army and drove Wade Hampton from his breakfast table. Sherman arrived on March 12 and remained two days, destroying war property.

In this vicinity was fought one of the most famous unimportant affairs of the war—the battle of Kilpatrick's Pants. All accounts seem to agree that the bantam, high-living Union cavalryman Judson Kilpatrick was overtaken in his nightshirt by Confederates, who, for the moment, were not taking off their hats to romance. When his camp near Solemn Grove was attacked, Kilpatrick retreated, leaving his companion to fend for herself. (Reportedly, a Southerner escorted her to a handy ditch where she reclined out of firing range.) Sherman has been quoted as saying: "I know Kilpatrick is a hell of a damned fool—" but valued his daring on the unprecedented march to the sea. The brigadier was young, reckless, and lustful, and his flight at Solemn Grove could have sup-

ported a Southern general's statement that he'd never seen a corpse with spurs on, but on occasions Kilpatrick's recklessness gained results. He was active in Republican politics after the war, died at Santiago in 1881.

Battle of Monroe's Crossroads, near Long Street Church on the old Yadkin Rd., on Fort Bragg Military Reservation. At this site Maj. Gen. Judson Kilpatrick opposed Lt. Gen. Wade Hampton. Confederates fell back when the Union troops were reinforced. Church cemetery has graves of unknown soldiers who were killed in battle here.

Confederate Earthworks, marker on US 15A.

Cross Creek Cemetery, Grove St. between Ann St. and Cross Creek. Confederate Monument, marking graves of soldiers, was erected in 1868.

The North Carolina Arsenal, 822 Arsenal Ave. Shortly after the fall of Fort Sumter, a contingent of elderly men and boys under C.S.A. Gen. Draughton took the arsenal, which furnished weapons for the Confederacy until Sherman's troops destroyed it in March 1865. Now a historical park with self-guiding tours.

Pemberton's Mill, Cool Spring St. A mill opposite the spring made gray cloth for Confederate uniforms.

Presbyterian Church, Bow and Ann streets. Confederate Gen. T. H. Holmes is buried in church cemetery, 1½ miles north of highway marker.

FLAT ROCK, Henderson County. US 25.

Connemara, Rock Hill, was built by C. G. Memminger, Confederate treasurer; later the home of poet Carl Sandburg, Lincoln biographer. Memminger is buried in the St. John-of-the-Wilderness churchyard.

Trenholm House, ½ mile east of US 25 in Flat Rock. Summer home of George A. Trenholm, who was Confederate secretary of the treasury in the last year of the war.

FORREST CITY, Rutherford County. US 74, 221A.

Baxter Birthplace, 4½ miles southeast of highway marker. Elisha Baxter was a Union colonel in the war; elected to the U.S. Senate in 1864 but not seated. Later he was governor of Arkansas.

FORT CASWELL, Brunswick County. Markers on State 130, about 2 miles west of Southport, and on State 40 at junction with Fort Caswell Rd. near Yaupon Beach. The fort was seized by state troops in January 1861 and abandoned by Confederates in 1865. Gov. Ellis had protested the seizure of the post as unlawful, informed President Buchanan of the event, and learned that Buchanan did not intend to garrison North Carolina forts.

FORT FISHER STATE HISTORICAL SITE, New Hanover County. Southeast terminus of US 421. The largest earthwork fort in the Confederacy kept Wilmington open to blockade runners until late in the war. In December 1864 and January 1865, heavy naval bombardment took place. On the night of January 15, some 1,500 Confederates surrendered at Battery Buchanan. Federal losses were about 1,300, but the Union fleet held Cape Fear. During World War II, when the site became an active military post, a landing strip altered the terrain. The visitor center has exhibits and a slide show.

FORT HATTERAS, Dare County. Hatteras-Ocracoke Ferry Landing at Hatteras Village, between Pamlico Sound and Raleigh Bay. Forts Hatteras and Clark were occupied by the Union after two days of heavy naval bombardment late in August 1861.

FORT HILL, Beaufort County. State 33. Confederate batteries on Pamlico River enabled Gen. Daniel Harvel Hill to approach Washington in the spring of 1863.

FORT JOHNSTON, Cape Fear was held by South until 1865 and kept Wilmington open to blockade runners until the last months of the war. Masonry in good repair.

FORT MACON STATE PARK, Carteret County. On Bogue Bank near Atlantic Beach. The brick fort was built in 1826–1834 to protect the Beaufort Inlet. It was occupied by Confederates during the early part of the war. On April 26, 1862, the garrison surrendered to Gens. John C. Parke and Ambrose Burnside.

FORT POINT, Craven County. US 70. Marker on highway southeast of New Bern for Confederate fort, then known as Fort Lane, taken by U.S. in March 1862.

GATESVILLE, Gates County. State 37.
Confederate Monument, opposite courthouse, honors William P. Roberts, one of the youngest generals in the Confederate army.

GOLDSBORO, Wayne County. US 70.
The town was raided on December 17, 1862, by Union Gen. J. G. Foster. In March 1865, the armies of Gens. Sherman, Schofield, and Terry converged here. Bummers were informed at this point that they must rejoin their regular outfits; many preferred to head for the far West instead.

Dortch House, N. William and E. Mulberry St. The home of Col. William T. Dortch, Confederate senator, later became a Masonic home. Marker on US 70 gives direction to home and to gravesite, five blocks farther south.

GREENSBORO, Guilford County. IS 40, 85, US 70. Jefferson Davis and his cabinet met at the home of J. T. Wood in April 1865; marker at site. Marker also at site of railroad car occupied by Confederate cabinet members in mid-April 1865. A Confederate hospital was set up in the First Presbyterian Church, on US 29, for soldiers wounded in the battle of Bentonville.

Blandwood, 447 W. Washington St., was the home of Gov. John Motley Morehead. Beauregard and his staff were guests here in 1865.

Dunleith, 677 Chestnut St. Union Gen. William R. Cox occupied the house; soldiers tented on the lawns.

Greensboro Historical Museum, 130 Summit Ave., has a War Memorial Room.

GRIMESLAND, Pitt County. Marker on US 264 about one mile southeast. Plantation of Confederate Gen. Bryan Grimes. Grimes commanded a regiment at Seven Pines where 462 of 500 men and all officers but himself were killed or wounded. In 1880 Gen. Grimes was shot from ambush by an assassin.

GUILFORD COLLEGE STATION, Guilford County. US 421.
Coffin Birthplace. Marker on highway. Levi Coffin, who was considered the president of the Underground Railway, was born near here in 1789,

HALIFAX, Halifax County. US 301.
Colonial Churchyard, State 113, has marker. Confederate Gen. Junius Daniel is buried here.

The Grove, southwest part of town, was an encampment for Col. McRae and his Confederate troops; later Union soldiers occupied the house.

HENDERSONVILLE, Henderson County. IS 85, US 25, 64. Stoneman's raiders passed here April 23, 1865.

HIGH HAMPTON, Jackson County. Marker on US 64 near State 107, for summer house of Confederate Gen. Wade Hampton.

HIGH POINT, Guilford County. Off IS 40, 85, US 70.

High Point Museum, 1 mile east on US 70A, has Civil War relics.

Oakwood Cemetery, north end of Steele St., has graves of Confederate soldiers and the grave of Laura Wesson, called the Florence Nightingale of the Confederacy. She was a nurse at the Wayside Hospital when a smallpox epidemic broke out. She served the quarantined patients until she contracted the disease and died of it on April 25, 1865.

JACKSON, Northampton County. US 158.
Boon's Mill, west of town, marker on highway. A Confederate force repulsed a Union march on the Wilmington and Weldon Railroad on July 28, 1863. Breastworks are just off highway to the southwest.

Bragg House, marker on US 158, was the home of Gov. Thomas Bragg, a Confederate attorney general. He is buried in the family cemetery.

Ransom House, about 5 miles west of town, marker on highway. Home of Confederate Gen. Matt W. Ransom. After the war he served as U.S. senator and as minister to Mexico.

JACKSONVILLE, Onslow County. US 17. Marker for the raid of November 23, 1862, when the Union gunboat *Ellis* attacked the town, ran aground downstream, and was abandoned.

JAMES CITY, Craven County. US 70. A Union victory here by forces under Gen. Ambrose Burnside on March 14, 1862, contributed to the fall of New Bern, an important Confederate stronghold.

KENANSVILLE, Duplin County. State 11.
Confederate Arms Factory. Marker on highway denotes site of factory which made bowie knives, saber-bayonets, and other small arms, and was destroyed by Union cavalry on July 4, 1863.

KINSTON, Lenoir County. US 70.
Battle of Kinston, marker on highway southeast of town. Confederates under Gens. Bragg, Hoke, and Hill delayed Union troops under Gen. Cox here in March 1865.

Foster's Raid. Union troops under Gen. J. G. Foster passed through en route to New Bern from Goldsboro, December 14, 1862.

Ram Neuse, on US 258, marker at site. Confederate ironclad, built at White Hall, was grounded and burned by the Confederates in 1865. A museum in the *Governor Caswell Memorial*-CSS Neuse *State Historic Site,* US 70A, has the remains of the *Neuse.* The iron-

clad was built farther up the river at White Hall. It was raised in 1963. Interpretative exhibits and a slide show.

LAUREL HILL, Scotland County. US 74. Several units of Sherman's army camped near here on March 8–9, 1865.

LAURINBURG, Scotland County. US 15, 501.
Confederate Monument, in courthouse yard.

Sherman's March, marker about 4 miles north of town. Some of Sherman's men, en route from Savannah to Goldsboro, camped at Laurel Hill Presbyterian Church. (*See* LAUREL HILL.)

LEASBURG, Caswell County. US 158.
Thompson Birthplace, marker denotes site. Jacob Thompson was U.S. Secretary of the Interior in 1861, became a Confederate secret agent in Canada, later was a U.S. representative from Mississippi.

LEE MARKER, Warren County. State 59. Annie Carter Lee, daughter of Gen. Robert E. Lee, died in 1862 at age 23. Her grave is ½ mile west of marker.

LENOIR, Caldwell County. State 13. Stoneman's Union cavalry passed through town March 28 and again on April 15–17, 1865.

LEXINGTON, Davidson County. Off IS 85, US 29, 70.
Confederate Monument, in midtown, is on site where public well was formerly situated.

Davis Camp, marker on highway 4 miles east of town. President Davis and cabinet members spent the night of April 16, 1865, in a pine grove near here.

LINCOLNTON, Lincoln County. US 321. Mary Boykin Chesnut, wife of the Confederate general James Chesnut, aide to Jefferson Davis, had fled to Lincolnton when the Union army advanced upon Columbia, South Carolina. Mrs. Chesnut's *A Dairy from Dixie* is a superlative account of affairs during wartime written by an exceptionally well-read and perceptive Southern woman who was intimately acquainted with the leading personalities of her day. One entry in her diary for February 1865 states that Mrs. Wigfall, in Lincolnton, exchanged a Yankee dollar for 28,000 Confederate dollars. An editor of the diary makes the footnote that Mrs. Chesnut probably meant a $10 goldpiece, and that in rural Carolina at the time this would not have been an impossible rate of exchange.

Confederate Laboratory, marker on highway. Part of a building used by Dr. A. S. Piggott for manufacturing drugs is 2 miles south.

Hoke House, US 321. Confederate Maj. Gen. Robert F. Hoke lived in house 50 yards east of marker. Hoke was wounded at Chancellorsville but returned to active duty, capturing Plymouth on April 20, 1864.

Ramseur Gravesite, State 27, 150. Grave of Confederate Maj. Gen. Stephen D. Ramseur is 2 blocks north of marker. Ramseur, a West Point graduate, was wounded at Malvern Hill, Chancellorsville, and mortally wounded at Cedar Creek, Virginia, October 19, 1864. He was 27.

United Daughters of the Confederacy Memorial Hall is 1 block east of marker on US 321, at E. Pine and N. Academy St. Library and historical relics.

LOWESVILLE, Lincoln County. State 273.

Morrison House, marker on highway about 2½ miles northwest of town. Site of house where Stonewall Jackson married Anna Morrison, July 16, 1857, was just east of highway.

LYNN, Polk County. State 108.

Lanier House, marker at site where poet and Confederate soldier Sidney Lanier died, September 7, 1881.

Stoneman Raid, marker on highway. Union cavalry and Confederates fought at Howard's Gap, 4 miles north, April 22, 1865.

MANTEO, Dare County. US 64.

Battle of Roanoke Island, marker near intersection of US 64 and 158. Gen. Burnside won a victory here on February 8, 1862, which led to Union control of the Albemarle Sound area.

MOCKSVILLE, Davie County. US 64. Hinton Helper, author of *The Impending Crisis,* which denounced slavery and U.S. consul at Buenos Aires during the war years, was born near here. Marker on highway.

MORGANTON, Burke County. IS 40, US 64, 70.

Burke County Courthouse was raided by Stoneman's men in February 1865; records were thrown into the square and burned. Marker on State 18, 2 miles north of town, for site of skirmish between Stoneman's cavalry and Southern troops on April 17, 1865.

Camp Vance, US 64 and 70, 3 miles east of town. Training camp for state militia, named for war governor Vance, was raided by Federal troops in 1864.

MOUNT AIRY, Surry County. US 601. Stoneman's cavalry passed through here April 2–3, 1865.

MULBERRY GROVE, Hertford County. State 305. Marker on highway near Minton's Store denotes site of birthplace of John W. Moore, historian, novelist, and Confederate major.

MURPHY, Cherokee County. US 64.

Cherokee County Courthouse is on site of earlier building which was burned in 1865 by local soldiers who had deserted the Confederate army for a Federal unit. Papers related to cases pending against them were in the courthouse.

Hanging Dog Creek, about 4 miles northwest of town, was site of a battle on May 6, 1865, when Confederates led by Maj. Stephen Whitaker routed the turncoats who had burned the courthouse.

NEW BERN, Craven County. US 70, Many antebellum houses remain because the town was occupied by the Federals after Gen. Ambrose Burnside defeated Gen. L. O'Bryan Branch on March 14, 1862.

Altmore-Oliver House, 511 Broad St., is headquarters for the historical society and has Civil War artifacts.

Captain's Walk House, southeast corner of Johnson and Craven St., served as hospital for the 9th New Jersey Infantry and as barracks for a company of the 45th Massachusetts.

Cedar Grove Cemetery, northeast corner of Queen and George St. Confederate monument is at site of a mass Confederate grave.

Fireman's Museum, 410 Hancock St., has firefighting equipment from antebellum times. Civil War relics.

First Presbyterian Church, New St. near Middle St., was built after a Christopher Wren design. It was a hospital for part of the war.

Fort Totten, west edge of town between US 17 and 70. After the Union forces took the town, trenches were built from the Neuse to the Trent River, with a fort at each end and in the center of the line.

Jarvis-Slover House, E. Front at Johnson St. Gen. John G. Foster and staff had headquarters here.

Jones-Lipman House, southwest corner of Pollock and Eden St., was used as a Federal prison.

National Cemetery, north end of National Ave., has graves of more than 3,500 Union soldiers.

New Bern Civil War Museum, 301 Metcalf

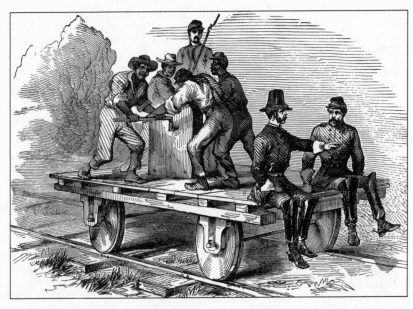

General Burnside "traveling in state" from New Berne to Beaufort.

St., has an extensive show of Civil War items. Among relics are the folding chair Gen. U. S. Grant used in the field, uniforms from the North and the South, camp furnishings, and weapons.

Rains House, 411 Johnson St., was the birthplace of Gen. Gabriel J. Rains, superintendent of the Confederate Torpedo and Harbor Defense Bureau. A veteran of the Seminole and Mexican wars, Rains is credited with first use of land mines and booby traps. He was severely criticized by a number of Confederates as well as Yankees for using the mines. Col. George Washington Rains, brother of Gen. Rains, was also a veteran of Seminole and Mexican wars. In August 1862, he was put in charge of all munitions operations in Augusta.

Simpson-Duffy House, southeast corner of E. Front and Pollock St., was used by the Federal provost marshal as office and guard house.

Slover-Guion House, southwest corner of E. Front and Johnson St., was headquarters for Gen. Burnside.

Stanly House, New St. between Middle and Hancock St. Birthplace of Brig. Gen. Lewis Addison Armistead, a West Pointer who served in the Mexican War and led his brigade in Pickett's charge at Gettysburg with his cap on the tip of his upraised sword. His monument marks the high tide of the Confederacy at Gettysburg.

Stevenson House, George and Pollock St. A Federal hospital during the war.

Taylor-Ward House, 228 Craven St. Headquarters of the 45th Massachusetts.

PITTSBORO, Chatham County. US 15, 501. James I. Waddell, commander of the Confederate cruiser *Shenandoah,* lived in house 3 blocks west of marker.

PLYMOUTH, Washington County. US 64. The town was shelled frequently during the war.

Battle of Plymouth Marker, on courthouse lawn, honors Confederate soldiers. In 1864, Gen. R. F. Hoke captured Plymouth after a three-day engagement. The ram *Albemarle,* anchored in the Roanoke River, was sunk by torpedo on the night of October 27, 1864. Union Lt. William Barker Cushing placed the torpedo and escaped by swimming down river. Marker near site.

Grace Episcopal Church donated its pews and gallery to make coffins for soldiers.

RAEFORD, Hoke County. US 15A. Marker on highway.

Monroe's Crossroads. Gen. Kilpatrick's cavalry of Sherman's army repulsed Gen. Wade Hampton's Confederates 10 miles north on March 10, 1865. Site is now in Fort Bragg area.

Sherman's Camp, marker on highway about 4 miles south of town. Part of the Union army camped at Bethel Presbyterian Church on March 9–10, 1865.

RALEIGH, Wake County. IS 40, US 70.

Archives and History Bldg., Jones and Wilmington, has Confederate exhibits in the Museum of History.

Branch Home, marker on US 1. Confederate Brig. Gen. Lawrence O'Bryan Branch, who was tutored by Salmon P. Chase, later U.S. Secretary of Treasury, fought under Stonewall Jackson and was killed at Antietam, September 17, 1862. His home was here, grave ⅔ mile east.

Confederate Breastworks. Marker on US 1 in Raleigh. Gov. Vance ordered fortifications thrown up in 1863 against Federal raiders.

Dorothea Dix Hospital, US 64 and 70A. Miss Dix was a crusader for prison reform and the care of the mentally ill, helped to establish a hospital here in 1849. During the war she was the Union's superintendent of women nurses. Union troops frequently gathered on the lawn during the occupation of Raleigh.

Governor's Palace, US 15A, 64, and 70, marker. Vance was the last governor to occupy mansion, 1862–1865. Grant conferred with Sherman here in April 1865, on new terms for surrender of Johnston's army. Stanton and others in the government had disapproved of Sherman's agreement with Johnston.

Hall of History, Edenton and Salisbury St., has extensive exhibits pertaining to the Confederacy, including the stack of the ironclad *Albemarle,* which was built near Scotland Neck on the Roanoke River and destroyed at Plymouth.

Haywood House, 127 E. Edenton St., was headquarters for Maj. Francis P. Blair, Jr. Grant and Sherman visited there. Grant came to Raleigh to have a secret conference with Sherman after the latter's terms of surrender had aroused Stanton and other Northerners.

Johnson House, 123 Fayetteville St. Marker at site of Andrew Johnson birthplace. The house was moved to the campus of the North Carolina University, restored with period furnishings.

National Cemetery, southeast corner of E. Davie St. and Rock Quarry Rd., has the graves of more than 1,000 soldiers.

Oakwood Cemetery, marker on US 1. Six governors, other notables, and Confederate

soldiers are buried in cemetery is 3 blocks east of marker.

Pettigrew Hospital, US 64. Confederate hospital, U.S. army barracks, and later Confederate soldiers' home at this site.

State Capitol, Capitol Square, was completed in 1840. Among statuary on grounds are monuments to Andrew Johnson, the women of the Confederacy, Confederate soldiers, Zebulon B. Vance, and Henry Lawson Wyatt, first North Carolina soldier killed in the war, at Bethel Church, June 10, 1861.

Surrender Site, on old US 70, just south of town. City commissioners surrendered the capital to Sherman's army near this spot on April 13, 1865.

REIDSVILLE, Rockingham County. US 29, State 87. Mrs. Stephen A. Douglas, first wife of the Illinois senator, is buried in the Settle family cemetery here. There is a marker on State 704 denoting site of house where Martha D. Martin was married to Sen. Douglas in 1847.

Reid House. Marker on US 29 for home which stands 2 blocks east. David S. Reid was governor, U.S. senator, and member of the Peace Conference of 1861.

Scales House, Marker on State 87, 2 miles south of town. Birthplace of Confederate Gen. Alfred M. Scales was 3½ miles east. He was wounded at Chancellorsville and Seminary Ridge, Gettysburg. In 1885, he was elected governor.

RIDGECREST, Buncombe County. US 70. Stoneman's cavalry was turned back by Southern troops at Swannanoa Gap on April 20, 1865.

ROCKINGHAM, Richmond County. US 1. Kilpatrick's cavalry, en route from Savannah to Goldsboro, passed through town on March 7–8, 1865.

ROCKY POINT, Pender County. US 117, north of town.

Ashe House, 1 mile west of highway marker. William S. Ashe was in charge of Confederate railroad transportation in 1861–1862.

ROXBORO, Person County. US 501.

Confederate Monument, in courthouse yard, honors Person County soldiers and Capt. E. Fletcher Satterfield, who was killed at the battle of Gettysburg.

SALISBURY, Rowan County. IS 85.

Confederate Monument, Innis and Church St.

Dr. Josephus Hall House, 226 E. Jackson,

served as Union commander headquarters after the war.

Ellis House, marker on US 70 and 601. Gov. John W. Ellis was a leader in the secession movement.

National Cemetery has the graves of nearly 5,000 Union soldiers who died in Salisbury prison.

Rowan Museum, 116 S. Jackson. Confederate relics.

Site of Salisbury Prison, Horah St. When Gen. George Stoneman captured the town in April 1865, he used the stockade for Confederates, later burned most of the area. Among a number of well-known Yankees who were imprisoned here were newspaper correspondents Junius H. Browne and Albert Deane Richardson, who were captured while trying to run the Vicksburg batteries to reach Grant's headquarters in May 1863. They were sent here from Richmond where they'd been kept at Libby and at Castle Thunder. On first arrival they preferred Salisbury to the other prisons. They were authorities on Confederate incarceration by the time they arrived; other newspapermen had been exchanged, but the *Tribune* correspondents were not returned to their much-hated editor, Horace Greeley. Richardson later wrote: "Captain Swift Galloway, commanding, though a hearty Confederate, was kind and courteous to the captives. . . . The yard of four acres, like some old college grounds, with great oak trees and a well of sweet, pure water, was open to us during the whole day. There, the first time for nine months, our feet pressed the mother earth, and the blessed open air fanned our cheeks." The correspondents found friends among the Salisbury citizens who visited the prison. A Luke Blackmer lent books and Richardson expected, like the Count of Monte Cristo, to emerge from prison a "very well-read man." All this respite was changed in October 1864, when 10,000 more prisoners were brought in. Increased filth and disease necessarily came with them. The sometimes rather precious Junius Browne was moved to remark of his cell: "I can give no idea of its repulsiveness and superlative squalor. A gentleman seemed more out of place there than the Angel Gabriel would in a prize ring." The correspondents escaped early in 1865; both wrote of their experiences in books that became best-sellers.

SANFORD, Lee County. US 421.

Egypt Coal Mine, marker on highway 6 · miles northwest of town. Mine supplied coal for Confederate blockade-runners. Shaft is 2 miles north.

SCOTLAND NECK, Halifax County. US 258.

Albemarle, marker on highway about 6 miles northeast of town for site where the Confederate ironclad *Albermarle* was built in 1863–1864. It was used in the recapture of Plymouth, April 1864.

SCOTTS HILL, New Hanover County. US 17.

Davis Birthplace, marker on highway south of town. George Davis, Confederate senator and attorney general, was born in house that stood 3 miles east.

SHELBY, Cleveland County. State 150.

Durham House. Home of Plato Durham, Confederate captain and legislator. Marker at site.

SMITHFIELD, Johnston County. IS 95, US 301. Marker on highway indicates site where Sherman's army on April 12, 1865, celebrated the news of Lee's surrender. In an unpublished diary, Col. John S. Jones, of the 174th Ohio Volunteer Infantry (later brevetted brigadier general), described how he heard the news on the march to Raleigh: "I can see the long column now as it moves along the dusty road through the pine forest. Halt! Halt! is rapidly passed along the line and we stand in great expectancy to learn what is the matter. Away in the distance we see the column opening to make way for a rapidly approaching horseman; he stops, says something, and we hear cheers; on he comes, stops again, more cheering, on he still comes, stopping at intervals, and the shouts become a mighty roar; he finally reaches us, reins in his steed, rises in his stirrups and announces at the top of his voice, 'General Lee and his entire army surrendered to General Grant on the 9th at Appomattox!' Never, never, until the sounding of the Angel's trumpet that shall wake the dead, do we expect to hear a more soul-thrilling announcement. On he went until the news was proclaimed along the entire column. Caps, knapsacks, blankets, and haversacks were thrown into the air in an instant. Men jumped, shouted, played leapfrog, turned somersaults and the whole army was in a delirium of excitement. The General commanding decided to move his corps into a field nearby and spend a few hours in rest and rejoicing. . . . Fifers and drummers and brass bands were assembled; guns placed in position; the infantry stood behind stacked arms; field officers, mounted, marched behind the musicians up and down the lines, and 20,000 veteran voices sang war songs to the accompaniment of fifes, drums, brass bands and salvos of artillery."

SOUTH MILLS, Camden County. US 17.
Battle of South Mills, 3 miles southeast of marker. Confederates prevented the blowing up of Dismal Swamp Canal locks on April 19, 1862.

STATESVILLE, Iredell County. IS 77, US 64, 70.
Vance House, 501 W. Sharpe, marker on highway, is now a historical museum. Gov. Zebulon Vance had temporary quarters here after the Union army occupied Raleigh in April 1865.

STONEMAN'S RAIDS: It is possible to follow the course of Gen. George Stoneman's raids through northwestern North Carolina by highway markers, not all of which have been listed here. In brief, Stoneman, with 6,000 cavalrymen, had the main objective of destroying railroads; in North Carolina the principal target was the Danville-Greensboro line. Gen. A. C. Gillem arrived in Boone with an advance guard on March 28, 1865, and destroyed some public buildings; Stoneman went from here to Deep Gap and Wilkesboro. Gillem and a lesser force went to Blowing Rock and Lenoir. The force reunited at Wilkesboro, March 29. Stoneman moved on to Mount Airy, Danbury, Germantown, and Salem, from which point detachments were sent out in all directions to destroy railroad and military property. Salisbury was an important port of call; the cavalry hoped to liberate the thousands of Union prisoners crowded into a one-time cotton factory. By the time Stoneman arrived, however, the Confederate government had transferred the prisoners elsewhere. Stoneman went back to Tennessee via Statesville, Taylorsville, and Lenoir. Gen. Gillem's detachment went to Morganton, Marion, Hendersonville, and Asheville, still ransacking Confederate property without knowledge that an armistice had been signed.

TARBORO, Edgecomb County. US 258.
Calvary Episcopal Church, Church and David St., marker on US 64, has the graves of Maj. Gen. William Dorsey Pender, West Point graduate, mortally wounded at Gettysburg, and of W. L. Saunders, Confederate colonel and editor.
Clark Marker, US 64 and 258, denotes site of grave of Gov. Henry T. Clark who helped organize the state for war.
Tarboro Common has monument to Confederate soldiers of Edgecomb County and to

Henry L. Wyatt, who was killed at Bethel Church, June 1861.

TIMBERLAKE, Person County. US 501.
Reade Birthplace, 2 miles southeast of highway marker. Home of Edwin G. Reade, Confederate senator and North Carolina Supreme Court justice.

WAGRAM, Scotland County. US 401.
Temperance Hall, 1½ miles west of marker. The meeting place of the Richmond Temperance and Literary Society was sacked by Sherman's army in 1865.

WARRENTON, Warren County. US 401.
Bragg House, N. Bragg St. Gov. Thomas Bragg, Confederate Gen. Braxton Bragg, and U.S. congressman John Bragg lived here.
Bridle Creek, US 401 south of town, was birthplace of two Confederate major generals, Matt W. and Robert Ransom.
Emmanuel Episcopal Church, 229 N. Main St. Horace Greeley, editor of the *New York Tribune,* married Mary Youngs Cheney here on July 5, 1836.
White House, 300 Halifax St. Marker on State 59. John White was a Confederate commissioner sent t buy ships and supplies in England. Gen. Lee visited the home in 1870.

WASHINGTON, Beaufort County. US 17. Town was taken by Federals in March 1862, burned by evacuating Union troops in April 1864.
Fowle House, 203 W. Main St. Gov. Daniel G. Fowle served as Confederate officer and legislator. Plaque at site.

WAYNESVILLE, Haywood County. Off IS 40, US 19. Gen. James G. Martin surrendered the last North Carolina Confederate force here on May 6, 1865.

WILLIAMSTON, Martin County. US 64.
Biggs House, 1 block north of highway marker. Asa Biggs was a U.S. senator, later a Confederate judge.
Fort Branch, State 125, 11½ miles northwest of town. Confederate fort at Rainbow Banks was built to guard railroads and the upper Roanoke River valley. Earthworks are about 3 miles northeast of highway marker.

WILMINGTON, New Hanover County. US 17. Historical markers will be found on US 421 for home and gravesite of Confederate senator George Davis; birthplace of Maj. Gen. William W. Loring; birthplace of John A. Winslow, captain of the USS *Kearsage;* early home of Judah P. Benjamin, Confederate cabinet officer; and gravesite of Confederate secret service agent Rose Greenhow. Marker for gravesite of John N. Maffitt, Confederate naval captain, on US 17, 74, and 76. On US 74 and 76, 8 miles east of town, is marker for salt works of 1861–1864.

Bellamy Mansion, northeast corner of Market and 5th St. Antebellum home was occupied by Federal forces.

Confederate Headquarters, northwest corner of Market and 3rd St., were at this site when Wilmington was still a Southern-held port. Building was razed during World War I.

Confederate Memorial, Dock and 3rd St., was designed by Francis H. Packer. Gabriel James Boney gave the memorial in honor of his comrades.

Confederate Navy Yard, across Cape Fear River from U.S. Customhouse. The ironclad *North Carolina* was built here in 1862.

Davis Monument, Market and 3rd St., honors George Davis, Confederate senator and attorney general. It is the work of Francis H. Packer.

First Presbyterian Church, Orange and 3rd St. The Bible in the sanctuary was borrowed by a Union soldier during the war and returned in 1928. If not the soldier at least the descendants must have got some use from it.

Fort Anderson, built near the old town site by the Confederacy, managed to hold out for a month after the fall of Fort Fisher *(which see).* Earthworks remain. A visitor center has exhibits and a slide show.

MacRae House, E. Market, between 7th and 8th St. Used by Federal troops as a hospital.

National Cemetery, Market at 20th St., on US 17N. Union soldiers, chiefly from Michigan and Wisconsin, who fell at Fort Fisher are buried here.

New Hanover Courthouse, Princess at 3rd St. The county museum has Confederate relics.

Oakdale Cemetery, Market St. to 15th St., north to cemetery. Among some rather curious burials here (a man and his dog, the last man killed in a political duel, a young lady seated in a chair and enclosed in a casket of rum) are Henry Baker, designer of the Lincoln Memorial, and Mrs. Rose O'Neill Greenhow, Confederate secret agent, who was credited for the Confederate lack of surprise at First Manassas. Mrs. Greenhow was arrested by Allan Pinkerton, imprisoned for a time; she later drowned near Wilmington.

Orton Plantation, south via US 17 and State 133. During the war the plantation was taken over as a smallpox hospital and escaped destruction by fire. Owner Thomas Miller, however, was bankrupted, and the estate was abandoned until the 1880s when it was bought by Confederate Col. Kenneth M. Murchison, who restored house and fields.

WILSON, Wilson County. US 301A.

Confederate Hospital, 1½ blocks southeast of highway marker. Dr. S. S. Satchwell operated hospital in building of the Wilson Female Seminary.

Maplewood Cemetery has the grave of Rebecca M. Winborne, who is said to have been the maker of the original Stars and Bars. The flag, designed by Maj. Orren R. Smith, was displayed on March 19, 1861, at Louisburg.

Pender Birthplace, State 42 about 8 miles east of town. Confederate Gen. W. D. Pender was mortally wounded at Gettysburg.

WINSTON-SALEM, Forsyth County. IS 40, US 52.

Joshua Boner House, 723 S. Main St. Union headquarters during occupation.

WINTON, Hertford County. US 13. Marker on highway. The first town burned in North Carolina during the war, February 20, 1862.

Potecasi Creek, US 158 between Winton and Murfreesboro, was scene of skirmish between Union and Confederate troops July 26, 1863. Breastworks southwest of highway marker.

NORTH DAKOTA

Dakota Territory was created shortly before the fall of Fort Sumter. Territorial Gov. William Jayne tried to raise a regiment when Lincoln called for volunteers, although a census showed only 2,402 white settlers. A few cavalry companies were mustered but were needed for frontier duty when the Sioux uprising in Minnesota spread west bringing increased Indian troubles.

Gov. Jayne, an abolitionist and a former neighbor of Abraham Lincoln in Springfield, asked the first session of the legislature meeting in March 1862 to pass a law prohibiting slavery in the territory. The assembly, which was largely Democratic, defeated the measure.

In 1863 the territory was opened for homesteading; boundaries were changed in 1864 when the Montana Territory was established, and again in 1858 with the Wyoming boundary settlement. North Dakota entered the Union on November 2, 1889. Indian troubles that began during the Civil War were not ended until December 1890, at the battle of Wounded Knee.

ANTELOPE, Stark County. US 10.
Site of Gen. Sully's Camp, 8 miles south. En route to the Yellowstone River in 1864, Gen. Sully bivouacked at this spot and made a surprise attack on 5,000 Sioux at the battle of Killdeer Mountains.

BIG MOUND BATTLEFIELD. *See* McPHAIL'S BUTTE.

BISMARCK, Burleigh County. IS 94, US 83.
North Dakota Heritage Center, on the Capitol mall, houses the state historical society and state historical museum, with historical displays, relics of pioneer and military interest, and Indian artifacts.

BUFFALO CREEK, Cass County. US 10.
Bronze tablet on highway marks site where Gen. Sibley and troops marched on August 16, 1863, on return from driving the Indians across the Missouri River.

BURMAN HISTORIC SITE, Kidder County. US 10. Ten miles north of Tappen. Monument marks site of an engagement between Sioux Indians and Sibley's troops, July 24, 1863. Army surgeon Dr. J. S. Weiser was killed during the engagement at Big Mound.

CAMP ARNOLD, Barnes County. State 32, 4 miles north of Oriska. Gen. H. H. Sibley camped here in 1863. Graves of James Ponsford and Andrus Moore have been marked with marble headstones. Bronze marker at site.

CAMP ATCHESON HISTORIC SITE, Griggs County. State 1. This camp on Lake Sibley was named for Capt. Charles Atcheson of Sibley's staff. On a tip from friendly Chippewas, Sibley learned the whereabouts of the Sioux, and chased them across the Missouri near Bismarck. In the fortification built at this site, all sick men, weak horses, and supplies were left in the protection of two infantry companies. There is a marble marker on a private's grave on hill near the lake.

CAMP CORNING, Barnes County. State 1. Named for one of Sibley's officers, the camp was established by the Sibley expedition on July 16, 1863. Granite monument.

CAMP GRANT, Stutsman County. State 36. A bronze tablet marks the site of Gen. Sibley's camp in 1863.

CAMP JOHNSON, Barnes County. State 1. Also known as *Birch Creek Historic Site,* 2 miles east of Hastings. Site of Gen. John Frémont's camp in 1839, later Camp Johnson established by Col. McPhail in 1863.

CAMP KIMBALL HISTORIC SITE, Wells County. State 30, 8 miles southwest of Carrington. A military camp established by Gen. Sibley in 1863.

CAMP SHEARDOWN HISTORIC SITE, Barnes County. State 32, 3 miles southeast of Valley City. Bronze marker for site of Sibley camp of 1863.

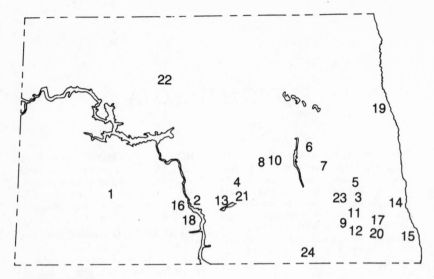

NORTH DAKOTA

1 — Antelope	7 — Camp Corning	13 — Chaska	19 — Grand Forks
2 — Bismarck	8 — Camp Grant	14 — Fargo	20 — Lisbon
3 — Buffalo Creek	9 — Camp Johnson	15 — Fort Abercrombie	21 — McPhail's Butte
4 — Burman Historic Site	10 — Camp Kimball	16 — Fort Abraham Lincoln	22 — Minot
5 — Camp Arnold	11 — Camp Sheardown	17 — Fort Ransom	23 — Valley City
6 — Camp Atcheson	12 — Camp Weiser	18 — Fort Rice	24 — Whitestone

CAMP WEISER HISTORIC SITE, Ransom County. State 46, 13 miles west of Enderlin. A small granite monument marks Sibley camp.

CHASKA HISTORIC SITE, Burleigh County. US 10, 3 miles north of Driscoll. The camp was named by Gen. Sibley for one of his Indian scouts who died while returning from the Missouri River expedition. Granite stone column with bronze tablet.

FARGO, Cass County. IS 29, 94.

The Forsberg House, 815 3rd Ave., has historical collection.

FORT ABERCROMBIE STATE HISTORIC SITE, Richland County. Off IS 29, US 75, in the town of Abercrombie in the southeast corner of the state. The fort was the first Federal military post in North Dakota; it was besieged by the Sioux for two months in 1862. The stockade and blockhouses have been restored. The museum has an extensive collection of historical items; caretaker is on duty during summer months.

FORT ABRAHAM LINCOLN STATE PARK, Morton County. State 6. Old Fort

McKeen is also on this site. Gen. George A. Custer and the 7th Cavalry were based at Fort Abraham Lincoln in 1873. The Custer house and infantry post blockhouses are open to visitors. Museum has military history.

FORT RANSOM, Ransom County. State 1. Fort was named for Gen. Thomas Ransom, wounded at Fort Donelson and Shiloh and mortally wounded in Georgia in 1864. The post guarded immigrant trains as thousands of Civil War veterans headed west after release from the service.

FORT RICE STATE PARK, Morton County. State 24. Site of fort established by Gen. Alfred H. Sully on his expedition of 1864.

GRAND FORKS, Grand Forks County. IS 29.

Grand Forks County Historical Society, 2405 Belmont Rd., has museum exhibits and photographic collection from 1850 to 1950.

Soldiers Monument, 6th St. S. and Belmont Rd. Memorial to 168 North Dakota Civil War soldiers. Names are engraved on bronze tablet.

LISBON, Ransom County. State 32, 27.

Oakwood Cemetery has statue of bugler sounding taps, a memorial to Civil War dead.

McPHAIL'S BUTTE HISTORIC SITE, Kidder County. US 10. About 10 miles north of Tappen. From this hill Col. Samuel McPhail sent his Minnesota Rangers against Sioux in the battle of Big Mound, July 24, 1863. During a peace talk a young Indian shot Dr. J. S. Weiser without warning or, apparently, explanation. The doctor is buried at the Burman Historic Site, northeast of the battlefield.

MINOT, Ward County. US 83, 52.

Rosehill Cemetery, 3rd St. SE at 11th, has a Civil War memorial erected by the Daughters of Union Veterans.

VALLEY CITY, Barnes County. IS 94, US 10.

Barnes County Courthouse, 7th St. between 6th and 7th Ave., has historical and Indian items.

WHITESTONE BATTLEFIELD HISTORIC PARK, Dickey County. State 56. Off US 281. On September 3 and 5, 1863, the battle that broke the power of the Sioux in this area was fought by troops commanded by Gen. Alfred Sully. The museum contains relics of the battle and of Indian and pioneer days. A caretaker is on duty during summer months. The battle monument to soldiers killed here is considered one of the best in the West.

OHIO

Ohio has been called the "Mother of Presidents." It also could be called the "Mother of Union Generals." Among Ohio-born commanders were Gens. Ulysses S. Grant, William T. Sherman, Joseph Warren Keifer, Benjamin Harrison, and James A. Garfield. Among major generals were Jacob D. Cox, George Armstrong Custer, George Crook, James Birdseye McPherson, Ormsby McKnight Mitchel, and William Starke Rosecrans. Rutherford B. Hayes was a brigadier general and William McKinley a major. Gen. Phillip Sheridan, born in Albany, New York, is considered an Ohioan, having arrived in the state at the age of one. Ohioans can also claim a rear admiral: Henry Walke, then a commander, was captain of the gunboat *Carondelet* in the daring and dramatic dash past Island No. 10 that helped to open the Mississippi for Union ironclads in April 1862.

The only engagements fought on Ohio ground occurred during the Morgan raid in the summer of 1863. The Confederate cavalry leader, Gen. John Morgan, and his raiders were defeated by Union troops at Buffington Island near Portland and surrendered near West Point, south of Lisbon. For a number of years prior to and throughout the war, however, Ohio was the scene of a bitter struggle between leading abolitionists and ardent Southern sympathizers. Both Clement L. Vallandigham, head of the Peace Democrats—more widely known as Copperheads—and Levi Coffin, the so-called "president" of the Underground Railroad, were Ohioans. The state supplied about 319,200 men to the Union army, far more than its quota. Meanwhile, the Confederates stepped to the tune of "Dixie," written by Ohio's Daniel Decatur Emmett of Mount Vernon.

AKRON, Summit County. IS 76, 77.

John Brown Home, 514 Diagonal Rd. Remodeled residence where John Brown lived from 1844 to 1846; he was a sheep raiser and wool broker in partnership with Col. Simon Perkins, son of Akron's founder. After Brown raided Harpers Ferry and was sentenced to death, Akron friends came to his defense; when he was hanged, city flags were flown at half-mast.

Perkins Mansion, Copley Rd. and S. Portage Path, was built in 1831 by Gen. Simon Perkins, founder of Akron and father of John Brown's onetime business partner. The Summit County Historical Society operates both the mansion and the Brown home as museums.

Perkins Woods Park, south of Copley Rd. and west of Edgewood, has the John Brown Monument, an eagle-crowned shaft built of stone from old courthouses.

ASHTABULA, Ashtabula County. US 20, north of IS 90. State 45, from Warren, has been called Freedom Road. Many fugitives escaped along this route to Ashtabula Harbor, where they took boats for Canada.

Hubbard Homestead, northwest corner of Lake Ave., and Walnut Blvd., was an Underground Railroad station. Now a community house.

ATHENS, Athens County. US 50, 33. Charles Cardwell McCabe was born here in 1836; he is credited with giving national popularity to "The Battle Hymn of the Republic." McCabe was chaplain of the 122nd Ohio Volunteers when he first read in the *Atlantic Monthly* a poem written by Julia Ward Howe for the tune of "John Brown's Body." Few Ohioans could have escaped hearing the melody often. McCabe taught the new words to Ohio soldiers. When captured at Winchester he was taken to Libby Prison, Richmond, where he again taught the song. Once, in Washington, Lincoln himself asked the chaplain to "sing it again."

BUFFINGTON ISLAND STATE MONUMENT, Meigs County. State 124 and Ohio River, at Portland. A four-acre plot with a freestone pillar marks the July 1863 battlefield where Morgan's raiders fought Union forces, some of whom were entrenched while others

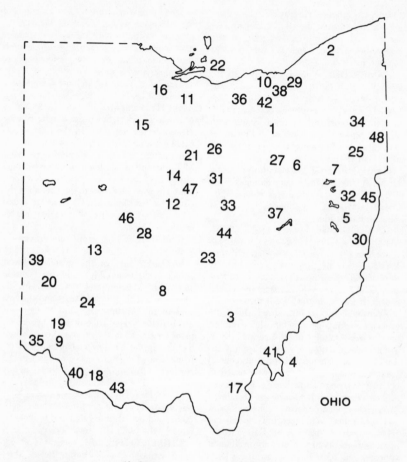

1 — Akron	13 — Dayton	25 — Lisbon	37 — Old Washington
2 — Ashtabula	14 — Delaware	26 — Mansfield	38 — Orange
3 — Athens	15 — Findlay	27 — Massillon	39 — Oxford
4 — Buffington Island	16 — Fremont	28 — Mechanicsburg	40 — Point Pleasant
5 — Cadiz	17 — Gallipolis	29 — Mentor	41 — Portland
6 — Canton	18 — Georgetown	30 — Mount Pleasant	42 — Richfield
7 — Carrollton	19 — Glendale	31 — Mount Vernon	43 — Ripley
8 — Chillicothe	20 — Hamilton	32 — New Rumley	44 — Somerset
9 — Cincinnati	21 — Iberia	33 — Newark	45 — Steubenville
10 — Cleveland	22 — Johnson's Island	34 — Niles	46 — Urbana
11 — Clyde	23 — Lancaster	35 — North Bend	47 — Westerville
12 — Columbus	24 — Lebanon	36 — Oberlin	48 — Youngstown

were aboard gunboats. On July 19, some 700 Confederates were captured. Morgan and about 1,200 escaped to the north. Morgan fought another skirmish near Salineville and surrendered near West Point, below Lisbon.

McCook Monument, erected in honor of Maj. Daniel McCook, is in a two-acre plot near Portland. (*See* CARROLLTON.)

CADIZ, Harrison County. US 22, 36-250. John A. Bingham, Civil War statesman; Bishop Matthew Simpson, noted abolitionist; Edwin M. Stanton, Lincoln's Secretary of War; and Clark Gable, whose most memorable role was that of Rhett Butler in the motion picture *Gone With the Wind,* were Cadiz citizens. There is a statue of Bingham in front of the Harrison

County Courthouse. He was elected to Congress in 1855, sat at the trial of Lincoln's assassin, and took an active part in the impeachment proceedings against President Johnson in 1868.

CAMBRIDGE, Guernsey County, IS 70, 77, US 22, off IS 70. There is a Civil War monument on Main St. that has full-size uniformed figures representing all branches of service and a seated, full-bosomed beauty who seems to represent the Muse of History and is extending a hand in appeal to a young man still in civilian clothes.

CAMP DENNISON, Hamilton County. US 50. A Union training camp during the war.

The Christian Waldschmidt House, 7567 Glendale-Milford Rd., has a Civil War museum room. Tours.

CANTON, Stark County. IS 77, US 62, State 8. Major William McKinley opened a law office here after the war. His wife's grandfather, John Saxton, brought out the first edition of the *Ohio Repository,* now the *Canton Repository.* Because of McKinley's fondness for the red carnation, it was made the state flower.

Archibald McGregor edited the *Stark County Democrat* opposing Lincoln, abolition, and the war. At midnight on August 22, 1861, a mob broke into his office and sacked it. Canton Democrats demanded that the city council reimburse McGregor. McGregor published an open letter saying that he knew every member of the mob and that the leader was Lt. Edward Meyer, son of Canton's mayor. The lieutenant and eight others were taken into custody but released when "prominent Republicans" brought bond money. The Canton council appropriated $3,000 to repair the plant. McGregor fought another sideline skirmish in October 1862, when Provost Marshal Anson Pease of Massillon, Postmaster W. K. Miller of Canton, and a file of Union soldiers marched into his office on a Sunday morning and took him into custody. To the crowd gathered outside the newspaper plant, McGregor shouted an invitation to witness "another instance of Abolition tyranny!" The editor was taken to Camp Mansfield, an army training center; meanwhile, his wife took up the editorial pen, asking Democrats to stand firm: "Falter not, for our cause is just and conquer we must." McGregor, having been treated more as a guest than prisoner, was released in November and was welcomed home by joyful Canton Democrats.

Canton Public Library, Cleveland Ave. and 3rd St. McKinley manuscripts.

First Methodist Church, southeast corner of W. Tuscarawas St. and Cleveland Ave. A silver plate marks the McKinley pew. Four stained-glass windows were presented to the church shortly after the death of the president, whose funeral services were held here.

McKinley National Memorial, McKinley Monument Dr. NW, includes a statue and the tomb of President McKinley and the McKinley Museum of History, Science and Industry. One viewer, greatly impressed by the tomb, compared it favorably with the Taj Mahal and "to a less degree, the tomb of Hadrian." Mrs. McKinley and two children are entombed here also. There are four memorial windows presented by Mrs. McKinley to the Church of the Savior United Methodist, Cleveland Ave. and W. Tuscarawas St., where the president and his family worshiped.

CARROLLTON, Carroll County. State 43, 9, 39.

McCook House, on the square, southwest corner, is the restored home of the "Fighting McCooks." Major Daniel McCook, with his nine sons ("The Tribe of Dan") and the five sons of his brother, Dr. John McCook of Steubenville ("The Tribe of John"), were famous for service in the army and navy before and during the Civil War. Thirteen were officers. Daniel died of wounds received in the battle of Buffington Island, and three sons lost their lives. The brick home, built in 1837, was the birthplace of the four youngest McCooks. It was acquired by the state in 1941; it has memorabilia and period furnishings and is administered by the Ohio Historical Society.

CHILLICOTHE, Ross County. US 50, 35, 23. The town had a scare during the war when word was spread that Gen. John Morgan was coming. Guards, hastily stationed at a covered bridge on Paint Street, mistook local scouts for raiders and burned down the bridge in their confusion. There was only one foot of water in Paint Creek at the time, but Morgan never appeared.

Ross County Historical Society Museum, 45 W. 5th St., has exhibits of firearms, costumes, and relics in a Civil War room.

CINCINNATI, Hamilton County. IS 71, 74, 75. Located on the Mason-Dixon line, and with the South an important factor in its trade, the city was as divided as the state in loyalties and interests. At the outbreak of war, merchants felt mortally wounded but began to recover as government contracts came in. While many remained loyal to the Union, others continued to smuggle goods south. A number of

Cincinnatians were closer emotionally as well as geographically to the slave-holding Kentuckians across the river than to the abolitionists of Akron who had draped the flags at half-mast for John Brown. Hamilton County had the largest black population of any county in the state. Many felt that the city had become a "dumping ground" for slaves, that it was becoming "Africanized." Riots were common, and free blacks had anything but a free and easy time of it.

In the summer of 1862, when Confederate forces under Gen. Kirby Smith were advancing toward the city from central Kentucky, Gen. Lew Wallace took over the town's defenses, throwing a pontoon bridge across the Ohio, putting in miles of entrenchments, and deploying artillery in key positions. Nearly 16,000 civilians came to the defense during the "Siege of Cincinnati." Many wore coonskin caps and homespun. Maj. Malcolm McDowell, an army paymaster, dubbed them "the Squirrel Hunters," a title made official by resolution of the Ohio General Assembly in March 1863. Kirby Smith never arrived. When Wallace departed in September, he announced that it had been the spades and not the guns that had saved the city. Cincinnati was bypassed again after a scare in July 1863, when Morgan and his raiders wheeled eastward away from the hastily remanned defenses. Serving as headquarters for the Department of the Ohio, the city remained a military center though it never again was threatened by invasion.

Beecher Home-Harriet B. Stowe Memorial, Gilbert and Foraker Ave., in Walnut Hills. In a house later known as the Edgement Inn, Rev. Dr. Lyman Beecher and his family lived when Beecher was president of Lane Seminary. Levi Coffin, "president" of the Underground Railroad, lived around the corner at 3131 Wehrman Ave. One room is dedicated to Mrs. Stowe and the Beecher family. Others have displays on Negro life and contributions to the American heritage.

Burnet House, northwest corner of 3rd and Vine St. On this site stood the city's leading hotel, the Burnet House, where Lincoln stopped en route to Washington in February 1861. In March 1864, Gens. Grant and Sherman met in Parlor A to plan Sherman's invasion of Georgia and South Carolina. For many years Sons of Union Veterans held meetings in Parlor A. The building was razed in 1926.

Burnside Headquarters, 24 E. 9th St. A three-story red brick house served as Gen. Burnside's quarters during war days. Following his defeat at Fredericksburg, the general was sent to Cincinnati to command the Department of the Ohio. Opposing Copperhead propaganda, Burnside issued his Order 38 from this house on April 13, 1863: "The habit of declaring sympathy for the enemy will not be allowed."

Chase Law Office, northeast corner of E. 3rd and Main St. The site of the office where Salmon P. Chase, later Lincoln's Secretary of the Treasury, practiced law. He was known derisively as "attorney general for runaway Negroes." His defense of James G. Birney, abolitionist editor accused of harboring a runaway, brought him national fame.

Civil War Fortification, along Fort View Pl., southwest from Hatch St., in Mount Adams. Cannon were placed on parapets and strong garrisons of troops were on duty at this vantage point overlooking the Ohio River.

Grant's Headquarters, 739 W. 8th St. Gen. Grant stayed at this site in March 1864. Since his table was too small for maps, Grant, Sherman, and others adjourned to the Burnet House to work out strategy.

Hayes Office, 127 E. 3rd St. president Rutherford B. Hayes was a city solicitor before he became a Civil War general.

Lincoln Statue, Lytle Park, 421 E. 4th St. The land once belonged to the Lytle family. Brig. Gen. William Haines Lytle was killed at the battle of Chickamauga. The Lincoln statue in bronze is beardless; it is the work of George Grey Barnard.

Rosecrans Home, 2935 Lehman Rd. in Price Hill, was the residence of Gen. William Starke Rosecrans when he commanded the military in the Cincinnati area.

Union Army Headquarters, southeast corner of Arch St. and Broadway, was in a four-story brick building at this site. Recruiters must have been somewhat surprised when 33 members of the "Literary Club" joined up in a body, with Rutherford B. Hayes leading the gallant group.

Waldschmidt House, 18 miles northeast on US Bypass 50 and State 126, at 7567 Glendale Milford Rd. The house, built in 1804, served as headquarters for the Union army at Camp Dennison. The camp was named for Gov. William Dennison who, by taking control of transportation and communication facilities and using public funds without special appropriation, managed to outfit the state for the war. He was Postmaster General in Lincoln's second term, served also under President Johnson. Restored house with Civil War room.

CLEVELAND, Cuyahoga County. IS 77, 90, US 20. An important point on the Underground Railroad, the city sent lawyers to defend John Brown during his trial, tolled city bells for half an hour at news of his death. Clevelanders gave an immediate response to Lincoln's call for volunteers; within two days the first Cleveland Grays were on the march.

Garfield Memorial, Lakeview Cemetery, Euclid Ave. at E. 123rd St. Tomb and monument of James Abram Garfield, Union general and 20th president. Mark Hanna and John Hay are also buried here.

Leggett Monument, Lakeview Cemetery, at grave of Maj. Gen. Mortimer D. Leggett, whose troops captured Bald Hill, from which Atlanta could be shelled; site became known as Leggett's Hill.

Public Square, center of business district. The Soldiers' and Sailors' Monument. Bronze figures depict infantry, cavalry, artillery, and naval detachments.

Weddell House, southwest corner of W. 6th St. and Superior Ave. From its second-floor balcony, Lincoln addressed a street crowd on February 13, 1861, when he was en route to his inaugural ceremonies. The Lincoln Sesquicentennial Committee has placed a plaque at the site now occupied by the Rockefeller Building.

Western Reserve Historical Society Museum and Library, 10825 East Blvd., has exhibits and printed material. Costume collection from 1800s.

CLYDE, Sandusky County. US 20, State 101.

McPherson Cemetery, junction of US 20 and State 101, is named for Brig. Gen. James Birdseye McPherson, who was killed in action at the battle of Atlanta by Confederates under the command of his West Point classmate John Bell Hood. The McPherson statue is in the southwest corner of the burial ground.

McPherson House, Maumee Pike and Maple St. The home where McPherson lived from 1833–1864 is not open to the public.

COLUMBUS, Franklin County. IS 70, 71, US 40. The city was created as Ohio's capital. The legislature first met here in 1816.

Camp Chase Confederate Cemetery, Sullivant Ave., west of Powell Ave., is the site of Camp Chase, once a training camp and prisoner camp. Buried are Confederates who died while prisoners. Near the entrance is a stone arch surmounted by the statue of a Confederate soldier. A Union soldier, William H. Knauss, contributed money and effort to have the monument erected.

Fort Hayes, Cleveland Ave. and Buckingham St., formerly known as Columbus Barracks, was established as a military post in 1863. It was named for President Rutherford B. Hayes. The shot tower was built to make Union bullets.

Franklin Park has marker at site where Gen. W. T. Sherman spoke in 1880, saying that war is "all hell."

McKinley Memorial, west entrance to Capitol grounds. Bronze statue of President McKinley.

Ohio History Center, 17th Ave. at IS 71. The Ohio State Historical Society is housed here. The museum has war and John Brown relics, also extensive Ohio periodical files, diaries, photographs, regimental histories, and letters.

Ohio State Capitol, High, Broad, State, and 3rd St. At northwest corner are bronze statues by Levi T. Schofield of Grant, Sherman, Sheridan, Stanton, Garfield, Chase, and Hayes, surrounding a shaft which bears a statue of Cornelia, the Roman matron. Her words, "These Are My Jewels," stand out in relief at the top of the shaft. The Capitol building has tablets, sculpture, regimental flags, and murals pertaining to Ohio's participation in the war. The Lincoln Sesquicentennial Committee has placed a plaque in the chamber of the house of representatives commemorating Lincoln's February 13, 1861, address to a joint session of house and senate.

DAYTON, Montgomery County. IS 75, US 35. The city was a battleground of Copperhead skirmishing. On November 1, 1862, J. F. Bollmeyer, editor of the states' rights advocate the *Dayton Empire,* was shot down in the street. In May 1863, Copperheads wrecked the pro-Lincoln *Dayton Journal* office when Clement L. Vallandigham was arrested. The Copperhead leader was banished to the South after a trial and great controversy.

Carillon Park, 2001 S. Patterson Blvd. on US 25, has museum with historical exhibits.

Dayton Library, Cooper Park, E. 3rd, and St. Clair St. Historical museum and Lincoln portrait. A McKinley monument was paid for by the contributions of schoolchildren.

The Paul Laurence Dunbar House State Memorial, 219 N. Summit St., is a national historical landmark. Paul Laurence Dunbar, whose parents were former slaves, wrote of black life in the Old South from tales told by his relatives and acquaintances who had outlived the system.

Woodland Cemetery, east end of Woodland

General Negley's Pennsylvania Brigade passes down the Ohio River.

Ave. Clement L. Vallandigham, Union Gen. Robert C. Schenck, and Paul Laurence Dunbar are buried here.

DELAWARE, Delaware County. US 23, 36.

Hayes Birthplace, E. William St., between Sandusky and Union St. Monument marks site of birthplace of Rutherford B. Hayes, Union general and 19th president.

Ohio Wesleyan University, US 23, was founded in 1840. An 1855 graduate, John Sills Jones, enlisted as a private soldier in April 1861, after resigning as prosecuting attorney of Delaware County. He was brevetted brigadier general in June 1865, after serving throughout the war. He was later a congressman.

FINDLAY, Hancock County. IS 75, US 224. Home town of David Ross Locke who, as Petroleum V. Nasby, was a popular Civil War humorist. His satirical letters attacking slavery appeared in the *Findlay Jeffersonian.* The town was an important stop on the Underground Railroad in the 1850s.

FREMONT, Sandusky County. State 53, South of IS 80-90.

Hayes Presidential Center, Spiegel Grove State Park, at junction of Hayes and Buckland Ave. The graves of President and Mrs. Hayes are in a small grove on the grounds. Hayes memorabilia, Lincoln and Confederate items, and period exhibits are in museum. Hayes was commissioned major of the 23rd Ohio Volunteer Infantry and was brevetted brigadier general in 1865 for gallantry and courage in battle. Whenever possible his wife, Lucy, lived at headquarters. The soldiers called her "our mother"; she nursed, cooked for them, and wrote their letters home. At her death the regiment escorted her body to the burial in Spiegel Grove.

The museum is, for its size and scope, outstandingly well arranged and maintained. Displays cover an amazing range of 19th-century memorabilia.

Memorial Monument, in the Birchard Library Park, commemorates Sandusky County soldiers and sailors.

GALLIPOLIS, Gallia County. US 35, State 7. Camp Carrington was located here as well as a hospital, which at one time housed 4,000 wounded soldiers. There is a marker on the public square at the site of the first mustering of Ohio troops for early western Virginia campaigns.

GAMBIER, Knox County. State 229.
Kenyon College. Lorin Andrews, president of the college, was the first Ohio volunteer.

GEORGETOWN, Brown County. US 68, State 125.
General Ulysses S. Grant lived here as a boy and went to school on South Water St. There is a monument in his memory in Confederate Cemetery.

GLENDALE, Hamilton County. IS 275, 75. An Underground Railroad station. It is said the real Eliza, model for Harriet Beecher Stowe's character, stopped here en route to Canada, staying in a brick house on Oak Road in the southeast part of town. During a night in July 1863, Morgan's Raiders also passed this way.

GRANVILLE, Licking County. State 16, 661.
Welsh Hills Cemetery has grave of sculptor T. W. Jones whose bust of Lincoln in the statehouse is said to be the only sculpture for which Lincoln posed. The president-elect said of the clay model: "I think it looks very much like the critter."

HAMILTON, Butler County. US 127, State 4.
Soldiers', Sailors' and Pioneers' Monument Building, southwest corner of High St. and Monument Ave. A 17-foot brass figure of a Civil War private stands atop the monument, which contains a library with the names of Ohioans who served in the Civil War.

HUDSON, Summit County. IS 80, State 91, 303. Jesse Grant once worked at a tannery here for Owen Brown, whose son John was learning the tannery business. The area has many Brown family associations. John and his first wife, Dianthe, were married here. The Brown farm was an Underground Railroad stop.

IBERIA, Morrow County. US 30S. An abolitionist stronghold, the town once resisted a U.S. deputy marshal and posse who were attempting to reclaim three runaway slaves. Iberians clipped the deputy's hair and whipped other members of the posse. The Rev. Mr. Gordon, president of Ohio Central College, was arrested though he was an innocent bystander. Indignant Iberians won a pardon for Gordon from President Lincoln, but Gordon died soon after release from prison.

JACKSON, Jackson County. US 35.
Buckeye Furnace, 10 miles east on State 124, then 3 miles south following signs. One of the last 19th century iron ore furnaces, active during the Civil War, has been restored. Buildings include the ironmaster's home, casting house, company store, charging house, and blacksmith's shop.

JEFFERSON, Ashtabula County. State 46.
Wade-Giddings Law Office has boulder with plaque in front of building. Benjamin Wade served as chairman of the Committee on the Conduct of the War. Joshua R. Giddings is said to have written the first Republican platform at his stand-up desk here.

JOHNSON'S ISLAND, in Sandusky Bay, ½ mile from Marblehead Peninsula. Site can be reached from Lakeside or Sandusky by speedboat. A stockade and prison camp covering 18 acres were built here in 1861; by war's end more than 15,000 Confederates, many of them officers, had been confined on the island. The Confederate cemetery has the graves of more than 200 who died as prisoners. Civil War financier Jay Cooke of Sandusky almost alone carried the burden of financing the Union war operations. His summer home was a castle on Gibraltar Island, Put-in-Bay.

LANCASTER, Fairfield County. US 22, 33.
Ewing House, 163 E. Main St., was the home of the Thomas Ewing family. On the death of his father, Judge Charles Sherman, William Tecumseh was taken into the Ewing home; he married Ellen Ewing in 1851.
Sherman House, 137 E. Main St., is a state-maintained memorial and museum, renovated in 1951 by the Ohio Historical Society which now administers the property. Rooms are furnished with pieces from the period when the house was occupied by the Sherman family. Relics and memorabilia. Tecumseh, later baptized William, was born here February 8, 1820; John, who was U.S. senator during the war years and later Secretary of the Treasury and Secretary of State, was born here May 10, 1823. In 1940, the house was in danger of being razed for the construction of an apartment building; the property was purchased in 1946 by the Lancaster city council. In 1950 it was deeded to the state.

LEBANON, Warren County. Off IS 71, US 42, State 48. Maj. Gen. Ormsby M. Mitchel lived here as a boy; he walked most of the way from here to West Point to enter the military academy.

Golden Lamb, Broadway north of Main St., was built in 1816. The inn sign has been described as a golden dropsical sheep. Among guests have been Charles Dickens, William Henry Harrison, Rutherford B. Hayes, James G. Blaine, DeWitt Clinton, and William McKinley. On the second floor is a room occupied by Clement L. Vallandigham, who came to the inn from Dayton to defend a Mr. McGehan, charged with murdering a man named Myers. Vallandigham concluded, perhaps rightly, that Myers had shot himself accidentally; the Copperhead lawyer may have tried to prove his point by pulling the trigger of a supposedly unloaded pistol. He died in this room from the accidental wound the next day. The Golden Lamb is now an inn and a restaurant. The inn is also a Shaker Museum.

Thomas Corwin House, corner of Main and Corwin St. The home of Corwin, who was minister to Mexico under Lincoln. He is buried in Lebanon Cemetery.

LISBON, Columbiana County. US 30, State 45.

Birthplace of Clement L. Vallandigham, 431 W. Lincoln Way. The leader of the Peace Democrats seldom met indifference or found any great degree of peace. He left school (Jefferson College at Cannonsburg, Pennsylvania) after an argument with the president over a point of law, was twice defeated for Congress, was eventually elected to the House of Representatives, and made scores of enemies and a small army of devoted followers when he advocated peace at the start of the Civil War. He was later jailed, banished to the Confederacy, escaped to Canada, was defeated in a correspondence campaign for governor of Ohio, and in 1871 accidentally shot and killed himself. (*See* LEBANON.)

Site of Morgan's Surrender, on State 518 south of Lisbon. A monument commemorates the surrender of Gen. John Morgan to Union forces on July 26, 1863. This was the northernmost point reached by Confederate troops engaged in battle during the war (see ST. ALBANS, Vermont). Morgan's raiders made some 49 raids in Ohio from Harrison to West Point. Many points are marked.

MANSFIELD, Richland County. IS 71, US 30, State 13. John Sherman began law practice here in 1844, was elected to Congress in 1855.

His Victorian-style home has been torn down. Mansfield was a station on the Underground Railway. The Richland County Lincoln Society first endorsed Lincoln for President in 1858 and worked in his behalf from that time. South Park and Middle Park were donated to the city by John Sherman and A. J. Heineman.

MANTUA, Portage County. State 44.

Hillside Cemetery has the grave of Newton Goodall, one of the famed "Squirrel Hunters" in the defense of Cincinnati.

MASSILLON, State County, Off IS 77, US 30, State 548. In West Brookfield Cemetery is the tombstone of Mary Owens Jenkins, who served in Company K, 9th Pennsylvania Volunteer Cavalry, under the name of John Evans. Mary served alongside her lover, William Evans. When William was killed and "John" wounded at Gettysburg, her disguise was discovered and her enlistment ended.

MECHANICSBURG, Champaign County. State 29, 4. Underground Railroad stations here received fugitives from three regular routes and had "switch" connections with other lines of escape. At one time most of the town turned out to chase the law enforcement officers who had come to reclaim Addison White, possibly the most famous fugitive in Ohio history.

MENTOR, Lake County. IS 90, US 20, east of Cleveland.

Lawnfield, 8095 Mentor Ave., was the last home of James A. Garfield, 20th president. It has been restored as a memorial with Garfield memorabilia on display. There is a replica of the log cabin that was Garfield's birthplace. A carriage house contains five period carriages.

MOUNT PLEASANT, Jefferson County. State 150, east of US 36-250. The Quaker settlement here was a refuge for fugitive slaves from the early part of the 19th century. The first abolitionist newspaper was the antislavery paper *The Genius of Universal Emancipation.* An abolition convention was held in 1837.

Free Labor Store was established in 1848 by the village Quakers; no products of slave labor were permitted to be sold.

Friends Meeting House, State 150, has been restored by the Ohio Historical Society and is maintained as a state memorial.

MOUNT VERNON, Knox County. US 36, State 13.

Bickerdyke Birthplace, State 13 toward Fredericktown. House where Mary Ann Ball (Bickerdyke) was born stood across from the Zenas Ball homestead. Zenas was Mary Ann's uncle. "Mother Bickerdyke," the widow, was a tireless Sanitary Commission worker, one who could hold her own with fellow Ohioan William T. Sherman.

Birthplace of Daniel Decatur Emmett, near center of town on N. Gay St., is marked by a plaque. Emmett was the northern composer of the South's, and Lincoln's, favorite song, "Dixie."

Cooper's Church, N. Main St., served as an Underground Railroad station. The saints in the stained-glass windows have Negroid features. The story is that the Presbyterian congregation differed on the slavery question and split—one section being known thereafter as "Cooper's Church." The building was moved here from the original site. It is now a Congregational Church.

Mound View Cemetery has a monument to Emmett at his gravesite. The inscription reads: "Daniel Decatur Emmett, 1815–1904, whose song 'Dixie Land' inspired the courage and devotion of the Southern people and now thrills the hearts of a reunited nation."

NEWARK, Licking County. US 16, State 13. With less than 5,000 residents at the outbreak of war, the village quickly secured a city charter and recruited almost a dozen companies. Johnny Clem ran off to become the famous "Drummer Boy of Shiloh." Johnny was born here August 13, 1851; his mother died by accident the day before Fort Sumter fell, and Johnny went with Newark's Wide Awake unit to Camp Dennison, where the outfit was redesignated Company H, 3rd Ohio Volunteer Infantry. Later in the war the boy joined the 22nd Michigan Volunteer Infantry, shot a Confederate officer who survived and apparently bore no hard feelings, as the two became friends years later. Johnny was made sergeant, became orderly for Gen. George Thomas who, with other officers, sent him to school after the war. President Grant commissioned him second lieutenant. As major general in 1917 he retired—peeved that President Wilson refused him permission to accompany the AEF to France. He is buried in Arlington National Cemetery.

NEW CALIFORNIA, Union County, US 33, 42.

Soldiers' Monument at highway intersection lists 396 men who went to service from the small community.

NEW RUMLEY, Harrison County. State 646.

Custer Monument is a state memorial marking the birthplace of Lt. Col. George Armstrong Custer, Union cavalry officer. Custer, who was born here December 5, 1839, was graduated at the foot of his class at West Point, but he became at 25 the youngest major general in the Federal army. He was killed at the battle of Little Big Horn in 1876. Exhibits depict a soldier's life.

NILES, Trumbull County. State 46, northwest of Youngstown.

National McKinley Monument, Main St. at Park St., houses a collection of McKinley relics. The 25th president was born here in 1843.

NORTH BEND, Hamilton County. US 50 and Ohio River.

Harrison House, southwest corner of Symmes and Washington Ave. President Benjamin Harrison was born here in the house in which his grandfather, William Henry Harrison, lived until he moved to the White House as ninth president. Benjamin's father, John Scott Harrison, who became a congressman, is the sole American who was the son of one president and the father of another. Benjamin raised and commanded the 70th Indiana. He was made brigadier general after the battles of Atlanta and Nashville.

Harrison State Memorial has the tombs of William Henry Harrison and his wife. The 14-acre park overlooks the Ohio River, just off US 50.

OBERLIN, Lorain County. State 58, south of IS 80-90. Oberlin College was the first coeducational institution to adopt a policy against discrimination because of race, creed, or color. It was a point of honor with Oberlin townspeople and college students to see that no slave arriving there was recaptured. In an incident known as the Wellington Rescue, some 20 persons from town and college were jailed for taking a slave from federal agents who were returning him to his Kentucky owner. Three Oberlin blacks were with John Brown at Harpers Ferry.

Oberlin Cemetery has a monument to John A. Copeland, a black man who was executed after Harpers Ferry.

Shurtleff Statue, south of campus, honors Brig. Gen. Giles W. Shurtleff, a theological student who was captain of the Monroe Rifles, composed of 100 Oberlin students.

OLD WASHINGTON, Guernsey County. US 40, east of Cambridge. Gen. John Morgan, in July 1863, stopped at the Pine Tree Inn for refreshments before galloping on, chased by Union troops. Cemetery has graves of some Morgan followers and of Union defenders.

ORANGE, Cuyahoga County. IS 271, State 174, about 13 miles east of Cleveland. James A. Garfield, 20th president, was born here in 1831.

OXFORD, Butler County. US 27, 40 miles northwest of Cincinnati. Home of Miami University, established 1809, and Western College for Women, 1853. Civil War participants were reared on McGuffey's readers, which William Holmes McGuffey compiled while a professor at Miami in the 1830s. There is a McGuffey museum on campus.

Beta House, northeast corner of High and Campus St., was the home of Lottie Moon, who left Gen. Burnside standing at the altar. On the second floor of a High Street building, Lottie's sister, Jennie, once scratched "Hurrah for Jeff Davis" on the windowpane with a diamond ring. On another occasion, Jennie popped a pistol into the folds of her hoop skirt, went to the square, and shot out all the stars of the Union flag. Jennie and her mother and sister served as Southern spies; Jennie and her mother were arrested and confined in the Burnett House in Cincinnati. As if Dame Fate had one eye on Hollywood, Lottie was arrested a bit later and taken before the commandant of the Cincinnati Military District: her rejected suitor, Ambrose Burnside. He promptly sentenced her to confinement in the Burnett House. In three months the ladies were released. Lottie married James Clark, an Ohio attorney.

Harrison Hall, site of Old Main, where prewar debates were held by Benjamin Harrison and Benjamin Piatt Runkle, both of whom became generals; Minor Milliken, killed as a colonel; and Whitelaw Reid, Civil War reporter.

POINT PLEASANT, Clermont County. US 52 and Ohio River.

Grant Birthplace, a state memorial, has been restored and is furnished in the period and administered by the Ohio Historical Society. Many personal belongings of Gen. Grant, who was born here April 27, 1822, are in the museum.

Grant Memorial Bridge, on US 52, has stone pillars mounted with guns cast in 1861 and used in the war.

PORTLAND. *See* BUFFINGTON ISLAND.

RICHFIELD, Summit County. US 21, south of Cleveland. John Brown lived here during the early 1840s, trying his hand at sheep raising and wool selling. Four of his children are buried beneath one headstone in Fairview Cemetery.

RIPLEY, Brown County. US 52, 62, 68.

Rankin House State Memorial, north off US 52 on Liberty Hill, was home of the Rev. John Rankin, abolitionist and Underground Railroad agent, who used to place a lighted lantern in an attic window to guide fugitive slaves across the Ohio River. Here, legend says, the original Eliza of *Uncle Tom's Cabin* found temporary refuge after being rescued from the river by Rev. Rankin. Grant once attended the Ripley Academy directed by Rankin. Bronze bust at Rankin gravesite in Ripley Cemetery.

SALEM, Columbiana County. US 62. This was a station on the Underground Railroad and headquarters for the Western Anti-Slavery Society.

Coppock Monument, Hope Cemetery, N. Lincoln St., honors Edwin Coppock, abolitionist hanged after the Harpers Ferry raid.

SANDUSKY, Erie County. US 250 at Lake Erie.

Follett House Museum, 404 Wayne St., south of US 6, has items from the Confederate officers' prisons on Johnson's Island.

SOMERSET, Perry County, US 22, State 256.

Sheridan House, Columbus St., was built by Gen. Philip Sheridan for his parents. Red granite monument.

Sheridan Monument, on US 22 and State 13, honors Sheridan, who came to Somerset at the age of one. His boyhood home, on State 13, had a great oak tree north of the house where William Henry Harrison made a speech during his presidential campaign in 1840.

STEUBENVILLE, Jefferson County. US 22 and Ohio River.

Edwin M. Stanton Monument, courthouse yard, sculpted by Alexander Doyle of Steubenville. Stanton was born on December 19, 1814, at 524 Market Place; a plaque was erected by schoolchildren of the country.

Jefferson County Historical Association Museum, 426 Franklin Ave., has the desk of Edwin Stanton among displays.

Union Cemetery, 1720 W. Market St. Among those buried here are the Edwin Stanton family and three of the "Fighting McCooks"—Gen. Anson McCook, Col. George McCook, and Capt. Francis McCook, grandfather of Woodrow Wilson.

TIFFIN, Seneca County. US 224.

Gibson Monument, courthouse grounds,

honors Gen. William W. Gibson, colonel of the 49th Ohio Volunteer Infantry in 1861.

URBANA, Champaign County. US 68, 36.

Soldier's Monument, Monument Square, is the work of John Quincy Adams Ward. It is the bronze figure of a Civil War soldier returning home. Ward was born at 335 West College St. He is buried in Oak Dale Cemetery.

WELLSVILLE, Columbiana County, State 7.

Henry Aten Museum, 1607 Buckeye, has Civil War relics.

WESTERVILLE, Franklin County. State 3, north of Columbus.

Hanby House, 160 W. Main, is the restored home of Benjamin Hanby, author and composer of "Darling Nelly Gray," which has been called the *Uncle Tom's Cabin* of song; it was also highly popular with the Union army. The house, which was moved to its present site, is maintained as a state memorial by the Ohio Historical Society.

WEST LIBERTY, Logan County. US 68.

Castle Piatt and Chateau Piatt, also known as Mac-O-Cheek (1864) and Mac-O-Chee (1879) were the homes of brothers who served in the Civil War. The castles are 1 and 2 miles east on State 245. Col. Donn Piatt was a colonel of the 14th Ohio Volunteer Infantry.

XENIA, Greene County. US 35, 42.

Greene County Historical Society Museum, 74 W. Church, has flag sent by Lincoln in 1864 to honor Ohio's leading all other states in Union enlistments. Greene led all other counties. War correspondent Whitelaw Reid was born near here.

YOUNGSTOWN, Mahoning County. IS 76, 80, US 62.

Soldiers' Monument, Public Square, honors soldiers from the community who lost their lives in the war. Four cannons at the base are a gift from Gen. Garfield, then a member of Congress from the Youngstown district.

Poland is a suburb, south on State 616, where William McKinley lived as a student at 210 Main Street. From the Sparrow Tavern, or Stone Tavern, a stagecoach stop, McKinley enlisted in the Union army in April 1861.

ZANESVILLE, Muskingum County. IS 70, US 22, 40. H. D. L. Webster, a local minister, wrote the ballad "Lorena," a favorite song of both armies. He later moved to Elkhorn, Wisconsin.

Alva Buckingham House was a key station on the Underground Railroad.

OKLAHOMA

From the 1820s to the mid-1840s Oklahoma, known as Indian Territory, was settled by the Five Civilized Tribes—the Cherokee, Chickasaw, Choctaw, Creek, and Seminole. Except for the Seminole, nearly all had lived in peace with white men for most of a century. Relatively few Indians were slaveholders, but the majority had come from Southern states, some had intermarried, and most Indian agents were pro-Southern. A report issued by the Oklahoma Civil War Centennial Commission offers the view that "in all the annals of warfare, it is questionable if a more senseless happening has ever been recorded than the participation of the Five Civilized Indian Tribes in the American Civil War. . . . They were independent nations with nothing at stake in the White Man's embroilments." In effect, their culture, which had reached a level comparable with the East, was destroyed by the war. Their chief contribution to the Confederacy was indirect but valuable. By protecting the Red River area from Northern invasion, they enabled the state of Texas to send most of her troops and supplies to Confederate armies in the East.

The last Confederate general to surrender was Stand Watie, Cherokee brigadier, at Doaksville on June 23, 1865.

ANADARKO, Caddo County. US 62-281.
Southern Plains Indians Arts and Crafts Museum, east edge of town on US 62. The museum, operated by the Department of the Interior, has dioramas and displays of costumes, weapons, artifacts. Adjoining museum is the National Hall of Fame for American Indians.

ARMSTRONG ACADEMY, Bryan County. US 69, 75. The academy was founded in 1844 as part of the Choctaw Indian school system. From 1863 to 1883 it served as capital of the Choctaw Nation. Confederates camped here in 1863. Ruins may still be seen.

BIG CABIN, Craig County. US 69.
Battles of Cabin Creek. Where the old Texas Road crosses Cabin Creek, which parallels the highway, Confederates attacked a Union supply train on July 1 and 2, 1863. The Federals were en route to Fort Gibson; some 1,500 Confederates under Gen. Stand Watie were repulsed and the train reached the fort safely. Confederates managed to capture a supply train in the same spot the following year on September 19. Gens. R. M. Gano and Stand Watie took supplies valued at $1.5 million.

BOGGY DEPOT, Atoka County. State 48A, 15 miles southwest of Atoka. Confederate army post here maintained a flagpole in midtown around which Confederate Indians liked to gallop, whooping, hollering, and singing the Choctaw war song. The Boggy Depot cemetery has a row of Confederate graves; markers indicate historic sites.

CADDO, Bryan County. US 69.
Fort McCulloch, at Nail's Crossing on south bank of Blue River. The fort, established in 1862 by Gen. Albert Pike, was named for Brig. Gen. Ben McCulloch, who commanded Confederates in Indian Territory in 1861 and was killed at Pea Ridge. In July 1862, denouncing 250 Texans who had decided to leave the fort to return home because they were over 35 years of age, Pike issued a proclamation to the citizens of Red River County, Texas: "The enemy is in the Indian country. It is worth a hundred millions, and there are thirteen hundred mounted white men in it to defend it." On July 12, Gen. Pike received orders to move to Fort Smith; he chose to resign.

DOAKSVILLE, Choctaw County. US 70.
Site of Fort Towson, US 70 east of town, preserves the ruins of the 1824 post. Confederate troops occupied the post, which had been abandoned some years after the Mexican War. Gen. S. B. Maxey had headquarters here in 1864. Gen. Stand Watie surrendered his Indian troops at this site in June 1865. The sutler's building has been reconstructed. Museum.

FORT ARBUCKLE, Garvin County. State

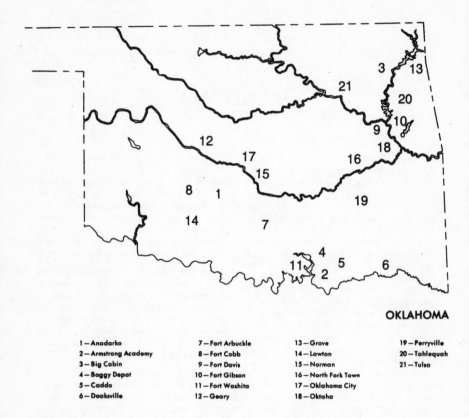

OKLAHOMA

1 — Anadarko	7 — Fort Arbuckle	13 — Grove	19 — Perryville
2 — Armstrong Academy	8 — Fort Cobb	14 — Lawton	20 — Tahlequah
3 — Big Cabin	9 — Fort Davis	15 — Norman	21 — Tulsa
4 — Boggy Depot	10 — Fort Gibson	16 — North Fork Town	
5 — Caddo	11 — Fort Washita	17 — Oklahoma City	
6 — Doaksville	12 — Geary	18 — Oktaha	

19A. Marker on highway. Ruins of bachelor officers' quarters remain. The fort was established in 1851 under the supervision of Capt. Randolph B. Marcy, whose daughter was once engaged to A. P. Hill and later became the wife of George B. McClellan. Confederates were quartered here during part of the war.

Arbuckle Historical Museum, in the old Santa Fe Railroad Depot, has artifacts from the fort.

FORT COBB, Caddo County. State 58. Confederates garrisoned the post in 1861. In October 1862, Kansas Indians united with Caddos in a massacre of the Tonkawas in this area. The Tonkawas were accused of cannibalism; the Confederates were not, but were driven out also and the fort was burned.

FORT DAVIS, Muskogee County. State 16. Site of the Confederate fort is near campus of Bacone Indian College. Southern forces were garrisoned here in the summer of 1862.

FORT GIBSON, Muskogee County. State 80, 1 mile north of US 62. Established in 1824, the fort was occupied during the war by both armies. It is now a state monument with a military park on the site of the first log fort. The national cemetery is 1 mile north. In July 1862, Union forces led by Col. William Weer bivouacked on the Grand River about 12 miles north of Fort Gibson. Weer noted: "Water, timber, grass, salt-works, and coal banks are all convenient." On July 14, a detachment under Maj. W. T. Campbell broke camp and scouted Confederate positions south of the Arkansas River, driving in the Confederate pickets at Fort Gibson. Next day, reinforced Federal troops entered the post, finding the Confederates had evacuated it during the night. Four days later, Col. Frederick Salomon of the 9th Wisconsin Volunteers arrested Col. Weer on a charge of indecision in command and habitual drunkenness. In a general court-martial later, all witnesses appeared to be partisan supporters of either Salomon or Weer; the presiding officer could not sort out charges and countercharges, dissolved the court and restored Weer to the rank of colonel. Within the reconstructed log stockade are officers' and enlisted men's quarters, blockhouses, and a guardhouse.

Fort Gibson National Cemetery, 1 mile east of Fort Gibson on US 62, has graves of veterans from every war.

FORT SILL (*See* LAWTON.)

FORT TOWSON, Choctow County. US 70.

Fort Towson Historic Site, 1 mile northeast of town. Ruins of the early army post are featured with artifacts on display.

FORT WASHITA, Marshall County. State 199, 16 miles northwest of Durant on State 78, 199. Confederate forces took the post on May 1, 1861, from four troops of Union cavalry, who rode away apparently without a backward glance. It remained in Confederate hands throughout the war. In 1962 the Oklahoma Historical Society purchased the site of 117 acres; it has been restored. The post was one of the fancier frontier fortresses, so elegant, indeed, that Congress launched an investigation to learn why elaborate officers' quarters were needed in the wilderness. Douglas Cooper, Indian agent here at the outbreak of war, served as Confederate general. He is buried here. The ruins feature Gen. Cooper's cabin and reconstructed south barracks.

GEARY, Blaine County. Off IS 40, US 81.

Memorial Tree Lane honors Jesse Chisholm, a half-Cherokee trader, pathfinder, and salt manufacturer, who remained loyal to the Union, accompanying Union troops to Wichita, Kansas. Some say the route he took on his return to Indian Territory in 1865 was the original Chisholm Trail, which approximately follows US 81. Chisholm died at Left Hand Spring; his grave is nearby overlooking the North Canadian River.

GROVE, Delaware County. US 59.

Polson Cemetery has the grave of Confederate Brig. Gen. Stand Watie.

LAWTON, Comanche County. US 62, 277.

Fort Sill Military Reservation and National Historical Landmark, 4 miles north on US 277. In the 1850s Capt. Marcy camped here, but the fort was not established until after the Civil War when Gen. Philip Sheridan moved his troops here from an encampment at the site of burned and abandoned Fort Cobb. The name of Camp Wichita was changed by Sher-

idan to honor his West Point classmate, Brig. Gen. Joshua W. Sill, who was killed at the battle of Stones River. Geronimo spent his last days imprisoned at the fort and is buried in Apache Cemetery, 2 miles northeast. The old post is a national historic landmark. On the grounds are the post commandant's quarters, where in 1871 an Indian added the name of Stumbling Bear to the long and illustrious list of those who made unsuccessful attempts on the life of Gen. William Tecumseh Sherman. (The general died in bed 20 years later.)

The museum in the old post buildings depicts the history of area and of artillery. There is a stone corral with relics and the Geronimo Guardhouse with exhibits. The visitor center also has exhibits and a slide program.

NORTH FORK TOWN, McIntosh County. US 69. Marker on highway for Creek community, where in 1861 Confederates made a treaty with the Creeks, Choctaws, and Chickasaws.

OKLAHOMA CITY, Oklahoma County, IS 35, 40, 44.

State Museum of History, 2100 N. Lincoln Blvd., has history of the state from prehistoric Indians to the present, including the Civil War era.

OKTAHA, Muskogee County. US 69.

Site of the Battle of Honey Springs, north of town. On July 17, 1863, Union forces under Gen. Blunt opposed Confederates under Gen. Cooper at Honey Springs. The Southern forces had two Cherokee and two Creek regiments, one regiment made up of Choctaws and Chickasaws, and the 20th Texas Cavalry. Other cavalry was in reserve at Honey Springs. Gen. Blunt had two cavalry and two Indian regiments, the 2nd Colorado Infantry, and the 1st Kansas Colored Infantry. The North drove the South across Elk Creek in a near rout.

PERRY, Pittsburg County. IS 35, US 69. Confederate military post and supply depot to which Gen. Douglas H. Cooper retreated after the battle of Honey Springs, 50 miles north. Brig. Gen. Steele brought reinforcements but Blunt's Union troops again routed the Confederates in August 1863. Before retreating, Cooper's troops dumped salt in the wells. Union troops salvaged what they could and then burned the town.

TAHLEQUAH, Cherokee County. US 62. **Park Hill Mission,** 4 miles south. The mission was a religious and educational center of the Cherokee Nation and was destroyed by the

Civil War. The Cherokee Female Seminary ruins remain. The Murrell House, built in 1845, is the restored residence of George M. Murrell, who came west with the Cherokee. It was invaded and robbed during the Civil War but escaped destruction. Period furnishings with some original pieces.

TULSA, Tulsa County, IS 44.

Thomas Gilcrease Institute of American History and Art, 1400 Gilcrease Museum Rd. An important collection of artifacts and documents pertaining to western Americana from earliest times through the 19th century.

OREGON

Oregon became the 33rd state on February 14, 1859, with a constitution that prohibited slavery but also prohibited the admission of any blacks, free or slave, into the state. Edward Dickinson Baker, who was born in London, later became a friend of Lincoln's in Illinois, lost a congressional race in California, and then won a U.S. senatorial seat in Oregon. He served briefly and eloquently in Congress before he joined the army and was killed while leading a charge during the battle of Balls Bluff.

In Oregon's first year of statehood, Democrats were in the majority but were divided by the slavery question. Douglas Democrats advocated popular sovereignty, interpreting this as the right of territories to decide for or against slavery within their boundaries; Buchanan Democrats held that the Constitution protected slavery rights. Horace Greeley, editor of the *New York Tribune,* was one of several who advocated that Republicans unite with antislavery Democrats to win public office. California Republicans had chosen not to follow his advice, but in Oregon Douglas Democrats helped to elect Sen. Baker, stating afterwards: "In voting for Colonel Baker, we were influenced, to some extent, by his well-known position upon the question of Slavery in the Territories—a position different but little from that of our own party." Gov. F. F. Low of California, who had bet Baker a suit of clothes that Oregonians would not put him in office, had to pay off.

Gov. John Whiteaker, said to be sympathetic to the South, responded slowly to Lincoln's call for troops in the spring of 1861. By the following year, however, Oregon had six companies in the field. Neither these troops (the 1st Oregon Volunteer Cavalry) nor the 1st Oregon Infantry, raised in 1864–1865, served in the East. They built forts, occupied posts on Indian reservations, provided escort duty, checked marauding Indians, and kept a watchful eye on activities of pro-secessionist groups, the Knights of the Golden Circle. All regular Federal troops were withdrawn from the state,

although a few regular officers were reassigned to the area. Gen. Benjamin Alvord commanded the Military District of Oregon throughout most of the war.

In 1866, Gen. Frederick Steele took command of the Pacific Northwest Military District which was renamed the Department of the Columbia. Many posts established by the Oregon cavalry and infantry were discontinued, regular army troops returned, and Oregon Volunteers were mustered out.

ASHLAND, Jackson County. IS 5, US 99. *Lithia Park,* entrance just off main business street, has a marble statue of Abraham Lincoln. Markers indicate sites of early industries.

BAKER CITY, Baker County. IS 84, US 30. Marker on highway east of town named for Sen. Edward D. Baker, who was killed at Balls Bluff. Henry Griffin, looking for the "lost" Blue Bucket Mine, discovered gold here in 1861, starting a stampede that lasted for years.

CAMP WATSON, Wheeler County. South of US 26 near Mitchell. The camp was established in 1864 by Oregon Volunteers and named for Lt. Stephen Watson of the 1st Oregon Cavalry. It was occupied by the cavalry from 1864 to 1866, having been set up to protect the Dalles-to-Canyon City route from Snake Indian raids.

CANYON CITY, Grant County. US 395. The town was established in 1862 following the discovery of gold on Whiskey Flat. There were frequent clashes between Unionist Oregon miners and pro-Southerners who had migrated to the gold fields from California. When the latter raised the Stars and Bars on "Rebel Hill" on July 4, 1863, Oregon men lowered it with far less ceremony than was used to hoist the Union flag that same day in Vicksburg. By 1872, $26 million worth of gold had been mined from Canyon Creek. The village was connected with the Dalles by the old Military Road, protected by the 1st Cavalry stationed at Camp Watson.

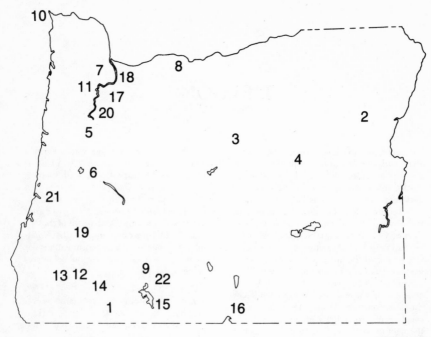

OREGON

1 — Ashland	7 — Forest Grove	13 — Grant's Pass	
2 — Baker	8 — Fort Dalles	14 — Jacksonville	
3 — Camp Watson	9 — Fort Klamath	15 — Klamath Falls	19 — Roseburg
4 — Canyon City	10 — Fort Stevens	16 — Lakeview	20 — Salem
5 — Corvallis	11 — Fort Yamhill	17 — Oregon City	21 — Scottsburg
6 — Eugene	12 — Gold Hill	18 — Portland	22 — Williamson River

Grant County Historical Museum, 101 S. Canyon City Blvd. Joaquin Miller's cabin is next to the museum.

EUGENE, Lane County. IS 5, US 126. The pro-Union *State-Republican* was first printed on January 1, 1862. Soon after, Southern sympathizers founded the *Democratic-Register,* which Cincinnatus Heine Miller, known as Joaquin Miller, purchased and published as the *Eugene City Review.* Miller, forbidden use of the mails because of his Southern proclivities, sold out. He later became a judge in Grant County and published a number of prose and poetical works, including *Songs of the Sierras.*

University of Oregon, Franklin Blvd., 11th and 18th avenues, and Alder and Moss streets. Henry Villard, Civil War correspondent who later became a railroad magnate, gave the university several thousand dollars in cash and $50,000 in Northern Pacific Railway bonds.

Lane County Historical Museum, 740 W. 13th Ave., has displays that interpret the area from its first settlement. Period rooms and 19th-century vehicles.

FOREST GROVE, Washington County. State 8, 47.

Pacific University, College Way, founded in 1849, is one of the oldest schools in the Pacific Northwest. Old College Hall, 1850, is the oldest building west of the Mississippi River in use for higher education. It contains a museum of pioneer relics.

FORT DALLES, Wasco County. US 30. Fort site is on southwest corner of 15th and Garrison St. in the Dalles. The garrison at the end of the Oregon Trail was first known as Fort Lee and served as military headquarters for central and eastern Oregon. Philip Sheridan served out of Fort Dalles in 1856. The post was garrisoned during the Civil War, abandoned in 1867. The former surgeon's quarters are now a museum, owned by the Oregon Historical Society and maintained by the Wasco County-Dalles City Museum Commission.

FORT KLAMATH, Klamath County, State 62, was established in 1863, mainly to protect settlers from Modoc, Klamath, and Shasta Indians. Museum is housed in a log replica of the original guardhouse.

FORT STEVENS, Clatsop County. Located at the mouth of the Columbia River, US 101, in Hammond. The post, now in Fort Stevens State Park, was built in 1862 and named for Gen. Isaac Ingalls Stevens, first governor of Washington Territory, later a highly regarded Union general who was killed at Chantilly. The fort, built to protect the river, was surrounded by a moat with an entrance tunnel. There were emplacements for 29 guns, but 20 of these were never mounted, and no hostile shots were ever fired. Gun batteries and a guardhouse remain. Interpretive center in a war games building.

FORT YAMHILL BLOCKHOUSE, Dayton, Yamhill County. US 99W, State 18. Lt. Philip Sheridan was stationed at Yamhill when Fort Sumter fell. In his memoirs he explains why he did not go east with his regiment: ". . . my company went off, leaving me . . . in command of the post until I should be relieved by Captain James J. Archer, of the Ninth Infantry. . . . Captain Archer, with his company of the Ninth, arrived shortly after, but I had been notified that he intended to go South, and his conduct was such after reaching the post that I would not turn over the command to him for fear he might commit some rebellious act." Nothing remains of the original fort, but the blockhouse stands in Dayton's city park. A plaque tells of the four Civil War generals who were stationed at Yamhill: Sheridan, William B. Hazen, D. A. Russell, and J. P. Reynolds. Russell was killed at the battle of Winchester, Reynolds at Gettysburg.

GRANTS PASS, Josephine County. IS 5. The Rogue River town was a stopping place on the California stage route. It was named by roadbuilders at the pass when news came of Grant's victory at Vicksburg.

JACKSONVILLE, Jackson County. Off IS 5, State 238.

This historic gold rush town is a well-preserved example of a busy Northwest settlement in the years just preceding and during the Civil War. It was founded in 1852 when mining was the main aim. Nearly 100 buildings have historical markers reflecting the prosperity that lasted until the Oregon and California Railroad bypassed the town in 1884. Information on self-guiding walking tours is available at the Jacksonville Museum, 5th and C streets, or at the U.S. National Bank on Main St. An information center is open during summer months in the Rogue River Valley Depot, Oregon and C streets.

OREGON CITY, Clackamas County. IS 205, US 99E.

John McLoughlin House, 7th and Center St., is a national historic site. Dr. John McLoughlin, known as the "Father of Oregon," did much to save the state for the Union.

PORTLAND, Multnomah County. IS 80N, 205.

Lincoln Statue, on square at Main and Madison.

Oregon Historical Society, 1230 S.W. Park St. State headquarters for museum exhibits and library research material about Oregon and the Pacific Northwest. Library includes extensive collection of military information in addition to one of the largest general collections on the West Coast.

ROSEBURG, Douglas County. IS 5. Home town of Oregon's first territorial governor, Joseph Lane, who was a candidate for U.S. vice president in 1860 on the John C. Breckinridge ticket. Lane, a Senator, was sympathetic to the South and at one time threatened to fight to defend South Carolina against a Federal invasion. One of his sons resigned from West Point to join the Confederate army. Lane served until March 1861 and returned to Oregon, having failed to secure reelection. Some Oregonians wanted to jail him during the war years, but tempers cooled and he was mourned widely upon his death in 1881. He is buried in the Masonic Cemetery in Roseburg.

SCOTTSBURG, Douglas County. State 38. Col. Joseph Hooker, later famous as "Fighting Joe" in the Civil War, directed military road building in southern Oregon and stayed at the Lyon's Hotel, owned by a blind Kentuckian, Daniel Lyon, who had sung and played a guitar in the gold camps until he collected enough gold to purchase the hotel.

WILLIAMSON RIVER, Klamath County. US 97. Marker at Collier Park denotes the site where the Pacific Railroad survey party, including Lt. Phil Sheridan, searched for a connecting route from the Sacramento Valley to the Columbia River in 1855.

PENNSYLVANIA

Slavery in Pennsylvania was inhibited in 1780 by an act which provided that no child born within the state should be a slave. The second state of the original 13 was a haven for runaway slaves; Quakers manned the Underground Railroad, citizens and legislature opposed the Fugitive Slave Act. The state responded promptly to Lincoln's call for troops; within two weeks, 25 regiments were organized. Gov. Andrew Gregg Curtin called a special session of the legislature which negotiated a $3 million loan to be used for war measures.

Pennsylvania troops, arriving in Washington on April 18, 1861, were called the "First Defenders." The Pennsylvania Reserves were the only division in the Union army composed entirely of men from one state. The state was invaded in October 1862, when Confederate Gens. J. E. B. Stuart and Wade Hampton, with some 2,000 cavalrymen, rode around McClellan's army. Gen. Robert E. Lee's invasion in July 1863 led to the battle of Gettysburg in which 34,530 Pennsylvanians took part. The third and last invasion occurred in July 1864, when Gen. Jubal Early sent the cavalry brigades of McCausland and Bradley Johnson into Chambersburg to demand $100,000 in gold in repayment for Gen. David Hunter's destructive raid into Virginia. Nearly two-thirds of the town was burned.

The state supplied about 338,000 men to the Union army and more than 14,000 to the navy. Gens. Meade, Hancock, Haupt, and McClellan were Pennsylvanians, as was Confederate Gen. J. C. Pemberton, the defender of Vicksburg. Naval leaders were Adm. David D. Porter and Rear Adms. Charles Stewart, Sylvanus W. Gordon, and John A. Dahlgren. Simon Cameron was first Secretary of War. The state spent more than $4 million in the war effort but gained in prosperity, having a treasury balance of more than $2 million at war's end.

ALLENTOWN, Lehigh County. IS 78.
Soldiers' and Sailors' Monument, Center Square, 7th and Hamilton St. Life-size figures of Civil War veterans surround the base.

ALTOONA, Blair County. US 22, State 36.
Baker Mansion Museum, 3500 Oak Lane, home of an early ironmaster, now housing the Blair County Historical Society, has Abraham Lincoln memorabilia.

BLOOMSBURG, Columbia County. IS 80, US 11. Federal troops crushed a "Fishing Creek Confederacy" of draft dodgers here.

BOALSBURG, Centre County. Just off US 322, east of State College. The town claims the first Memorial Day observance was held here on May 30, 1864. A number of other communities make the same claim.
Pennsylvania Military Museum, US 322. Displays pertain to the history of servicemen from the Revolution through WW II.

CALEDONIA STATE PARK, Adams and Franklin counties. US 30. Site of the Caledonia charcoal iron furnace, established by Thaddeus Stevens in 1837. Gen. Jubal Early's cavalry destroyed all but the furnace stack in an 1863 raid.

CARLISLE, Cumberland County. IS 76, 81.
Carlisle Barracks, ½ mile east on US 11. Army War College with fine museums and library. Washington reviewed troops here. Civil War soldiers were also stationed here. The Hessian Guardhouse is now a museum.
Dickinson College, W. High St., was the 12th college chartered in the United States President James Buchanan was a graduate. During the Confederate invasion of June 1863, troops of Ewell's corps camped on the college grounds. From here Confederates were planning to move on Harrisburg until Gen. Robert E. Lee ordered them to Cashtown.

CASHTOWN, Adams County. US 30. On June 28, 1863, Gen. Lee sent his army across the mountains from Chambersburg to this vil-

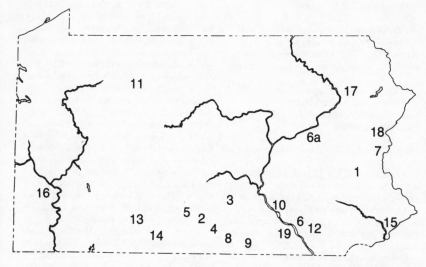

PENNSYLVANIA

1 — Allentown	6 — Columbia	10 — Harrisburg	15 — Philadelphia
2 — Caledonia	6a — Bloomsburg	11 — Kane	16 — Pittsburgh
3 — Carlisle	7 — Easton	12 — Lancaster	17 — Scranton
4 — Cashtown	8 — Gettysburg	13 — McConnellsburg	18 — Stroudsburg
5 — Chambersburg	9 — Hanover	14 — Mercersburg	19 — York

lage. Gens. R. E. Rodes, at Carlisle, and Early, at York, were also ordered to this assembly point. Gen. Henry Heth's division reached Cashtown on June 29. On July 1, A. P. Hill, acting in Lee's absence, sent the brigades of Archer and Davis, of Heth's division, to advance toward Gettysburg.

CHAMBERSBURG, Franklin County. IS 81, US 30. The town was invaded three times during the war. Lee was here late in June 1863 when he learned that Gen. George Meade was following him; plans to invade Harrisburg were altered as Lee decided to concentrate his troops in the eastern foothills of the mountains. In the invasion of 1864, more than 500 buildings were burned by troops under the command of Gens. McCausland and Johnson. Chamberfest is a weeklong festival commemorating the town's participation in the Civil War. Late July.

Civil War Monument, in center of town traffic circle, has no safe space for visitors to linger long enough to read the inscription.

Confederate Conference, plaque in midtown at site where Lee and staff arrived for meeting with A. P. Hill.

John Brown's Headquarters, 225 King St. Brown collected arms for the raid on Harpers Ferry while posing as a prospector in the summer of 1859.

Lee's Headquarters, US 30, east edge of town. Messersmiths' Woods, where Lee camped June 26–30, 1863, were just south of highway.

Soldier's Monument, 10 miles south of town on US 11, commemorates the spot where the first Union soldier was killed in action on Northern ground.

Susseratt House, Washington and Main St. Marker at site where the fire started by Confederate cavalry June 30, 1864, was arrested.

COLUMBIA, Lancaster County. US 30. A bridge over the Susquehanna River between Columbia and Wrightsville was burned on June 28, 1863, by Col. J. G. Frick, 27th Pennsylvania Volunteers, on orders from Maj. Gen. D. N. Couch. Southern invaders here turned westward toward Gettysburg instead of continuing toward Harrisburg.

CORNWALL, Lebanon County. US 322.
Cornwall Iron Furnace, off 322; route is marked. The 1742 furnace operated until the 1880s. Visitor center in the Charcoal House.

EASTON, Northampton County. IS 78.
Soldiers' and Sailors' Monument, 3rd and Northampton St. Dedicated to Northampton Civil War veterans.

GETTYSBURG, Adams County. US 15, 30.
The Conflict, US 15, has programs that cover the battle and the entire war, also a live one-man performance, "A. Lincoln's Place."
Gettysburg College, Stevens and Washington St. The oldest Lutheran college in the U.S. was part of the battlefield. The seminary served as a hospital. Pennsylvania Hall was used as a hospital by both armies.
Gettysburg Battle Theatre, 571 Steinwehr. Miniature battlefield and multimedia program.
Hall of Presidents, US 140 next to national cemetery. American presidents in wax, life-size and handsomely costumed, in period settings.
Lee's Headquarters and Museum, on Chambersburg Pike, US 30W. The stone house on highway has relics and souvenirs. Lee's headquarters was in the house. Lee set up his headquarters here on July 1, 1863. Exhibits include Union and Confederate military equipment, photographs, and documents.
The Lincoln Room, Wills House, Center Square, 12 Lincoln Square. Room where Lincoln completed the Gettysburg Address has been preserved; museum has Lincoln memorabilia.
Lutheran Theological Seminary, Confederate Ave. Old dorm served as hospital. Cupola was used as a Confederate lookout tower.
National Gettysburg Battlefield Tower, US 140, affords general view of battlefield, with taped description. Privately operated.
Soldiers' National Museum, 777 Baltimore. Gettysburg Tour Center. Dioramas.
Wax Museum, Steinwehr Ave. at Culp St. Aside from the fact that Sherman looks about as loony as Murat Halstead's newspaper once called him, the figures here are incredibly lifelike. Among the scenes are: Brown on the gallows, Clara Barton at Antietam, firing on Fort Sumter, and Lincoln in debate with Douglas, delivering the Gettysburg Address, and at Ford's Theatre.

GETTYSBURG NATIONAL MILITARY PARK. US 15, 30. The battle of Gettysburg, fought on July 1, 2, and 3, 1863, may well be the most written-about engagement of the Civil War. The visitor center, on State 134, has information for a self-guided auto tour, as well as licensed guides for a two-hour tour of the major points of the battle that left some 51,000 men dead, wounded, or captured in those grim three midsummer days. The center has an electric map with colored lights to show the battle movements where Lee led his Confederates into their greatest invasion of Northern territory and where the Union, with 92,000 men under Gen. George Gordon Meade, fell back or rallied to win the bitter conflict at an unforgettable cost. Also in the center is the Rosensteel Collection of Civil War artifacts. Adjacent is the Cyclorama Center which features the renowned "Battle of Gettysburg," painted by Paul Philippoteaux in 1884. A sound and light program accompanies the viewing.

The park has more than 35 miles of roads through its nearly 6,000 acres. There are more than 1,300 monuments, statues, and markers, 3 observation towers, and 400 cannon. The park is open daily except Thanksgiving, Christmas, and New Year's Day.

Among the chief points of interest are Little Round Top, High Water Mark, Seminary Ridge, Spangler's Spring, the Peach Orchard, and Culp's Hill. Among farm buildings that survived the conflict are the McPherson barn where the battle began, the Codori House on the site of Pickett's charge, the Trostle buildings, and the Hummelbaugh House where Barksdale died. Park employees or local farmers use the buildings; some of the farms are still cultivated under the park superintendent's direction.

The site where Lincoln made the Gettysburg Address is marked by the Lincoln Address Memorial; this is near the west entrance to the cemetery. Confederate dead were removed in the 1870s for reburial in the South. Northwest of town is the Eternal Light Peace Memorial, dedicated in 1938, on the 75th anniversary of the battle. Its legend: "Peace Eternal in a Nation United."

Eisenhower National Historic Site. The only home ever owned by the 34th president, Dwight D. Eisenhower, the Eisenhower farm is open daily from April 1 through Oct. 31; Wednesday through Sunday the rest of the year, with closings Thanksgiving, Christmas, New Year's Day, and four weeks in January/February. Visits are by shuttle bus from Gettysburg National Military Park visitor center. Entrance fee.

HANOVER, York County. State 116. Scene of an engagement between Union troops under Gen. Hugh Judson ("Kill Cavalry") Kilpatrick and Custer and Confederates under Gen. J. E. B. Stuart, June 30, 1863. This conflict delayed Stuart from arriving at Gettysburg in time for the battle.

HARRISBURG, Dauphin County. IS 81, 83, US 22. Camp Curtin, the first concentration camp for Union forces, was named in honor of Gov. Andrew Curtin. T. F. Dornblaser, of the Pennsylvania Dragoons, tells of his arrival in Harrisburg in October 1861, and marching to Camp Cameron: "This was our first march, and in some respects it was a *forced march,* as some of the boys preferred to go in hacks, but that was unsoldier-like and contrary to orders. With a huge bundle on each shoulder, and an occasional umbrella raised to break the rays of a warm October sun, we footed it through the dusty highway to Camp Cameron, three miles south of the depot."

Dauphin County Historical Society, 219 S. Front St. Historical collections are housed in the Harris Mansion, said to be the oldest house in town. It was built about 1766. Gen. Simon Cameron, Lincoln's first Secretary of War, bought the house in 1865.

State Museum, north of Capitol Building, 3rd and North, has one of the world's largest framed paintings, Rothermel's "Battle of Gettysburg."

LANCASTER, Lancaster County. US 230, 30.

Fulton Opera House, 12 N. Prince St. The theater was built on the foundation of the old jail and served as convention site, armory, and hospital during the war, again has year-round entertainment.

Site of Thaddeus Stevens Home, 45 S. Queen St. Bronze plaque marks location where the famous abolitionist once lived. During the Civil War Stevens was majority leader in the national House of Representatives.

Wheatland, 1120 Marietta Ave. The home of President James Buchanan has been restored with period furnishings. Guided tours are conducted by a hostess in period costume.

McCONNELLSBURG, Fulton County. US 30, 522. Marker on US 30, east edge of town, tells of three invasions by Confederates, chiefly cavalry, in June 1863.

Buchanan Birthplace, on State 16, at Cove Gap. Site is marked by a stone pyramid. It is located in the James Buchanan State Forest Monument.

Confederate Dead, marker on State 16 south of town, at site where two Confederate soldiers were buried by local residents. They were killed in a skirmish on June 29, 1863, said to be the first battle on Pennsylvania soil.

MERCERSBURG, Franklin County. State 16. (*See* McCONNELLSBURG.) The Buchanan log cabin birthplace is now on the campus of Mercersburg Academy. It is furnished in Early American style. Another Buchanan home is now the James Buchanan Hotel on N. Main St. Across the street is the Lane House, birthplace of Harriet Lane, Buchanan's niece who became White House hostess during her bachelor uncle's administration. House has marker but is not open to public.

PHILADELPHIA, Philadelphia County. IS 76, 95, 96.

Civil War Library and Museum, 1805 Pine St. nineteenth-century four-story townhouse has some 12,000 books and periodicals pertaining to the war and Reconstruction, and a large collection of memorabilia gathered by Union officers, beginning in 1865.

Grant's Cabin, Sedgely and Lemon Hill drives, in Fairmount Park, was built in 1864 on a bluff overlooking the James River at City Point, Virginia, and served as Grant's headquarters from November 1864 to March 29, 1865. After the war Grant gave it to G. H. Stuart whose heirs gave it to Philadelphia.

Historical Society of Pennsylvania, 1300 Locust St., has Lincoln items, rare books, paintings, and prints.

Independence Hall, 6th and Chestnut St., Independence Square. Lincoln spoke here on February 22, 1861, en route to his first inaugural.

Laurel Hill Cemetery, Ridge Ave., has the grave of Confederate Gen. John C. Pemberton. Marker placed by United Daughters of the Confederacy. Pittville Cemetery, Germantown, has 426 Confederate graves.

PITTSBURGH, Allegheny County. IS 79, 376.

Allegheny Arsenal, northwest corner of 40th and Butler St. Site of a leading Civil War arsenal.

Allegheny County Soldiers' and Sailors' Memorial Hall, 5th Ave. and Bigelow Blvd. Civil War relics, including flags, weapons, and uniforms.

SCRANTON, Lackawanna County. IS 81, US 11.

Courthouse Square, Spruce St. and Washington Ave. Monument to Gen. Philip H. Sheridan and Civil War dead.

Federal troops at the Union Volunteer Refreshment Center in Philadelphia.

STROUDSBURG, Monroe County. IS 80, US 209. J. Summerfield Stapels, who was Lincoln's substitute serving in the 2nd Regiment, D.C. Volunteers, is buried here.

TOWANDA, Bradford County. US 220.
Riverside Cemetery, William St. between Chestnut and Walnut streets. David Wilmot, senator in 1861–63, leader of the Free Soil Party, who introduced the Wilmot Proviso, is buried here.

Tioga Point Museum, State 199, 15 miles off US 220, 724 S. Main in Athens, has Civil War and Stephen Foster items among historical displays.

YORK, York County. IS 83, US 30. The town was one of the stops in Gen. Jubal Early's fund-raising campaign of 1863. He demanded $100,000 in cash and supplies but accepted $28,000, as he was due at Cashtown.

RHODE ISLAND

Rhode Island, last of the original 13 states, responded quickly to the first call for volunteers in April 1861. On April 16, Gov. William Sprague, out of his personal funds, contributed $100,000 to help raise a regiment of infantry. Two days later, the first detachment of 1,000 men, picked from 2,500 volunteers, was organized under Col. Ambrose E. Burnside. A second detachment was formed within four days under Lt. Col. Joseph S. Pitman. Rhode Islanders made up the first volunteer artillery battery of the war. Captained by Charles H. Tompkins, they arrived in Washington on May 2.

Gov. Sprague, as colonel of the state militia, led a regiment and a battery of light horse artillery at the first battle of Bull Run, where his horse was shot from under him. He declined a commission of brigadier general but served at Williamsburg and Yorktown. He was U.S. senator in 1864. His stormy marriage to the Washington belle, Kate Chase, daughter of Salmon P. Chase, Lincoln's Secretary of the Treasury, was a much talked-of affair, as was Mrs. Lincoln's dislike of Mrs. Sprague. Ambrose Burnside, born in Indiana, was considered an adopted son of Rhode Island. His whiskers, however, were somewhat more distinguished than his performance in command at Fredericksburg. The facial adornment became known as sideburns; and Burnside became a subordinate commander.

Out of a population of 100,000, Rhode Island sent 23,778 volunteers to the service. More than 1,200 died of wounds or disease; another 1,200 were injured. The last Rhode Island whaler at sea, the *Covington* of Warren, was destroyed in the Bering Straits by a Confederate raider, the *Shenandoah*, in June 1865, two months after the war had ended.

BRISTOL, Bristol County. State 114.

Burnside Memorial Building, southwest corner of Court and Hope St., was built and named in honor of Gen. Burnside. On south side of hall is a soldiers and sailors monument.

Ambrose Burnside had a factory in Bristol for manufacturing a breech-loading rifle of his own invention. He entered the Civil War as colonel of the 1st Regiment of Rhode Island Volunteers and commanded a brigade at the first battle of Bull Run. He was a major general at Antietam, succeeded McClellan as commander of the Army of the Potomac, and at Fredericksburg was badly repulsed and removed from high command. He served ably in lesser commands throughout the war and was governor of Rhode Island from 1866 to 1869, U.S. senator, 1875–1881.

Cranston, 1351 Cranston, home of William Sprague; governor, 1860–1863; U.S. senator, 1863–1875.

MIDDLETOWN, Newport County. State 138.

Holmes Burial Ground, Vaucluse Ave. Abraham Lincoln is descended from the Rev. Obadiah Holmes who is buried here.

NARRAGANSETT PIER, Washington County. US 1.

St. Peter's by-the-Sea Church has a memorial stained glass window in honor of Winnie Davis, "Daughter of the Confederacy," who vacationed summers here and died here September 18, 1898.

NEWPORT, Newport County. State 138. Newport was the site of a naval academy during the Civil War.

Fort Adams, at entrance to Newport Harbor. The fort may be seen from the Jamestown-Newport ferry. Among Federal officers who served here were Gens. Burnside, Rosecrans, and Anderson; Confederate Gen. Magruder, known as "Prince John," had duty at the fort.

Naval War College Museum, in Founders Hall on Coasters Harbor Island, is reached by Gate 1 of the Naval Education and Training Center. Founders Hall is the original site of the college. Exhibits depict the history of naval warfare.

Newport Artillery Company Armory, 23

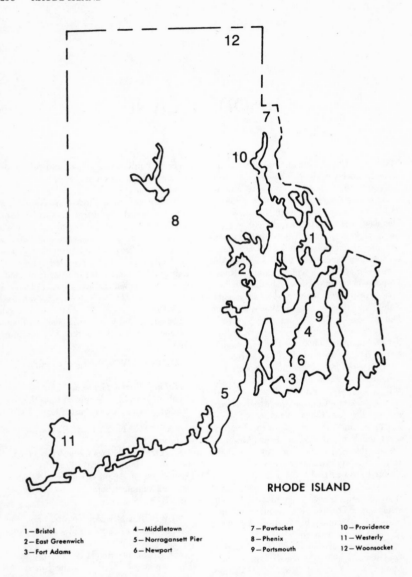

RHODE ISLAND

1 — Bristol	4 — Middletown	7 — Pawtucket
2 — East Greenwich	5 — Norragansett Pier	8 — Phenix
3 — Fort Adams	6 — Newport	9 — Portsmouth

10 — Providence
11 — Westerly
12 — Woonsocket

Clarke St., is the oldest active military organization in America; Civil War items.

Old Colony House, Washington Square, has a secession flag taken from the steamer *Eagle* in 1863 as a prize of the Union steamer *Victoria.*

St. Mary's Church, Spring St., has a memorial stained-glass window in honor of Gen. Rosecrans, who helped to build the church when he was a lieutenant at Fort Adams.

Touro Park, Mill St., off Bellevue. Midshipmen from the U.S. Naval Academy trained here during the Civil War. The academy was temporarily located at Newport from May 1861 to August 1865. Fort Adams was occupied for a time. At Goat Island, the USS *Constitution* (Old Ironsides) and the yacht *America* were moored.

PAWTUCKET, Providence County. Off IS 95, Alt. 1.

Slater Mill Historic Site, downtown on Roosevelt Ave., has been restored to its 19th-century appearance. "Cotton Is King" was a Southern slogan; here are displays of early cotton gins and hand-processing methods and implements.

Wilkinson Park, Park Place, has a memorial dedicated to soldiers and sailors of the Civil War; it is named "Liberty Arming the Patriots," was executed by W. Granville Hastings.

PORTSMOUTH, Newport County. State 138.

Julia Ward Howe, author of "The Battle Hymn of the Republic," as a summer resident in Portsmouth often occupied the pulpit of the Christian Sabbath Society here. At Portsmouth Grove, in about the area later occupied by the U.S. Navy at Melville, a large Civil War hospital, known as Lovell General Hospital, was established. Gov. Sprague directed the building and equipping of the quarters; the War Department sent the first contingent of 1,724 patients on July 6, 1862.

PROVIDENCE, Providence County. IS 95, US 1, State 146.

Annmary Brown Memorial, Brown St., built in 1907 by Gen. Rush Hawkins in memory of his wife, contains Civil War relics.

Burnside House, 314 Benefit St. Gen. Ambrose Burnside lived here for a time. The house was built by Nicholas Brown about 1850.

Exchange Place, Exchange Terrace and Dorrance St. In the eastern section is the Burnside equestrian statue by Launt Thompson. At the far end is the monument to Maj. Henry Harrison Young, who was Sheridan's chief of scouts.

Federal Building, east end of Exchange Place, has a plaque honoring the occasion of February 28, 1860, when Lincoln gave a pre-election speech in the city.

John Hay Library, 20 Prospect St., Brown University, across Prospect St. from university gates. Named for John Hay, who was Lincoln's secretary and biographer, the library has an excellent collection of Lincoln manuscripts.

Old Arsenal, 176 Benefit St., was used by state troops during the Civil War.

Providence Public Library, Washington and Empire St., has a Civil War collection.

Rhode Island Historical Society, 110 Benevolent St., has relics and manuscripts of Civil War interest.

Soldiers' and Sailors' Monument, in the Mall, was designed by Randolph Rogers, cast in Munich, dedicated in 1871.

State House, Smith, between Francis and Gaspee streets, north of Civic Center, has a large collection of Civil War flags in cases on the main floor of the rotunda area. Included in the collection are two regimental flags that were used on the USS *Sarah Bruen* and the U.S. mortar schooner, *Rachael Seamen.* In front of the State House, on Smith Street, is the "Gettysburg Cannon." The bronze Napoleon 12-pounder was used by the Rhode Island Light Artillery, Battery B, at the point where Pickett's division made its famous charge upon the Union lines. William Jones and Alfred G. Gardiner were killed by a shell while placing the shot now in the muzzle.

Swan Point Cemetery, off Blackstone Blvd., has grave of Gen. Ambrose E. Burnside.

WESTERLY, Washington County. IS 95, US 1, State 3.

Westerly Memorial Building and Library, Broad St., was erected in 1894 as a memorial to Civil War veterans. Has memorabilia.

WOONSOCKET, Providence County. State 122.

City Hall has plaque commemorating a speech made here by Abraham Lincoln on March 8, 1860.

SOUTH CAROLINA

At noon on December 17, 1860, a convention assembled in Columbia's Baptist Church to consider secession from the Union. The blue silk flag suspended over the rostrum carried on its reverse a palmetto, an open Bible on its trunk, and the words: "God is our refuge and strength—ever present to help in time of trouble, therefore will we not fear, though the earth be removed, and though the mountains be carried into the sea. The Lord of Hosts is with us; the God of Jacob is our refuge." From the reception given the speech made by D. F. Jamison, president of the convention, it was clear the delegates meant to remove South Carolina from the United States. Because smallpox was prevalent in the capital, the delegates voted to transfer the convention to Charleston. There, on December 20, the Ordinance of Secession was unanimously adopted.

On January 8, 1861, cadets of The Citadel, a Charleston military academy, fired upon the sidewheeler *Star of the West*, which was bringing supplies and secret reinforcements to the garrison at Fort Sumter. Federal forces evacuated the fort on April 12, 1861, after bombardment by Confederates under the command of Gen. P. G. T. Beauregard. On November 7, 1861, Flag Officer Samuel F. duPont, with the largest fleet then commanded by an American, captured Forts Beauregard and Walker. The harbor became a base for Union blockade of Confederate ports. Charleston was under heavy attack throughout the war. Naval bombardment on Fort Sumter and land attacks failed, 1862–1865.

Troops led by Gen. William T. Sherman blazed a destructive path to Columbia in the last months of the war. The flames that burned the capital have long since died out, but not the controversy. Gen. Wade Hampton accused Sherman of deliberately setting the torch to the city; Sherman blamed Hampton for having left burning cotton in the streets on a windy day. Beyond doubt the conquering army had a grievance against the state held to be "precipitator of the rebellion," and both regulars and stragglers had grown practiced in the fine art of plundering.

South Carolina furnished about 63,000 troops to the Confederacy and lost at least one-fourth of them. The state was readmitted to the Union on June 25, 1868, but Federal occupation forces remained almost nine more years. A complexity of motives propelled carpetbaggers, scalawags, Red Shirts, and the Ku Klux Klan to violence nearly as devastating as wartime's. President Rutherford B. Hayes authorized withdrawal of federal troops in April 1877, formally, at least, ending the Reconstruction period.

ABBEVILLE, Abbeville County. State 72, 20. The town is often called "the Cradle and the Grave of the Confederacy." It is claimed that the meeting which began the secession movement was held here November 22, 1860, as well as the last Confederate cabinet meeting, May 2, 1865. The district sent six delegates to the secession convention.

Burt Mansion, Main and Greenville St., later called the Stark House, was the home of Maj. Armistead Burt. It was built about 1850. Davis, hurrying southward and looking for a haven where he could carry on the Confederate cause, held a cabinet meeting here before going on to Georgia.

Perrin House, directly across the street from Burt House, was the home of Thomas Chiles Perrin, the first to sign the Ordinance of Secession. He served as "president of the day" at one of the first secession meetings held here in November 1860. Members of the Confederate cabinet stayed at the Perrin House when President Davis was the guest of Maj. Burt. Secretary of State Judah P. Benjamin left the president's party at Abbeville and went alone to Florida.

Trinity Episcopal Churchyard has the grave of John Alfred Calhoun, signer of the ordinance, lawyer, and planter. His residence was at Rosdhu plantation, about 2½ miles from the village.

Upper Long Cane Cemetery, near Pres-

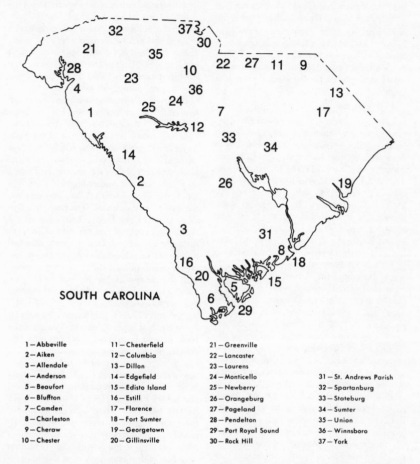

SOUTH CAROLINA

1 — Abbeville	11 — Chesterfield	21 — Greenville	
2 — Aiken	12 — Columbia	22 — Lancaster	
3 — Allendale	13 — Dillon	23 — Laurens	
4 — Anderson	14 — Edgefield	24 — Monticello	31 — St. Andrews Parish
5 — Beaufort	15 — Edisto Island	25 — Newberry	32 — Spartanburg
6 — Bluffton	16 — Estill	26 — Orangeburg	33 — Stateburg
7 — Camden	17 — Florence	27 — Pageland	34 — Sumter
8 — Charleston	18 — Fort Sumter	28 — Pendelton	35 — Union
9 — Cheraw	19 — Georgetown	29 — Port Royal Sound	36 — Winnsboro
10 — Chester	20 — Gillinsville	30 — Rock Hill	37 — York

byterian Church on State 20. Thomas Chiles Perrin and David Lewis Wardlaw, delegates to the secession convention of 1860, are buried here. Wardlaw in 1866 was one of a committee sent to Washington to petition for the release of ex-President Davis. Chancellor Francis Hugh Wardlaw, a brother of David Lewis Wardlaw and a native of Abbeville, prepared the original draft of the secession ordinance. He died in 1861 and is buried in Edgefield.

AIKEN, Aiken County. Off IS 20, US 1, 78. Local mills provided equipment for Southern troops. In February 1865, Sherman ordered Gen. H. J. Kilpatrick to destroy the Graniteville mills. Forces led by Gen. Joe Wheeler met the Yankees on Aiken's main street. An engineer ran his locomotive almost into the midst of the fight, had to back out and retreat to Graniteville. Recently the Aiken County Historical Society has erected a monument on the battlesite.

Confederate Park, Mayfields. The South Carolina Confederate Centennial Commission has erected a marker in memory of Gen. Joe Wheeler, commanding officer at the battle of Aiken. Also in the park are a Confederate museum and restored monuments to Mary Ann Bowie, Confederate nurse, and to Rev. S. P. T. Fields, Confederate chaplain.

Sweetwater Cemetery, in Aiken County, has a monument in memory of Pvt. Sidney Weeks, the first South Carolinian killed in the war.

ALLENDALE, Allendale County. State 641.

Rivers Bridge State Park, 15 miles east, off State 641. A museum houses relics of the battle of February 4, 1865, when troops under Maj. Lafayette McLaws, numbering less than 1,500, are said to have held off 22,000 men of Sherman's army for two days. In 1876, bodies interred along the battle site were reburied in a single grave.

ANDERSON, Anderson County. IS 85, US 29, 178. Anderson district sent five delegates to the secession convention. Gen. Joseph Newton Whitner was one of the founders of Anderson; his five sons served in the Confederate army. Maj. Richard Franklin Simpson, also a senator, had two sons in the army; Cpl. Taliaferro Simpson was killed September 20, 1863, at Chickamauga. B. F. Mauldin was a farmer, soldier, and minister; after the war he became paymaster of the Greenville and Columbia Railroad, died in Anderson in 1886. Delegate James Lawrence Orr seems to have had a look at both sides of the states' rights fence. He edited the *Anderson Gazette,* later went into politics, was speaker of the 35th Congress, was a National Democrat at the 1856 state Democratic convention, of which he was president. In 1860 he withdrew from the national Democratic convention and signed the Ordinance of Secession later that year. He organized Orr's Regiment of Rifles and served for a time in the army, later was a Confederate senator until the fall of Richmond. He quarreled with President Davis and advocated a negotiated peace. After the war he served in the Reconstruction administration of President Johnson and was the first governor of South Carolina chosen by popular election. In 1868, he joined the Radical party, supported President Grant's Ku Klux Klan policy at the Republican convention of 1872, and was appointed minister to Russia. He died of pneumonia in St. Petersburg in 1873. Delegate Jacob Pinckney Reed, judge and a founder of Johnson Female University, is buried in the old cemetery of the First Baptist Church.

The Old Reformer, at the courthouse, Main and Whitner St., a cannon used by both British and Americans in the Revolutionary War, was fired when the ordinance was signed in 1860.

BEAUFORT, Beaufort County. US 21, State 170. Union Gen. Isaac I. Stevens occupied the town on the evening of December 11, 1861. His brigade was astonished to find the beautiful village deserted by its white residents and looted by freed slaves. The general ordered his staff to clear out the looters and restore order. The town became a leave center for soldiers and sailors of the Department of the South. Mansions were used for hospitals, quarters, and commissaries. Many homes have been restored and can be seen on a walking tour.

Baptist Church, Charles St. between King and Prince St., built in 1844, had a slave membership of more than 3,000. The church served as a hospital during the war.

Barnwell House, northwest corner of Carteret and Washington St., was built by Elizabeth Barnwell Gough whose descendant, Robert Barnwell Rhett, a signer of the ordinance, was born Smith. The family name was changed in 1837 to carry on the name of Rhett. Delegate Rhett, a fiery secessionist, had served as a U.S. senator, succeeding Calhoun. His son, Robert, Jr., edited the *Charleston Mercury;* the senior Rhett often used the newspaper columns to attack the Davis administration.

Beaufort Arsenal, Craven and Carteret St., sustained a basic loss. Gen. Stevens, who had graduated first in his class at West Point, was an officer of exceptional ability and a gentleman with the greatest disdain for looters. He gave orders to have the library restored and assigned men to catalogue the books and open the building for use. A U.S. Treasury agent, William H. Reynolds, had other ideas. He demanded the books be sold as captured Rebel property. Stevens threw him out, but Reynolds returned in a month with a formal demand from the Secretary of the Treasury, endorsed by Gen. Thomas West Sherman (who was taking a long coffee-and-bakery break at Hilton Head; *see* PORT ROYAL SOUND). Stevens balked again, but the books eventually were sent north. Salmon P. Chase stopped the sale; the remaining books were sent to the Smithsonian Institution until the "authority of the Union should be reestablished in South Carolina." Before that authority was achieved most of the volumes were destroyed by a Smithsonian fire in 1868. In 1940, Congress passed a bill appropriating $10,000 to reimburse Beaufort for the books. Now a museum.

Chaplin Court, Washington and New St., was built by John Chaplin who sent eight of his 22 children into Confederate service.

The Fripp House, Short St. between Prince and Duke St., was sold for taxes while its owner, just returned from the war, looked on in despair. It is said that a Frenchman who had been living in the house bought it, gave Fripp the deed, and disappeared.

George P. Elliott House Museum, Bay and Charles, was used as hospital.

John Mark Verdier House, 801 Bay St., once entertained Lafayette; served as Union headquarters during occupation of the town.

McLeod House, west corner Bay and Wilmington St., served as a Union hospital, then as headquarters for an agent of the U.S. Treasury; in 1865 it was Maj. Blair's headquarters, later was again used as a hospital.

National Cemetery, Boundary St. at northwest entrance to town. Twelve thousand Union soldiers are buried here with a small group of Confederate soldiers.

The Oaks, Short St. between King and Prince St., was built in 1856 by Col. Paul Hamilton. The family deserted the home in 1861, and on its return in 1865 the colonel's brother-in-law had to pay the rent. When the house was auctioned off, a Northern merchant helped the Hamiltons raise the money to buy it.

St. Helena Episcopal Church, 507 Newcastle St. at North St. Tombstones from the burial ground were used as operating tables when the church served as a hospital during the war. Among notables buried here: Lt. Gen. R. H. Anderson who served during the bombardment of Fort Sumter, succeeded Beauregard in command at Charleston, led a brigade under Longstreet, served with Lee and A. P. Hill, and led Bushrod Johnson's division at Saylor's Creek. Financial hardships of the war reduced his circumstances at one time to the status of a day laborer. Also buried here is Robert Woodward Barnwell, once president of the University of South Carolina, U.S. senator, a member of the secession convention, and a member of the Confederate senate.

Smith House, 400 Wilmington St., served as headquarters for Gen. Stevens. His wife and daughter occupied the mansion with the general in the spring of 1862. He was killed in action a short time later in Virginia.

University of South Carolina, Beaufort Branch, is housed in the former Beaufort College, used as a contraband hospital during the war.

Weymouth House, now the mayor's home, was headquarters of the special U.S. Treasury agent in 1864.

BENNETTSVILLE, Marlboro County. US 401.

Jennings-Brown House Restoration, 121 S. Marlboro St., was headquarters for Union army when the town was captured in 1865. Antebellum furnishings.

BLUFFTON, Beaufort County. State 46. The village was shelled by a Federal gunboat, but a Confederate detachment arrived in time to save the Episcopal Church from burning.

CAMDEN, Kershaw County. IS 20, US 1, 521. Six Confederate generals were born in Camden. The city was a Confederate storehouse, hospital, and refugee center until burned by Sherman's troops, February 24, 1865. Mary Boykin Chesnut, in one of the most memorable accounts of life in the Confederacy, *A Diary from Dixie,* has many references to Camden throughout the war. One of her observations, in May 1865: "We are shut in here, with our faces turned to a dead wall; no mails except that a letter is sometimes brought by a man on horseback travelling through the wilderness made by Sherman. All the railroads are destroyed, the bridges gone. We are cut off from the world, to eat out our own hearts."

Camden Archives and Museum, 1314 N. Broad St., has Civil War memorabilia.

Confederate Generals Monument, Rectory Square, Chestnut St. and Lyttleton. A fountain with six columns in honor of James Cantey, James Chesnut, Zack Cantey Deas, John D. Kennedy, Joseph B. Kershaw, and John B. Villepigue.

Court Inn, Mill and Laurens St., was bought in the 1830s by Richard Lloyd Champion for his daughter, wife of John M. de Saussure. Mary Boykin Chesnut, in leaving Camden temporarily in June 1861, speaks of being "touched" when Mrs. John de Saussure bade her goodbye and God bless her. "Camden people," wrote Mrs. Chesnut, "never show any more feeling or sympathy than red Indians, except at a funeral. It is expected of all to howl then." Legend has it that on an evening in April 1865, young people were dancing in this house when news came of Lee's surrender. The de Saussure daughter then lit the gas with Confederate money.

Greenleaf Villa, 1307 Broad St., was the home of Gen. R. E. Lee's cousin, Dr. Lee, who used it as a Confederate hospital. Fired by Federal soldiers in 1865, it was rescued by Mrs. Lee, servants, and neighbors, who formed a bucket brigade.

Hampton Park, Lyttleton near US 1, is named for Gen. Wade Hampton. When Hampton held a Red Shirt campaign meeting here in 1876, he was greeted by Revolutionary cannon shot. In the northeast corner at DeKalb and Lyttleton streets is a marble horse trough, erected by Camden schoolchildren and the National Humane Society in memory of Richard Kirkland, Confederate soldier, who carried water to suffering Union soldiers under

State authorities seized the U.S. Arsenal at Charleston.

gunfire at Fredericksburg in 1862. He was killed at Chickamauga at the age of 20. (*See* LANCASTER.*)

Mulberry Plantation, south of Camden about 3 miles, was the boyhood home of James Chesnut, Jr., Confederate statesman and general, the husband of Mary Boykin Chesnut. He was a U.S. senator, a member of the secession convention, later an aide to Gen. Beauregard and to President Davis. Life at Mulberry during the war years is described in *A Diary from Dixie.*

Quaker Cemetery, Wyly, Campbell, Wateree, and Meeting St. Among those buried here are Dr. George Todd, brother-in-law of Abraham Lincoln, and Alexander Hamilton Boykin, a Camden planter who served with distinction as captain of the Boykin Rangers, 2nd South Carolina Cavalry.

CHARLESTON, Charleston County. IS 26. A city of firsts—in secession, shots, and submarine warfare—Charleston was heavily bombarded during the years of siege but was not evacuated until Sherman had demolished Columbia in February 1865.

Charleston Museum, 360 Meeting St.

Oldest city museum in North America has a full scale replica of the ill-fated CSS *Hunley.*

Citadel Museum, 25 Elmwood Ave., has two large Confederate flags among its exhibits.

City Hall, Broad and Meeting St., was erected in 1801 for a branch of the First Bank of the United States. Marker on building. Picture gallery on second floor. City Hall Park has monuments honoring the Washington Light Infantry and Beauregard.

Confederate Museum, Meeting at Market St., built in 1841 and known as Market Hall, is now a museum maintained by the United Daughters of the Confederacy, exhibiting articles pertaining to the Charleston-Fort Sumter area.

County Courthouse, Broad and Meeting St., was completed in 1800 on the site of State House built in 1752 and burned in 1788. Records date back to 18th century.

Hibernian Hall, 105 Meeting St., served as headquarters for Stephen A. Douglas and his followers during the ill-fated Democratic convention in April 1860. Marker.

Institute Hall, 134 Meeting St. On this site the Ordinance of Secession was signed, December 20, 1860. It had been adopted at St.

Andrews Society Hall, 118 Broad St., but two delegates moved here for more room.

Magnolia Cemetery, just off US 52 and 78, was established in 1850. A number of Confederate soldiers are buried here. Among noted South Carolinians who were delegates to the secession convention and signers of the ordinance of secession: Charles Pinckney Brown, killed at Drewry's Bluff, Virginia, May 14, 1864; Andrew William Burnet, planter and legislator who had five sons in the Confederate army; Benjamin F. Dunkin (a South Carolinian by adoption; he was born in Massachusetts), lawyer and a chief justice of the state supreme court; Robert Newman Gourdin, a colonel of reserves; William Gregg (born in western Virginia), industrialist and legislator; and Benjamin Huger Rutledge, captain of the Charleston Light Dragoons, later a colonel. The Charleston County Centennial Commission has erected a marker on the plot known as "Hunley Circle," where Horace L. Hunley and his crew are buried. The unlucky submarine, the *H. L. Hunley*, was sunk twice, suffered a number of other "accidents." On an evening in August 1863, Lt. John A. Payne prepared to take the undersea vessel for a dive. When all the crew but Payne were below, the submarine became entangled with lines from the *Etiwan* nearby and was drawn on her side, filled, and submerged. Five seamen were drowned and the vessel was known henceforth as the "Peripatetic Coffin." Horace Hunley came up from Mobile with what he hoped was a more experienced crew. On the morning of October 15, 1863, after making a few successful dives, the *Hunley* failed to surface. Lost on this occasion were Robert Brookbank, Joseph Patterson, Thomas W. Park, Charles McHugh, Henry Beard, John Marshall, and Charles L. Sprague. The *Hunley* eventually sank the *Housatonic*, losing still another crew in the process.

Magnolia Plantation and Gardens, 9 miles northwest on Ashley River Rd. (State 61), has Civil War memorabilia on second floor of plantation house.

Marion Square, Calhoun between Meeting and King St., also known as Old Citadel Square, has monuments to John C. Calhoun and Gen. Wade Hampton.

Old Citadel Buildings, facing Marion Square, once called "The Arsenal," were built in 1822, after an attempted slave uprising, to house state troops and arms. Later used by the military academy; The Citadel cadets fired on the Union vessel *Star of the West* in January 1861. From 1862 to 1864, The Citadel was occupied by Union soldiers.

Old Exchange Building, East Bay, foot of Broad St., was built in 1771. It was badly damaged during the Federal bombardment.

Old Slave Market, 6 Chalmers St., is a museum on the site of a warehouse where slaves were sold. A Charleston guide, written some 60 years ago, listed a "Mythical Slave Market, 6 Chalmers St.," commenting, "Authorities are positive in saying that nowhere in Charleston was there a constituted slave market. . . . Several houses in this vicinity were used in olden times to quarter slaves who were to be sold on the block."

Parker House, 10 Legare St. Dr. and Mrs. Francis Simons Parker, who also owned Mansfield, a rice plantation on the Black River, lived here during the war. Dr. Parker was a delegate to the secession convention and signed the Ordinance of Secession. His great-grandfather had signed the Constitution of the United States. He served as provost marshal for Georgetown while four sons fought for the Confederacy.

Petigru Law Office, 8 St. Michael's Alley. James Louis Petigru, a Unionist, heard the bells ringing at the adjournment of the secession convention and asked a friend where the fire was. He disputed the answer that there wasn't one: "They have this day set a blazing torch to the temple of constitutional liberty and, please God, we shall have no more peace forever." Petigru also observed that South Carolina was too small to be a republic and too large to be an insane asylum. A cousin, James Johnston Pettigrew, became a lawyer in the Petigru firm, served in the war, and became a brigadier general in 1862. He led his brigade in Pickett's charge at Gettysburg, was mortally wounded at Falling Waters in a rearguard action, and died July 17, 1863.

Pringle House, 27 King St., also known as the Miles Brewton House, was built about 1765. It was headquarters for British troops in 1781, for Federal troops in 1865. Two Pringle sons were killed in the Confederate service. Maj. Robert Pringle, after being carried home from battle, died on the front steps.

Roper House, 9 E. Battery, was the home of Robert William Roper. More recently it was the winter home of Solomon R. Guggenheim, donor of the Guggenheim Museum in New York, who found a 1,000-pound piece of cannon lodged in the rafters. The weapon had exploded at the Battery during the bombardment of Fort Sumter, sending its tailpiece into the Roper attic where it seems likely to remain as the stairs are too narrow for its removal. On the other hand, some of the cast-iron lions' heads used as bolt ends on the outside of the house have been dislodged by the impact of jet planes breaking the sound barrier.

St. Andrews Society Hall, 118 Broad St., site of the hall where the secession convention met in December 1860. Marker on fence. Building burned in 1861,

St. John Hotel, 115 Meeting St., is Charleston's oldest hotel; part of the building dates back to 1801. Gen. Robert E. Lee was a guest here in December 1861 when the hotel narrowly escaped a fire that imperiled part of the city. Lee watched the conflagration from the rooftop.

St. Michael's Protestant Episcopal Church, southeast corner of Broad and Meeting St. The bells of St. Michael's are not only much vaunted but much traveled. Originally brought from England, they were seized by the British during the Revolution, carried back to England in 1784, and later returned to Charleston. In 1862 they were shipped to Columbia for safekeeping and stored in a shed on the State House grounds, where they were partially destroyed in 1865. Somewhat the worse for wear and war, they were returned to England in 1866; the chimes were recast in the original molds which luckily had not been within range of Sherman's guns. They were returned to Charleston in 1867. During Charleston's "Night on the Rooftops," while Fort Sumter was under bombardment, Mary Boykin Chesnut recorded: "I count four by St. Michael's chimes . . . At half past four, the heavy booming of a cannon! . . . I prayed as I had never prayed before."

In the church vestibule is a memorial tablet to Theodore Dehon Wagner, who signed the Ordinance of Secession. Among many notables buried in St. Michael's graveyard are Robert Y. Hayne, nullification statesman; James Louis Petigru, leading Unionist of Charleston; and Henry Workman Conner, intimate friend of John Calhoun and delegate to the secession convention who signed the Ordinance of Secession as the last public act of his life.

St. Philip's Protestant Episcopal Church, Church St., north of Queen, has the graves of many distinguished South Carolinians in its two cemeteries. John C. Calhoun is reburied here in the west side ground. During the war his body was removed for safekeeping but later reinterred. Also here is Edward McCrady, who took the Union side in the nullification struggle, later signed the Ordinance of Secession, and still later opposed the Sequestration Act of the Confederate government, then represented black soldiers taken prisoner under the

black insurrection laws. At the time of his death in 1892, McCrady was the oldest living graduate of Yale. The chimes of the church were cast into Confederate cannon.

CHERAW, Chesterfield County. US 1, 52.

St. David's Episcopal Church, 1st and Church St. The Confederate monument in the cemetery was made possible by the efforts of Mrs. Alexander McLeod, who taught school in Marlboro County for more than 50 years; she raised funds and supervised the reburial of soldiers in the memorial plot. Dr. McLeod, physician and planter, was a delegate to the secession convention from Marlboro District. His plantation, Groveton, is 5 miles south of Bennettsville. He is buried in the family plot at Groveton.

Washington Square, Broad and Meeting Streets, has a statue of P. G. T. Beauregard.

CHESTER, Chester County. US 321, State 9. State records sent to Columbia for safekeeping were packed in freight cars and dispatched to Chester before Sherman's arrival in the capital. Later, Jefferson Davis and members of the government who were fleeing from Richmond discarded some Confederate records that were found scattered about the Chester depot. John McKee, oldest signer of the Ordinance of Secession, was a watchmaker and merchant here. His son, John, Jr., served in the first company raised in Chester. A grandson presented McKee's portrait and framed copy of the ordinance to the town library.

CHESTERFIELD, Chesterfield County. State 9, 102.

Courthouse, Main St., has a marker asserting that the first secession meeting was held here. Abbeville disputes the claim. The original courthouse and public buildings were razed in one of Gen. Sherman's last raids.

COLUMBIA, Richland County. IS 20, 26, 77, US 1, 378, 176. Except for the unfinished State House and the French consulate, no antebellum buildings remained on Main St. after Sherman's occupation of the city. Almost all of the older houses in town have a story of how they escaped destruction. Sherman's army was met by Mayor Goodwin in surrender at Fifth St. and River Dr. A granite slab marks the spot.

Archives Building, 1430 Senate, has a Confederate Relic Room and Museum.

Chestnut College, 1718 Hampton St. The house where Gen. James Chesnut, Jr., and Mrs. Chesnut entertained Jefferson Davis in 1864. In A Diary from Dixie, Mary Boykin Chesnut writes, for July 1864: "We are in a cottage rented from Dr. Chisholm. . . . The girls were at my house. Everything was in the utmost confusion. We were lying on a pile of mattresses in one of the front rooms while the servants were reducing things to order in the rear. . . . Suddenly Buck [Sally Buchanan Campbell Preston, daughter of Gen. John S. Preston, chief of the Conscript Bureau] sprang up. 'Mrs. Chesnut, your new house is very hot. I am suffocated. It is not so oppressingly hot at home, with our thick brick walls!' Isabella came soon after. She said she saw the sisters pass her house, and as they turned the corner there was a loud and bitter cry, and both of the girls began to run at full speed . . . [someone] had come to tell Mrs. Preston that Willie was killed. Willie, his mother's darling!" In October 1864, when President Davis sat on the Chesnut piazza, some little boys passing called out, "Come here and look! There is a man on Mrs. Chesnut's porch who looks just like Jeff Davis on a postage stamp."

Crawford-Clarkson House, 1502 Blanding St. John A. Crawford put a guard on duty to protect his home from arson, but a mahogany secretary was scarred by bayonet thrusts. Mrs. John Preston, wife of the general, is quoted in *A Diary from Dixie* as saying: ". . . there are Crawford, Judge O'Neal, Governor Perry and Mr. Petigru. They openly condemn this war, but no hand is lifted to turn them aside from any public praise or honor."

DeBruhl-Marshall House, 1401 Laurel St. The house is believed to have been used as Confederate Col. James Johnstone's headquarters prior to 1865. Mrs. John S. Wiley persuaded Sherman's men to extinguish flames they had set.

De Saussure Home, southeast corner of Washington and Sumter St. On this site stood a beautiful house which was burned by Sherman's troops; it was the home of William Ford de Saussure, U.S. senator, delegate to the secession convention, and signer of the Ordinance of Secession. A son, William Davie de Saussure, was a colonel of the 15th Regiment, South Carolina Volunteers, and was killed at Gettysburg, July 2, 1863.

Duncan Home, 1615 Gervais St. Col. Blanton Duncan's house served as Sherman's headquarters. A new building occupies the site.

First Baptist Church, 1306 Hampton St. The first secession convention met here December 17, 1860. It is said that the black sexton deliberately misdirected Sherman's soldiers, who were bent upon destroying the "Rebel Convention" site, to an older frame church which was burned instead.

First Presbyterian Church, Marion and Lady St. Among notables buried in the churchyard, the city's first cemetery, are: Henry William de Saussure, first director of the U.S. Mint; Woodrow Wilson's parents, Dr. and Mrs. Joseph R. Wilson; and Gen. Maxcy Gregg, one of the signers of the Ordinance of Secession, who was killed at Fredericksburg, December 14, 1862. A cenotaph in the burial ground was erected to Col. John Hugh Means, who is buried in the Means cemetery in Fairfield County. Means, who owned 127 slaves in 1860, was a delegate to the secession convention, later colonel of the 17th South Carolina Infantry, and was mortally wounded at Second Manassas.

Governor's Mansion, Richland and Gadsden St., was built as officers' quarters for the Columbia Academy and was the only building left by Union soldiers on the arsenal grounds.

Guignard House, 1527 Senate St., reputedly was saved from fire by the slave cook, Dilcie, who went to face Sherman after the household had fled, offered the best cooking in Columbia, and then served it to Union officers who quartered here. The soldiers "presented" Dilcie with the house and its contents intact on departure.

Hampton-Preston Mansion, 1615 Blanding, was headquarters for Union Gen. Logan in 1865. Many Hampton family furnishings. Logan had planned to burn the mansion on his departure but was dissuaded by the Ursuline Sisters, who used the house as a refuge after their convent was burned.

Millwood, 4 miles out of town on US 76, was the home of Wade Hampton, burned by Sherman's troops. Columns and outlines of the garden remain.

Monument to the Confederate Dead, directly north of the State House, was carved by Nicoli, an Italian sculptor.

Monument to the Women of the Confederacy, on State House grounds, was executed by F. W. Ruckstuhl. Columbia women, led by Miss Isabella Martin, established the first "Wayside Hospital" in 1861. It cared for more than 1,000 soldiers the first year.

Old Slave Market, southwest corner of Senate and Assembly St., is the site where slaves were auctioned in antebellum days. They were confined in a small brick building with high barred windows at the rear of the residence of slave dealer Samuel Mercer Logan. The court and driveway were paved by slave labor.

Palmetto Tree, near the State House west portico. An iron tree monument to the Palmetto Regiment, which served in the Mexican War. Sherman's soldiers destroyed the pedestal plates engraved with names of regiment members; they were replaced, but the statue was shattered by a tornado in 1939. It has again been restored.

Pinarea, below the falls on Lightwood Creek, was the home of Gen. Paul Quattlebaum, legislator and a signer of the Ordinance of Secession. The general took part in the defense of Columbia, fighting on the Capitol grounds. A detachment of cavalry was sent to burn his home, but plantation slaves managed to save it. Quattlebaum's father operated a rifle works; the entire output went to the Confederate army.

Shaw House, 1502 Hampton St., was saved by its resident, Alexander Herbemont, Italian consul, who raised the Italian flag. Henry Timrod, unofficial poet laureate of the Confederacy, worked here as governor's clerk.

Sherman's Battery, off US 378 at 321 Moffat Dr. A boulder marks the location of guns that shelled the city.

South Carolina Confederate Relic Room and Museum, 920 Sumter St., has a military collection. Guide service is available.

State Archives, 1430 Senate St., has extensive Confederate relics collection.

State House, Main and Gervais St. Bronze stars on west and south walls mark shell holes made by Sherman's artillery. Confederate statues, tablets, and portraits are in the building; statues are also on the grounds.

Trinity Episcopal Church, 1100 Sumter St. Lead finials from church roof were used to make bullets during the war. Among those buried in the churchyard are seven South Carolina governors, the poet Henry Timrod, and three Confederate generals. Joseph Daniel Pope, signer of the Ordinance of Secession, who was head of the revenue department in charge of the printing and issuance of Confederate currency, is also buried here.

University of South Carolina, 900 block of Sumter St., was used as a hospital by both Union and Confederate armies, and thereby saved from burning. Francis Lieber, a liberal German, taught many of the state's leading Unionists. C. G. Memminger, Confederate secretary-treasurer, was a student here. Harper College, on the north quadrangle line, was used by a Federal garrison as a military prison. Rutledge College, southeast end of quadrangle, was used as Union staff headquarters in 1865 and its chapel housed the state legislature, 1865–1868.

DILLON, Dillon County. IS 95, State 9, 34. A memorial light honoring Confederate soldiers at South of the Border Motel, IS 95.

EDGEFIELD, Edgefield County. US 25, State 23.

Baptist Cemetery has the grave of Robert Gill Mills Dunovant, who with his brother, Alexander, signed the Ordinance of Secession. Gen. Dunovant was in charge of Charleston until the appointment of Beauregard. After the war he published a history of the Palmetto Regiment.

D. A. Tompkins Memorial Library, northeast corner of square, has books and papers of John R. Abney, colonel under Wade Hampton.

Oakley Park Museum, US 25, has Confederate relics.

Willowbrook Cemetery, Church St. Buried here are Preston Brooks, U.S. congressman who caned Charles Sumner, senator from Massachusetts, because of a slavery dispute; and "Douschka," the daughter of Francis W. Pickens, an American minister to Russia. Her full name was Andrea Dorothea Olga Liva Lucy Holcombe Douschka Francesca Pickens Dugas. The czar and czarina were her godparents, and legend says she once rallied 1,500 men under the Red Shirt banner and rode at the head of a Wade Hampton parade clad in a scarlet gown. Francis Wardlaw, author of the Ordinance of Secession, also is buried here.

EDISTO ISLAND, Colleton County. State 174. Joseph Evans Jenkins, signer of the Ordinance of Secession, reputedly rallied delegates at the secession convention by declaring, "If South Carolina doesn't secede, Edisto Island will." He is buried in *Trinity Churchyard.* Ephraim Mikell Seabrook, also signer of the ordinance, was a colonel on Gen. Ripley's staff. His third wife was the widow of Gen. Bartow. G. W. Seabrook, Ephraim's cousin, also a native of Edisto Island and a signer of the ordinance, was a wealthy planter who is said to have served in the Confederate army in spite of his age, as did his sons. During the war he sold his vast holdings for Confederate money.

ESTILL, Hampton County. US 321. George Rhodes, signer of the Ordinance of Secession, sent two sons to the war. Sgt. Theodore Rhodes was killed at Gettysburg. The Rhodes home was burned during the war and the family lived in the carriage house. There is a memorial to Rhodes in the *Baptist Church* here. He is buried at *Lawtonville Cemetery* 2 miles west of town.

FLORENCE, Florence County. IS 20, 95, US 76, 301. The town was founded by William Wallace Hardee, later a Confederate general, and named for his daughter. A shipping center, point of embarkation, hospital center, and finally a prison, the village was overrun with incoming prisoners before a stockade was completed 3 miles south. Improvised and imperfect camps were set up in midtown, typhoid broke out, and wagons daily hauled the dead off for burial, often as many as 100 corpses in one load. Coffin makers could not keep pace; the dead were buried in blankets. The surviving prisoners were inadequately guarded by old men and boys; when a detachment of Sherman's cavalry arrived to free them in March 1865, none was on hand to be liberated. Confederate cavalrymen, led by Gens. Wheeler and Colcock, rushed their horses off loaded boxcars, skirmished behind Gamble's Hotel, and drove the Yankees back towards Darlington.

Florence Museum, Graham and Spruce streets, has "The Hall of South Carolina History," which traces the state's development.

National Military Cemetery and Stockade Site, 1 mile east off US 76.

Public Library, 319 S. Irby St., has the propellers of the *Pee Dee* cruiser on the grounds. The *Pee Dee* was a Confederate gunboat constructed on the Pee Dee River, eventually sunk by its crew to avoid capture.

Timrod Park, Timrod Park Dr. and Colt St., was named for Henry Timrod, known as the Poet Laureate of the Confederacy. He taught school nearby.

FORT SUMTER NATIONAL MONUMENT consists of two historic forts. Fort Sumter, in Charleston Harbor, is accessible by tour boat from the City Marina in Charleston and from Patriot's Point in Mount Pleasant. Fort Moultrie is on Sullivan's Island and is easily visited by following Route 703 from Mt. Pleasant.

Due to difficulties in defending Fort Moultrie, Maj. Robert Anderson moved his federal troops from that location to Fort Sumter in December 1860. Confederate batteries fired the first shots of the war on Fort Sumter at 4:30 A.M. on April 12, 1861. Fort Sumter surrendered 34 hours later. On April 14, 1861, Maj. Anderson lowered the flag to a fifty gun salute. The fort was held by Confederate forces until the end of the war. However, due to almost constant bombardment by Federal forces, its walls had been reduced to rubble, which proved quite resistant to further bombardment.

The trip to Fort Sumter affords a view of *Fort Johnson,* from which the first shot was fired at Fort Sumter; *Fort Moultrie,* the original base of Maj. Anderson's troops; and *Castle Pinckney,* the first Union-held area captured by Confederates just before the outbreak of the war.

GEORGETOWN, Georgetown County. US 17, 701.

Belle Isle Gardens, 4½ miles south off US 17. Site of a Confederate fort captured by the Federal navy in 1865.

Market Building, Front and Screven St. Site of old slave market. Federal troops attempting to take the town came ashore on the dock at rear of building. Museum.

Prince George Winyah Church, Broad and Highmarket St. Confederate soldiers are buried in church cemetery.

GILLINSVILLE, Jasper County. State 128. Every building except the Baptist Church and one residence was burned by Sherman's army. Richard James Davant, legislator who had four sons in the Confederate army, is buried in the Baptist churchyard.

GREENVILLE, Greenville County. IS 85, 26. There were many Unionists in this area, but wayside hospitals were established for Confederate soldiers. The surrounding mountains were infested with deserters who organized in bands to prey upon the town. At one time Maj. A. D. Ashmore requested a cannon to use in striking back. Greenville County Centennial Commission has erected a marker honoring its delegates to the secession convention. Delegate Perry Emory Duncan was also Greenville's representative in the state legislature; his wife was president of the Hospital Relief Corps during the war, directing a small army of assistants, with special trains at her disposal. She collected and distributed hospital supplies at all points east of the Mississippi River. Delegate William Hans Campbell, legislator and editor of the *Greenville Mountaineer,* raised a company for Confederate service and served as captain in Gregg's Regiment; later he was a lieutenant colonel of the Palmetto Light Infantry. Delegate William King Easley, lawyer, planter, and railroad promoter, raised a company of cavalry, served as major in the Confederate army and as adjutant general in the reorganization of state militia. The town of Easley was named for him.

Furman University, about 7 miles north of town. Delegate Dr. James Clement Furman was first president. During the war he resigned as pastor of the Brushy Creek Baptist Church when some members regarded him as instrumental in bringing on hostilities. The university closed during the war, and Furman taught at the Greenville Female College, later helped to reopen the university in 1866.

Greenville Woman's College, College St., 3 blocks west of N. Main St. Greenville Female College during the war, the library building served as a hospital. James Furman taught here when Furman University was temporarily closed. The college is now part of Furman University.

Site of Harrison House, North St. where county courthouse stands. Delegate James Perry Harrison was one of the first doctors in Greenville District. Dr. Harrison was disfranchised for having signed the Ordinance of Secession, was restored to citizenship by a pardon from the president of the United States. His home was moved a short distance from this site and is now the Greenville Women's Club.

HILTON HEAD ISLAND, off the southern coast of South Carolina, was used by Union troops as a base to blockade Confederate ports.

LANCASTER, Lancaster County. US 521. Dr. Robert Lafayette Crawford, delegate to the secession convention, served as assistant surgeon to the 9th South Carolina Volunteers, later raised Company D, Waxhaw Guards. Capt. Crawford was wounded at Second Manassas, again at Antietam, and was killed at Suffolk, Va., April 20, 1863. He is buried in *Lancaster Presbyterian Church Cemetery* on W. Gay St. Dr. William Columbus Cauthen, also a delegate to the secession convention, was a victim of tuberculosis. Long hours during the war broke his health completely. During Sherman's invasion, Union soldiers dragged the ailing doctor from his bed and flogged him in a fruitless effort to learn the family hiding place for valuables. The "bummers" did not discover the secret panel behind the doctor's bed, nor the fact that he had signed the Ordinance of Secession. He died on May 4, 1865, and was buried in the *Hanging Rock Methodist Church Cemetery,* Kershaw County.

A Lancaster resident, Richard Kirkland, aided wounded Federal soldiers at Fredericksburg and was killed at Chickamauga at age 20.

LAURENS, Laurens County. IS 26, US 76, 221.

Site of Andrew Johnson Tailor Shop, north side of square. Lincoln's successor once worked as a tailor's apprentice here. At times he designed coverlets to help young women quiltmakers.

Laurens City Cemetery has the graves of several delegates to the secession convention

and other Confederate patriots. Among them Henry William Garlington, who was the first merchant in Laurensville, later owned more than 100 slaves, and was president of the Laurens Railroad. Col. Garlington lost two of his three sons and two brothers in the war. His third son, Dr. William Hunter Garlington, was a surgeon in the Confederate army. Other delegates were William Dendy Watts, tax collector and later ordinary of Laurens District; John Drayton Williams, merchant and planter; Henry Clinton Young, legislator and a director of the Laurens Railroad.

National Guard Armory, opposite courthouse, was the scene of an 1870 riot when armed blacks, reputedly led by a "scalawag," set out to burn the town. The affair caught national attention, arousing champions for both parties in the controversy.

MONTICELLO, Fairfield County. State 215. The town suffered heavily when Sherman's army passed this way in 1865. A preparatory academy chartered before 1804 was burned. The mansion of William John Alston, signer of the ordinance, was destroyed; and a brick church on the banks of Little River lost its flooring after Union soldiers had camped there. The departing soldiers left a note explaining that the floor planks were needed to rebuild a bridge burned by escaping Confederates.

NEWBERRY, Newberry County. IS 26.

Newberry College, College St. Simeon Fair, signer of the ordinance, helped to organize the college and gave to the trustees the land on which the institution stands. He also gave ten acres for *Rosemont Cemetery.* John P. Kinard, signer of the ordinance, was the first treasurer of the college. He was a captain of Company F, 20th South Carolina Volunteers.

Newberry County Courthouse, on square, erected in 1850, has a pediment added in 1880 which bears a bas-relief symbolizing the spirit of the state during Reconstruction: an uprooted palmetto held in the talons of the U.S. eagle; on the palmetto roots, a gamecock with a gold dollar for his right eye. A dove in the top branches holds an olive branch. An irate judge once denounced the sculptor Osborne Wells, who responded that had he possessed a likeness of the judge, he'd have been happy to have included it.

Rosemont Cemetery, Robert Moorman, signer of the ordinance, is buried here, as is Simeon Fair. Moorman was a member of the Soldiers' Relief Board and a lieutenant in the 3rd South Carolina Volunteers.

ORANGEBURG, Orangeburg County. IS 26. Thomas Worth Glover, planter and jurist, signed the Ordinance of Secession. Sherman later used the Glover mansion as headquarters. Gen. David Flavel Jamison, president of the secession convention, was born in Orangeburg District, served in the House of Representatives from Orange Parish. In his fourth term he introduced the bill for the formation of the military academy which became The Citadel. He served as presiding judge for the military court of Beauregard's Corps until his death from yellow fever in 1864. He is buried in Orangeburg.

Presbyterian Church, corner Russell and Doyle St., lost its communion service in 1865 when Union soldiers used the church basement as their stable.

PAGELAND, Chesterfield County. State 9, 151.

Five Forks Cemetery, on State 9, has the grave of James H. Miller with stone engraved "Murdered in Retaliation." Miller, cavalryman under Gen. Hampton, was executed by a firing squad on Sherman's orders. The story is that Hampton's men fired on Union foragers after the burning of Columbia. Sherman announced that the next Union man killed would mean a Confederate prisoner's death. Soon after, raiders under Sgt. Woodford, 46th Ohio, kidnapped a slave who retaliated when Woodford took an after-dinner nap by crushing the sergeant's head with a lightwood knot. Sherman ordered prisoners to cast lots to be shot, in accordance with his warning. Miller was buried with a lightwood knot at his head.

PENDLETON, Anderson County. IS 85, US 76-123.

St. Paul's Episcopal Church, Queen's St. Among notables buried in the church graveyard are: Gen. Barnard E. Bee, killed at Manassas, the officer who gave Gen. Jackson the sobriquet "Stonewall"; Mrs. John C. Calhoun and children; and Thomas G. Clemson and his wife, Anna. Clemson, a son-in-law of John C. Calhoun, was Supervisor of Mining and Metal Works in the Trans-Mississippi Department of the Confederacy.

PORT ROYAL SOUND. The estuary can be reached by State 46 east from Bluffton. During the war, Fort Walker was established on Hilton Head, Fort Beauregard on Bay Point. Confederates here were commanded by Gen. Thomas F. Drayton, brother of Percival Drayton, commander of the *Pocahontas* in the Union fleet which attacked and took posses-

sion of the area. Under Union occupancy Fort Walker became Fort Welles. William Seabrook Drayton and John Edward Drayton served under their father, Thomas, in the defense of Hilton Head. William later became a captain in the Army of Northern Virginia. Percival of the Union navy, who had to fire on relatives and homeland, later became captain of the *Hartford,* Adm. Farragut's flagship at the battle of Mobile Bay. It was Capt. Drayton to whom the admiral shouted: "Damn the torpedoes. Full speed ahead!"

Gen. A. W. Sherman seems to have spent part of his time, during the occupation of Hilton Head, at the garrison bakery, watching the bakers work, strolling along the beach, or watching his staff make out endless reports. Although the Union officer had served with distinction in the battle of Buena Vista, his inaction after the capture of Fort Walker was puzzling to a fellow Mexican War veteran, Robert E. Lee, then headquartered at Coosawatchie. In a letter to his son on January 4, 1862, after a skirmish, Lee wrote: "Enemy quiet and retired to his Islands. The Main seemed too insecure for him, and he never went 400 yards from his steamers. . . . After burning some houses, three, on the river bank, and feeling our proximity unpleasant, he retreated to Port Royal again."

ROCK HILL, York County. IS 77, US 21, State 322. A transfer point for Confederate troops and supplies, the town suffered one skirmish and one casualty when a detachment of Stoneman's cavalry came from Charlotte to destroy bridges and railroads.

Confederate Park, Confederate Ave. The park was named for a monument to Confederate dead which has since been removed to *Laurelwood Cemetery.*

ST. ANDREWS PARISH, Charleston County. State 61, 12 miles from Charleston.

Drayton Hall was the only Ashley River home not vandalized by Union soldiers in 1865. It was saved because an alert Confederate, learning of the enemy's approach, transferred a number of slaves with smallpox into the "Big House."

Magnolia Gardens, adjoining Drayton Hall. The second mansion here was razed by Sherman's army in 1865. The gardens are internationally famous.

SPARTANBURG, Spartanburg County. IS 26, 85. The district sent six delegates to the secession convention, and the war brought a boom. County plants worked overtime to provide cotton and wool yarns, corn, wheat, arms and tools, and—during the latter part of the conflict—wooden shoes.

Mt. Zion Baptist Cemetery, northwest of town, has the grave of John Gill Landrum, signer of the ordinance and chaplain of the 13th South Carolina Volunteers. The town of Landrum was named for him.

Spartanburg Regional Museum, behind the library at 501 Otis Blvd., has regional history displays and a model of an early plantation, Walnut Grove, which is open to the public, on US 221, 9 miles south of jct. with IS 26. Pre-1830 furnishings.

STATEBURG, Sumter County. US 75, 378.

Borough House, opposite Episcopal Church of the Holy Cross, was the birthplace of Lt. Gen. Richard Anderson and Maj. William Wallace Anderson, Confederate surgeon. Union soldiers left bayonet scars in the house.

SUMTER, Sumter County. US 15, 76-378. The city had only minor skirmishes during the war, but a Sumter boy, George E. Haynesworth, a Citadel cadet, fired the first shot on January 9, 1861, at the *Star of the West* in Charleston harbor. Gen. Richard H. Anderson, who lived here, has been called South Carolina's ranking officer. (Some say Wade Hampton ranked him.) Rev. John Leighton Wilson, a pioneer missionary to Africa who was once offered the governorship of Liberia, endeavored to abolish slave traffic. Thomas Reese English, signer of the ordinance, is buried in *Mt. Zion Churchyard.*

UNION, Union County. US 176, State 49. When Sherman was marching on Columbia, Gov. Magrath and other officials brought valuable papers and records here. They were guests of Judge Dawkins. The town was the scene of many Reconstruction struggles between Democrats and Radicals. Klansmen, taking the several-eyes-for-an-eye view, killed a number of black militiamen in retaliation for the death of a one-armed Confederate veteran. Benjamin Franklin Arthur, who taught school here, was clerk of the secession convention and copied the Ordinance of Secession in beautiful script, using a quill pen. William Henry Gist, who as governor requested the call for the secession con-

vention, lived at Rose Hill (just off US 176), which was acquired by the state as a historic park in 1960. Gist is buried in the family cemetery there.

Carnegie Public Library, southeast corner of S. Mountain St., has war relics.

Culp House, 28 N. Mountain St. From the front porch Mrs. Ann Hill presented a flag to the Union's first company of volunteers, the Johnson Rifles. In 1876, Gen. Hampton made an address here.

General William Wallace House, 97 E. Main St. Jefferson Davis was entertained here, and Union citizens brought dishes for the feast.

Presbyterian Church. The graveyard has a monument at the burial site of Col. James M. Gadberry, signer of the ordinance, who raised the 18th South Carolina Volunteers and was killed while leading his regiment at Second Manassas, August 30, 1862. A Union street is named for him.

WINNSBORO, Fairfield County. US 321, State 200. Sherman burned part of the town after leaving Columbia in 1865.

Confederate Monument, Congress and Washington St. An antebellum clock in the tower was brought here from Charleston in an oxcart. It was once mortgaged to a citizen who lent money to the town—which gave him the clock when unable to pay off the debt. The creditor, finding the timepiece impractical, returned it to the city.

Site of Mount Zion Institute is on land occupied by the Mount Zion High School. Sherman burned the building after occupying it for a time. Eustace St. Pierre Bellinger, signer of the ordinance, was a former student of the institute.

Presbyterian Church cemetery has the grave of John Buchanan, signer of the ordinance and a former student of Mount Zion Institute. He was a lawyer and owner of the plantation Malvern Hill.

YORK, York County. US 321, State 5. York furnished the background for Thomas Dixon's novel *The Clansman,* which was adapted for the motion picture *The Birth of a Nation.* The Ku Klux Klan of South Carolina is said to have been organized here. Archibald Ingram Barron, the last delegate to sign the Ordinance of Secession, is buried in Rose Hill Cemetery.

SOUTH DAKOTA

When the territory of Nebraska was organized in May 1854, and the state of Minnesota in May 1858, an expanse of territory lying to the north and west was left without a title or government. Undaunted settlers in what is now the eastern part of South Dakota spread themselves thin in order to give Congress the impression of a fairly well-populated area. Some 30 or 40 residents of Sioux Falls split into groups of three or four and rode off in all directions except east. Wherever they stopped to water their horses, they set up election precincts, appointed themselves judges, clerks of election, and voters. They voted for themselves, relatives, and auld acquaintance. An unorthodox legislature convened soon after and elected a delegate to Congress. Congress kept a straight face but looked the other way. In 1859 the settlers held another election, tried another delegate to Washington, as well as a governor and a legislature. Congress still refused to set up a territory. That same year, however, the Indians were persuaded to vacate the land between the Big Sioux and Missouri rivers, leaving it open for settlement. As the Indians moved west to Yankton Reservation, settlers poured in from Nebraska establishing the towns of Bon Homme, Yankton, and Vermillion. One of President Buchanan's last official acts was to sign the bill creating Dakota Territory on March 2, 1861.

Lincoln appointed Dr. William Jayne, his family physician in Springfield, as the first territorial governor. Jayne chose Yankton as temporary capital. The first legislature, called the "Pony Congress," a comment on its size, convened on St. Patrick's Day, 1862, choosing Yankton as permanent capital of the Dakota Territory. A company of militia was raised and offered to Lincoln, but the unit remained in South Dakota for protection against Indian uprisings. The Santee Sioux wasted little time in launching the offensive. Full-scale war broke out in Minnesota that August and spread through the Northwest. Though most of the fighting took place outside South Dakota, a skirmish occurred near Sioux Falls; Gov. Jayne sent soldiers to evacuate the inhabitants and bring them to Yankton for safety. Indians pillaged and burned the deserted settlement and Fort Dakota was built there in 1865. A council in 1865 officially ended the War of the Outbreak.

BLUNT, Hughes County. US 14.

Mentor Graham House, west edge of town, a half-block off the highway. The last home of Lincoln's teacher, Mentor Graham, has been restored by the South Dakota Historical Society. Lincoln once lived for a time in the Graham home in Sangamon County, Illinois. Graham was invited to sit on the platform at Lincoln's first inauguration.

CUSTER, Custer County. US 16. The town was first named Stonewall in honor of Gen. Jackson, renamed Custer by miners.

Custer City Courthouse Museum, 411 Mount Rushmore Rd., has historical memorabilia.

Log Cabin Museum, Main St., in City Park; historical exhibits in oldest cabin in the Black Hills.

DEADWOOD, Lawrence County. Off IS 90, US 85, 385.

Adams Memorial Museum, Sherman and Deadwood St., has historical collection featuring pioneer life in the Black Hills.

Ghosts of Deadwood Gulch, old Towne Hall, Lee St., has costumed wax figures representing life in the territory from the arrival of the first white man through the gold rush. From June through September, there is a nightly reenactment of the *Trial of Jack McCall;* McCall shot Wild Bill Hickok.

Mount Moriah Cemetery, Van Buren Ave. Wild Bill Hickok, once a Union soldier, is buried here in Deadwood's "Boot Hill." The funeral notice in August 1876 announced that J. B. Hickok had died from the effects of a pistol shot. Not mentioned in the notice, but told ever after, is the "Dead Man's Hand" Hickok was holding at demise—aces and eights.

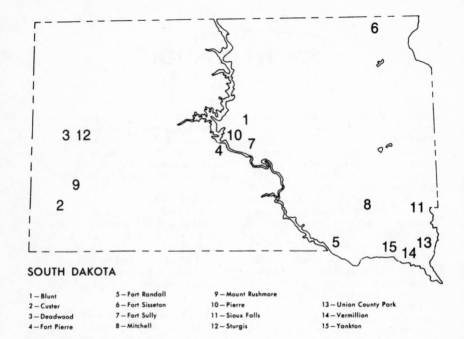

SOUTH DAKOTA

1 — Blunt
2 — Custer
3 — Deadwood
4 — Fort Pierre

5 — Fort Randall
6 — Fort Sisseton
7 — Fort Sully
8 — Mitchell

9 — Mount Rushmore
10 — Pierre
11 — Sioux Falls
12 — Sturgis

13 — Union County Park
14 — Vermillion
15 — Yankton

FORT PIERRE, Stanley County. North of US 14. An important early trading post, the fort was bought by the government in 1855. William Lass, in writing of steamboating on the upper Missouri, tells of a dispute between Gen. Pope and Gen. Sully during the summer of 1863. Sully's army, organized at Sioux City, was to be supplied by steamers which had been so long arriving from St. Louis that the expedition into the Dakotas was delayed until mid-June. A drought had not helped matters; Sully's boats rested on sand bars between Fort Randall and Fort Pierre through June and July. By the second week of August, Sully had his river fleet at Fort Pierre and had sent two mountain steamers ahead with supplies for Swan Lake, about 100 miles upriver. Pope, however, was outraged by the delay and wrote to Sully: "I never dreamed you would consider yourself tied to the boats if they were obstacles in going up the river. . . . It seems to me impossible to understand how you have staid about the river, delaying from day to day . . . and when you had wagons enough to carry at least two months' subsistence for your command." The chastened Sully eventually

moved up the Missouri and defeated the Sioux at the battle of Whitestone Hill.

FORT RANDALL, Charles Mix County. US 18. (*Also see* FORT PIERRE.) In the summer of 1861 only one company manned the post, but by summer of 1862 more than half the men on duty in the Northwest Military Department were stationed here. Gen. Sully used the fort as a base for his expeditions against the Sioux in 1863, 1864, and 1865.

FORT SISSETON, Marshall County. Off State 25, in Fort Sisseton State Park. Established in 1864 by Maj John Clowney, commander of troops recruited in Wisconsin, the post was originally Fort Wadsworth, for Gen. James S. Wadsworth of New York who died in the battle of the Wilderness. It was renamed in 1876 for the local Sisseton tribe. Visitor center.

FORT SULLY, Hughes County. State 34. Site of Old Fort Sully has marker 4 miles east of Pierre on the highway. The post was established in 1863, named for Gen. Alfred Sully. Sully's troops wintered here after the battle of Whitestone Hill.

HURON, Beadle County. US 14.

Dakotaland Museum, W. 3rd St., on state fairgrounds, has Civil War memorabilia.

KEYSTONE, Pennington County, US 16A.

Parade of Presidents Museum, on highway, depicts U.S. presidents and other notable historical figures.

Rushmore-Borglum Story, southwest on Main St. (US 61A), exhibits many works of sculptor Gutzon Borglum, including a full-size reproduction of the Lincoln carving's eye.

MITCHELL, Davison County. IS 90.

Israel Greene Monument, Graceland Cemetery, Lakeshore Dr. A red stone marker is at the grave of Israel Greene who captured John Brown at Harpers Ferry in 1859. Greene was a lieutenant serving under Gen. Robert E. Lee. He came to Mitchell as a surveyor after the war.

MOUNT RUSHMORE NATIONAL ME-MORIAL, Pennington County. Twenty-five miles south of Rapid City off US 16. The world's largest sculpture is carved in solid granite. Lincoln's face measures 60 feet from chin to forehead; the nose is 18 feet long, the mouth 22 feet wide. Dedication of the Lincoln bust took place September 17, 1937, on the 150th anniversary of the signing of the Constitution. In 1939 Congress designated Rushmore as a national memorial. It is administered by the National Park Service; evening programs are given during the summer in the Rushmore amphitheater.

PIERRE, Hughes County. (Pronounced Peer.) US 14-83.

Cultural Heritage Center, 900 Governor's Dr., is an excellent new facility that houses the State Historical Society's archives, library, and a museum. The society also maintains museums in Brookings, Vermillion, and Madison, and a research center in Rapid City.

Robinson State Museum, 1500 E. Capitol Ave., has historical exhibits including Civil War uniforms and weapons.

SIOUX FALLS, Minnehaha County. IS 29, 90. In April 1862, Company A, Dakota Cavalry, was organized here. News of massacres in Minnesota brought orders from the governor for Sioux Falls settlers to leave the area. Soldiers were sent to escort civilians to stockades at Fort Randall and the Yankton Agency. The Indians burned the town after it was evacuated. The trail over which settlers fled to Yankton is marked.

Fort Dakota was established May 1, 1865, in a log and stone barracks on what is now Phillips Ave., between 7th and 8th streets.

Minnehaha County Courthouse, 200 W. 6th, has murals depicting early historical views of Sioux Falls.

Pettigrew Museum, N. Duluth and 8th St., has historical exhibits. When Indians burned the village they also threw the Smith press into the river and carried the type away with them, using the metal for inlaid decorations on pipes. Long after, the press was retrieved from the Big Sioux River; the platen is in the museum.

Sioux Falls College, 22nd St. and Prairie Ave. A marker on the campus points out the Yankton Trail used by the settlers fleeing town during the Indian scare of 1862.

Smith Printing Press, west end of 8th St. bridge, has marker for the site of the first newspaper in the Dakota Territory. The Smith printing press came to town from Dubuque, Iowa, by way of Lancaster, Wisconsin, and St. Paul, Minnesota. On July 2, 1859, the *Democrat* was first issued. Indians disrupted publication in 1862.

STURGIS, Meade County. IS 90, US 34. Alt. 14.

Black Hills National Cemetery, south on US 14 and State 79.

Old Fort Meade County Museum, State 34. Some original fort buildings remain from the 1878 post. The horse Comanche, sole survivor of the 7th Cavalry massacre at Little Big Horn, retired here. Fort cemetery nearby.

UNION COUNTY STATE PARK, Union County. US 77. This area was surveyed in 1861 at the request of President Lincoln, prior to the opening of Dakota Territory for homestead settlement. Mahlon Gore took out the first claim at 12:01 A.M. on January 1, 1863.

VERMILLION, Clay County. IS 29, US 15, 90.

University of South Dakota, Dakota St. on State 50. The W. H. Over Museum in the administration building has historical exhibits. Near the building is the site of the first permanent schoolhouse in South Dakota. It was built by soldiers of the U.S. Cavalry, Company A. A reproduction has been built of the old log building which also served as the town's first church, community hall, and voting place.

YANKTON, Yankton County. US 81.

Dakota Territory Capitol Building, Riverside Park. A replica of the original territorial Capitol of 1862. In 1861 the first meetings were held in two places: the upper house in William Trapp's home, the lower house in the Episcopal chapel.

Territorial Museum in Westside Park, Summit Ave., on Missouri River, was the home of William Tripp and served as the meeting place for the upper chamber of the Dakota territorial legislature. It has been restored.

TENNESSEE

Admitted to the Union on June 1, 1796, as the 16th state, Tennessee was the last to secede. In answer to Lincoln's call for two regiments for immediate service, Gov. Isham Greene Harris had responded that the state would not furnish a single man for purposes of coercion, "but 50,000, if necessary, for the defense of our rights and those of our southern brothers." Although eastern Tennessee had many Unionists, a special session of the legislature drew up a declaration of independence which was approved in election on June 8, 1861, thereby making the state a part of the Confederacy although the word *secession* was not used.

Many of the major battles of the war in the West were fought within the state, among them Fort Donelson, Shiloh (Pittsburgh Lndg.), Chattanooga, Stones River, Franklin, and Nashville. Tennessee sent 186,652 men to the Confederate army, 31,092 to the Union. Forrest's cavalry corps, surrendered as part of Gen. Richard Taylor's command on May 9, 1865, was the last Confederate unit to surrender east of the Mississippi.

After Union successes had established military control in the western part of the state, Andrew Johnson served as military governor. He was inaugurated as president on April 15, 1865. In June he declared the rebellion in Tennessee ended, but a congressional group opposed efforts to readmit the state. After stormy debate, on July 24, 1866, Tennessee, last to secede, was first to be readmitted to the Union.

ADAMS, Robertson County. US 41.

Camp Cheatham, at crossroads leading into Cedar Hill. Named for B. F. Cheatham, first camp commander of the Provisional Army, Independent State of Tennessee, in 1861. A number of Confederate units trained here.

ALEXANDRIA, DeKalb County. State 26, 53.

Morgan's Raid into Indiana and Ohio began at this point. Marker at highway junction.

ALTAMONT, Grundy County. State 56, 108.

Forrest Bivouac. Marker at highway junction for site where Forrest camped en route to Murfreesboro, July 10, 1862.

ANDREW JOHNSON NATIONAL HISTORICAL SITE, Greene County. US 11E, State 35, 70, 93, 107 in Greeneville. The 16-acre site administered by the National Park Service includes the tailor shop where Johnson worked, his restored home, and the national cemetery where he is buried. Andrew Johnson remained loyal to the Union, and some 13,000 "Andy Johnson Democrats" enlisted in the Union army. The visitor center, with monument office, tailor shop, and museum, is situated at the corner of Depot and College St., 1 block east of Main. The home is on Main St., 1 block south of Summer. Cemetery is at end of Monument Ave., 1 block south of Main.

ASHWOOD, Maury County. US 43.

Forrest and Capron Encounter, near St. John's Church. Forrest's cavalry, screening the advance of Stewart's Corps on Columbia, chased Capron's cavalry back to Columbia from this locality.

ATHENS, McMinn County. IS 75, US 11, State 30.

Grand Army of the Republic Memorial, southeast corner of courthouse square. Names of veterans are inscribed on monument with a quatrain composed by Dr. R. A. Brock.

Morgan Birthplace, US 11 near railroad overpass. Marker denotes site of house where John Tyler Morgan, Confederate brigadier, was born in 1824.

BEARDEN, Knox County. US 11, 70.

Reynolds Home, about 1½ miles west of Bearden. Maj. Robert Reynolds, veteran of the Mexican War, built the house in 1848. It served for a time as command post of Maj. Gen. James Longstreet, just before the siege of Knoxville. Confederate units camped in the adjoining fields.

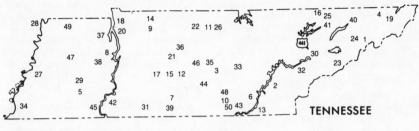

1 — Andrew Johnson
    Monument
2 — Athens
3 — Beechgrove
4 — Blountville
5 — Britton's Lane
6 — Brown's Ferry
7 — Buford
8 — Camden
9 — Camp Boone
10 — Camp Harris
11 — Castalian Springs
12 — Chapel Hill
13 — Chattanooga

14 — Clarksville
15 — Columbia
16 — Cumberland Gap
17 — Davis' Ford
18 — Dover
19 — Elizabethton
20 — Fort Donelson
21 — Franklin
22 — Gallatin
23 — Gatlinburg
24 — Greeneville
25 — Harrogate
26 — Hartsville
27 — Henning

28 — Island No. 10
29 — Jackson
30 — Knoxville
31 — Lawrenceburg
32 — Lenoir City
33 — McMinnville
34 — Memphis
35 — Murfreesboro
36 — Nashville
37 — Paris
38 — Parker's Crossroads
39 — Pulaski
40 — Rogersville
41 — Rutledge

42 — Savannah
43 — Sewanee
44 — Shelbyville
45 — Shiloh
46 — Stone's River
47 — Trenton
48 — Tullahoma
49 — Union City
50 — Winchester
(See chapter for other
sites and cities.)

BEECH GROVE MEMORIAL STATE PARK, Coffee County. US 41, State 64.

Confederate Cemetery has monument erected to unknown Confederate soldiers buried here, or elsewhere, who fell in the Beech Grove and Hoover's Gap engagements of June 24–26, 1863. The cemetery was established after the war.

Watterson Marker, about 40 yards south of post office on opposite side of road. Henry Watterson spent most of his boyhood in a house 100 feet west of here. He was a Confederate soldier, journalist, political leader, and founder of the *Louisville Courier-Journal.*

BEERSHEBA SPRINGS, Grundy County. State 56. Marker for Forrest's Murfreesboro raid of July 10, 1862.

BETHEL SPRINGS, McNairy County. US 45.

Hurst Nation Marker, on highway 5 miles west of town. Among the many Hursts, Unionists living in a Confederate area, was Col. Fielding Hurst, commanding the 6th Tennessee Cavalry. The unit skirmished and scouted for Federal commanders in the area.

BLOUNTVILLE, Sullivan County. IS 81, State 37.

Battle of Blountville Monument, courthouse yard, is dedicated to Sullivan County soldiers in the battle of September 22, 1863.

BOLIVAR, Hardeman County. US 64, State 18, 125.

Confederate Monument, in courthouse yard, in honor of Hardeman County soldiers.

Magnolia Manor had 4 Union generals as "guests" during the war. En route to Shiloh, Grant, Sherman, Logan, and McPherson stayed here. House has been restored and used as guest house.

The Pillars, Bills and Washington streets, restored 1826 home, was owned by Maj. John Bills in 1831. Among his guests: Davy Crockett, James Polk, his cousin Sam Houston, and Gen. Grant.

BRENTWOOD, Williamson County. IS 65, US 31.

Hood's Retreat, in roadside park. Marker for site where Hood reorganized his army for withdrawal after defeat at Nashville, December 16, 1864.

BRITTON'S LANE, Madison County. Off State 18.

Battle of Britton's Lane. Site of engagement that took place on September 1, 1862, is marked by a monument to the unknown soldiers who fell in the conflict; many are buried here. Descriptive marker at Medon, State 18 and Collins Rd.

BROWN'S FERRY, Hamilton County. US 27, at overpass south of junction with State 27.

At the ferry 1½ miles north, Hazen's brigade made an amphibious surprise attack on the west bank of the river. A pontoon bridge opened a river supply route to the Federal base at Bridgeport, Alabama, in October 1863. Turchin's brigade reinforced Hazen.

BROWNSVILLE, Haywood County. US 70, State 19.

Monument, in courthouse yard, to the Confederate dead and the faithful women of Haywood County, 1861–1865.

BUFORD, Giles County. US 31.

Hood's Retreat. Marker in roadside park. Here on December 24–25, 1864, Wilson's cavalry was checked by an engagement with the Army of Tennessee rear guard, composed of Forrest's cavalry and Walthall's infantry.

BULL'S GAP, Greene County. IS 81, US 11E. Marker on highway for scene of several heavy skirmishes; traces of fortifications remain.

CAMDEN, Benton County. US 70, State 69.

Courthouse Square. Marker in northeast corner tells of action at Johnsonville Landing, 8½ miles east, on November 4, 1864. Forrest's cavalry destroyed the Union naval base: four gunboats, 14 steamboats, 17 barges, and many tons of quartermaster stores.

Nathan Bedford Forrest State Historic Area, 8 miles northeast of town via Eva Rd. In November 1864 Forrest attacked and destroyed the Union supply and munitions depot at Old Johnsonville on the river, achieving the first defeat of a "naval force" by cavalry. A monument on Pilot Knob honors Forrest's victory. The Tennessee River Folklife Center now occupies the battle site and is worth a stop.

CAMP BOONE, Montgomery County. US 79, State 13. Marker on highway about 3½ miles south of Kentucky line. Site of staging and training camp for Kentuckians enlisting in the Confederate army. Gen. Simon Bolivar Buckner was an early camp commander. Both North and South violated Kentucky's neutrality. About the same time Camp Boone was established, the Union set up Camp Joe Holt near Jeffersonville, Indiana, just across the Kentucky border, to lure Kentucky recruits.

CAMP CHEATHAM, Robertson County. US 41. Marker at crossroads leading into Cedar Hill. Training camp established June 1861 was named for its first commander, Benjamin Franklin Cheatham.

CAMP HARRIS, Franklin County. State 16. Marker on highway at crossroads 1½ miles south of Estill Springs. Early training camp of the Confederacy. The area was heavily fortified to protect roads and bridges over Elk River. Gen. Braxton Bragg, commanding the Army of Tennessee in 1863, established his command post here for a brief time in June.

CAMP SMARTT, Warren County. State 108. Marker at road fork about 2 miles south of McMinnville. Staging and training area established in summer of 1861. Benjamin Hill was camp commander. Later in war camp was used chiefly as a center for Confederate conscripts.

CAMP TROUSDALE, Sumner County. US 31W, State 109. Marker on State 109, 3 miles south of junction with US 31W, State 41. Early training camp for Tennessee Confederate units.

CARTHAGE, Smith County. US 70, State 25.

United Daughters of the Confederacy Monument in courthouse yard.

CASTALIAN SPRINGS, Sumner County. State 25. Marker on highway for site where Col. John H. Morgan, with the 2nd Kentucky cavalry, met Brig. Gen. R. W. Johnson and a Union task force in a four-hour engagement. The Federals were defeated; the commander and about 175 men were captured.

Bate Birthplace. Marker on highway west of bridge in west part of town. William Brimage Bate was born here October 7, 1826. He was a major general in the Confederate army, later served as governor and U.S. senator.

CHAPEL HILL, Marshall County. US 31A, State 99.

Forrest Birthplace. Monument and plaque denote site of pioneer cabin where Nathan Bedford Forrest was born on July 13, 1821.

CHATTANOOGA, Hamilton County. IS 24, 59, 75.

Chattanooga Battlefields. Visitors are urged to go first to Point Park. Highways 41, 64, 72, and 11 combine at outskirts of city. Turn off on Scenic Highway at base of Lookout Mountain. Buses from the city connect with the Lookout Mountain Incline Railway which takes passengers within a short distance of park entrance. A panoramic view of the battlefields is available from terrace of Adolph S. Ochs Observatory and Museum. Markers identify important landmarks. A National Park Service attendant is on hand to assist visitors. *The Chickamauga and Chattanooga National Mil-*

itary Park is the oldest and largest of military park areas. It includes Chickamauga Battlefield in Georgia, Point Park and Lookout Mountain Battlefield, and reservations on Missionary Ridge, Orchard Knob, and Signal Point. Chickamauga visitor center is at the north entrance to battlefield on US 27. Free information is available for self-guided tours; trained historians are on duty. Missionary Ridge, so-called because it was the westernmost point Christian missionaries were allowed to advance into Cherokee Indian territory, is traversed by Crest Drive, which is well marked with informative tablets. Orchard Knob, between Mc-Callie Ave. and East 3rd St., is a seven-acre reservation on the site where Gen. Grant had his field headquarters. Signal Mountain, southernmost point on Walden's Ridge, 9 miles north on State 127, was used by the Indians as a signaling point and then by the Confederates. The road leading to Signal Point may be reached via Cherokee Blvd.

Baird Headquarters, south side of W. 9th St., between E. Terrace and Cedar St. A post marks site of quarters occupied by Brig. Gen. Absalom Baird, commanding 14th Army Corps.

Bragg's Headquarters, 407 E. Fifth St. Gen. Braxton Bragg stayed here in 1862.

Brannan Headquarters, 302 Walnut St. Brig. Gen. John M. Brannan was chief of artillery, Army of the Cumberland.

Breckinridge Headquarters, 415 Poplar St. Maj. Gen. John C. Breckinridge commanded a Confederate division.

Bridge Burners, marker on State 58 near bridge over Chickamauga Creek, denotes site where Unionists burned two railroad bridges, November 9, 1861.

Cameron Hill, marker on freeway at Olgiatti Bridge. Confederates fortified the hill; when Federals took over, they built a reservoir along its side.

Chattanooga Daily Rebel, 523 Market St. Franc M. Paul established a newspaper for the Confederate armies here on August 2, 1862. It was published in three states, five towns, and in a boxcar traveling with the army. Last issued at Selma, Alabama, April 11, 1865.

College Hospital, northeast corner W. 11th and Cedar St. A college building here was used to care for 100 wounded soldiers.

Confederama, 3742 Tennessee Ave., re-creates the battles with 6,000 miniature soldiers; 650 flashing lights show battle movements.

Confederate Cemetery, E. 3rd to E. 5th St., between Lansing and Palmetto. Commem-orative tablets line the walks. There is another Confederate cemetery on US 11 and 64 at Silverdale, about 10 miles northeast of the city. (*See* SILVERDALE.)

Cravens House, on Lookout Mountain, is the only remaining structure of the Civil War period on the battlefield. It has been restored.

Crutchfield House, W. 9th St. between Broad and Chestnut. The building which stood here in 1861 was used as a military hospital during the war. Bronze tablets are in the 9th St. entrance of Read House.

Fort Milhalotzy, 221 Boynton Terr., on Cameron Hill.

Fort Phelps, 1706 Read Ave.

Fort Sheridan, 1219 E. Terrace. Site marked by a shell pyramid.

Fort Wood, site marked by standpipe of City Water company.

Garfield's Headquarters, northeast corner of 4th and Walnut St. Gen. James A. Garfield was chief of staff to Gen. Rosecrans. Gen. Joseph J. Reynolds, Thomas's chief of staff, also was quartered here.

Grant's House, 110 E. 1st St. Grant and later Gen. Sherman had headquarters here.

Hill's Headquarters, 309 W. 6th St. A post marks the site of quarters for Lt. Gen. Daniel H. Hill of the Confederate command; later the site was used by Maj. Gen. John M. Palmer, commanding the 14th Army Corps, Army of the Cumberland.

Incline Railway, at foot of Lookout Mountain, 3 blocks south of US 11, 41, 64, and 72. The Cloud High Station at the top is 2 blocks from Point Park.

Lookout Mountain Museum, near entrance to Point Park. Dramatic displays of Civil War weapons and diorama.

National Cemetery, main entrance at south end of National Ave. About one-third of the graves are unknown dead from Chickamauga and Missionary Ridge. The Andrew's Raiders are buried beneath a monument bearing a re-production of the captured locomotive, the General. For about three months after the battle of Chickamauga, both Union and Confederate dead were buried in trenches at the battlefield. Union soldiers were reburied here; Confederates were reburied at Marietta, Georgia.

Sherman's Hideout, Hickson Pike near junction with Ozark Rd. Concealed by the hills, Gen. Sherman moved four divisions across the Tennessee River on November 24, 1863, preparatory to the attack on Missionary Ridge. Confederates mistakenly thought he had gone to Knoxville to relieve Burnside.

Stewart Monument, in yard of county courthouse, was erected by the United Daughters of the Confederacy in honor of Lt. Gen. Alexander Peter Stewart.

Tennessee Valley Railroad Museum, 4119 Cromwell Rd. A 6-mile train trip passes through a historic Civil War tunnel. Passengers can also board at 2200 N. Chamberlain Ave.

10th Ohio Volunteer Infantry Camp, 654 Houston St., was site where the first shell from Lookout Mountain exploded.

Wagner Headquarters, 407 E. 5th St. A post marks the site where Brig. Gen. George D. Wagner lodged when Union troops first occupied the city.

Wheeler Headquarters, 515 Douglas St. Maj. Gen. Joseph Wheeler commanded the Confederate cavalry corps in 1863.

Wood Headquarters, 504 Vine St. Brig. Gen. Thomas J. Wood commanded the 3rd and 4th Federal Army Corps.

CHESTERFIELD, Henderson County. State 20.

Forrest's Raid. Marker on highway west of town. Along Beech River to the south, Forrest and Col. Robert G. Ingersoll engaged in a running fight which ended 4 miles from Jackson. Forrest captured most of the Federal forces, including its commander, December 18, 1862.

CHRISTIANA, Rutherford County. US 241.

Army of the Cumberland marker on highway. McCook's Corps was stopped at Liberty Gap, 6 miles southeast, by the 5th and 15th Arkansas Infantry of Liddell's Brigade, later reinforced by Cleburne's Division, June 24–26, 1863.

CLARKSVILLE, Montogomery County. US 41A, 79, State 12.

County Historical Museum, 200 S. Second St., has Civil War displays.

Don E. Pratt Museum, 9 miles north of US 41A in Fort Campbell, depicts the history of the U.S. Army from the Civil War on.

Emerald Hill, north suburbs, was the home of Gustavus Adophus Henry, who represented Tennessee in the Confederate senate.

Greenwood Cemetery has a Confederate monument erected by United Confederate Veterans and a committee of other Montgomery County citizens.

Kennedy and Glenn's Bank. Marker on wall of Northern Bank of Tennessee. Bank funds and securities were smuggled to England for safekeeping, returned at war's end.

Riverview Cemetery has monument to unknown Confederate soldiers buried here.

CLEVELAND, Bradley County. US 11, 64, State 60.

Confederate Monument, junction of N. Ocoee and Broad St.

Fort Hill Cemetery has monument to "The Boys in Blue in the War of 1861–1865, Who Lived in Bradley County."

CLIFTON, Wayne County. State 114, 8 miles south of US 64.

Forrest's Raid, marker at highway junction. Forrest crossed the river at Clifton with 1,800 cavalrymen and four guns, led a 200-mile raid into West Tennessee, and recrossed on January 1, 1863, having delayed Grant's Vicksburg campaign, torn up three railroads, and taken more prisoners than he had soldiers.

Hood's Command Post, on US 31, 3 miles south of town. Lt. Gen. Hood occupied house November 24, 1864. Forrest was here December 20; the next day, Maj. Gen. Schofield, pursuing Hood and Forrest, occupied the house.

COLUMBIA, Maury County. US 31, 43, and State 7.

The Athenaeum, 808 Athenaeum St., served as headquarters for Union generals J. S. Negley and Schofield.

Hood and Schofield Marker, south edge of town. Gen. Schofield built Union entrenchments here November 24, 1864. Hood attacked the position two days later while the rest of the Army of Tennessee crossed Duck River at Davis's Ford, 3 miles east, planning to cut Schofield off at Spring Hill.

Rose Hill Cemetery has monument to "Our Fallen Heroes" with a handsomely mustachioed soldier standing at funeral "parade rest," in Confederate Square.

St. John's Episcopal Church, 1842, is said to be the state's only remaining plantation church. One of the builders was George Polk, owner of *Rattle and Snap,* a restored antebellum mansion. This and many other fine homes can be visited on tour.

Zion Presbyterian Church has burials from three early wars, including 47 Civil War soldiers, in the churchyard.

COOL SPRING CHURCH, Giles County. State 11.

Forrest-Wilson Marker on highway denotes site where Forrest stopped the Union advance on December 26, 1864.

CORRAL ROAD, Hamilton County. Route 8. Marker at road junction about ½ mile from Sequatchie County line. In fall of 1863, when Federal signal station was located at Signal Point, the draft stock of troops was kept in two corrals about 4 miles northeast.

COVINGTON, Tipton County. US 51, State 54.
Confederate Monument, in Courthouse Square. The variety of headgear on Tennessee Confederate statuary is worth noting. Brims on all war bonnets except forage caps seem to have been worn to suit the individual soldier.

COWAN, Franklin County. US 64.
Site of Turney Home, marker on highway west of town. The home of Peter Turney was burned by Federals in 1863 in reprisal for his secessionist activities. He was organizer and commander of the 1st Tennessee Infantry, later became governor.

CRONANVILLE, Lake County. Route 22.
Confederate Cemetery contains about 75 who were killed during the siege and capture of Madrid Bend and Island No. 10.

CUMBERLAND CITY, Stewart County. State 149. Marker at southwest edge of town is descriptive of Gen. Hylan B. Lyon's raid, December 9, 1864.

CUMBERLAND FURNACE, Dickson County. State 48.
Cumberland Iron Works, marker on highway. A half-mile north is the site of the first iron works west of the Alleghenies. It was operated by A. W. Van Leer during the war.

CUMBERLAND GAP NATIONAL HISTORIC PARK, Claiborne County. US 25E. Marker ½ mile south of railroad underpass. The national historical park is in Virginia, Tennessee, and Kentucky. A strategic point during the war, the gap changed hands several times. Union forces under Gen. Ambrose E. Burnside captured the area in September 1863. A visitor center has museum and information desk.

DANDRIDGE, Jefferson County. IS 40, US 25W, 70.
Battle of Dandridge. Marker in courthouse yard for action of December 24, 1863.

DAVIS'S FORD, Maury County. State 50. Marker ½ mile from Fountain Creek, at intersection of county road. About 1½ miles northeast, the Army of Tennessee, except for Lee's Corps and most of the artillery, crossed here on a pontoon bridge, November 25, 1864. Hood was attempting to intercept and destroy Schofield's force before it could unite at Nashville with Thomas.

DOVER, Stewart County. US 79, State 49.
Surrender House, State 49, south of courthouse. On February 16, 1862, Brig. Gen. Simon B. Buckner surrendered Fort Donelson to Brig. Gen. Grant. Brig. Gen. Floyd, having been Buchanan's Secretary of War, feared execution as a traitor, passed command to Brig. Gen. Pillow who passed it to Buckner. Forrest, refusing to surrender, took his cavalry out through backwaters. Buckner found his old friend Grant friendly enough once the firing had stopped. The same man whose terms were "unconditional surrender" offered the Southerner money from his own pocket in case Buckner as a war prisoner might be in need of funds. Now part of Fort Donelson National Battlefield, the Dover Hotel has been restored and is open to the public during the summer.

DRESDEN, Weakley County. State 54, 89.
Confederate Monument, in Courthouse Square, commemorates Weakley County soldiers.

DYER, Gibson County. US 45W, State 5.
Forrest Raid Marker for site where a cavalry detachment captured Co. K, 119th Illinois Infantry.

DYERSBURG, Dyer County. IS 155, US 51, State 20.
Confederate Monument, in courthouse square, erected by United Confederate Veterans, dedicated 1905.

ELIZABETHTON, Carter County. State 91.
Andrew Johnson Marker, north of bridge over Watauga River. About 1 mile southwest, Andrew Johnson died at the home of a daughter, Mary Johnson Stover, in 1875.
Green Hill Cemetery, outskirts of Elizabethton at junction with road leading to ball park. The Tipton family cemetery has soldiers of all American wars, from the Revolution to World War I, buried here.

ELKTON, Giles County. US 31.
Brown Birthplace. Marker north of town. John Calvin Brown was born here June 1, 1827. He commanded a division in the Confederate army at the war's end. He became governor in the 1870s.

ERWIN, Unicoi County. US 19W, 23, State 107.
Bell Cemetery, State 107, has graves of nine Unionists killed while trying to escape to Kentucky, November 1863.
Confederate Monument, in courthouse yard, erected by the United Daughters of the Confederacy, also honors World War I soldiers.

FAIRFIELD, Bedford County. State 64.
Hardee's Campsite. Marker on highway denotes area where Hardee's corps camped from January to June 1863.

FARMINGTON, Marshall County. US 31A, State 64.
Confederate Cemetery. Inscription near gate commemorates members of Maj. Gen. Wheeler's cavalry who fell at this site, October 7, 1863.

FAYETTEVILLE, Lincoln County. US 64, State 50.
Courthouse Square has three Confederate monuments.

FORT DONELSON NATIONAL BATTLEFIELD, Stewart County. US 79, State 49. Descriptive markers on both highways.
Visitor Center has exhibits and slide show describing the campaign of February 1862, which was Grant's first major victory of the war, opening a path into the Confederacy by way of the Cumberland and Tennessee rivers. Roads and footpaths are well marked. Earthworks are well preserved. There is a Confederate monument, erected by the United Daughters of the Confederacy, dedicated June 3, 1933, near earthworks on the west. The National Cemetery was established in 1867. Among the 655 Federal dead, 512 were unknown; they were taken from battlefield graves and reburied in the cemetery.

FORT HENRY, Stewart County. US 79, State 76. Marker on US 79 about 2 miles east of bridge over Tennessee River. On February 6, 1862, the fort was surrendered by Brig. Gen. Lloyd Tilghman to the naval task force led by Flag Officer A. H. Foote.

FRANKLIN, Williamson County. IS 65, US 31, 431. The battle of Franklin, November 30, 1864, was one of the bloodiest of the war. Five Confederate generals were lost, six others wounded (one mortally), and one captured. Lost were Gens. Adams, Carter, Cleburne, Gist, Granbury, and Strahl. Hood's frontal attack was repulsed; Schofield withdrew to Nashville during the night.
Carnton Mansion, end of Carnton Lane, off US 431, is being restored over a period of 20 years; visitors can see progress. During the battle of November 30, 1864, Carnton was on the Confederate rear lines. Before the smoke of the intense conflict cleared away, the bodies of four fallen C.S.A. generals lay on the back porch.
Carter House, 1140 Columbia Ave. The command post of Union Maj. Gen. Jacob D. Cox was located here. The Carter family had three sons in the Confederate army. The youngest, Capt. Theodoric (Tod) Carter, saw his home for the first time in three years when he reached a hill above Franklin with Hood's army. Using field glasses he could see the house was about 50 yards beyond Federal lines; after the battle he was found mortally wounded near the home. House is now a museum, restored with outbuildings and video presentation.
Confederate Cemetery, about 1½ miles south of town on US 431. Col. John McGavock, owner of Carnton, donated the land and supervised the burial here of 1,496 Confederates after the war. The bodies of five generals were brought to the house but interred elsewhere. Other Confederates were later buried here, among them Brig. Gen. Johnston K. Duncan.
Confederate Monument, in public square, erected by United Daughters of the Confederacy, unveiled November 30, 1899.
Fort Granger. Union breastworks were on hills to the east. The largest was named for Gen. Gordon Granger; at the battle of November 30, 1864, it contained 8,500 men and 24 pieces of artillery.
Harpeth Academy, south of north city limits. Marker on US 431. Federal forces burned the boys' school in 1863.
Harrison House, 3½ miles south of town on US 31. On September 2, 1864, Confederate Brig. Gen. John H. Kelly was brought here, having been mortally wounded in an engagement with Union troops under Brig. Gen. James D. Brownlow. Kelly was buried in the garden; after the war he was reinterred in Mobile. In this house, Gen. Hood held his last staff conference before the battle of Franklin. Wounded Brig. Gen. John C. Carter was brought here, died December 10, 1864, and was buried in Columbia.
Hood's Retreat. The line of retreat in November and December 1864 is well marked at intervals along US 31 to Pulaski, then along State 11 to Alabama line.
Maury's Home. Marker on US 431, north edge of Franklin. About 1½ miles west was the home of Matthew Fontaine Maury, officer in the U.S. Navy, later in the Confederate navy.
St. Paul's Episcopal Church was used as barracks and hospital and so damaged it had to be rebuilt in 1869.
Winstead's Hill, 2 miles south on US 31. Site of Hood's command and observation post, November 30, 1864. Battle map shows major action.

GAINESBORO, Jackson County. State 53, 56.

Gillem Memorial, on public square. Alvan Cullen Gillem, born nearby on July 29, 1830, was graduated from West Point in 1851, during the war served as Union provost marshal of Nashville, then as adjutant general of Tennessee. As major general, Gillem commanded the expedition that killed John H. Morgan at Greeneville.

GALLATIN, Sumner County. US 31E, State 25.

Confederate Monument, on lawn of Trousdale mansion, erected by United Daughters of the Confederacy, dedicated September 19, 1903.

Morgan's Cavalry. Marker on US 31 near junction with State 25. On August 12, 1862, Col. John H. Morgan, with the 2nd Kentucky Cavalry, captured a Federal garrison of 200 men under Col. Boone. According to the *Atlanta Confederacy,* Morgan had a lively time at Gallatin earlier that year: on Sunday, March 16, Morgan and 40 men had captured a group of Union men, stored them in the guardhouse, then, dressed in borrowed blue uniforms, had taken the telegraph office at the depot and awaited the Bowling Green train. "In due time the train came thundering in. Capt. Morgan at once seized it, and taking five Union officers who were passengers and the engineer of the train prisoners, he burned to cinders all of the cars, with their contents, and then filling the locomotive with turpentine, shut down all the valves, and started it toward Nashville. Before it had run eight hundred yards, the accumulation of steam caused it to explode, shivering it into a thousand atoms."

GATLINBURG, Sevier County. US 441.

American Historical Wax Museum, 544 Parkway, devoted to Tennessee history.

Reagan Birthplace. Marker on highway. John H. Reagan was born near here October 18, 1818. He was postmaster general of the Confederacy and for a time acting secretary of the Confederate treasury.

GREENEVILLE, Greene County. US 11E, 411, State 70. In 1861, Unionists of the area held a convention here which proposed that East Tennessee be made a separate state.

Andrew Johnson Home, W. Main St. Johnson completed the house in 1851. (*See* ANDREW JOHNSON NATIONAL HISTORIC SITE.)

Dickson-Williams Home, downtown, has been restored. It is the mansion where John

Hunt Morgan's body was laid out after he was killed almost outside the door.

Johnson Tailor Shop, northwest corner of Depot and College St. The frame structure is now enclosed in a brick building. In the late 1820s, Johnson was the only tailor in Greeneville. He married Eliza McCardle in 1827.

Morgan Monument, on courthouse lawn. Gen. Morgan was betrayed by Union sympathizers who reported his whereabouts to Gen. Gillem. He was shot September 4, 1864, by Pvt. Andrew G. Campbell of the 13th Tennessee Cavalry.

Union Monument, in courthouse yard, erected by the G.A.R. to the memory of Greene County Union soldiers.

HARROGATE, Claiborne County. US 25E.

Lincoln Memorial University has the largest collection of Lincolniana in the South. The institution was founded in 1897 as a memorial to Abraham Lincoln. There are exhibits and an extensive library in Duke Hall.

HARTSVILLE, Trousdale County. State 10, 25.

"Hartsville Races" Marker, on State 10, west edge of town. Morgan's cavalry, in a running fight, killed, wounded, or captured 2,200 Federals of DuMont's Brigade, December 7, 1863.

HENDERSON, Chester County. State 100.

Cox's Raid, marker at junction of State 5, 100. Confederates under Maj. N. N. Cox made a successful attack here on October 25, 1862.

HENNING, Lauderdale County. US 51.

Fort Pillow State Historic Area, State 207, off State 87, 18 miles west of town. In 1862, Federal forces captured the fort, 18 miles west; on April 12, 1864, Forrest retook the fort, which was then held by 262 black and 295 white troops. A Committee on the Conduct of the War concluded that the Confederates were guilty of atrocities committed after the fort had surrendered; Southerners maintained that the House report was Northern propaganda, that the Federal loss (231 killed and 100 seriously wounded) was the result of the troops having refused to surrender. Breastworks and remains of large fort at site. Visitor center.

HERMITAGE, Davidson County. US 70.

Confederate Cemetery has graves of soldiers who died in the Tennessee Confederate soldiers' home.

HICKERSON, Coffee County. State 55.

The Confederate massacre of Federal troops at Fort Pillow.

Marker on highway near town denotes site of Bobo's Crossroads where Confederate Col. James Starnes was killed in a cavalry skirmish, June 30, 1863.

HUMBOLDT, Gibson County. US 45W.
Forrest's Raid. Marker on highway south of town. Starnes's detachment captured both railroads and burned supplies and munitions on December 20, 1862, while Forrest passed northward and took Trenton.
Gibson County Confederate Monument, in Bailey Park. Erected by the United Daughters of the Confederacy, dedicated in 1912.

HUNTINGDON, Carroll County. US 70.
Oak Hill Cemetery has graves of soldiers from all American wars; 38 from the Civil War.

ISLAND NO. 10, Lake County. State 78. Markers for the capture of the island on April 8, 1862, by Federal forces under the command of Maj. Gen. John Pope, are on State 22 and 78 and in courthouse yard at Tiptonville.

JACKSON, Madison County. IS 40, US 45, 70.
Camp Beauregard, US 70, State 20, was activated in May 1861 under Confederate Col. W. H. Stephens.

Confederate Monument, in courthouse yard. Dedicated in 1884.
Grant's Command Post, marker on building at 512 E. Main St. Grant occupied the home of James S. Lyon at this site in the weeks preceding the battle of Shiloh.
Riverside Cemetery, Bolivar St., has Confederate graves.

JASPER, Marion County. Off IS 24, US 41, 64.
Turney Birthplace, west of Lankester Hotel. Peter Turney, born here September 27, 1827, raised and commanded the 1st Tennessee Infantry. He was wounded at Fredericksburg, promoted to brigade command, and after the war served on the state supreme court and as governor.

JOHNSON CITY, Washington County. 11E, 19W, 23
Confederate Training Campsite, on Lamont St. at intersection with Tennessee St. Monument for 1861 camp erected by United Daughters of the Confederacy, 1904.
Tipton-Haynes Historical Site, Erwin Hwy., US 19W, south of town. Restored home built by the father of Landor Carter Haynes, C.S.A. senator. Visitor center and museum.

KENTON, Obion County. US 45W.

Forrest's Raid Marker, on highway south of town. A cavalry detachment captured a Federal garrison of 250 men, including Col. T. J. Kinney, 122nd Illinois Infantry, on December 21, 1862.

KNOXVILLE, Knox County. IS 40, US 11, 25W, 70. Confederates withdrew from Knoxville in August 1863; soon after, the town was occupied by Union forces led by Gen. Burnside. Confederates under Longstreet began a siege of Knoxville on November 19. Having heard that Sherman was en route to relieve Burnside, Longstreet attacked Fort Sanders on November 29 but was repulsed with heavy loss to troops and to the town. Marker for east side of Federal lines is on Tennessee River side of Riverside Dr. and McCammon Ave., west end of lines, on Neyland Dr. west of Second Creek.

Battery Wiltsie, Vine Ave. between Market and Walnut St. Marker for Federal earthworks and defense line.

Brownlow Home, Mulvaney Ave. across from City Auditorium. Marker for homesite of Unionist editor W. G. Brownlow.

Cherokee Heights, marker on Neyland Drive. The heights across the river were seized by Longstreet on November 23, 1863, in order to bombard Federal Fort Sanders, 2,400 yards north. Poor powder made firing at such range ineffectual.

Civil War Hospital, marker on City Hall lawn. Building was used as a Confederate hospital until September 1863; thereafter, it was used by Union troops.

Confederate Cemetery, Bethel Ave. Descriptive marker at gate.

Confederate Memorial Hall, formerly Bleak House, 3148 Kingston Pike. Headquarters for Longstreet and McLaws during the siege of Knoxville. From the tower a Southern sharpshooter fatally wounded Brig. Gen. W. P. Sanders. House contains period furnishings and historical displays.

Confederate Monument, 17th and Laurel Ave., erected by United Daughters of the Confederacy in memory of the four brigades that made a bayonet charge on Fort Sanders, November 29, 1863.

Fort Byington, at main entrance to University of Tennessee, Cumberland Ave., west of stop light. "The Hill" was held by a battery of Federal cannon and an infantry brigade during the siege. Entrenchments ran across the west and south slopes of the hill, connecting Fort Sanders and Second Creek.

Fort Dickerson and Fort Stanley, on Chapman Highway south of Tennessee River.

Marker on highway at Woodbine Ave. Forts Dickerson to the west and Stanley to the east were the center two of four fortified heights held by the Union during the siege. Maj. Gen. Joe Wheeler, coming from Maryville, made an unsuccessful attempt to seize the hills on November 15–16, 1863. A Fort Dickerson descriptive marker is on Fort Dickerson Hill, off State 71.

Fort Sanders, on campus of University of Tennessee, marker on lawn of Sophronia Strong Hall. The fort was located on a ridge 2 blocks north. Longstreet made an unsuccessful assault at dawn on November 29, 1863.

Fort Huntingdon Smith, Payne Ave. Marker on lawn of Green School denotes site of Federal earthworks.

Knoxville College, 1400 College St., occupies the site where Confederates under Gen. Longstreet camped during the siege.

National and Old Gray Cemeteries, Broadway between Tyson and Cooper St. National Cemetery was founded in 1863 for Union soldiers killed in East Tennessee. Unionist editor W. G. ("Parson") Brownlow is buried in Old Gray.

Second Presbyterian Church, Kingston Pike. On November 18, 1863, Brig. Gen. Sanders, U.S.A., was fatally wounded on the church lawn, died the following day.

Union Headquarters, First Tennessee Bank Building, has plaque denoting the site of J. H. Crozier home where Maj. Gen. Ambrose Burnside made his headquarters during the siege.

Union Pontoon Bridge, marker at end of Central Ave. in Chisholm Tavern Park. The Union pontoon bridge here enabled Burnside to hold the heights on the south side of the river; they were, from left to right, Sevierville Hill, Fort Stanley, Fort Dickerson, and Fort Higley.

LA GRANGE, Fayette County. State 57. Marker for Grierson's Raid, April 17, 1863.

A major Union base for most of the war, the town also served as background for the John Wayne–William Holden movie *The Horse Soldiers,* about Grierson's raid. Many old homes remain and are considered antebellum treasures. Pilgrimages are held every few years; meanwhile, friendly and proud homeowners have been known to invite shutter-snappers indoors.

LA VERGNE, Rutherford County, Off IS 24, US 41, 70S. Marker here mentions Wheeler's ride around Rosecrans, December 30–31, 1862. Others are on US 241 and 41A.

LAWRENCEBURG, Lawrence County. US 43.

Army of Tennessee Marker, at roadside park, 5 miles north of town. Forrest's cavalry moved north past this point on November 19, 1864; Stewart's Corps passed here on November 22, following Hood's plan to concentrate at Columbia. There is a marker on US 64, 10 miles west of town, near Red Hill, denoting route Lt. Gen. Stephen D. Lee took toward the concentration point at Columbia. Hood hoped to destroy Schofield's force before it could unite with Thomas at Nashville.

LEBANON, Wilson County. IS 40, US 70A, 231.

Cedar Grove Cemetery. A monument erected in 1899 by United Daughters of the Confederacy and United Confederate Veterans has a statistical inscription which, in part, reads: THE CONFEDERACY WITHOUT AN ARMY, NAVY OR GOVERNMENT, 600,000 VOLUNTEERS SUSTAINED THE ASSAULT OF 2,778,304 MEN, SUPPORTED BY THE STRONGEST GOVERNMENT IN THE WORLD FOR FOUR YEARS. ITS DESTRUCTION RENDERED NECESSARY A PUBLIC DEBT OF $2,708,393,885, THE SACRIFICE OF 349,944 LIVES AND OF 1,366,443 PRISONERS. Also in the cemetery is a monument to Gen. Robert Hatton, who was killed while leading his brigade in the battle of Seven Pines, Virginia.

Confederate Monument, in public square, was dedicated May 20, 1912.

LENOIR CITY, Loudon County. Off IS 75, US 11.

Battle of Lenoir's Station, marker on highway in midtown. Longstreet attacked Burnside here on November 15, 1863. Burnside retreated next morning to Campbell's Station, now Farragut.

LEWISBURG, Marshall County. US 31A, State 50.

Confederate Monument, in courthouse yard, dedicated 1904.

MADISONVILLE, Monroe County. US 411.

Vaughn Birthplace. Marker on highway south of junction with Tellico. St. John Crawford Vaughn was born in a house at this site on February 21, 1824. He was captured at Vicksburg on July 4, 1863; after exchange he commanded the cavalry which escorted Jefferson Davis on his flight from Richmond.

MANCHESTER, Coffee County. IS 24, US 41. Marker on highway north of bridge.

Rosecrans concentrated his army here in June 1863 preparatory to moving against Chattanooga.

MARYVILLE, Blount County. US 129.

Sam Houston Schoolhouse, 6 miles north off State 33, where Houston taught early in the century has been restored. Visitor center.

Sherman's Camp. Marker in yard of municipal building denotes area where Sherman's troops camped en route to relieve Burnside at Knoxville in December 1863.

McKENZIE, Carroll County. US 79.

Forrest Raid. Marker south of town. Forrest's brigade captured a 100-man garrison here on December 24, 1862. The men spent Christmas Eve destroying railroad trestles and bridges.

McMINNVILLE, Warren County. US 70S, State 8.

Confederate Monument, in courthouse square, in memory of 16th Tennessee Infantry Regiment Confederates killed in battle, was erected by their colonel, John H. Savage, in 1904.

Forrest Bivouac, marker on State 1, on east approach to town. Cavalry units, combined to make a brigade about 1,400 strong, camped here on July 11, 1862, along Mud Creek.

Morgan's Headquarters, marker in front of Central Church of Christ. Morgan brought his bride, the former Martha Ready of Murfreesboro, to the house of Dr. W. C. Armstrong, which stood here. The house served as command post until the summer of 1863.

MEMPHIS, Shelby County. IS 40, 55, US 51, 61, 64.

Civil War Capitol, northeast corner, 2nd St. and Madison Ave. After Nashville fell, Gov. Isham Harris convened the legislature at this site, February to March 1862. The wartime post office stood at the northeast corner, 3rd and Jefferson Ave. When Memphis surrendered to Union forces, June 5, 1862, the only citizen resistance was a shot fired here, aimed at soldiers raising the Union flag.

Confederate Park, Front St., has tablet with Confederate history of Memphis. There is also a monument to Capt. J. Harvey Mathes.

Court Square, N. Main St. between Jefferson and Court Ave., has marker denoting site of the Federal prison which was located in the Irving Block from 1862 to 1865. Women as well as men were imprisoned; conditions were so wretched, Lincoln ordered an investigation and later abolished the institution.

Elmwood Cemetery, northeast corner of

Walker Ave. and Neptune St., was the official burial ground for Confederate dead.

First Methodist Church, 2nd Ave. and Poplar St. During Federal occupation of the city, a minister was detailed by the Union commander to occupy the pulpit.

Forrest's Artillery Positions, 1327 Mississippi Blvd. A section of artillery under Lt. Sale was located here on August 21, 1864.

Forrest Homes. An early home stood on the south side of Adams Ave., between 2nd and 3rd St. Forrest was a Memphis alderman before the war; he enlisted June 14, 1861. In his brother's house (Col. Jesse Forrest) at 693 Union Ave., the general died on October 27, 1877.

Forrest Park. An equestrian statue is at the gravesite of Gen. Forrest and his wife, Mary.

Fort Pickering, Crump Blvd. west of intersection with Pennsylvania Ave. Federal defenses were extensive at this site.

Freedman School, northeast corner S. Main and Beale Street. The first school for freed blacks, it opened early in a barracks on government order. By 1865 there were nine schools. All were burned in a May 1866 riot and reopened in 1868–69.

Gayoso Hotel, Front St. between McCall and Gayoso Ave. Marker on Front St. states that Capt. William H. Forrest, raiding under his famous brother at dawn on August 21, 1864, rode into the lobby searching for Maj. Gen. Stephen A. Hurlbut, quartered in the hotel but sleeping elsewhere. Plaque in hotel lobby, erected by the Confederate Dames, has a slightly different version of the early morning doings: A DETACHMENT . . . RODE INTO THE ROTUNDA OF THE ORIGINAL GAYOSO HOTEL, AND SOUGHT TO CAPTURE THE FEDERAL COMMANDER, BUT SAID GENERAL, AND HIS BROTHER OFFICERS, FLED IN THEIR NIGHT CLOTHES AND ESCAPED. A bit of poetry concludes the message:

Never was cause more holy,
Than defending home and right;
Never were soldiers braver
Than those on duty that night.

Jefferson Davis House, 129 Court Ave. Tablet marks site where Davis lived from 1867 to 1875.

Memphis Daily Appeal. Marker on wall of Union Planters' National Bank on Madison Ave., west of intersection with Main St. From here the press and type of the Appeal were loaded on a freight car, June 6, 1862, the day before Memphis was occupied by Federal forces. Co-editors Benjamin Franklin Dill and John McClanahan took the plant to Grenada, Mississippi, and began republishing under the

Memphis masthead. Later the newspaper moved to Jackson, and further south, keeping ahead of Sherman's troops. Union men called it a "moving Appeal." The last stop was Columbus, Georgia, where three editions were issued before the Federals smashed the boiler and scattered type. On November 5, 1865, the newspaper was back in business in Memphis.

Memphis Museum, Tilton Rd. at Central Ave. Museum is owned by the city and operated by the Memphis Park Commission. Document room contains letters, newspapers, pictures, and documents of the Civil War period.

Mud Island, in Mississippi River, is easily reached by monorail, from Front St. It displays part of a Union gunboat and other Civil War items; the museum is well worth a visit to learn more about the Mississippi of yesterday and today.

National Cemetery, on Raleigh Rd., has monument with reclining figure erected by the state of Illinois in 1928 to Illinois soldiers of 1861–1865.

The Pink Palace, 3050 Central Ave., is an excellent museum (at a cost of $5.5 million) that has a fine Civil War section.

Sherman's Headquarters, Tennessee St. between Butler and Nettleton. Sherman stayed here after becoming commandant in July 1862 of nearby Fort Pickering.

Washburn's Quarters, 206 Union Ave. Marker here tells of Maj. Gen. C. C. Washburn escaping from the back door in his night clothes on the morning of Forrest's dawn raid. His uniform and sword, seized by raiders under Lt. Col. Jesse Forrest, were returned next day under a flag of truce.

MINOR HILL, Giles County. State 11.

Sam Davis Monument, erected by the Tennessee Historical Commission, dedicated 1925, on site where Sam Davis, Confederate courier, was captured by Union troops in November 1863. (Also see SMYRNA.)

MOUNT PLEASANT, Maury County. US 43.

Confederate Monument, in public square, dedicated 1907.

MULBERRY, Lincoln County. State 50.

Confederate Monument, in public square in memory of 300 Mulberry Confederate soldiers, erected by United Daughters of the Confederacy, 1908.

MURFREESBORO, Rutherford County. IS 24, US 41, 70S.

Army of the Cumberland Route, in June 1863, is well marked along US 41.

Battle of Murfreesboro (Stones River). Marker on State 96, Gresham's Lane, about 3 miles west of town, at site where the Confederate assault began December 31, 1862. Marker on US 41 and 70S, at Van Cleve Lane, denotes site of final action which took place on January 2, 1863. Union Capt. John Mendenhall set up 58 guns on a hill commanding a ford over Stones River and broke up the assault led by Maj. Gen. John C. Breckinridge. Monument on hill, ½ mile north of Military Park.

Cannonsburgh, S. Front St., downtown, is original name of town. The area is now a living museum village, with a display of relics from the Battle of Stones River.

Confederate Monument, in courthouse square, in memory of soldiers who fell in the battle of Murfreesboro and in minor engagements in this vicinity.

Courthouse has plaque on south wall to the memory of Gen. Forrest. Marker on lawn.

Evergreen Cemetery has monument to unknown Confederate soldiers, most of whom fell at battle of Murfreesboro.

Morgan's Wedding, marker on front of Jordan block, E. Main St. In a house that stood here Gen. Morgan was married to Miss Martha Ready on December 14, 1862. Bishop and Lt. Gen. Leonidas Polk, of the Confederate army, performed the ceremony; Col. Basil Duke served as best man. Among the groomsmen were Gen. Braxton Bragg, Lt. Gen. W. J. Hardee, Maj. Gens. J. C. Breckinridge and B. F. Cheatham, and Col. G. St. Leger Grenfell. The best man later wrote a history of Morgan's cavalry and recalled that St. Leger Grenfell was in a high state of delight after the affair ". . . although he had regretted General Morgan's marriage—thinking that it would render him less enterprising—he declared, that a wedding, at which an Episcopal bishop-militant, clad in general's uniform, officiated, and the chief of an army and his corps commanders were guests, certainly ought not to soften a soldier's temper. On his way home that night he [Grenfell] sang Moorish songs, with a French accent, to English airs, and was as mild and agreeable as if some one was going to be killed."

Oaklands, N. Maney Ave., off US 41. Among noted guests of Dr. James Maney, owner of Oaklands in antebellum years, were Matthew Fontaine Maury, who became a Confederate naval commander; John Bell, presidential candidate who ran against Lincoln in 1860; and Leonidas Polk, bishop-general. During the war the house was headquarters for Union Col. W. W. Duffield, who surrendered Murfrees-

boro to Gen. Forrest. President Jefferson Davis visited here in 1863 to inspect his troops and confer with Gen. Braxton Bragg. A medical museum has a large number of wartime instruments. A marker in the front yard describes the Union surrender on July 13, 1862.

Union University, marker west of Central High School entrance. The buildings were used by both armies as a hospital.

NASHVILLE, Davidson County. IS 24, 40, 65, US 70N, 31.

Battle of Nashville, which took place December 15–16, 1864, between Hood's Confederate army and Thomas's Federal forces, is marked throughout the city with descriptive plaques. A number of markers will be found on 21st Ave. S., Granny White Pike, 12th Ave. S., US 31, State 106, and State 6. The Tennessee Historical Commission has issued a booklet with the complete texts of the more than 1,000 markers erected by the commission.

Belle Meade, 110 Leake Ave., US 70S, is the 1853 mansion of a one-time 5,300-acre plantation. During the battle of Nashville, it served as headquarters for Confederate Gen. James R. Chalmers; some fighting took place on the lawn. The carriage house displays 20 carriages. Guided tours available.

Bell Home, 413 Broadway. Site of home of John Bell, who opposed secession and helped to keep Tennessee in the Union until Fort Sumter was fired on. In 1860, Bell was nominated for president on the Constitutional Union party ticket, won the votes of Tennessee, Kentucky, and Virginia. Bell was born near Nashville on February 15, 1797. Marker in Davidson County on US 41A for birthplace site.

Centennial Park, W. End Ave., between 25th and 28th Ave. N., has monument to the private Confederate soldiers, also battle marker.

Cunningham House, 221 6th Ave. S. Site of headquarters for a succession of Union commanders, among them Maj. Gens. Buell, Rosecrans, Grant, and Thomas.

Downtown Presbyterian Church, 5th Ave. and Church St., served as a hospital for Federal troops.

Driver Home, 511 5th Ave. S. Capt. William Driver, shipmaster, was presented with an American flag by his mother and some neighbors in Salem, Massachusetts. It is said that when the flag was unfurled from the masthead, Driver said, "I'll call her 'Old Glory.'" During the war Driver lived in Nashville, hid the flag by having it sewn into a quilt; it was flown from the capitol when Union forces occupied the city.

Fort Negley, Chestnut St. and Ridley Blvd., was named for Federal Gen. James S. Negley of Pennsylvania, who commanded here in 1862. During Reconstruction the fort was a gathering place for the Ku Klux Klan.

Mount Olivet Cemetery, northeast of Nashville on US 70N. Confederate Memorial, in Confederate Circle, was erected through the efforts of the women of the South, 1892.

National Cemetery, US 31E, has monument erected by Minnesota, 1920.

State Capitol, north of Legislative Plaza on Charlotte Ave. On grounds are a Civil War cannon and a statue of Sam Davis, boy hero of the Confederacy, sculpted by Julian Zolnay.

Tennessee State Museum, 505 Deaderick Street, has a large collection of Civil War items, as well as exhibits of antebellum and Reconstruction days.

Travellers Rest, off US 31, 6½ miles south of town. Headquarters for Gen. John Hood during the battle of Nashville. The "battle of Peach Orchard Hill," an important part of the battle of Nashville, was fought on the grounds.

War Memorial Building, 7th Ave. facing Legislative Plaza, houses the Military Branch of the state museum. Legislative Plaza has monuments of Civil War interest.

PALMYRA, Montgomery. State 149.
Streight's Raid. In April 1863, Col. Abel D. Streight came here by transport from Nashville and marched his task force to Fort Henry, where he re-embarked for Eastport, Mississippi. His 1,500-man force was captured near Rome, Georgia, by Forrest's cavalry.

PARIS, Henry County. US 79, 641.
Battle of Paris, marker on State 54. On this ridge on March 11, 1862, Confederates under Maj. H. Clay King were attacked by Federal troops from Fort Henry. Twenty Confederates and 60 to 80 Federals were killed or wounded before the Federals withdrew.

City Cemetery, Ruff St. Marker at gate for James Davis Porter, chief of staff to Gen. B. F. Cheatham. After the war Porter held many high offices, including the governorship.

Confederate Monument, courthouse yard, erected by United Daughters of the Confederacy and United Confederate Veterans.

Harris Home, N. Washington St., 3 blocks from square. Isham G. Harris was governor from 1857 to 1861. When Nashville was taken by Union forces he joined the staff of the Army of Tennessee; after the war he fled to Mexico for two years, later served as U.S. senator. His birthplace near Tullahoma has marker on old highway east off US 41A, north of Elk River.

PARKER'S CROSSROADS, Henderson County. State 22, 1½ miles south of county line. Forrest had an all-day engagement here on December 31, 1862, with two Federal brigades who were unsuccessful in their attempt to prevent his recrossing the Tennessee River.

PHILADELPHIA, Loudon County, IS 75, US 11. Marker on highway tells of cavalry action October 20, 1863.

PULASKI, Giles County. US 31, 64, State 11.
Adams Marker, at junction of E. College St. and S. Sam Davis Ave. John Adams was killed leading his brigade at Franklin, November 30, 1864. He is buried in the cemetery to the south.

Sam Davis Memorial, on Sam Davis Ave. Items in museum were collected by United Daughters of the Confederacy and W. B. Romine of Pulaski. The memorial was erected by the Tennessee Historical Commission, dedicated in 1950.

Sam Davis Monument, in courthouse square, erected by United Daughters of the Confederacy, 1906.

Tarpley's Shop, US 31, State 7, south of town. Marker is descriptive of Forrest's raid in September 1864. Monument in cemetery on west side of highway just north of crossroads was erected by Col. V. Y. Cook of Arkansas, a veteran of the engagement.

RIDDLETON, Smith County. State 25.
Morgan's Raid. Marker on highway. Morgan's cavalry bivouacked about 3 miles southwest on June 12, 1863, before leaving Tennessee en route to Ohio.

ROGERSVILLE, Hawkins County. US 11W.
Big Creek Skirmish, 2 miles east of town on north side of road. Scene of action on November 6, 1863, when two Confederate cavalry brigades captured the 2nd Tennessee Mounted Infantry and a detachment of the 7th Ohio Cavalry.

Hale Street Inn (1824) is the oldest continuously operating hotel in the state and was Union headquarters during the war. Confederate headquarters were across the street. Both buildings still stand. The inn has been restored.

Stewart Birthplace, marker on front of Lyons Hospital. Alexander Peter Stewart was born here October 2, 1821. As a brigadier general in the Army of Tennessee, he was twice wounded. He finished the war as a lieutenant general and corps commander.

RUSSELLVILLE, Hamblen County. US 11A.

Longstreet's Billet. Marker across from post office. Longstreet stayed here during the winter of 1863–1864. The general and his staff occupied this house. Brig. Gen. Kershaw's troops were north of the road; McLaws' division to the south.

RUTLEDGE, Grainger County. US 11W.

Johnson's First Tailor Shop. Marker at southwest corner of courthouse yard. Johnson had his first establishment in a small brick building which was also the sheriff's office.

SAVANNAH, Hardin County. US 64.

Approach to Shiloh. Marker at corner of Main and Pickwick St. On April 5, 1862, Buell's army turned south at this point and marched up river to a point opposite Pittsburg Landing.

Cherry Mansion, west edge of town where road branches north. Maj. Gen. C. F. Smith had headquarters here, died of a foot infection which he received in leaping from one boat to another early in the Shiloh campaign. He was succeeded by Gen. Grant, who was breakfasting here when the cannons began to fire at Pittsburg Landing. Maj. Gen. Buell used the house for a short time while commanding the Army of the Ohio. Maj. Gen. W. H. L. Wallace, mortally wounded at Shiloh, died here.

SEVIERVILLE, Sevier County. US 441.

McCown Birthplace. Marker south of bridge at south city limits. Maj. Gen. John Porter McCown was born here on August 19, 1815. In the fall of 1862, he commanded the Department of Eastern Tennessee and fought at Stones River.

SEWANEE, Franklin County. US 64.

University of the South. Leonidas Polk laid the cornerstone for the central building in October 1860. When Federal troops occupied the area, the cornerstone was broken up into "keepsakes" and carried off in Union pockets. The last full Confederate general, Kirby Smith, and the last Confederate naval officer, Capt. Jack Eggleston, both died at Sewanee and are buried here.

SHELBYVILLE, Bedford County. US 241, 41A.

Andrews's Raiders. Marker on State 64, about 1½ miles east of town. The Federal raiders assembled here in 1862 before their capture of the Confederate locomotive, the General.

Army of the Cumberland. Descriptive plaques regarding the army's movements in June 1863 will be found on US 41A, west of town, and on US 231, at Guy's Gap.

Confederate Monument, county courthouse lawn, in memory of the Shelbyville Rebels. Erected by the United Daughters of the Confederacy.

Davidson Birthplace. Marker on N. Main St. Henry Davidson was born here on January 28, 1831. During the war he was captured at Island No. 10, promoted after being exchanged, given a brigade in Wheeler's cavalry.

Willow Mount Cemetery has a memorial in Confederate Square and a monument at the grave of Sumner A. Cunningham, founder and publisher of *The Confederate Veteran.*

SHILOH NATIONAL MILITARY PARK, Hardin County. US 64, State 22, 142. Shiloh has been called a place of ghosts and echoes and long memories. There are hauntingly quiet areas where it is possible to picture how it is must have been at dawn on April 6, 1861, with one vast army, tense and waiting, and another just coming awake and thinking of breakfast. Shiloh was a country church, not a well-populated area, and progress (custard stands and Japanese art goods) has not marched too heavily here—which accounts for some of the respectful hush still lingering in these fields; but mainly it was the nature of the terrible engagement, involving more than 80,000 young men, many of whom were untrained farm boys, some of whom had never fired a gun, "Not knowing," writes Bruce Catton, "as much about military matters as so many high school cadets . . . and many thousands of them died or were maimed simply because it was their hard fate to come out and take charge of a little history."

Visitor Center has a well-stocked library and an exhibit room with relics and maps. Trained historians are on duty and a film is shown throughout the day. All points of interest have numbered markers to correspond with free map and direction guide available at the center. The park comprises about 3,600 acres. The national cemetery is located on a bluff overlooking Pittsburg Landing and the Tennessee River.

SILVERDALE, Hamilton County. US 11.

Confederate Cemetery, north of junction with Route 2A. Army of Tennessee soldiers who died in hospitals during the mobilization for Bragg's Kentucky campaign of September 1862 are buried here. Graves which once had wooden markers are now unidentified.

SMYRNA, Rutherford County. Off IS 24, US 70.

The charge of General Negley's division at Stones River.

Sam Davis State Memorial, Sam Davis Rd. Sam Davis, a member of Shaw's cub scouts, was captured by Union troops in November 1863. Under his saddle and in his boots were papers with information on Federal fortifications, movements, etc. He was convicted as a spy and hanged at Pulaski after refusing a pardon which would have meant the betrayal of his informer. He was buried here on December 24, 1863. Home has many original furnishings. Museum and family cemetery.

SPRING HILL, Maury County. US 31.

Cheair's House, south edge of town, east of and facing US 31. Maj. Gen. Earl Van Dorn was assassinated on May 8, 1863, in the colonial house here, now part of an orphanage. It has long been disputed whether he was shot by an outraged husband or for political reasons. There is no marker, and none is planned.

Ewell Farm, marker on highway at junction with Depot Rd. The last home of Lt. Gen. Richard S. Ewell.

Hood and Schofield. On highway at north edge of town is one of several state markers denoting troop movements in the Hood Campaign against Schofield, November 1864.

STONES RIVER NATIONAL BATTLEFIELD. IS 24, northwest of Murfreesboro. Park headquarters and visitor center are across the road from the national cemetery. The 344-acre area includes parts of the battlefield and the cemetery which contains about 6,100 graves. Free literature is available at the visitor center. The battle of December 31, 1862–January 2, 1863, was fought by Confederate forces under Gen. Braxton Bragg and Union troops under Maj. Gen. William S. Rosecrans. Bragg moved out from Murfreesboro to meet Rosecrans, who was then advancing from Nashville. On January 2, Bragg's army had the Federals in retreat when Capt. John E. Mendenhall, Union artillery chief, brought his guns to bear on the Southerners. By firing at the rate of about 100 rounds a minute, Union artillery killed or wounded 1,800 Confederates. The next day Bragg withdrew to Tullahoma, some 40 miles away.

The Hazen Brigade Monument, erected in 1863, is considered to be the oldest Civil War memorial in the U.S.

TRENTON, Gibson County. US 45W, State 54.

Confederate Monument, in public square, erected by United Daughters of the Confederacy.

Forrest Marker, on US 45W south of town. On December 20, 1862, Forrest captured the Federal garrison at Trenton.

Oakland Cemetery has graves of 141 Confederates, most of whom survived the war. Forrest's men who fell at the battle of Trenton were buried here originally.

TRIUNE, Williamson County. US 31A.

Jobe Marker, about 2½ miles south of Sanford Rd., between Triune and Nolensville. Dewitt Smith Jobe, of Coleman's Scouts, was captured in a nearby cornfield on August 29, 1864, by a patrol from the 115th Ohio Cavalry. He swallowed his dispatches, was tortured, and dragged to death by a galloping horse. He is buried in the family cemetery 6 miles northeast.

TULLAHOMA, Coffee County. State 55.

Bragg's Quarters. Marker in northwest suburbs. Bragg established his command post here after the battle of Stones River, in January 1863.

Confederate Cemetery. Marker at southwest corner of Carroll and Jackson St. One mile southwest are buried 407 unknown Confederates, many of whom died in hospitals here when the town was headquarters for the Army of Tennessee from January to June 1863.

UNICOI, Unicoi County. State 107.

Bell Cemetery on highway east of town. Nine Union sympathizers, victims of a massacre by a detachment of Confederate cavalry, are buried here. Names on gravesite marker.

UNION CITY, Obion County. US 45W, 51.

Confederate Monument, in public square, has a specialized inscription: TO THE CONFEDERATE SOLDIER OF OBION COUNTY WHO WAS KILLED IN BATTLE, WHO WAS STARVED IN FEDERAL PRISON AND WHO HAS PRESERVED ANGLO-SAXON CIVILIZATION TO THE SOUTH.

Forrest Raid Marker, south of town. Forrest captured the Federal garrison of Union City on December 23, 1862, and destroyed railroad lines.

Unknown Confederate Dead Monument is in Confederate Cemetery.

VALLEY FORGE, Carter County. State 67. Marker on Doe River north of town is descriptive of the activities of Unionist Dan Ellis who guided recruits along a "Federal Underground Route." Trail is marked at two other points in Sullivan County on State 36 (US 23).

WILLIAMS'S ISLAND, Hamilton County. State 27A. Marker on highway at junction with road to Baylor School. James J. Andrews, leader of the Andrews's Raid, was captured here on May 31, 1862, following his escape from jail in Chattanooga.

WINCHESTER, Franklin County. US 64.

Secession Marker, in courthouse yard. Franklin County seceded from Tennessee at a mass meeting on February 24, 1861, and petitioned Alabama to annex it. The secession of Tennessee, June 24, 1861, made further action needless. The restored Old Jail, 400 1st Ave. NE, is now a museum with war relics.

WOODBURY, Cannon County. US 70S, State 53.

Forrest Rest, east edge of town. On July 12, 1862, Gen. Forrest and his newly organized brigade of about 1,400 cavalrymen rested here before making a raid on Murfreesboro.

Hutchenson Monument, ½ mile west of town. Boulder marks spot where Lt. Col. John B. Hutchenson (spelled Hutchinson in *Official Records*) of Morgan's cavalry was killed in battle, January 1863.

WOODLAWN, Montgomery County. State 57. Marker west of junction with Route 18. Sherman made his headquarters here for a time; the house was also used as a hospital by both armies.

TEXAS

In the presidential election of 1860, Texans voted 3 to 1 for John C. Breckinridge, Southern Democrat, over conservative John Bell, of the Constitutional Union party. When a man whose name wasn't even on the Texas ballot won the election, a good part of the state went into mourning. Although Gov. Sam Houston tried to block secession movements, a convention met in Austin, January 28, 1861, and passed an ordinance of secession which was later ratified by popular election. Houston, who has been quoted as saying a drop of Jefferson Davis's blood would freeze a frog, refused to take an oath of allegiance to the Confederate constitution and was removed from office. Lt. Gov. Edward Clark served the remaining nine months of the term.

One hitch in recruiting was that all Texans wanted to fight on horseback, although the Confederacy had enough cavalrymen and needed foot soldiers. Few Texans ever walked anywhere they could gallop, but ten regiments were ready for service by September. About 2,000 Texans joined the Union army. The state gave to the Confederate army one general, Albert Sidney Johnston; an "adopted son," Lt. Gen. John Bell Hood; three major generals, S. B. Maxey, John A. Wharton, and Tom Green; 32 brigadier generals, and nearly 100 colonels. There were few major engagements within state borders, but Texas units fought in campaigns from Maryland to Arizona and from the Potomac to the Rio Grande. The state furnished to the Confederacy foreign supplies brought in through Mexico. The last battle of the war was fought at Palmito Hill on May 12–13, 1865.

The 1860 assessed valuation of slave property in Texas was $64,000,000. On June 19, 1865, Gen. Gordon Granger arrived in Galveston to proclaim all slaves free and all laws enacted since 1861 null and void. Riots and violence soon set in; military rule was established and maintained until 1869. The 1870 legislature ratified the 13th, 14th, and 15th Amendments to the U.S. Constitution, and on March 30, 1870, Texas was readmitted to the Union.

ANDERSON, Grimes County. FM (Farm Rd.) 149. During the war, local arms factory produced weapons and gunpowder.

Fanthorp Inn Historic Structure, Main St., built during the Republic of Texas era, hosted Sam Houston, Jefferson Davis, Grant, Lee, and Stonewell Jackson. Tours.

ANTHONY, El Paso County. IS 10, at New Mexico State Line. Texas Highway Tourist Bureau has free maps, literature, and road condition data.

ARANSAS PASS, San Patricio County. State 35 at Gulf of Mexico. W. A. Jones, deputy custom collector, seized the Union coast guard schooner *Twilight* on April 20, 1861. The Union navy attacked the garrison on February 22, 1862, and in April Confederates captured U.S. Navy launches off Aransas Pass.

ARLINGTON, Tarrant County. IS 20, 30, US 80, State 360.

Six Flags Over Texas, amusement center on turnpike midway between Dallas and Fort Worth. One section of the park represents the history of the state under the Confederacy.

AUSTIN, Travis County. IS 35, US 183, 290.

Daughters of the Confederacy Museum, in Old State Land Office Building on Capitol grounds. Texas regimental flags, Confederate history, relics, uniforms, and paintings. Rosters of Confederate veterans' camps.

Daughters of the Republic of Texas, 11th and Brazos St. Second floor of Old Land Office Building. Relics of the Republic; among exhibits are items pertaining to Confederate Gen. Albert Sidney Johnston, who was killed at the battle of Shiloh.

Governor's Mansion, 11th and Colorado St., has Sam Houston's bed, other historical furnishings.

State Capitol, Congress Ave. Among ex-

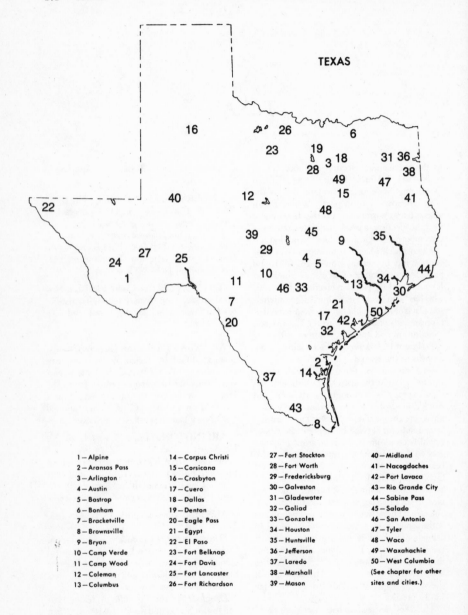

TEXAS

16   26   6
23   19
28 3 18   31 36
49   38
40   12   15   47   41
22   48
39   45   35
29   4 9
24 27 25   5   44
1   11 10   13 34
7   46 33   30
20   17 21
32 42   50
2
37   14
43
8

1 — Alpine	14 — Corpus Christi	27 — Fort Stockton	40 — Midland
2 — Aransas Pass	15 — Corsicana	28 — Fort Worth	41 — Nacogdoches
3 — Arlington	16 — Crosbyton	29 — Fredericksburg	42 — Port Lavaca
4 — Austin	17 — Cuero	30 — Galveston	43 — Rio Grande City
5 — Bastrop	18 — Dallas	31 — Gladewater	44 — Sabine Pass
6 — Bonham	19 — Denton	32 — Goliad	45 — Salado
7 — Bracketville	20 — Eagle Pass	33 — Gonzales	46 — San Antonio
8 — Brownsville	21 — Egypt	34 — Houston	47 — Tyler
9 — Bryan	22 — El Paso	35 — Huntsville	48 — Waco
10 — Camp Verde	23 — Fort Belknap	36 — Jefferson	49 — Waxahachie
11 — Camp Wood	24 — Fort Davis	37 — Laredo	50 — West Columbia
12 — Coleman	25 — Fort Lancaster	38 — Marshall	(See chapter for other
13 — Columbus	26 — Fort Richardson	39 — Mason	sites and cities.)

hibits is the Texas Ordinance of Secession. State Archives and Library are in Capitol complex. On Capitol grounds: *Confederate Dead Monument,* center walk, erected 1901, designed by Pompeo Coppini and executed by Frank Teich; *Monument to Hood's Texas Brigade,* east lawn, sculpted by Coppini; *Terry's*

Texas Rangers Monument, center walk, erected 1907, sculpted by Coppini; *Twin Cannons,* south entrance of Capitol, presented to the Republic of Texas in 1836 by Maj. Gen. T. J. Chambers, used in the Texas Revolution and in the Civil War.

State Cemetery, 7th and Cornal St., has

graves of many noted Texans. A reclining marble figure of Gen. Albert S. Johnston was executed by Elizabeth Ney.

Texas Memorial Museum, 2400 Trinity St., has historical exhibits as well as archaeological and others.

BASTROP, Bastrop County. State 95, 21. Although the majority of residents were Unionists, B. F. Terry gained a good many recruits here for his Texas Rangers.

Bastrop County Museum, 702 S. Main St. Historical manuscripts, newspapers, and miscellany of the pioneer period.

BONHAM, Fannin County. US 82. The town was headquarters of the Northern Military Sub-District of Texas with Brig. Gen. Henry E. McCulloch commanding.

BRACKETVILLE, Kinney County. US 90, State 674. An army post established here in 1852 as Fort Riley was renamed Fort Clark. It was abandoned by Federal troops in March 1861, occupied for a short time by Confederates, then was without a garrison until 1866. Indians took advantage of the withdrawal of troops to raid; when the post was regarrisoned, soldiers had a rough time establishing order. Some buildings remain from early days. The post was abandoned by the army in 1949.

BROWNSVILLE, Cameron County. US 77. Benjamin Franklin McIntyre of the 19th Iowa Infantry found duty in Brownsville more tiresome than dangerous in December 1863: "I am sick of the sights . . . hairless mexican dogs, bare breasted women, naked children, dirty orange women sitting on the ground with their fruit spread before them—tired of wide baskets of dirty looking sugar plumbs. . . ." His mood was not improved greatly by the following July when Union forces were evacuating the post; McIntyre may be speaking for all foot soldiers of all wars: "There is not a shadow of excuse for the officers in command not furnishing means of conveyance. . . . Teams and steamboats have been running regularly . . . and could have carried every soldier and his load and saved a sacrifice on the part of the soldier of clothing which must be replaced from his meagre wages. This march has been no loss to the government—no loss to officers who ride on horses and whose things are nicely packed and furnished a conveyance. . . ."

Fort Brown, southeast end of Taylor Ave. Federal troops under Capt. B. H. Hill abandoned the fort on March 20, 1861, after burning military supplies. Confederates occupied the post until November 1863, when Union forces in a combined land and naval action took over Brownsville and Brazos Island. Gen. H. P. Bee, Confederate commander, believed himself outnumbered and retired without resistance after burning military supplies and cotton. In July 1864, Confederates were back in residence and Federals had again lost their lease. Texas Southmost College now occupies the site. Original hospital has become an administration center.

Miller Hotel, 1309 S.E. Elizabeth St., was a social center for Brownsville. Gens. Grant, Sheridan, and Robert E. Lee were guests here.

Palmito Hill (or Palinetto), marker on State 4, 14 miles east of town. The last land battle of the Civil War was fought by Confederates un-

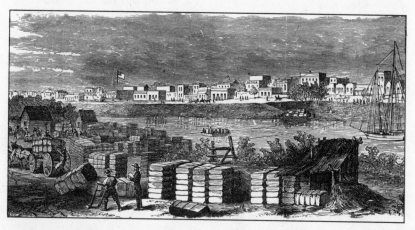

The port of Brownsville was occupied by Federal troops.

der Col. John ("Rip") Ford and Union forces under Lt. Col. David Branson. There are several versions of the engagement which took place more than a month after Lee's surrender. Some say one side, others say both sides, knew the war was over when the shooting started. Reportedly, Lt. Col. Branson maintained the battle was getting underway when he received news of the surrender, and he was unable to send immediate word to the Confederate commander; therefore he fell back slowly, maintaining a rear-guard action until he could find a Texan for message bearer. A Texas version says that the Federals tried to ambush a Confederate outpost near Palmito Ranch; when the Southerners under Col. Rip Ford gave chase, the Northerners broke ranks and fled. Col. Ford is quoted as saying: "Some of them Yankees could outrun our horses."

BRYAN, Brazos County. US 190, State 6. Hood's Brigade was organized here in 1862.

CAMP VERDE, Kerr County. State 689. The post, established in 1858, was a home for Jefferson Davis's camel corps, used in an experiment to transport military supplies in semiarid regions of the Great Plains. When the post was surrendered to the Confederates in March 1861, the camels were left without trained supervision. Many wandered into surrounding hills, where survivors were found for years afterward. Confederates kept prisoners in a "prison canyon" near Camp Verde. This was a pitlike gully where Union soldiers were allowed to build shacks and to exercise in fresh air with no chance to escape. There were as many as 600 prisoners in the handy canyon at one time. No camp buildings remain.

CAMP WOOD, Real County. State 55. A military post was established here in 1857 and abandoned by U.S. troops on March 15, 1861. Northwest of the present town is Military Mountain, so named because the garrison kept a lookout on its peak.

CLEBURNE, Johnson County, US 67, is named for the gallant Gen. Pat Cleburne, born in Helena, Arkansas, who died in the battle of Franklin, Tennessee, after giving his boots to a barefoot soldier.
Layland Museum, 201 N. Caddo, has a Civil War exhibit.

COLEMAN, Coleman County. US 69, 283. Camp Colorado 9 miles northeast of town on Jim Ned Creek was abandoned by Federal troops on February 26, 1861. The city park has a reproduction of the old camp.

COLUMBUS, Colorado County. IS 10, US 90, State 71.
Confederate Memorial Hall Museum, Milam and Spring St. Items depicting Colorado County during the Civil War, also documents, books, photographs, and artifacts.
Old Water Tower/United Daughters of the Confederacy Museum, in brick tower, features early Texas life. U.D.C. members conduct tours.

COMFORT, Kendall County. IS 10. Monument near high school recalls when the German settlers, who were chiefly Unionist, left in a party of 65 to head for Mexico. They were attacked by Confederate cavalry on the west bank of the Nueces about 20 miles from Fort Clark. Nineteen died in the battle, nine were wounded and executed later.

CORPUS CHRISTI, Nueces County. IS 37, US 181. The town was shelled in August 1862. Legend says that some of the shells failed to explode because they were filled with liquid instead of powder. Union Capt. Kittredge missed a barrel of bourbon, found out too late that some of his men had decanted it into shells in place of the charge. Presumably, the day it rained whiskey was one of the liveliest of the war.
Corpus Christi Museum, 1900 N. Chaparral St., N. Water St., has local history displays.
Site of Gen. Taylor's Camp, Mesquite St. at drawbridge. Zachary Taylor's army roster in 1846 contained a good many names who gained added fame in the Civil War. Among them: Don Carlos Buell, Jefferson Davis, Ulysses S. Grant, Joseph Hooker, Robert E. Lee, Albert Sidney Johnston, James A. Longstreet, John Bankhead Magruder, George Gordon Meade, and George B. Thomas. Franklin Pierce, later to become president, was also stationed here.

CUERO, DeWitt County. US 183, Alt. 77. Town was an origin point for a leg of the famous Chisholm Trail. The courthouse is a Texas Historical Landmark.
St. Mark's Lutheran Church has one of three bells that once tolled in the now vanished town of Indianola. The bell was stolen by Union soldiers, retrieved by Confederates, and buried beneath the sand of Matagorda Bay for years until it was saved again and placed atop the church.

DALLAS, Dallas County. IS 20, 30, 35E, 45. Offices of the quartermaster and commissary departments of the trans-Mississippi were located here.

Old City Park, 1717 Gano St., just south of downtown business district, has furnished historic buildings. The *Millermore Mansion* was completed as the Civil War began.

Texas Hall of State, in Fair Park, 2 miles east of downtown Dallas. Civil War items, including weapons and clothing, are among the extensive displays of Texas life.

Visitor Centers are in the restored Union Station, 400 S. Houston, and the Renaissance Tower, 1201 Elm St.

DENISON, Grayson County. US 75, 69N. Texas Highway Department Tourist Bureau has free maps, literature, and road information.

DENTON, Denton County. IS 35.
D.A.R. Museum, Home Economics Building of Texas Woman's University, 117 Bell St. Historic inaugural gowns worn by governors' wives are featured.

North Texas University Museum, W. Mulberry and Ave. A, has Texas and general historical collections.

EAGLE PASS, Maverick County. US 277, State 131. One of the main wartime outlets for Confederate cotton blockaded elsewhere. Camp Eagle Pass, established during the Mexican War, was named for an eagle that took a daily flight across the river to and from its nest in a cottonwood tree on the Mexican bank of the Rio Grande. The post, known as Fort Duncan during the Civil War, was garrisoned by Confederates. Fort Duncan Park has some of the original buildings of the garrison.

EDINBURG, Hidalgo County. US 281.
Hidalgo County Historical Museum, 121 E. McIntyre St. Exhibits include the Civil War period.

EL PASO, El Paso County. IS 10, US 62-180. The Federal garrison surrendered Fort Bliss on March 31, 1861. Brig. Gen. H. H. Sibley had his headquarters here during the unsuccessful campaign to conquer New Mexico. Union troops reoccupied the post in August 1862.
Fort Bliss Replica Museum, Pleasanton Rd. facing main parade grounds of Fort Bliss, east of US 54. The 1848 post served as Confederate headquarters in the Southwest. It was reactivated later when the U.S. cavalry chased the elusive Geronimo, the great Apache chieftain. The site is now occupied by an army air defense center for rocket research and combat training, but four adobe buildings facing the main parade ground display early cavalry, infantry, and artillery exhibits, 1848 to 1948.

McGinty Cannon, southwest corner of W. Missouri and N. Santa Fe St., was used during the battle of Valverde. The cannon was named after the social club that acquired it long after the war—a club whose name was taken from a popular song of the day, "Down Went McGinty to the Bottom of the Sea." The cannon itself went down to Mexico to be used in the Madero uprising and was returned to El Paso after the fall of Juarez.

Mills Memorial Shaft, N. Oregon St. in Carnegie Square. A memorial to seven El Pasoans who tried to prevent property of the Southern Overland Mail, where they were employed, from falling into Confederate hands at the beginning of the war. They were killed at Cook's Spring, New Mexico, by marauding Indians.

Museum of the Noncommissioned Officer, Briggs Army Airfield, Bldg. 11331, Barksdale and 5th streets. Artifacts date from the Revolutionary War.

Site of Southern Overland Mail Station, southeast corner of Overland and S. El Paso St. The stage station and its stables occupied the entire block in 1857–1861.

FORT BELKNAP, Young County. State 251, 24. The fort is 1 mile south of the highway junction. Albert Sidney Johnston, Earl Van Dorn, George H. Thomas, and George B. McClellan were stationed here at various times. When Gen. William Sherman visited the garrison in 1871, he just missed being killed by Kiowa raiders who massacred the personnel of a wagon train following Sherman's party. Union troops evacuated the post early in the Civil War; it was used by Texas troops as a base for operations against hostile Indians, reoccupied by U.S. troops after the war. Six original buildings and one replica remain. It is now a county park, with museum, three miles south of Newcastle.

FORT DAVIS NATIONAL HISTORIC SITE, Jeff Davis County, State 17, 118. To protect the Overland Trail here, the fort was established in 1854 and named for Secretary of War Jefferson Davis; it was the largest and most important garrison in western Texas. U.S. troops evacuated the fort on March 13, 1861. In August 1861, Lt. Reuben E. Mays and 14 soldiers pursuing an Apache raiding party were ambushed; only the Mexican guide escaped. After the unsuccessful campaign to conquer New Mexico, Confederates abandoned this and other western posts.

Some postwar troopers were black, known as the "buffalo soldiers," many of whom had been in slavery earlier. Little remained of the original fort when troops returned in 1867, but rock and adobe buildings soon housed 12 companies of cavalry and infantry. Ruins and restorations can be visited today. A museum, open daily, interprets frontier military life.

Fort Davis Historical Society Museum, on the grounds of the post, has military weapons, photographs, and regiment records.

Neill Museum, 7 blocks west of Fort Davis Courthouse, has historical items, featuring Texas-made antique toys.

Treasure Trove, Davis and Murphy St. Among the relics on display are Camel Corps and Cavalry Corps bells, tools used at old Fort Davis, and music books written for the post string band.

FORT LANCASTER, STATE HISTORICAL SITE, Crockett County. US 290. The fort, which guarded the Pecos crossing of the San Antonio-El Paso Rd., was abandoned by U.S. troops on March 19, 1861. Stone ruins of the buildings remain. Marker erected by Texas Centennial Commission.

FORT STOCKTON, Pecos County. IS 10, US 67, 285, 290.

Old Fort Stockton, Williams St. between 4th and 5th. Many original buildings of adobe and hand-hewn limestone remain, including Officers' Row and the old guardhouse. The fort was established in 1859.

FORT WORTH, Tarrant County. IS 20, 30, 35W. The town, a U.S. army patrol post, was only 11 years old when the war came, and it was a year after the fall of Sumter before Fort Worthians, divided in loyalties, organized enough to put a military unit into the field.

Amon Carter Museum of Western Art, 3501 Camp Bowie Blvd. Western art and history. Paintings and sculpture by Frederic Remington and Charles M. Russell are featured.

Site of Fort Worth, northwest corner of Houston and Belknap St. Bronze plaque on Criminal Courts Building.

FREDERICKSBURG, Gillespie County. US 290. German settlers in the area formed a 500-man Union Loyal League to defy the draft and to promote sympathy for the Union. State militia took control of the town and gave the citizens six days to take an oath of loyalty to the Confederacy. Most complied, some did not and were arrested, still others fled to Mexico.

Pioneer Museum and Country Store, 309 W. Main St., has historical displays pertaining to the community.

GAINESVILLE, Cooke County. IS 35, US 77. Texas Highway Department Tourist Bureau has free maps, literature, and information on road conditions.

GALVESTON, Galveston County. IS 45. The city was blockaded by the Union navy. Cmdr. William B. Renshaw took command of the fleet in October 1862, giving city authorities four days to surrender. Federals occupied the town without resistance. On January 1, 1863, Gen. John Magruder retook Galveston for the Confederacy and captured the *Harriet Lane,* a sidewheeler. A naval engagement took place near Galveston on January 11 between the Union *Hatteras* and the Confederate *Alabama.* Adm. Raphael Semmes, commander of the *Alabama,* in his lively *Memoirs of Service Afloat During the War Between the States,* tells of nearing Galveston early in 1863 intending to attack Union forces, but Semmes's lookout reported no Union fleet of transports at the port. Semmes writes: "Here was a damper! What could have become of Banks? . . . Presently a shell . . . was seen to burst over the city. 'Ah ha!' exclaimed I to the officer of the deck who was standing by me, 'there has been a change of program here. The enemy would not be firing into his own people, and we must have captured Galveston since our last advices.' 'So it would seem,' replied the officer. And so it turned out."

Rosenburg Library, 2310 Sealy Ave., has papers signed by Gen. Houston, Gen. Grant, and Jefferson Davis.

Ursuline Convent, Ave. N, between Rosenberg Ave. and 27th St., was shelled by the Union navy, which mistook it for a Confederate stronghold. Gen. Magruder sent a message to the sisters to hoist a yellow flag, the signal for quarantine. Legend says a yellow skirt was found and a soldier waved it from the belfry, whereupon the bombardment ceased. Mother St. Pierre Harrington, superior of the convent during the Civil War, is buried here. Her grave was decorated yearly by Confederate veterans and the G.A.R. Her name and the names of five sisters of the Galveston Ursulines are inscribed on the Nuns of the Battlefield Monument in the District of Columbia.

GLADEWATER, Gregg County. US 183. See TYLER for *Site of Camp Ford.*

GOLIAD, Goliad County. Alt. 77. Goliad's Aranama College closed its books in 1861 when the entire student body enlisted in the Confederate army.

Market House Museum, Franklin and Market streets, is one of the most unusual looking museums you're likely to find. The Chamber of Commerce housed here has facts about the many historical sites in the area.

GONZALES, Gonzales County. US 183, 90A.
Confederate Square and *Texas Heroes Square* are downtown plazas. The earthworks of a Confederate fort are near the intersection of US 90A, 183.

HILLSBORO, Hill County. IS 35.
Confederate Research Center, Gun Museum, campus of Hill College, has more than 3,000 books, many rare, as well as maps, photographs, letters, and dioramas of the Civil War. Hood's brigade is featured. The research center offers symposia on eras in American history including the Civil War.

HOUSTON, Harris County, IS 10, 45. The famous Terry's Texas Rangers assembled at Houston in 1861. One observer said that every man in the outfit had "a six-shooter and a bowie knife in his belt as well as a rifle or a double barrel shotgun to be slung to the saddle bow."
Dick Dowling Monument, Hermann Park, erected by the United Daughters of the Confederacy.
San Jacinto Historic Park, 22 miles east on State 134. A museum in the memorial has many fine exhibits on the history of the area: documents, maps, broadsides, photographs, costumes, and other memorabilia.
United Daughters of the Confederacy Monument, Sam Houston City Park, downtown. The memorial is named "The Spirit of the Confederacy."

HUNTSVILLE, Walker County. IS 45, US 75.
Oakwood Cemetery, about 3 blocks north of courthouse, has Sam Houston's grave.
Sam Houston Memorial Museum Complex, 1836 Sam Houston Ave. Memorabilia of Sam Houston and his family. His residence, the Steamboat House where he died in 1863, a log museum housing relics of major U.S. wars, and a blacksmith shop are on the grounds.
Texas Department of Corrections, 12th St., 3 blocks east of courthouse, held Union prisoners during the war. Cloth made here was used for Confederate military clothing, blankets, and equipment.

JEFFERSON, Marion County. US 59, State 49.
Excelsior House, 211 W. Austin St. Hotel has been in operation since the 1850s. Period furniture; old guest registers and documents on display. Gen. Grant, Rutherford B. Hayes, and Jay Gould have been guests.
Gould's Private Railroad Car, Austin St., across from Excelsior House. The private "palace on wheels" belonging to the Civil War financier Jay Gould is on display.
Hotel Jefferson, 124 W. Austin, was a cotton warehouse in 1861.
Jefferson Historical Society Museum, 223 W. Austin, in library, has newspapers, documents, and historical relics.

KERRVILLE, Kerr County. IS 10.
Hill County Museum, 226 Earl Garrett St., has memorabilia of Capt. Charles A. Schreiner, who was born in France, became a Texas Ranger after serving with the Confederacy, and later was a very rich landowner and philanthropist.

LA GRANGE, Fayette County. US 77. It is said that more companies were organized for the Confederacy here than anywhere else in Texas. Museum has war relics.

LAREDO, Webb County. IS 35.
Fort McIntosh Museum, Washington St. at the banks of the Rio Grande. The post was evacuated by Union soldiers on April 11, 1861, after Gen. David E. Twiggs surrendered the Department of Texas. Texas troops garrisoned the post. The Federals made an unsuccessful attack in 1863, approaching up the Rio Grande from Fort Brown. It was reoccupied by U.S. forces on October 23, 1865. The old guardhouse, chapel, warehouse, and commissary remain and are now the Nuevo Santander Museum.

MARSHALL, Harrison County. IS 20, US 80, 96. W. W. Heartsill, who joined the Lane Rangers here in April 1861, recalled that his horse "Pet" carried: ". . . myself, saddle, bridle, saddle-blanket, curry comb, horse brush, coffee pot, tin cup, 20 lbs ham, 200 biscuit, 5 lbs ground coffee, 5 lbs sugar, one large pound cake . . . 6 shirts, 6 prs socks, 3 prs drawers, 2 prs pants, 2 jackets, 1 pr heavy mud boots, one Colt's revolver, one small dirk, four blankets, sixty feet of rope, with a twelve inch iron pin attached; with all these, and divers and sundry little mementoes from friends."
Governor's Mansion, 109 E. Crockett. "Gov." Thomas C. Reynolds rented both the mansion and the Capitol.
Harrison County Historical Society Museum, in former courthouse, has Civil War items.
Site of the Capital of Missouri, 402 S. Bolivar. When Gov. Claiborne F. Jackson died in Little Rock in December 1862, Lt. Gov.

T. C. Reynolds, who succeeded Jackson, moved to Marshall and set up the Confederate capital of Missouri here.

Trans-Mississippi Agency of the Post Office Department had offices in the 900 block on W. Grand Ave. The quartermaster and commissary departments and ordnance departments were housed in Marshall. Military supplies were stored in the basement of the First Methodist Church and the Odd Fellows Hall. A house at 109 W. Grand Ave. served as a Confederate hat factory.

MASON, Mason County. US 87.

Site of Old Fort Mason is at Post Hill. The roster had the names of Hood, Thomas, Lee, Longstreet, Johnston, Van Dorn, and Kirby Smith. Reconstructed building on original foundations. This was Lee's last command in the U.S. Army. He was called to Washington where he refused a command with the Union. The museum at 300 Moody St. was built in part from Old Fort Mason materials. It was then a schoolhouse.

MIDLAND, Midland County. IS 20, US 80, State 349.

Midland County Museum, 301 W. Missouri. Civil War articles and Indian artifacts as well as saddles, trunks, glassware, and musical instruments.

NACOGDOCHES, Nacogdoches County. US 59, State 21.

Old Stone Fort Museum, Stephen F. Austin College campus. Historical collections, guns, coins, flags, and pressed glass.

ORANGE, Orange County. IS 10, Louisiana State Line. Texas Highway Department Tourist Bureau has free maps, literature, and road condition information.

PALESTINE, Anderson County. US 79. the home town of John H. Reagan, Confederate cabinet member, has a monument to him, and a museum.

PORT LAVACA, Calhoun County. US 87. In 1861, Federal troops under Gen. Twiggs gathered here to embark for the North after having surrendered the Texas forts. The port was bombarded by the Union navy in October 1862. It was occupied by a limited force toward the end of 1863, then evacuated as the Union needed regiments for a massive invasion of the Red River Valley.

RICHMOND, Fort Bend County. US 90A, 59.

Confederate Museum, 2740 FM, 359 N, has weapons and other artifacts.

Fort Bend County Historical Museum, 500 Houston St. Exhibits include the Civil War period.

RIO GRANDE CITY, Starr County. US 83.

Fort Ringgold, east side of town on US 83. Also known as Ringgold Barracks, the post was established in 1848; it was a base for many young officers who gained prominence in the Civil War. Among them were Robert E. Lee, Ulysses S. Grant, Jefferson Davis, and Stonewall Jackson.

SABINE PASS BATTLEGROUND STATE HISTORICAL PARK, Jefferson County. State 87. Gen. Nathaniel Prentiss Banks succeeded Gen. Benjamin Butler in command of the Department of the Gulf; late in the summer of 1863 he was ordered to invade Texas. Banks chose to land an expedition at Sabine Pass, defended by an earthwork named Fort Griffin. The fort had six guns, manned by an artillery company composed of Irish stevedores who had been recruited in Houston and Galveston. Lt. Dick Dowling, in command, held off fire until three Union gunboats had been lured within close range. In 45 minutes the Confederates had sunk two gunboats, damaged a third, and driven off the remaining ships. There is a monument to Dick Dowling at Sabine Pass with an inscription written by Jefferson Davis.

Adm. Semmes later wrote, "He [Banks] was here met by General Dick Taylor [Semmes is in error; Taylor was absent and Dowling was in command], who, with a much inferior force, demolished him, giving him such a scare that it was with difficulty Porter could stop him at Alexandria to assist him in the defence of his fleet until he could extricate it from the shallows of the river where it was aground. The hero of Boston Common had not had such a scare since Stonewall Jackson had chased him through Winchester, Virginia."

SALADO, Bell County. IS 35, US 81.

Central Texas Area Museum. Exhibits include Southern Confederate home life; war years, 1861–1865; Reconstruction and birth of cattle empire.

Stagecoach Inn, off IS 35, hosted such 19th century luminaries as Gen. George Armstrong Custer, Gen. Robert E. Lee, Sam Houston, and, though it seems unlikely, Jesse James.

SAN ANTONIO, Bexar County. IS 10, 35, 37

Robert E. Lee once stopped at the Menger Hotel on the NE corner of Alamo Plaza. Lee reportedly arrived in town the afternoon of the same day Texans had taken over the Alamo. He was en route from Fort Mason to Washington and was told by local military authorities that unless he joined the Confederacy his baggage would be withheld. Lee chose to leave his gear rather than pledge any allegiance to a revolutionary government of Texas. Lt. Col. James Fremantle, of the Coldstream Guards, who visited the Confederacy in 1863, stopped at the Menger in April and recorded: "Menger's Hotel is a large and imposing edifice, but its proprietor (a civil German) was on the point of shutting it up for the present." Coffee was $7 a pound, most essential articles were at "famine price," and trade was very slow.

The Alamo, Alamo Plaza, was captured by Texans on Feb. 16, 1861. U.S. troops surrendered to the forces, known as the Committee of Public Safety, commanded by Col. Ben McCulloch, without firing a shot.

TEXARKANA, Bowie County. IS 30. US 67W. Texas Highway Department Tourist Bureau has free maps, literature, and road advice.

TYLER, Smith County. US 69, 271. A factory near the town, erected in May 1862, produced weapons known as the "Texas rifle," the "Australian Rifle," and the "Enfield Rifle." The arsenal was bought by the Confederate government in 1863.

Camp Ford, at its high point in spring 1864, held some 6,000 Union men. The largest POW compound west of the Mississippi. Marker on US 271, 2 miles northeast. The camp was named for Col. John S. Ford. Federal soldiers and sailors imprisoned here dug caves in the hillside or constructed huts of sticks, tin, and mud for shelter.

Carnegie History Center, 125 S. College. Displays include Civil War items.

Old Courthouse Museum, on Peter Whetstone Square, is the restored former courthouse. There are 20 Civil War display rooms and Civil War artifacts among exhibits.

Smith County Historical Society and Survey Committee Museum, 624 N. Broadway. Civil War items.

WACO, McLennan County. IS 35, US 84. Six Confederate officers came from Waco: Hiram Granbury, J. E. Harrison, Thomas Harrison, W. H. Parsons, L. S. Ross, and J. W. Speight.

Earle Museum, 814 S. 4th. John Earle manufactured Confederate uniforms. House restored.

WASKOM, Harrison County. IS 20. Texas Highway Department Tourist Bureau has free maps, literature, and road directions.

WAXAHACHIE, Ellis County. IS 35E, US 77. A powder mill was operated here by the Confederate government but exploded in 1863. Frank X. Tolbert in *An Informal History of Texas* claimed for Waxahachie the honor of having had the world's oldest 4-F: Frank Oliveras, at 22, was pronounced unfit for Confederate service. He served as a government teamster during the war and died at 114.

WEST COLUMBIA, Brazoria County. State 35, 36.

Verner-Hogg Plantation State Park, 2 miles northeast of town. Home of Texas' first native governor, James Stephen Hogg, the plantation houses relics of pre-Civil War days, mementos of Sam Houston and Gov. Hogg.

UTAH

In 1850 Congress established the territory of Utah with boundaries far wider than present state lines. President Millard Fillmore appointed Brigham Young first territorial governor, but petitions for statehood were refused because of the polygamy issue. President Buchanan in 1857 appointed Alfred Cummings to replace Young as governor and sent troops the following year to enforce the appointment. The Utah cold war was waged, without actual fighting, between Brigham Young followers and troops at Camp Floyd under the command of Col. Albert Sidney Johnston, until the outbreak of the Civil War.

The Pony Express began operation in 1860, with Salt Lake City a key stopping place. In 1861 the first transcontinental telegraph was completed when lines from Washington, D.C., and California met at Salt Lake City. Congress again refused to grant statehood to Utah in 1862 and passed a law forbidding polygamy. More concerned with military events nearer home, legislators made no great effort to enforce the new law but sent California troops under Col. Patrick Edward Connor to keep watch on Mormon activities. The century was nearly ended before Utah came up with a constitution outlawing polygamy and was finally admitted to the Union as the 45th state, January 4, 1896.

CAMP FLOYD AND STAGECOACH INN STATE PARK, Utah County. State 73.
This was the largest army encampment in the United States from 1858 to 1861 when the start of the Civil War depleted its ranks. Col. Albert Sidney Johnston (who was to die at Shiloh) and some 6,500 troops were here to keep down a Mormon rebellion that never got under way. Some legends say that William Quantrill was Johnston's cook, but there is no record that he helped to fill the cemetery here as he did in the border wars. The Stagecoach Inn was a rest stop for Pony Express riders. Restored, has historical exhibits.

FILLMORE, Millard County. IS 15.
Old State House, Fillmore City Park. The building, intended to serve as territorial Capitol, was never completed. It now houses a pioneer museum with relics, costumes, and furnishings.

Territorial Statehouse State Park, US 91, at 50 W. Capitol Ave., was the site of the 1st territorial government. Only one wing was completed, for lack of funds. Pioneer relics and papers are exhibited in the 1851 structure.

FORT DOUGLAS, Salt Lake County. (*See* SALT LAKE CITY.)

OGDEN, Weber County. IS 15, 84, US 89.
John M. Browning Armory, in the Union Station, 25th and Wall St., has a trophy room featuring original models of Browning firearms.
Daughters of Utah Pioneers Relic Hall, 2148 Grant Ave., has historical displays pertaining to early Utah.

PLEASANT GROVE, Utah County. IS 15. The town was the site of a non-Hollywood type engagement between Ute Indians and California troops in April 1863. Historian Ray Colton describes the attack: ". . . the cannon was hidden in an adobe house. At 6:00 A.M. on April 12, a band of about one hundred belligerent Utes approached the soldiers' camp. The concealed howitzer went into action. The first shell of grapeshot missed the Indians and killed five government mules. The second cracked the walls of the house. No more artillery shots were attempted. The Indians, firing from behind an adobe fence, kept up the siege until 8:00 P.M., when they withdrew, taking the soldiers' provisions and seven surviving mules."

PROVO, Utah County. IS 15, US 91.
Pioneer Museum, 500 N. West St., has Utah historical exhibits, including a replica of a pioneer cabin.

SALT LAKE CITY, Salt Lake County. IS 15, 80. Information concerning the city and the Latter-Day Saints Church is available at the Convention and Visitors Bureau, in the Salt Palace, also at major hotels and information centers, east entrance to Heritage Square, and west entrance to Trolley Square.

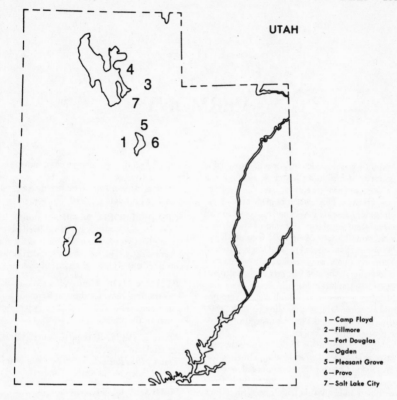

UTAH

4
3
7
5
1 6

2

1 — Camp Floyd
2 — Fillmore
3 — Fort Douglas
4 — Ogden
5 — Pleasant Grove
6 — Provo
7 — Salt Lake City

During the spring and early summer of 1862, Utah Volunteers raised by Brigham Young guarded the Overland Mail and telegraph routes from Green River to Salt Lake City. The troops, who were stationed at Fort Bridger, Wyoming, supplied their own horses and equipment. Historian Orson F. Whitney pointed out that Capt. Lot Smith, in command of the volunteer Union cavalry, was operating in the same area where five years earlier he had burned U.S. wagon trains in an effort to keep the column led by Col. Johnston from entering Utah Territory.

Beehive House, 67 E. South Temple St. From a widow's walk where a telescope was mounted, Utah citizens watched activities at Fort Douglas. When a cannon was shot off at the fort one midnight, there was hasty mobilization at Beehive House. It was soon learned the big bang was to celebrate the news that Patrick Connor had been brevetted brigadier general. The house, which served as official residence of presidents of the Mormon church, has been restored.

Fort Douglas Memorial Military Museum,

east of University campus on Wasatch Dr. Museum is on fort grounds. The fort was established in 1862 by Col. Connor and the California Volunteers to protect the Overland Mail route and to maintain observance upon Mormons, whose loyalty was never taken quite for granted by Washington though no hostility occurred. Regular soldiers replaced volunteers at the war's end, and the post remained active. There is a monument to Connor and his volunteers in the post cemetery.

Lion House, 63 E. Temple St. The residence of Brigham Young for more than 20 years. Guide service.

Pioneer Memorial Museum, 300 N. Main St., west of Capitol, has pioneer relics and is itself a replica of the old Salt Lake Theater. Headquarters of Daughters of Utah Pioneers here.

Pony Express Monument, 147 S. Main St., is a seven-foot granite marker erected in 1931.

Utah State Capitol, Capitol St., has historical exhibits and an excellent collection of art.

Utah State Historical Society, 603 E. South Temple, has state archives and a library of Utah and western history.

VERMONT

Vermont was an independent republic until it entered the Union on March 4, 1791, as the 14th state. From its earliest days the state opposed slavery. The legislature made annual resolutions protesting slavery and sent copies to all other state legislatures. Some of the replies were equally outspoken. The Georgia legislature, in 1856, offered to send the governor of Vermont a proslavery resolution wrapped in a lead bullet. Another Georgia suggestion was put into a resolution asking President Pierce to hire enough men to dig a ditch around Vermont and float the "thing" into the ocean. In 1860 the state supported Lincoln instead of native son Stephen A. Douglas.

Vermont sent about 35,000 men to the war; more than 5,000 died in service. The state was invaded in October 1864 by a Confederate raid on St. Albans. Vermonters took to the defense with fists and guns that hadn't been fired since the War of 1812. The raiders made off with more than $200,000, but were caught and tried in Canada. When the Canadian court acquitted the Confederates on the ground that the invasion was a legitimate act of warfare, Congress abrogated the reciprocity treaty and both countries guarded the frontier for some time afterward.

BELLOWS FALLS, Windham County. IS 91, US 5. At one time the home of Edwin H. and Charles B. Stoughton, brothers who became brigadier generals in the Civil War. Edwin Henry Stoughton had served on garrison duty and scouted in the western territories before being commissioned colonel of the 4th Vermont. In March 1863 he was captured at Fairfax Courthouse by Mosby's raiders. His commission as brigadier general expired while he was a prisoner at Libby. After the war he practiced law.

BRANDON, Rutland County. US 7, State 73.
Douglas Birthplace, 2 Grove St., US 7. Stephen A. Douglas was born here in 1813. He attended Brandon Academy before moving to Illinois at the age of 20.
Soldiers' Monument, in midtown, is a granite shaft with figure of Civil War soldier.

BRATTLEBORO, Windham County. IS 91, State 9. Sculptor Larkin Mead lived here. During the Civil War he was staff artist for *Harper's Weekly.* The town was a station on the main line of the Underground Railroad.

BURLINGTON, Chittenden County. IS 89. A training camp for the 2nd Vermont was located here. The regiment lost 40 percent of its men in the war.

FAIR HAVEN, Rutland County. US 4, State 22A.
Zenas Ellis House, S. Main St., was an important Underground Railroad station.

GEORGIA CENTER, Franklin County. US 7.
Stannard Birthplace, on highway about 1 mile north of town. Monument marks the site of the birthplace of Gen. George Stannard. Stannard's counterattack on Pickett's right flank broke up the famous charge at Gettysburg.

GROTON, Caledonia County. US 302.
William Scott Memorial, granite marker on highway west of town. The "Sleeping Sentinel" of the Civil War was born here in 1839. Scott, who was court-martialed for sleeping at his sentry post at Camp Lyon, was pardoned by Lincoln. He was killed in action at Lee's Mill, Virginia, April 16, 1862.

MANCHESTER, Bennington County. US 7. Robert Todd Lincoln died here on the Lincoln estate south of Dellwood Cemetery.
Hildene, 1½ miles south on US 7A, was the summer home of Robert Todd Lincoln and the home of his descendants until 1975. Original furniture and personal memorabilia in mansion. Visitor center in the carriage barn has exhibits and a slide show.

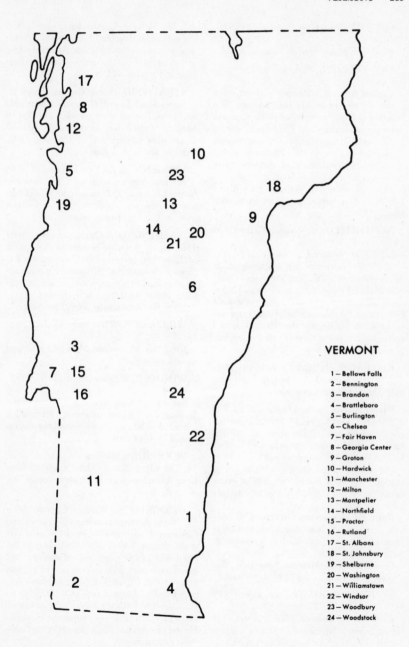

VERMONT

1 — Bellows Falls
2 — Bennington
3 — Brandon
4 — Brattleboro
5 — Burlington
6 — Chelsea
7 — Fair Haven
8 — Georgia Center
9 — Groton
10 — Hardwick
11 — Manchester
12 — Milton
13 — Montpelier
14 — Northfield
15 — Proctor
16 — Rutland
17 — St. Albans
18 — St. Johnsbury
19 — Shelburne
20 — Washington
21 — Williamstown
22 — Windsor
23 — Woodbury
24 — Woodstock

MILTON, Chittenden County. Off IS 89, US 7.
Civil War Monument, in business center.

MONTPELIER, Washington County. IS 89.
Capitol, State St. Near main entrance is the Larkin Mead bust of Abraham Lincoln. The building also has a display of battle flags and silver plaques listing Civil War engagements in which Vermont men participated. Lincoln sent a telegram to Gov. Erastus Fairbanks asking what could be expected from Vermont. "Vermont will do its full duty," was the reply.
Vermont Museum, Pavilion Office Bldg., 109 State St., has weapons, uniforms, and relics.

NORTHFIELD, Washington County. Off IS 89, State 12.
Civil War Memorial, in town square.
Norwich University, 6 miles north off IS 89. Among famous alumni: Maj. Gen. Grenville Mellen Dodge. After graduating, he surveyed for railroads and was active in the Iowa home guard. At the outbreak of war Dodge was commissioned colonel of the 4th Iowa, served throughout the war though twice wounded. Museum has war relics.

RUTLAND, Rutland County. US 7, 4. This was the home of Gov. John B. Page, state treasurer during the Civil War.

ST. ALBANS, Franklin County. IS 89, US 7, State 105. On October 19, 1864, 22 Confederate soldiers held up the three St. Albans banks and fled into Canada with about $200,000 in loot. The only casualty, E. J. Morrison, was a luckless visiting workman from Manchester; he was shot. St. Albans eventually recovered about $70,000 of the lost funds.
Brainerd Monument, Greenwood Cemetery, S. Main St., is a father's vengeful commemoration of his son's death as a prisoner at Andersonville.
Franklin County Museum, Church St., has displays pertaining to the Confederate raid.

ST. JOHNSBURY, Caledonia County. IS 91, US 5.
Civil War Monument, Main St., in Court House Square. The figure carved in Carrara marble is by Vermont sculptor Larkin Mead.

SHELBURNE, Chittenden County. US 7.
Shelburne Museum, 1 mile south. A 45-acre reconstruction of early American life, including buildings, locomotives, sleighs, buggies, and a sidewheel steamer.

STRATFORD, Orange County, State 132.
Justin Smith Morrill Homestead, State 132, is a Gothic Revival house completed in 1851 by Senator Morrill, who authored the Morrill Land Grant College acts of 1862 and 1890. Exhibits and guided tours.

VERGENNES, Addison County. US 7.
Rokeby, 2 miles north on US 7, was the home of Rowland T. Robinson, an abolitionist who provided a safe house for escaped slaves en route to Canada. Family relics.

WASHINGTON, Orange County. State 110. Home town of Napoleon Bonaparte McLaughlen, brevetted for Chancellorsville, Gettysburg, and Fort Stedman. He was captured at Fort Stedman, Virginia, and sent to Libby Prison until the end of the war.
Civil War Monument, in village center.

WILLIAMSTOWN, Orange County. State 14.
Civil War Monument, Main St., is topped by a stone eagle.

WINDSOR, Windsor County. IS 91, US 5, State 44.
Salmon P. Chase, who was Secretary of the Treasury in Lincoln's cabinet, attended a school for girls here. He was a small boy accompanied by his sisters.

WOODBURY, Washington County. State 14. The village claims to have furnished more Civil War troops per capita than any other Vermont town.

WOODSTOCK, Windsor County. State 12, 100A. Among eminent citizens was Jacob Collamer, close friend of Lincoln, who as Vermont senator drafted the bill which gave the Civil War its first congressional sanction and gave Lincoln new military powers. The bill was enacted July 13, 1861. George P. Marsh was appointed by Lincoln first U.S. Minister to Italy. Joseph Anthony Mower, a graduate of Norwich University, was wounded at Corinth. He was promoted to major general in the Carolinas campaign.

VIRGINIA

In 1860, Virginia had a population of more than 1½ million. When the state seceded from the Union on April 17, 1861, 50 counties in the northwest section separated from the commonwealth and in 1863 became the state of West Virginia. About 60 percent of all Civil War military engagements were fought in Virginia. The highway marker system makes it possible to follow most campaigns as well as many less severe actions. About 300 descriptive plaques, text prepared by the Virginia State Library, pertain exclusively to the Civil War. The Department of Highways has erected warning signs in advance of markers and provided parking turnout space where possible.

From May 1861 to April 1865, Richmond was the capital of the Confederacy. Danville served briefly as the seat of government in the last days of the war. Virginia, like Ohio, has been called "Mother of Presidents" and could also be called "Mother of Generals"; Robert E. Lee, Stonewall Jackson, Joseph E. Johnston, J. E. B. Stuart, and George E. Pickett were Virginians. Major conflicts took place at Manassas (or Bull Run), Fredericksburg and Spotsylvania, Chancellorsville, Petersburg, the Richmond area, Saylor's Creek, and Appomattox, where Lee surrendered on April 9, 1865.

Because of the manifold military events, space does not allow a listing of all major historic sites in the state. The major battlefields have been preserved and are maintained by the National Park Service and the state government. Trained historians are on duty; maps, literature, and displays are illustrative of events. Self-guided tours are aided by directional markers and orientation discs. A handbook has been prepared by the Virginia Department of Conservation and Development, Richmond, with code letters and descriptive texts of some 1,400 markers which pertain to all phases of Virginia history.

ABINGDON, Washington County. US 11, 19. Home town of Gen. Joseph E. Johnston. In 1862, church bells were melted for cannon.

The town was partly burned in Stoneman's raid, December 1864. New courthouse built 1869.

ACCOMAC, Accomack County. IS 81, US 13.

Onley, marker 2 miles south of town, was the home of Henry A. Wise, governor from 1856–1860 and Confederate brigadier general.

ALEXANDRIA, Fairfax County. IS 95, US 1.

Alexandria Convention and Visitors Bureau, 221 King St., for tour information.

Alexandria Gazette-Packet, 717 Asaph St., has been published continuously since 1784, except for a few days during the Civil War when the news—at least the type—was too hot to handle. Federals had burned the building. When the government suppressed the newspaper for secessionist sympathies, the publication continued undercover as *Local News.*

Alexandria National Cemetery, end of Wilkes St., has graves of more than 3,500 Union soldiers.

Christ Church, 118 N. Washington. Robert E. Lee was confirmed here. It has been said that it was after church service on the morning of April 21, 1861, that he met with representatives of the governor who offered him command of Virginia forces.

City Hall Council Chamber, 100 block on N. Royal St. Mural on second floor depicts Alexandria in 1863 with military installations.

Confederate Memorial, Washington and Prince St., marks the place where the 17th Virginia Regiment assembled on May 24, 1861.

Confederate Museum, 806 Prince St., open by request, is headquarters for units of the United Daughters of the Confederacy and the Sons of Confederate Veterans. Lee's camp chair is among exhibits.

Defense Forts, marker on US 1, just south of town. Forts O'Rorke, Weed, Farnsworth, and Lyon were to the north, Fort Willard to the east; they provided the southern defense line for Washington, 1862–1865.

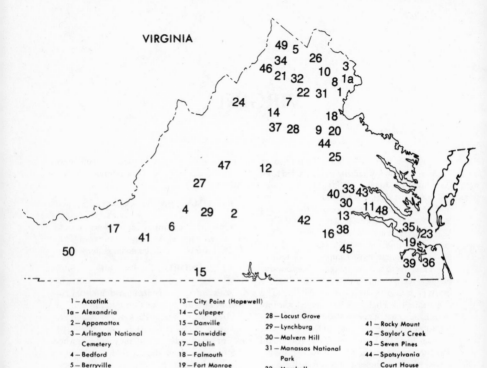

VIRGINIA

1 — Accotink
1a – Alexandria
2 — Appomattox
3 — Arlington National
    Cemetery
4 — Bedford
5 — Berryville
6 — Booker T. Washington
    National Monument
7 — Brandy Station
8 — Centerville
9 — Chancellorsville
10 — Chantilly
11 — Charles City
12 — Charlottesville

13 — City Point (Hopewell)
14 — Culpeper
15 — Danville
16 — Dinwiddie
17 — Dublin
18 — Falmouth
19 — Fort Monroe
20 — Fredericksburg
21 — Front Royal
22 — Gainesville
23 — Hampton
24 — Harrisonburg
25 — Ladysmith
26 — Leesburg
27 — Lexington

28 — Locust Grove
29 — Lynchburg
30 — Malvern Hill
31 — Manassas National
    Park
32 — Marshall
33 — Mechanicsville
34 — Middletown
35 — Newport News
36 — Norfolk
37 — Orange
38 — Petersburg
39 — Portsmouth
40 — Richmond

41 — Rocky Mount
42 — Saylor's Creek
43 — Seven Pines
44 — Spotsylvania
    Court House
45 — Stony Creek
46 — Strasburg
47 — Waynesboro
48 — Williamsburg
49 — Winchester
50 — Wytheville

(See chapter for other
sites and cities.)

Fort Ward Museum and Historic Site, 4301 W. Braddock Rd. Fort Ward was one of the defense posts forming a ring around the capital during the Civil War. Changing exhibits, interpretive programs, lectures, and tours.

The Free School, 400 block of S. Washington St., next door to Chamber of Commerce. Lee received his primary education here.

Green's Mansion House, 121 N. Fairfax St. Lee visited Alexandria in May 1869, after having called on President Grant. He stayed at the Fitzhugh House on Washington, but so many old friends came to call that a reception was held at the Mansion House. The line of well-wishers took two hours of handshaking.

Hallowell School, 609 Oronoco St. A

Quaker, Benjamin Hallowell, opened the school in 1824; Lee attended the following year to prepare for West Point.

Lee Homes: Lee's parents moved to 611 Cameron St. from Stratford in 1810; the family moved to 407 N. Washington St. in 1816, were living here when Lee's father, Lighthorse Harry Lee, died in Barbados. He had been away from home for five years, trying to regain his health. Lee's home from 1818 until he went to West Point was at 607 Oronoco St.; 220 N. Washington St. was the home of the Lloyds, cousins whom Lee often visited; 428 N. Washington was the home of Lee's uncle, Edmund Jennings Lee.

Lee's boyhood home, 607 Oronoco, is open most of the year, with period furnishings.

The Lyceum, 201 S. Washington St. Historical museum for the city of Alexandria. Exhibitions and travel information.

Old Christ Church Cemetery, Wilkes St., has the graves of Samuel Cooper, adjutant general and ranking general officer of the Confederate army, and James Murray Mason, commissioner to Great Britain, who was captured with John Slidell in the Trent Affair.

Stabler-Leadbeater Apothecary Shop, 107 S. Fairfax St., is said to be the place where Lee received orders carried by Lt. J. E. B. Stuart to command the troops sent to stop the John Brown raid, and here that he learned Virginia had seceded. The shop has been restored, has historical exhibits.

AMELIA, Amelia County. US 360. Markers on highway southwest of town follow Lee's line of retreat in April 1865.

Amelia Courthouse just missed being the surrender site. Lee was delayed here, having expected to find provisions arriving from Richmond by train. His men had to spend a day foraging, had clashes with Union cavalry, lost some 200 wagons. The present courthouse dates from 1924. Confederate memorial is in courthouse square. From here, on April 5, Lee moved toward Jetersville.

APPOMATTOX, Appomattox County. US 460, State 24.

Appomattox Court House National Historic Park, on State 24, 3 miles northeast of town. The visitor center is in the reconstructed courthouse. Exhibits and audio-visual programs every half-hour. In summer there are living history programs with a soldier from each army dressed in period costume who converse with visitors as if it were 1865. The McLean house was dismantled in 1893 to be re-erected as a war museum in Washington; plans were not carried out, but wood and bricks of the original structure were carried away. National Park Service historians also regret that many of the original furnishings were carried away by some of those present at the surrender. Some have been returned; other pieces are at the Smithsonian Institution in Washington and at the Chicago Historical Society. The village contains 27 historic structures. There are a number of markers along State 24, indicating Grant and Lee headquarters, Lee's farewell to his troops, a North Carolina regiment's last stand, the Confederate cemetery, the apple tree where Lee waited for Grant's call to the surrender conference. Some of these have parking turnoff areas. A map giving locations is available at the park headquarters.

New Appomattox County Courthouse, in the village, has descriptive plaque, Civil War monument, and cannon.

AQUIA CREEK, Stafford County. US 1. Marker about 3½ miles north of Stafford for site where the Army of the Potomac, coming from the James, landed in August 1862. The creek was a supply base for campaigns in 1862–1863.

ARLINGTON NATIONAL CEMETERY, Arlington County. IS 66, 395. Established in 1864, is the largest of national cemeteries. Civil War personages are among the 100,000 buried here.

Arlington House, the Custis-Lee Mansion, was the home of Robert E. Lee and the girlhood home of Mary Ann Randolph Custis, who became Mrs. Lee. Six of their seven children were born here. Federal troops occupied the area soon after the war began. The mansion served as headquarters for the general commanding the nearby forts. It has been restored under the administration of the National Park Service to its 1861 appearance. Some original furnishings have been returned. A new visitor center, which accommodates 3,000 visitors, has first-aid facilities as well as a Tourmobile Sightseeing information booth.

Confederate Memorial, off McPherson Dr. on the west side of the cemetery, was erected by the United Daughters of the Confederacy in 1914. Graves are arranged in concentric circles around the monument.

Tomb of the Unknown Dead of the Civil War marks a mass grave of 2,111 soldiers who died in the area during the war.

ASHLAND, Hanover County. IS 95, US 1. Three markers on highway north of town trace the movement of Lee's troops from May 22 to May 27, 1864. His army faced Grant along the North Anna River. Town was raided by Stoneman, May 1863; by Kilpatrick, March 1864; by Sheridan, May 1864.

Chickahominy Battles, marker on US 1, 5 miles south of town.

Jackson's March, marker on US 1, south edge of town, for Jackson's route to Gaines Mill, June 1862.

Lee's Headquarters, US 1, 4½ miles south, on May 27, 1864.

Stuart's Camp, US 1, about 2 miles north of town. J. E. B. Stuart camped at Winston's Farm, June 12, 1862.

AYLETT, King William County. US 360. Cavalry raiders apparently liked this route. Kilpatrick came in from the east long enough to burn Confederate stores on May 5, 1863. Dahlgren, from Richmond, crossed the Mattapony River here on March 2, 1864. Sheridan came through town on his way back from Richmond, May 22–23, 1864, and again on June 7, on his Trevilian raid.

BALL'S BLUFF. See LEESBURG.

BEDFORD, Bedford County. US 460. *Bedford City/County Museum,* 201 E. Main St., has Civil War relics.

Bedford County Courthouse has Confederate monument on grounds. Present building dates from 1930, is the third courthouse since 1782. Bedford was the home of John Goode, member of the secession convention, Confederate Congress, and U.S. Congress. Union Gen. David Hunter came this way en route to and coming from Lynchburg, where in 1864 he was repulsed by Early. He followed the Peaks of Otter Road, which is marked.

Hunter's Bivouac for night of June 18, 1864, is 3 miles west of town on US 460. His retreat into West Virginia left the way open for Jubal Early's raid on Washington. Hunter resigned his command in August.

BELLONA ARSENAL, Chesterfield County. US 60. Marker on highway 5½ miles west of Richmond denotes site of arsenal ruins. It was used by Confederates in 1861.

BERRYVILLE, Clarke County. US 340, State 7, 12.

Anderson and Crook Skirmish, on State 7 just west of town. R. H. Anderson, marching to join Lee at Petersburg in September 1864, attacked and drove back Gen. George Crook, who had succeeded Hunter as commander of the Department of West Virginia. Crook was once captured in a hotel bed by enterprising Confederates. In later years he became known as one of the best Indian fighters in the army and was called Gray Fox by his opponents.

Crook and Early, markers on State 7, 4½ and 7½ miles east of town. Early, coming back from Washington, was attacked here by Crook on July 16, 1864. Early lost some wagons but captured a cannon.

Lee and Longstreet Camp, US 340, 1 mile north of town. The Confederate generals camped here June 18–19, 1863, en route to Gettysburg. In the same area on August 13, Mosby attacked Sheridan's supply train, captured horses, mules, and 200 prisoners.

BLACKSTONE, Nottoway County. US 460. Union Gen. Wilson passed through on a raid in June 1864. Gen. Ord camped here early in April 1865.

BLAND, Bland County. IS 77, US 21. Gen. George Crook fought a skirmish at Rocky Gap in his May 1864 raid against the Virginia and Tennessee Railroad.

BOOKER T. WASHINGTON NATIONAL MONUMENT, Franklin County. Sixteen miles north of Rocky Mount on State 122, or 22 miles south of Roanoke by State 116. Since 1956, the area has been administered by the National Park Service. Booker Washington was born to Jane Ferguson, slave and cook on the James Burroughs plantation, in April 1856. After emancipation, the family moved to Malden, West Virginia, where Booker worked at a salt furnace and in coal mines. As an adult he gained national prominence as an author and in the field of education. The 200-acre monument includes the Burroughs plantation. James Burroughs had 14 children. Four of the six boys served in the war; two died in service—one is buried in the family cemetery on park grounds. Monument is operated as a living historical farm with costumed demonstrations and replicas of 19th-century farm buildings. Self-guiding plantation trail; visitor center has exhibits and slide show.

BOTTOMS BRIDGE, New Kent County. US 60. McClellan crossed the Chickahominy here May 23, 1862, on his march toward Richmond. About 5 miles southeast, marker denotes site of Long Bridge, where Longstreet crossed the river in the Peninsular campaign of May 1862. Grant's 2nd and 5th corps used the bridge en route to Petersburg in June 1864.

BRANDY, Culpeper County. US 15. *Battle of Brandy Station,* marker on highway, northeast edge of town. One of the greatest cavalry battles occurred here on June 9, 1863, between J. E. B. Stuart, who was screening Lee's advance toward Gettysburg, and Hooker's cavalry. There was much saber action. Gen. Lee's son, Rooney, was among the wounded; Wade Hampton's brother, Frank, and Stuart's scout, Will Farley, were mortally wounded.

Lee's Review, ½ mile southwest of town on US 15. Gen. Lee reviewed his cavalry here on June 8, 1863. Ewell's corps broke camp here on June 10 for the march to Pennsylvania.

Pelham's Mortal Injury occurred at Kelly's Ford on March 17, 1863. The young major, known as the "Gallant Pelham" and as "Lee's Boy Artillerist," was shot during a cavalry charge and died soon after. Marker on US 15, 2 miles northeast of Brandy.

BUCKINGHAM, Buckingham County. US 60.

Lee's Tent, 1 mile east of town. Monument marks spot where Lee camped after Appomattox on the night on April 12, 1865.

BURKEVILLE, Nottoway County. US 360. Jefferson Davis and cabinet went south through town on April 3, 1865. Federals in pursuit camped here three days later.

Richmond and Danville Railroad lost tracks when Union cavalryman Kautz came by in June 1864, on a raid to cut off Confederate supplies to Richmond and Petersburg.

BURROWSVILLE, Prince George County. State 10.

Coggin's Point, marker on highway 8, 3 miles northwest of town. From the bluff on the James River, Gen. D. H. Hill shelled McClellan's camp on the north bank, July 31, 1862.

Flowerdew Hundred, just over 5 miles northwest on State 10, was named for Temperance Flowerdew Yeardley, the governor's wife, in 1619. In June 1864, Grant's army crossed the James here. At Powell's Creek in the same area, Grant turned toward Petersburg.

CARET, Essex County. US 17.

Fonthill, marker 3 miles northwest, denotes site of home of R. M. T. Hunter, Confederate secretary of state. The home was raided by Union troops in 1863. Hunter was arrested here in 1865 and taken to Fort Pulaski.

CARMEL CHURCH, Caroline County. US 1.

Long Creek, about 2½ miles south. Grant's troops took Confederate earthworks here on May 23, 1864. Lee's army was on the south side of the river; marker ½ mile south in Hanover County.

Mount Carmel Church was Grant's headquarters in May 1864.

CEDAR MOUNTAIN. See CULPEPER.

CENTREVILLE, Fairfax County. IS 66, US 211. Descriptive plaques on highway denote sites pertaining to the first and second battles of Manassas, or Bull Run. Cub Run, about 2 miles west of town, was the point where an upset wagon caused a traffic jam on a bridge and panicked fleeing soldiers as well as civilians who were heading back to Alexandria. At Bull Run, Gen. Sherman had what may have been the first brush of his private four-year war with Northern civilians, most of whom were newspapermen. In this case, the Illinois abolitionist Lovejoy thoughtfully offered the general a pair of field glasses in the midst of battle. Sherman, in astonishment, asked, "Who are you, sir?" Response: "My name is Lovejoy and I'm a mem-

ber of Congress." A boiled-down version of Sherman's comment reads: "What are you doing here? Get out of my lines, sir! Get out of my lines!" Confederate Gen. Joseph E. Johnston had quarters here in the winter of 1861–1862, built fortifications which kept McClellan from marching upon Richmond from the north in the spring of 1862.

CHANCELLORSVILLE, Spotsylvania County. State 3. (*Also see* FREDERICKSBURG.) The battlefield is named for a family place rather than a town; it is on the Orange Turnpike, about 10 miles west of Fredericksburg and is part of the Fredericksburg and Spotsylvania National Military Park. Markers for the site where Gen. Stonewall Jackson was wounded and for the tent where his arm was amputated are on State 3. The visitor center has a film program, exhibits, literature, and maps.

CHANTILLY, Fairfax County. US 50. Stonewall Jackson reached a crossroads here, sometimes known as Ox Hill, on September 1, 1862, and had a skirmish with Federal troops under Gen. Pope in which the very able Gen. Philip Kearny was killed. One of Pope's contemporaries said he preferred the general no more than "a pinch of owl dung." Pope liked to say his headquarters were in the saddle—which inevitably led to someone's saying that was where his hindquarters should be.

CHARLES CITY, Charles City County. State 5.

Berkeley Plantation, on State 5, 7 miles west. Birthplace of President William Henry Harrison. McClellan's headquarters in the summer of 1862. Union Gen. Daniel Butterfield composed "Taps" while stationed here. Plantation was also used as hospital and signal tower. Estate then known as Harrison's Landing.

Charles City Courthouse. Grant's army was here in June 1864.

Evelynton, 5 miles east on State 5. Edmund Ruffin, who fired the first shot at Fort Sumter, carried on agriculture experiments here. During the war, ramparts were built across the field to the north of the main house. Longstreet camped nearby and J. E. B. Stuart fought a skirmish in the neighborhood.

Salem Church, about 6 miles west on State 5, was used as a field hospital in June 1864, after a skirmish at Nance's Shop; Union cavalryman Gregg was guarding a wagon train when attacked by Wade Hampton. Some of the dead were buried in church cemetery.

Sherwood Forest, 3½ miles east. The home

General Frémont's division crossing the pontoon bridge over the Shenandoah River.

of President John Tyler, who died here in 1862, was damaged during the war years.

Shirley, 9½ miles west, was the birthplace of Anne Hill Carter, mother of Gen. Robert E. Lee. The general's parents were married here in 1793. House has Lee memorabilia. Confederate soldier Beverly Carter, youngest of six sons of Hill Carter, owner of Shirley, came home to see his sick mother in 1863. A slave reported to Union headquarters across the river that there was a spy in the house. Young Carter was cornered in the attic by a searching party but escaped by climbing down a lightning rod.

Upper Weyanoke, 5 miles south. Most of Grant's army crossed the James at Weyanoke on a pontoon bridge in June 1864.

Wilcox's Wharf, about 2½ miles west. Marker denotes site where part of Grant's army was ferried across the James to Windmill Point, June 14–16, 1864.

CHARLOTTESVILLE, Albemarle County. IS 64, State 29, Business 250.

Jackson Statue, in Jackson Park near courthouse. The general on "Little Sorrel," by Charles Keck, is considered one of the finest equestrian statues in the country.

Lee Monument, in Lee Park, Jefferson St. between 1st and E. 2nd St., honors Gen. Robert E. Lee.

University of Virginia, west end of Main St. The Rotunda was used as a Confederate military hospital. Confederate ranger John Mosby was a student here.

CHATHAM, Stafford County. State 3, just east of Fredericksburg. Robert E. Lee courted his wife here. During the battle of Fredericksburg, the house was occupied by Gen. Sumner; later it was Gen. Hooker's headquarters for a time in 1863.

CHESTERFIELD, Chesterfield County. State 10.

Chesterfield County Museum, on State 10 in the Courthouse Complex, has Civil War artifacts.

CHRISTIANSBURG, Montgomery County. IS 81. Marker about ½ mile east on US 11. Union Gen. W. W. Averell raided the town on May 10, 1864. Union Gen. George Stoneman came here on April 5, 1865, during his raid to destroy railroads in Virginia and North Carolina.

CITY POINT, Prince George County. Marker for City Point and Hopewell on State 36 east of Petersburg.

Appomattox Manor can be reached by State 10 into Hopewell, where there are directional signs, or by Hopewell Ferry from State 5. Grant established headquarters here in June 1864. Lincoln often visited City Point on the *River Queen.* The famous conference held by Lincoln, Grant, and Sherman in March 1865 was at City Point aboard the presidential steamer. After the first day's meeting, Sherman dined with the Grants. Julie Grant asked if the generals had seen Mrs. Lincoln. They confessed they hadn't asked for her. Mrs. Grant said, "Well, you are a pretty pair!" Next day they dutifully inquired about the President's wife, but were not received. Mrs. Lincoln was feeling unwell. Three rooms of manor are open to the public.

National Cemetery, in east end of town off sidestreet, is a small, well-tended, quiet place with lovely shade trees and an unpretentious monument.

COLONIAL HEIGHTS, Chesterfield County. IS 95.

Violet Bank Civil War Museum occupies the site of Lee's headquarters from June to November 1864. Weapons, flags, and memorabilia displayed.

COLUMBIA, Cumberland County. State 27.

Flannagan's Mill, also known as Trice's Mill, about 19 miles south of Columbia, was a stopping place for Gen. Lee on the night of April 13, 1865, returning to Richmond from Appomattox.

CONCORD, Campbell County. US 460. Union Gen. David Hunter burned the railroad station and the Confederate commissary here in 1864.

COURTLAND, Southampton County. US 58. Marker on highway about 2 miles southeast denotes site of George H. Thomas birthplace. The "Rock of Chickamauga" was born July 13, 1816.

CRIGLERSVILLE, Madison County. State 670. 1 mile northwest is site where Stonewall Jackson camped on November 25, 1862, en route to join Lee at Fredericksburg.

CROZIER, Goochland County. State 6. *Dahlgren's Raid,* 2 miles east. Union Col. Ulric Dahlgren came this way in February 1864 on a raid toward Richmond in which he burned mills, barns, and destroyed railroad property.

Sabot Hill, 2½ miles east of Crozier, was the home of James A. Seddon, Confederate secretary of war. Union Gen. Ulric Dahlgren burned the barn on March 1, 1864.

CULPEPER, Culpeper County. US 15.

Battle of Cedar Mountain. Marker 6 miles south for site where Stonewall Jackson formed line of battle and received attack of Banks's Corps of Pope's army, August 9, 1862. Banks

was defeated. When Union reinforcements arrived late in the day, Jackson withdrew southward.

Clark's Mountain, marker about 5 miles south. Lee's army was behind the mountain on August 17, 1862, and Lee observed Pope's army from the signal station. Pope, realizing that he was in danger of attack, retired northward.

Culpeper Cavalry Museum, 113 W. Davis St., has an excellent collection of weapons and cavalry equipment.

Virginia Hotel in Culpeper was headquarters for Confederates and later for Union officers. Grant stayed here in April 1864. The wounded from the battles of Cedar Mountain, Kelly's Ford, and Brandy Station were treated in Culpeper homes, churches, and empty buildings in makeshift conditions.

DANVILLE, Pittsylvania County. US 58, 360, 29.

Confederate Memorial, Sutherlin Ave. and Main St. The home of Maj. W. T. Sutherlin, where President Davis stayed April 3–10, 1865, and held the last full cabinet meeting, except for Breckinridge, is regarded as the last Capitol of the Confederacy. News of Lee's surrender arrived here on April 10, 1865, ending the government. Now Danville Museum of Fine Arts and History.

DERWENT, Powhatan County. Here is the house where Gen. and Mrs. Lee stayed for part of the summer after Appomattox. Mrs. Elizabeth Randolph Cocke realized that Lee needed quiet but had to receive an endless line of visitors in his Richmond home, so she offered a cottage on her property. The general was here when Judge Brockenbrough brought the news that Lee had been elected president of Washington College. The nearest marker is about 10 miles south of State 13, 2 miles east of Tobaccoville.

DINWIDDIE, Dinwiddie County. IS 85, US 1.

Chamberlain's Bed, 1 mile south. On March 31, 1865, Pickett and W. H. F. Lee, coming from Five Forks, crossed the stream here, driving back Sheridan's troops to Dinwiddie Courthouse.

Confederate Monument, courthouse grounds, has a granite soldier at rest that has been described as looking "aloof." Pickett's men were anything but remote in attitude or behavior on March 31, 1865, when they drove Sheridan's troops to the courthouse. Sheridan was saved by darkness but rallied next day to defeat Pickett at Five Forks.

Scott's Law Office. Lt. Gen. Winfield Scott, commander of the Union army at the outbreak of war, was born here June 13, 1786, had a law office slightly to the west of highway marker.

Vaughan Road, US 1. Grant came west on this road to attack Lee's right wing. For Union Gen. Hancock, it was a road to defeat—at Burgess Mill, October 27, 1864. Sheridan took this route to town on March 29, 1865.

DRANESVILLE, Fairfax County. State 7. Marker for Stuart's route north before Gettysburg is on highway 2½ miles west of town. In town is a marker for an action of December 20, 1861, when Stuart attacked Union Gen. Ord; both forces were on foraging expeditions. Also marker for Lee's route toward Leesburg in the Antietam campaign, September 1862.

DREWRY'S BLUFF, Chesterfield County. US 1. Markers are located on highway at points about 1½, 4, and 4½ miles south of Richmond. The battle of Drewry's Bluff took place on May 16, 1864. The Union troops under Gen. Butler advanced north, but were held back by Confederate troops and home guards, reinforced by Gen. Beauregard, and Butler withdrew. Earthworks remain. Halfway House, which was Butler's headquarters, is now a restaurant.

DUBLIN, Pulaski County. Off IS 81, State 100.

Battle of Cloyd's Mountain, 5 miles north of town, west of highway. May 9, 1864, Union Gen. George Crook, on a raid against the Virginia and Tennessee Railroad, repulsed Gen. A. G. Jenkins, who was mortally wounded in the encounter. Jenkins, a graduate of Harvard Law School, had been a U.S. and Confederate congressman; as a brigadier general he had led a raid through West Virginia and into Ohio, captured Chambersburg, Pennsylvania, during the Gettysburg campaign, and was wounded at Gettysburg.

DUMFRIES, Prince William County. IS 95, US 1. Marker just over 3 miles north indicates site of Leesylvania, home of Robert E. Lee's grandfather. In Dumfries on December 12, 1862, Wade Hampton surprised a Federal detachment and captured wagons; on December 27, Stuart had a brush with Union troops occupying the town. Marker on highway about 4½ miles south for site where Fitz Lee captured wagons on the same day as Stuart's skirmish.

DUTCH GAP, Chesterfield County. US 1. Just over 6½ miles south of Richmond. Marker denotes site where Gen. Butler cut a canal through the neck of the James, shortening the river 5 miles, in August 1864.

EDINBURG, Shenandoah County. IS 81, US 11. Gen. Turner Ashby made the town a base for operations in 1862, engaging in 28 skirmishes in one month. Sheridan is said to have set the local mills on fire but doused the flames when appealed to by two young women. The area was called the "Granary of the Confederacy."

ELKWOOD, Culpeper County. US 15. Marker on highway for Kelly's Ford, where Maj. John Pelham was mortally wounded. (Also see BRANDY.)

FAIRFAX CITY, Fairfax County. IS 66, US 50. Marker on highway about 7 miles west of town for action of September 1, 1862, between Jackson's troops at Ox Hill (Chantilly) and Pope's men. Gen. Philip Kearny was killed. Pope retreated to Alexandria. Marker just west of town for Lee's movements in Antietam campaign, September 3, 1862. Courthouse has monument to Capt. John Q. Marr, Confederate soldier killed in battle.

St. Mary's Catholic Church, has plaque presented by the Red Cross commemorating the services of Clara Barton.

FALLS CHURCH, Fairfax County. IS 66, US 29. Marker on US 211 for church which was used as a stable by Union troops, 1862–1864.

The Falls Church, 115 E. Fairfax St., was used as a Federal hospital, later as a stable. Restored.

FALMOUTH, Spotsylvania County. Off IS 95, US 1.

Cavalry Encounters, State 17, 8 miles northwest of Falmouth. Hampton captured officers and men of the 3rd Pennsylvania Cavalry here on November 28, 1862. On February 25, 1863, Fitz Lee drove back Federal cavalry toward the Union encampment at Falmouth.

Lee's Headquarters, on US 1, about 5½ miles south of town. Winter quarters, 1862–1863.

Sheridan's Raid, just over 5 miles south of town. In May 1864, Sheridan's cavalry filled Telegraph Road for several miles, advancing toward Richmond.

Stuart's Headquarters, about 5½ miles south of town. J. E. B. Stuart camped in this area in December 1862.

FARMVILLE, Prince Edward County. US 15, 460.

Prince Edward Hotel has marked the rooms occupied overnight by Lee and Grant when the armies moved toward Appomattox.

FIVE FORKS, Dinwiddie County. US 460. Five miles west of Sutherland marker on highway. Battleground is to the south. Sheridan attacked Pickett on the afternoon of April 1, 1865. A Confederate defeat here broke Lee's line of defense around Petersburg, forcing him to withdraw. Union officers had quarters in the Gilliam farmhouse.

FORT LEE, Dinwiddie County. 2 miles east of Petersburg.

Quartermaster Museum, 1 block inside the main gate, has Civil War memorabilia.

FORT MONROE, Elizabeth City County. US 60. One of the few forts in the South not taken by Confederates at the start of the war. Gen. McClellan had headquarters here in the spring of 1862. Lincoln came to the fort in May 1862 and helped to plan operations which resulted in the fall of Norfolk and the blowing up of the *Merrimac* by her own crew. Grant was here in April 1864. The Army of the James was organized at the fort.

Jefferson Davis Casemate (a casemate is a chamber in the wall of a fort) is on display. The outer room, used by Davis's guards, is now a gallery with pictures depicting events in the Confederate president's life. When his health suffered, he was transferred to Carroll Hall in the fortress and remained there until parole in May 1867, when he was released on bail. He was never brought to trial.

Monitor and Merrimac Casemate contains scale models, maps, photographs, and documents pertaining to the naval engagement of March 9, 1862, at Hampton Roads.

FORT MYER, Arlington County. US 50, across Arlington Memorial Bridge. The only Civil War fortification still in use near the Capitol was established in 1863. The "Old Guard" 1st Battle Group, 3rd Infantry Regiment, protects the president and the national Capitol, guards the Tomb of the Unknown Soldier, and provides ceremonial units for Arlington National Cemetery. Open daily.

FRANKLIN, Southampton County. US 258.

Mahone Birthplace, marker on highway just over 2 miles south of town. Maj. Gen. William Mahone ("Little Billy") was born at Monroe, 3½ miles southwest. A graduate of V.M.I., he rose rapidly in the Confederate service, commanded the Norfolk district, then commanded

Drewry's Bluff defenses. He was wounded at Second Manassas and given an on-the-field promotion for his performance at the Petersburg crater.

FREDERICKSBURG, IS 95, US 1.

Fredericksburg, Area Museum and Cultural Center, 905 Princess Anne St. Old town hall and marketplace contains exhibits illustrating area's history from prehistoric times to the 20th century, including Civil War displays.

Confederate Cemetery, Washington Ave. and Amelia St., has graves of 2,640 Confederate soldiers and officers who fell on nearby battlefields.

Courthouse, Princess Anne St. Union Gen. D. N. Couch had headquarters here during the battle of Fredericksburg, used the tower as a signal station.

Kenmore, Washington Ave. between Lewis and Fauquier St. House was used as hospital and military headquarters during Civil War.

Presbyterian Church, southwest corner of Princess Anne and George St. Clara Barton took care of wounded here. Two cannon balls have been built into the left column of the portico, struck during the bombardment of the town.

Slave Block, Charles and William St.

Visitor Center, 706 Caroline St., has much literature pertaining to the historic city. Has slide presentation, maps, and other items.

FREDERICKSBURG AND SPOTSYL-VANIA NATIONAL MILITARY PARK, Spotsylvania, Stafford, Orange, and Caroline counties and city of Fredericksburg, IS 95 and Route 3. The park is located in and around the city of Fredericksburg. It covers more than 5,000 acres and includes parts of the battlefields of Fredericksburg, Salem Church, Spotsylvania Court House, Chancellorsville, and the Wilderness. Two visitor centers offer exhibits and slide presentations: the Fredericksburg Battlefield Visitor Center at 1013 Lafayette Blvd. at the foot of Marye's Heights, across the Sunken Road from the national cemetery; and the Chancellorsville Battlefield Visitor Center on Route 3 west of IS 95, near the site of Stonewall Jackson's wounding. Free literature, inexpensive brochures, and tapes are available for self-guided tours to the battlesites. Narrative markers and maps are located at key points. Included in the park area is the Stonewall Jackson Shrine at Guiney's Station, the building in which the general died. The national cemetery has graves of more than 15,000 Union soldiers; about 13,000 are unknown.

FRIENDS MISSION, Patrick County. State 773.

Stuart's Birthplace, marker on highway 4 miles south of town for site where James Ewell Brown Stuart, Confederate major general, was born February 6, 1833.

FRONT ROYAL, Warren County. US 340, 522. The 1st Maryland Regiment, U.S.A., under Col. Kenly, was attacked here by the 1st Maryland Regiment, C.S.A., under Stonewall Jackson, May 23, 1862. Jackson captured the town.

Belle Boyd and Jackson Marker, 3 miles southwest on US 340. The literally dashing Belle is said to have raced across the embattled field of Front Royal to give Jackson helpful details regarding the size and disposition of the Federal force.

Mosby's Men. Marker on US 522 just north of town. Gen. Custer executed several of Mosby's raiders on September 23, 1864. In November, Col. Mosby executed an equal number of Custer's men near Berryville.

Warren Rifles Museum, 95 Chester St., has relics, flags, arms, uniforms, documents, personal memorabilia.

GAINESVILLE, Prince William County. IS 66, US 211. Ten markers in the town and on highway both east and west are situated at key points of the first and second battles of Manassas.

GERMANNA FORD, Orange County. State 3, about 5 miles west of the Wilderness. This crossing of the Rapidan was used by the Army of the Potomac on April 30, 1863, before Chancellorsville, by Meade's army en route to Mine Run, November 26, 1863, and by part of Grant's army early in May 1864, before the Wilderness campaign.

GLOUCESTER, Gloucester County. US 17.

Gloucester Courthouse was the scene of a cavalry skirmish, January 29, 1864.

Gloucester Point was fortified by Confederates in 1861, occupied by Federals in 1862.

GROTTOES, Rockingham County. IS 81.

Grand Caverns Regional Park, 6 miles east on State 256. Both Federal and Stonewall Jackson's troops were quartered at different times in the Great Cathedral and the Grand Ballroom.

HALIFAX, Halifax County. US 501.

Confederate Monument, courthouse grounds.

St. John's Church, Main St. Rev. Charles Dresser, rector from 1823 to 1831, moved to Illinois where he performed marriage ceremony of Abraham Lincoln and Mary Todd in 1842.

HAMPTON, Elizabeth City County. IS 64, US 60. Marker at west entrance of town, which was burned by Confederates in August 1861 to prevent its use by Union troops. The *Monitor* and the *Merrimac* (the C.S.S. *Virginia*) fought here, in Hampton Roads. The *Merrimac* destroyed two other vessels before being badly shaken, though not pierced, by *Monitor* shells.

Big Bethel, the first regular battle of the war was fought here on June 10, 1861. The area is now within the city of Hampton. Cemetery has Civil War soldiers. Marker on US 60 at Morrison.

Camp Hamilton. Marker on highway. Union camp established here May 1861. Hampton Hospital was also here.

Hampton Institute, east end of Queen St., was established on the farmland where Hampton Hospital had been maintained during the war. The Collis P. Huntington Memorial Library has an extensive collection of books and documents pertaining to black history. Booker T. Washington is among the distinguished graduates of the institute.

St. John's Church, northwest corner of Court and Queen St., was partially burned in 1861. Monument in church cemetery.

Syms-Eaton Museum, Cary St., has exhibits and relics pertaining to Hampton history.

HARRISONBURG, Rockingham County. IS 81, US 11, State 33.

Ashby Marker, on US 11, 1½ miles south of town. Turner Ashby, Jackson's cavalry commander, was killed in a rear guard action at a point 1½ miles east on June 6, 1862.

Caverns of Melrose, 6 miles northeast, were used for encampment during the war; names of hundreds of soldiers are inscribed on the walls. There is a Civil War museum at the site.

Cross Keys, marker on US 33, 5 miles east. June 8, 1862, Ewell, commanding Jackson's rear guard, was attacked by Frémont. Trimble, of Ewell's command, drove the Federals back.

Jackson's Campaign. Descriptive marker at Harrisonburg for events in the area pertaining to the end of Jackson's Valley campaign in June 1862.

Lincoln Family Graves, 4 miles north of town, near Edom. The gravesites of "Virginia John" and Rebekah Flowers Lincoln, great-grandparents of Abraham Lincoln, are in the family cemetery and are marked. Two Lincoln family homesteads are near the cemetery; one is the home of Jacob Lincoln, the only son of

"Virginia John," who remained in Rockingham county after the Revolutionary War; the other is the home of Jacob Lincoln, Jr. Marker on US 11, at Lacey Spring, denotes site of Thomas Lincoln birthplace. President Lincoln's father was born about 1778 and taken to Kentucky about 1781.

Pritchett Museum, on campus of Bridgewater College, 7 miles southwest of town, on State 42, has Confederate relics.

Rosser-Custer Engagement, US 11, 7½ miles north. Rosser's Confederate cavalry attacked Custer's camp, December 20, 1864. The two cavalry leaders had been West Point roommates.

Warren-Sipe Museum, 301 S. Main, has Civil War exhibits and an electric map with narration featuring the Valley campaign of 1862.

HAYMARKET, Prince William County. US 15.

St. Paul's Church was used as hospital, barracks, and stable during the war.

HOPEWELL, Prince George County. Off IS 95, State 10, 36. (*Also see* CITY POINT.)

Fort Lee, 3 miles west of town, is the largest quartermaster installation and training center in the country. A museum has historical Quartermaster Corps documents, relics, and memorabilia.

Merchants Hope Church, off State 10, 5 miles east of town, south on 641. Church was used as a picket station during the war; the building, which dates from 1655, has been restored. (*Also see* CITY POINT.)

JARRATT, Sussex County. US 301.

Jarratt's Station, ½ mile south. Depot on the old Weldon Railroad burned by Union cavalryman Kautz on May 8, 1864. Union Gen. Wilson camped here June 29, 1864, retreating from Reams Station. Union Gen. Gouverneur Kemble Warren, on his raid to destroy the railroad, camped here in December 1864.

JETERSVILLE, Amelia County. US 360.

Lee's Retreat. Markers on highway from Amelia, in town, and on highway to the southwest, are placed along Lee's line of retreat toward Danville in the first week of April 1865. Sheridan arrived at Jetersville on April 4 and entrenched his corps across Lee's intended route to Danville. Lee detoured to Amelia Courthouse.

JONESVILLE, Lee County. US 58. On January 3, 1864, Confederate Gen. William E. Jones, aided by Col. A. L. Pridemore, defeated a Federal force and captured a battalion. Union troops burned the courthouse in 1864.

KERNSTOWN, Frederick County. US 11.

Battle of Kernstown, about 2 miles south. In the afternoon of March 23, 1862, Jackson attacked Shield's troops on a hill to the west of the highway. After severe fighting in which the Confederates were outnumbered, Jackson withdrew southward. Citizens of Winchester next day buried the dead.

KING GEORGE, King George County. State 3.

Lamb's Creek Church, 5½ miles west. Kilpatrick's Union cavalry skirmished near here on a raid to destroy gunboats at Port Conway on September 1, 1863.

Port Conway, about 3 miles east. Kilpatrick's cavalry shelled two gunboats captured by Confederates, September 1, 1863. John Wilkes Booth crossed the river at this point on April 24, 1865.

LADYSMITH, Caroline County. US 1.

Dickinson's Mill, just over 2 miles south, is the site where Lee camped on May 21, 1864, en route to North Anna. Ewell's and Longstreet's corps were here that night.

Doctor Flippo's, 1½ miles north of town. Warren's corps of the Army of the Potomac camped here May 22, 1864, en route to the North Anna River.

Nancy Wright's, 5 miles north of town, was site of Union encampment, May 22, 1864.

LEE HALL, Warwick County. US 60. Confederate Gen. John B. Magruder had headquarters here in April and May 1862.

Lee's Mill, or battle of Dam No. 1, 2 miles southeast, was scene of the opening engagement of the Peninsular campaign, April 16, 1862.

LEESBURG, Loudoun County. US 15, State 7.

Battle of Ball's Bluff, marker on US 15. October 21, 1861, Edward Baker, close friend of Lincoln's, attempted to make a demonstration against Confederate forces opposite Potomac fords near Poolesville. The Federals were ambushed by Evans's troops; Baker and 48 others were killed. The smallest national cemetery is on the wooded bluff that overlooks the Potomac.

Confederate Monument, on courthouse grounds.

Early's Route, State 7, 2 miles west of town. Jubal Early came this way, returning to the Shenandoah Valley, July 16, 1864.

Jackson Camp, US 15, about 3 miles north of town. Stonewall Jackson's bivouac on September 4, 1862.

Loudoun Museum, 16 Loudoun St. SW, has Civil War memorabilia.

Potomac Crossings, just over 4 miles north of town. Lee crossed the river at White's Ford, September 6, 1862, in his invasion of Maryland. Early, coming back from Washington, crossed here July 14, 1864.

LEXINGTON, Rockbridge County. IS 81, US 11, 60.

Houston Birthplace, marker on State 10, just over 5 miles north of town. Sam Houston, governor of Texas who tried to hold the state in the Union at the time of secession, was born in a cabin on a hilltop to the east, March 2, 1793.

Stonewall Jackson House, 8 E. Washington, was the general's home before the war. Slides, memorabilia, and guided tours.

Stonewall Jackson Memorial Cemetery, east side of Main St., has the graves of Gen. Stonewall Jackson and many other Confederate soldiers.

Maury Monument, northwest of town on State 39, in Goshen Pass. Anchor monument honors Confederate Commodore Matthew Fontaine Maury, who was an instructor at V.M.I. after the war.

Thorn Hill, marker on US 11. Home of Gen. E. F. Paxton, commander of the Stonewall Brigade, killed at Chancellorsville, May 3, 1863.

Virginia Military Institute. Jackson, Maury, and John Mercer Brooke, Confederate chief of naval ordnance, were faculty members. The V.M.I. Museum, on campus, has Jackson and Maury memorabilia. A bronze statue of Gen. Jackson overlooks the parade grounds.

Washington and Lee University, west end of Henry St., was closed during the war. Gen. Robert E. Lee became president of the institution after the war; it was then known as Washington Academy. After Lee's death, it was renamed. The Lee Memorial Chapel is now a National Historic Landmark and has been restored. Lee is buried in the chapel, which was designed by him and built under his supervision. Also buried here: his wife, Mary Custis, a descendant of Martha Washington; his father, Lighthorse Harry Lee; his mother, Anne Carter Lee; and other members of the Lee family. Above the tomb is the Valentine recumbent statue of the general. The chapel also contains family and Civil War memorabilia. The President's House was built when Lee was head of the university. Adjacent is the stable of his horse, Traveller.

LOCUST GROVE, Orange County. State 20.

Battle of the Wilderness, marker 3 miles east of town. Ewell's corps engaged Warren's Union troops here on May 5, 1864. Two miles south on the Orange Plank Road, Lee's right wing was opposed to Grant's left wing on May 6.

Robinson's Tavern, marker on highway. Meade gathered his troops at this point in November 1863, hoping to surprise Lee in winter quarters to the west. One corps arrived so late his plans were altered and Lee was able to entrench on Mine Run. (Marker for Lee's position on State 20, 6½ miles east of Unionville.) Ewell, in May 1864, camped near Robinson's Tavern.

LONG DALE, Alleghany County. US 60.

Lucy Selina Furnace was taken over by the Confederate government in 1861 and run by Gen. Jospeh R. Anderson; the furnace supplied much of the iron used for Confederate cannon and cannon balls.

LORTON, Fairfax County. Off IS 90. West of Mount Vernon.

Pohick Church, 10651 Gunston Rd., had pews removed during the war when it was used as a stable. Years later the baptismal font was discovered being used as a trough in a neighboring farmyard.

LOUISA, Louisa County. US 33.

Battle of Trevilians, 4½ miles west of town. June 12, 1864, Sheridan's cavalry attacked Wade Hampton. Fitz Lee joined Hampton to drive back the Unionists, who retired eastward.

Green Springs, 7 miles west of Louisa, is site where Wade Hampton's cavalry camped on June 10, 1864.

LOVINGSTON, Nelson County. US 29.

Rives Birthplace, 4 miles south of town. William Cabell Rives was born at Oak Ridge, 2 miles east of highway marker. He was a U.S. senator and a member of the Confederate congress.

LYNCHBURG, Amherst County. US 29.

Battle of Lynchburg, marker at 9th and Church St. The city was a main military supply center. Confederates under Gen. Jubal Early defeated Gen. David Hunter, June 18, 1864. Markers for defense sites are located at Bedford Ave. and Holly St.; 12th St. between Fillmore and Floyd St.; Rivermont Ave. near Krise St.; Rivermont Ave. and Fitzhugh Pl.; 9th St. between Fillmore and Floyd St.; and 5th St. between Wise and Floyd St. Two Confederate earthworks are on Madison Heights, ½ mile southeast of US 29, 1 mile north of town.

Confederate Monument, Monument Terrace, 9th St. between Church and Court St. Bronze Confederate infantryman was designed by James O. Scott of Lynchburg, erected in 1898.

Daniel Monument, 9th, Floyd St., and Park Ave., honors John Warwick Daniel. The Confederate major is seated, holding a crutch. He was wounded at the battle of the Wilderness and known as the "Lame Lion of Lynchburg."

Fort Early, Fort and Vermont Ave. The earthwork has been restored. It was part of the outer defenses in June 1864, built by Gen. Jubal Early. Monument honors the Confederate general. He lived in Lynchburg from 1869 until his death.

Fort McCausland, Langhorne Rd. west of Clifton St. Fortifications were built by Gen. Early to protect the approach from the west. A cavalry skirmish took place on the road immediately to the west. Federals were repulsed by Gen. McCausland's men.

Miller Park, US 460, Park Ave. Marker at Park Ave. entrance. The 2nd Virginia Cavalry was mustered into service here on May 10, 1861. Disbanded here April 10, 1865.

Old Lynchburg College, Wise St. between 10th and 11th St., went out of existence in February 1861; buildings were being used as a Confederate hospital and as Federal barracks after the war.

Sandusky, US 29. Headquarters of Union Gen. Hunter in mid-June 1864. Future presidents Hayes and McKinley, then serving under Hunter, roomed together in this house.

Spring Hill Cemetery, Fort Ave. between Lancaster St. and Wythe Rd., has the graves of Confederate Gens. Jubal A. Early and Thomas Taylor Munford, V.M.I. graduate who served from First Manassas through Appomattox; James Dearing, who was mortally wounded at High Bridge and died a few days after the surrender at Appomattox; Sen. John W. Daniel; and a child of Gen. J. E. B. Stuart.

MADISON, Madison County. State 231.

Jackson's March, marker in town. Jackson, en route from Winchester to Fredericksburg, camped here November 26, 1862.

Stuart-Kilpatrick Encounter, 5½ miles south. J. E. B. Stuart was fighting Union cavalry under Buford when attacked from the rear by Kilpatrick's men. Stuart turned and cut his way out on September 22, 1863.

MALVERN HILL, Henrico County. State 5. Marker on highway 13½ miles southeast of Richmond. Last of the Seven Days' battles of the Peninsular campaign. McClellan, with-drawing from Richmond, was attacked by Lee on July 1, 1862. Federal gunners had the advantage, having had time to take positions on the hill. Lee was unable to storm the hill, but McClellan, against the advice of Porter and Hunt, withdrew that night to a new base at Harrison's Landing.

MANASSAS, Prince William County. Off IS 66, US 211.

Manassas City Museum, in Baldwin Park. Exhibits depict the history of this famous little railroad junction, including a celebration in 1911 when veterans of both sides reunited at a "Peace Jubilee."

MANASSAS NATIONAL BATTLE-FIELD PARK, Prince William County. US 29, 211, State 234. First battle of Manassas (or Bull Run) was fought July 21, 1861, between Federals under Gen. Irvin McDowell and Confederates under Gens. Beauregard and Johnston. Jackson won his nickname when he awaited attack behind the eastern crest of Henry House Hill and Gen. Bee shouted: "Look! There stands Jackson like a stone wall! Rally behind the Virginians!" The Confederates were fighting a desperate defense when reinforcements turned the battle tide, routing the Federals. The battle of Second Manassas took place on August 28–30, 1862. Lee led the Confederates, Pope was in command of Federals. The Southerners again were victorious; Pope retreated to Washington, and Lee prepared to invade Maryland.

The visitor center, on State 234 between IS 66 and US 29, has a museum with slide programs and a three-dimensional map of the battle formations. Key points of interest are well marked; the Jackson equestrian statue and the Stone House are major landmarks. In the Henry House yard is the grave of Mrs. Judith Henry, an 85-year-old widow who was carried to a nearby gully during the first part of the battle by her son and daughter, but was brought back to the house where she was killed when the tide of battle again came her way. Descriptive highway markers pertaining to both campaigns will be found in the surrounding area at Centreville, Gainesville, Fairfax, Massies Corner, Warrenton, Marshall, and Orange.

MANNBORO, Amelia County. State 38. Marker 7 miles east of town. On April 3, 1865, Custer, with an advance guard of the Army of the Potomac, drove back Fitz Lee, commanding the left flank guard of the Army of Northern Virginia.

MARION, Smyth County. IS 81, US 11.

Scene of cavalry action, December 1864, during Union Gen. George Stoneman's raid. Stoneman occupied Seven Mile Ford, 3 miles east of Chilhowie.

MARKHAM, Fauquier County. State 55. *Lee's Headquarters* were here on June 17, 1863, before the invasion of Pennsylvania.

MARSHALL, Fauquier County. State 55. Confederates frequently tore up tracks of the Manassas Gap Railroad, which was controlled by the Federals after 1863. Col. Henry Dixon of Marshall was said to be the only man in the county who voted for Lincoln in 1860; reportedly, he carried a gun in one hand and a ballot in the other. He was killed in a gunfight in Alexandria after the war. Stonewall Jackson took a rest stop near here in August 1862, en route to Bristoe Station. At Rectortown, 4 miles north, McClellan was relieved of command, November 7, 1862, and turned over the Army of the Potomac to Ambrose Burnside.

McDOWELL, Highland County. US 250. *Battle of McDowell,* May 8, 1862. Jackson beat off attacks of Frémont's advance troops under Milroy from a position on hills to the south of highway.

MECHANICSVILLE, Hanover County. US 360, State 156. The battle of Mechanicsville, June 26, 1862, was part of the campaign known as the Seven Days' battles and is now part of the Richmond National Battlefield Park. At this town, Union outposts were driven back to a position on Beaver Dam Creek by A. P. Hill; then D. H. Hill, followed by Longstreet, crossed the Chickahominy here and joined A. P. Hill. At Cold Harbor Visitor Center are maps for tours of the whole campaign. The National Cemetery has Union dead. It is said to have the only mass grave for U.S. military dead.
Ruffin's Grave, at Marlbourne, about 10 miles northeast of Mechanicsville. Edmund Ruffin, agriculturist and ardent secessionist, fired the first gun at Sumter and served in the Confederate army for a time.

MIDDLEBURG, Fauquier County. US 50. *Atoka* (Rector's Crossroads), 3½ miles west, was the site where Company A, 43rd Battalion of Mosby's Rangers was organized June 10, 1863, under Capt. James William Foster.

MIDDLETOWN, Frederick County. Off IS 81, US 11. *Battle of Cedar Creek* markers are located just north and just south of town. Gen. Jubal Early opposed Sheridan's cavalry on October 19, 1864. The Federals were driven back until Gen. H. G. Wright stopped the retreat. T. Buchanan Read's poem "Sheridan's Ride" was based on Sheridan's return to the field; although Wright actually had the situation under control, Little Phil was a great morale booster. The knoll where the cavalry leader rejoined the army is marked on US 11 just over 3 miles south of Stephens City. The poet may be forgiven for putting Sheridan 20 miles away; it reads better than 14 miles. At Cedar Creek in 1862, Ohioan John S. Jones, aide to Gen. James Shields, recorded a small personal victory in his diary (unpublished): "At Cedar Creek Ashby made a stand and fired the Bridge on the evening of the 14th of March. It was dark when the Gen'l ordered the cavalry across; they failed to go and gave as a reason that they would be exposed to the fire of the enemy on account of the light from the burning bridge. The Gen'l was out of patience with them and I volunteered to lead a squad across. I crossed but no cavalry followed. It was just as well, however, as I accomplished all that was desired. I found Ashby had retreated and that the stream was fordable. . . . After that I stood higher in the estimation of the Gen'l than did his cavalry."
Belle Grove, 1 mile south on US 11, then west on County Rd. 727, was Gen. Philip Sheridan's headquarters during the battle of Cedar Creek. House museum on working farm.
Signal Station. Marker denoting site is on US 11, 1 mile south of town. Mountain top to the southeast was used as signal station by both armies. There is the grave of an unknown soldier at the site.

MOUNT CRAWFORD, Rockingham County. US 11. Marker on highway for engagement of March 1, 1865, in Sheridan's last raid.

MOUNT JACKSON, Shenandoah County. US 11.
Cavalry Engagement occurred 1 mile south on November 17, 1863, between the 1st Virginia and the 1st New York.
Confederate Cemetery, in village, has graves of 500 soldiers, 112 unknown.

NARROWS, Giles County. US 460. Confederate troops under French and Jackson occupied the area in May 1864. A fort was built on the heights, with guns ranged on the gorge, and a signal corps station was located on East River Mountain. Gen. McCausland had about 1,000 soldiers here; these, with the men under French and Jackson, drove Union Gen. George Crook to evacuate Blacksburg.

NEW KENT, New Kent County. IS 64, State 33.

New Kent Courthouse. Part of Joseph Johnston's army came through here in May 1862, retiring to Richmond.

NEW MARKET BATTLEFIELD PARK, Shenandoah County. US 11.

Battle of New Market marker just north of town. May 15, 1864, on hills to the north, Union Gen. Franz Sigel faced Confederate John C. Breckinridge, who was forced to order the boys from V.M.I. to join in the battle. All cadets of military age were already in service, but those still at the school, oldest 20 and youngest 14, took to the field under Gen. Schott Shipp, captured a battery, took from 60 to 100 prisoners, and left nine dead. Hall of Valor Visitor Center has film program.

NEWPORT NEWS, York County. IS 64, US 60, 17.

Army Transportation Museum, on Mulberry Island, has a Civil War earthwork fort; the museum depicts army transportation from 1776 to the present.

First Battle of Ironclads marker at Chesapeake Ave. between La Salle and East Ave. The *Merrimac* (*Virginia*) and the *Monitor* fought in Hampton Roads, to the south, on March 9, 1862. On the previous day, the *Merrimac* had destroyed the *Cumberland* and *Congress,* wooden Union ships.

Mariners Museum, entrance off US 60, has an extensive collection of Civil War naval items. Among exhibits are the trailboards from Farragut's flagship, the *Hartford,* models of the ironclads, diorama of the first ironclad battle, maps, charts.

War Memorial Museum of Virginia, 9285 Warwick Rd., Huntington Park, features relics of World Wars I and II, but also has items pertaining to the Civil War on permanent display. These include swords, rifles, medals, flags, uniforms, and prints.

NEW POST, Caroline County. US 17.

Jackson's Headquarters, about 6 miles southeast of town. Stonewall Jackson had headquarters at Moss Neck from December 1862 to March 1863. He was guarding the Rappahannock.

Skinker's Neck marker on highway about 7 miles southeast of town denotes site. Jubal Early prevented Burnside from crossing the river at the point in December 1862.

NORFOLK, Norfolk County. US 60.

Camp Talbot, corner of Oak Grove Rd. and Granby St. The Confederate camp was ½ mile west of marker. Georgia and Virginia troops camped there from April 1861 until evacuation of the city on May 10, 1862.

Confederate Flag, Market St. and Monticello Ave. The first Norfolk Confederate flag was flown from a housetop about 1½ blocks east of marker on April 2, 1861.

Confederate Monument, Main St. and Commercial Pl., has statue designed by William Couper of Norfolk.

Fort Norfolk, west end of Front St., was abandoned by the U.S. garrison when Virginia seceded and evacuated by Confederates in 1862. In May, President Lincoln, discouraged by McClellan's lack of progress in the Peninsular campaign, went to Hampton Roads with Secretaries Stanton and Chase to confer with Maj. Gen. John E. Wool. Sec. Chase, in a tug, looked over the Norfolk side of the river and located a landing site; then Lincoln had a look at it and decided Chase had a practicable plan. On May 10, an assault was ordered. When the Federals arrived they found the Southerners had evacuated; the mayor surrendered the city. The *Merrimac,* cut off from supplies, was abandoned and her magazine fired. New York newspapers hailed Lincoln's first military and naval operation as a "great success." Marker at Ocean View for site where Wool landed 6,000 Union troops on May 10, 1862.

Hampton Roads Naval Museum, on the Norfolk Naval Base at Farragut Ave. and Dillingham Blvd. Paintings, documents, and memorabilia relate to the naval history of the area. The *Merrimac* and the *Monitor* had a major engagement on March 8, 1862, in Hampton Roads.

Indian Pool Bridge, New Granby St. Bridge. The bridge spanning Tanner's Creek, now Lafayette River, at Indian Pool Point was burned by Confederates on May 10, 1862, to retard Union advance upon the city.

Merrimac and Monitor. Descriptive marker at Newport News Ferry Wharf pertaining to the engagement of March 8, 1862.

Ryan Home, corner of Lafayette Blvd. and Cottage Toll Rd. Marker denotes site of home of Father Ryan, poet-priest of the Confederacy.

Selden's Home, southwest corner of Freemanson and Botetourt St. The house, built in 1807 as the country home of D. William B. Selden, was seized during Federal occupation of city in 1862 and used as a headquarters. In April 1870, Gen. Lee visited his friend, Dr. Selden, Confederate surgeon, at the home.

U.S. Customhouse, Main and Granby St., was used as Federal prison during the war and then burned.

Whittle House, southeast corner N. Duke and W. Freemason St. Col. Walter H. Taylor, who served on the staff of Gen. Lee, was born here.

NOTTOWAY, Nottoway County. US 460.

Nottoway Courthouse. Cavalry action occurred nearby on June 23, 1864, when Confederate W. H. F. Lee came between Union raiders Wilson and Kautz, who were headed for Burkeville. Grant passed here in pursuit of Lee, April 5, 1865; he received word at this point that Sheridan was entrenched across Lee's line of retreat at Jetersville.

OCCOQUAN, Prince William County. IS 95. The town was a busy port until silt built up in the Occoquan River so that vessels no longer could reach the cotton mills. General Wade Hampton had headquarters in the Hammill Hotel, now converted to shops and offices.

Visitor Information Center, 200 Mill St., has a self-guided walking tour of the historic district.

ORANGE, Orange County. US 15, State 20.

Jackson's Crossing, marker on US 15, in Madison County, 7½ miles north of Orange. Jackson crossed the river at Locust Dale, moving north, where the battle of Cedar Mountain was fought on August 9, 1862.

Lee's Headquarters, marker on State 20, 1½ miles east of town. Lee's winter quarters from December 1863 to May 1864.

Montebello is one of the most beautiful mansions in the Piedmont country. Gen. Lee's army camped on the grounds in 1862–1863. Lee and his staff were entertained in the house.

PARIS, Loudoun County. US 50.

Jackson's Bivouac, east edge of town. Jackson's men, en route to First Manassas, took a rest break here on July 19, 1861. Jackson dispensed with pickets and guarded the camp himself.

Signal Station, about 1 mile west of town. Hilltop south of highway was signal station used by both armies.

PEARISBURG, Giles County. US 460. In May 1862, Federals under Col. Rutherford B. Hayes were defeated by Confederates under Gen. Henry Heth.

PETERSBURG, Dinwiddie County. IS 85, 95, US 1. A number of descriptive markers pertaining to troop movements and actions of the Petersburg campaign will be found on US 1, both north and south of the city, and on Graham Rd. The place where Ambrose Powell

Hill was killed, April 2, 1865, is about 3 miles southwest of town.

Petersburg, which fell to the Federal forces after a grim 10-month siege that began in June 1864, seems to have fallen again, at least in part, to time and "progress." Several of the sites which had historic interest have been replaced with modern structures. They are listed, however, for the original sites; and some are still standing.

Bolling-Zimmer House, 244 S. Sycamore St., was the home of Mary Tabb Bolling, who married Gen. William Henry Fitzhugh Lee in 1867. Gen. Robert E. Lee, the groom's father, was present at the wedding.

Centre Hill Mansion, Centre Hill Court, entrance from Adams and Tabb streets. The 1823 Federal-style mansion has been restored and beautifully furnished with period antiques. Three presidents—Tyler, Lincoln, and Taft—were among the many distinguished guests here at various times.

City Hall, N. Sycamore St., formerly was the U.S. Custom House and Post Office, occupied by Confederates. A signal station was established on the roof, to which Petersburg residents sometimes climbed to have a look at the fighting to the east.

Courthouse, N. Sycamore St. The first group of Petersburg volunteers left here on April 20, 1861. The bell rang a warning on the morning of June 9, 1864, that the city was about to be attacked by raiders from Gen. Butler's Army of the James. Federal troops east of Petersburg could tell the time of day by the courthouse clock.

Lee Memorial Park, Johnson Rd. Some fortifications remain.

Lee's Headquarters, Violet Bank, 1 mile north of town off Route 1, was Lee's headquarters from June to October 1864. Museum open to public. Beasley-Williamson House, 558 High St., was Lee's residence during most of November 1864; from here he moved to the Turnbull House, Edge Hill, which stood opposite the present Central State Hospital on US 1 and 460, west of town. The house was burned soon after Lee left it on April 2, 1865. Later that day, he established headquarters at Cottage Farm, where he planned the evacuation of the area. Violet Bank (which see) in Colonial Heights, was Lee's headquarters from June to November 1864. He moved from this site when the house became visible to Federal batteries south of the Appomattox River—the protecting trees were becoming bare with the approach of winter.

Mahone House, 137 S. Sycamore St. Gen.

William Mahone, hero of the battle of the Crater, was host here to Gen. Lee in 1867. Now the Petersburg public library.

Niblo's Tavern, Bollingbrook and 2nd St., was a favorite resort of generals during the siege of 1864–1865.

North Carolina Hospital, northeast corner of Perry and Brown St., was one of several Confederate hospitals established in tobacco factories.

Old Blandford Church and Interpretation Center, 319 S. Crater Rd., is a Civil War shrine with 15 Tiffany stained-glass windows that are memorials donated by the Confederacy. The Old Blandford Cemetery contains some 30,000 Confederate graves. Shortly after the war's end, Mrs. Mary Logan, wife of Union Gen. John A. Logan, observed a group of schoolgirls placing flowers on the graves of Southern soldiers who fell at the battle of Petersburg. She saw this ceremony again the following year, discussed it with her husband, and, it is said, "took steps that ultimately led to the observance of Memorial Day as a national holiday"—an act that has been claimed by several other communities.

Pickett's Headquarters, southwest corner of Washington and Perry St. Before the opening of the Petersburg campaign, Gen. George E. Pickett was in command of the military Department of Southern Virginia.

Poplar Grove National Cemetery, State 675 (Vaughn Road), is situated on ground captured by the Federals in the fight for the Weldon Railroad in August 1864. More than 6,000 soldiers are buried here; more than 4,000 are unknown.

Poplar Lawn, later known as Central Park, corner of Filmore and S. Sycamore St. Volunteer companies enlisted here in April 1861. A hospital was here during the siege.

St. Paul's Church, N. Union St. Lee's pew is marked. After the war his son, W. H. F. Lee, was married here to Miss Mary Tabb Bolling. The building was damaged by shells.

Siege Museum, 15 W. Bank St., displays and a film narrated by Joseph Cotton relate to life in Petersburg during the siege. A National Historic Landmark.

Visitors Center, Sycamore St. and Old Towne Rd. Maps and brochures for self-guiding tours, and a bank museum with displays including original plates and press for printing Confederate money.

Wallace House, southwest corner S. Market and Brown St. Lincoln and Grant had a conference here on the morning of April 3, 1865. The Army of Northern Virginia had evacuated the city during the previous night.

PETERSBURG NATIONAL BATTLEFIELD, IS 95. Visitor center is 2 miles east of IS 95 off Route 36. A museum here has campaign exhibits, relics, models, and maps. Literature is available for a self-guided tour of the area; a full tour takes in a 27-mile circuit. Key points are well marked. The ten-month siege took place in and around Petersburg, covering about 170 square miles, the largest single battlefield in the United States. In June 1864, Lee had about 50,000 men defending the city; Grant had about 112,000 for besieging the fortifications. In July, men of the 48th Pennsylvania, many of whom had been coal miners, dug a tunnel under a Confederate battery and on July 30 exploded four tons of powder under the Confederates, leaving a crater about 170 feet long, 60 feet wide, and 30 feet deep. In the confusion that followed, the Southerners regained possession of the crater. The Union lost about 42,000 men and the Confederates 28,000 in the campaign. The battlefield tour is 4 miles long. There is a 23-mile Siege Line tour that begins where the Battlefield Tour ends and takes in park areas to the south and west. New units have been established at City Point, at the James and Appomattox Rivers junction, and at Five Forks, west of IS 85 on White Oak Road (Route 613).

PORT CONWAY, King George County. State 3. Union Gen. Kilpatrick shelled two gunboats captured by Confederates here in September 1863. John Wilkes Booth crossed the river here on April 24, 1865.

PORT REPUBLIC, Rockingham County. US 340, State 12.

Battle of Port Republic, marker on US 340, 3½ miles north of Grottoes. Jackson attacked Shields here on June 9, 1862, but was repulsed. Reinforced by Ewell, Jackson later drove Shields from the field, then burned the bridge to prevent Frémont from coming with Federal aid.

PORT ROYAL CROSSROADS, Caroline County. US 17. Union gunboats were driven back by D. H. Hill at this point in December 1862.

Garrett House, marker on highway. The farm (he supposedly was killed in the barn) where John Wilkes Booth was found and killed by Union cavalry on April 26, 1865, stood about 2 miles south.

PORTSMOUTH, Norfolk County. IS 264, US 60, 460.

Butt House, 327 Crawford St., was used as commissary headquarters for the Union.

Craney Island, about 3 miles west of town on State 337. Marker denotes site where Confederates destroyed site where the *Merrimac* in 1862.

Fort Nelson, near west edge of town, marker on State 337. The area was fortified in 1861.

Ironmonger House, northeast corner of Crawford and High St. Confederate soldier Frank M. Ironmonger was born here. He enlisted at age ten, acted as courier, then took part in battles and was captured in 1865; sentenced to be shot as a spy, he escaped.

Norfolk Navy Yard, south end of 1st and 4th St. Here in 1861–1862, the *Merrimac* was converted into the ironclad *Virginia.*

Porter House, 23 Court St., was the home of John L. Porter, who designed the ironclad *Virginia.*

Portsmouth Naval Shipyard Museum, on waterfront of the Elizabeth River, at the foot of High St. Ship models, uniforms, flags, maps, prints, and memorabilia. Displays portray the history of the CSS *Virginia,* originally the *Merrimac.*

Trinity Church, Court and High, has Confederate memorial window.

United States Naval Hospital, north end of Green St. Burial ground has graves of Confederate and Union sailors. The stone cairn is in memory of 300 men lost when the *Cumberland* and the *Congress* were sunk by the *Virginia* in 1862.

POUND GAP, Wise County. US 23. James A. Garfield, with Union troops, forced this gap in March 1862. John H. Morgan, with Confederates, forced the gap from the Virginia approach in his raid of June 1864.

POWHATAN, Powhatan County. State 13. Scene of skirmish in January 1865.

Lee's Last Camp, State 44, 9½ miles north of Powhatan. Lee, returning from Appomattox, pitched his tent here April 14, 1865. He stopped here to visit his brother, Charles Carter Lee, who lived nearby at Windsor.

PRINCE GEORGE, Prince George County. State 106, 609.

Courthouse was occupied by Union troops in the last year of the war. Part of Grant's army passed this way en route to Petersburg in June 1864.

Sycamore Church, marker on State 106 about 7 miles east of town. Wade Hampton attacked Federals guarding Grant's beef cattle on September 16, 1864, and escaped with 2,500 beeves.

REMINGTON, Fauquier County. US 29.

Pelham Memorial honors Confederate Maj. John Pelham who was mortally wounded March 17, 1863, at Kelly's Ford.

RICE, Prince Edward County. US 460.

High Bridge, marker on highway. Grant's 2nd Corps drove Lee's rear guard from bridgehead on west bank of the Appomattox River, April 7, 1865. The bridge was burned.

RICHMOND, Henrico County. IS 64, 95.

Frémont's division marching through the woods in the Shenandoah Valley.

Battle Abbey, 428 N. Boulevard Ave., is a Confederate museum with a vast collection of flags, portraits, arms, and equipment. Also contains renowned mural "Four Seasons of the Confederacy" commissioned in 1921. Home of the Virginia Historical Society.

The Capitol, in Capitol Square. In the Old Hall of the House of Delegates, Robert E. Lee accepted the command of the armed forces of Virginia from the convention that had also passed the Ordinance of Secession. Other famous Confederates represented in the hall are Gens. Fitzhugh Lee, Joseph Johnston, J. E. B. Stuart, and Stonewall Jackson; Matthew Fontaine Maury; President Jefferson Davis and Vice President Alexander H. Stephens. In Capitol Square are monuments to Gen. Jackson, wartime Gov. William Smith, and Dr. Hunter McGuire, Confederate surgeon. Volunteers who stood on the roof manning a water bucket brigade saved the Executive Mansion when the city fell.

City Hall, northwest corner of 11th and Capitol. City government was housed from 1816 to 1870 in a building that used to stand here.

Confederate Hospital No. 1, Hospital St. between 2nd and 4th St., later the Richmond Nursing Home.

Confederate Museum and White House of the Confederacy, 12th and Clay streets. The home of Confederate President Jefferson Davis and his family has been restored with many original furnishings and personal items. The museum, which is adjacent, contains the largest collection of Confederate artifacts in the nation: weapons, uniforms, documents, personal belongings of the Davis family, and an art collection with oil paintings by Conrad Wise Chapman depicting the Charleston defenses of 1863. The Great Seal of the Confederacy is among the relics. Lincoln visited the house during the occupation in April 1865 and conferred with Gen. Godfrey Weitzel, who had headquarters here as commandant of Military District No. 1. The reference library of the museum is a rich heritage of original material on the Confederate States and is available to students, historians, and scholars by appointment only.

Gamble's Hill Park, south end of 3rd and 4th St., gives an excellent view of the site of Tredegar Ironworks of the Confederacy.

Hollywood Cemetery, Cherry and Albemarle St. Among many notables buried here are Jefferson Davis and family; Gens. Fitzhugh Lee, J. E. B. Stuart, and George Pickett; Matthew Fontaine Maury; and Douglas Southall Freeman, biographer of Lee and other Confed-

erates. There is a memorial to the 18,000 Confederate soldiers buried here.

Lee House, 707 E. Franklin St., has been restored and refurbished by the Confederate Memorial Literary Society. During the war the house was rented to Gen. Custis Lee and fellow officers. In January 1864, Mrs. Robert E. Lee and her daughters took occupancy and Gen. Lee returned here after Appomattox. The general's camp bed and washstand are among relics on display. Part of the house is now used as a restaurant.

Libby Hill Park, 27–29 E. Franklin St., has monument to Confederate soldiers and sailors. At the foot of the hill is the site of the Confederate Navy Yard.

Libby Prison, 20th and Cary St. Site of Confederate prison. No longer standing.

Monument Avenue, a continuation of W. Franklin St., has statues of noted Virginians: J. E. B. Stuart, at Lombardy S., equestrian bronze by Fred Moynihan; Robert E. Lee, at Allen Ave., equestrian bronze unveiled by Gen. Joseph E. Johnston in 1890 (sculptor Jean Antoine Mercie thought Lee's brow should not be hidden by a hat and created the first equestrian statue with bared head in the United States); Jefferson Davis, at Davis Ave., monument sculpted by Edward V. Valentine; Stonewall Jackson, at Boulevard, equestrian bronze by F. William Sievers; Commodore Matthew Maury, at Belmont Ave.

Richmond National Cemetery, 1701 Williamsburg Rd. One of five national cemeteries in and around Richmond. Of the more than 6,000 soldiers buried here, more than 5,500 are unidentified.

St. John's Episcopal Church, 24 and Broad St., where Patrick Henry delivered his "liberty or death" speech, survived the conflict which Henry and his peers never foresaw. In the area surrounding the church more than 70 antebellum houses have been restored. Information is available at Shelton House, 2407 E. Grace St.

St. Paul's Church, 9th and Grace St. Davis and Lee attended services here. President Davis was here when he received word that Lee's line had been broken at Petersburg and that Richmond could no longer be defended.

Shockoe Hill Cemetery, north end of 3rd St., has the grave of Elizabeth Van Lew, Richmond woman who aided Unionists during the war.

Spotswood Hotel, southeast corner of 8th and Main. Jefferson Davis, on arrival in Richmond, had quarters in the elegant hotel that stood here.

Tredegar Ironworks, south end of 6th St.,

between the Canal and James River. The plant furnished munitions to the Confederacy. The plates that armored the *Merrimac* were rolled here.

U.S. Customhouse, now part of Richmond Post Office, was used for Confederate treasury offices.

Valentine Museum, 1015 E. Clay St., has displays, costumes, dioramas.

Van Lew House, Grace St. between 23rd and 24th. Site of the home of Elizabeth Van Lew, who helped Federal soldiers escape through a tunnel leading from her house. Gen. Grant appointed her postmistress of Richmond after the war.

Virginia State Library and Archives, 12th St. and Capitol Sq. in Finance Building, has extensive collection of rare manuscripts, charts, and maps.

RICHMOND NATIONAL BATTLE-FIELD PARK, 3215 E. Broad St. The visitor center and park headquarters are in Chimborazo Park, site of Chimborazo Hospital. Exhibits, literature, film, slide program, and a library here are helpful in understanding the Richmond battlefield area which extends well beyond the city. The complete tour is a 57-mile drive. Auto cassette tape tour available. Key points are well marked; recorded lectures provide background. There is an exhibit shelter at Cold Harbor, 8 miles northeast on State 156, and a visitor center at Fort Harrison, southeast on State 5. Among important sites are: Malvern Hill, Glendale (Frayser's Farm), Chickahominy Bluff, Drewry's Bluff, Fort Harrison, White Oak Swamp, Savage Station, Seven Pines, Cold Harbor, Gaines Mill, Beaver Dam Creek (Ellerson's Mill), and Mechanicsville. The Watt House, which served as Gen. Fitz-John Porter's headquarters, and the Garthright House, which was a Union field hospital, are on the battlefield. During the restoration of the Watt House, workmen found a cannon ball that had knocked off a chimney lodged in the rafters. Displayed at the Chimborazo Park headquarters is a brass valve which was used by Professor Lowe to inflate his reconnaissance balloon in 1862. J. Ambler Johnston, a Richmond architect, was looking over the Gaines Mill battle area when he observed a farm boy who was plowing pick up the valve. Johnston paid a quarter for it; it is now valued at more than $50,000.

RIVERTON, Warren County. US 522.

Guard's Hill, just north of town. Gen. Fitz Lee's cavalry attacked a detachment of Sheridan's cavalry, August 16, 1864. The Federals were reinforced and drove the Confederates back across the river.

ROANOKE, Roanoke County. Off IS 81, US 11. Gen. David Hunter came this way in June 1864, while retreating from Lynchburg.

ROCKY MOUNT, Franklin County. US 220.

Confederate Monument, in courthouse square.

Early Memorial, also in courthouse square, honors Gen. Jubal Early, who was born in Franklin County November 3, 1816. He was a member of the Virginia Secession Convention of 1861 and raised funds for his raid of Washington by exacting levies from a number of towns along the route.

Franklin County Courthouse has among its records a notation that "one Negro boy, Booker," was valued at $400. Booker T. Washington grew up to become a leader and educator. His birthplace is now a national historic site.

ST. STEPHENS CHURCH, King and Queen County. US 360. March 2, 1864, Col. Ulric Dahlgren, returning from his Richmond raid, was killed by Confederate soldiers and home guards about 12 miles southeast of highway marker.

SALTVILLE, Smyth County. US 11. Marker on highway about 4 miles west of Chilhowie. In December 1864, Confederate saltworks were destroyed by Gen. George Stoneman.

SAYLOR'S CREEK, also Sailor's Creek, Amelia County. State 617.

Battle of Saylor's Creek. On April 6, 1865, Ewell's corps of Lee's army, retreating toward Appomattox, was attacked by Sheridan's troops. Ewell and 11 other generals were captured with several thousand Confederate soldiers. This was the last major engagement between the armies of Lee and Grant. Hillsman House, on the battlefield, was used as a hospital.

SEVEN PINES, Henrico County. US 60, State 156. A number of descriptive markers for the Seven Days' battles will be found on State 156, south of Seven Pines. The action at Allen's Farm took place near town on June 29, 1862. Sumner's corps, forming the Union rear, was attacked by Magruder and driven back to Savage's Station. The actions at White Oak Swamp took place 7 to 8 miles south; at Glendale (Frayser's Farm), 10 to 11 miles south; and at Malvern Hill, 12 to 14 miles south.

SMITHFIELD, Isle of Wight County. State 10.
Cherry Grove Landing was the scene of a skirmish on April 13–15, 1864. Early in December 1864, Confederates captured a Union vessel near here.

SPERRYVILLE, Rappahannock County. US 522. The Union Army of Virginia was organized here June 26, 1862, from the troops of Frémont, Banks, and McDowell.

SPOTSYLVANIA COURT HOUSE, Spotsylvania County. Off IS 95, State 208, 613. The battlefield is part of the Fredericksburg and Spotsylvania National Military Park, located between the Po and Ny rivers. The opening engagement took place on May 8–10, 1864. On May 12, in the battle of the Bloody Angle, Union Gen. John Sedgwick was one of about 29,000 casualties.

SPROUSES, Buckingham County. US 15. Markers on highway about 9 and 11 miles south for route of Lee's army in retreat toward Appomattox, and Grant's army in pursuit.

STAUNTON, Augusta County. IS 64, 81, US 11. The Stonewall Brigade Band had headquarters here. It was mustered in as the 5th Virginia Regimental Band; Jackson raised its rank to the Stonewall Brigade. At Appomattox, Grant allowed the members to take home their instruments. Later, when he passed through town, the band serenaded him at the railroad station. The band appeared also at Grant's funeral and at the dedication of Grant's Tomb.

STEPHENS CITY, Frederick County. IS 81, US 11. Jackson's army, en route to Winchester, stopped to rest on the morning of May 25, 1862, at a point about 3 miles north of town. About 3 miles south of town is marker for site where Sheridan rejoined the Union army on October 19, 1864, in the battle of Cedar Creek.

STEVENSBURG, Culpeper County. State 3. Grant's 2nd Corps camped near here in the winter of 1863–1864. The Wilderness campaign began in May when the army moved from here to Germanna and Ely's Ford on the Rapidan River.

STONY CREEK, Sussex County. IS 95, US 301. Lee's supplies were carted from the Weldon Railroad here to Petersburg in 1864. Union Gen. Wilson fought a cavalry skirmish with Lee's troops June 28–29, 1864. Union cavalryman David McMurtrie Gregg, a former

Indian fighter, came through Stony Creek Station on a raid, December 1, 1864.
Nottoway River, about 3½ miles south. Union Gen. Wilson crossed here on June 28, 1864, recrossed June 29, to and from his Burkeville raid.

STRASBURG, Shenandoah County. IS 64, 81, US 11.
Banks's Fort, southwest of highway marker, was built by Union troops in 1862.
Battle of Cedar Creek, marker on highway at bridge, also at Hupp's Hill just north of town.
Battle of Fisher's Hill, about 2 miles south of town. Jubal Early was attacked here by Sheridan, September 22, 1864, and forced to withdraw. Confederate Adj. Gen. A. S. Pendleton was mortally wounded. Marker at site just over 3 miles south of Strasburg.
Strasburg Museum, State 55, 2 blocks east of junction US 11 and East King St., in the old Southern Railway depot, has Civil War items.

STRATFORD, Westmoreland County. State 214.
Stratford Hall is the Lee ancestral home and the birthplace of Gen. Robert E. Lee. The house has been restored, has period furnishings. Plantation outbuildings and gardens have also been restored.

STUART, Patrick County. US 58.
Patrick County Courthouse has statue on grounds which honors Gen. J. E. B. Stuart, who was born in the county.

SUFFOLK, Nansemond County. State 10. Marker on highway 1½ miles northwest of town, at site where the main line of Confederate works was built by Gen. Longstreet during his siege of Suffolk, April 1863.

TALLEYSVILLE, New Kent County. State 33. Gen. J. E. B. Stuart, on his ride around McClellan's army in mid-June 1862, arrived here on the night of June 13, coming from Hanover Courthouse. From here he went on to the Chickahominy River.

THORNBURG, Spotsylvania County. US 1. There are a number of markers along the highway for troop movements of May 1864. If you are driving south on US 1, turn left at Thornburg for the Jackson shrine at Guinea Station, the site where Jackson died, May 10, 1863. The area is a part of the Fredericksburg and Spotsylvania National Military Park.
Massaponax Church, 4½ miles north of Thornburg, was used as a troop shelter, then as a hospital.

TREVILIANS, Louisa County. US 33. (*Also see* LOUISA.) Sheridan and Wade Hampton fought an engagement here on June 12, 1864.

TURKEY ISLAND, Henrico County. State 5. A colonial home here—once the residence of William Randolph, ancestor of Jefferson, Marshall, and Lee—was destroyed by Union gunboats in 1862.

UNIONVILLE, Orange County. State 20. Marker on highway for site where J. E. B. Stuart was almost captured on August 18, 1862.

Mine Run, just over 6½ miles east of town. Meade and Lee skirmished here in late November 1863. Meade retired across the Rapidan.

WARRENTON, Fauquier County. State 613. Stuart began his ride around Pope's army on August 22, 1862, from a point 6 miles west of town. He destroyed supplies and captured Pope's headquarters' wagons.

WAYNESBORO, Augusta County. IS 64, US 250, State 12.

Early's Last Battle, west edge of town on US 250. Sheridan drove Early from the ridge west of town, capturing a number of his men, on March 2, 1865. It was the last important engagement in northern Virginia.

Tinkling Spring Church, 4 miles west of US 250. R. L. Dabney of Jackson's staff was minister here from 1847 to 1862.

WILLIAMSBURG, James City County. IS 64, US 60.

Battle of Williamsburg, marker on highway, was fought at Fort Magruder on May 5, 1862. Gen. Joseph Johnston and 65,000 Confederates withdrew from the Yorktown-Warwick River line toward Richmond, coming through Williamsburg on May 4. The army was pursued by Union Gen. McClellan. Johnston ordered Longstreet, commanding the rear guard, to hold off the Union attack until Confederate wagon trains, slowed by heavy rains and mud, were out of danger. In spite of heavy casualties, the holding action was successful. Johnston continued the withdrawal and Federals occupied the city on May 6.

Coke-Garrett House, east end of Nicholson St. The lawn was used for wounded soldiers during the battle. College buildings, the Baptist Church, and the courthouse were also used for the wounded.

College of William and Mary. The faculty suspended the college one month after the outbreak of hostilities. President Benjamin S. Ewell served in the Confederate army; 90 percent of the students became Confederate soldiers. Wren Building was partially burned in September 1862. Gen. Weiss, in a raid on September 9, 1862, captured 33 Federals who were sleeping on the college lawn and arrested Union Col. Campbell, who was sent to Libby Prison. Confederates, however, held the town for only a day.

Confederate Position, on Colonial National Parkway west of Jones Mill Pond, was site of Federal advance.

Magruder's Defenses, built in 1861–1862, are marked on US 60.

Palmer House, historic marker at site, was headquarters for Gen. Joseph Johnston, then headquarters for Gen. George B. McClellan, and remained occupied by Federals throughout the war.

Whitaker's House. Marker on US 60, 1½ miles southeast of town, for headquarters of Gen. W. F. Smith during the battle of Williamsburg.

WINCHESTER, Frederick County. IS 81, US 11, 50. The city changed flags 70 times during the four years of war and was the objective of six battles fought in Frederick County. Numerous historic markers are in the area. The Winchester-Frederick County Visitor Center, 1340 S. Pleasant Valley Rd., has a brochure for self-guided walking tours.

Baker's Lane House, east on Berryville Ave. to an Acme Supermarket on north side of avenue; house is just west of market. The home was squarely in the middle of battle lines during the third battle of Winchester; a cannonball is still imbedded in the west wall.

County Courthouse, corner of Rouss Ave. and N. Loudoun St., was described in the diary of Mrs. Cornelia McDonald after the battle of Kernstown, March 23, 1862. "The porch was strewed with dead men. Some had papers pinned to their coats telling who they were. . . . Soon men came and carried them away to make room for those dying inside. . . . The next day I passed the Court House and there was a banner 'Theatre Tonight.' The wounded men had been removed to prepare for the theatre to amuse the men." The building has historical relics.

First Presbyterian Church, 304 E. Piccadilly St., was used by Union troops as a stable.

Handley Library, corner of W. Piccadilly and N. Braddock St. The Winchester-Frederick County Historical Society Museum has collections from 1740 to the present including photographic materials.

Jackson's Headquarters, 415 N. Braddock

St. During the winter of 1861–1862, Gen. Stonewall Jackson and his staff occupied the home of Col. L. T. Moore. Mrs. Jackson visited here for three months. The house has period furnishings, Jackson items, and war relics. A visitor recently remarked that Jackson would be upset if he could see the Lincoln rocker in the bedroom; another visitor said, "Oh, I don't think the general would mind," and the guide agreed: "I don't either—he'd be too glad to be back!"

National Cemetery, Woodstock Lane, has the graves of more than 2,000 known and more than 2,000 unknown Union soldiers. Marker on State 7, near entrance, pertains to the third battle of Winchester, in which future presidents Hayes and McKinley took part.

Old Taylor Hotel, 225 N. Loudoun St., was used as headquarters at various times by officers of both armies.

Sheridan's Headquarters, southwest corner of Braddock and Piccadilly St. The building was occupied by Gen. N. P. Banks in 1862, by Gen. R. H. Milroy in 1863, and by Gen. Phil Sheridan in the autumn and winter of 1864–1865.

Stonewall Cemetery, Greenwalt Ave., Cork St. E., and Woodstock Lane, has a Confederate monument to unknown dead, honoring 829 unidentified Confederates. More than 3,000 unknown Confederate soldiers are also buried here.

Stonewall Jackson's Headquarters, 415 N. Braddock St., was the general's headquarters from November 1861 to March 1862. Many of his possessions and the original furnishings are here. Also Civil War relics include items that belonged to the Confederate cavalry general Turner Ashby, who had been an influential grain dealer, planter, and politician in the Shenandoah Valley. He was named cavalry commander by Jackson in October 1861, became a brigadier general in May 1862, and was killed June 6, 1862, near Harrisonburg.

WISE, Wise County. US 23. The courthouse was burned by Union troops. An action was fought here in July 1863.

WOODBRIDGE, Prince William County. IS 95, US 1.

Leesylvania State Park, 16236 Neabsco Rd., was the birthplace of "Light Horse Harry" Lee, Robert E. Lee's father. The former home-site is on 500 acres of grassland, now a park; also here are the relics of dependencies and the family burial site. Remains of gun emplacements that were active in the Civil War are on the bluff overlooking the Potomac River.

WOODS MILL, Nelson County. US 29.

Mosby House, marker on highway 3 miles north. Thoroughfare Gap, 5 miles south, was the boyhood home of Confederate raider Col. John Singleton Mosby. He went to school near Murrell's Shop, east of Elmington.

WYLIESBURG, Charlotte County. US 15.

Staunton Bridge. Marker on highway denotes site which is 9 miles west. The bridge was held by Confederate reserves and citizens from surrounding counties against Union cavalry raiders who were destroying railroads in June 1864. The Federals were repulsed here and retreated to Petersburg.

WYTHEVILLE, Wythe County. IS 81, US 11, 21. In July 1863, Toland's raiders captured the town. Averell's raiders came in May 1864, and Union troops again occupied the town in December 1864 and April 1865. Lead and salt mines made this town important to North and South. One Union takeover attempt was foiled by a Molly Tynes, who is said to have ridden 40 miles over the mountains to alert the home guard to return and save the town.

Ingleside, east edge of town, marker on US 11. Home of Confederate Col. R. E. Withers, who also served as U.S. senator and consul at Hong Kong.

Shot Tower Historical Park, southeast of town on US 52. Shot was made here during the war by dropping molten lead from top of tower to water tank at base.

YELLOW TAVERN, Henrico County. US 1. Marker on highway 2½ miles north of Richmond. Site of old inn, near which a cavalry engagement occurred on May 11, 1864, between Sheridan, on a raid to Richmond, and Gen. J. E. B. Stuart, defending the city. Stuart was mortally wounded and died the next day.

YORKTOWN, York County. US 17. Visitor center and museum of the National Historical Park open daily. Gen. J. B. Magruder built up fortifications here during the war. The national cemetery has 2,200 Union dead. There is also a small Confederate burial ground.

WASHINGTON

The bill creating the Oregon Territory, which included the present state of Washington, was approved in 1848. Abraham Lincoln was offered the governorship but declined; Gen. Joseph Lane, later a U.S. senator and candidate for vice president, took office at Oregon City as territorial governor in March 1849. Settlers north of the Columbia River soon began a movement for a new division of the area. In 1853, President Fillmore signed a bill creating Washington Territory; part of present-day Idaho and Montana fell within the boundaries. Stephen A. Douglas suggested the name of Washingtonia to avoid confusion with the national capital, but his proposal was not adopted. Isaac Ingalls Stevens, later a Union general, was appointed governor, and Olympia was selected as capital. The white population of the new territory was not quite 4,000.

By 1860 the population had almost tripled and the prevailing sentiment was pro-Union. At the outbreak of the war ten companies of volunteers garrisoned army posts, releasing army regulars for active duty in the East. Union generals Frémont and Bonneville were among early explorers of Washington territory. Grant, Sherman, Sheridan, and McClellan, of the Federal command, and Confederate Gen. Pickett served before the war in Pacific Coast posts.

The transcontinental telegraph line was completed in 1864. Gov. William Pickering sent a message to the president who replied two days later: "GOV. PICKERING, OLYMPIA, W.T. YOUR PATRIOTIC DISPATCH OF YESTERDAY RECEIVED AND PUBLISHED. A. LINCOLN."

BELLINGHAM, Whatcom County. IS 5, US 99.

Captain George Pickett House, 910 Bancroft St. The house where Capt. Pickett lived with his Indian wife and son while he was stationed at Fort Bellingham has a marker. Widower Pickett married LaSalle Corbell shortly after he gained his greatest fame at Gettysburg.

Pickett Memorial Bridge, Dupont St. and Prospect Ave. A tablet at the north end of the bridge over Whatcom Creek commemorates Capt. Pickett, who built Bellingham's first bridge in 1856.

CENTRALIA, Lewis County. IS 5. In 1850 a Missourian brought a young slave, George Washington, to this stagecoach stop, filed a donation land claim on the townsite, later freed the servant and sold him his claim for $6,000.

George Washington Park, Main and Pearl St., is named for the former slave who donated the land to the city.

FORT CANBY, Pacific County. US 101. The post, originally known as Fort Cape Disappointment, was established in April 1854 and named for Maj. Gen. Edward Richard Canby, who later commanded the Department of New Mexico, holding the territory for the Union and checking a Confederate invasion of California. The garrison guarded the mouth of the Columbia River. Now a state historic park.

FORT COLVILLE, Stevens County. US 395. Troops stationed here apparently fought tedium by tiresome pranks and worse in the town of Colville. In 1861 soldiers raided the town laundry and ran off with the Chinese proprietor and most of the stock. In 1862 a lieutenant killed a civilian but was acquitted, according to local legend, because no one dared to testify against him. Maj. Curtis, commanding officer, dismantled the Colville distillery in a move perhaps to cut down on high and bottled spirits.

FORT SIMCOE STATE PARK, Yakima County. State 220, about 27 miles west of Toppenish. Original buildings have been restored and furnished in period. Gen. George B. McClellan visited the site in 1853 as a lieutenant. Commandant John Garnett was killed at Chantilly. Museum and interpretive center.

FORT STEILACOOM, Pierce County. (Pronounced *Still-a-kum.*) West of IS 5. Fort

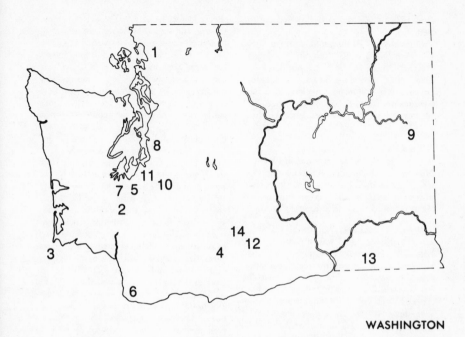

WASHINGTON

1 — Bellingham	5 — Fort Steilacoom	9 — Spokane	13 — Walla Walla
2 — Centralia	6 — Fort Vancouver	10 — Sumner	14 — Yakima
3 — Fort Canby	7 — Olympia	11 — Tacoma	
4 — Fort Simcoe	8 — Seattle	12 — Toppenish	

site is on the grounds of Western State Hospital, 4 miles from Steilacoom. Capt. George B. McClellan supervised the building of a military road from this point to Walla Walla. O. O. Howard and George Pickett were officers here. In the fort cemetery is a marker for William H. Wallace, governor of Washington and the Idaho Territories and delegate to Congress from each.

FORT VANCOUVER NATIONAL HISTORIC SITE, Clark County. E. Evergreen Blvd., Vancouver. The National Park Service has reconstructed some of the fort. A visitor center with museum has slides and video shows, arranges tours.

OLYMPIA, Thurston County. IS 5, US 99.
Site of the First Legislative Hall, Capitol Way between State and Olympia Ave. Bronze tablet marks the site where the first territorial legislature met on February 27, 1854.
State Capitol Museum, 211 W. 21st Ave., has historical exhibits featuring early days in the Northwest.

SEATTLE, King County. IS 5, US 10. Asa Mercer, instructor at the Territorial University which opened in Seattle in 1861, offered young men $1.50 a cord for split wood as credit against tuition charges. Courses had to be adjusted to student comprehension as only one student managed to qualify above high school level. The first issue of the *Seattle Gazette* (later the *Post-Intelligencer*) was published by J. R. Watson in 1863 from an office in the Gem Saloon. The enterprising Prof. Mercer went east in 1864 to persuade unmarried women to settle in the territory; two years later he brought another group, many of them Civil War widows. The professor himself married one of the "Mercer girls."
Lakeview Cemetery has monument to the Confederate veterans buried here.
Museum of History and Industry, 2700 24th Ave. E., has pioneer artifacts and historical exhibits.
Pioneer Square, 1st Ave. and Yesler Way, site of Yesler's Mill where early settlers congregated. A 140-year-old totem pole stood here

until 1939; it was the model for its replacement.

University of Washington, main entrance, 17th Ave. NE and NE 45th St. The largest university in the Pacific Northwest developed from Prof. Mercer's classes in a wooden building hemmed in by a white fence on land cleared by townspeople. The original site on Seneca St., between 4th and 5th avenues, is marked by a plaque.

TACOMA, Pierce County. IS 5.

Washington State Historical Society Museum, N. Stadium, N. 3rd and 4th St. Historical exhibit includes memorabilia associated with Gen. Isaac Ingalls Stevens. Illuminated photo murals depict the history of the state.

WALLA WALLA, Walla Walla County. US 410. In 1861 gold was discovered in the Salmon River territory, bringing boom times to the settlement. Prospector Herman Francis Reinhart went west to the gold regions in the decade preceding the war and seems to have dipped his pen into an inkstand almost as often as he dipped his pan into the streams of the far western territories. As he recalled Walla Walla in the winter of 1861: ". . . it was a lively little place . . . mostly transient miners, teamsters, packers and land-seekers. There were two or three hotels and a lot of boarding houses, some four or five restaurants, eight or ten saloons, three or four bakeries; at least 8 or 10 general stores, dry goods and groceries, boots and shoes, doctors, lawyers, two breweries, one nice theatre, and several churches (not very costly buildings) and some five or six livery, feed, and sale stables, some nice billiard rooms, and several large gambling saloons with all kinds of games and gaming tables where they had singing every night free, and one or two dance houses of evil repute, and one or two hurdy-gurdy dance houses of fair repute—taken altogether Walla Walla was a fast place, and a great outfitting place for the mines all over."

Fort Walla Walla Museum Complex, adjoining Fort Walla Walla Park, was garrisoned from the 1850s through the Indian wars. The post was rebuilt in 1857 by Col. George Wright; it is situated on the east bank of the Columbia, about ½ mile above the mouth of the Walla Walla River. Reinhart recalled it as being on a stream called "Garrison Creek" because it ran by the garrison which had fine buildings, farm, barns, sheds, and sawmill. "It was on a high sort of a hill and laid off very nice with parade grounds in the center . . . and they had long stables to stable several thousand head of cavalry horses and teams of mules to haul supplies." The post cemetery is within the city park grounds.

YAKIMA, Yakima County. IS 82.

Yakima Valley Museum and Historical Association, 2105 Tieton Dr. in Franklin Park, has period costumes, weapons, household furnishings, replicas of pioneer rooms, and a large collection of carriages, coaches, and wagons.

WEST VIRGINIA

A Virginia convention, meeting at Richmond, passed the Ordinance of Secession in April 1861 over the opposition of delegates from the western counties. This section of the state voted against the ordinance approximately ten to one. In June, delegates meeting at Wheeling declared the ordinance void and the offices of the state government vacant. A convention met in November and formed a constitution, which was ratified by popular vote in April 1862. The state entered the Union June 20, 1863.

The first skirmish took place at Philippi on June 3, 1861. During the next four years about 600 engagements occurred within the new state, but few were of major proportion; guerrilla fighting constituted most of the conflict. One naval battle was fought at Buffington Island on July 19, 1863, when U.S. steamers in West Virginia waters supported Ohio land forces in an attempt to capture Morgan's raiders.

The state sent 32,000 men to the Union army and about 10,000 to the Confederacy. Fourteen Union generals and seven Confederate generals were West Virginians. Many West Virginia families suffered a division. Representative of the emotional rift that existed was Laura Jackson Arnold, who remained loyal to the Union though she was the wife of a secessionist and sister of one of the Confederacy's greatest generals. West Virginia's swing to the Union was a chancier matter in the early days of the war than was generally acknowledged.

ALLEGHENY MOUNTAIN, Pocahontas County. US 250. Marker at Virginia line for Camp Allegheny. Confederates entrenched in this area repulsed a Federal attack led by Gen. Robert J. Milroy, but soon after retreated to the Shenandoah Valley.

ALTA, Greenbrier County. US 60.
Unknown Soldiers Marker, 4 miles from Alta at junction of highways.

ALVON, Greenbrier County. US 60, State 15.

Dry Creek Battle. Marker by West Virginia Historic Commission describes two-day engagement in August 1863 between Gen. Sam Jones's Confederates and Gen. W. W. Averell's Federals.

ANSTED, Fayette County. US 60. Markers on highway.
Contentment, US 60, houses the Fayette County Historical Society. The house, now restored, was the home of Confederate Gen. George W. Imboden. Period furnishings. There also is a one-room schoolhouse on the grounds.
Westlake Cemetery has the grave of Julia Neale Jackson, mother of Stonewall Jackson. A marble monument was erected after the war by Capt. Thomas D. Ranson of the Stonewall Brigade.

ARNOLDSBURG, Calhoun County. US 33, 119.
Arnoldsburg Skirmish. Historic Commission marker for site of Camp McDonald. Scene of May 6, 1862, engagement; Federals under Maj. George C. Trimble held off Moccasin Rangers under Capt. George Downs.

BARTOW, Pocahontas County. US 250.
Blue and Gray Marker, on highway. A skirmish was fought here in December 1861.
Traveler's Repose Marker, junction of US 250 and State 28. Confederate trenches are to the south.

BEALLAIR, Jefferson County. US 340. Marker on highway. On October 16, 1859, John Brown and his men kidnapped Col. Lewis Washington, a great-grandnephew of George Washington, who had a sword that Frederick the Great had given to Gen. Washington, saying it was a gift from the oldest general to the greatest. Brown wanted the sword to use in what he considered his fight for liberty; he was wearing it at the time of his capture.

BECKLEY, Raleigh County. IS 77, US 19, 21. The town was occupied by both armies early in the war. Federals shelled it in 1863.

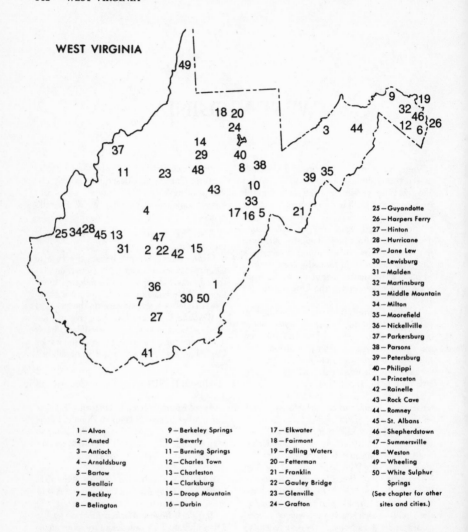

WEST VIRGINIA

25 — Guyandotte
26 — Harpers Ferry
27 — Hinton
28 — Hurricane
29 — Jane Lew
30 — Lewisburg
31 — Malden
32 — Martinsburg
33 — Middle Mountain
34 — Milton
35 — Moorefield
36 — Nickellville
37 — Parkersburg
38 — Parsons
39 — Petersburg
40 — Philippi
41 — Princeton
42 — Rainelle
43 — Rock Cave
44 — Romney
45 — St. Albans
46 — Shepherdstown
47 — Summersville
48 — Weston
49 — Wheeling
50 — White Sulphur
    Springs
(See chapter for other
sites and cities.)

1 — Alvon
2 — Ansted
3 — Antioch
4 — Arnoldsburg
5 — Bartow
6 — Beallair
7 — Beckley
8 — Belington
9 — Berkeley Springs
10 — Beverly
11 — Burning Springs
12 — Charles Town
13 — Charleston
14 — Clarksburg
15 — Droop Mountain
16 — Durbin
17 — Elkwater
18 — Fairmont
19 — Falling Waters
20 — Fetterman
21 — Franklin
22 — Gauley Bridge
23 — Glenville
24 — Grafton

Honey in the Rock, Civil War drama, is presented in summer in the Grandview Amphitheatre; curtain time at dusk. Kermit Hunter wrote the play.

BELINGTON, Barbour County. US 250.
Laurel Hill, east of town. Markers on US 250 and Old Beverly Pike. In July 1861, Confederates under Gen. R. S. Garnett unsuccessfully attempted to halt Gen. Thomas A. Morris's advance eastward.

BERKELEY SPRINGS, Morgan County. Off IS 70, US 522. The war halted the growth of this popular spa where even George Washington once "took the waters." It rebounded.

Pau Pau, 22 miles west of Berkeley Springs. Marker on State 29. Concentration point of Union Army, 1861–1865, with 16,000 men encamped here at one time.

Strother House, southeast corner of Washington and Warren St. Gen. David Hunter Strother bought the house in 1861 and lived here with his second wife. Union troops occupied the house for a time. Strother wrote under the pseudonym of Porte Crayon. He was adept at sketching as well as writing; his account of John Brown's trial, with drawings, is memorable. In the prewar years Berkeley Springs was a fashionable spa; its official name, Bath. Strother's father ran a popular hotel where generals, statesmen, presidents, literary lights, and even exiled royalty came to relax. A Strother biographer saw great social contrasts in the town: "On Saturdays during the summer, nabobs, fops, and mountaineers gathered on the square to hear the band concerts. . . . Bear steak was washed down with the best champagne, distances were sometimes measured by the number of 'barks of a dog' . . ." Strother's decision to join the Union army, though he was a Virginian by birth, alienated many of his relatives forever.

BEVERLY, Randolph County. US 219, 250.

Battle of Rich Mountain. Marker on Old Staunton-Parkersburg Pike, 5 miles west of town, also on US 219 and 250 at Beverly. Confederates were entrenched on Rich Mountain after retreating from Grafton and Philippi. Rosecrans attacked on July 11, 1861, and routed the Southerners, who were commanded by Gen. Robert Garnett. The Hart House on the battlefield was built by Joseph Hart, son of a signer of the Declaration of Independence. It was used as a hospital.

Mount Iser Cemetery has a Confederate monument erected by the United Daughters of the Confederacy.

BOLIVAR, Jefferson County. US 340.

Bolivar Heights, opposite cemetery, Washington St., has series of markers relating to the Confederate capture of Harpers Ferry on September 15, 1862.

Jackson's Headquarters, Washington St. Marker for site where Stonewall Jackson stayed in September 1862.

St. John's Lutheran and *Bolivar Methodist Churches,* Washington St., were used as hospitals by both armies.

BURNING SPRINGS, Wirt County. State 14.

Rathbone Well Marker. In 1863, Confederates under Gen. William Jones raided the oil field here, destroyed machinery and barges.

CHARLESTON, Kanawha County. IS 64, 77, 79, US 60, 35.

Cultural Center, Greenbrier and Washington streets, in Capitol complex, has Civil War and John Brown displays.

State Capitol, E. Kanawha Blvd. On west lawn is a statue of Stonewall Jackson by Sir Moses Ezekill, and a mountaineer statue dedicated to the men and women who saved West Virginia for the Union. Southwest corner of Capitol grounds has a monument to Union soldiers.

CHARLES TOWN, Jefferson County. US 340, State 9, 31. Residents were pro-Southern; the city was heavily shelled. By 1863, no able-bodied males were left in the community. The town was named for George Washington's youngest brother. Many antebellum homes here have been restored. *Falling Spring* was the home of Confederate Col. William Morgan. *Locust Hill* was the scene of a skirmish in August 1864. Gen. Philip Sheridan had taken possession of the estate; Gen. Jubal Early attacked from breastworks back of the stone fence. A cannon ball went down the chimney; rear wall of house has bullet holes.

Jefferson County Courthouse, George and Washington St. The room where John Brown was tried is part of the present courthouse which was rebuilt after being shelled in the war. Museum.

Jefferson County Museum, 200 E. Washington, in lower level of the Charles Town Library, has John Brown memorabilia and many Civil War items.

Site of John Brown Gallows, S. Samuel St. between McCurdy St. and Beckwith Alley. Maj. T. J. Jackson commanded a howitzer unit at the hanging. John Wilkes Booth was a militiaman.

Zion Episcopal Church, E. Congress St. between S. Mildred and S. Church St. The church cemetery contains graves of Confederate soldiers. John Yates Beall, who attempted to capture Johnson's Island, Lake Erie, and was hanged on Governor's Island, N.Y., is buried here.

CLARKSBURG, Harrison County. Off IS 79, US 19, 50, State 20. Gen. George B. McClellan had his headquarters here until First Manassas. The town served as a supply depot for the Union throughout the war.

Jackson Birthplace, 328 W. Main St. Bronze tablet marks site where Thomas Jonathan Jackson was born on January 21, 1824. He was one of four children and was three years old when his father died of an undiagnosed fever. Mrs. Jackson operated a small private school and took in sewing until she married Capt. Blake Woodson, a lawyer.

Jackson Cemetery, E. Pike St. between Cherry St. and Charleston Ave., has the graves of Gen. Jackson's grandparents, father, and sister, Elizabeth Jackson.

Jackson Monument, in northeast corner of courthouse plaza. Equestrian statue of Gen. Jackson by Charles Keck.

Lowndes Hill Park has remains of Union earthworks.

DROOP MOUNTAIN BATTLEFIELD STATE PARK, Pocahontas County. US 219. Park commemorates battle of November 6, 1863. Gen. William W. Averell defeated Gen. John Echols, ending the last major Confederate resistance. There are monuments, graves, and breastworks.

DURBIN, Pocahontas County. US 250.
Cheat Summit Camp, marker on highway near Cheat Bridge. Union camp at summit of mountain was also known as Fort Milroy.
Gaudineer Fire Tower, on Shavers Mountain, off highway to the north, gives excellent view of terrain. Visitors welcome.

ELKWATER, Randolph County. US 219.
Monument to Col. Washington, on highway. Col. John Augustine Washington, aide-de-camp to Gen. Robert E. Lee, was killed here on September 13, 1861.

FAIRMONT, Marion County. US 19.
Jones's Raid, marker on highway at county line of Marion and Monongalia. On April 29, 1863, Confederate Gen. William E. Jones and cavalry attacked the city, took 260 prisoners, and destroyed the railroad bridge across the Monongahela River.
Pierpont House, northeast corner of Pierpont Ave. and Quincy St. Site of former home of Gov. Francis H. Pierpont, which was raided by Jones's troops. Pierpont was active in the Wheeling conventions. He was elected governor of the Restored Government of Virginia at the second Wheeling convention; after the state was admitted to the Union, he moved the government to Alexandria, Virginia, until the end of the war.
Woodlawn Cemetery has the grave of Gov. Pierpont. His statue is in the Hall of Fame in Washington.

FALLING WATERS, Berkeley County. US 11.
Battle of Falling Waters took place in July 1863, when Lee's army, retreating from Gettysburg, was attacked by Meade's troops. The Confederates managed to cross the Potomac and escape. There were a number of cavalry skirmishes in the area because the river was swollen with heavy rainfall and bridges had been destroyed by the Union. Lee had warehouses torn down, used the timber to make pontoon bridges. Gen. J. J. Pettigrew of North Carolina was mortally wounded in the battle on July 14. Monument on highway denotes site of house in which Pettigrew died. Another marker commemorates site where Gen. Stonewall Jackson was seated under an oak tree on

July 2, 1861, when fired on by the Federals. A cannonball brought down a limb of the tree, but not the general.

FAYETTEVILLE, Fayette County. US 19, 21. Marker on highway. The town was fortified by both armies. On May 19, 1863, Confederates shelled the Union entrenchments. Here the military tactic of shooting over the heads of friendly troops into the enemy lines was introduced in the Civil War.

FETTERMAN, Taylor County. US 50.
Brown Monument. T. Bailey Brown possibly was the first casualty of the war; he was shot by Confederate sentries on May 22, 1861.

FLAT TOP, Mercer County. US 19, 21.
Camp Jones, marker on highway.

FRANKLIN, Pendleton County. US 33, 220. Markers erected by the West Virginia Historic Commission are on US 220 for:
Smoke Hole, where saltpeter was mined in caves during the war.
Trout Rock Fort, end of Gen. Jackson's pursuit of the Federals after the battle of McDowell, May 12, 1862. At this site saltpeter was mined at a nearby cave to make gunpowder for Confederates.

GAULEY BRIDGE, Fayette County. The town was the gateway to the Kanawha Valley and the scene of heavy fighting. Gen. W. S. Rosecrans defeated Gen. John B. Floyd here in November 1861.
Miller Tavern, Main St. northeast of railway overhead crossing, was headquarters for Union army officers. Among them were two future presidents, William McKinley and Rutherford Hayes.
Old Gauley Bridge, junction of US 60 and 19. Confederates destroyed the bridge in 1861. Stone piers remain.

GLENVILLE, Gilmer County. US 33, 119.
Battle of Tank Hill, a minor skirmish took place here. Remains of Union trenches are on Tank Hill.

GRAFTON, Taylor County. US 50. The railroad town had strategic importance and was occupied by both armies. In June 1861, Gen. Thomas A. Morris camped here with some 4,000 Union troops before marching south to Philippi. Also in 1861, Gen. McClellan had headquarters here. (*See* FETTERMAN for *Bailey Brown Marker.*)
Andrews Methodist Church claims the first official Mother's Day service. The idea grew out of post-Civil War days when Mrs. Ann Reeves Jarvis wanted to reunite family ties that

had been severed by the conflict. All Union and Confederate soldiers and their families were invited to a friendship day at Pruntytown. Years later Mrs. Jarvis's daughter, Anna M. Jarvis, inaugurated Mother's Day to commemorate the anniversary of her mother's death.

Latham Print Shop, 35 W. Main St. Twenty-eight days after Fort Sumter fell, Gov. Letcher of Virginia ordered Col. Porterfield to capture Grafton. On May 10, 1861, Porterfield arrived in town to seize the railroad and enlist men. George R. Latham defiantly nailed the American flag over his print shop door and began to recruit Union troops. By the middle of May he was captain of the Grafton Guards and was drilling in Main Street.

National Cemetery has the graves of more than 2,000 Union and Confederate soldiers. Pvt. T. B. Brown's grave has a ten-foot monument.

West Main Methodist Church was allotted $490 by the U.S. government on March 4, 1915, for damages inflicted by Union soldiers who were quartered here.

GUYANDOTTE, Cabell County. State 2. Marker on highway at Huntington. Nearly two months before the Confederacy was formed and four months before Fort Sumter was fired on, Cabell County formed a military unit, the Border Rangers, to protect a Virginia flag hoisted at Guyandotte. Albert Gallatin Jenkins was elected captain. The Confederate town was burned by Union troops after the raid by Confederate Rangers on November 10, 1861, when recruits of the 9th West Virginia Infantry were massacred. Marker for Greenbottom, home of Gen. Albert Jenkins, is located on State 2 at site of mansion.

HARPERS FERRY, Jefferson County. US 340. John Brown and his men marched on the town in October 1859, captured two watchmen, and took the armory and arsenal. The marines arrived next day, commanded by Robert E. Lee and J. E. B. Stuart. When Brown refused to surrender, the troops stormed the armory. Brown lost ten men, the town lost four, and the marines one. Brown was tried and hanged. At the outbreak of war, Virginia militia moved to seize the armory and arsenal. Union troops fired the buildings before retreating. The town was caught between the two armies a number of times and was virtually a ghost town at war's end.

Harpers Ferry National Historical Park, situated at the confluence of the scenic Potomac and Shenandoah Rivers, is steeped in more than 250 years of history. The four parts

themes are: Industry, John Brown's Raid, the Civil War, and African-American History, particularly Storer College.

Exhibits, audio-visual presentations, walking tours, and scenic hikes all help visitors to experience the past. Entrance fee: $5 per vehicle; $2 per person for cyclists, walk-ins, bus groups.

John Brown Wax Museum, High St., is designed to relive the career of the abolitionist who captured the Federal arsenal and rifle works on October 16, 1859. It is housed in an old building not far from the engine house in which Brown and some of his men were besieged and captured.

HILLSBORO, Pocahontas County. US 219. Union Gen. William Averell camped here before the battle of Droop Mountain. Marker on highway.

HINTON, Summers County. State 20.

Confederate Monument, 1st and James St., honors soldiers of Greenbrier and New River valleys who followed Robert E. Lee and Stonewall Jackson.

Mike Foster Monument, Forest Hill Cemetery, commemorates a Confederate soldier of New River Valley.

HUNTERSVILLE, Pocahontas County. State 39. Markers on highway.

Presbyterian Church was used as a hospital and garrison for both Confederate and Union troops.

HURRICANE, Putnam County. IS 64, US 60.

Hurricane Skirmish. Marker on highway. The Baptist church was burned in the affair that took place at Hurricane Creek Bridge on March 20, 1863. Civil War soldiers are buried in the First Baptist Church graveyard.

HUTTONSVILLE, Randolph County. US 219, 250.

Fort Milroy, marker on highway southeast of town. The fort, used by Union troops, was established at the summit of White Top Mountain.

IRELAND, Lewis County. US 19.

Fort Pickens. Marker at junction of US 19 and Sec. Rd. 50 denotes site of Civil War fortifications.

JACKSON MILL, Lewis County. US 19. Marker on highway at 4-H State Camp. The 1837 mill was built on the farm of Col. Edward Jackson, grandfather of Thomas Jackson. When Jackson's widowed mother remarried, Thomas and Laura were sent to stay with their grandmother. Thomas, who was six years old, stayed here until he went to West Point in 1842. Museum.

JANE LEW, Lewis County. IS 79, US 19.
General Lightburn Marker, west of town. Gen. Joseph Andrew Jackson Lightburn had ambitions to go to West Point, but the appointment for his district went to a neighbor, Tom Jackson. Lightburn served in the Mexican War, was commissioned colonel of the 4th West Virginia in August 1861, served at Vicksburg, Chickamauga, and Atlanta, and was wounded in August 1864. After the war he became a Baptist minister; he is buried in the Broad Run Baptist Church cemetery.

KEYSER, Mineral County. US 220, State 46. Marker on highway. Town was captured and recaptured 14 times. The town was known as New Creek during the Civil War.
Fort Fuller, campus of Potomac State College, was a Federal barricade.

LEWISBURG, Greenbrier County. IS 64, US 60.
Battle of Lewisburg, marker on highway east of US 219. In May 1862, Confederates attempted to drive out Federals but were unsuccessful. Library Park also has descriptive marker. A cross-shaped mass grave on McIlhenny Rd. holds the remains of 95 unknown Confederate soldiers killed in the battle.
Greenbrier County Library and Museum, US 60, is in a building used as a hospital in the war.
Old Stone Church, Church St., was used as emergency hospital and later for billeting troops.

MALDEN, Kanawha County. IS 77, US 60.
Washington Homesite. Marker denotes site of cabin where Booker T. Washington, educator and author of *Up From Slavery,* lived as a boy.

MARTINSBURG, Berkeley County. IS 81, US 11, State 9. Marker on highway. In Jackson's raid of 1861, captured locomotives were drawn by horses to Winchester.
Berkeley County Courthouse, King and Queen St. Belle Boyd, Confederate spy, was imprisoned here several times during the war.
Boydville, Queen St. between South and Buxton St., was saved from destruction by a presidential order signed by Abraham Lincoln.
Everett House, southwest corner of Burke and Queen St. Stonewall Jackson had headquarters here and reviewed his troops from the veranda; Gen. Phil Sheridan later had quarters here.
Flick House, southwest corner of King and Queen St., is said to have been invaded by a Union officer who rode his horse up the circular staircase on a spy hunt.
Norbourne Hall, West Race St., was the home of David Hunter Strother (Porte Crayon), who became a brigadier general in the Union army. (*Also see* BERKELEY SPRINGS.)
St. John's Lutheran Church, southwest corner Martin and Queen St., served as a Union hospital.

McCAUSLAND, Mason County. State 17.
McCausland Homestead. Marker on highway. Gen. John McCausland commanded a detachment of cadets at John Brown's hanging, fought in many Confederate campaigns, burned Chambersburg, Pennsylvania, refused to surrender at Appomattox and led his brigade through Union lines. Another McCausland marker is located on highway below cemetery near Henderson, where he is buried.

MIDDLEBOURNE, Tyler County. State 18. Home town of Arthur Ingraham Boreman, wartime governor. He took the oath of office on June 20, 1863, in front of Linsly Military Institute at Wheeling. The crowd gave three cheers for the state and three for the Union, and 35 schoolgirls sang "The Star Spangled Banner."

MIDDLE MOUNTAIN, Randolph County. US 219.
Lee's Headquarters during summer of 1861 was on lower slopes of mountain. Lee also had temporary headquarters at an old toll house on highway at junction with State 28.

MILTON, Cabell County. IS 64, US 60.
Covered Bridge was guarded by the Union army against Confederates. On April 5, 1863, Capt. P. M. Carpenter attempted to seize the bridge but was repulsed by troops under Capt. Dove. Sign on bridge.
Union Baptist Church. Descriptive marker has been placed by the West Virginia Historic Commission, on old James River and Kanawha turnpike in front of church. It was garrisoned by Federal troops who were protecting the covered bridge.

MOOREFIELD, Hardy County. US 220, State 28.
McNeill's Raid. Marker at junction of highway. Capt. Hanson McNeill and his son Jesse led the McNeill rangers on raids from a base at Willow Hall, off US 220. The mansion was

built in 1818 by Capt. Daniel McNeill. The raiders were well acquainted with the territory and inflicted great damage on Union forces. They burned railroad cars, tore up tracks, and captured prisoners, horses, and cattle throughout the eastern panhandle and into Maryland.

NICKELLVILLE, Fayette County. Alt. US 19.
Indirect Firing Marker, where Cpl. Milton Humphreys, Bryan's Battery, 13th Virginia Light Artillery, made first use of indirect artillery fire in warfare.

PARKERSBURG, Wood County. IS 77, US 21, State 14.
City Park, Park and 23rd streets, has Centennial Cabin with historical relics.
Morgan's Raiders. Marker on junction of highways. Some of Morgan's men escaped to West Virginia after the battle of Buffington Island. Morgan was captured in Ohio.
Nemesis Park, south of the mouth of Little Kanawha River, was the site of Fort Boreman, a Union fortification established in 1863.

PARSONS, Tucker County. US 219.
Battle of Corrick's Ford Monument, on courthouse lawn. Gen. Robert Selden Garnett was killed while conducting the Confederate retreat from Laurel Hill on July 13, 1861. Garnett died in the arms of Union General T. A. Morris; they had been West Point classmates.

PAW PAW, Morgan County. State 29.
Union Barracks and Blockhouse were located along the tracks of Baltimore and Ohio Railroad.

PETERSBURG, Grant County. US 220, State 4.
Federal Trenches overlooked the town, 1863–1864.
Greenland Gap, 19 miles west of State 42. Scene of skirmish between Gen. Jones's cavalry and Federal troops.
Smoke Hole Caverns, 8 miles west on State 4, 28. Marker at entrance to Smoke Hole Gorge. Ammunition was stored in caverns during war.

PHILIPPI, Barbour County. US 119, 250.
Alderson-Broaddus College has memorial on site of cannon emplacement at first land battle of the war.
Covered Bridge, on highway over Tygart River, was used by both armies during the engagement of June 3, 1861. Federals under Col. B. F. Kelley routed Confederates under Col. G. A. Porterfield. The prize was control of the Baltimore and Ohio Railroad.

PRINCETON, Mercer County. IS 77, US 19, 21, 219. Marker on highway. The town was the scene of several engagements. In 1862 Capt. Jennifer's Confederate troops set fire to the courthouse and the entire town burned.

RAINELLE, Fayette County. US 60.
Lee's Headquarters. Marker on highway. Robert E. Lee had quarters near the summit of Big Sewell Mountain. His warhorse, Traveller, came from the Andrew Johnston farm in Greenbrier County, near Blue Sulphur Springs. Lee refused to accept the horse as a gift but paid for it with 200 Confederate dollars.

ROCK CAVE, Upshur County. State 4, 20.
Upshur Militia Marker. Seventy militia members were drilling without arms under Capt. Daniel Gould when surprised and captured by Confederates.

ROMNEY, Hampshire County. US 50. The town changed hands 56 times. Early in the war the Hampshire Guards and the Frontier Riflemen joined the Confederate army.
Confederate Monument, Indian Mound Cemetery, was dedicated in 1867.
Wallace Headquarters, on road to the south, at east end of bridge over South Branch River, US 50, west edge of town. Not only Wallace, however, but the McNeill Rangers found the place. The rangers surrendered here at the end of the war.

ST. ALBANS, Kanawha County. IS 64, US 60.
Battle of Scary Creek, marker on State 17 about 15 miles west of Charleston. On July 17, 1861, Confederates won their first victory in the Kanawha Valley. Capt. Albert G. Jenkins of Cabell County led the counterattack against the Union forces of Gen. Jacob Cox.

SHEPHERDSTOWN, Jefferson County. State 45. The river crossing was a strategic point in the war. A wooden toll bridge was destroyed by Confederate forces fearing Union invasion. In September 1862, after the battle of Antietam, Lee retreated to Shepherdstown, crossed the river at Pack Horse Ford. Marker on Sec. Rt. 17, 1 mile east of town.
Elmwood Cemetery has a monument to 577 Confederates killed at Antietam.

SUMMERSVILLE, Nicholas County. US 19.
Carnifex Ferry Battlefield State Park, 10 miles southwest. Museum has relics, exhibits pertaining to the battle of September 10, 1861. Federals under Gen. Rosecrans encountered Confederates under Gen. John B. Floyd.

Cross Lanes Battle Marker, erected by the West Virginia Historic Commission on State 39, at site of Confederate surprise attack on August 26, 1861, against the 7th Ohio under Col. E. B. Tyler. The engagement was also known as the battle of Knives and Forks.

Nancy Hart Marker, on courthouse lawn. The beautiful Confederate spy led a surprise attack on the town, was captured, bewitched her guard reportedly to the extent that the fellow let her examine his gun. This, however, was his last mistake. Nancy shot him and escaped.

UNION, Monroe County. US 219.

Echols Monument, courthouse lawn. Gen. John Echols fought in the Stonewall Brigade, was severely wounded at Kernstown, later fought at Droop Mountain and New Market.

Salt Sulphur, headquarters of Gen. A. J. Jenkins and other Confederate leaders during campaigns.

WESTON, Braxton County. IS 79, US 19, State 4.

Bulltown Battle, marker on US 19 and State 4, between Weston and Sutton. Sharp skirmish in which Union troops were victorious.

WHEELING, Ohio County. IS 70, US 40.

Mansion Museum, Oglebay Park, has historical exhibits.

Soldiers' and Sailors' Monument, grounds of City-County Building, Chapline between 15th and 16th St.

West Virginia Independence Hall, 16th and Market streets, was once the customhouse. From 1861 to 1863 the government for the restored state of Virginia and the independence convention that declared the state's separation from Virginia met here. Restored, with interpretive files.

Wheeling Park, US 40, has memorial to Gen. Jesse Lee Reno, who was killed at South Mountain.

WHITE SULPHUR SPRINGS, Greenbrier County. US 50.

Old White was a hotel here during the war years. It served as headquarters for both armies as the battle lines shifted across the valley. After the battle of White Sulphur Springs it was a hospital. Dead and wounded were laid in rows in ballroom and dining room. A photograph taken in 1869 shows a reunion of Gen. Lee with Southern and Northern military leaders at Old White. Among those at the gathering: Gens. John W. Geary, John B. Magruder, Robert D. Lilly, P. G. T. Beauregard, Lew Wallace, Henry Wise, Joseph L. Brent, and James Connor.

WINFIELD, State 17. Marker for 1864 skirmish between Confederate and Union troops. Confederate Capt. Philip Thurmond was killed here. Union rifle pits are visible.

WISCONSIN

Wisconsin became the 30th state on May 29, 1848. In 1854, the state supreme court declared the Fugitive Slave Act unconstitutional. The decision drew together Whigs, Democrats, and Free Soilers in the beginnings of the Republican party, voting first for Frémont, then for Lincoln.

Within a week after war began, the state had organized 36 companies. In the first year of conflict, 16 regiments were raised, but the call for more troops in August 1862 led to a draft in Wisconsin as elsewhere. Gov. Louis P. Harvey, who took office in 1862, was drowned in the Tennessee River while returning from a trip to aid Wisconsin soldiers wounded at Shiloh. His widow, Cordelia P. Harvey, worked ceaselessly to aid soldiers and to establish hospitals. She was known as the Wisconsin Angel and even pleaded with Lincoln to get hospitals established in a healthful climate. Three were set up: at Milwaukee, Prairie du Chien, and at Madison, where more than 600 Wisconsin soldiers were treated before the war's end.

Wisconsin men served in every major campaign of the war. More than 91,000 were in the Union army; more than 11,000 were lost. The Iron Brigade, also known for a time as the Black Hat Brigade for their army dress black hats, was composed of the 2nd, 6th, and 7th Wisconsin Volunteers, plus the 19th Indiana and the 24th Michigan. It was probably the North's most famous fighting unit.

BARABOO, Sauk County. State 33.
Sauk County Historical Museum, 531 4th Ave. Military Room on second floor of museum has Union photographs, Confederate currency and bonds, Civil War books and records.

BEAVER DAM, Dodge County. US 151.
Dodge County Museum, 105 Park Ave. Historical items, railroad exhibits.

BELOIT, Rock County. IS 90. Abraham Lincoln visited here twice. He camped in Riverside Park when he was in the Illinois militia during the Black Hawk War, came again when campaigning in 1859, and spoke at Hanchett Hall.

CASSVILLE, Grant County. State 81, 133.
Dewey Home, in Nelson Dewey State Park, has Civil War artifacts. Dewey was Wisconsin's first governor.

DELAFIELD, Waukesha County. One mile north of the town there was a little memorial park to honor three interesting brothers who served in the Civil War. Unfortunately the park is gone, but the memory lingers on.

William B. Cushing became a lieutenant commander in the navy; Maj. Alonzo B. Cushing served in the artillery, won honors at Chancellorsville, and was killed at Gettysburg; Howard B. Cushing was transferred at his own request to his dead brother's artillery company, served throughout the war, and was transferred to Arizona Territory where he was killed in action in the Apache wars, having been ambushed by Cochise and a war party.

ELKHORN, Walworth County. State 11.
Webster House, Corner of Washington and Rockwell St., 1 block south of square. Home of Joseph Philbrick Webster, composer of "Lorena" and other popular songs of the Civil War period. Guided tours available.

FORT ATKINSON, Jefferson County. US 12.
Hoard Historical Museum, 407 Merchants Ave. (US 12), has Civil War firearms.

GREEN BAY, Brown County. IS 43.
Hazelwood, 1008 S. Monroe Ave. The 1837 home of Morgan L. Martin, a major in the Civil War and president of the state's constitutional convention.

GREENBUSH, Sheboygan County. State 23.
Old Wade House, on highway, midway between Sheboygan and Fond du Lac. A stopping point in stagecoach and plank road days. The inn is maintained by the state historical society. Guided tours available.

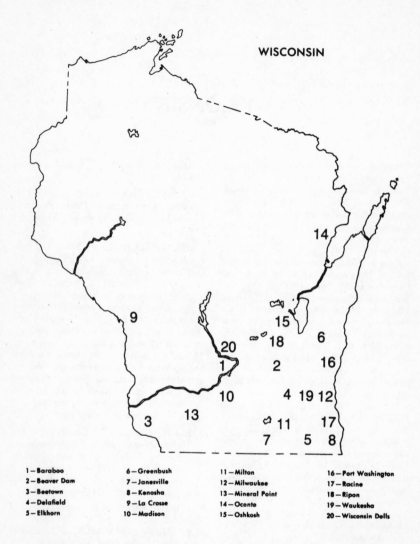

WISCONSIN

14

9

15

18

20

1

2

6

16

10

4 19 12

3   13

11   17

7   5   8

1 — Baraboo	6 — Greenbush	11 — Milton	16 — Port Washington
2 — Beaver Dam	7 — Janesville	12 — Milwaukee	17 — Racine
3 — Beetown	8 — Kenosha	13 — Mineral Point	18 — Ripon
4 — Delafield	9 — La Crosse	14 — Oconto	19 — Waukesha
5 — Elkhorn	10 — Madison	15 — Oshkosh	20 — Wisconsin Dells

JANESVILLE, Rock County. IS 90.

Lincoln-Tallman Homestead. 440 N. Jackson. Lincoln spent a weekend here in 1859. Period furnishings and relics. Guided tours. Visitor center and museum in the horse barn.

KENOSHA, Kenosha County. IS 94, State 32.

Civil War Museum, in Lentz Hall, Carthage College, has an excellent collection gathered by Frank A. Calumbo, a dedicated student of the war. There are ten showcases with Confederate and Union uniforms, many rare prints, a currency collection, and other relics.

Kenosha County Historical Society, 6300 3rd Ave. War artifacts and frontier items, Indian and county history exhibits.

Library Park, 7th Ave. between 59th Pl. and 61st St. Lincoln Monument is a replica of statue sculptured by Charles H. Niehaus at Muskegon, Michigan. Soldiers' and Sailors' Monument in north part of park honors Civil War veterans.

LA CROSSE, La Crosse County. IS 90. Mark M. ("Brick") Pomeroy of the *La Crosse Democrat* was anti-abolition and anti-Lincoln; when Lincoln sought reelection, Pomeroy put the candidate's photograph on the front page with a caption: "The Widow Maker of the 19th Century and Republican Candidate for the Presidency." Local legend says that a mob intent upon hanging Pomeroy, after the President's assassination, stopped at a brewery en route and never got the job done.

MADISON, Dane County. IS 90, 94.

Site of Camp Randall, University Ave. to Monroe St., Randall Ave. to Breese. Seventy thousand men were quartered here during the war. Some recruits claimed to be reading their Bibles nightly; local newspaper accounts complained of the "rowdies" who led brewery raids. A memorial arch was dedicated to Civil War soldiers in 1912, in a section of the land set aside as the Camp Randall Memorial Park. Pvt. John Brobst wrote home from Columbus, Kentucky, that times were dull but "we are not penned up like a pack of hogs as we were at Madison."

Forest Hill Cemetery contains the graves of 140 Confederate soldiers who were members of the Alabama Volunteer Regiment captured at Island No. 10. Of the noncommissioned officers and privates, 1,156 were taken prisoner and sent to Camp Randall, where many died.

State Historical Society, 816 State St., has period rooms giving a chronological history of Wisconsin life. Civil War exhibits.

Wisconsin Memorial Union, Park and Langdon St., a recreational and cultural center of the University of Wisconsin, was erected in memory of Wisconsin men and women who served in American wars.

Wisconsin State Capitol, Capitol Park. Daily tours in summer months. G.A.R. Memorial Hall on fourth floor contains Civil War relics. Replicas of Old Abe, the War Eagle, are in Memorial Hall and the Assembly Chamber. In 1861 a band of Flambeau Indians of the Chippewa tribe caught a young eagle which they traded to Mrs. Dan McCann, who kept the bird as a family pet until it was offered to a new regiment organized at Eau Claire. With Old Abe as mascot, the 8th Wisconsin was known as the Eagle Regiment. The eagle was present in 42 battles and skirmishes, riding on a standard to the left of the colors. Confederates tried repeatedly to capture the "Yankee Buzzard" but did not succeed. He was presented to the state in September 1864 and lived in the Capitol until 1881 when his health was imperiled by a fire near his cage: he suffered from smoke inhalation and died a month later. His mounted body was consumed in a Capitol fire in 1904, but his legend is so bright he might have been a phoenix instead of an eagle.

MILTON, Rock County. State 26.

Milton House Museum, State 59, 26. Inn and log cabin were stations on the Underground Railroad. A restored general store is part of display. Tunnel from inn to cabin.

MILWAUKEE, Milwaukee County. IS 43, 94.

Court of Honor, a three-block area just off the business district containing library, churches, and YMCA, is dedicated to Milwaukee's Civil War dead.

Milwaukee County Historical Center, 910 N. Old World 3rd St., exhibits and a slide presentation depicting Milwaukee's past.

Milwaukee Public Museum, 800 W. Wells St., features natural and human history; outstanding American Indian and weapons exhibits.

MINERAL POINT, Iowa County. US 151.

Site of Mineral Point Bank, 324 High St. One of the founders of the bank was Gen. Cadwallader Colden Washburn, an early Republican congressman and a delegate to the Washington Peace Conference in 1861. Gen. Washburn raised the 2nd Wisconsin Cavalry, commanded the District of Eastern Arkansas, and later commanded the District of Western Tennessee; after the war he was a congressman and governor of Wisconsin.

OSHKOSH, Winnebago County. US 45.

Camp Bragg Memorial Park, northeast corner of Hazel and Cleveland St., is the site of a military camp used in the Civil War. Cannon mark areas where the 21st and 32nd Wisconsin regiments were organized and drilled. Park was named for Gen. E. S. Bragg of the Iron Brigade. Bragg once told his wife he was fighting for a star or a coffin. He didn't get the second until the 20th century.

Oshkosh Public Museum, 1331 Algoma Blvd., has extensive collections of regional history, river steamboat history, firearms, and paintings.

PORT WASHINGTON, Ozaukee County. IS 43, US 141.

Pors House, 405 Wisconsin St., was the site of a draft riot in 1862, when Gov. Edward Salomon ordered all able-bodied men to enroll for service. In November a mob of citizens stormed the courthouse and reportedly threw Draft Commissioner Pors down the steps. After ransacking the Pors house, they took a cannon used for 4th of July celebrations, loaded it, and retired to South Bluff, armed with farm tools and the cannon. Government troops, arriving by boat, came ashore and circumvented and captured the 80 draft dodgers.

PRAIRIE DU CHIEN, Crawford County. US 18.

Villa Louis, 521 Villa Louis Rd., has memorabilia of Union Gen. Samuel Sturgis and of his son, Capt. Jack Sturgis, who died with Custer at Little Big Horn. Jefferson Davis was once a guest here. Home is owned and operated by the state historical society.

RACINE, Racine County. IS 94, State 32. *East Park.* Statue by Frederick C. Hibbard is the first monument to a president and his wife and the first statue of Mary Todd Lincoln.

Mound Cemetery has the grave of Capt. Gilbert Knapp of the U.S. Revenue Marine Service, who was active in coast and blockade duty during the war.

Racine County Historical Museum, 701 S. Main St., has some Civil War items; changing exhibits feature local history. A replica of Old Abe, the famous eagle mascot of the Civil War, is here.

RIPON, Fond du Lac County. State 49, 23.

Little White School House, on State 23, State 44, and State 49, was the scene of a mass meeting on March 20, 1854, where a new party was advocated—to be called "Republican."

VIROQUA, Vernon County. US 14.

Vernon County Historical Museum, 50(W. Broadway, has Civil War artifacts.

WATERFORD, Racine County. State 36.

Historic Heg Memorial Park, 4 miles northeast on Loomis Rd., commemorates Col. Hans Christian Heg who emigrated from Norway and raised a regiment of Norsemen for the Union army. He died of wounds at Chickamauga. There is a statue of Heg here and an identical one on the Capitol grounds in Madison. Museum.

WAUKESHA, Waukesha County. US 18. There is a marker in Cutler Park that honors a resident who escorted the first slave through the state to Canada. An abolitionist paper was published in this important station on the Underground Railroad.

Waukesha County Historical Society Museum, in Courthouse Annex, 101 W. Main St. at N. East Ave. Among the historical displays is one of the first Civil War uniforms issued in the North. Pioneer and Indian exhibits are featured as well as Civil War.

WISCONSIN DELLS, Columbia County. IS 90, 94, US 12, State 23. Confederate spy Belle Boyd is buried in the Spring Grove cemetery. She was scheduled to give a recital for the Grand Army Post here on July 13, 1900; she died on July 11.

WYOMING

Wyoming is the only state put together from land acquired in the four principal annexations to the original United States. Five nations have laid claim to parts of the state; boundaries have been altered 30 times. The Organic Act creating Wyoming Territory was not approved until July 25, 1868. The government took office in April 1869. Sections of Idaho, Dakota, and Utah made up the new territory which chose Cheyenne as territorial capital.

The Civil War years were a time of increasing Indian strife. As regular army soldiers left outposts to head for southern battlefields, the Shoshone and Sioux depredations grew more frequent. New posts were set up and garrisoned to protect stage and telegraph lines, but hostilities were not really ended until more than a decade after Appomattox. Wyoming became the 44th state on July 10, 1890.

CHEYENNE, Laramie County. IS 25, 80.
State Archives Department and Historical Museum, Barrett Building, Central Ave. and 24 St. Indian and pioneer mementos. Fine collection of historical manuscripts on Wyoming history and state and local archival records.
State Capitol, Capitol Ave. between 24th and 25th St. There are guided tours of the gold dome, affording a panoramic view of the area. Portraits and murals of early Wyoming statesmen and pioneer life are in legislative halls.

CODY, Park County. US 14-20.
Buffalo Bill Historical Center, 720 Sheridan Rd., has personal belongings of Col. Cody, who was a scout during the Civil War, serving also as a private with the 7th Kansas Cavalry. Buildings include his boyhood home, brought from LeClaire, Iowa.
Buffalo Bill Statue, Sheridan Ave., is in bronze, executed by Gertrude Vanderbilt Whitney.
Cody Firearms Museum, part of complex, has more than 5,000 weapons, many historical.

FORT BRIDGER STATE HISTORIC SITE, Uinta County. US 30S, in Fort Bridger

Park. At the beginning of the Civil War the garrison consisted of a sergeant's guard and a volunteer company of mountain men mustered by Judge W. A. Carter, post sutler. Later, California and Nevada volunteers and ex-Confederates, known throughout the western territories as "Galvanized Yankees," were posted here. Many of the buildings remain. They are closed in winter; in summer there are living history interpretive programs. Museum in barracks of partially restored fort.

FORT CASPAR, Natrona County. IS 25. (Also known as Platte Bridge Station.) In Casper. Restored fort has museum. In the summer of 1865, Indians from three tribes came from the Powder River country to harass the Oregon Trail. At this point they ambushed Lt. Caspar Collins and his cavalry troop, also wiped out a wagon train.

FORT LARAMIE NATIONAL HISTORIC SITE, Goshen County. US 26, 3 miles southwest of Fort Laramie. The fur-trade center was bought by the government in 1849 and was an important base during the Indian wars through the 1870s. The National Park Service has restored the buildings and parts of the grounds. Guardhouse, hospital, officers' quarters, and cavalry barracks are among those to be seen, as is sutler's store built 1849, the oldest building in Wyoming. A museum has artifacts.

FORT RENO, Johnson County. Twenty-seven miles northeast from Kaycee, near Sussex Schoolhouse. Originally known as Fort Connor, the post was a temporary base for the Powder River campaign in 1865. It was manned by troops under Gen. Connor and Indian volunteers. There is a monument on the fort site.

FORT SANDERS, Albany County. US 287. Site of fort is 2 miles south of Laramie. Known at first as Fort John Buford, established by troops from Fort Halleck, it was renamed for Gen. Sanders, who died in the battle of Campbell's Station, Tennessee, November 1863.

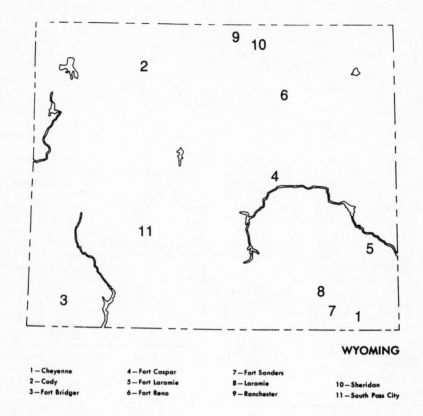

WYOMING

1 — Cheyenne   4 — Fort Caspar   7 — Fort Sanders
2 — Cody   5 — Fort Laramie   8 — Laramie   10 — Sheridan
3 — Fort Bridger   6 — Fort Reno   9 — Ranchester   11 — South Pass City

Gens. Grant, Sherman, and Sheridan met here in 1868 to discuss the railroad with Union Pacific officials.

LARAMIE, Albany County. IS 80.

Abraham Lincoln Memorial Monument, 10 miles southeast on IS 80. A 3½ ton bronze bust, sculpted by Robert I. Russin, is said to be the world's largest bronze head. It commemorates the sesquicentennial of Lincoln's birth and is situated at the highest point on the Lincoln Highway.

Western Historical Collection and University Archives, in the University of Wyoming library at 13th St. and Ivinson Ave., has an excellent collection of manuscripts pertaining to western history.

RANCHESTER, Sheridan County. IS 90.

Connor Battlefield State Park, on US 14. A stone marker is at the site of the August 1865 engagement of Gen. P. E. Connor's troops from Fort Laramie with Arapahoes under Black Bear and Old David. Many women and children were killed during the hand-to-hand combat.

SHERIDAN, Sheridan County. IS 90.

Fetterman Massacre Monument, 20 miles south on US 87. The site where in 1866 Chief Red Cloud and warriors ambushed and killed a force of 80 men under Capt. W. J. Fetterman.

SOUTH PASS CITY, Fremont County. State 28. Capt. B. L. E. Bonneville, later a Civil War general, first took wagons over the pass in 1832; it later became a stage and Pony Express route. The telegraph line came through in 1861. During Indian uprisings in 1862, stage and mail routes were shifted to the south to what became the Overland Trail. The village of South Pass is now a restored ghost town, with museum.

NATIONAL PARK SERVICE
CIVIL WAR AREAS

Abraham Lincoln Birthplace National Historic Site
RFD 1
Hodgenville, KY 42748

Andersonville National Historic Site
Andersonville, GA 31711

Andrew Johnson National Historic Site
Depot Street
Greeneville, TN 37743

Antietam National Battlefield Site and Cemetery
P.O. Box 158
Sharpsburg, MD 21782

Appomattox Court House National Historic Park
P.O. Box 218
Appomattox, VA 24522

Arlington House
c/o National Capital Parks—West
1100 Ohio Drive, S.W.
Washington, D.C. 20242

Brices Crossroads National Battlefield Site
c/o Supt., Natchez Trace Parkway
RR 1, NT-143
Tupelo, MS 38801

Chickamauga and Chattanooga National Military Park
P.O. Box 2126
Fort Oglethorpe, GA 30742

Ford's Theatre National Historic Site
c/o National Capital Parks—West
1100 Ohio Drive, S.W.
Washington, D.C. 20242

Fort Donelson National Military Park
Box F
Dover, TN 37058

Fort Jefferson National Monument
c/o Supt., Everglades National Park

Box 279
Homestead, FL 33030

Fort Pulaski National Monument
Box 98
Savannah Beach, GA 31328

Fort Sumter National Monument
Drawer R
Sullivan's Island, SC 29482

Fredericksburg and Spotsylvania County Battlefield Memorial National Military Park and Cemetery
Box 679
Fredericksburg, VA 22401

General Grant National Memorial
Riverside Drive at 123rd Street
New York, NY 10027

Gettysburg National Military Park and Cemetery
P.O. Box 70
Gettysburg, PA 17325

Harpers Ferry National Historical Park
P.O. Box 65
Harpers Ferry, WV 25425

Kennesaw Mountain National Battlefield Park
P.O. Box 1167
Marietta, GA 30061

Lincoln Boyhood National Memorial
Lincoln City, IN 47552

Lincoln Home National Historic Site
413 South Eighth Street
Springfield, IL 62701

Lincoln Memorial National Monument
c/o National Capital Parks—West
1100 Ohio Drive, S.W.
Washington, D.C. 20242

Manassas National Battlefield Park
P.O. Box 350
Manassas, VA 22110

Pea Ridge National Military Park
Pea Ridge, AR 72751

Petersburg National Battlefield
Box 549
Petersburg, VA 23803

Richmond National Battlefield Park
3215 East Broad Street
Richmond, VA 23223

Shiloh National Military Park and
Cemetery
Shiloh, TN 38376

Stones River National Battlefield and
Cemetery
Box 1039
Murfreesboro, TN 37130

Tupelo National Battlefield
c/o Supt., Natchez Trace Parkway
RR 1, NT-143
Tupelo, MS 38801

Vicksburg National Military Park and
Cemetery
Box 349
Vicksburg, MS 39180

Wilson's Creek National Battlefield
Route 2, Box 75
Republic, MO 65738